THE RATITE ENCYCLOPEDIA
Ostrich • Emu • Rhea

Claire Drenowatz
Editor

RATITE RECORDS
INCORPORATED
SAN ANTONIO, TEXAS

Copyright © 1995 Charley Elrod & Helen Wilborn
Published by Ratite Records, Inc.
Post Office Box 790365
San Antonio, TX 78279-0365

First Edition

Reproduction or translation of any part of this work beyond that permitted by section 107 or 108 of the 1976 United States Copyright Act without the permission of the copyright owner is unlawful. Requests for permission or further information should be directed to Ratite Records, Inc.

Unless otherwise noted, drawings and illustrations are by Brian Wessels.

Unless otherwise noted, photographs were supplied by the author of the chapter or by the publisher.

Designed and typeset by Alphabet Soup, San Antonio, Texas.

Cover design by John Bader.

Photo in upper left of cover courtesy Jerry and Susan Jones, JJ Rheas, Bergheim, Texas.

Printed on acid-free paper, in accordance with the standards of the American National Standard of Permanance of Paper for Printed Library Materials.

Library of Congress Catalog Card Number: 95-72092
Includes bibliographical references and index.

ISBN 0-0642940-2-8

Printed in the United States of America

10 9 8 7 6 5 4 3 2 1

This book is dedicated to the authors who
unselfishly gave their time to make
The Ratite Encyclopedia possible.

TABLE OF

PREFACE vii
Charley Elrod

HISTORY & GEOGRAPHY 3
Claire Drenowatz
James Sales, Ph. D.
Daniel V. Sarasqueta
Andy Weilbrenner

ANATOMY OF OSTRICHES, EMUS & RHEAS 31
Brett A. Hopkins, MS, DVM
Gheorghe M. Constantinescu, DVM, Ph. D.

RATITE GENETICS 63
Benny Gallaway, Ph. D.
John C. Patton, Ph. D.
Ken Coldwell
Wayne Sealey

RATITE REPRODUCTION 79
Paul C. Smith, Ph.D., DVM

THE RATITE EGG 93
D. C. Deeming, Ph. D.

INCUBATION & HATCHING 103
John Brake, Ph. D.
Bruce Rosseland

CANDLING 117
Lisa Kinder, MS

1995 HOUSTON lIVESTOCK SHOW 123

OSTRICH BREEDER MANAGEMENT 129
Sharon Barron

OSTRICH CHICK REARING 139
Susan Dunn

OSTRICH CHICK REARING 149
William C. Sutton, MD

OSTRICH MEAT 159
Craig Morris, Ph. D.

INTERVIEW WITH JAMES LEDDY, BOOTMAKER ... 167

OSTRICH FEATHERS 173
James Sales, Ph. D.

EMU BREEDER MANAGEMENT 183
Vern Brackett

EMU CHICK REARING 191
Pat Jodoin

WORKING EMUS 201
Kent Robinson

EMU MEAT 209
Leslie Thompson, Ph. D.

INTERVIEW WITH N.B.A. TRAINER DOUG ATKINSON 217

EMU OIL 223
Stephen Birkbeck

CONTENTS

RAISING RHEAS 227
    Mary Lee Stropes
    Chris Ramsey

FREE-RANGE RHEAS 239
    Kathy Bader

RHEA OIL 245
    Donna Fezler

RATITE MEAT 251
    Chef Hubert Schmieder
    W. J. Stadelman, Ph. D.
    R. L. Adams, Ph. D.
    R. F. Ghiselli, Ph. D.
    K. W. McMillin, Ph. D.
    Joe Berry, Ph. D.

FARM DESIGN & LAYOUT 257
    Scotty Flowers
    Rollo Gurss

TRANSPORTATION & HANDLING 267
    Lyle Hague

MICROCHIP IDENTIFICATION 273
    John R. Wade, DVM
    Jean Anne Mayhall

DISEASES OF RATITES 277
    Amy Raines, DVM

WORKING WITH YOUR VETERINARIAN 281
    Teresa Coble, DVM

BASIC NUTRITION FOR RATITES 287
    Dennis H. Sigler, Ph. D.

BIOSECURITY 295
    Rocky Terry, DVM

RECORD-KEEPING & MANAGEMENT 299
    Charley Elrod

INSURANCE 317
    Alex Fairly

TAX CONSIDERATIONS 323
    Walter G. Miller, CPA
    Dennis L. Sisson, CPA

LEGAL ASPECTS 337
    Jack W. Ledbetter, Attorney at Law

GLOSSARY 351

CHARTS 377

BIBLIOGRAPHY 429

INDEX 435

THE AUTHORS 455

RESOURCES 471

PRODUCTS & EQUIPMENT 473

PREFACE

Since earliest recorded history, man has used birds as symbols. The ostrich and feather has been a symbol of justice, power, authority, status, and fashion. The emu is used on currency and extensively in trademarks in Australia. Ratites are unique as avian species because they do not fly, and because of physical characteristics which set them apart from all other orders of birds.

This book was published for ratite producers, veterinarians (as a helpful handbook), students, bird enthusiasts, and all who want to know about domestic ratites and the emerging worldwide commercial industry. Extensive research went into the compilation of this information. It was surprising to us to find so little in libraries about the past, present and future of ratites and how they have affected, are affecting, and will affect the economics of our world.

Because the industry in the United States is new and many ratite producers come from non-agricultural backgrounds, an extensive glossary introduces the terminology of veterinary medicine, ratite ranching, and general agriculture.

Although we realize there are other ratite species, we have addressed only ostriches, emus and rheas because these are the ones with potential in the worldwide commercial industry.

American author Henry David Thoreau wrote of man's tendency always to complicate things. As the scientific community continues to research ratites, I often think there is much to be learned by observing these birds in their natural environment, their lives uncomplicated by the "help" of man. Studying how ratites live in the wild can give us tremendous insight into how better to raise them in a controlled environment.

Even if you raise ostriches or emus, I highly recommend that you read the chapter on range-raised rheas. The author has come closest of any producer I know to letting nature take its course, while still raising alternative livestock for profit.

At the same time, it is of the utmost importance that producers support, in whatever way they can, research by the scientific community. Without continued research by universities, colleges and private companies, the industry will stagnate and growth will be minimal.

The ratite industry is just emerging as an economic force in the United States and around the world. Early stages of marketing have put ostrich and emu meat into restaurants and grocery stores.

In traditional meat and livestock industries in the United States, individual producers accept the price the market offers at the time they sell their products. The ratite industry has a unique opportunity not to be placed in this predicament.

If the national ratite organizations and cooperatives, working through their state and local affiliates, make a concerted effort at marketing, they can assure that their producer members will control the market, rather than letting the market control them.

This is a tremendous opportunity for the ratite industry. Requirements for a good co-op management team are good financial backing, expertise in marketing, knowledge of the industry (e. g., leather goods and how to capture a market share for them), how to process products, delivery of products to final destinations, keeping abreast of market trends, and knowing how and when to get the best price. These are just a few examples of what will be required of a co-op to process and market the products of your ratite species.

Anyone who has had the experience of selling a crop or livestock through a cooperative understands its value. As with any commodity, some years your co-op check will be higher than others. However, receiving a second check—your share of the profits made by the co-op through their know-how in selling your product—is a great bonus.

Do we want Hunt Foods, Coca-Cola, Kraft Foods, Tyson, or other industry giants to control our livelihood and destiny? This is a great challenge, an unbelievable opportunity for the ratite industry. The decision time is now.

Throughout the book you will find that the authors do not agree on every subject. They have expressed their views on raising ratites and reported the results of their scientific research. Because the industry is in its infancy, there is still much research to be done.

The ratite ranchers who have written chapters have shared what works best for their operations. We have printed two chapters on raising ostrich chicks because of the challenges sometimes presented by raising them. The producers have shown you their best scenarios, what would be optimum conditions for any producer, but I have known people who have incubated and hatched ratites in spare bedrooms and garages when they first got started in the business.

As someone who has been actively involved in agriculture for twenty-five years, I know that not everyone will agree on the best way to brand or work cattle, or when to plant wheat or oats. Please do not think that one author is absolutely right and another is absolutely wrong. This is rarely the case.

We are aware that material of a scientific nature normally undergoes peer review before publication. For a small publisher, however, the cost would have been prohibitive and would have taken another year to accomplish. We hope that *The Ratite Encyclopedia* is a good starting point from which the industry can go forward in coming years.

When and how God made these birds, I don't know. I do know they have benefited mankind for thousands of years and will continue to benefit us in the future.

- Charley Elrod, Publisher
December, 1995

In our effort to better understand the many facets of the ratite industry, we have been avid readers of published materials and articles written on the subject for several years. Recognizing the need for a compilation of information pertinent for the newcomer to the industry, veterinarians, and seasoned producers to make reasonable decisions, we have made an effort to include a discussion of each subject important to the decision-making process.

There are many variables which can affect the success that individual ratite ranchers can expect from their efforts. Certain principle apply almost universally, but ranchers must also consider the variables which apply to a specific operation before and during its life.

For these reasons, because our knowledge and understanding are progressing so rapidly, and since we are living in a constantly-changing economic environment, it is critical that the ratite producer be diligent in his efforts to remain current and seek competent professional assistance whenever it is required.

The Ratite Encyclopedia provides a compilation of useful information, but the many variables associated with the industry make it necessary for the individual rancher to make decisions based on the conditions which pertain to his specific operation. Therefore, the publisher assumes no liability for the information contained herein as it pertains to the success or failure of specific operations.

- ce

THE RATITE ENCYCLOPEDIA

HISTORY & GEOGRAPHY

Claire Drenowatz

James D. Sales, Ph. D.
University of Stellenbosch

Daniel V. Sarasqueta
Instituto Nacional de
Tecnologia Agropecuaria

Andy Weilbrenner
Southwind Ostrich Ranch

If you paid attention to the dialogue in the film *Jurassic Park*, you might have gained the impression that the theory of birds evolving from dinosaurs is a new idea.

It isn't. T. H. Huxley wrote in 1870:

> . . .And if the whole hindquarters from the ilium to the tail, of a half-hatched chicken could be suddenly enlarged, ossified, and fossilized as they are, they would furnish us with the last step of the transition between Birds and Reptiles; for there would be nothing in their characters to prevent us from referring them to the Dinosauria.

The books and research papers we were able to find in researching the origins of ratites go back to the middle of the last century, but many are clustered from 1974 to 1995.

Read the works more or less in chronological order, and it's fascinating to digest the reasoning behind one writer's argument that modern ratites originated in what eventually became Africa, spread to other portions of the ancient supercontinent Gondwanaland, and rode with their respective southern continents as the landmass broke up.

Pick up the next book or journal article, and the first author is being taken to task by the second, who insists that ostriches originated in Eurasia and only later spread to Africa.

We'll take a look at some of the rationales behind the arguments shortly, but first a short review of evolutionary theory in general.

French naturalist Georges Buffon published his multi-volume *Historie Naturelle* between 1749 and 1767. In it, he estimated that the time of creation was hundreds of thousands of years, and foreshadowed the development of evolutionary theory.

In 1788, James Hutton, called the father of geology, published a paper (expanded in 1795 to his *Theory of the Earth*) which ended with this sentence: "The result, therefore, of our present enquiry is that we find no vestige of a beginning—no prospect of an end."

Back to France, and to Georges Cuvier, Professor of Comparative Anatomy at the National Museum of Natural History. In 1795 he examined an enormous jawbone which had been dug up twenty-five years earlier by construction workers in Maastricht, The Netherlands.

He correctly identified it as belonging to a marine lizard, and called it *Mosasaur*. He had previously identified bones found in the vicinity of Paris as belonging to an extinct elephant, a mastodon.

Cuvier reasoned that extinctions were caused by catastrophes such as mountain-building, floods and earthquakes (Gould, 1991).

While scientists such as Cuvier (catastrophe) and Charles Lyell (uniform rates of change) argued their theories of evolution in geology, others were looking more closely at change in animals.

Charles Darwin published *On the Origin of Species by Means of Natural Selection* in 1859. His was the book which raised the most ruckus. Most scientific debates and arguments had more or less been kept within the scientific community. But *Origin of Species* was sensationalized by the press—the last century's equivalent of the *National Enquirer*.

One reason for continued resistance to Darwin's theory is its shortened title. To people whose educations do not include hard science, it is easy to interpret it to mean a theory of creation. But that's not what the book is about.

The word *species* has a very definite meaning to scientists. It is very far down the ladder in terms of defining the position of an animal within its line of descent: phylum, class, order, family or genus, species. *Origin of species by means of natural selection* refers to the origination of *new* species from *existing* ones.

The other reason Darwin's theory is controversial, as pointed out by countless writers since 1859, is the use of the term *natural selection*, which many have taken to mean *intentional change* by the organism involved.

But Darwin never stated that natural selection was intentional. He simply proposed, and demonstated by examples, a *mechanism for change*—that organisms evolve by countless small changes which help them adapt to changing conditions or take advantage of resources no one else is using.

BIRDS AND DINOSAURS

The first time the word *dinosaur* (*deinos* - terrible; *sauros* - lizard) was used was in 1841, when Sir Richard Owen proposed that the term *Dinosauria* be used to cover the whole family of fossils for which people were now starting intentionally to dig.

Shortly thereafter, the terms *Ornithischia* (bird-hipped) and *Saurischia* (lizard-hipped) were coined to separate dinosaurs into two very distinct orders, one of which recognized early on their similarity to birds.

ARCHAEOPTERYX

In 1861, a fossilized feather was found in a limestone quarry in Solnhofen, Germany. A few months later, a complete fossil skeleton was found in the same quarry.

It's not a fossil you can hold in your hand, like a dinosaur bone. It's the impression of a creature which, 155 million years ago, fell into a quiet marine lagoon, settled into fine sediment, and was covered by more fine sediment.

The soft parts—flesh and tendons—rotted away, but bones and, in this case, feathers take longer. The sediment, the remnants of small marine creatures, eventually turned into limestone.

When the rock was quarried, it split to reveal an imprint of the complete skeleton and feathers of a bird which lived in the Jurassic era, at the same time as dinosaurs.

Indeed, fossils of a dinosaur called *Compsognathus* have been found in the same quarry as the bird, now famous, called *Archaeopteryx lithographica*.

The name is derived from *archaios* (old) and *pteryx* (wing). *Lithographica* (stone, drawing) refers to the quarry's very fine limestone, into which artists etched illustrations as part of the printing process (lithography).

Archaeopteryx. Note the toe claws and toothed jaw. Note also the fully-aerodynamic feathers of modern birds. (After Heilmann, 1926)

The first specimen found its way in 1863 to the British Museum, where it was identified by its director, Sir Richard Owen, as belonging to the class *Aves*, or birds.

T. H. Huxley, however, thought that *Archaeopteryx* had many similarities to reptiles. According to Cracraft (1986):

> He identified the theropod *Compsognathus* as that reptile most closely approaching the avian level of organization.
>
> His observation is all the more remarkable for someone in 1868, especially when it is realized paleontologists a century later were reindentifying specimens of "*Compsognathus*" as those of *Archaeopteryx* (Mayr, 1973; Wellnhofer 1974).

Gill (1995) states flatly, "Birds evolved from reptiles." He points out characteristics shared by birds and modern reptiles, including

- articulation between the neck and skull,
- similar skull structures
- similar middle ear structures,
- similar numbers of bones in the lower jaw (mandible),
- the location of the ankle in the tarsal bones, rather than between the tibia and the tarsi,
- and the very obvious similarity between scales in reptiles and feathers in birds.

According to Olson (1985), "The specimens of *Archaeopteryx* are as yet the only certain birds known from the Jurassic."

Since then, in 1987, fossils of *Sinornis santensis* were discovered in China. From the early Cretaceous, *Sinornis*, like *Archaeopteryx*, had a toothed jaw. But *Sinornis* was smaller, the size of a sparrow.

Sereno and Chenggang (1992) report that *Sinornis* displayed many characteristics of theropod dinosaurs, placing it close to the root of the tree in evolutionary terms. At the same time, *Sinornis* was considerably closer to birds than *Archaeopteryx*, with many changes that made it a better flyer.

It also had an opposable hallux, which improved its grasping and therefore perching ability.

As we go to press, Hou et al (1995) report the discovery of *Confuciusornis sanctus*, from the Jurassic, the same era as *Archaeopteryx*.

Unlike *Archaeopteryx*, it was found in fresh-water sediments, indicating early evolution in continental interiors. *Confuciusornis* has many features similar to *Archaeopteryx*, such as large curved claws on the wings, body size, and many skeletal features.

But there are enough significant differences (*Confuciusornis* is the earliest known bird to have a true beak rather than teeth, for instance) to show that this type of bird was widespread and evolving rapidly during the Jurassic.

Confuciusornis is also the earliest bird proven to have body contour feathers.

Compsognatus, a theropod dinosaur whose fossils have often been confused with those of Archaeopteryx, some of which were found in the same quarry in Bavaria. (After Heilmann, 1926)

BUT COULD THEY FLY?

Olson (1985) notes, "One of the most striking features of *Archaeopteryx* is that its feathers appear in every respect to be like those of modern birds." Others have made the observation that they are fully aerodynamic.

The asymmetry of the size of the vanes on either side of the quill is familiar to anyone who has ever looked at an aircraft wing. The thickest part of the wing is well forward, where the airflow is divided above and below to provide lift, just as in flight feathers. The air then flows backward over the longer part of the wing, or the longer vanes of the feather, to rejoin at the trailing edge.

Whether or not *Archaeopteryx* was capable of flight as we know it is still the subject of debate, but there is little doubt that it could at least glide, much as flying squirrels and foxes climb a tree and

WHY ALL THE LATIN?

Do we really need Latin names? Maybe a brief excursion into how they came about will explain why they are useful. Actually, many of the names aren't Latin at all. They are what word scientists refer to as *learned borrowings* from Greek, including many of the words used to describe dinosaurs (*deinos* and *sauros* = terrible lizard).

For most of human history, animals and plants were known by local names. Which was fine, until the invention of the printing press in 1459 AD and the explosion of knowledge which it brought. By 1500 AD, Europe was flooded with books, many of them reprints of manuscripts in the libraries of monasteries, universities, and wealthy families all over the continent.

The universal language of educated people, particularly scientists, was the Latin of the church. It provided, as English does today, a common tongue in which people from different countries could share knowledge. It was so widespread that scientists often Latinized their names. Mikolaj Kopernik of Poland was known, for instance, as Copernicus.

Many of the first books printed were of a more or less scientific nature, such as volumes on herbs from which one could make medicinal compounds. But even though books were printed in Latin, the Latin names used were merely translations of local terms for flowers, animals, and anything else worth writing about. When a book printed in Italy got to Sweden, the Swedish reader didn't have a clue. The addition of illustrations helped, but the confusion remained, particularly when scientists tried to compare notes.

Carolus Linnaeus (Carl von Linné), a Swedish botanist, is generally credited with codifying the system of Latin names. In his *Systema Naturæ*, published in the mid-1700s, he named "everything in the known world," only a slight exaggeration. While many of his assertions as to the unchanging nature of, well, nature, were quickly disputed, his basic system is still in use. It is based on features which distinguish one type of creature from similar ones. (The name for emus, *Dromaiidae*, comes from the Greek *dromos* = running.) Many changes, of course, have been made to classifications as research has clarified the erroneous assumptions—or incomplete knowledge—of early scientists.

For instance, thirty years ago, emus were referred to as *Dromiceidae*. In the interim, researchers have added to, rearranged, and fine-tuned much of what is known about the world around us.

---

glide from branch to branch or to other trees. Gill (1995) and others point out that *Archaeopteryx* probably could not take off from the ground because it lacked the skeletal support for flight muscles strong enough for a quick upstroke, necessary to continue the momentum of the lifting force of the downstrokes.

Olson and Feduccia (1979) argue that *Archaeopteryx* could have been capable, once airborne (as in a glide from a tree branch), of flapping its wings to continue or prolong flight.

THE ORIGINS OF FLIGHT

Within twenty years of the discovery of *Archaeopteryx*, scientists had accepted the theory that it was a missing link between reptiles and birds, and had started the arguments which still continue, about which line of dinosaurs they may have descended from.

Very quickly, of course, debate started over the origin of flight: cursorial (from the ground up), as proposed by Williston in 1879, or arboreal (starting from trees), according to Marsh in 1880 and Ostrom as late as 1984.

As Walter J. Bock (1986) points out, much of the early discussion was limited by the lack of knowledge of the physics of flight.

He also refers to the 1926 work of Gerhard Heilmann, who argued for arboreal origin in which ". . . an initially terrestrial runner became an arboreal climber, then a leaper between branches and from trees to the ground, a glider, and finally an active flyer."

Bock points out:

Partly because Heilmann's study was so complete, relatively little was published on *Archaeopteryx* for the next 30 years. The modern period of *Archaeopteryx* studies was ushered in with the publication of de Beer's monograph on the London specimen and his discussion of the pertinence of evolutionary ideas.

He then reviews discoveries or recognition of additional *Archaeopteryx* fossils, and concludes, "The result has been much new information on the morphology of this primitive bird and numerous ideas on many aspects of avian evolution."

ARBOREAL THEORY

One idea bound to be reviewed was the theory of the arboreal origin of flight. Bock states that arboreal flight requires less-well-developed flight structures, in that flight is toward the direction of gravity.

A cursorial origin implies a more-well-developed flight apparatus, since the evolving bird must act against gravity in taking off from the ground. In beginning his review of the theory, he states:

The two key features of the arboreal theory are that

protobirds lived in trees and that flight originated by locomotion through the air from the trees downward toward the ground.

The starting point was a terrestrial ancestral reptile, presumably with quadruped locomotion. At some point, protobirds went up into trees and spent part of their life in trees and part of their life on the ground. Protobirds could climb up the tree trunks, scramble about on branches, and leap from one branch to another nearby branch as do present-day squirrels.

Protobirds could also climb down the tree trunks or otherwise reach the ground. Possibly they leaped from a low branch, or from the trunk, to the ground.

With evolutionary change and specialization, protobirds probably first parachuted (unspecialized glide with a steep angle of descent) to the ground and subsequently became more and more specialized gliders. Gliding led to active flight.

During the early stages of flight (e.g., gliding and primitive flapping flight) most of the energy for flight came from the downward pull of gravity. Only in the more specialized stages of flapping flight did much of the energy for flight come from flight muscles.

During the entire period of the evolution of flight, protobirds spent much of their life on the ground, probably for feeding.

Bock discusses support for the arboreal theory, including homoiothermy (ability to aid maintain body temperature), evolution of feathers from scales (originally as a device to aid in regulating body temperature), size, three dimensional orientation, bipedalism and the hind limbs, body shape and structure, and wing and tail structure.

Homoiothermy seems to be a prerequisite for flight, in that the flight muscles need to be warm *before* the bird begins to fly. There is no time for warmup if the muscles are to develop the force needed either to hold the wings out in a glide or to flap them.

In small animals (*Archaeopteryx* was about the size of a crow) heat loss is a problem, which lends support to the theory that, in protobirds, feathers developed from scales as thermoregulators before being used in flying.

Bock also hypothesizes that homoiothermy developed in protobirds as a result of an at least partly arboreal lifestyle.

Reptiles, as a rule, sun themselves in the morning to warm up sufficiently to go about their daily business. But it's significantly cooler in trees due to more wind and shade, and less heat reflected from the ground.

Why Climb Trees?

Bock points out two strong arguments for terrestrial animals to become arboreal: to escape from or stay out of the way of predators, and to protect their young from them by building their nests in trees.

Again, development of homoiothermy is a success strategy, in that a warm-blooded animal could heat the eggs in the cooler climate above the earth's surface.

To a pilot, Bock's argument for development of flight in an animal which is already oriented in three dimensions is particularly interesting.

I must disagree with his statement that "synthetic devices (e.g. artificial horizons) are required to provide information on the relationship to the horizontal." In all but very-high-altitude or very-high-speed flight, pilots normally refer to flight instruments only in poor weather conditions. But his argument against developing flight from the ground up is persuasive:

Three-dimensional orientation is an absolutely essential precondition for the evolution of flight of any sort, including primitive downward jumping and gliding.

Three-dimensional orientation would not evolve in a ground-dwelling form, not even in a leaping organism. A long jump from the ground is still in the realm of the terrestrial, two-dimensional world.

I know of no examples in which specialized, three-dimensional orientation has been demonstrated in a primary terrestrial vertebrate, one that did not have an immediate arboreal or flying ancestor. A three-dimensional orientation can, and almost always does, evolve in arboreal tetrapods [four-limbed creatures] because life in trees is in a three-dimensional world.

I doubt that three-dimensional orientation would evolve in cliff dwellers. These tetrapods still live in a two-dimensional world—one that is turned on its side.

Bock also discusses the physiological changes which point to an arboreal, rather than terrestrial, orientation. He points out that it is not clear whether the pubic structure is fully reversed in *Archaeopteryx*, as it is in modern birds.

But it is clear that the hallux, or avian version of the big toe, is fully reversed, and that its foot "functioned as a grasping one. Specialized ground-dwelling birds tend to reduce and lose the reversed hallux." He disagrees with Peters (1984), who "argues that the evolution of the hallux in protobirds was associated with the need to grasp food while tearing it to pieces before swallowing it." Bock argues "It is not clear why the food must be grasped by a foot using the reversed hallux, and not simply held against the ground as is done by most modern birds..."

Bock's analysis of the body and wing structures is extremely long and complex, but his conclusion is that the fully-feathered wings and tail, while lacking many of the structures associated with flapping flight, would have allowed *Archaeopteryx* to be "an excellent flyer, with fine control of the direction and duration of the flight and fine control of landing."

But, even assuming that protobirds took to the trees for protection, why fly in the first place?

Development of protobirds occurred during the Jurassic, but flowering plants, and therefore edible seeds and fruit, did not develop until the Cretaceous. *Archaeopteryx*, at least, was almost certainly carnivorous (its toothed jaw is not representative of plant eaters) and it and other protobirds would likely have hunted on the ground.

Once having formed an arboreal habit for protection, the easiest way to the ground for hunting is in a controlled fall (or parachuting), leading to gliding, and eventually to flight. It's also the easiest way to get around for an animal which must cover ground to hunt or feed.

Climbing a tree and gliding to the next requires less energy than either walking or running to a feeding area (and puts the animal in less danger from predators). And it takes less exertion than climbing a tree, climbing back down, scampering to the next tree, and climbing it.

CURSORIAL THEORY

John H. Ostrom, however, in a paper published in the same book as Bock's, disagrees and argues for a cursorial origin of birds.

He notes "it is doubtful that climbing skills were part of the repertoire of primitive birds, or even of early bird ancestors. The clawed hands of *Archaeopteryx* might have been adapted for climbing, but there is disagreement on this."

Ostrom reviews—and rejects—proposals from various other authors as to how a running animal could have evolved into a flying one.

Baron Franz Nopcsa (1907) suggests "... we may quite well suppose that birds originated from bipedal long-tailed cursorial reptiles which during running oared along in the air by flapping their free anterior extremities."

Ostrom points out that the "minuscule amount of additional thrust produced by those earliest enlarged 'protofeathers' could hardly have produced any measurable selective advantage."

However, while Ostrom points out what he sees as problems with the arboreal theory, he does not propose a mechanism by which flight would have originated from the ground up.

He cites a paper by Russell Balda (1983) which supports his theory, noting,

> ... they propose that avian flight began with a bipedal cursorial ancestor that used its arms to help maintain balance and active control of body attitude while running and leaping. They point out that control of changes in body attitude (roll, pitch, and yaw) is paramount for any animal that becomes airborne, even if such aerial excursions are just simple leaps.

Ostrom also notes, however, "control of body attitude is just as critical for the airborne hypothetical arboreal 'proavis' that launched itself from the tree tops." In other words, he points out the hole in what appears to be his best argument.

MECHANICAL CONSIDERATIONS

C. J. Pennycuick (1986) explored the mechanics of flight in terms of power-to-weight ratios, glide angles, wing loading, and aspect ratios, terms more familiar to engineers than to ornithologists. He even considers weight and balance, as critical to birds as to airplanes.

In discussing the transition from gliding to powered flight, he states:

> To develop powered flight in an animal that can already glide at a reasonably flat angle, further adaptations are required to develop a small amount of forward thrust, which in turn requires some muscle power to be supplied.
>
> The easiest entry point is to exert thrust while gliding at the minimum power speed, since the power required is least for an animal that can already glide at that speed.
>
> It is much less likely that flight would originate in a running and leaping animal, ... since this would involve a direct transition to strenuous low-speed flight, besides requiring difficult coordination requirements to be met *de novo*, without an existing basis of flight adaptations.
>
> A gliding animal can already control itself in a steady glide, and has only to build on this by supplying a minute amount of power from its muscles, so slightly flattening the glide angle...
>
> until the glides finally merge imperceptibly into horizontal, powered flight.

Remember that the word *dinosaur* does not necessarily mean a huge, lumbering beast. Many were small animals no larger than domestic cats, or even birds. Thinking of them as small animals makes the mental leap from dinosaurs to birds somewhat easier.

In his discussion of the origin of birds, Gauthier (1986) states flatly, "Birds are living dinosaurs, and as such they have extended the preeminence of Dinosauria among terrestrial vertebrates from the late Triassic to the present day."

But not all dinosaurs which are included by researchers in the lineage of birds were small. In one of the scenes from *Jurassic Park*, a herd of stampeding dinosaurs flees from *Tyrannosaurus rex*, and indirectly threaten our hero and the kids. The species of dinosaur, identified by the boy as *gallimimus*, is seen by some researchers as a precursor of a line which eventually led to ratites.

THE TELLTALE HEART

Pennycuick (1986), in his engineering approach to flight, notes an anatomical hint to development from what he calls "a tall ancestor:"

> The best living examples of cursorial bipedal animals are the ratites, which are all much too large to fly. Most of the known cursorial dinosaurs were at least as large as modern ratites, and many were considerably larger. . . . fast bipedal or quadrupedal running seems to work best at these large sizes.
>
> The ratites have evidently relinquished the power of flight as a necessary consequence of evolving the large size best suited to this mode of locomotion. . . . a prospective proavis needs to be in the mass range 10-100 grams to have the best chance of evolving powered flight, and this is not a favorable range for cursorial locomotion.
>
> However, there is one characteristic of birds that indicates they are descended from a tall ancestor, which may also have been ancestral to dinosaurs and pterosaurs. This feature is the fully divided ventricle.

Pennycuick explains that, because the capillaries of the lungs are not surrounded by tissue as are the capillaries in other organs, they cannot take high pressure.

However, an animal which stands upright needs blood in its brain, and it takes high pressure to deliver it. Modern amphibians and reptiles all have an undivided ventricle, which limits their ability to function in a heads-up position. The ancestors of birds, Pennycuick explains, solved the problem:

> A large animal that stands upright for extended periods has no alternative but to divide the ventricle fully, accepting the inconvenient consequence that the volume rate of flow through the lungs then has to equal that through all other organs combined.
>
> The divided ventricle of birds thus indicates that they are descended from a tall ancestor. This could well have been a common ancestor of birds, pterosaurs, and dinosaurs and may be assumed to have been a tall, bipedal, cursorial animal.
>
> If that were the case, all three groups would have inherited the divided ventricle from the same source. Similarly, mammals no doubt inherited their fully divided circulation from a tall ancestor in the Permo-Triassic radiation of synapsid reptiles.

However, the argument for the divided heart is not proof of the origin of birds from a tall ancestor. Crocodiles also have divided hearts, yet they never stood erect (the hip structure is proof of this). More on crocodiles later.

If the ancestors of birds were dinosaurs the size of ostriches and larger, how did they then become small enough to fly?

Simply put, a lot can happen in 150 million years, which is generally accepted as the time line connecting modern birds with their dinosaurian ancestors. In that time, according to this theory, not only did they become small enough to fly, they also lost the ability to fly and once again grew large.

WHY STOP FLYING?

There are several reasons to give up the ability to fly, including the fact that it's expensive in terms of energy requirements. If a line of birds has no reason to continue flying, the ability will eventually disappear.

Feduccia (1980) states that when dinosaurs disappeared at the end of the Cretaceous, a niche for bipedal flesh-eaters was left open, and several birds moved into that niche. He mentions two in particular which he and other writers cite as coming from the same ancestral stock as ostriches, the Gruiformes.

Diatrymas were huge birds which were widespread over North America and Europe before the continents separated at the end of the Eocene. They had small wings, massive legs, wicked claws on their toes, and a keelless sternum. Their huge heads and powerful hooked beaks led Feduccia to consider them carnivores.

A lighter, probably faster flightless family of birds of South America, which was isolated during the Cenozoic, were the phorusrhacids, which dated from the Oligocene to the end of the Pliocene. More crane-like than diatrymas, they were from 5 to 8 feet tall, and also had beaks which indicate that they were carnivorous.

Modern descendents of the Gruiformes include rails (many of which evolved into flightless forms, some only a few thousand years ago), cranes (all modern forms fly), and bustards (which can fly, but by habit are ground birds).

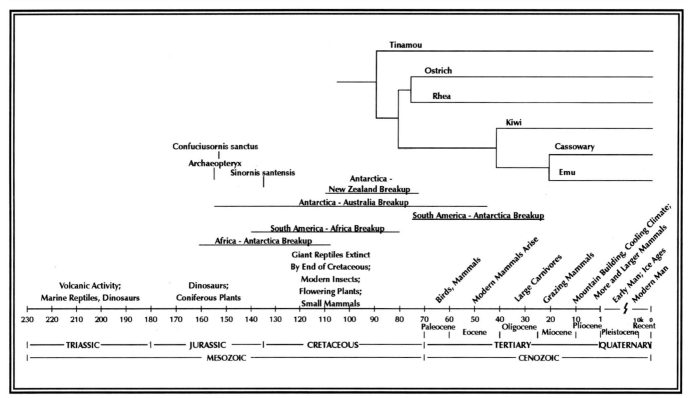

Figure 1. An aid to the visualization of paleohistory, with the breakup of the supercontinent Gondwanaland (Figure 2) and the development of the ratite line superimposed on a generalized geological time scale. (After Cracraft, 1973 & 1974, Olson, 1985, Hou et al, 1995, Sereno & Chenggang, 1992, Gallaway, in press)

As noted above, flightlessness is an energy-saver. The keel, flight muscles, and associated structures constitute as much as 20 to 25 per cent of a bird's total body weight. Since flightless birds no longer need such adaptations, these and other specialized features gradually disappear.

Because they no longer need to be light in weight, flightless birds also tend to grow larger than their flying ancestors (Feduccia, 1980).

While ostriches, emus and rheas evolved into fast runners to evade predators, Feduccia points out that the recently extinct moas of New Zealand and the elephantbirds of Madagascar grew to great size, which protected them until the arrival of man.

The huge digestive system required to digest grasses and other plants would be impossible for a flying bird to carry around, and flying birds eat foods which are easy to digest and which provide quick energy. Unlike their flying relatives, birds such as ostriches can afford to become herbivorous.

Another effect of the savings in energy is the ability to produce more offspring. No large flying birds equal the reproductive capability of the large ratites, which even in the wild produce as many as a dozen eggs in a season.

To the layman, it is the lack of a keeled sternum which is usually thought of as separating ratites from other birds. But as Feduccia (1980) points out, the keelless sternum is not an exclusively ratite feature. It is a characteristic also of other flightless birds.

Various authors cite other features such as the fused scapula and coracoid (which in ratites form an extremely wide angle similar to many dinosaurs), number of toes and structure of the metatarsus, and sutured skull bones, which are unlike the fused skulls of other birds.

Indeed, it is the skull, and particularly the palate, which places ratites in the superorder *Paleognathus* (old jaw). All other living birds belong to the superorder *Neognathus* (new jaw).

Soon after Charles Darwin, in his *Origin of Species* (1859), made an attempt to explain how species evolve, Thomas H. Huxley was the first to suggest that all living ratites are related. He started an argument which has not yet been fully resolved.

The scientists are no longer arguing, however, *whether* birds are related to dinosaurs. Only the evolutionary path is being argued.

WHERE *DID* THEY COME FROM?

In a long paper published in 1973, Joel Cracraft explored the relationship of the relatively new theory of continental drift (now usually called plate tectonics) to the evolution of birds.

In doing so, he explained why the idea of continents moving

around the globe was not taken seriously for so long, even though it had been proposed near the turn of the century. The main objection was that a mechanism had not been proposed which would explain it.

The theory finally gained acceptance with the discovery that continents rode on plates surrounded by fracture zones, with sea-floor spreading at one edge of a plate while the other edge was either being plowed under a neighboring plate or pushed up against it, raising mountain ranges.

With propulsion by currents in the earth's molten core as the driving force, the idea of movement made more sense than when the earth's crust was assumed to be solid and seamless.

The theory was of interest to people other than geologists, of course, because it helped explain anomalies in the fossil records related to climate and the evolution of all manner of animal and plant life. When one knows that the positions of the continents have shifted, it's easier to understand finding fossils of ancient tropical or temperate-zone forests in now-polar locations.

Cracraft's emphasis was on the breakup of the southern supercontinent of Gondwanaland into South America, Antarctica, Australia, New Zealand, Africa, and Madagascar.

The breakup of South America and Africa is probably easiest to visualize, since the apparent fit of their coastlines is what gave rise to the idea of continental drift in the first place.

But the rift did not happen all at once along the full length of the coast. Rather, it was a rotation away from each other, with the split starting at the southern end by the end of the Jurassic, and complete separation by the middle to late Cretaceous.

Antarctica and Africa appear to have separated between the middle Jurassic and middle Cretaceous, along what is now the northern coast of Antarctica and the lower east coast of Africa.

Prior to breakup, the southern coasts of Antarctica and Australia were joined. After breakup, with rifting beginning in the middle Jurassic and complete by the late Eocene, Antarctica rotated about 90 degrees clockwise and Australia 90 degrees counter-clockwise with respect to each other.

The hollow bones and small bodies of birds tend not to be preserved well, and, until the very recent discoveries of *Confuciusornis* in China, the impressions of *Archaeopteryx* are the only bird fossils from the Jurassic.

According to Cracraft (1973), however, from the Cretaceous period around 40 species in 20 families have been identified. He mentions:

- feather impressions from 135 milllion-year-old (myr) Koonwarra claystones in Australia;
- *Gallornis*, an extinct flamingo-like family, from about the same time period in Europe;
- from the British Isles, *Enaliornis*, related to loons and grebes.

According to Cracraft, this distribution by the early Cretaceous suggests that birds were well developed and widespread, having evolved into recognizable birdlike form during the Jurassic.

The discovery of *Confuciusornis* strengthens that argument immeasurably, given the differences between it and *Archaeopteryx*, and the fact that they were apparently nearly contemporaneous with each other.

Many of the other fossils known from the Cretaceous were of water birds, which further suggests that the fossil record will always be incomplete, due to the poor preservation of the delicate bones of birds from that era.

However, climatic conditions changed in the early Cenozoic,

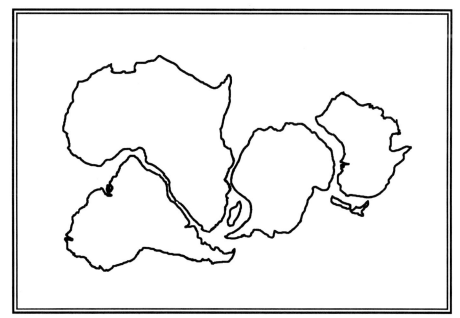

The continents comprising Gondwanaland, shown in their present outlines for clarity, but they would not have been separate in this form at any time. For instance, South America and Africa started breaking up from the south, and over a period of perhaps sixty million years finally completed separation at the north as South America rotated, rather than simply sliding away. Similarly, Antarctica has rotated roughly 90 degrees clockwise and Australia 90 degrees counterclockwise with respect to each other. See Figure 1 for approximate geological time scales. (After Cracraft, 1973)

and avian fossils are common. As Cracraft (1973) notes:

> ... the great diversity and morphologic specialization of many Paleocene and Eocene birds suggests that many of these groups originated in the Cretaceous. Most importantly, we can infer that the class Aves, much as we know it today, was present on all continents in the Cretaceous and thus would have been readily susceptible to changes in global paleogeography and climatology.

Cracraft (1973, 1974) prefers a southern-continent origin for the ratites, before the breakup of Gondwanaland. His hypothesis is that the center for dispersal was South America, in several stages.

- Tinamidae branched off from the main lineage, which at that time was capable of flight, and remained isolated in South America.
- The main line stopped flying.
- The ancestor of kiwis and moas moved through what was is now western Antarctica (but was then southern) into New Zealand, no later than 80 myr ago, when New Zealand started breaking away from Antarctica.
- Aepyornithidae, elephant birds (only recently extinct), moved through Africa and into what is now Madagascar, which separated from Africa in the middle to late Cretaceous, 80-90 myr ago. Fossils of related species have been found in the Canary Islands, supporting the idea of dispersal from South America.
- The ancestor of emus and cassowaries moved across then north Antarctica (now east) into Australia, prior to the late Eocene, when Australia separated from Antarctica.
- Finally, after South America and Africa split in the late Cretaceous (Turonian), the ratites diverged further into the rheas in South America and ostriches in Africa.

Cracraft states that the struthionids dispersed from Africa to Eurasia, but due to changes in climate, became extinct there.

Feduccia (1980) questions Cracraft's assertions. He wanted to know why fossils of ostriches aren't found in South America and Africa.

He argues that, unlike the bones of small birds, ostrich bones are large and easily recognized (because of the tarsometatarsus, which has a distinct shape due to its structural fit with a two-toed bird).

He postulates that the ancestors of ostriches originated in the Eocene in Eurasia, that ostriches appeared in Eurasia, and only in the Pleistocene spread into Africa. His argument is the same as Olson's five years later, allying ostriches with the gruiforms, especially the Ergilornithidae.

Storrs L. Olson (1985) comes down firmly on the origination of the ostrich lineage in central Asia. He has extensively studied the fossil record of three families which he considers to be related and forebears of present-day ostriches: the *Geranoididae* (from the early and middle Eocene in North America), *Eogruidae* (cranelike birds from the late Eocene and early Oligocene of central Asia), and *Ergilornithidae* (large two-toed running birds from the early Oligocene of Asia and the late Miocene and Pliocene of Asia and Europe).

By the late Miocene, fossils show that a true *Struthio* had appeared, but there is a gap in the fossil record of some 20 million years.

Olson attributes this to the "near absence of early and middle Miocene sediments in Asia." He notes,

The earliest ostrich ... *Struthio orlovi*, from the late Miocene of eastern Europe, was smaller than any of the later forms, as were its Oligocene ancestors.

Kurochkin and Lungu (1970) point out that the ancestors of *Struthio orlovi* would not have occurred in eastern Europe in the early Tertiary, as this area was then forested; an open steppe environment did not prevail here until the late Miocene.

Such environments were present throughout most of the Tertiary in central Asia, however, where the eogruid and ergilornithid presumptive ancestors of ostriches are found.

Olson disputes Cracraft's (1973) opinion that "ostriches were derived from a common ancestor with other ratites that inhabited Gondwanaland in the Mesozoic. If so, then how does one explain *Struthio* appearing in the Miocene of Europe and Asia with no known antecedents?"

WHICH DINOSAURS

Gill (1995) explains conflicting theories of the evolution of birds from dinosaurs. In the Mesozoic, a line of small reptiles called thecodonts evolved into small arboreal dinosaurs, as well as pterosaurs and crocodiles.

Some researchers point to the similarity of fourteen characteristics of crocodilian thecodonts and birds as an argument in favor of birds having evolved from the crocodilian line by the middle Triassic. But then why is there a 90-million-year gap in the fossil record before *Archaeopteryx* appears? Gill considers it most likely that theropod dinosaurs evolved from the thecodonts, and that birds later evolved from the theropods.

Many theropods were small, and they included *Compsognathus*, the dinosaur which was found in the same quarry as *Archaeopteryx*. As noted above, they are so similar that specimens of *Archaeopteryx* have for years been misidentified as *Compsognathus*.

The fact that theropods and early birds existed at the same time points to a closer relationship than that of thecodonts and birds.

But the ratites... John Patton (personal communication, September 29, 1995), co-author with Benny Gallaway of the **Genetics** chapter, agrees with the general theory of the dispersal of ratites, but believes that the main lineage never developed flight.

It is his opinion that the *Tinamidae*, weak flyers at best, developed flight only *after* breaking off from the rest of the ratites. This, Patton says, also relieves researchers of having to explain how the ratite line developed and then lost the keeled sternum.

Finally, remember the discussion about the divided heart and the tall ancestor? It is also found in crocodiles, almost unchanged since the Triassic. More importantly, the leg structure of crodilians is lizard-like throughout all that time—crocodiles never stood on their hind legs.

So why did they develop a divided ventricle? Good question. Crocodiles also have all the equipment necessary to be homoiothermic, but they're cold-blooded. Why? Another good question.

But for this discussion, according to Patton, what it means is that it is possible that some ancestral crocodile developed into the reptiles called thecodonts, then into theropod dinosaurs, and from there directly into the ratite line, without ever having gone through a flying stage.

By the end of the Cretaceous, the giant reptiles were extinct, but their descendants the birds—and small mammals—were coming along nicely.

And with that, let's get into the modern history of the ratites.

TABLE 1. TAXONOMIC CLASSIFICATION OF RATITES

Phylum	Chordata
Subphylum:	Vertebrate
Class	Aves
Sub-class	Neornithae
Superorder	Paleognathae

ORDER	FAMILY	SPECIES	SUB-SPECIES
Struthioniformes			
	Struthionidae (ostriches)		
		Struthio camelus	
			S. c. camelus
			S. c. massaicus
			S. c. molybdophanes
			S. c. australis
Rheiformes			
	Rheidae (rheas)		
		Rhea americana	
			R. a. albascens *
			R. a. araneipes *
			R. a. americana *
			R. a. intermedia *
			R. a. nobilis *
		Pterocnemia pennata	
			P. p. pennata *
			P. p. tarapacensis *
			P. p. garleppi *
Casuariiformes			
	Dromaiidae (emus)		
		Dromaius novaehollandiae	
	Casuariidae (cassowaries)		
		Casuarius casuarius	
		Casuarius unappendiculatus **	
		Casuarius bennetti	
Apterygiformes			
	Apterygidae (kiwis)		
		Apteryx australis	
		Apteryx owenii owenii	
		Apteryx owenii haasti **	
Tinamiformes			
	Tinamidae (tinamous)		
		Tinamous major	
		Crypturellus soui	
		Crypturellus cinnamomeus	
		Nothoprocta pentlandii	
		Eudromia elegans	
		and 42 more species	

We compiled this chart primarily from Perrins (1990), with additions as noted.
* Added from Sarasqueta (1995). He notes that some authorities consider there are only two subspecies of *Rhea americana*, *R. a. albascens* and *R. a. araneipes*. With respect to *Pterocnemia pennata*, he notes that some consider *P. p. tarapacensis* and *P. p. garleppi* to be a single subspecies.
** Added from Hopkins (1995).
Like some other authorities, Perrins classifies only ostriches, rheas, emus, and cassowaries as ratites. He lists tinamous separately, with a comment that they have features which link them to ratites.

TABLE 2. TAXONOMY AND CHARACTERISTICS OF OSTRICHES

COMMON NAME	SCIENTIFIC NAME	NOTABLE	RANGE	DESCRIPTION
Syrian, Arabian, Aleppo	S. c. syriacus	Finest feathers	Arabian deserts, Palestine (now Israel & Jordan), Syria, Persia (now Iran)	Extinct
North African, Barbary, St. Louis, Mogodor, Algerian, Sudanese	S. c. camelus	Taller, longer legs & neck, thicker legs, more robust, larger feet, than S. c. massaicus or S. c. australis	Formerly throughout Northern Africa, now in a band from Mauritania to Ethiopia	Crown: bald patch with short brown feathers. Skin: all juveniles & mature hen creamy yellow; mature cock red/pink body, scarlet head, neck & leg during breeding season. Male: collar of white feathers between upper & lower neck, body black, tail & wings white. Female: body feathers dark brown, edges paler, paler tail & wing feathers.
Masai, East African	S. c. massaicus	Narrow neck ring	Tanzania, Kenya	Crown: partially bald or completely feathered. Neck & thighs pink-grey, breeding season bright red. Body feathers similar to S. c. camelus.
Somali	S. c. molydbdophanes	Tallest of wild ostriches	Somalia, Ethiopia, Kenya	Crown bald, broad white neck ring. Neck & thighs blue-grey. Male: black and white. Female, grey.
South African	S. c. australis	Original southern Africa native	South Africa, Namibia, Botswana, Zimbabwe, now limited to parks and some parts of northern Namibia	Crown feathered. Neck bluish grey, red in breeding season; in male tarsal scutes also bright red. Tail is dull to bright cinnamon-brown, other plumage similar to other species. No neck ring.
Domestic, African Black, Israeli Black, Oudtshoorn	S. c. var. domesticus	Hybrid of australis, camelus, and syriacus; smaller than wild subspecies; shorter legs & neck; broader, longer bodies; often shorter bill. Broader barbs, rounded not pointed. More white plumes in hens.	None known in wild	Generally same as S. c. australis

Chart prepared from Medeiros, 1993.

OSTRICHES

THE EARLY RECORD

Editor's note: The following is from Greenway, 1967.

There can be no doubt that ostriches have disappeared from a large part of their range and have been disappearing for perhaps a million years. No reason can be given for this, for there is no evidence.

There are no more ostriches in southern Europe, in India, or in China, where fossil remains have been found. Presently they are confined to the drier parts of Africa, which excludes the forested Congo region. They are nowhere common and have disappeared from the neighborhood of human habitation over the range of the species.

Fossil remains of ostriches have been found:
- in lower Pleistocene beds near Odessa, west coast of the Black Sea, and near Cherson, on the north coast;
- in rocks of the lower Pliocene on the island of Samos;
- in Algeria and Egypt, in beds thought to be the Tertiary and the second late-Pleistocene or Recent;
- in Tanganyika, now Tanzania, also lower Pleistocene;
- in the Siwalik Hills of India, lower Pliocene;
- in Lower Pliocene formations in Pao Te Hsien, Northwest Shansi, on the Yellow River, China; and
- fossil eggs have been found in a region from north-northwest to south-southwest of Kalgan, on the border of Shansi and Inner Mongolia.

The living species include *Struthio camelus camelus*, which occurs sparingly in the Sahara desert, Egyptian Sudan, and the west coast of the Red Sea; *S. c. molybdophanes*, which is still to be found in Ethiopia and Somalia; *S. c. massaicus*, a rare bird of eastern Kenya and Tanzania; *S. c. australis* still to be seen in the wilder parts of South Africa south of the Zambesi and Cunane Rivers.

The Arabian ostrich, *S. c. syriacus*, went extinct when the last specimen was, according to anecdotal evidence, killed and eaten near the oil pipe line north of Bahrein between 1940 and 1945.

SOUTH AFRICA

We received two excellent contributions on the origin of the ostrich industry in South Africa. Together, they filled in the history over the last century very nicely, so we combined them. The bylines of the authors appear at the end, and their names appear at the end of each of their sections of text.

Most of the African continent was at one time or another home to the ostrich, the only exception being part of the Ivory Coast and the Congo basin of central west Africa.

As an emblem of authority and nobility, the ostrich plumage has few if any peers. This fact is verified as even the tombs of the Egyptian pharaohs were inscribed with pictures and held plumage and eggs of the stately ostrich. Roman generals and Zulu warriors alike adorned themselves with ostrich feathers.

The Bushman of the Kalahari relied heavily on the ostrich as a source of food. Paintings in their holy places clearly show their use of ostrich eggs as water vessels, a practice still in use today.

Bushmen, after killing an ostriches with their poison arrows, would take the "cape" of the bird and adorn themselves with the plumage, extending one arm through the neck skin, thereby making themselves decoys to approach other ostriches. Their attempts using this device were very successful.

As time progressed, the plumage became more in vogue and was worn in Europe by much of the aristocracy. During the Middle Ages, Edward, Prince of Wales, known as the Black Prince, emblazoned his shield with three ostrich feathers.

Elizabeth I of England and Marie Antoinette of France are given credit for establishing ostrich plumage as high-fashion articles in their respective centuries. Most of the early feathers came from wild birds in northern Africa.

Rock painting found near Fort Djanet in the Sahara.
(Photo taken at C. P. Nel Museum, South Africa, by James Sales)

INCUBATION TRIVIA

In *The Incubation Book* (1979), Dr. A. F. Anderson Brown describes incubation and hatching techniques dating back at least four millenia. In cylindrical brick ovens set in double rows, facing a corridor, as many as ninety thousand eggs would be incubated at a time. With the eggs on the floor of the incubating ovens, fires burned continuously in troughs circling the inner walls. Continuous airflow was assured by an inlet opening at ground level and an exhaust through the roof. Additional ventilation was provided by openings in the connecting corridor roof and walls.

Anderson Brown also mentioned methods used by the Chinese circa 1000 BCE. In one, heat for the eggs was supplied by rotting manure. The second was similar to the Egyptian method in that it utilized cylindrical buildings, but the eggs were suspended in baskets above a fire on the floor.

He notes that the Chinese used candling, and that Aristotle described in detail an incubation method which also used rotting manure.

It's a tale often told that in South Africa, feather merchants paid native girls to hatch ostrich eggs with their body heat.

Modern hatching techniques began in Paris in 1749, with a hatching box invented by Réamur, and a special room invented by Campion in 1770. The ostrich-egg hatcher, as noted in the text, was developed in South Africa by Douglass in the late 1800s.

Not until around 1838 did the South Africans export plumage to Europe.

When the Dutch led by Jan Van Reibecck landed at what is today Cape Town, South Africa, in 1652, the area literally swarmed with animal life, including ostriches. As man moved inland from the first few settlements along the African coast, and with the advent of more modern firearms, the herds of wildlife were slaughtered. Ostriches were no exception, as the feathers were highly prized and very valuable.

As the white settlers advanced inland, due primarily to political strife between Dutch and English settlers, soon there were few wild birds left. With these events, ostrich farming had its advent and has literally been attempted in every continent which has a suitable climate (Weilbrenner).

As early as the 1770s, a Swedish traveller, a Dr. Sparrman, found that many farmers at the Cape kept a number of tame ostriches on their farms. The birds supplied their owners with plumes that were used in brooms and in fans to drive away the mosquitoes.

Hunting ostriches and selling ostrich eggs were prohibited by Governor Yonge during his term from 1799 to 1801. In the very early days of the industry, the first ostrich feathers were exported from the Cape Colony in 1826. Approximately 31,000 ostrich feathers were sold from 1827 through 1833 at the Cape Market.

The origin of ostrich farming in South Africa as anything other than a sideline, however, seems unclear. According to Mosenthal and Harting (1877) it would seem that the first hatching of eggs from domesticated ostriches occurred in the Beaufort and Oudtshoorn districts at about 1866. During a census taken in 1865 there were only 80 tame ostriches in the Cape Colony.

The profitability of the ostrich industry was aided in 1869 by the invention of a simple but effective incubator for ostrich eggs by Arthur Douglass, the pioneer ostrich farmer of Grahamstown. It was now possible to remove eggs from the nest and hatch the chicks under controlled conditions.

By 1870 auctions of feathers were launched on a regular basis at Mosselbay. A census taken in 1875 indicated the presence of a total of 32,247 tamed ostriches in the Cape Colony.

Although Oudtshoorn, in the Little Karoo region, was not the original leader of the ostrich industry, census figures of 2,519 ostriches in Oudtshoorn and 1,802 in George in 1875 showed that the ostrich industry was established in the Little Karoo.

When the farmers of Oudtshoorn discovered that lucerne (alfalfa) was an ideal fodder for ostriches, some of the first lucerne fields in South Africa were established there.

Due to a severe depression in Europe after 1873 and the fickleness of fashion, feather prices started to vary according to demand and sometimes overproduction.

The year 1878 was a high point for prices for ostrich feathers. 253,953 pounds of ostrich feathers were exported in 1882. Demand increased again in 1886, mainly due to the use of ostrich feathers at the opening of parliament by Queen Victoria, but by 1888 the value had dropped to one-fourth of 1882 prices.

In 1891 18 per cent of the ostriches in the Cape Colony were found in the Oudtshoorn district. It seemed that the ostrich industry in this area was firmly established.

From the earliest times in the development of the ostrich feather industry the procedures for harvesting the feathers received attention. The question was whether the feathers should be plucked or cut.

According to Douglass (1881) in the first days of the ostrich industry the feathers were plucked every six months. It was soon found that plucking before the feather was ripe caused successive growth to become shorter and the quill stiffer. Feathers of birds five or six years old were thus of little value. Since Douglass's time, cutting the feathers after six months growth has become a universal practice.

Douglass (1881) prescribed the following procedure for the removal of feathers: The quill feathers should be cut when the chick is seven months old as near the wing as possible without letting the stumps bleed; pull out two rows of the brown feathers above the quill; also two rows above and below the arm of the wing; do not remove the floss feathers; pull out the tail. Two months afterwards pull out the quill stumps. Feathers from the wings and tails were then sorted separately for males and females.

Despite a major slump from 1894 to 1899 the ostrich feather industry grew steadily. After the Anglo-Boer War (1899-1902), until 1914 the so-called second ostrich feather boom took place.

The industry was based solely on the feathers of the birds, and little if any value was reaped from the leather or meat.

During this time the district of Oudtshoorn experienced ultimate wealth. "Ostrich feather palaces" arose everywhere, as the town homes and ranch houses of wealthy ostrich farmers (Sales).

Many of them remain today, refurbished as a tribute to the success of the industry. Some became historical monuments. Others are homes of the affluent. The most famous are Pinehurst C. P. Nel Museum, and Welgeluk Homestead (Weilbrenner).

By 1910 there were 746,736 breeding birds in the Cape Colony, producing 741,078 pounds of feathers annually. In 1913 ostrich plumes ranked fourth on the list of South African exports after gold, diamonds and wool.

During this time scientific research was also conducted on ostriches. It was the task of Professor J.E. Duerden of the Department of Zoology at the University of Rhodes, Grahamstown, to investigate the problem of rale (small breakages) in ostrich feathers.

With the establishment of the Agriculture College at Grootfontein came an Ostrich Division, with Professor Duerden as researcher on aspects of feathers and breeding.

Even before 1890 it was realized by ostrich farmers that Cape feathers were not perfect (Sales). Competition from other areas became fierce to develop the bird with the finest feathers. The South Africans knew of the Barbary species of ostrich, which had a very high quality feather, fuller and closer with greater breadth of fluff at the lower part and lower crowns.

They believed that cross breeding with their own stock would produce a feather of extremely high quality. They were right. A joint venture was undertaken and an expedition was sent to north Africa to secure some of these scarce wild birds.

After a long and arduous journey, determination finally prevailed. The birds were transported from Timbuctoo to the Cape Colony (Weilbrenner).

In all, there were three expeditions, in 1886, 1888 and 1903. With effective selection, cross breeding, and culling a good-quality feather was obtained by 1910 (Sales).

The result of the cross breeding remains today in what is commonly called in the United States the South African Black. The Black was the only variety of ostrich ranched for commercial purposes in any numbers. So specific was the breeding of these birds that farmers named the type of feather produced after themselves. The most famous was the Evans feather, which became internationally renowned for density, gloss, curl, and strength.

The ability to successfully produce plumage of this quality established Oudtshoorn as the hub of the ostrich industry (Weilbrenner). At the beginning of the 20th century there was even an ostrich section registered at the South African Studbook. The best birds were from Evans, Barber and Riempie strains. Cross breeding was actively done between wild birds from Barbary and tamed Cape birds at Grootfontein.

And then, in 1914, with close to a million ostriches in South Africa, the feather industry collapsed overnight.

There were several reasons for this collapse. Certainly the worldwide socio-economic effects of World War I was one. Some fashion experts say that the advent of the motor car was another. With the speed of this machine ladies were no longer interested in the kind of wide hats they had worn with ease in the slower horse-drawn carriages.

There was also an anti-plume campaign abroad, due to the indiscriminate wholesale slaughter of egrets and other plume-bearing wild birds. Then there was the overproduction of plumes and disorganized marketing locally.

Ostrich numbers decreased to fewer than 400,000 in 1916 and only 23,528 in 1930. Ten shillings was the top price for an ostrich. Many farmers just let their ostriches out in the veldt where most of them died. Unfortunately it was also the end of promising and interesting breeding experiments at Grootfontein.

In 1924 there was a slight revival in the ostrich industry. The South African Ostrich Farmers Co-operative was established to regulate the market, stabilize prices and develop the industry.

TABLE 1. SALES OF THE KLEIN KAROO AGRICULTURE CO-OPERATIVE

MILLIONS OF 1995 US DOLLARS

Year	Hides	Meat	Feathers	Total
1989	18.7	4.4	3.2	26.3
1990	21.1	5.2	2.9	29.2
1991	28.8	6.8	4.8	40.4
1992	36.4	7.2	3.9	47.5
1993	39.7	8.6	3.9	52.2

The price of feathers, however, had slumped to a third of their boom-time value.

This price decreased even more during the years of the World Depression. Although there was a brief revival of demands for feather fashions and ostrich skin in the late 1930s, World War II intervened. This was also the end of the South African Ostrich Farmers Co-operative.

The modern ostrich industry dates back to 1945. The Klein Karoo Agriculture Co-operative (KKLK) was founded on May 25, 1945 by 120 farmers from the Little Karoo region.

The Queen of England, now the Queen Mother, visited South Africa in 1947, and favored ostrich feathers. In 1959 the KKLK gained control over all ostrich products.

The industry no longer relies on fashion. The world's first ostrich abattoir was erected by KKLK in 1963/64 at Oudtshoorn, mainly for the production of biltong (dried meat) and fresh meat for local consumption.

The marketing of leather processed from ostrich skin started in 1969/70 when a leather tannery was built near the abattoir. This tannery was expanded in 1974 to double its original capacity.

A new abattoir was built in 1980/81 due to the overseas demand for ostrich meat. The tannery and abattoir both were expanded again in 1989 because of the popularity for both leather and meat.

The *single channel* cooperative marketing system of the KKLK definitely organized and promoted ostrich product sales in the best interest of the producers and protected the South African industry. See Table 1 for sales figures for the five years thru 1993 (Sales).

The co-op set up regular auctions of the feathers, and stringently controlled sales and production through selection and by construction of its own processing plants.

Klein Karoo is very tightly held, and is sometimes compared to the DeBeers diamond cartel in steadfastly protecting their product from outside influence by monopolizing their industry.

The market for ostrich products continued to expand tremendously as the market tried to keep pace. Americans began to recognize the great potential for supplying low-fat, low-cholesterol red meat to replace beef in large quantities at reasonable prices. Americans came into the ostrich picture in the mid-1980s.

The South Africans, recognizing the potential threat of the American ostrich grower, had years earlier pre-empted much potential exportation of the Oudtshoorn commercial ostrich by tightening export laws.

The powerful KKLK forced through legislation eliminating the export of eggs and chicks capable of reproduction. With the monopoly tightened, the movement of the domestic ostrich was curtailed and remained centralized in the Oudtshoorn.

Man is indeed ingenious when told he is not allowed to do something. Someone will find a way. The breed slowly spread across the Little Karoo and into Namibia, and later into Botswana and Zimbabwe.

Settlers emigrating away from political strife in South Africa in

A clutch of unhatched eggs in an ostrich nest in Tanzania. Note the shell fragments and dirty eggs. (Photo courtesy Dr. Brett Hopkins)

the 70s covertly brought some very high quality eggs into Israel. The Israelis named their ostrich *African Black,* coining the name prevalent today in all but South Africa (Weilbrenner).

After severe droughts that led to crop failures at the beginning of the 1990s, more and more farmers outside the Little Karoo region started ostrich farming. These farmers began to object to the restrictive regulation of the South African ostrich industry through legislation sponsored by Klein Karoo.

A major sore spot was KKLK's abattoir, the only one licensed to slaughter ostriches. Due to the difficulty of transporting ostriches over long distances, the industry was effectively limited to an area of about a 100-kilometer (62 miles) radius around Oudtshoorn.

Another problem was marketing. Only buyers selected by the KKLK had the right to buy skins at prices determined by the co-op. Other potential buyers found it difficult, if not impossible, to obtain ostrich skins.

Prohibiting the export of breeding stock and eggs to protect the industry from potential competitors abroad did not succeed. In 1991 there were enough breeding birds outside South Africa to develop long-term industries in other countries.

All of these problems led to the lifting of the single channel marketing scheme by the KKLK on October 26, 1993. This meant that ostrich and ostrich products could be marketed freely in South Africa. Ostrich producers would be able to make their own marketing strategies. The embargo and control measures on the export of ostrich breeding material, however, would be retained.

At this time a National Ostrich Breeders Association was also founded. It included breeders from Little Karoo, Eastern Cape and Transvaal. Since then, abattoirs and tanneries have been established at Magaliesburg in the Transvaal and at Graaff-Reinet, Grahamstown and Uitenhage in the Eastern Cape (Sales).

The modern ostrich industry in America began basically in the mid-1980s, and today the market remains in the breeder mode. Prices are still generally above slaughter prices.

But just as the first Herefords were very expensive, as the breed became numerous enough for a slaughter market to be initiated, so will the price of ostriches and ostrich products inevitably come down (Weilbrenner).

*- James D. Sales, Ph. D.
University of Stellenbosch
Stellenbosch , South Africa*

*- Andy Weilbrenner
Southwind Ostrich Ranch, Inc.
Mount Vernon, Indiana*

OSTRICHES IN AMERICA

We found this unsigned article in Live Animal Trade & Transport Magazine, *June 1993.*

There are conflicting claims as to the first ostrich farmer in America, but the most authoritative source we found was the *Report of the Commissioner of Agriculture - 1888* in a chapter entitled "Ostrich Farming in America" by T. C. Duncan, Ph. D.

He reported the Commissioner of Agriculture had tried to create interest in ostriches for a number of years. America at that time was using half the world production of feathers. He reasoned that since the U. S. had successfully introduced seeds such as Kaffir corn, why not introduce ostriches.

In 1881 and 1882, the American consuls in Algeria, Cape Town and Buenos Aires collected a mass of facts on ostrich production.

In 1882, a Dr. Charles J. Sketchly, who had been one of the largest ostrich farmers in Africa before the Boer Wars, started from Capetown with 200 carefully selected ostriches. They traveled to Buenos Aires, then to New York by ship, arriving in December. He then shipped them by rail overland via Chicago and Omaha to California. After this arduous journey, 22 arrived in Anaheim in fair condition. The California Ostrich Company was formed with Dr. Sketchly as superintendent.

The birds were placed on a 600-acre farm and confined with 3' x 12' plank fences four feet high since ordinary fences would not hold them.

From April 12 to October, the hens produced 270 eggs and the first chick was hatched July 28, 1883. The second year Dr. Sketchly reared 58 young. He felt the number of eggs was low and that the reproductive powers of the birds were impaired by the difficult trip.

In another effort, the American Ostrich Company was formed in Maine with a Mr. E. J. Johnson as manager. He went to Africa and spent a year studying ostrich husbandry. He started with 23 birds and landed at New Orleans in December, 1884, after a voyage of 53 days with no losses . . . even for today. After several offers to locate in the South, he shipped the birds to San Diego via the Southern Pacific Railway, and located in the Valley of San Luis Rey.

This farm was described by a writer later: "Eight miles from Fall Brook is a bit of Africa dropped down between the hills. . . .The birds seem to take kindly to their adopted home. There are about 40 on the ranch . . . The old birds are placed in pairs in their several pens, and the young are allowed to wander over the grounds. One pair have a nest hallowed [sic] out in the ground, and are patiently sitting on a dozen eggs, the male bird taking charge nineteen hours out of the twenty-four."

Thomas Cockburn, a Scot, formed a partnership around 1880 with Edwin Cawston. Duncan reported on the origin of this enterprise: "In July, 1986, parties leased

Washington Gardens, Los Angeles, and Mr. Cawston started at once to Africa and selected a troop of 44 birds. He brought them in a sailing vessel, via St. Helena and Barbadoes, to Galveston. He shipped them via Southern Pacific Railroad, reaching his destination with about 40 fine birds.

"Mr. Cawston says in a letter to the writer (Duncan) that he lost 25 per cent, but was favored with particularly good weather. A friend of his who imported a troop lost abut 50 per cent. These birds do not seem to bear the confinement of shipboard. There is no direct line of steam-ships from this country to South Africa, consequently all importations have come in sailing vessels via South America, and thence to New York, New Orleans, or some Gulf port."

Cockburn later moved to San Antonio, Texas where he established a 300-bird farm. In 1903, he moved his birds to his Hot Springs Ostrich Farm in Arkansas. The facility became a great showplace and visitors flocked to see the great birds. All these operations would be classed as show farms with great attention to the tourist side of the trade.

. . . At that time, everything looked rosy for ostrich farmers. The Report of the Commerce and Navigation for 1908 (Bureau of Statistics) showed that $3,568,152 worth of feathers were imported into the U. S. that year. Tariff on raw feathers was 20% and 60% on dyed or prepared feathers.

In a 1911 USDA Bulletin, A. R. Lee commented on the economics of ostrich growing in the United States:

"The profit to be derived from the business will depend on the management, on the success secured in the raising of the young birds, and on the production of feathers of good quality. The average yearly yield of feathers from an ostrich is 1¼ pounds. Birds produce from 12 to 20 ounces at each plucking, with an average of 16 ounces. The weight of an average yield divided about as follows: wings, 48 per cent; short stuff, 25 per cent; and tails 27 per cent.

"The amount received from the feathers of each bird varies from $20 to $30, depending on their yield and the price of the product. The average return during the year 1909 was $25.93 per bird.

"While both ostrich eggs and flesh may be used for human consumption, the amount to be derived from these products is hardly worth considering.

"As each pair of breeding birds is worth about $800, and chicks 6 months old are valued at $100, any deaths from accidents or any inability to raise chicks greatly lessen the profit to be derived from the business. Allowing for some loss in these ways, and charging a fair interest on the investment, the business can be operated at a profit."

All of this changed with the advent of WWI, and references to ostrich production disappeared. By 1920 only 231 birds remained in the US.

However, in the mid-1980s demand for ostrich leather developed and with the United States ban on South African trade, prices soared. Businessmen again began to consider the ostrich as a profitable venture.

AMERICAN OSTRICH ASSOCIATION (AOA)

The AOA was co-founded, after an inaugural meeting in Kerrville, Texas on March 15, 1988, by Tom Mantzel and Jerry Henderson. The Articles of Incorporation were filed on July 29.

The first officers, elected in the fall of 1988, were President, Kevin Owen, DVM; Vice President, Pat Sutton; and Jerry Henderson, Secretary/Treasurer. The first board members were Tom Mantzel (Executive Director), Cooper Hamilton, C. C. Killian, Bill Haney, Jim Terrell, and Albert Durham.

The first directory was printed in November 1989, and listed 503 members. Membership at December 31, 1994 is 3750.

The objectives of AOA "are to foster exchange of information among ostrich breeders and others interested in the birds and in ostrich products, and to encourage development of a sound basis for the ostrich industry."

To that end, AOA has been active in sponsoring legislation or regulations such as:

On October 28, 1994, USDA announced ostrich inspection guidelines. As of March 1, 1995, 17 packing plants had received USDA approval.

AOA routinely monitors egg and chick imports, and lobbies for regulations that assure the continued health of the domestic ostrich flock.

On January 18, 1995, the General Conference Committee of the National Poultry Improvement Plan voted to include ostriches. This program was designed to improve breeding and production qualities of poultry.

Today, 95% of US poultry breeders and hatcheries participate in the NPIP. The ostrich industry must now develop regulations and contract with state agencies and other organizations for enforcement.

AOA has participated in discussions with the USDA regarding the use of nutrient composition data from AOA-sponsored research projects.

AOA has approached the Census Bureau about capturing ostrich data in the Agriculture Census to be conducted in 1997.

AOA has sponsored research projects at research laboratories and universities around the country on meat, nutritional requirements, egg storage and incubation procedures, reproductive endocrinology, disease pathogens, skeletal growth, maternal antibodies in eggs and hatchlings, and others.

INTERESTING FACTS & TALES

. . . An ostrich produces about 1.25 pounds of plumes every year, and about 2 - 4 pounds of feathers when slaughtered.
- Duewer, Madison & Christensen, 1994

Editor's note: In an 1897 book, C. A. Cronwright Schreiner describes some of his experiences in nine years of ostrich farming in the Karoo region of South Africa.

One striking point of interest is Schreiner's term for a breeding male: vicious cock. The two words are repeated endlessly, and one must wonder if the book reflected current attitudes—or contributed to attitudes about ostriches over the years.

It's also curious that Schreiner devoted several pages to defending the morals of ostriches. He makes it clear that in his experience, ostrich males are strictly monogamous, and if the cock strays, it's an interloper hen that is at fault!

Ostriches have been known to have swallowed oranges, small tortoises, fowl and turkey chickens, kittens, tennis balls, fencing wire, brass cartridges, soda pop bottles, and money.

I was on one occasion, struck by the remarkable behavior of a setting hen on a terrible hot still day. I found her sitting, with raised body, over the nest; that is, she had her feet and torso along the ground among the eggs as usual, but her body did not rest upon them; she had raised it above them and was sitting on her "knees" (like a rolling cock) and a free current of air passed between her body and the eggs; her wings were held a little away from the body and slightly drooped, the feathers over the whole body being on end, admitting the air to every part; her neck and head were raised up in the manner of a non-sitting bird, and she was panting with beak slightly open.

This attitude is not uncommon among ostriches in very hot weather: they can remain in it for a considerable time; but I have not seen it assumed by a sitting bird on the nest on any other occasion.

One result of the hen assuming this attitude was that all the eggs were completely in the shadow cast by her body and wings; but although this was one of its effects, I should think she assumed it to cool herself because she was so intolerably hot in the scorching sun on the baking ground in the still air; but the incident is remarkable (apart from the question of whether there was any deliberate intention of cooling the eggs, which I doubt) as indicating the importance she attached to the nest being covered and protected while she was responsible.
- Schreiner, 1897

It was noted that the birds seldom entered enclosed barns, even in the worst of climates, but would utilize wind breaks effectively. Many of the early birds were quite wild and reluctant to enter a closed shelter. Their natural mode of protection is sight, thus enclosures which blocked their wide-angle view of an already alien environment were avoided.
- Peters, 1993

Ostriches sleep with their necks upright most of the night, however if they do extend their necks to the ground it is only one to four times a night and never longer than 16 minutes at a time. Only then is the ostrich in really deep sleep; it can be photographed with a flash and one can knock on the floor or speak loudly without waking it up.

The birds also like to stretch their legs, which have been in a sitting posture under their bodies, out behind themselves.

Ostriches live between 30 and 70 years.

Ostriches will wake up a dozen times a night to defecate and urinate.

The typical ostrich shell is thick as china; it sometimes takes a saw and hammer to open it.

Ostriches can run fifty kilometers per hour for a quarter to almost half a hour without obvious signs of exhaustion.
- Grzimek, 1972

One would think that by 1968 writers would have stopped attributing human qualities to birds, but in Ostrich Country, Fay Goldie attributes problem-solving intelligence to the ostrich. Her explanation for finding them in among herds of grazing animals is that:

". . . the ostrich is conscious of its often fatal tendency to run in wide circles, and consequently looks to its companions to keep it on the straight and safe way when a common danger threatens."
- Goldie, 1968

Cautious creatures, ostriches avoid forested areas and keep to open country where their long necks and excellent vision enable them to detect distant danger.

As a result, zebras and various species of antelope frequently associate with these birds, which act as "watchdogs" for the animals. The ostriches also benefit—they dine on the insects, reptiles, and rodents flushed by the hoofs of the grazing zebra and antelope.
- Lavine, 1981

. . . Each ostrich may provide 12 - 16 square feet of hide, selling for $400 - $600 in the US after processing. At least one industry source estimates that as more ostrich hides become available, prices in the US may drop.
- Duewer, Madison & Christensen, 1994

The Search for the Perfect Feather

Several times in the history of ostrich farming in South Africa, expeditions were launched to search for wild ostriches to cross-breed with domestic stock to improve the quality of the feathers.

Goldie relates the following story as a search for the perfect feather. (In her story, the search was in the southwest Sudan, which seems unlikely, given the location of Timbuctoo in the southwest Sahara.)

In order for South Africa to remain the first in feather sales, a search was launched in 1911 to locate a superior feather.

After a parcel of feathers arrived from Tripoli in which one perfect feather was found, the British Consul in Tripoli was asked to trace from which part of the country the feather originated. The answer was vague: Somewhere probably in the southwest Sahara.

Four men set out for the Sahara in strictest secrecy, for an American expedition was set on the same objective.

They traveled 500 miles up the Niger river to the native village of Baro where they recruited 80 carriers to transport their supplies on the 70-mile foot trek to Kano, the central feather market for the whole of the southwest Sahara.

The search went on until they bought a small, perfect white feather in a market place. It had come in a parcel from north of Timbuktu, not only in the middle of the Saraha, but deep in French territory. A permit was required from the French so the party set out on horseback across the desert to Fort Zinder to apply for it.

The French Government refused to give them a permit. If they were caught hunting wild ostriches without one they could be thrown in prison or even killed.

But now their secret was out. Their American rivals were moving closer. On the positive side, the Americans still did not know that the South Africans had reliable information as to the location of the ostriches they sought. The South African team bought up all kinds of feathers to confuse the issue, and the Americans had no choice but to buy the same feathers.

The South Africans were offered an opportunity to join a large party of Arab hunters. Mounted on camels they headed into the desert to capture these wonderful feather producers. This was fraught with danger. Not only must they evade the French Legionnaires but also the savage, pitiless, Taureg Arabs.

Capturing the ostriches was one thing but transporting them quite another. The transport officer devised a four-sided cage of light palm cane with no tops or bottoms. The ostriches were herded into the cages, and four Arab bearers would pick up the poles and start to walk. The ostriches in the cage had no choice except to walk also.

Birds were transported safely for over 100 miles to the headquarters at Kano. Spies were everywhere and plans had to constantly be changed in order to evade the French Legionnaires.

Finally 150 priceless birds were transported by train and arrived at Cape Town to a wildly enthusiastic welcome. The birds were taken to Grootfontein Agricultural College to be cross-bred with South African birds.

- Goldie, 1968

Interesting Trivia:

The Roman Emperor Heliogabalus [204-222 AD] had the brains of six hundred ostriches served up in one dish at a feast.

On her statue on Helicon, the Egyptian queen Arsinoe, who lived some time before Cleopatra, is shown riding an ostrich and miraculously contriving to look regal and comfortable, and not at all ridiculous, in the saddle.

Apparently she wasn't the only one. "Moore recorded in *Travels into the Inland Parts of Africa (1738)*, having seen 'an Englishman at Joar travelling long distances on a bridled ostrich.'"

The ostrich feather has barbs of equal length on either side of the central quill. Because of this the ostrich feather was regarded by the ancient Egyptians as a symbol of justice.

Ostriches are mentioned in the pages of the Bible and the earliest recorded stories of man.

Hundreds of years B.C., Pliny and other ancient writers described warriors sporting ostrich plumes in their helmets.

Dancing is a love shared by all ostriches, adults and chicks. It is an essential part of their nature. They whirl about in one direction like waltzing in ecstasy. The mating dance is done in measured steps with grace, beauty and dignity. Waltzing flocks of ostrich in full plumage is a sight to behold.

A Bushman on trek will carry a dozen or more ostrich eggshells, filled with water, in a net bag slung on his back.

Ostrich eggs shells filled with water and sealed with beeswax are carefully buried underground for use during the periods of prolonged drought in the Kalahari.

In South Africa farmers employed native women to act in relays as ostrich foster-mothers. Wearing the voluminous, colorful skirts of those days the women would squat on nests of eggs. Immobile, they would chatter among themselves until their patience would eventually be rewarded by the queer-looking chicks that hatched out under them.

- Goldie, 1968

South Africa has prohibited the export of ostriches or ostrich eggs since 1959. And while the US has allowed the import of ratites since 1990, quarantines are required. Although eggs can also be imported from approved overseas farms, hatchability has been low.

. . . South Africa exported a record 1 million pounds of feathers in 1913-14, from about 1 million birds on 1,300 farms. There were an additional 20,000 birds in the Northern Hemisphere.
Duewer, Madison & Christensen, 1994

Ostriches don't stick their heads in the sand, they lay their necks very close to the ground for camouflage.

A single pair of tame ostriches in 1913 was worth $1000.
- Wallace, 1963

An ostrich egg weighs about as much as 25 to 30 chicken eggs.

An ostrich can be as tall as 9'.

The Kalahari bushman of today makes beautiful jewelry from ostrich shells.

The male ostrich is father in no uncertain terms. He builds the nest, he guards the nest before and after the eggs are laid. The male sits on the nest at night to hatch the eggs.

If it were not for the ostrich farmers, the ostrich would have disappeared altogether. Otherwise like other wild animals with valuable fur, feathers, skins, etc., they would have been hunted and possibly exterminated.
- Grzimek, 1972

It takes approximately one hour to boil an ostrich egg.

In Africa ostrich pets follow children around like dogs do.

Ostriches like to play in water.

Ostriches run faster than most antelopes.
- Martin, 1987

The ostrich was introduced to Australia in the nineteenth century because of the value of the feathers. After the collapse of the feather market they were turned to the wild where there is now only a small feral population.
- Marchant & Higgins, 1990

The social life of ostriches is one of the most complex in the animal world. In drought periods, when wandering, and in the common grazing grounds at watering places, they often form peaceful aggregations of up to 680 birds. However, the individual flocks remain recognizable. To make social contact, between birds of different groups, they approach the other in a submissive posture, with lowered head and tail down. The chicks or young of one herd will often be adopted by a family of another herd. Single cocks may form schools of half-grown ostriches, with whom they wander about for days or weeks. For the communal sand bath each flock seeks out its own sandy depression.
- Grzimek, 1972

The cry of the ostrich is very correctly described as a *boom*. The word in use among all ostrich farmers at the Cape is the Dutch verb *brom*; in English, an ostrich broms or is bromming
- Schreiner, 1897

Commercial Uses
Aside from their fashion appeal, feathers are currently used in the electronics manufacturing industry, since they are static free.
- Duewer, Madison & Christensen, 1994

The largest purchaser for ostrich feathers at the present time are producers of feather dusters. According to two manufacturers of feather dusters in the US, the demand is larger than the supply.

There is a company in the US that manufactures for the automotive industry a machine which uses ostrich feathers to clean and dust the outsides of automobile bodies before the paint is applied.
- C. E.

EMUS

THE EARLY RECORD

The following is from Greenway, 1967. The year should be remembered in reading some of the statements.

Emus (*Dromaius novahollandiae*) are still to be found throughout most of their range, the semiarid regions of Australia excluding the deserts. They are much reduced in numbers, and the subspecies that once lived on Tasmania and Kangaroo and King Islands of Bass Strait are extinct.

These large flightless "ostriches of Australia" appear to be ill fitted for adaptation to human beings [in the wild]. The birds were removed from the protected list in parts of Western Australia because of their inroads on the wheat crops as long ago as 1923. At that time a bounty was paid in certain districts.

So great was the outcry against the birds in 1932 that soldiers were sent against them armed with machine guns. Although this adventure met with no great success the bounties have continued; as much as 4 shillings a beak plus sixpence for an egg was being paid in 1948 by local "vermin boards." The great rabbit fences stretching from north to south are a hindrance, and many birds are found dead on the desert side of them.

It seems unlikely that the emus can survive once men have actually declared war on them. We may hope that sanctuaries will be adequate (See Serventy and Whittell, 1951).

The Tasmanian birds (*Dromaius novahollandiae diemenensis*) became extinct in the early part of the 19th century. The exact date cannot be determined because of the introduction of *novahollandiae* from Australia.

Two specimens upon which the subspecies is based were presented to the British Museum in 1938, and there is a third in the museum at Frankfurt, Germany. These lack the black feathers on the fore neck of *novaehollandiae*.

Bones have been found (H. H. Scott, 1924, 1932) but they do not reveal any size difference between this form and its mainland relative.

Dromaeius n. minor of King Island, between Tasmania and Australia in Bass Strait, is known only by bones found in post-Pliocene sand dunes. Most of these are smaller than those of other forms, but there is more individual variation than was at first suspected. Perhaps it is not a recognizable subspecies.

However that may be, the birds of that island are gone . . . There is no explanation for the disappearance of this species. Although men made their way to the islands in Bass Strait in late Pleistocene, there is no reason to believe that these few negritos killed all the birds. It is possible that fires started by men or by lightning on so small an island may have been responsible.

Forest fires were probably the cause of the extirpation of the Kangaroo Island birds (*D. n. diemenianus*), in the opinion of the Australian naturalists Morgan and Sutton (1928). The island was discovered in 1802 by Flinders, who saw many. Except for a few seal hunters, there were no inhabitants until 1836, when a few settlers arrived from England. The birds were gone by that time.

It is unlikely that a few men could have extirpated the entire population from an island 90 miles long by 35 miles wide, even though they depended on the country for food, according to those authorities.

Only one specimen is known, and that is in Paris. François Péron and other naturalists of the naval expedition captured three birds on Kangaroo (Decrés) Island in 1803 and brought them alive to Paris, where they lived for a time.

The skin in the Muséum National, Paris, is one of these. It is the type of *D. ater Vieillot* (see Berlioz, 1929, 1935). It is darker and smaller than the other subspecies. Skeletal material is in Paris, Florence, and Adelaide, South Australia.

These allied forms have been described from bones found in post-Pliocene beds in Queensland and New South Wales. In the opinion of De Vis, one form (*patricius*) had shorter, stouter legs than the living birds and the coracoid is said to differ.

A second (*graciliceps*) had longer and more slender legs. A third species (*Dromaius queenslandiae*) is known only by a fragment, but so large that De Vis identified it as a moa (*Dinornis*). Hutton (1894) pointed out that this resembles both the emu and a larger species, *Dromornis australis* Owen, which also inhabited Queensland in post-Pliocene. Recently (C. Anderson, 1937) a sternum had been found in Wellington Caves, Queensland, but no other such bone had been identified as a member of the genus, and apparently no other bird bones were found with it. It was a larger bird than *novahollandiae*.

Because of the considerable individual variation in the size of the leg bones of the living emus, it seems probable that there were three species in Pleistocene times (F. S. Colliver, in Morrison, 1942): *D. patricius*, the possible ancestor of the living *novahollandiae*; *Dromornis australis* Owen, 1872; and *Genyornis newtoni* Sterling and Zeitz, 1894.

Both of the latter were large, robust species, and it is likely that because of their relatively large heads their feeding habits were specialized. Any change in their environment would jeopardize their existence. Undoubtedly men were present at that time, but it is doubtful that they contributed to the extinction of the species.

BEGINNINGS IN AUSTRALIA

The following is from a report to the Western Australia Department of Agriculture.

Interest in emu farming was first stimulated by two Swiss families who established a farm at Kalannie in 1970.

Despite problems with nutrition of the birds, incubation of the eggs, and the removal of fat from the skins, some progress was made and prospects for commercial leather production were identified. The farm never built up sufficient numbers of birds to approach commercial production and closed in 1973.

In 1976, Applied Ecology, a company established by the Commonwealth Government to promote enterprises for Aboriginal communities, established an emu farm on the site of the old Western Australia Department of Agriculture Research Station at Wiluna.

The farm faced the difficulties of a remote location and was often short of equipment, food, spare parts and trained staff. Despite this, useful work was carried out by a number of workers and stock numbers increased.

The farm was handed over to the Ngangganawili Aboriginal Community in 1981 and by 1986 they were raising some 600 emu chicks a year.

At this time a private enterprise group, Dromaius Pty Ltd, was authorised to capture 500 chicks from the wild to establish a second experimental farm.

In 1987 emu farming was recognized as being technically feasible in a report prepared by the Department of Agriculture under its New Export Initiatives Programme established by the Minister for Agriculture in 1986.

An interdepartmental Committee was formed and commercial emu farming became possible when the Government approved the sale of 500 chicks reared by the Ngangganawili Community in August 1987.

A similar auction was held in 1988 and some 1500 chicks were sold from commercial farms.

A major condition for the granting of approval to farm emus was that only captive or farm reared stock was permitted to be farmed.

This was necessary to comply with the International Convention for the Trade in Endangered Species, CITES, or more specifically Australian Commonwealth legislation, the Regulation of Exports and Imports Act which requires all products from native animals to come from animals bred in captivity unless it has been taken under an Approved Mangement Programme.

Emu numbers throughout Australia are relatively low and estimated to be only 400,000 nationally, with the WA population being somewhere between 100,000 and 200,000.

- O'Malley, 1990

AMERICAN EMU ASSOCIATION

The American Emu Association (AEA) was founded in 1989 in Brenham, Texas, with fifty members, and has grown to 6500 members. The first board meeting was held in Whitney, Texas, on June 24, and was attended by Al Jodoin, Sally Weiner, Joe Gordy, Janice Castleberry, Jerry Hopkins, Jody Lewis, Philip Minnaar, James McDonald, Andre Lombard, and Stan Weiner.

The first annual convention was held in Austin, Texas, in May of 1990. The first issue of *AEA News*, the association's magazine, was published in January 1991.

The AEA has supported state legislation when requested by state affiliate chapters. In Texas, AEA supported the Theft Astray Bill, affording emus the same protection as other livestock.

AEA also worked with the Texas Emu Association in calling for health certification and identification with the Texas Animal Health Commission, principles which were adopted by the Animal Plant Health Commission Service for importation purposes on a national level.

Research studies have included fatty acid analysis of emu oil, a census of US farmed emus, a membership survey, chemical restraint techniques, blood reference values, anesthesia for emus, moisturizing and cosmetic properties of emu oil, anti-inflammatory properties of emu oil in treatment of burn wounds, and passive immunity in emus following vaccination for equine encephalitis.

A major success for the industry was announced in October, 1995, when the USDA approved voluntary inspections to plants that slaughter emus.

Future goals of the AEA include development of the world emu market, using the American emu as the standard of the world, and working in cooperative efforts with emu associations in other countries and other ratite organizations to establish the ratite family as an accepted food and multipurpose species.

INTERESTING FACTS & TALES

In 1801, three live emus reached England on the Buffalo. Lieutenant Kent, who had charge of the birds, wrote to Sir Joseph Banks from Portsmouth, saying, "I have pleasure in informing you that the emus were safely landed . . . and set off immediately for town [London]. We had much trouble with the Custom-house people."

- Hindwood, 1966

Although the vast numbers of migrating emu ate untold millions of beetles, caterpillars, and grasshoppers, as well as consuming tons of the burrs that catch on sheep's wool during their cross-country treks, cattlemen, farmers, and sheepmen did not consider them as allies. The birds competed with cattle and sheep for grass, drank at the watering tanks built for stock in arid regions, broke fences, and caused tremendous economic loss to those who raised wheat in Western Australia.

In the 1930s the government placed a fifty-cent bounty on the emu. Thousands of the birds were slaughtered. But still they flourished. Finally, in 1932, the authorities declared all-out war on the birds. They ordered a company of the Royal Australian Artillery—equipped with two machine guns and ten thousand shells—into the field to decimate the emus.

The plan was to drive them along fences until they were within range—a tactic that had proven successful in the state of New South Wales. But the operation in Western Australia was a military disaster. Only twelve birds were killed. Not only did the emus outwit the soldiers by breaking up into small bands, but also the machine guns jammed at the one time great numbers were within point-blank range.

Because of these mishaps, the offensive, known to Australians as the "Great Emu War," came to a sudden end. Some thirty years later, the government of Western Australia was still paying a bounty on emus. Eventually it was decided not to attempt to exterminate them but rather to confine them to the northern part of the state. To limit the movement of the emus and to protect the wheatlands and sheep farms in the southwest from an invasion, an emu-proof fence some five hundred miles long was erected and wardens were assigned to patrol it.

Meanwhile, ranchers and farmers continued to shoot and poison emus and to smash their eggs. This, plus the inroads of civilization, drastically reduced the size of the herds. Fearful that the emu might become extinct, the Australian government established sanctuaries where the birds could breed unmolested.

Because the emu thrives in these sanctuaries and also readily breeds in captivity, there is little danger of its becoming an endangered species at the present time, even though the birds are still treated as pests on their natural range.

- *Lavine, 1981*

The loose, filamentary plumage of the emu is composed of "double" feathers formed by the extension of the aftershaft, which is almost as long as the main feather. When running the emu presents a slightly comical appearance because its dense but loose feathering sways from side to side, like a bustle.

The rather ungainly emu figured prominently in the lives of the aboriginal population, primarily because it was good to eat. As part of their culture, the Aborigines chipped the outlines of this bird on rock-faces and drew it on walls of caves and shelters, or on bark. Its actions were mimed in their dances and it was the totem bird of some tribes. Today, without thought of the past, we carry on the tradition by using the image of the emu on coins, stamps, emblems and crests, and even as a trademark.

Apart from grasses and other herbage, which are staple foods, the birds eat native fruits, berries, and insects, including large numbers of grasshoppers. The stomach of one bird examined contained about 3,000 injurious caterpillars each about two inches in length. In general, emus are practically omnivorous—they can and do swallow almost anything at all edible.

- *Hindwood, 1966*

Incubation is by the males alone, which do not normally eat, drink, defecate or leave the nest during a period of about 55 days.

Only the male broods and guards up to one month; the male calls to the chicks as soon as they are active beneath him.

Males do not allow broods to mix until chicks are at half-grown immature stage.

Longest recorded movement by banded emu 324 miles ; travels at up to 8.1 miles per day.
- *Marchant & Higgins, 1990*

Early emu farming in Australia: "to give you an idea of how sensitive things were . . . a wildlife inspector once drove approximately 500 miles to ask me to explain why he'd found oats in wild emu droppings outside our pens."
- *Venn, 1994*

RHEAS

HISTORY OF THE RHEA

The article below was graciously contributed by Daniel V. Sarasqueta, of INTA, Bariloche, Argentina.

The Ñandúes (family Rheidae) have been considered by man as an animal to be hunted since the earliest pre-Hispanic times until the present. In recent times, the frequency and intensity of the hunt have diminished, but the motives remain.

Men chose ñandúes as birds to be captured or hunted in the total area of their distribution. They were hunted for the meat and fat, the eggs were gathered, and the feathers and skin were used to fabricate products. The degree of dietary importance varied among different Indian tribes.

People in subtropical and temperate areas (for example, Mocovies, Tobas, Abipones) had a diversity of game to select from, much greater than people in the south.

The Tehuelches, for example, who lived in the Patagonian region, based their diet almost exclusively on the hunting of two species: Ñandú petiso or choique (Darwin's rhea) and guanaco (Lama guanicoe).

Their meat was considered to be the most nutritious and tasty of all known animals. Consumption of choique gordo (fat adult rhea) was one of the favorite foods.

One means of cooking the ñandú was to place hot rocks in its interior. For this purpose the bird was eviscerated, bones of legs and lower spine were extracted, and hot rocks were placed inside. The bird was tied up as a sack with the skin and leg tendons, and then placed on hot coals until well cooked.

The meat was also broiled in sections, or dried in the sun and then covered with salt for preservation. The heart and gizzard were eaten, and the blood was mixed with salt. The spine, with

A rhea at INTA, Bariloche, Argentina. (Photo courtesy Daniel V. Saresqueta)

much fat, was reserved for women and children. The fat was highly prized, providing an important supplement to a diet based on lean meats. Fat from the breast and spine was refined and stored in skin bags, to be used later to be rubbed into lean meats, such as the guanaco, for roasting.

Eggs of the ñandú were cooked on coals. The eggs were placed in coals with an opening at one end into which salt was added. The interior yolk was stirred with a stick until well-cooked. Eggs containing embryos (charitos) were also consumed.

The skins were used to make bags to transport processed fats. Skin from the neck was removed in tube form and sewed at the bottom for transport of salt or tobacco (tabaqueras) that were decorated with colors and paintings.

Feathers were used as body ornaments for religious ceremonies or as filling for leather balls used in traditional games. Capes were made with skin and feathers, or with the skins of charitos.

Tendons of the choique were braided and used to make the cords of boleadoras. These consisted of two round rocks wrapped in skin and joined by a thin flexible cord of 1.8 to 2 meters in length.

Boleadoras for hunting ñandú were made with two balls, and for hunting guanaco three balls were used. The tendons were also used to secure capes worn as hunting decoys.

Fat and bone marrow were used for cooking and for preparing a cream mixed with paint to decorate the face and to protect from wind and sun. Aruacanos Indians used the fat to cure muscular and joint pains.

In northwest Argentina, bones of the ñandú were used to make musical instruments.

The interior coating of the gizzard was dried and ground to a crystalline appearance, and taken internally to cure gastro-intestinal disturbances such as indigestion.

Many of these customs have persevered to the present in rural populations, such as consumption of roast or cooked meat of flank (picana) and wings, or consumption of the eggs.

It is worth noting that during pre-Hispanic times the Diaquitas and Comechigones kept ñandúes in captivity.

Hunting guanacos and rheas. Note the men on horseback closing in from all sides. (Etching courtesy Daniel V. Sarasqueta, provenance unknown)

Methods of Hunting

The method of hunting ñandúes has varied with time, according to the availability of horses or firearms, bows and arrows or boleadoras, or if hunted by lone hunters or a collective hunt.

Solitary hunters used disguises of skin and feathers or branches and approached the animals until close to arrow range. They were also taken in swamps, in traps, or were tracked by dogs.

The collective hunt much utilized by the Tehuelches Indians of Patagonia was based on encircling. This method was utilized on foot or on horseback to hunt either ñandúes (choiques) or guanacos.

Game was circled while they were feeding, and the circle was tightened until the attack order was given. Then the Indians on horseback hunted with great efficiency. Many times this method served to hunt ñandúes, guanacos, and pumas at the same time.

In winter the Tehuelches herded choiques into rivers where cold water numbed their legs and they were captured as the current pushed them to shore.

The most-used weapon was the boleadora of two balls (ñanducera), that was thrown at the neck of the animal, choking it.

From the beginning of the nineteenth century until the start of the present century, capture of ñandúes on ranches was directed to extraction of feathers.

They were herded on horseback toward a wired corner and driven into nets where they were captured and defeathered. Some were killed for food and sale of the skin.

These practices have continued sporadically with time, depending on the price paid per kilo of feathers.

There no longer exist the large flocks as in the past century, but they continue to be hunted as a source of food, sport hunting (illegal), for commercial purposes with rifle (illegal), or to illegally sell the feathers, skin, and feet. The skin is utilized for leather goods for making purses, shoes, ropes and wallets. Feathers are sold to make dusters or for artistic purposes (vedettes, costume disguises for the carnival in Brazil, etc.) The feet are used by artisans to make knife handles.

During the years 1976-1984 there were exported from Argentina 204,222 Nandú skins without determination of species, and 7,745 kilos of unworked feathers. All of this was the product of hunting wild animals.

Actually, export of wild animals from Argentina is prohibited. It would facilitate the export of these animals and their products if they were provided from a legally-established commercial farm.

The common ñandú (American rhea) in international legislation, is listed in Appendix II of CITES (species not in danger of extinction, with controlled commercialization), while the ñandú petiso or choique (Pterocnemia pennata) is listed in Appendix I of CITES (animals in danger of extinction, therefore their commercialization is prohibited). However, if they are raised in captivity or on farms they will be treated the same as species in Appendix II.

At present there are no breeding farms for ñandúes in commercial operating condition in Argentina. There is one commercial operation, BAT-IANA, part of the Don Elias Sociedad Ganadera, in Salto, Uruguay

There are breeding farms in formation in Argentina that will surely begin production which will meet CITES requirements within the next few years. All have started from the capture of wild adult, young, or eggs of these animals.

In the particular case of the breeding farm at Bariloche (INTA), which started in 1991 with collecting fertile eggs from wild animals and later artificial incubation, the species being raised is the choique or Darwin's rhea (*Pterocnemia pennata*).

The first birds raised at Bariloche laid their first eggs between 20 to 24 months of age. In order to carry out comparative investigations between the two species of ñandú, samples of each were raised.

It was decided to begin raising these starting with the eggs, instead of from the capture of adult animals. In that way animals free of parasites and more docile would be obtained.

We foresee that in the short time span of 2 or 3 years, there will emerge an important quantity of breeding farms in Argentina, Uruguay, Chile, and Brazil.

In brief it can be said that captive raising of ñandúes with the philosophy of beginning a viable ratite industry, South America is taking its first steps. It is not yet seen as a productive alternative for the future, as there is resistance. Others only see export opportunity of a product at a good price on a short term. The situation today in South America is more or less comparable to that of the USA at the stage of the 80s.

I believe that for countries such as Argentina and others in South America commercial rhea farming will constitute a good productive alternative for diversification as concerns all marginal ecological areas.

The family Rheidae or Ñandúes are native to South America (the neotropical zoogeographic region). Its evolutionary history is difficult to reconstruct because of the lack of fossil records. Bird bones, as opposed to mammals, disintegrate rapidly.

Fossils of four species of genus Rhea have been found in deposits of the Upper Pliocene (10 million years) in Argentina.

- Daniel V. Sarasqueta
Instituto Nacional de Tecnologia
Agropecuaria (INTA)
Bariloche, Argentina

NORTH AMERICAN RHEA ASSOCIATION

The North American Rhea Association (NARA) was founded in January of 1992, at a meeting in Round Mountain, Texas.

The organizers were Clyde Castleberry and John Poehling. The first officers were President Diane Poehling; Vice President Jim Curbo; Treasurer Mary Lee Stropes; Secretary Edna Williams; and directors Mark Wright, Wally Caviness, and Larry Benson.

NARA was founded to encourage and promote the products, marketing, sales, and commercial use of rheas and rhea products; to encourage laws, regulations and programs agreeable to develop a viable rhea industry both domestically and internationally and within the legal and lawful guidelines and state statutes and/or guidelines; and to promote the common business interests of the member and the industry. The association has sponsored research on rhea oil and meat.

A major goal, obtaining USDA slaughter approval, was met when the US Department of Agriculture announced in October of 1995 that it would provide voluntary inspections to plants that slaughter and process the meat of rheas.

The next step is development of a market for rhea meat and products.

INTERESTING FACTS & TALES

In 1992, rhea feathers sold for $70 (Uruguayan) per kilo. Large feathers are used in costumes for carnival all over South America.

In 1985, eggs taken from wild rhea nests were sold to bakeries for 5 cents each (Uruguayan currency).

- Daniel V. Sarasqueta

Rhea can make strides of up to 1.5 meters.

Rheas were named after the mother of Zeus, who was the chief god in the pantheon of the ancient Greeks.

Like ostriches, rheas often are found in association with other herd animals. In the wild they live in large flocks. While they don't migrate, like all herd animals they move considerable distances while feeding.

Rheas when running raise one wing and lower the other rather like the [ailerons] of an airplane, creating a steering effect.

The wing span of the rhea may reach 250 cm.

Rheas generally live in groups of one cock and several hens within a distinct territory.
- Grzimek, 1972

In South American the skins of rheas are used for rug making.
- Wallace, 1963

A full-grown rhea is 5 feet tall and weighs approximately 60-80 pounds.

There were 250 to 500 rhea farms in the United States in 1993.
- USDA, 1993

Sixty tons of rhea feathers valued at $137,689 were exported from Argentina in 1874.
- Goldie, 1968

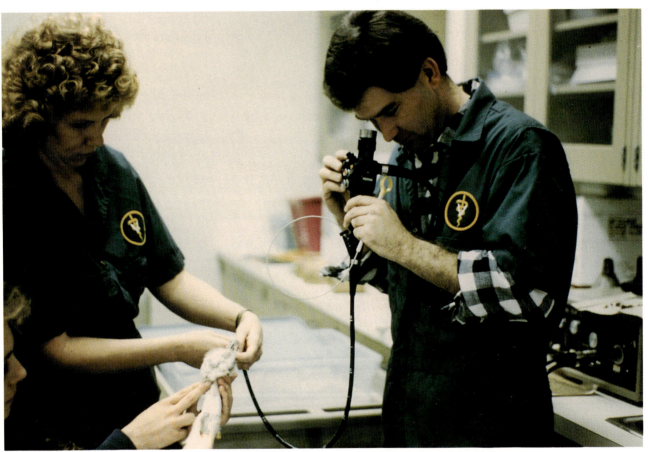
Dr. Brett Hopkins, using an endoscope inserted through the esophagus into the ventriculus of a rhea to remove a foreign object such as a nail.

ANATOMY OF OSTRICHES, EMUS, AND RHEAS

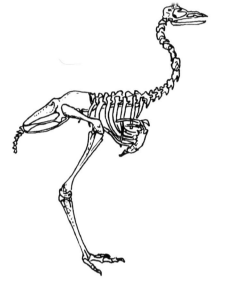

Brett A. Hopkins, MS, DVM, ACPV (Text and Photos)
University of Missouri
Columbia, Missouri

Gheorghe Mircea Constantinescu, DVM, Ph. D. (Illustrations)
University of Missouri
Columbia, Missouri

To understand ratites, one must become familiar with their anatomy. Ratites are avians, but it is their unusual anatomy that taxonomically places them together into the ratite group. Each ratite group or order (ostrich, emu, cassowary, kiwi, rhea, and the now-extinct elephant bird) has its own unique anatomy, although there are many similar structures between each order.

All ratites are flightless, have toe claws on the end of the digits of their wings, feathers without barbules, and they do not have a crop, major breast muscles, uropygial gland, or a pygostyle. But this group of anatomic features does not classify them as ratites.

The term *ratite* is derived from the Latin word *Ratitae*, which refers to a figure similar to a raft. A raft is a flat floating structure without a keel. All ratites have a broad, smooth, *bowl*-shaped breast plate or sternum without a keel, which in other birds is an adaptation for attachment of the breast or flight muscles. It is the lack of a keel on their sternum or breast that gives ratites their name.

This chapter provides practical information identifying the location, function, and structure of the major organs, glands, bones, and veins of ostriches, emus, and rheas for use by the producer, veterinarian, and student. Detailed information is purposely omitted, as well as discussion of the muscles, vessels, nerves, tendons, ligaments, and feathers.

The contents of this chapter are organized into six categories: 1) skeletal structures, 2) external organs and tissues, 3) digestive system, 4) internal organs and tissues, 5) selected veins, and 6) a table of major anatomical differences between ostriches, emus and rheas.

SKELETAL STRUCTURES

SKULL

The skull includes the upper and lower jaws, the palate, orbits and brain case. These bones interact to provide protective locations in which the eyes, brain, and mouth reside, and also to support the jaws, and nasal and auditory canals.

The upper jaw includes the nasal, premaxillary, and maxillary bones. In ostriches, the rostral half of the upper jaw is movable. In ratites, the nasal bars that connect to the brain case are incomplete. The lower jaw, or mandibular bone, articulates with the movable quadrate bone. The lower jaw is very mobile.

The palate is formed by the palatal processes of the premaxillae and maxillae bones, and the palatine, vomer, pterygoid, quadrate, and jugal arch bones. This complex of bones forms the support for the roof of the mouth.

The brain case houses the brain and provides the canals for the ears and the orbits for the eyes. The brain case is a complex of fused bones. The fusion lines or sutures can be seen in an adult skull.

Ostriches have laminated facial bones but otherwise the bones are pneumatic and positioned in a similar fashion as other avians. The pneumatic spaces communicate with the nasal and tympanic cavities and not the air sacs associated with the lungs. The exact shape of each ratite skull is slightly different from the other species, and within species.

GLOSSARY

For readers unfamiliar with the technical language of anatomy, here are some definitions of terms which will be found in this chapter.

callosity: a hard or thickened part of the skin.
caudal: of, at, near or toward the tail end of the body.
distal: away from the point of origin or attachment, as of a limb or bone.
dorsal: of, pertaining to, or situated on, the back.
endocrine gland: any of various glands, as the thyroid, adrenal, or pituitary glands, that secrete certain substances or hormones directly into the blood or lymph; ductless gland.
endogenous: growing or proceeding from within; originating within.
exocrine gland: any of several glands, as the salivary glands, that excrete externally through a duct.
exogenous: having external origins; derived externally.
glomerulus: a tuft of convoluted capillaries in a nephron, that filters certain substances from the blood and passes a protein-free filtrate into the associated tube.
ilium: the broad, upper bone which with the ischium and pubis, form the pelvis.
ischium: the lower bone which forms the floor of the pelvis.
lumen: the canal, duct, or cavity of a tubular organ.
mesentery: the membrane that surrounds the intestines, attaching them to the posterior wall of the abdomen, maintaining them in position and supplying blood vessels, nerves, and lymphatics.
nephron: a functional structure of a kidney.
orbit: the bony cavity of the skull which contains the eye; eye socket.
osmoregulation: the mechanism that controls the rate at which fluids pass through a membrane or porous partition.
papilla: any small, nipple-like projection; one of certain small protruberances concerned with the senses of touch, taste, and smell.
phalanges: plural of phalanx; any of the bones of the fingers or toes.
pneumatic: containing air or air cavities.
pygostyle: the bone at the posterior end of the spinal column in birds, formed by the fusion of several caudal vertebrae.
rostral: beaklike; toward the beak.
sesamoid bone: shaped like a sesame seed, as certain small nodular bones and cartilage.
uncinate: hooked, bent at the end like a hook.
uncinate process: a curved, bony projection on certain ribs of birds that projects backward and overlaps the succeeding rib, serving to strengthen the thorax.
ventral: situated on the abdominal side of the body; of, pertaining to, or situated on the lower side or surface, as an organ or part.

HYOID APPARATUS

This structure is located in the floor of the mouth, attached to the tongue and larynx. The hyoid physically supports the tongue, larynx, and proximal trachea. This structure is very mobile, allowing the tongue, larynx, and trachea to be manually pulled forward, if desired.

The shape and parts of hyoid vary between ratites, but it is basically a rod-shaped combination of bone and cartilage, in the form of the *wish bone* from a chicken. It consists of a rostral bone or cartilage called the paraglossum or entoglossal that is the internal part of the tongue, and two small bones or cartilage directly caudal to the tongue that support the ventral larynx and trachea. A *rod* of bone and cartilage extends off each side near the larynx in a caudoventral direction.

In ostriches, these two rods are very long and usually curve upward, ending behind the external ear. They can be seen moving the skin behind the ear when the bird moves its tongue and/or its mouth. The length is shorter in emus and rheas.

VERTEBRAL COLUMN

The vertebral column consists of the bones of the spine beginning at the skull and ending at the tip of the tail. Ratites and swans have the greatest number of vertebrae of all vertebrates.

There are five regions of vertebrae, named in descending sequence: 1) cervical, 2) thoracic, 3) lumbar, 4) sacral, and 5) caudal. In ratites, as in most birds, the last few thoracic, all the lumbar and sacral, and most of the caudal vertebrae are fused to form the synsacrum. The ilium is also fused to the synsacrum, forming the lateral walls.

Each vertebra is bilaterally symmetrical but the size and shape of each vertebra varies. Since their structure is similar to other avian vertebrae, they will

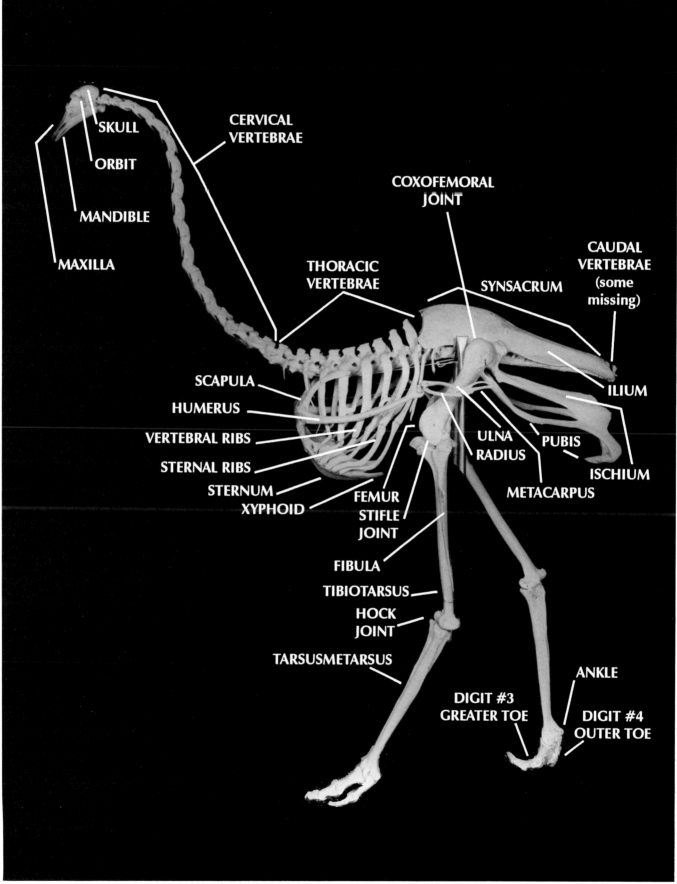

Figure 1. Ostrich skeleton at Auburn University. (Photo courtesy A. E. Marshall, DVM, Ph. D. Skeletal component identification by Brett A. Hopkins, DVM)

not be described here. Each vertebral region is discussed below.

Cervical Vertebrae

There are 18 cervical vertebrae in ostriches and emus and 15 in rheas. The cervical vertebrae support the head, neck, and associated structures: the muscles, nerves, vessels, esophagus, and trachea. Their mobile articulations allow the neck to be very flexible.

Thoracic Vertebrae

There are ten thoracic vertebrae in ostriches, emus and rheas. The vertebrae are immobile because the articulations are rigid, thus providing support for the thoracic cavity and ribs. Most of these vertebrae have paired articulations with a rib.

The first, second, ninth and tenth thoracic vertebrae in ostriches have short ribs called floating—or asternal—ribs that do not attach to the sternal ribs. The ninth and tenth thoracic vertebrae are fused to the synsacrum. The third through eighth thoracic vertebrae have ribs that attach to sternal ribs.

In emus, the first, second, third and ninth thoracic vertebrae have asternal ribs. The tenth thoracic vertebrae lacks a visible rib. The ninth and tenth vertebrae are fused into the synsacrum.

The first, second, sixth, seventh and eighth thoracic vertebrae in rheas have asternal ribs. The eighth, ninth, and tenth thoracic vertebrae are fused to the synsacrum. The ninth and tenth thoracic vertebrae lack a rib.

Synsacrum

Located over the caudal half of the body, the synsacrum consists of fused thoracic, lumbar, sacral and caudal vertebrae. The lateral sides are fused with the ilium. This structure is extremely rigid and strong, and provides support for the limbs and associated back muscles.

In ostriches and emus, the last two thoracic vertebrae, all the lumbar and sacral vertebrae, and only some of the caudal vertebrae are fused along with the ilium, to form the synsacrum.

In rheas, the last three thoracic vertebrae and all of the lumbar and sacral vertebrae and only some of the caudal vertebrae are fused to form the synsacrum.

Caudal Vertebrae

These vertebrae comprise the last region of the spine. The first few caudal vertebrae are fused together in the synsacrum and the last few extend beyond the synsacrum or pelvis to form the tail.

The tail was once used for balance, locomotion and protection, but now has little use except to cover the vent, help protrude the cloacal during coitus, and in ostriches wag like a dog's tail when they are happy or anxious.

The exact number of caudal vertebrae has not been determined, as they are easily confused with the fused sacral and lumbar vertebrae within the synsacrum.

Beyond the synsacrum, ostriches have eight caudal vertebrae. The first six are always free and the last two may be fused to form a structure similar, but not homologous, to a pygostyle.

Emus have eight vertebrae beyond the ilium. The first five are free and the last three are fused together.

Rheas have five or six fused vertebrae beyond the synsacrum and five free vertebrae beyond the ischium. The tail is distinct and very mobile in ostriches, less so in rheas. It is indistinct and immobile in emus except during coitus.

PELVIC GIRDLE

The pelvis is a paired, elongated structure consisting of the ilium, ischium, and pubis bones located in the caudal third of the body. This girdle of bone forms a platform for the attachment of large and small muscles used for locomotion, as well as providing structural protection for the abdominal viscera and in the female, the egg.

There is a pre- and post-acetabular ilium fused to the synsacrum, forming the lateral walls. The ilium is smooth surfaced, thin, wide, and forms the top of the pelvic girdle, sloping caudally downward. The degree of slope varies with each ratite group.

The ischium forms the middle portion of the pelvic girdle. It is a very narrow, round to flat bone. In ostriches, it cranially articulates to the ventral and caudal rim of the acetabulum; caudally it broadens to fuse with the dorsocaudal region of the pubis bone.

The ischium of emus articulates cranially as in ostriches, but it broadens caudally only slightly to fuse with the caudoventral end of the ilium. It does not contact the pubic bone.

In rheas, the cranial end of the ischium articulates with the ilium as in the ostrich, as well as the dorsocaudal end of the pubis. The ischium curves slightly upward to fuse at its mid point with the ventrocaudal region of the ilium. The ischium then curves slightly downward and broadens to fuse again with the dorsocaudal end of the pubis.

The pubis forms the ventral sides of the girdle. The bone is long and narrow, with the cranial end articulating to the ventral acetabulum, then sloping caudally downward at an approximate 45-degree angle in each ratite group.

In ostriches, the pubis turns to a near horizontal position halfway down the shaft, then broadens and fuses with the ventrocaudal region of the ischium. It curves downward, then sharply back cranially, forming a hook. This hook of the pubis supports the weight of the bird and protects the abdominal viscera from being compressed when the bird lies down.

The halves of the ostrich pubis are side by side, connected by cartilage, but are not fused together

Anatomy

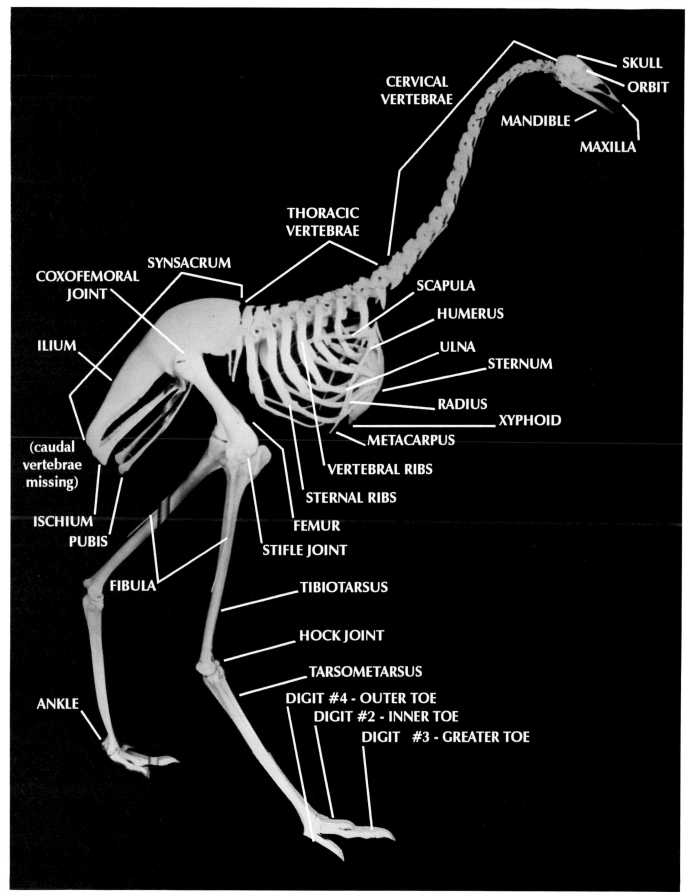

Figure 2. Emu skeleton at Auburn University. (Photo courtesy A. E. Marshall, DVM, Ph. D. Skeletal component identification by Brett A. Hopkins, DVM)

with bone—therefore this is not a true pubic symphysis.

In emus, the pubis bones are widely separated, slightly curved and broad at the end. The caudal ends are free.

The pubis bones of rheas are separated and relatively straight, but broaden upward at the end to fuse with the ventrocaudal end of the ischium.

In emus and rheas, the right and left ischial and pubis bones do not fuse together to form a pelvic floor or pubic symphysis.

STERNUM

The sternum, or breast plate, is a bilaterally-symmetrical structure that forms the front of the thoracic cavity. It is a very strong, broad, bowl-shaped bone convexed on the outside surface and concaved on the inside surface.

The sternum supports the thoracic girdle, wings, and ribs, and provides protection to the thoracic organs during sitting and when the bird fights or runs into stationary structures.

In ostriches and emus, the two halves of the sternum are fused. In rheas, the halves are articulated by cartilage in chicks, and the bones gradually fuse as the bird ages.

The sternum is divided into the costal sternum where the ribs attach, and the metasternum, the portion of sternum extending caudal to the attachment of the last sternal rib. A pair of cranial and caudal lateral processes are also present, and are most evident in ostriches. The sternum of each ratite group varies in size and structure.

RIBS

The ribs are paired, and articulate with either the thoracic vertebrae or sternum to form the lateral walls of the thorax. The ribs provide support for the sternum and protection for the thoracic organs.

There are vertebral or spinal, sternal, complete and floating ribs. The type of rib is determined by its origin and articulation site(s).

Vertebral or spinal ribs originate from the thoracic vertebrae. Sternal ribs originate from the sternum. Complete ribs are defined as having both a vertebrae and sternal rib joined together by cartilage at the costal-chondral junction in the middle of the thorax. Floating ribs are vertebral ribs that do not join a corresponding sternal rib and the end is free.

The size, shape, and number of each type of rib varies for each ratite group. There are nine or ten visible vertebral or spinal ribs in ostriches, emus and rheas. The number of sternal ribs varies, with five or six in ostriches, five in emus, and three in rheas. The number of complete ribs equals the number of sternal ribs for each ratite group.

In ostriches, the first, second, ninth, and tenth rib are floating. The third through eighth ribs are complete, although the sternal portion of the eighth rib may or may not attach to the sternum. The tenth rib is fused with the synsacrum. There is a small caudodorsal projection of bone on the fourth, fifth, and sixth ventral ribs called the uncinate process.

In emus, the first, second, third, and ninth ribs of emus are floating. The fourth through eighth are complete although the sternal portion of the eighth rib does not attach to the sternum. A very small uncinate process is visible only on the sixth rib. The tenth vertebral rib is not visible.

In rheas, the first, second, sixth, seventh, and eighth ribs are floating. The third, fourth, and fifth ribs are complete. The eighth and ninth ribs are fused to the synsacrum. The tenth vertebral rib is not visible. The third and fourth vertebral ribs have a large uncinate process.

It should be noted that there is variation of the ribs and vertebrae between individual specimens and especially on prepared collections that have been reassembled in error.

THORACIC GIRDLE

The bones of the thoracic girdle include the scapula, clavicle, and coracoid. Ostriches totally lack a clavicle, even embryologically, and the scapula and coracoid are fused together. The clavicle is free in emus and the scapula and coracoid are fused together. In rheas, all three bones are fused together.

WING

The wing is formed by articulation of the humerus, ulna, radius, metacarpal bone, and phalangeal bones. They are located on each side of the cranial sternum. In the flightless ratites, the major functions of the wing include balance, thermoregulation, intimidation, and mating rituals. The structure of the wing is similar between ratites, but size varies dramatically.

Ostriches and rheas have large wings. The humerus is the longest bone of the wing, articulating proximally with the scapula and distally with the ulna and radius. The ulna is positioned lateral and below the radius. Both are short bones. The ulna is slightly larger than the radius. A radial and an ulnar carpal bone are usually present. The metacarpals are fused into two bones, which fuse together on each end leaving an open space between them.

There are three very small digits. The medial digit is fused to the proximal metacarpal bone, and the central and lateral digits extend from the end of the distal metacarpal bone. The central digit has two phalanges and the lateral and medial digits have one phalanx. Toe claws can be seen on one or two of the digits, depending on the individual.

Most emus have extremely short vestigial wings, although some have only a thoracic girdle and others are totally wingless

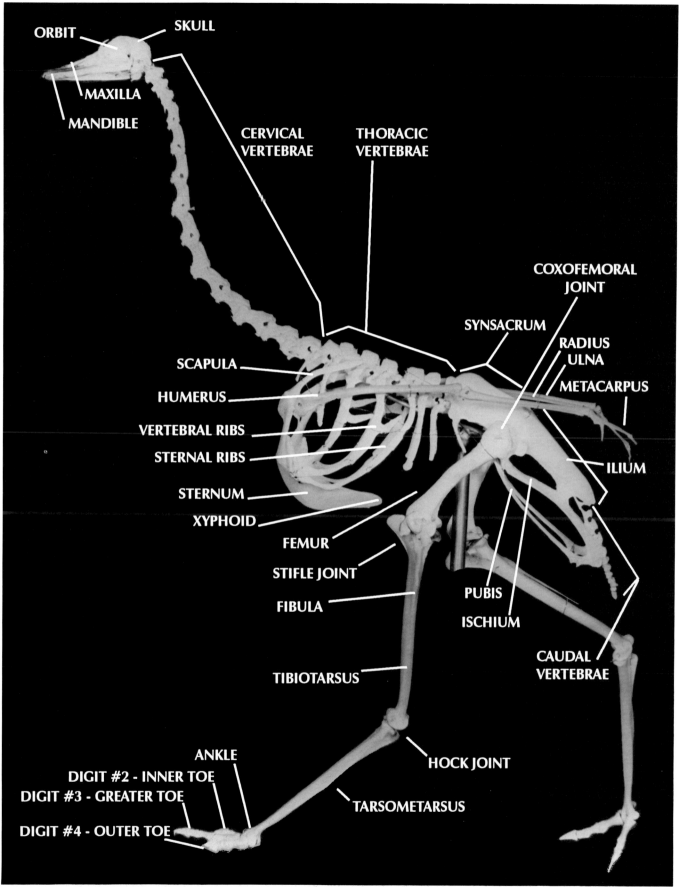

Figure 3. Rhea skeleton at Auburn University. (Photo courtesy A. E. Marshall, DVM, Ph. D. Skeletal component identification by Brett A. Hopkins, DVM)

and lack a thoracic girdle. The functions of the wing described for ostriches and rheas do not apply to the emu. Emu wings make very good handles to grasp while trying to restrain larger juveniles and adults.

The wing consists of a very short humerus, radius, and ulna. The metacarpal bones are fused into a single, solid bone.

Emus have only two digits. The medial digit is not visible and is fused to the proximal end of the metacarpal bone. A visible digit with three phalanges and a toe claw is attached to the end of the metacarpal bone.

LEG

The paired leg consists of the articulations of the femur, tibio-tarsus, fibula, and tarso-metatarsus bones. The proximal and distal row tarsal bones are fused to the tibia and metatarsal bones, giving rise to the tibio-tarsus and tarso-metatarsus bones, respectively.

The fourth tarsal bone is unfused in ostriches. Emus have a free tarsal or sesamoid bone caudal to the hock joint. The legs are very similar for each ratite group. The legs provide for locomotion, defense, and access to food.

The head of the femur articulates proximally within the acetabulum located on the side of the pelvic girdle, and articulates distally with the tibio-tarsus. The femur is a short pneumatic bone, with a large circumference.

The femur extends forward and downward at an approximate 45-degree angle to the spine, and is covered by very large muscles, making it difficult to see. The proximal articulation forms the hip joint and the distal articulation forms the stifle joint.

There is no true patella bone in ratites but in ostriches there is calcification of a 5- to 9-centimeter segment of a tendon.

The tibio-tarsus is a strong, long, straight bone with a wider irregular proximal end that articulates proximally with the femur and distally with the tarso-metatarsus, forming the hock joint.

The fibula is a very thin, straight bone with a wide irregular proximal end that articulates proximally to the lateral side of the proximal tibio-tarsus bone. The fibula extends one-half to three-fourths of the way down the tibio-tarsus bone, ending with a sharp unarticulated point.

In avians, all the metatarsal bones are fused into a single, very strong and long bone. It articulates proximally with the caudal tibio-tarsus and distally with the proximal end of the digits (toes). The proximal articulation is called the hock joint and the distal articulation is called the ankle joint.

FOOT

A paired structure that is a combination of various numbers of digits (toes) articulated to the distal end of the tarso-metatarsus bone, the foot provides friction so the bird can stand, walk, and run without slipping.

The foot has a major role in providing balance, as well as being used for defense, nest-building, scratching the neck or head, and finding food. Unlike most birds, all toes in the ratites are directed forward.

In ostriches, only two toes are present on each foot. There is a large medial toe, called the greater toe, which is embryologically the third digit. It is composed of four smaller bones called phalanges

Toe claws on the ends of the digits of the wing of an ostrich.

Sternum of an adult ostrich, viewed from back to front. The ribs attach to the opening on the right side. The projections are the xyphoid, or bottom of the sternum. The heart rests in the concave bowl.

and has a very large claw on the end. The lateral toe, which is embryologically the fourth digit, is very small and vestigial. It is composed of four phalanges, with the presence of a fifth phalanx representing a small toe claw.

In emus and rheas, there are three toes. Embryologically, the medial toe is the second digit, the central toe, which is the largest toe, is the third digit, and the lateral toe is the fourth digit. The end of each toe has a well developed toe claw.

The number of phalanges per toe varies. Emus and rheas have five phalanges in the lateral toe, four phalanges in the central toe and three phalanges in the medial toe. This is similar to other avian species.

HIP JOINT (COXOFEMORAL JOINT)

Located on the lateral side of the upper mid-back, the hip joint is formed by the articulation of the proximal head of the femur and the acetabulum of the pelvic girdle. This joint is difficult to see. It allows the leg to move forward, slightly backward, inward and outward.

STIFLE JOINT (KNEE JOINT)

The stifle is located on the lateral side of the body near the lower level of the sternum at approximately the seventh rib. This is variable as the bird moves, walks, or runs. It is formed by the articulation of the distal femur and proximal tibio-tarsus bones.

The stifle joint, often erroneously called the hip joint, is difficult to see as it is covered by feathers and has large muscles attached around it. It flexes forward and backward.

HOCK JOINT

Often erroneously called the knee joint, this is the most easily visualized joint in ratites, located one-half to two-thirds down the leg. It is formed by the articulation of the distal tibio-tarsus and proximal tarso-metatarsus bones.

Above the hock, feathers are present (except in ostriches). Below, feathers are missing and the skin changes color and becomes hard and scaly.

The hock joint is square in appearance and can flex forward only, moving the tarso-metatarsus bone and foot upward. The joint is in full extension when the bird is standing. It functions and moves opposite of the human knee joint.

ANKLE JOINT

The ankle is located above the toes and is formed by the articulations of the distal tarso-metatarsus bone and proximal end of the digits of the toes.

This joint is structurally different in each ratite because of the differences in the toes. This joint is in full extension when the bird is standing and can be flexed ventrally or caudally.

EXTERNAL ORGANS AND TISSUES

SKIN

The skin covers the entire outer body surface. It functions to aid in temperature regulation, prevention of dehydration, as a site of attachment for the feathers, and as protection from trauma and external parasites.

The character of the skin varies in thickness, elasticity, and hardness, depending on the body location. Avian skin does not have sweat glands.

The skin covering the head and neck is very thin. Over the lateral thorax, abdomen and back, it is thicker than on the neck and fairly uniform in character. The skin on the legs is thicker, less elastic, and harder.

The tarso-metatarsus bones and toes have several very hard plates of keratin called *scutes*, that cover the skin for added protection against trauma (see photo next page). The bottom of the toe in ostriches has special skin that provides protection and friction. This skin forms papilla that can be rough, and they grow very rapidly because they are continually being worn down by walking.

A special very thick, hard skin called a *callosity* is present on the bottom of the feet of emus and

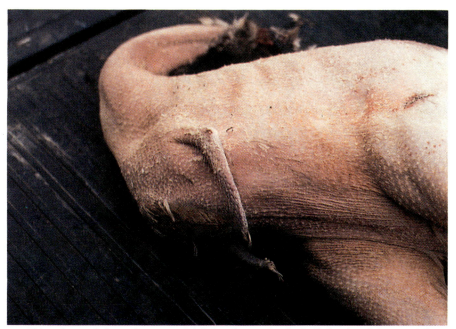

Skin of an adult male emu which has been plucked. Color is white to pink. Small wings, toe claw on end. Brown area is sternal callosity..

Skin over tarso-metatarsus bone in an adult male emu, illustrating the raised scutes on the back side. The foot is below the bottom of the photo.

rheas, and in all ratites on the sternum. Ostriches also have a callosity on the ventral pubis. These are present to prevent trauma when the bird walks or lies down.

The skin is the site of attachment of feathers. There are pterylae, or rows of feathers, in a given pattern in ostriches. There is apteria, or lack of feathers, on the skin over the thorax, midline, lateral abdomen, under the wings, legs, and feet in ostriches.

In emus and rheas, feathers cover the entire body except for the underside of the wing and from the hock joint down to the feet.

The toe claws and scutes are a special type of very hard keratinized skin that is present on the end of each toe and finger (tip of the wings). Look closely and you will see them. The outer toe of ostriches may or may not have a visible toe claw. The scutes on emu and rhea wings may or may not be present.

BEAK

The beak consists of the maxilla (upper) and mandibular bones (lower). The bones are covered by a layer of keratinized tissue.

Beak shape is associated with the type of diet, as the beak is the primary means of gathering food and water. The rostral end of the maxillary beak is longer and overlaps the tip of the rostral end of the mandible.

Ostrich beaks are long, flat, and rounded on the rostral end. Emu beaks are thick, triangular, and pointed at the rostral end. The occlusal edges of emu beaks are often slightly serrated. The serrations are the remnants of teeth which existed in distant ancestors of ratites and have disappeared as the birds evolved.

Rhea beaks are flat, long and rounded on the rostral end, having a shape similar to a combination of duck and ostrich beaks.

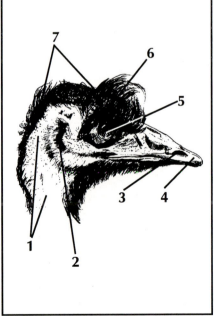

Head of an adult emu. 1: Apterylae on head and neck. 2: External ear. 3: Nares. 4: Beak. 5. Eye with golden iris. 6: Eyelid. 7: Feathers on top of head.

Anatomy

EGG TOOTH

Present in all ratite chicks, the egg tooth is used only during hatching to pip through the shell. It is a small, white, raised dot located on the rostral tip of the maxilla (upper beak). It is made of a special, very hard keratin. It disappears within the first week after hatching.

NARIS

Paired external opening in the nasal cavity located in the middle of the maxillary beak, the nares are the opening to the nose. The nares and nasal cavity, in association with the choanal opening in the roof of the mouth, allow the bird to breathe with its mouth closed. The shape of the naris is slightly different in each ratite group.

NASAL CAVITY

Located in the caudal ⅔ to ½ of the upper maxillary beak, the nasal cavity has sinuses made of trabecular bone and choanae.

The sinuses act as a barrier to inhaled debris and as a thermoregulatory organ that can conserve moisture from expired air by cooling it, causing condensation of water. Olfactory sensors are also located here, but the sense of smell is not very good. The structure of the nasal sinuses is slightly different in each ratite group.

CHOANAL OPENING OR CHOANAL SLIT

Located in the middle of the palate or roof of the mouth, the choanal opening communicates with the nasal passages. On each side of the opening there is a flap of soft tissue which surrounds the larynx when the mouth is closed, allowing direct air movement from the nares to the trachea.

NASAL OR SALT GLAND

This paired gland, located under the skin in a slight depression on either side of midline of the skull on the rim of each orbit (supraorbital position), is present in ostriches, but not in emus or rheas.

The gland is common in saltwater avian species, in which it excretes hypertonic sodium chloride, to allow them to maintain water balance even while eating high salt diets. For ostriches, the gland also plays a role in osmoregulation to maintain internal water balance.

One method of regulation may be by excreting the hypertonic sodium chloride fluid into the nasal sinuses to aid in preventing excess moisture from being lost during expiration.

The salt gland is an important adaptation to living in very arid climates with limited water sources. It is tan to slightly pink in color, oval to almond and flat shaped, with a rough granular to nodular surface.

The white raised spot on the end of the upper beak is the egg tooth of an emu chick (dead in the shell).

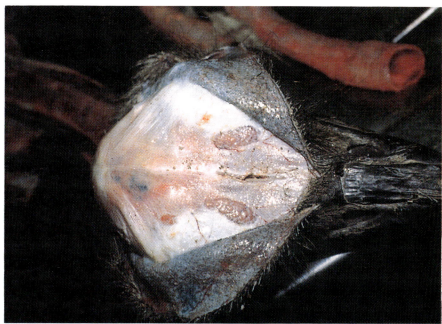
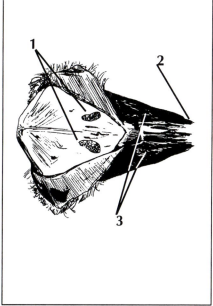

Yearling ostrich. Skin over top of head is retracted to expose the paired nodular salt or nasal glands. Pink tissue to one side of the skull is the trachea. 1. Salt or nasal glands. 2. Beak. 3. Nares.

EYE AND ASSOCIATED STRUCTURES

The paired organs of sight are positioned rostral and lateral to the calvarium (brain case) within the bony ocular orbits. Upper and lower eyelids with eyelashes are present and functional. The lower lid has greater mobility.

A third eyelid or nictitating membrane is present. This is what is usually seen as the bird blinks to protect its eye from trauma. The third eyelid is very thin and transparent. It is attached to the middle of the external globe and rests in the medial, dorsal aspect of the orbit and moves in a lateral ventral direction to cover the eye.

There is a small, pink third-eyelid gland on the caudomedial side of the globe. A small lacrimal gland is located on the lateral, caudoventral region of each orbit.

The structure of the eye is typical of avians. A pecten is present in the posterior chamber. Ocular muscles are small compared to the size of the eye. Ocular movement within the orbit is minimal. The eyesight is very keen and essential for survival.

PECTEN

A single structure found only in the avian eye, the pecten is located within the vitreous body of the eye attached to the optic disc.

The major role of the pecten is to provide nutrient and oxygen exchange to the vitreous and retina, and to maintain intraocular pressure. This is an important structure of the avian eye as there is no retinal artery.

The pecten is pigmented, usually black, raised, and conical in shape. In ostriches and rheas, there are 25 to 30 very thin vertical vanes encircling it. Emus have half as many vanes and they are much thicker. Within the vanes are a complex of venules and arterioles.

EXTERNAL EAR

The external ears are paired circular openings located on each

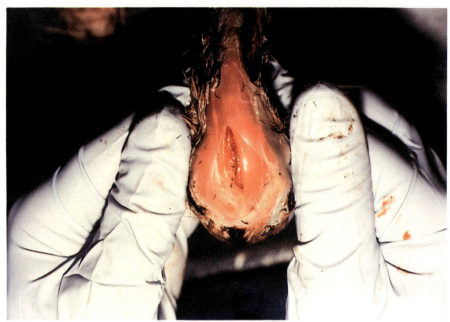

Pipping muscle in an ostrich chick. The skin is retracted from the neck behind the head, iillustrating the muscle and usual site of microchip placement.

side of the skull just behind the articulation of the maxillae and mandibular bones. The external ear is a canal through bone that directs sound waves into the tympanic membrane, then the inner ear. The canal, called the acoustic meatus, is very short and extends inward in a caudal and ventral direction from the external opening.

There are small, special feathers around the rim of the ear. In ostriches, the feathers are very short and do not cover the opening and bare skin is easily seen. In emus, there are black or tan feathers that are longer on the rostral rim and extend backward to cover the opening. The ear is difficult to see in rheas because the feathers around the rim are long enough to cover over the entire external ear opening and they are the same color as other feathers.

An ostrich eye, cut to show the black cone-shaped pecten.

Anatomy

PIPPING MUSCLE

The muscle is located just behind the base of the head, over the first through third cervical vertebrae. This is an enlarged muscle, present at hatching, that provides the strength to move the head and neck to aid the egg tooth in pipping through the shell.

The pipping muscle forms the hump seen in the dorsal, cranial neck after hatching. It decreases in size rapidly after hatching. This is one of the sites in which identifying microchips are placed.

UROPYGIAL GLAND

This gland is absent in ostriches, emus and rheas. In most birds it is a bilobed gland, located above the tail, with a single raised papilla that secretes a lipoid sebaceous material that the bird gathers with its beak, then places onto the feathers during preening for flexibility and waterproofing.

DIGESTIVE SYSTEM

MOUTH

The mouth is the internal space between the maxilla and mandible bones. The roof is formed by the palate and the floor by tissue between the paired mandibular bones.

The mouth contains the oral mucosa, choanal opening, tongue, larynx, proximal trachea, hyoid apparatus, and esophagus. It is used during eating, drinking, respiration, mating, preening, and noise production. The floor of the mouth may contain taste sensors.

TONGUE

Located on the floor of the mouth, as a rostral projection of the hyoid apparatus, which also attaches to the larynx and trachea, the tongue has very little mobility as it aids in the manipulation of food particles and drinking.

Experience indicates that birds can taste, but classic taste buds are not present. Taste sensors are likely to be present in the rear of the tongue and/or the floor and roof of the mouth.

Ostrich tongues are short, blunt, and rectangular, and have a fold of tissue over the rostral end of the cartilage. Emus have a longer, pointed tongue with serrated edges. Rhea tongues are thicker, and wide at the base and narrow at the tip.

ESOPHAGUS

The esophagus begins by forming the back of the oral pharynx (mouth), then extends down the neck, located between the right side of the trachea and right jugular vein. It begins ventral to the neck, then becomes right paramedian, then two to four vertebrae cranial to the thoracic inlet it returns to a ventral position.

After entering the thoracic inlet, the esophagus passes between the greater vessels of the heart and over or to the side of the liver, and ends at its junction with the proventriculus within the thoracic cavity.

The esophagus is an extremely flexible, tubular, muscular organ. The muscle contracts and relaxes, moving ingesta from the mouth to the proventriculus.

In male ostriches and rheas, the esophagus is inflated with air, which is released to create the booming sounds during mating season.

CROP

Unlike most avians, ratites do not have a crop.

PROVENTRICULUS

A single organ that begins as a dilated continuation of the end of the esophagus, the proventriculus ends at its junction with the ventriculus.

In ostriches, the proventriculus is located in the thorax and abdomen, dorsal to the liver and dorsal and caudal to the ventriculus. The proventriculus of rheas and emus is dorsal to the liver within the thorax.

The proventriculus is the *first* stomach and is also the glandular

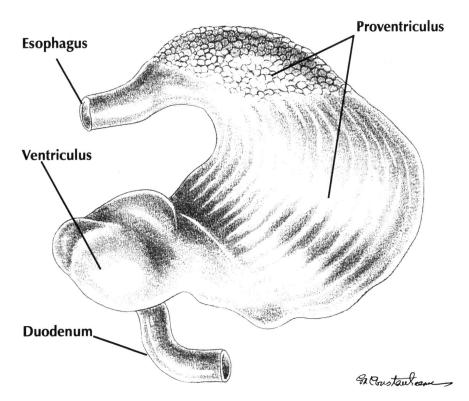

Figure 4. Ostrich proventriculus and ventriculus

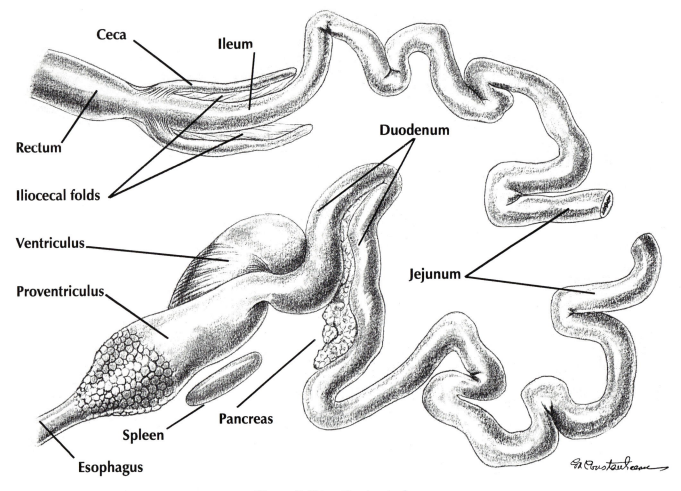

Figure 5. Digestive tract of an emu

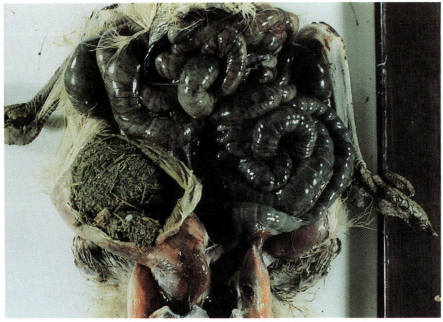

An ostrich chick that died because of grass overload. The proventriculus is open, showing the grass wad. The intestines are discolored and distended.

stomach. It coats ingesta with digestive enzymes. The structure is different in each ratite species. See Figures 4 and 5.

In rheas it is a raised nodular gland, present only on the dorsal half of the tubular ventriculus. It does not expand to store ingesta and enters directly into the cranial aspect of the ventriculus.

In emus, the proventriculus is a dilated, linear tube with the lumen enlarging, allowing for some storage of ingesta. The glands fully circumscribe the cranial 2/3 to 3/4 of the organ. The proventriculus empties directly into the cranial aspect of the ventriculus.

In ostriches, the proventriculus acts as a true stomach, having contractile forces for mixing, and a storage capacity with a tremendous ability for expansion and secretion of digestive enzymes. There is a wide strip of secretory glands located on the craniodorsal aspect extending to the greater curvature.

The proventriculus has the shape of a sideways horseshoe or backward "C," beginning as a large dilation of the esophagus, extending dorsal and caudal to the ventriculus, then curving back cranial to enter the caudal aspect of the ventriculus.

The junction between the proventriculus and ventriculus is called the isthmus. Most of the proventriculus is caudal to the ventriculus on the left of midline. It is easily palpated and identified on radiographs. This is the site of most impaction disorders. Surgical access to the proventriculus (proventriculotomy) can be obtained on the left side of the cranial abdomen or cranial ventral midline.

In contrast, in emus and rheas, the proventriculus is in front of the ventriculus and in the confines of the ribs and *can not* be externally palpated in an anatomically-correct patient. Surgical access to the proventriculus in emus and rheas is extremely difficult and is rarely, if ever, indicated for routine impactions.

VENTRICULUS

Also called the gizzard, in general the ventriculus is located behind the liver and ribs and in front of the intestines, separated by a thin membrane and attached to the ventral abdomen by membranes. The exact location varies with each ratite group.

The ventriculus is the *second* and also the muscular stomach. It is responsible for the grinding of hard, larger sized ingesta, such as seed, nuts, and coarse grass.

In all ratite groups, it is a hollow organ, round to elongated, with two large, thick, strong muscles on each side of the lumen and two smaller, thin, expandable muscles on each end. The lumen is lined with a cuticle made of a special secretion called koilin that

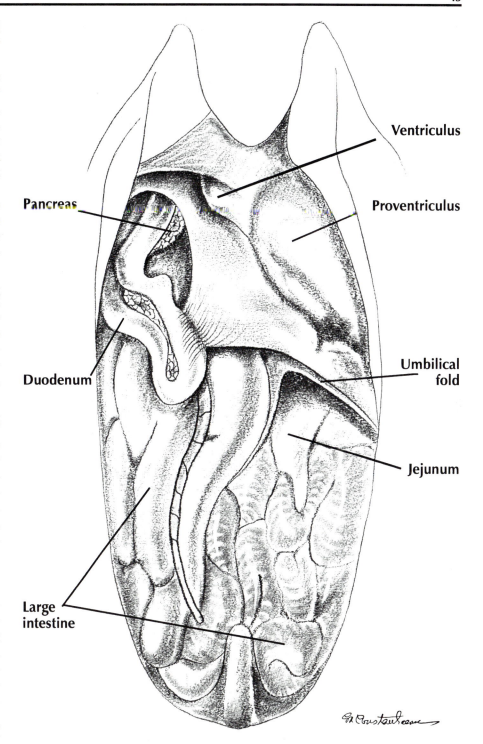

Figure 6. Ostrich abdomen, ventral view

is a complex of carbohydrates and protein. The ingesta exits the ventriculus through the pyloric valve, an opening on the right side, entering into the duodenum of the small intestine.

In rheas, the ventriculus is in a more caudal and midline position in the abdomen. It can expand, elongating its shape and increasing its lumenal volume to provide storage of ingesta. This feature allows rhea chicks to become impacted easily when they overeat on feed, grass, twigs, or other difficult-to-digest items. Surgical correction is performed by a ventriculotomy through the caudal thin muscle. In adults, the pyloric valve of the ventriculus will allow most large items, such as rocks and grass wads, to pass into the duodenum, preventing most ventricular impactions from occurring.

In emus, the ventriculus is smaller compared to rheas and ostriches. It is located slightly to the left of midline. The pyloric valve in the ventriculus is not very restrictive and can enlarge to allow passage of most food items into the duodenum. This is why impaction in emus is uncommon. Occasionally a bird will eat an excessive amount of grass, plastic, etc., that is stringy or flexible and which will not pass, leading to impaction.

In ostriches, the ventriculus is more rounded and is located either within the caudal thorax or just behind the ribs and sternum on the left side. It is in front of the proventriculus.

The pyloric valve in the ventriculus is well developed, having a sphincter muscle that is very sensitive and restrictive as to the size of particles it will allow to pass into the duodenum.

Small particles such as digested feed, grain, sand and water will easily pass, but items larger than 1 cm in size have a more difficult time getting past the valve, and items larger than 4 cm in size will rarely pass out of the ventriculus. This design ensures larger ingesta such as nuts, twigs and grass, etc. will be appropriately ground, so they will be digested and utilized in the intestine.

In captivity, the birds consume too much grass, rocks, carpet, plastic, etc., to be timely ground to a small size, the stomachs become full, and the passage of food dramatically slows or stops, creating an impaction.

In chicks, this is a critical state due to rapid starvation and bacterial overgrowth, but many adults overcome most partial impactions due to energy reserves that provide time for the ingesta to digest.

Rock overload is common in most domestic ostriches. This is because the rocks that are ingested, such as creek gravel, are too hard for the ventriculus to grind into small particles. As a result, they accumulate in the stomachs as the bird continues to eat additional rocks. Over twenty pounds of rocks can accumulate in the proventriculus and ventriculus of an adult ostrich.

Ostriches will rarely impact or get overloaded with rocks if they are provided *soft* rocks such as limestone, sandstone and some granites that can be effectively ground down by the ventriculus. Only a few, around 10, small rocks or gravel are needed for effective grinding of ingesta.

DUODENUM

The first segment of the small intestines, the duodenum begins at its attachment to the pyloric valve on the right side of the ventriculus and continues to the jejunum. The duodenum crosses between the right and left side of the cranial abdomen.

The liver and pancreas release their digestive enzymes into the duodenum via the bile and pancreatic ducts, respectively. The duodenum is the major site for protein, fat and carbohydrate digestion.

The duodenum is pink to purple in color with a smooth surface, and forms a duodenal loop in which the pancreas is located (Figures 5 and 6). In ostriches, a secondary loop of duodenum is present at the end of the ascending limb.

JEJUNUM

The second segment of small intestine is a continuation from the duodenum. There is no clear morphologic change between the duodenum and jejunum.

Most of the jejunum is coiled and located in the left and right dorsal abdomen in the ostrich and in the mid-abdomen in emus and rheas.

The jejunum is the site of nutrient absorption. The color is light pink and it has a smooth surface. The jejunum, by definition, ends where the distal tips of the ceca are attached. Distal to this is the ileum. In emus and rheas, the jejunum is the longest segment of intestines.

ILEUM

The third and last segment of small intestine, by definition, the

An accumulation of rocks from the ventriculus of one ostrich.

Anatomy

ileum begins where the distal tips of the ceca attach to the small intestine and ends at the ileo-cecal junction where the proximal end or beginning of the ceca are located.

The ileum provides for absorption and digestion of ingesta. It is pink to tan in color and has a smooth surface.

The ileum in emus is very short. In ostriches, most of the ileum is in the right caudoventral to caudal half of the abdomen, but does course cranially to the proventriculus and right kidney where it attaches to the ceca and proximal large intestine.

CECUM

The ceca are paired organs that are part of the intestines, arising at the ileo-cecal junction between the ileum and large intestine. By definition, distal to this junction are the large intestines. The ceca course forward and are attached along the ileum by the ileo-cecal ligament. They are blind sacs that aid in the digestion of fiber, water absorption and a few lesser-defined functions.

In emus, the ceca are very short, smooth-surfaced with a small lumen, and green to black in color.

The ceca in ostriches and rheas are very well developed, thin-walled, very long, and have a large lumen with surface ridges corresponding to mucosal folds or saccules.

In ostriches, the ceca originate in the right cranial abdomen, then course to the left side ventral to the proventriculus, then turning direction to dorsocaudal along the caudal greater curvature of the proventriculus on the left side, then becoming mid-abdominal.

The ceca will collect larger particles of ingesta that have not been previously digested, such as sticks, grass, straw, rocks and sand, etc., in an attempt to digest them. The ceca often become overloaded or impacted with sand and gravel, leading to malabsorption and bacterial imbalances.

LARGE INTESTINE

This is the last segment of intestine. It begins at the ileo-cecal junction and ends at its junction on the central, dorsal region of the coprodeum in the cloaca. The circumference is larger than the small intestine, thus the name large intestine. The primary role of the large intestine is that of water absorption.

Emus and rheas have a relatively short large intestine, colon and rectum.

Ostriches have a large intestine composed of two major segments. The first is described as the

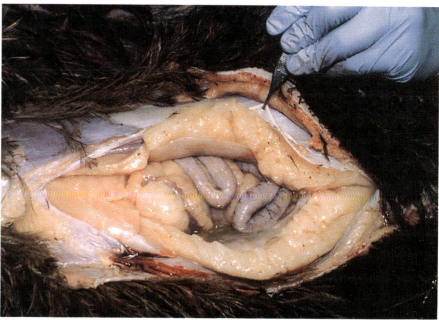

Adult emu, showing fat within abdominal wall, small intestines surrounded by mesenteric fat within the abdomen, and subcutaneous fat (behind the forceps).

Volvulus or twisting of the yolk sac and small intestine (jejunum) in an ostrich chick. The twist stops venous blood flow. Note pallor of the stomachs and duodenum and severe congestion of the yolk sac and jejunum.

proximal, thin-walled, sacculated segment, and the second, the distal, thick-walled, smooth, or non-sacculated segment.

The proximal segment occupies the caudal two-thirds of the right abdomen and the distal segment occupies the caudal one-third of the dorsal, mid, and left abdomen.

The large intestine is very long in ostriches. In hatchlings, the length of the small and large intestines are equal, but the length of the large intestine increases to be twice the length of the small intestine in adults. At necropsy the length ratio can be used to estimate age in chicks and juveniles less than 6 months of age.

The proximal large intestine has a very thin transparent wall with long, thin, mucosal fold or saccules. It appears to be an additional site for digestion and fermentation of ingesta, especially fiber.

There is a gradual morphologic change between the proximal and distal large intestine. The lengths of the proximal large intestine and distal large intestine segments are similar. The distal segment appears similar to the jejunum in color and size.

CLOACA

In ostriches and rheas, the external opening to the cloaca (the vent) is located under the base of the tail and is easily seen after lifting the tail.

The opening in emus is on the ventral side of the tail approximately halfway between the legs and end of the tail feathers.

The vent in emus is circumscribed with anal musk glands and feathers. These glands produce a very thick, peculiar smelling substance that cause the feathers around the vent to stick together, making the opening often difficult to locate.

The cloaca is a common collection pouch for the digestive, urinary and reproductive ducts, and also houses the bursa of Fabricius. There are three major compartments: the coprodeum, urodeum and proctodeum. A rectal pouch is present in ostriches (Figure 7).

The coprodeum receives feces from the rectum. The urodeum receives the urine from the ureters arising from the kidneys, and the semen from the vas deferens in the male or the egg from the oviduct in the female.

The proctodeum houses the phallus and bursa of Fabricius and communicates directly with the external opening or vent.

Ratites do not have a urinary bladder, but urine can accumulate in the urodeum and the large cavity of the coprodeum, with large volumes being expelled periodically.

INTERNAL ORGANS AND TISSUES

BRAIN

The brain is located within the skull, most of which is caudal to the orbits. The brain, as in vertebrates, is the Grand Central Station of the neurologic functions, including intelligence, locomotion, sensory responses, and autonomic activities of the body.

The brain has five major regions: olfactory lobes, cerebrum, optic lobes, cerebellum, and medulla oblongata.

The two olfactory lobes are rudimentary projections in front of each cerebral hemisphere. The two cerebral hemispheres are slightly bilobed with a smooth surface. The paired, large, round optic lobes lie behind the cerebral

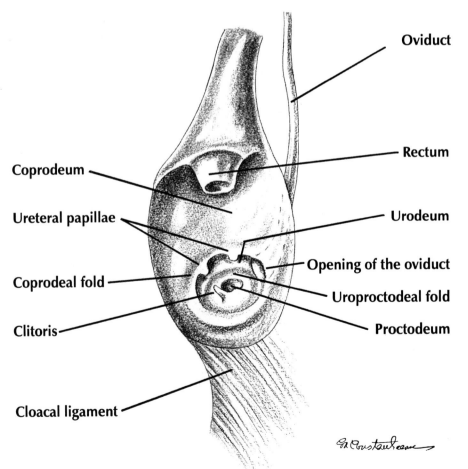

Figure 7. Cloaca, ventral view, of a 4-month-old female ostrich

Anatomy

hemispheres and lateral to the cranial half of the cerebellum. The cerebellum is oblong shaped, and positioned behind and between the caudal aspect of the two cerebral hemispheres. Its surface has horizontal folds or folia. The medulla oblongata is a wide segment of the brain stem extending caudally and ventral to the cerebellum, and continuing as the spinal cord.

PINEAL GLAND

A small, oval, tan-to-pink gland with a ventral stalk, the pineal gland is located in a triangle formed by the two cerebral hemispheres and the cerebellum. It is positioned dorsally and is often removed with the top of the skull.

The functions of the pineal gland have not been completely elucidated. It is hypothesized that the gland acts as a photoreceptor regulating reproduction, the mating season, circadian rhythm and perhaps other bodily activities.

Adult female tracheal worm, or gape worm, seen in young emus. The scientific name is Cyanthostoma (var).

TRACHEA

The trachea begins at an attachment to the larynx within the mouth. When the mouth is opened, the large hollow tube staring at you is the trachea. It extends down the neck in a ventral, then right paramedian, then returns to a ventral position prior to entering the thoracic inlet.

Inside the thorax, the trachea divides into two branches called major bronchi which supply air to the right and left lung.

A syrinx, a vocal organ in the trachea or bronchi in birds, is present only in rheas. Emus and ostriches have a thin membrane within the lumen of the bronchi, but it is debatable whether this can be considered a true syrinx.

The trachea is made of several cartilaginous rings, each with irregular widths that overlap adjacent rings, and they are connected by a thin membrane, giving great flexibility. In older adults, the rings become very hard and lose their flexibility as they become calcified.

In emus, the ventral trachea has a segment of incomplete rings forming a tracheal diverticulum, an open cleft covered by a very thin membrane. The segment involves 7 to 12 rings and is located just in front of the thoracic inlet.

The membrane covering the cleft enlarges during the mating season, creating a pendulous pouch easily seen in females during their first and/or second breeding year. In older females, the pouch is present but is not

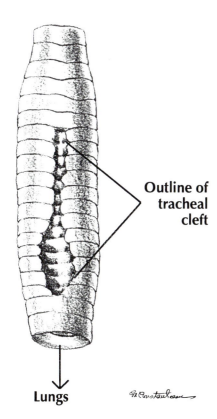

Figure 8. Emu trachea, showing outline of tracheal cleft.

Adult female emu. Note the general strutting appearance, the tracheal diverticulum and excess skin hanging below the neck, apterylae on head and upper neck. The dark spot behind the eye is the ear canal.

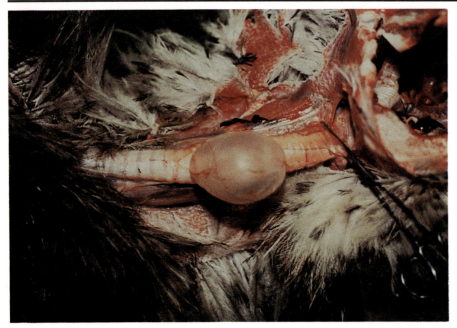
Juvenile emu ventral trachea, demonstrating the tracheal diverticulum as it is inflated.

seen as readily. Males also have the cleft, but the membrane doesn't enlarge as much.

The cleft is the source of the deep booming sound from female emus and the grunting sound in male emus. See Figure 8.

THYMUS

The thymus is a paired organ located on the right and left sides of the cervical spine, one to three vertebrae cranial to the thoracic inlet. The organ is attached to the subcutaneous tissue and is usually removed with the skin. It is a light tan color, with an oval to elongated shape less than 1 cm in diameter or up to 3 cm in length.

The thymus is the site of production and maturation of the T-lymphocytes which have an extremely important role in cell-mediated immunity. The function and size diminish after puberty, although they are often still present in aged adults.

THYROID

The thyroid is a paired endocrine gland attached to the right and left subclavian artery inside the thoracic inlet. It is oval, less than 1 to 2 cm in diameter, semi-translucent, and pink to red in color. It produces hormones such as thyroxine.

PARATHYROID

The parathyroid is a paired endocrine organ attached directly to the medial, cranial pole of the thyroid glands. They are tan in color and are 0.5 to 4 mm in size. They produce the hormone parathormone, which regulates calcium and phosphorous metabolism. These glands are often enlarged in cases of rickets.

HEART

The heart is located immediately behind the breast plate and the thoracic inlet, inside the thoracic cavity. It is a muscular organ comprised of four chambers, similar to human and mammalian hearts. The base is upward, with the apex in a ventral caudal position. The heart's contractions pump the blood throughout the vascular system. A thin, tough, semi-opaque fibrous membrane surrounds the heart, forming the pericardial space and pericardial sac that partitions the heart from other structures within the thoracic cavity.

LUNG

The lung is a paired organ, positioned in a vertical plane, attaching along the ventral spine and the second through seventh ribs. The lungs are thick dorsally where they fit between the ribs, and become thin ventrally.

The lungs are the site of air exchange with the blood. Oxygen is absorbed while carbon dioxide is released.

The lungs have a smooth, pink ventral surface with large openings from the bronchi into the thoracic openings of the air sacs. The dorsal lung has large grooves where the ribs are positioned. The internal lung structure is similar to other avian groups.

The lungs do not expand and contract as in mammals. Respiration is an active process during both inspiration and expiration, using the thoracic and abdomen muscles, as the lungs do not have elastic recoil.

The lungs can often be seen as a pink color through the skin of the thorax in chicks. Remember, ratites do not have major breast muscles, and injections in this area will probably be placed into the lung.

AIR SACS

The air sacs are very thin-walled, transparent sacs that originate from the bronchi on the ventral surface of the lung, and they are all interconnected via the lung. They are usually paired organs, but the clavicular air sac is unpaired and the left abdominal air sac appears to be slightly larger than the right in some specimens.

The air sacs occupy approximately 80 per cent of the respiratory volume and they provide added space for air passage to improve the efficiency of respiration by allowing fresh air to enter the lung during both inspiration and expiration. They also reduce the density of the body and bone to aid in flight, although ratites are flightless.

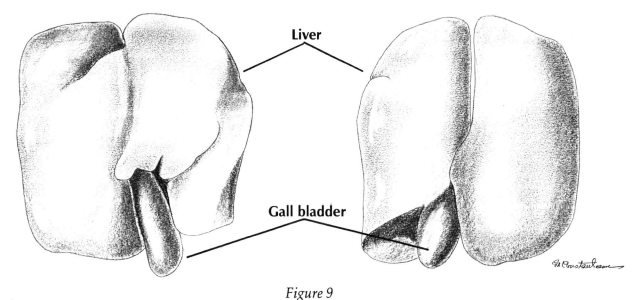

Emu liver and gall bladder, dorsal view.

Figure 9

Emu liver and gall bladder, ventral view.

The air flow is complex and not completely understood, but it appears all air sacs are emptying and filling at the same time. It is estimated that at least three complete respiratory cycles are required for a given unit of inspired air to be completely exhaled.

Each ratite group has slightly different sized and shaped air sacs. Although these differences have been noted, a detailed scientific evaluation of all air sacs is needed to provide an accurate description.

Basically, the air sacs are located 1) in front of and within the thoracic inlet (cervical and clavicular air sacs), 2) attached below to the lungs in the thorax (thoracic air sacs), and 3) within the abdomen (abdominal air sacs).

Air passages also communicate with some bones. These bones are called pneumatic. The femur is the largest pneumatic bone.

The breastplate, sternal ribs, humerus, and vertebrae also have some degree of communication with the air sacs, although the humerus is not pneumatic in all individuals.

The cervical air sac is paired, very small, and vestigial. It is located in front of the thoracic inlet on the ventral, cervical vertebrae.

The clavicular air sac is unpaired, very delicate, and complicated to define. It probably communicates with the breastplate, humerus, the sternal ribs and cervical vertebrae. It has two communications with the lungs.

The paired thoracic air sacs are positioned directly under the lungs. Depending on the ratite group, there are 3-4 divisions or compartments separated by a thin-walled membrane. These compartments are often termed cranial, middle, and caudal thoracic air sacs.

The caudal thoracic air sac (the largest air sac in the ostrich) communicates with the paired abdominal air sacs which communicate with the femur and synsacrum.

LIVER

The liver is a single organ located within the thorax immediately behind the heart, in front of and ventral to the proventriculus, and usually not extending caudal to the last rib. In the emu, the liver may extend slightly beyond the last rib.

The liver filters the blood, metabolizes foreign exogenous and endogenous substances, and synthesizes bile, many enzymes and proteins for bodily functions, as well as for the formation of the yolk. It also has a role in many metabolic processes such as carbohydrate utilization and storage.

The liver is the largest single organ in vertebrates, although comparatively small in the ostriches. In ratites, it has two large lobes that are separated from each other and the heart, lungs, proventriculus and abdomen by several strong, but thin, membranes.

In ostriches, the left major lobe has three small minor lobes. The color is dark reddish brown. The surface may appear silver to grey due to a thick surface capsule. In emus and rheas, the gall bladder is positioned between the two lobes on the caudal end (Figure 9).

GALL BLADDER

Ostriches do not have gall bladders. In emus and rheas it is located on the caudal surface of the liver, between the two lobes and attached to the common bile duct (Figure 9).

This is a storage pouch for bile produced by the liver. It is thin-walled and dark green in color due to the presence of bile. The size of the bladder varies according to bile production and utilization during, after, and between eating.

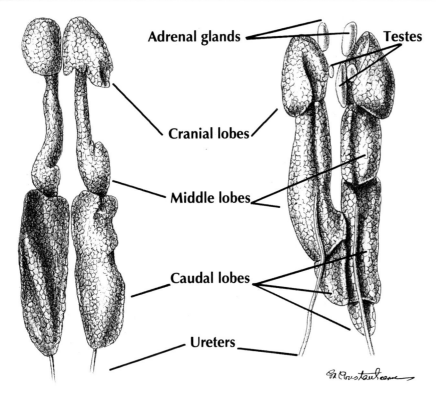

Figure 10
Ostrich kidneys, dorsal view *Emu kidneys, adrenals, and testes, ventral view*

SPLEEN

The spleen is located within the abdomen, attached by loose connective tissue to the right side of the proventriculus and ventriculus in ostriches and the ventriculus in emus and rheas.

The spleen is the site of red and white blood cell production during embryonic development.

After hatch, the spleen's primary role is lymphocyte and monocyte production, as well as acting as a filter removing bacteria, abnormal cells and/or cellular debris from the blood.

The shape varies but the color is usually reddish. In ostrich chicks, the spleen is often bean shaped, but can be tubular in older ostriches. In emus and rheas, the shape is almost always tubular. See Figure 5.

PANCREAS

A single gland, the pancreas is attached within the duodenal loop of the small intestines, just caudal to the ventriculus in the right side of the cranial abdomen. See Figures 5 and 6.

The gland has both exocrine and endocrine functions. The exocrine portion releases digestive enzymes into the duodenal portion of the small intestines through pancreatic ducts.

The endocrine portion produces hormones such as insulin and glycogen that aid in the regulation and metabolism of blood sugar or carbohydrates.

The gland is thin, narrow, and long with a flat or flared dorsal surface that is pink to tan in color.

KIDNEY

The kidney is a paired organ positioned within the caudal abdomen on the right and left of midline immediately ventral to the caudal spine or pelvis.

The kidneys filter the blood, creating urine. During filtration, they resorb substances back into the blood that are needed and excrete substances such as uric acid (the creamy white material in the urine) that are metabolic waste products, or are not needed to maintain a proper balance of water, electrolytes and pH.

The kidneys are red-brown in color and are long, thick, tubular organs. The shape varies between ratite groups, but all have three divisions of cranial, middle and caudal lobes. The internal structure is similar to other avians. See Figure 10 for a comparison of ostrich and emu kidneys.

ADRENAL

The adrenal is a paired gland located within the abdomen on the right and left of midline, adjacent to the cranial, medial pole of the kidneys and gonads.

The adrenal is a very important endocrine gland that produces hormones such as epinephrine, cortisol, aldosterone and several others. The hormones regulate body functions such as vascular tone, blood pressure, cardiac output, stress, carbohydrate and electrolyte metabolism. Almost all body functions are affected by hormones produced by this gland.

The gland is oval to elongated, usually 1 to 3 cm in size in chicks. The surface is tan in color with the cut surface being tan/yellow with a dark tan/brown center. The internal structure is similar to other avian groups. See Figure 10.

TESTIS

The testes are paired glands within the abdomen on the right and left of midline, below the spine, adjacent to the cranial pole of the kidneys and adrenal glands (Figure 10). They are present only in the males and produce spermatozoa and male sex hormones, such as testosterone.

Unlike mammals, ratite testes greatly enlarge to over 10 cm in length during the mating season, then regress in size to an inactive state at the end of the season.

In emus the right testis, or testicle, is round, often with secon-

Breeding male emu. Note 1) the long tubular spleen, brownish red in color; 2) paired green testes, the left being larger; 3) the paired kidneys under the testes. The fat and spleen are cranial.

dary nodules, and is much smaller than the oval-shaped left testis (Figure 10). Both emu testes are dark green in color.

Both testes are similar in size in ostriches and rheas, and they are oval to elongated in shape and tan in color. The internal structure is similar to other avians.

Testes from an ostrich which has recently begun to "redden up." The testes are not yet full-sized. They are located over the cranial lobe of the kidney, on the ventral lumbar spine.

OVARY

Present only in the females, the ovary is a single gland located within the abdomen, on the left side along the ventral spine, adjacent to the cranial pole of the left kidney.

The ovary produces the ova or yolks, as well as female hormones, such as estrogen. All the ova that a hen can produce are present at hatch.

These ova (or follicles) are microscopic in size and randomly enlarge during the mating season after reaching puberty. Once the follicle is mature, it is released into the oviduct where it is fertilized by the male spermatozoa, and the formation of an egg begins.

From hatch until puberty the ovary is a flat, elongated to almond-shaped pad of tissue, with a grainy surface that is tan in color in ostriches and rheas. Emu ovaries are dark green in color.

During the mating season, the ovary in a mature hen resembles a cluster of various sized grapes, with the smallest follicle being microscopic and the largest, most mature follicle being the size of a softball. The size of the egg is determined by the size of the follicle and yolk when it is released into the oviduct. See photo next page.

OVIDUCT

A single tubular organ, the oviduct is attached to the ovary and abdominal wall by thin mesenteric membranes, and extends down the left side of the abdomen, ending at its attachment to the left dorsolateral wall of the urodeum within the cloaca.

The oviduct is the canal that transports the yolk, manufactures the albumin, shell membranes, shell, and cuticle, and expels a formed egg into the cloaca, then into the world.

Like the gonads, the oviduct greatly enlarges in size during mating season to accommodate egg production.

The oviduct is organized into the following segments in descending sequence: ostium, ampulla, infundibulum, magnum, isthmus, uterus, and vagina, which opens into the urodeum of the cloaca.

In immature ratites, a thin, solid membrane covers the opening at the junction of the vagina

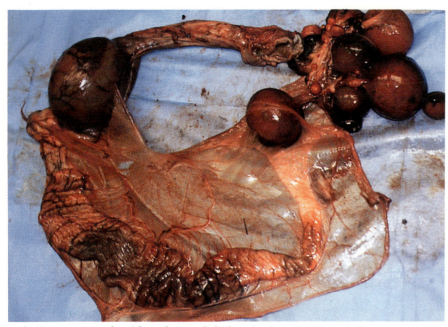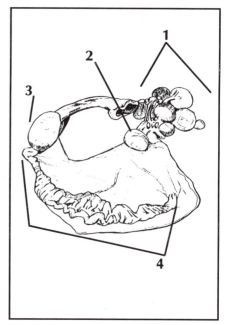

Active ovary and oviduct from adult female rhea. Redness is due to illness. 1: Follicle cluster in the ovary. 2: Follicle and pedicle attached to ovary, preparing for release. 3: Soft-shelled egg in oviduct, entering shell gland. 4. Oviduct.

and the urodeum. This membrane is torn open when the hen lays her first egg. The tearing of the membrane and enlargement of the opening often creates bleeding, the source of blood on the shell of the first few eggs that are laid.

Hens that are several years old that have not laid an egg still have the membrane, preventing insertion of swabs for culture unless it is torn, which is not recommended.

The ostium with fimbriae, in conjunction with the ampulla, acts as a funnel to catch the ovum, guiding it into the infundibulum as it is released from the pedicle of the ovary. The infundibulum is the site of fertilization of the ovum by spermatozoa, secretion of a membrane that covers the ovum or yolk, and albumen secretion.

The magnum is the longest section, where most of the albumin is secreted. The isthmus is where the inner and outer shell membranes are formed.

The uterus is the site of the shell gland, which forms the shell, adds the pigment, and places the cuticle on the shell surface.

The vagina is the site of the storage glands. They house the spermatozoa in many avians. It is assumed that ratites have similar storage glands for spermatozoa somewhere within the oviduct, although they have not yet been structurally identified. Vaginal glands are absent in ostriches.

The vagina is the last stage before oviposition (laying the egg) and it contracts to expel the egg.

PHALLUS

This is the copulatory organ of the male. In the female, the rudimentary organ is often called a vestigial phallus, but it is actually the clitoris. Both are positioned on the floor of the caudal proctodeum of the cloaca. Ratites have an intromittent-type phallus. This

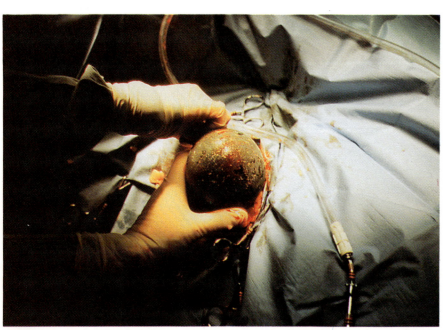

Surgical removal of an egg from the oviduct of a two-year-old emu hen. The tan spots on the egg are inflammatory debris due to an E. coli infection, which contributed to the hen becoming egg-bound.

Anatomy

type is found in only a few other types of birds as Tinamidae, Cracidae, Anseriformes, and the lone Passeriforme, the Black Buffalo Weaver. Most birds have a non-intromittent phallus.

The avian intromittent phallus functions only as a mechanical probe, and unlike the mammalian penis the intromittent phallus does not have a urethra and therefore does not have a role in voiding of urine or the internal transport of semen.

The phallus enlarges at puberty, then again during each mating season, after which it slightly reduces in size. The phallus allows the semen of the male to enter the vagina of the female during intromission. This is accomplished by an external shallow sulcus referred to as the seminal groove, or the *sulcus ejaculatorius* and a *sulcus phalli*.

The semen enters the seminal groove after accumulating in the ejaculatory fossa in the floor of the urodeum of the cloaca after being voided from the vas deferens. The semen then drains, by gravitational forces, down the seminal groove and sulcus phalli into the vagina during intromission.

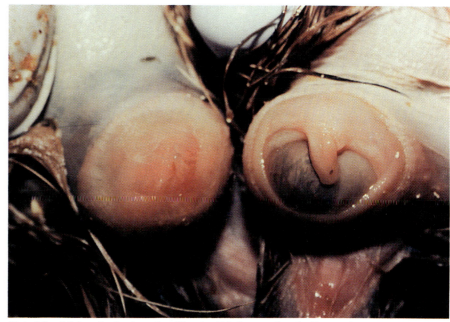

Ostrich chicks. Left: female clitoris. Right: male phallus. The male is photographed upside down to better illustrate the phallus.

The structure of the phallus is greatly different between ratite groups. The intromittent phallus has two major forms: 1) a solid phallus, and 2) a phallus with an ostium containing an invaginated portion of the phallus.

Ostriches have the simplest phallus. It is solid, firm, yet spongy, wide at the base and pointed at the end, with a rounded, triangle shape in cross section. The seminal groove is positioned on the dorsal surface when the phallus is everted.

In the sexually active male, the everted phallus curves sharply ventrally, then immediately in a left, cranial direction.

The phallus is bright pink to red and can be up to 40 cm in length. It consists of fibro-elastic

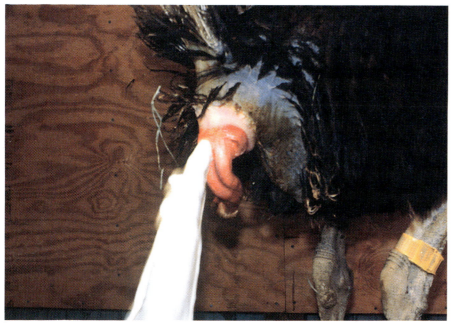
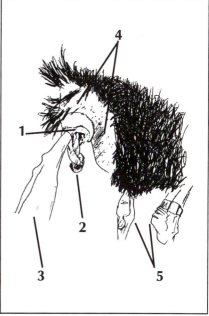

Adult male ostrich. 1. Cloaca. 2. Phallus. 3. White urine stream, containing urates. 4. Apterylae around vent. 5. Hock joints.

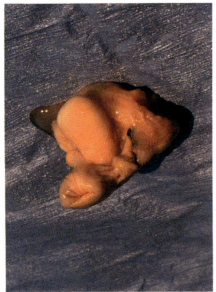
Breeding male emu phallus, illustrating the ostium in the tip and the pouch of erectile tissue.

Externalized non-erect phallus of adult male emu.

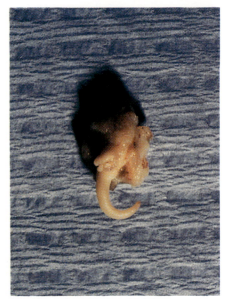
Phallus of male rhea chick.

tissue with lymphatic cavities. It is easily seen as it is everted during defecation, urination and mating.

In male emus, the phallus has a short, firm cartilage base that extends vertically only a few centimeters with a left twist that is covered with erectile tissue.

The non-erect phallus has an ostium or opening in the tip that contains an invaginated portion of non-cartilaginous phallus that extends to the base of the cartilage, forming a small pouch on the ventral surface. During coitus, and tumescence, this tissue is everted, greatly lengthening the phallus up to 7-12 cm.

The extended phallus has a seminal groove and sulcus phalli, is very soft and flexible, and has an internal elastic ligament that pulls the phallus into its invaginated position during detumescence. See Figure 11.

The structure of the phallus in rheas is very similar to emus, although the non-erect phallus is much longer and twisted. As emus, the rhea phallus has an ostium with an invaginated portion of non-cartilaginous phallus that is extended during tumescence to increase its length up to 10-15 cm.

Unlike a mammalian penis, where blood is utilized to enlarge the penis, avians, including the ratites, have lymph cavities in the erectile tissue of the phallus which fill with lymph from adjacent paracloacal vascular bodies to create an erection. The left vascular body is larger than the right, causing the erect phallus to curve to the left.

The clitoris of female ostriches is easily seen and often confused with the male phallus prior to puberty. The clitoris only slightly increases in size up to puberty. In adult females, it is usually less than 3 cm in length, pink in color, flat on cross section with a rounded tip, and has a small groove.

The clitoris in female emus is either a small grey to pink nodule of tissue appearing as a *wart,* or it may be a short vestigial cartilage covered with tissue, but NO ostium in the tip. The latter type is often confused with a male phallus or vice versa prior to puberty.

In female rheas, the clitoris is a very small nodule of grey to white tissue that is often so small it can be seen only after close scrutiny. The tissue of the floor of the proctodeum will "V" with a tiny groove pointing toward the clitoris. Distinguishing between male and female rheas by visually examining the phallus or clitoris is quite simple if the organs are properly everted.

BURSA OF FABRICIUS

A single organ, the bursa of Fabricius is located in the lateral and dorsal wall of the proctodeum in the cloacal pouch. It has a major role in humeral immunity, i.e. antibodies, and the production and

Clitoris (nodule over forefinger) of female rhea chick.

Anatomy

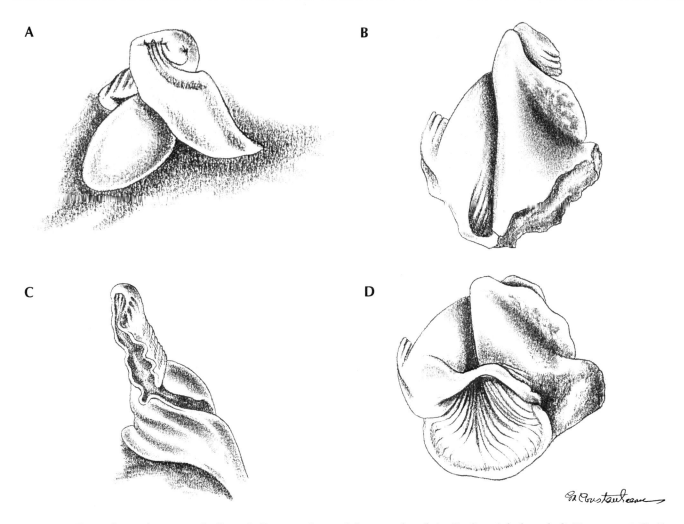

Figure 11. Four views of an emu phallus. A: Retracted, cranial, ventral and tip. B: Cranial, dorsal. C: Tumescent. D: Base.

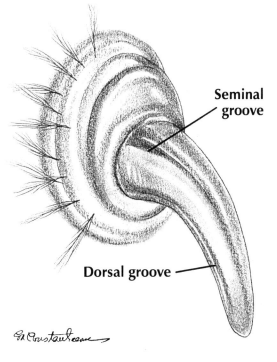

Figure 12. Partially protruded ostrich phallus.

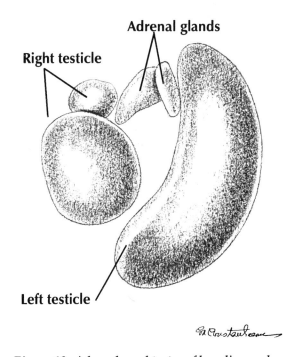

Figure 13. Adrenals and testes of breeding male emu.

Fat within abdominal wall of adult ostrich.

FAT

Called adipose tissue, fat is a special tissue designed for storage of excess energy and to provide insulation and protection from cold and trauma.

The fat is uniquely deposited under the skin (subcutaneous), on the surface of organs, especially the heart, ventriculus, intestine, internal pelvic muscles, and within the mesentery.

The major deposition sites are the breast plate, ventral abdomen, and over the rump or dorsal pelvic region. Subcutaneous fat as thick as 12 cm is not uncommon in overfed, breeding birds. The oil is derived from the adipose tissue.

maturation of B-lymphocytes and T-lymphocytes.

The organ is unique to avians. In most birds, it is an inverted sac or pouch with long, folded papillae inside. The papillae have follicles that produce T-lymphocytes in the cortex region and B-lymphocytes in the medullary region.

In ratites, the bursa of Fabricius is everted, forming a raised strip of lobulated follicles instead of a pouch. The B-lymphocytes and T-lymphocytes are also produced in the opposite locations, i.e., cortex and medulla, respectively. The bursa is tan to white in color, raised, linear and is very difficult to see. If a portion of the dorsal proctodeum is removed, it can be seen and evaluated histologically.

SELECTED VEINS

JUGULAR VEIN

Located just under the skin, the jugular vein courses from the lateral side of the skull near the ear, down the right side of the neck, closely positioned but dorsal to the esophagus, then entering into the thoracic inlet.

The jugular vein carries venous blood from the head and neck to the heart. It is a very good vein to use for blood collection and/or intravenous catheterization or injections. The vein is very large when occluded, has a very thin wall, and is very pliable and mobile.

Ostriches have only a right jugular vein. Emus have both right and left veins, although the right is slightly larger. Rheas have right jugular veins, and given individuals may or may not have left jugular veins.

BRACHIAL AND BASILIC VEINS

These veins are visibly located on the ventral side of the right and left humerus bone of the wings of ostriches and rheas only.

The brachial vein is lateral to the bone and basilic vein. The basilic vein overlies the humerus bone and is often larger than the

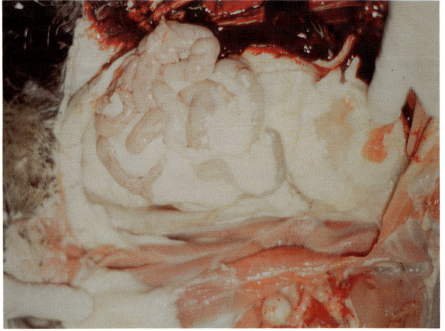

Excessive fat within the abdomen and mesentery, and surrounding the stomach of a six-week-old emu that died due to a ruptured fatty liver. Some fat is good. Excessive amounts are deadly.

brachial vein. Both can be easily seen if occluded, except in very dehydrated patients.

The size of the veins depend on the patient, but these veins are much less mobile and easier to see than the jugular vein. These two veins are excellent sites for blood collection and intravenous injections or catheterization.

The skin over the veins in adults is very tough and often crinkles the tip of the IV catheter during placement.

MEDIAL METATARSAL VEIN

This vein is located on the medial side of the right and left tarsometatarsus bone in all ratites. It carries venous blood from the foot to the femoral vein. It lies immediately beneath the very tough scaly skin, and is most easily seen in the middle of the bone and over the hock joint. This vein can be used for blood collection and intravenous injections or catheterization.

RENAL PORTAL VEINS

There are cranial and caudal renal portal veins and a renal vein associated with each kidney. These veins receive venous blood from both hind limbs, the pelvis, caudal portions of intestines, cloaca, and tail.

The cranial and caudal renal portal veins form a ring around each kidney. The cranial renal portal vein continues into the internal vertebral sinuses, and the caudal renal portal vein ends at an anastomosis with the coccygeomesenteric vein.

Both portal veins begin at an anastomosis with the external iliac vein. The external iliac vein becomes the common iliac vein, which has an anastomosis with the renal vein, then continues as the caudal vena cava.

The anastomosis of these veins, associated valves, and the caudal vena cava interact to form a renal portal system which can shunt blood to or away from the kidneys. The valves (described in more detail below) are located within the lumen of the common iliac vein, positioned after the anastomosis of the caudal and cranial renal portal veins, and prior to the anastomosis of the renal vein.

The valves are under autonomic control. When the valves are closed, additional venous blood is shunted from the common iliac vein into the kidneys, via the cranial and caudal renal portal veins and the associated peritubular capillaries. This venous blood passes through the proximal and distal tubules of all nephrons, but not the glomeruli.

When the valves are open, less venous blood enters the kidneys as it flows through the valves into the caudal vena cava, by-passing the cranial and caudal renal portal veins.

This is an important feature to consider when administering therapeutics or injectable tranquilizers or anesthetics. When additional blood is flowing through the kidneys, therapeutics with potential renal toxicity may need to be administered in lower than normal dosages, or not given. Anesthetic agents metabolized or excreted by the kidney will need to be given in higher dosages to attain the desired effect and the duration of effects is usually shortened.

The anatomy of the valves is usually slightly different between avian species, but most have only a single valve for each kidney, as present in emus and rheas.

Ostriches are unique in having a total of six valves, three for each kidney, located in a cranial to caudal row with the size of each valve decreasing caudally.

The valves are conical in shape and have cholinergic and adrenergic innervated smooth muscle fibers.

In ostriches, the valves are within a common wall between the dilated caudal renal portal vein and the more medial renal vein and common iliac vein. The base of the valves faces the caudal renal portal vein, and the large orifice in the apex opens into the common iliac vein.

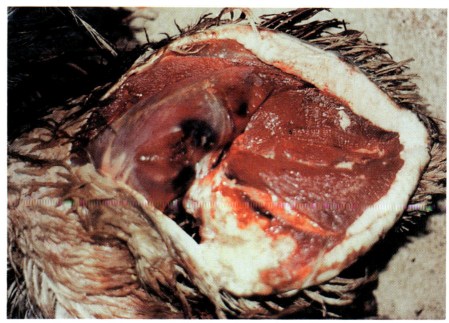

Cut section over side rump of adult female rhea. Note the red meat and the layer of white subcutaneous fat.

TABLE 1. MAJOR ANATOMICAL DIFFERENCES BETWEEN OSTRICHES, EMUS AND RHEAS

ANATOMICAL FEATURE	OSTRICH	EMU	RHEA
Body Size	Largest.	Second largest.	Smallest.
Proventriculus	Very large, located dorsal and directly caudal to the ventriculus, with a dorsal strip of glandular tissue.	Small, with glands encircling the cranial 2/3 to 3/4 of the organ.	Small dilation, with a nodular gland on the dorsal 1/3 of the organ.
Ventriculus	Large, round, and muscular with a restrictive pyloric valve.	Smaller, round, and muscular with a less restrictive pyloric valve.	Elongated, expandable and muscular, with a less restrictive pyloric valve.
Large Intestine	Very long, with proximal sacculated and distal non-sacculated segments.	Very short; non-sacculated.	Very short; non-sacculated.
Apterylae	Lateral thorax and abdomen, ventral wing, below the vent and legs.	Ventral wing, and leg below the hock joint.	Ventral wing, and leg below the hock joint.
Toes	The greater toe has four phalanges, the lateral has four or five.	Three toes, medial toe has three phalanges, central toe has four, the lateral toe has five.	Three toes, medial toe has three phalanges, central toe has four, the lateral toe has five.
Male and Female	Dimorphic: Male - black and white feathers, usually larger body size. The beak, lower legs, and skin turn bright pink to lavender during breeding season. Female - grey and white feathers.	Monomorphic - charcoal grey. Body size is not a distinguishing feature.	Monomorphic - white or grey and white, although the male has a distinctly larger body size.
Tail	Mobile and functional, with eight vertebrae caudal to the ilium. The first six are always free and the last two may be fused together.	Immobile, indistinct, consisting of eight vertebrae caudal to the ilium. The first five are free and the last three are fused together.	Small and slightly mobile, with five vertebrae caudal to the pubis.
Wings	Large.	Short and vestigial.	Large.
Jugular Vein	Only the right is present.	Both right and left are present.	Right is always present; left is absent in some individuals.
Pubis	Caudal ends are in close proximity and curve forward to form a pubic floor. Fused to the ischium.	Caudal ends are free and widely separated.	Caudal ends are widely separated and fused to the ischium.
Ceca	Long, with a large lumen, and sacculated.	Short, small lumen and non-sacculated.	Long, with a large lumen, and sacculated.
Clavicle	Absent.	Present.	Fused to thoracic girdle.

TABLE 1. (Continued)
MAJOR ANATOMICAL DIFFERENCES

ANATOMICAL FEATURE	OSTRICH	EMU	RHEA
Tracheal Diverticulum	Absent.	Present.	Absent.
Skin on Metatarsus	Grey/tan to pink in color, cranial scutes.	Black in color, cranial scutes and raised caudal scutes.	Grey in color, cranial scutes.
Sternum	Bilaterally fused together.	Bilaterally fused together.	Bilaterally unfused in chicks, becoming partially fused in adults.
# of Cervical Vertebrae	18	18	15
# of Complete Ribs	5 or 6	5	3
Number of Renal Portal Valves per Kidney	3	1	1
Testes	Paired, tan in color, similar in size.	Paired, green in color, left larger than the right.	Paired, tan in color, similar in size.
Phallus (male)	Long, large, solid with no ostium.	Short, cartilage base, with ostium, containing invaginated phallus.	Short cartilage base with long, non-erect phallus with ostium, containing invaginated phallus.
Gall Bladder	Absent.	Present.	Present.

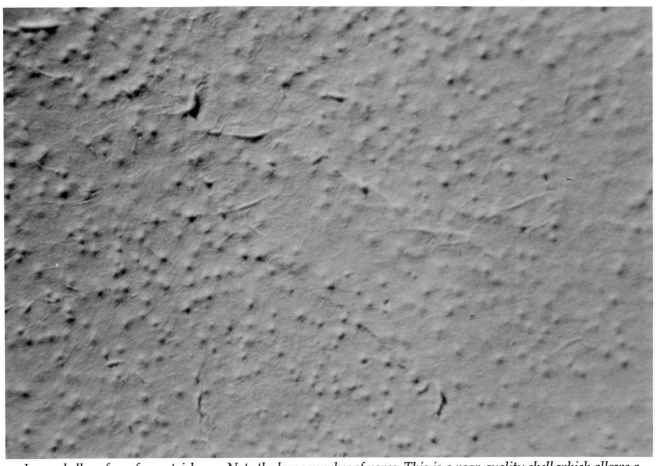

Inner shell surface of an ostrich egg. Note the large number of pores. This is a poor-quality shell which allows a greater risk of bacterial infection and increased moisture loss. Genetics will probably play an important role in eggshell quality in the future. (Photo courtesy Dr. Brett Hopkins)

RATITE GENETICS

Benny J. Gallaway, Ph.D. and John C. Patton, Ph.D.
LGL Ecological Genetics, Inc.
Bryan, Texas

Ken Coldwell and Wayne Sealey
C&S Ranch, GenLab, Inc.
Bellville, Texas

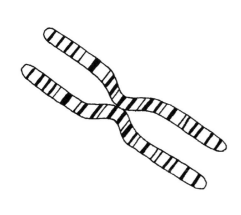

The ratite industry comes along at an opportune time in the history of agriculture. Scientific and technological advances in agriculture have developed to a point that was undreamed of only a few short years ago. Much of this new and emerging technology can be readily extended to ratites.

One such area is in the field of genetics. For more than three decades prior to the late 1980s and early 1990s, poultry geneticists and poultry breeders explored the use of genetic markers for evaluating the genotype of an individual and its breeding value. They achieved only limited success.

Then, in the mid 1980s, came the development of many new technologies, including DNA fingerprinting. These highly polymorphic molecular genetic markers opened the door to a wide range of possible applications, including marker-assisted selection of breeders to achieve greater and more uniform production.

Scientific and agricultural journals, indeed even newspapers, are now flooded with articles describing the use of these markers to improve quality and quantity of production. The ratite industry stands ready to inherit much of what has been learned by the genetic study of other animals and birds.

We begin this chapter with the unavoidable presentation of some basic terms and concepts in genetics as background for the following subjects.

We then describe the degrees of relatedness and evolutionary history of the various species of ratites as determined from genetic assays, and how genetics have enabled identifications or confirmations of sub-species within a species.

The emphasis of this chapter is placed upon describing genetic methods for identifying individuals and their relatedness, and how the application of this information results in demonstrable increases in production, at least for the emu (*Dromaius novaehollandiae*).

We next move to the matter of the use of genetics for gender identification, a topic of great importance and interest to ratite breeders. Some species (e.g., the emu) express little or no sexual dimorphism, especially at younger ages.

Lastly, we conclude the chapter with a discussion of the immediate future of ratite genetics: genome mapping and the identification of genetic markers associated with quantitative traits in ratites.

BASIC TERMS AND CONCEPTS

All living organisms have their genetic material in the form of DNA (deoxyribose nucleic acid). It is a complex molecule that gives living cells all the instructions needed to grow or reproduce. Ultimately, these instructions guide all living processes—all form and function of living things.

Segments of the DNA molecule that code for a given task are known as genes. DNA molecules occur in an array of discrete packages known as chromosomes.

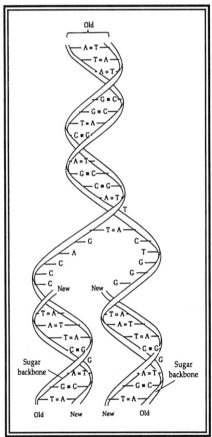

Figure 1. A diagrammatic representation of a section of the DNA molecule shown in the process of replication. The molecule occurs as a double helix or twisted-ladder form. The sides, or backbone, of the ladder (molecule) are comprised of sugar (deoxyribose) and the rungs are made of paired nucleotides bonded together: adenine (A) to thymine (T) and guanine (G) to cytosine (C).

Birds typically have 60 to 80 pairs of chromosomes; i.e., the genetic material of most higher organisms comes in duplicate.

Each chromosome is paired with a *sister* (or homologous) chromosome which contains a duplicate set of instructions to perform the tasks controlled by that chromosome. The purpose of this redundancy is generally thought to provide a genetic *fail-safe* or back-up system. However, this redundancy also serves as an important source of genetic variation, as will be discussed later.

The DNA in each chromosome is a single long, thin, continuous molecule which is actually composed of a chain of smaller subunits known as nucleotides. Each nucleotide consists of a phosphate, a sugar known as deoxyribose, and any one of four nitrogen bases: adenine (A), guanine (G), cytosine (C), and thymine (T).

The chain of nucleotides making up the DNA molecule is composed of two strands in the form of a double helix, somewhat resembling a long spiral ladder (Figure 1). The backbone strands, or sides of the ladder, are made up of alternating phosphate and sugar molecules.

The nitrogen bases, joining in opposite pairs, act as the rungs. Each base is attached to a sugar molecule, and is linked by a hydrogen bond to its complementary base on the opposite strand. Adenine always links to thymine, and guanine always links to cytosine (Figure 1).

If the DNA strands making up the entire genetic composition (genome) of a human were laid end to end, they would be about 3 feet long and there would be on the order of three billion base pairs.

To make a new identical copy of the DNA molecule, the two backbone strands need only unwind and separate at the weakly-linked bases comprising the rungs of the ladder (Figure 1).

New complementary bases are manufactured in the cell and link with their complementary base on each of the separated strands. Thus, two double helixes or chromosomes are formed, each identical to the original strand which served as a template or blueprint for replication.

Each segment on a DNA molecule coding for a particular task is specifically called a *locus*, a Greek word meaning the location that a set of instructions physically occupies on a chromosome. *Gene* is a more general term used as a synonym for locus. At each locus, the exact instructions might vary to some degree. Thus, genes come in different versions known as alleles.

Whereas many versions of a gene (allele) may occur in the population as a whole, each individual can have only two alleles, one from each parent (Figure 2). When the two alleles—one from each parent—at a locus are different, the individual is said to be heterozygous. If the two alleles are the same, that individual is said to be homozygous. Alleles are also classified as being either dominant or recessive.

When an allele is recessive, its instruction is masked by the dominant allele. Thus, the instruction from the recessive allele is not expressed when a dominant and recessive allele are paired at the same locus on sister chromosomes. The instructions coded by the dominant allele are all that is used by the cell in performing the task. To have the instructions of a recessive allele followed by the cell, both alleles must be the same.

The principles of genetic transmission of physical traits of organisms were first deduced in 1865 by the Augustinian monk, Gregor Johan Mendel. A summary of these principles, in modern terms, is shown by Figure 2. Each parent is shown to be heterozygous for a given gene, and can provide only one or the other of these alleles to each offspring. Three of the four possible gene combinations of the offspring produced by this pair will contain the dominant allele, which will be expressed in the offspring (phenotype). The phenotype of the recessive allele will be expressed in only one of the four offspring, those homozygous for the recessive allele.

However, the genotype distribution shows that two more of the offspring carry the recessive allele which can be expressed in future generations (Figure 2). One of the major ramifications of this to the ratite industry will be discussed later, in the context of inbreeding depression.

The sex of birds is believed to be determined by a single pair of chromosomes, called sex chromosomes. The sex chromosomes differ from all other pairs (called autosomes) in that they are usually not greatly alike or homologous as described above, but occur in two forms, Z and W.

Male birds carry the Z form only (ZZ) whereas the female carries both the Z and W, a state called female heterogamety. This is the opposite of the situation in humans and other mammals.

The Z chromosome in many birds is decidedly larger than the W chromosome, which over time has become specialized and reduced in size.

However, exact identification of Z and W chromosomes based upon size is quite difficult in many birds. The reduced size of the W chromosome results in it being similar to many of the other of the 80 or so small chromosome pairs.

There are other diagnostic tests for the W chromosome that are based on staining differences between the Z and W chromosomes. They work well with many bird species, but not ratites.

For ratites, the problem of identifying sex based upon examination of the sex chromosomes is compounded. Sex chromosomes

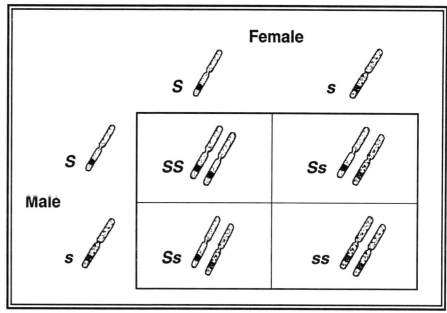

Figure 2. Diagram of a chromosome showing alleles (S or s) at a locus or gene. Each parent (shown outside the box) can give one of its chromosomes to the offspring (shown inside the box). The parents are shown to be heterozygous carrying both a dominant (S) and recessive (s) allele. The three possible genotypes of the offspring are shown. Note that one out of four will be homozygous for the recessive allele.

of ratites differ little, if any, in size and/or morphology. They are believed to remain in the primitive evolutionary state where only slight differences occur, probably at the nucleotide sequence level.

HISTORY AND TAXONOMY

Advances in DNA technology have enabled scientists to better understand the evolutionary history and taxonomy of animals, including ratites.

These aspects are often viewed as being of little value to ratite ranching; however, they should be given much more consideration. Evolutionary history and taxonomy of ratites are measures of relatedness. Differences among and within species have emerged as a result of alternative and adaptive solutions to problems encountered. Understanding the ratites in these terms has much to offer.

For example, the most genetically-divergent subspecies of the ostrich (*Struthio camelus molybdophanes*) readily occupies brushy habitats and is a browser of brush.

In contrast, its nearest geographically neighboring subspecies (*S. c. massaicus*) is remarkably different on a genetic basis. *S. c. massaicus* is strictly an open-savannah bird and a grazer.

The taxonomy of these birds reflects an adaptive difference that would be of value to know in setting up and stocking a ranching operation.

RATITE EVOLUTIONARY HISTORY

The evolutionary relationship of ratite birds, as indicated by DNA analysis, was described in 1981 by Charles G. Sibley and Jon E. Ahlguist, researchers from Yale University. They used a DNA-DNA hybridization approach to determine evolutionary and taxonomic relationships among the ratites.

The primary question they addressed was whether the various

kinds of ratites, now occurring on different continents, originated separately or were derived from a common ancestor. The fossil record had been of little help in solving this question—in some cases the same characters or data had been used to support opposing conclusions.

The living ratite birds are ostriches (*Struthio camelus* of Africa and Arabia); two species of South American rheas (*Rhea americana, R. pennata*); emus (*Dromaius novaehollandiae*) of Australia; three species of forest-dwelling cassowaries (*Casuarius sp.*) of New Guinea, nearby islands and northwestern Australia; and the three species of kiwis (*Apteryx*) of New Zealand.

The relationships of these birds and the 46 species of neotropical tinamous (*Tinamiformes*) of South America had been hotly debated. The basic argument was whether the birds shared a common ancestor (and were thus monophyletic) or whether they originated separately on the different continents.

The answer to this debate centered primarily on the relative positions of kiwis and tinamous, and the degree of relationships among all the ratite genera.

The DNA-DNA hybridization approach must first be described before presenting the results of the study. As we have seen above, the double-stranded DNA consists of two strands with complementary nucleotide sequences.

They can be artificially separated, by heating, into single strands which reassociate on cooling. If single strands from two related species are combined in conditions permitting reassociation, the mismatched base pairs (due to divergence of the species) reduce bonding strength so that the dissociation temperature is lower than for double-stranded DNA from the same species.

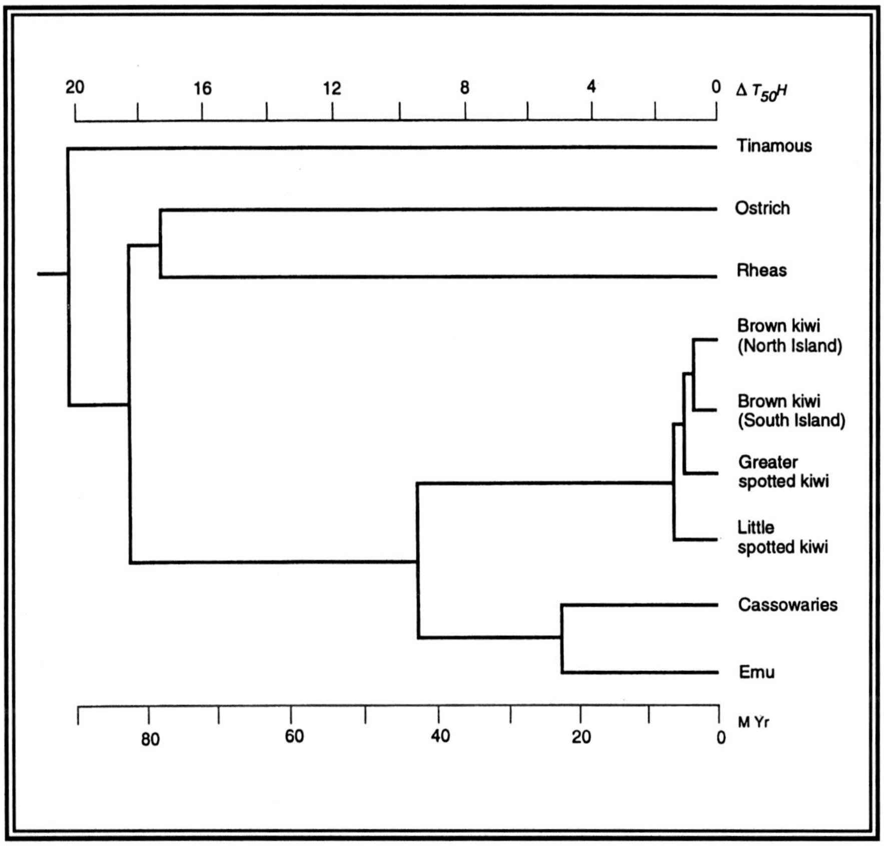

With this technique it turns out that a lowering of the dissociation temperature by 1°C corresponds approximately to a 1 percent difference between the nucleotide sequences of the two species under comparison.

Thus, the difference in temperature for 50 percent dissociation ($\Delta T50H$) of conspecific DNA and heterospecific DNA provides an average measure of similarity for the whole genome.

As a rough rule of thumb for birds, different species of the same genus yield a $\Delta T50H$ value of up to around 4°C; members of different genera but of the same family ~4-11°C; members of different families but the same order, ~11-20°C; and members of the same class but distantly related orders, about 25°C.

The results of the research of Sibley and Ahlquist were summarized in the journal *Nature* (Vol. 305, September 1983). The ratite group, including tinamous, were shown to have been derived from a common ancestor (Figure 3).

The tinamous were the first to diverge, an event that occurred on the order of 90 million years (Myr) ago. The reconstructed sequence of divergence among the ratites themselves showed remarkable agreement with the estimates of the breakup of Gondwanaland and subsequent continental drift (Figure 3).

It is thought by geologists that, at one time, the present southern continents of the planet comprised a single land mass in the southern hemisphere, called Gondwanaland.

This land mass broke apart, with the resulting continents gradually drifting to the positions they occupy today.

The first rift was between present-day Australia (and surrounding land masses), and the other

Figure 3. The family tree of ratites and the closely-related tinamous of South America. The top scale shows the dissociation temperatures for the DNA-DNA hybrids used to construct the family tree (see text for explanation). The bottom scale shows the appropriate time in millions of years ago that the divergences occurred.

southern continents, Africa and South America. Africa and South America were separated by the opening of the Atlantic Ocean shortly thereafter. These events served to isolate ostriches (Africa) and rheas (South America) from the emu-cassowary-kiwi assemblages of ratites in Australia-New Guinea and New Zealand.

The Tasman Sea between Australia (emus, cassowaries) and New Zealand (kiwis) opened about 80 million years (Myr) ago. However, kiwis did not diverge from emu-cassowaries until much later, about 40 to 45 Myr ago (Figure 3).

Thus, the ancestor of the kiwis must have reached New Zealand from Australia via intervening islands or emergent land that occurred earlier along the rises that bear Norfolk and Lord Howe islands today. The three species of kiwis have diverged within New Zealand in the last 10 Myr and the two subspecies of Brown kiwi even more recently (Figure 3).

SUBSPECIATION

In the section on **Basic Terms and Concepts** above, we focused on DNA found in the nucleus of each cell which is transmitted to the offspring, half from each of the parents. DNA is also found in a cytoplasmic structure of the cell found outside the nucleus, the mitochondria.

Mitochondrial DNA (mtDNA) is a much smaller molecule than nuclear DNA. It is comprised of only about 16,000 nucleotides and differs further in that it is arranged in a circle. The genes comprising this molecule are reasonably well known and the order of the mtDNA genes in birds is different from mammals.

Mitochondrial DNA is self-reproducing and maternally inherited. Compared to nuclear DNA, mitochondrial DNA undergoes rapid evolutionary changes in nucleotide sequence. Once a variant or an allele is established in a female, all descendants of that individual carry it, and, therefore the inheritance pattern is clonal through the matriarchal lineage.

These characteristics make mtDNA analysis particularly appropriate in determining relatedness at the breeding-population or subspecies level, or for determining recently divergent species. MtDNA analysis offers great potential to the ratite industry in that it may be the ideal way to classify maternal bloodlines.

The analysis of mtDNA is straightforward, once it has been extracted from tissues and purified. The molecule can be cut into pieces or fragments using molecular scissors called restriction enzymes. Restriction enzymes recognize and digest specific, short sequences of nucleotides at every locus where they occur on the mtDNA molecule.

These fragments can be sorted by length using an electrical current, which causes the fragments to migrate through an electrophoresis gel. The smaller fragments migrate farther than larger ones.

When the fragments are stained, a banding pattern is revealed, showing the location of the fragments in the gel. The sum of the fragment lengths should be about

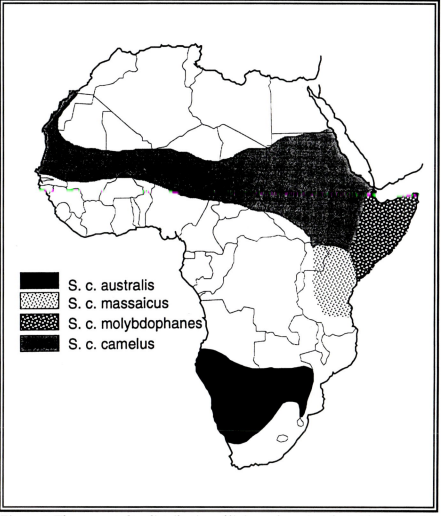

Figure 4. The present-day distribution of living subspecies of ostriches (Struthio camelus). As shown in Figure 5, S. c. australis and S. c. massaicus are genetically very similar despite being very separated geographically at present. Conversely, S. c. molybdophanes is the most genetically divergent of all the subspecies despite the fact that it occurs in close proximity to both S. c. massaicus and S. c. camelus populations.

16,000 bases, the total size of the mtDNA molecule.

This type of analysis is generally termed *Restriction Fragment Length Polymorphism* or RFLP. Differences in the banding patterns between individuals result, in this case, from the gain or loss of restriction enzyme recognition sites. The fewer shared bands there are between two samples, the less closely related they are. RFLP analysis will be discussed in more detail in the context of DNA fingerprinting in a later section.

RFLP studies of ostrich mtDNA were reported by Stefanie Freitag and Terence Robinson of the University of Pretoria in 1993, in volume 110, issue 3 of *The Auk*, a scientific journal.

At present, there are four subspecies of ostrich (Figure 4, preceding page). One of these (*Struthio camelus australis*) occupies a range in southern Africa which is widely disjunct from the more northerly range of the other three subspecies.

The northern population, from east to west, consists of *S. c. molybdophanes*, *S. c. massaicus*, and *S. c. camelus*. Samples were drawn from a total of 97 specimens representing these subspecies, and subjected to RFLP analyses using a battery of 15 different restriction enzymes.

The results showed that the specimens could be grouped into 10 discrete maternal lineages, labeled A through J (Figure 5).

Only 6 maternal lineages were represented among the 78 *australis* samples, a surprisingly low number compared to mammals. The subspecies *massaicus* was represented in the study by 10 specimens which showed only 2 maternal bloodlines; and the subspecies *molybdophanes* showed 2 bloodlines in 8 specimens. *S. c. camelus* was represented by a single specimen.

Little genetic diversity was evident among samples drawn from localities throughout southern Africa (*S. c. australis*), while deep divisions in the mtDNA gene evolutionary tree were found between representatives of eastern (*molybdophanes* and *S. c. massaicus*) and western African subspecies (*S. c. camelus*) (Figure 5).

The low mtDNA variability within *australis* and the presence of widespread mtDNA genotypes in this subspecies suggest considerable historical interconnectedness among populations, either through gene flow and/or recent colonization from smaller source populations (e.g., introductions).

The strong phylogeographic structuring evident in eastern and western north Africa aligns with the currently-accepted subspecies designations. Data indicate that the Ethiopian system of the Great Rift Valley has been effective in disrupting east-west gene flow between *molybdophanes* and *camelus*, while ecological differences and behavioral/reproductive cues have contributed to maintaining the genetic and phenotypic discreteness of *molybdophanes* and *massaicus* in east Africa.

Although contemporary ostrich populations are effectively divided into southern and northern populations by a belt of *Brachystegia* woodland, arid-corridor links in the recent evolutionary past appear to have allowed periodic contact between *australis* and *massaicus* populations. Consequently, the development of subspecific differences between these

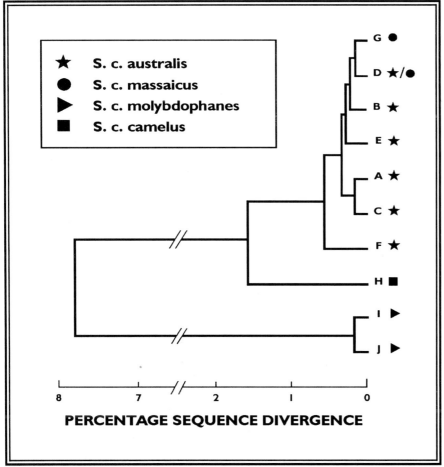

Figure 5. The family tree showing relatedness of the four living subspecies of ostrich (Struthio camelus). The letters A-J denote maternal bloodlines followed by symbols to denote the subspecies of each bloodline. The closer the splits are to 0, the more genetically similar the bloodline. S. c. australis is genetically very similar to S. c. massaicus, and these two subspecies differ distinctly from S. c. camelus. S. c. molybdophanes is the most genetically divergent of all subspecies.

two taxa has occurred within the context of shallow evolutionary separation.

DNA FINGERPRINTS AND PROFILES

From the above descriptions, we have seen that even the most diverse of the commercially-raised ratites (the ostrich) is characterized by a relatively small number of bloodlines, even in the wild.

The emu population in the U.S. was derived from a small number of birds constituting the original stock (probably only a few thousand) and the same is likely true for rheas and cassowaries.

These observations suggest that the ratite industry may be particularly susceptible to inbreeding depression, resulting in significant levels of lost production.

Below we provide a background about inbreeding depression and its effects, and the methods available to determine relatedness of individuals. We then discuss how molecular genetics can be applied to avoid these effects.

INBREEDING DEPRESSION

New alleles arise originally by mutation. A mutation is essentially a mistake that is made in the DNA molecule when the molecule replicates.

During reproduction, the DNA molecules make copies of themselves so that the offspring can inherit a full set of genetic instructions. During replication, mistakes can occur in the sequence of instructions coding for a particular task.

These mistakes are generally quite rare, typically occurring once in a million new copies of DNA, although mutation rates can be either higher or lower, depending on the locus.

Most mistakes in the molecular instructions of genes are harmful, in fact disastrous, to the organism. This is not surprising. The complexity of most organisms (even simple organisms) is astounding, and every cellular function must be working correctly for an organism to stay alive.

Even if the genetic instructions are off by only one subunit (nucleotide) in the DNA sequence, the result can be biochemical nonsense and the whole function of that task breaks down.

Thus, by far most mutations are deleterious, and in fact, most are outright lethal. Fortunately, most mutations are recessive. The harmful qualities of deleterious, recessive alleles can therefore only be expressed in a homozygous state.

This fact makes perfect sense from an evolutionary point of view: If the *normal* or *good* allele is dominant, it will be expressed properly even if mistakes are made in the transcription of the DNA molecule during reproduction. Eventually mistakes are inevitable, but if the normal instructions are always dominant to those mistakes, the costs of those errors can be avoided.

The disadvantage of this evolutionary trick is that deleterious recessive alleles can build up in a population. If a mutant allele is rare (and a new mutation will always be rare), then the mutant allele will virtually always be masked by a dominant allele. As a result, the deleterious recessive allele will not be removed by natural selection.

Natural selection favors some traits over other traits through the differential survival and reproduction of individuals with those traits.

Individuals with *good* traits (coded by particular alleles) should survive and reproduce at a faster rate (by definition) compared to individuals with *bad* traits. In this way, genes coding for good traits occur more frequently in a population with each generation.

Conversely, genes coding for bad traits should become less common, because individuals with those traits will survive and reproduce less well, and fewer copies of those harmful genes will be passed to the next generation.

The problem is that natural selection can work only on genes that are actually expressed. If a deleterious recessive allele is in a heterozygous state, which it nearly always is at first, it is not expressed and therefore cannot be removed from the population by natural selection.

Thus for a long time, recessive deleterious alleles can gradually build up in a population. If they become common enough, two recessive deleterious alleles are more likely to be paired up in a single individual.

This homozygous recessive trait will then be expressed and that individual will produce fewer offspring with the harmful trait, compared to the average number of offspring for that population.

Eventually, the frequency of a harmful recessive allele in a population reaches equilibrium—a balance between how many harmful alleles can hide by being heterozygous, versus how often homozygous individuals are produced and how bad the trait is when expressed.

This buildup is often called genetic load. The more such alleles build up at increasing number of loci, the lower the average fitness in that population, evolutionarily speaking. All diploid species (those having two similar complements of chromosomes) have a certain amount of genetic load.

Geneticists express the size of a species' genetic load in terms of lethal equivalents. Some recessive deleterious alleles are lethal 100% of the time; others have lesser degrees of harmful effects. However, if you add all the partially harmful effects, you can still wind up with lethal genetic combinations.

Genetic load leads to inbreeding depression. Inbreeding by itself would not be harmful if it were not for the recessive deleterious genes hidden in heterozygous form.

Inbreeding exposes harmful recessive alleles because inbreeding leads to homozygosity. For exactly this reason, inbreeding is a powerful tool of animal and plant breeders who want their lines to express desirable alleles that also happen to be recessive. The loss of heterozygote *hybrid vigor* is also a possible mechanism of inbreeding depression.

So how does inbreeding cause homozygosity? Relatives share genes—specifically alleles—that they inherited from a common ancestor. That is why they are relatives—they have a close ancestor in common. When two individuals are related and inherit the same genes from a close ancestor, they share a large proportion of the same alleles, taken over all their thousands of loci.

Offspring share 50% of their alleles with each parent, because they get half their chromosomes from their father's sperm and half from their mother's egg. It is easy to prove with genetic theory that brothers and sisters share 50% of their genes on average, at least in diploid organisms. That is a high proportion of alleles to have in common, when you consider how many alleles you might share with a complete stranger.

Uncles and aunts share about 25% of their alleles with nieces and nephews, as do grandparents with their grandchildren. First cousins share 12.5% of their alleles, and so on.

The more distant the common ancestor, the fewer alleles shared that are identical by descent. Moreover, the proportion drops off very rapidly, as you can see from the above—halving with each outbred mating.

If a recessive allele—good or bad—is rare, then two individuals taken randomly from a population are unlikely both to have the same rare allele. As mentioned above, rare recessive alleles will nearly always appear in heterozygous form and are therefore not expressed.

However, here is where inbreeding comes in. Two relatives are much more likely to share the same alleles compared to two unrelated individuals. So if two relatives mate and have offspring, the odds of the same recessive allele pairing up are greatly increased.

Put another way, while an allele might be rare in the whole population, it will be common in a family, because they all got this *rare* allele from a shared ancestor.

Genetic theory and supporting experiments have shown that generations of repeated inbreeding gradually increase the proportion of loci that are homozygous. Because inbreeding causes homozygosity, it will cause rare deleterious alleles to be expressed in homozygous form.

This process occurs quickly, with severely harmful effects often occurring in the first generation of close inbreeding. In ratites, these effects can be expressed as early embryonic death, poor hatch rates, deformed chicks and low survival rates. Therefore, it is important for the serious breeder of ratites to understand the relatedness of his/her flock.

DNA FINGERPRINTS

DNA fingerprinting of birds, available for all the ratites, is a straightforward but technically-sophisticated RFLP procedure much like that described earlier.

DNA is isolated from blood or another tissue and digested with restriction site enzymes. The resulting fragments are then sorted by length using gel electrophoresis. The next step is to break the hydrogen bonds holding the two strands of each fragment together,

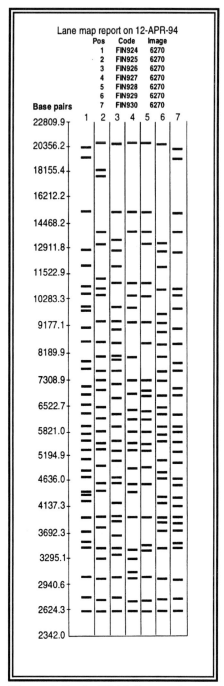

Figure 6. Ratite DNA fingerprints derived from RFLP analysis showing individual-specific banding patterns. The original autoradiograph was scanned into a computer, which also determined the size of fragments constituting the visible and scorable bands. As described in the text, the strength of this analysis lies in identifying individuals. However, the bands do not necessarily reflect the products of a given locus. This precludes the ability to estimate levels of heterozygosity or homozygosity. (Figure courtesy of Zoogen Inc.)

and bind the strands onto a supportive membrane. This membrane is then placed in a solution containing radioactive probes. These probes attach to any of the complimentary strands found on the fragments.

The probes are typically what are called Variable Number Tandom Repeats (VNTR's) or mini-or microsatellite loci. These loci are characterized by a particular core sequence of nucleotides which are almost perfectly repeated from ten to several hundred times. Regions of DNA containing these elements will vary in length depending on how many times the core sequence is repeated.

The radioactively-labeled membrane is then used to expose a strip of film, called an autoradiograph, which reveals the image of the membrane which is then scored.

The product is a series of bands, much like a grocery store bar code. The banding pattern is complex; typically some 20 to 30 fragments of different sizes can be visualized (Figure 6).

Usually, each individual shows at least some differences in its banding pattern as compared to all other individuals. This is because 1) a large component of the DNA molecule has been assayed and 2) at the absolute level, each bird is unique in terms of its DNA sequence. An index to the relatedness of individuals can be estimated based upon the number of bands that are shared.

The strong point of this RFLP method lies in the identification of individuals, but it also has limitations. The first limitation is that while labeled fragments can be very accurately assigned to the proper band, the bands can include a range of different-sized fragments.

Usually the median size is given, but the band can also include fragments about ±5% of the median or mean size. This grouping of fragments is called binning, i.e., assigning fragments of similar size to a common bin.

The second, and in our view the more serious limitation, is that the bands in an RFLP analysis of this sort do not necessarily reflect products of individually-identifiable loci. Levels of heterozygosity or homozygosity, therefore, cannot be estimated with certainty.

In humans, this limitation of RFLP fingerprinting has been overcome, in large part. Research has uncovered minisatellite probes that are locus-specific, and some have been found to have a large number of alleles (10 to 30) at each locus in the overall population. Most alleles of these loci are uncommon or rare.

One consequence of this rarity is that the majority of the individuals are heterozygous. Another is that the probability of even a single-locus genetic match between randomly chosen individuals is low.

If the genotype frequencies of alleles from several loci are combined to calculate the multilocus probabilities, the odds of observing a given DNA profile from a random draw of the population become astronomically low, one in a billion or more. To our knowledge no locus-specific minisatellite probes are available for ratites.

MICROSATELLITE DNA PROFILES

A different approach to identifying individuals and their relatedness has been developed which is based upon the Polymerase Chain Reaction. The PCR method, as it is called, enables identification of the alleles found at specific loci. These alleles vary in length due to the number of repeats of a microsatellite element found at a specific locus.

The core sequence of a microsatellite VNTR is only 2 or 4 nucleotides long, and is typically repeated 10 to 40 times. This compares to minisatellite VNTRs which are 10 to 30 nucleotides long, and are repeated 100 to 1000 times. As a result, microsatellite loci are much smaller than minisatellite loci. This is important because PCR analysis is presently restricted to small fragments.

PCR is a method for selecting and repeatedly replicating a defined DNA sequence from an overall mixture of DNA. This process, called amplification, works only with short fragments and requires beginning sequence information so that primers can be made. Primers consist of specific sequences of nucleotides that will attach at each end of the DNA segment of interest, in our case a microsatellite-bearing locus.

DNA from the sample is extracted and the two strands are separated using heat. Primers are introduced to mark the ends of the region of interest. The polymerase enzyme and a solution of the four nucleotides are added, which enables the region between the two primers to be replicated when the solution is allowed to cool.

A chain reaction of repeatedly duplicating the small DNA segment of interest is maintained by alternatively heating and cooling the mixture. In a matter of a few hours, the starting soup of primers, nucleotides, polymerase and a small amount of sample DNA has been converted to millions of copies of the DNA sequence being analyzed.

The primers for these fragments are labeled with fluorescent dyes, which allows identification and sizing of these dye-labeled fragments (Figure 7). Their size can be accurately measured using an autosequencing machine linked to computers.

The fluorescent-dyed fragments and size standards migrate through an electrophoresis gel, which is scanned with a laser beam to record the size of the fragments as they pass. The data are sorted and analyzed in the autosequencer and are stored electronically while the analysis is being conducted.

A: LOCUS AND ALLELE FREQUENCY DATA

LOCUS NUMBER	1	2	3	4	5	6	7
NAME	EMU 14	EMU 12S	EMU 9	EMU 2S	GATA 11	EMU 3L	EMU 5
Allele							
1	0.005	0.289	0.046	0.052	0.020	0.626	0.655
2	0.127	0.185	0.735	0.112	0.259	0.372	0.345
3	0.122	0.163	0.095	0.540	0.372	0.001	
4	0.380	0.127	0.073	0.099	0.343	0.001	
5	0.016	0.107	0.008	0.094	0.002		
6	0.078	0.064	0.042	0.042	0.004		
7	0.160	0.045	0.001				
8	0.074	0.020					
9	0.020						
10	0.005						
11	0.005						
12	0.005						
13	0.001						
14	0.001						
	0.999	1.000	0.999	1.000	1.000	1.000	1.000
	n=1096	n=1096	n=1096	n=1096	n=1096	n=1096	n=1096

B: EXAMPLE CALCULATIONS OF THE POWER TO IDENTIFY AN INDIVIDUAL

Hypothetical Genotype from Above Data

Locus	Allele	Frequency	Multiplied Frequencies	If Heterozygous x2	Individual Locus Value
1	2	0.127	0.04826	0.09652	0.09652
	4	0.380			
2	5	0.107	0.01145	0.01145	
	5	0.107			
3	2	0.735	0.06983	0.13965	0.13965
	3	0.095			
4	3	0.540	0.29160	0.29160	
	3	0.540			
5	2	0.259	0.06708	0.06708	
	2	0.259			
6	1	0.626	0.23287	0.46574	0.46574
	2	0.372			
7	1	0.655	0.42903	0.42903	
	1	0.655			

Probability of single allele values are from table above. For heterozygous birds, the probability of having a pair of alleles is 2 times the product of the individual allele frequencies. For homozygous birds the probability is the square of the individual allele frequency. The probability of another emu having the same genotype as our hypothetical bird is obtained by multiplying the probability for all loci together. For our bird, that probability is 6.0×10^7, approximately 1 in 1.7 million.

Table 1. Allele frequencies observed at 7 PCR loci in emus as of October 1994 (Part A). Part B shows how these data are used to determine the probability of there being another emu with the same genotype as a hypothetical individual with a multilocus profile consisting of common alleles. (Source: LGL Ecological Genetics, Inc.)

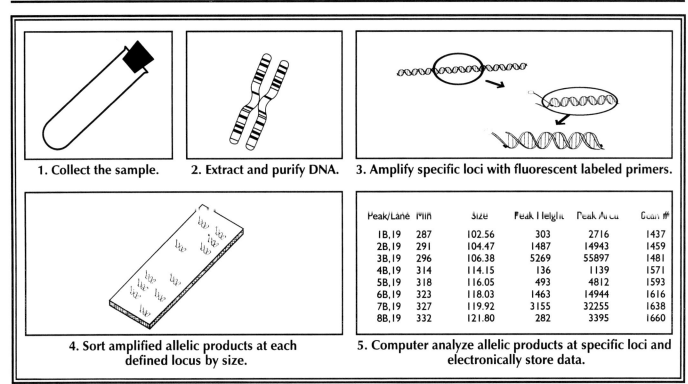

Figure 7. The process of determining alleles at a specific locus using the Polymerase Chain Reaction. When multiple loci are analyzed, the multilocus profile obtained can be used to identify individuals and estimate levels of heterozygosity and homozygosity. (Figure courtesy of GenLab, Inc.)

This procedure allows for rapid, highly-accurate measurements of fragment length, eliminating the need for binning of alleles. The bands yielded are locus-specific alleles which can be used to generate multilocus profiles. These profiles enable the identification of individuals, determinations of parentage, and the degree of relatedness. Heterozygosity of individuals can also be accurately determined.

The results obtained by the PCR method might better be called AMPFLP (Amplified Fragment Length Polymorphism). Likewise, the RFLP analysis can be referred to as the Southern Blot Method. The terms are commonly used interchangeably, leading to some confusion.

In humans, RFLP analyses are generally said to be much more powerful tools than AMPFLP or PCR analysis. This is because forensic work has historically focused on RFLP (the first technology available) and locus-specific probes have been identified that have a high diversity of alleles in the overall population.

In legal applications, only four or so standard loci are usually analyzed but these, having many (10 to 30) distinguishable alleles, are indeed very powerful tools for discriminating individuals and relatedness.

In contrast, the PCR method is new and fewer data are available for humans. At present, even though some six PCR loci are routinely analyzed, these loci exhibit relatively few (2 to 6) distinguishable alleles. This makes PCR a less powerful tool in human legal applications, at least for the present.

PCR primers have been developed for only one species of ratite, the emu. At present, 7 loci are being analyzed, and these exhibit from 2 to 14 alleles, many of which appear to be rare in the overall emu population. Consequently, the multilocus profiles generated have great power for distinguishing individuals and their degrees of relatedness, even those individuals having a preponderance of alleles common in the overall population (Table 1).

When one or more rare alleles occur, the odds of a match increase astronomically—as much as one in trillions.

REDUCING INBREEDING EFFECTS

We, the authors of this chapter, conducted a study in 1993 and 1994 under contract to representatives of the emu industry (C&S Ranch). This study addressed the application of DNA profile analyses to identify and reduce the possible adverse effects of inbreeding.

In this study, we first developed PCR primers for some 10 loci and assayed a sample of 200 emus from around the country to estimate allele frequencies at these loci. For some 36 pair of these emus, detailed production records were available dating back to 1990.

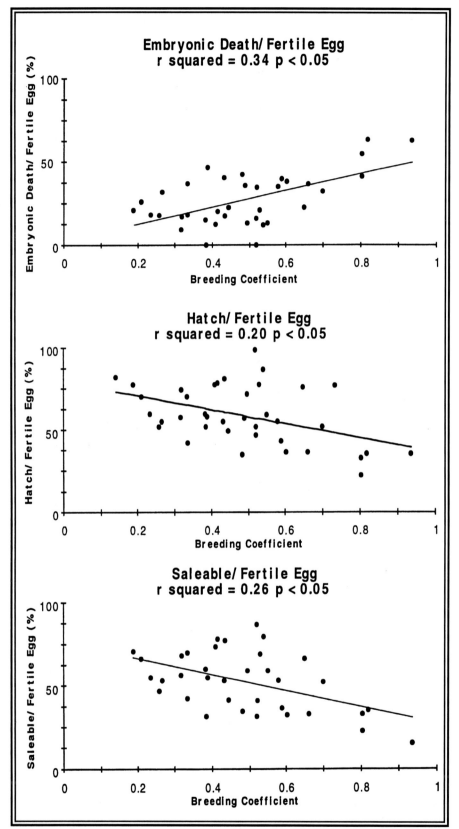

Figure 8. The observed statistical relationship between PCR-derived breeding coefficients and production measures for the emu. The r-squared value shows the amount of variance in the production measure explained by the relatedness of the test pairs as estimated by the breeding coefficient. The p level shows the probability that the observed association might occur due to chance. (Unpublished data, LGL Ecological Genetics, Inc.)

The degree of relatedness of the pairs, called a Breeding Coefficient, was calculated based upon the number of shared alleles held by the pair at 7 of the 10 loci, weighted by frequency of those alleles in the overall population.

These values were then regressed against production parameters, including rates of early embryonic death (EED) in the egg, hatch rates and percent saleable chicks (those without observable physical deformities).

For 16 of these 36 test pairs, RFLP fingerprints were also available, from which a historical breeding coefficient had been calculated, independent of our laboratory, based upon percent bands shared in the RFLP fingerprints of the pairs.

The results showed that the PCR breeding coefficient was statistically correlated to production parameters (Figure 8). Degree of relatedness accounted for some 34% of the observed variation in early embryonic death (EED), with the rates of EED increasing with the degree of relatedness of the parents.

Hatch rates and percent of saleable chicks per fertile egg produced declined with increasing relatedness, and the statistics showed that some 20 to 26% of the observed variance in these relationships were accounted for by relatedness alone.

These findings provide strong evidence for reduced productivity of closely-related pairs of emus, and the findings are probably reflective for ratites as a whole, at least the U.S. population.

The PCR-based and RFLP-based breeding coefficients were not significantly correlated to each other, perhaps due to small sample size. The RFLP band-sharing coefficient did not exhibit a significant relationship with either EED or hatch rates, but did show an obvious trend of association with number of saleable chicks produced (Figure 9).

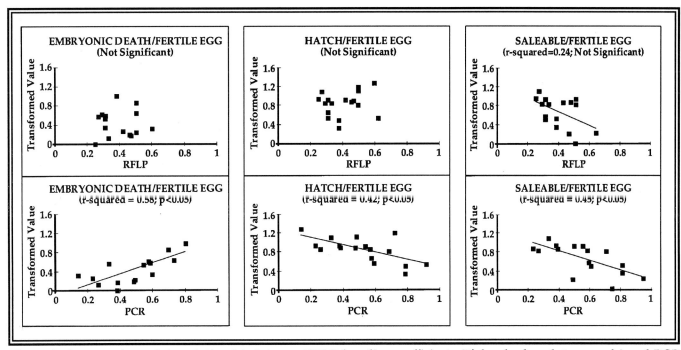

Figure 9. A comparison of the relationship between RFLP breeding coefficients (% bands shared, top panels) and PCR breeding coefficients (bottom panels) and production measures for the emu. Sample size was small, consisting of 16 pairs for which both RFLP and PCR coefficients were available in conjunction with known production histories. R-squared and p values are defined in the legend for Figure 8. (Unpublished data, LGL Ecological Genetics, Inc.)

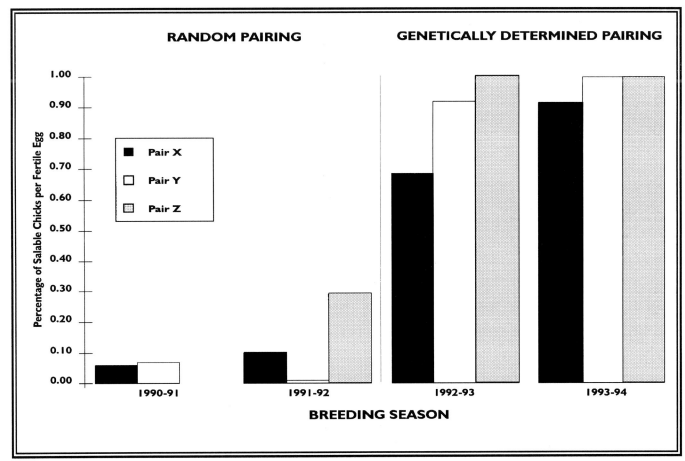

Figure 10. The observed increase in production levels (saleable chicks per fertile egg) achieved following genetic-based selection of new mates for three pairs of emus with previously poor production histories. (Figure courtesy of GenLab, Inc.)

While not statistically significant at the 5% level, this relationship accounted for 24% of the observed variance, about half that explained by the PCR breeding coefficient (45%) for this sample of 16 pairs.

While field trials are limited, the results of using breeding coefficients to better pair emus having poor production histories have yielded dramatic increases in production (Figure 10).

The described technologies are improving almost daily and offer great potential to the industry for maximizing production, as well as insuring that genetically-viable populations of ratites can be maintained in the U.S. over the long term.

GENDER IDENTIFICATION

Many of the ratites are not sexually dimorphic on a morphological basis at early ages when the breeder wishes to pair the birds. Historical techniques available to sex these birds from blood or tissue samples based upon physical and staining differences associated with the Z and W chromosomes do not work well with ratites.

However, DNA probes which yield sex-specific bands in ratites have been developed by the private sector. The RFLP procedure is followed, and using the probes which have been developed, males show a pattern of banding different than females (Figure 11). In laboratory tests, such probes have accurately distinguished up to several hundred control ratites of known sex.

In the field, one sometimes hears doubt expressed about the accuracy of this method, but most claims appear to be unsubstantiated. Further, apparent errors can result from the misidentification of birds during sample collection, mislabeled sample containers, etc.

Nevertheless, biological variation in ratites remains as another reason for test inaccuracies. Ratites, from the beginning, have posed special problems due to the primitive nature of their sex chromosomes. The genetic determination of sex in ratites, even most birds, is very complex and not well understood.

In poultry, intersexes (birds displaying the characteristics of both sexes) and sex-reversed birds (birds that are genetically one sex but physically the opposite sex) are not uncommon. In poultry, the frequency of intersexes alone regularly exceeds one in a thousand.

This rate may be higher in ratites. Much more work is needed regarding sex-determining processes in the ratites.

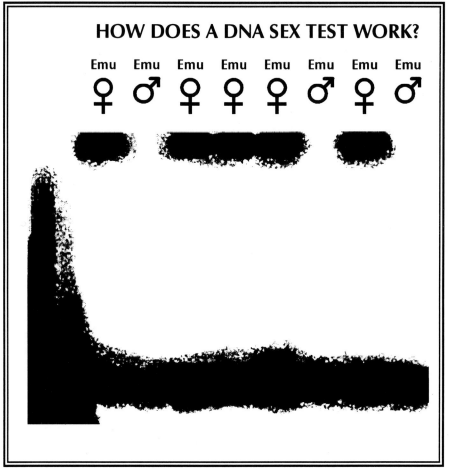

Figure 11. Differential banding patterns yielded by ratites following RFLP analysis with sex-specific probes. (Figure courtesy Zoogen Inc.)

THE FUTURE

What does the future hold? It should include the development of a ratite genome map which will show the relative positions and function of genes on the chromosomes.

Studies need to be conducted to evaluate the functions of these genes, particularly those whose tasks relate directly to production characteristics or those whose malfunction are responsible for disease or death.

Genetic markers, such as locus-specific RFLP probes and PCR alleles (and others), have already contributed greatly to the development of detailed genome maps in human and other animals groups, and the same will likely ultimately be true for ratites.

Using a variety of available markers, specific alleles have been identified by trial and error in humans and other animal and plant groups that always co-segregate with an uncharacterized disease-causing locus in a family or population under study.

Put another way, all individuals in a family which have the disease will have the allele. Those individuals without the disease have other alleles.

In summary, genetic marker loci have been found that are tightly linked to some disease-associated or production-related locus, although the location of these genes are unknown.

Most of these discoveries of the relationships between DNA markers and quantitative traits in animals and plants have been fortuitous and have not resulted from a systematic survey of the entire genome using predetermined sets of mapped markers.

Because of this, as seems to be the case for the human genome map, it is unlikely that very many molecular geneticists will be willing to lock themselves away and devote their time to assembling an overall detailed map of the ratite genome on a step-by-step basis. Few monks practice genetics these days.

More likely, different research groups will spend time in a race to develop markers for particular desirable traits of the breeding stocks being studied, and then market these to the ratite industry.

Most of these markers will likely be of the microsatellite variety amenable to PCR. The minisatellite RFLP markers have been found to be clustered near the ends of chromosomes, as compared to microsatellites, which are not only more numerous, but are also more widely distributed throughout the chromosome.

Further, RFLP analysis methods are slow relative to the automated methods of PCR. The advent of PCR has marked a turning point in the strategies used for detecting polymorphic markers.

Genetic advances and understanding are increasing at remarkable rates, even in little-studied creatures such as ratites. The experimental framework for conducting new studies has been established from the study of other species.

A major problem that molecular biologists and the ratite industry must overcome is that of communication between the two groups.

Better understanding of the role that molecular biology can play in the ratite industry is needed by breeders.

Scientists need to keep in mind that the breeder's interests are restricted to the availability of new, cost-effective tools that will improve selection strategies and develop lines of birds with commercially valuable characteristics.

This will require a concentrated effort, and, for the ratite breeders, will involve a commitment toward learning and understanding a new, complex and changing language.

The problem is no less difficult for the scientists, for many will be required not only to think in new ways, but also become accountable for practical application of their research interests.

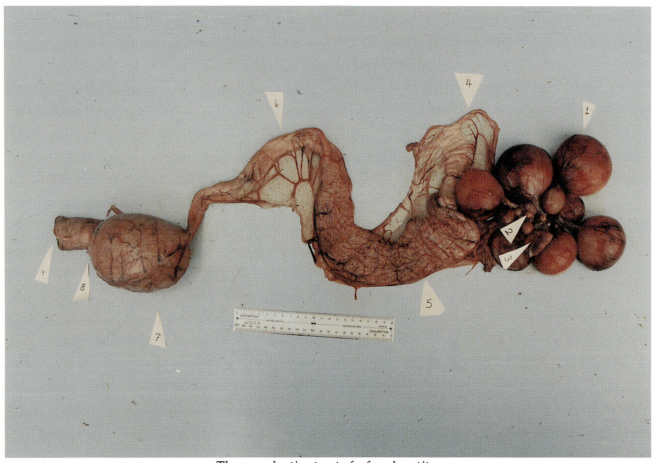

The reproductive tract of a female ratite.

RATITE REPRODUCTION

Paul C. Smith, DVM, Ph. D.
Auburn University
Auburn, Alabama

The success of any domestic animal production enterprise is directly dependent upon the potential reproduction capacity of mature breeding stock.

Ratites have many of the same reproductive characteristics and problems found in other birds, yet some of the reproductive features of these large flightless birds are unique and must be understood by ratite owners or producers if they are to be successful in this rapidly expanding enterprise.

The measure of success reflected in the margin of profit may be severely impacted by the producer's knowledge of the basic aspects of ratite reproduction.

In this chapter the sexual, anatomical, physical, biochemical and social features of ratite reproduction will be discussed.

Details of the essential parts of the egg, its development and role in the reproductive process will also be described.

Finally, the impact of disease and nutrition on reproductive health will be emphasized.

GENERAL CHARACTERISTICS

The dusty gray-brown feathering of the mature ostrich female or hen (Photo 1) is thought to be of value in camouflage during the daytime incubation of the eggs.

Occasionally, mature ostrich hens may exhibit a degree of black body feathering that varies from a few dull black feathers to nearly complete coverage of black feathers over the body. Coloring in ostriches is influenced by sex hormones in that a lack of estrogen produces black feathering in the male, whereas a high concentration of the hormone in the female causes the feathers to be gray or brown. Therefore, the rare black-feathered hen may not be as prolific as other hens because of low estrogen levels.

The male ostrich, sometimes called the cock or rooster, is a curious, rather docile but sometimes aggressive bird. Black body feathering and long white tail and wing feathers are characteristics of the male (Photo 2). This coloring of pigmented feathers is thought to serve as an effective camouflage because, in the natural environment, the male incubates the eggs at night and subsequently assists in raising the young chicks.

There are few secondary or visible sexual features that distinguish male and female emus. Some have suggested that coloring of the eyes and bluish skin of the neck distinguish female from male, but this is not dependable.

The female usually makes a booming or drumming sound that resonates in a large subcutaneous air pouch that is a diverticulum of incomplete tracheal rings at the base of the neck. The same, though smaller, pouch limits the male to characteristic grunts. In general the male often appears to be more docile than the female.

Adult rheas exhibit few secondary characteristics that are distinguishing features but the male often has a more bulky frame and dark feathers around the neck.

Photo 1. Ostrich female. Grey-brown feathers provide camouflage while she is on the nest during the daytime.

Photo 3. Courtship display, or cantling.

Photo 2. Male ostrich, showing considerable reddening, indicating readiness to breed.

BREEDING BEHAVIOR

OSTRICHES

When the young ostrich hen reaches maturity she will usually begin to *flutter* at the beginning of longer days. This posturing activity is an indication of the sexual receptivity toward the male. In this sexual display the hen lowers her head and neck to body height, snaps her beak, spreads her wings and begins a rhythymical wing trembling or fluttering.

This sexual posturing activity is sometimes called *clucking* but this is perhaps a poorly chosen term, for in other avian species this term may indicate broodiness. This activity becomes very frequent at the beginning of breeding season and indicates her continued receptiveness toward the male.

Ostrich hens may begin to lay eggs at 24 to 30 months of age, though some hens do not lay until the age of 3 to 4 years.

The flashy white wing and tail feathers play a prominent role in the courtship ritual or sexual display (cantling) of the ostrich rooster (Photo 3). The neck and head feathers are short, sparse and usually gray to dull white.

Red-pigmented skin develops rapidly on the beak, neck and lower legs at the beginning of the breeding season (Photo 2). These skin and attitude changes are hormonally induced and are influenced by light, seasonal and environmental changes.

The regal and rhythmical movements become more aggressive during the breeding season and the male will defend the nest, eggs and female very vigorously. The single large nail on the main toe of the two-toed foot is a formidable weapon backed by powerful leg muscles.

Mature male ostriches also may have a distinct enlargement (Photos 4 and 5) around the vent, especially during the mating season, due to the enlargement of the phallus in its natural position on the floor of the proctodeum.

A young ostrich rooster may mate with a female by two years of age, but may prove incapable of producing viable sperm. Most males produce fertile sperm by three years of age; however, in their natural environment they may not be sexually mature until four years of age.

EMUS

Sexual activity and egg laying begins in emus when days begin to shorten. Subsequently the lengthening of days and decreasing length of night ushers in broodiness in the male. This is a highly unusual phenomenon in birds. Usually quite the opposite is true.

RHEAS

Young rhea males begin to dig or build a nest usually between 18 and 20 months of age if environmental conditions are conducive. At this time their aggressiveness is very prominent.

The male digs a rather deep depression in the soil for a nest, and may drag or collect grass,

Photo 4. Enlargement around the vent of a sexually-mature male ostrich.

leaves and other fibrous material into the nest. He will then sit on the nest and defend it against all intruders, especially other male rheas. He attracts females by fluffing his feathers to appear larger. He then mates with these females, who lay eggs in the area of the nest. The male collects the eggs laid by three to five females and incubates a clutch of 20 to 25 eggs, and raises the chicks in a small brood.

THE REPRODUCTIVE SYSTEM

MALES

The male gonads (testicles or testes) of ostriches are located at the anterior or caudal pole of the kidney, above the abdominal air sacs and immediately adjacent to the spinal column. Normally they are light tan in color and oblong in shape. They are normally reduced

Photo 5. A closer view of the enlargement around the vent.

Photo 6. Phallus of breeding ostrich male.

The male gametes or sperm are carried or suspended in a milky white to clear or light tan fluid (semen). The color of ratite semen is influenced by the amount of fluid provided by the ampullae. During ejaculation the semen is deposited through the posterior opening of the vas deferens at the papillae into the cloaca onto the spermatic groove at the base of the phallus.

The phalli (Photos 6, 7, and 8) of male ratites are sometimes thought to be analogous to the mammalian penis. However, since it has no complete central channel or urethra and serves no urinary function, the phallus of birds is distinctly different from the penis of mammals. The phallus is composed primarily of erectile tissue and serves as an organ of intromission during breeding.

The non-erected phallus of the adult ostrich rooster rests in the floor of the cloaca and is usually curved downward and forward. Since the organ is quite large (13-20 cm, non erected), it causes a distinct visible enlargement of the tissues surrounding the vent or cloaca. During erection and mating the phallus reaches an average length of 35 to 40 cm (Photo 6) and may be 20 cm in circumference.

The erectile tissue adjacent to the seminal groove that courses the dorsal or upper surface of the phallus directs the semen into the cloaca of the hen in the area of the terminal opening of the reproductive tract or vagina in the cloaca.

The long tail-piece of the sperm cell provides each spermatozoa with a vigorous swimming motion that assists in movement of the sperm cell in its long journey up through the reproductive tract of the female to the infundibulum.

Evaluation of ostrich sperm for concentration, mobility and viability is seldom attempted because of the difficulty of collection during the breeding season. The rapid shrinkage of the testes and

in size during the resting or non-breeding season of the year.

At the onset of sexual maturity, however, ostrich testes will enlarge by 400 to 600 per cent within a few weeks. Often the left testicle will be larger in length and diameter than the right, but this seems to cause no reduction in sperm production, motility or viability.

In the process called spermatogenesis, the spermatozoa mature in the cells of spermatogonia (or Leydig epithelial cells). They are stored in the epididymis until ejaculation.

Mature sperm are stored along the entire length of the respective paired spermatic cords or vas deferens that course along the kidney surface with the ureters. The ampullae, an enlargement at the posterior end of the vas deferens, apparently produces fluids that nourish and extend the life or viability of the spermatozoa.

Photo 7. Phallus of breeding emu male.

Reproduction

reduced sperm production make any attempt to do such an evaluation other than during the breeding season of no value.

The normal reproductive system in the ratite male is illustrated in the schematic in Figure 1. The paired testes in young males are small and poorly developed until sexual maturity is reached.

The reproductive anatomy and physiology of emus and rheas are essentially the same as that described for ostriches in the paragraphs above, except that the testes of emus are more tubular, and have a greenish bronze color and a thick capsule (Photo 9).

The phallus also is different since during the non-erected state the organ recedes into a subepithelial space.

In the erected phase (Photo 7) the broad base everts, and the body of the phallus has a distinct spiral ejaculatory groove. The fully erected phallus of emus is seldom more than 10 cm in length and varies in circumference from 10 to 25 cm at the base to 2 to 3 cm at the tip of the organ.

The phallus of rheas is smaller in diameter, slightly longer and appears to be more flexible than that of the emu (Photo 8). However, both emu and rhea phalli contain a distinct palpable cartilage center that assists in differentiating the male from the female from sub-puberty onward.

FEMALES

The anatomical arrangement of the female ostrich reproductive tract is shown in Figure 3. The female has only one ovary, since the right embryonal ovarian tissue development is suppressed and only the left ovary develops. This is the case in practically all birds.

As many as 2,000 primordial cells for egg (oocyte) development exist in the very young and juvenile female. As maturity begins the follicles and various sizes of early surrounding yolk material hang in grapelike clusters (Photo 10) at

Photo 8. Phallus of breeding rhea male.

the anterior pole of the left kidney immediately adjacent to the spinal column. Sequential follicular development of the oocyte-carrying yolk material is manufactured by the liver and is laid down in concentric rings around the oocyte (the true egg).

The mature yolk and oocyte (now referred to as the germinal disc or blastoderm, Figure 2) mature under hormonal influence and rupture from the follicle (ovulation) to enter the abdominal or peritoneal cavity. The free-floating yolk is then trapped in the finger-like projections of the infundibulum or the anterior-most part of the fallopian tube or reproductive tract.

Viable sperm that have traveled up the female reproductive tract from the cloaca following mating are nurtured and preserved by the secretions of the epithelial cells of the infundibulum.

Photo 9. Emu testes. Note the color and thick capsule.

They are essentially *lying in wait* for the entry of the oocyte-bearing yolk into the infundibulum. Within 10 to 15 minutes the active spermatozoa seek out the tiny oocyte or germinal disc on the yolk, attach to the capsule of the oocyte and a single spermatozoa penetrates and fertilizes the true egg or oocyte. (The *table egg* is not the true biological egg ((oocyte)) that should be referred to as the ovule.)

All other sperm are then rejected by the egg. In some bird species it is known that spermatozoa may remain viable in the infundibulum for approximately three weeks. Though little information is known relative to sperm viability in the infundibulum of ratites, it is known that in chickens fertility is highest in eggs 2 to 3 days following copulation but some eggs may be fertilized months after copulation.

Following a short stay of only a few minutes in the infundibulum where it has been fertilized, the yolk and now developing zygote or embryo descend into the next portion of the reproductive tract called the magnum. The epithelial cells of the magnum secrete a specialized substance called the thick albumen (sometimes called the white of the egg or egg whites) which envelopes the yolk. This process may require several hours.

Another critical structure which is added in the magnum is referred to as the chalazae. The chalazae are made up of a number of shrouds of white high-protein, fiber-like strands that hold the yolk and the developing embryo suspended in the thick albumen. The early slow revolutions of the yolk in the reproductive tract give a slight twist to these strands (chalazae) that further fixes the yolk in tight suspension within the thick or dense albumen.

The developing egg then descends to the short portion of the reproductive tract referred to as the isthmus, where the inner and outer shell membrane are added to confine the albumen, yolk and developing embryo or germinal disc.

The first or inner shell membrane is in rather close proximity to the albumen, but then is enveloped in the thicker or outer shell membrane. The two membranes adhere tightly together except at the large end of the egg where they divide to form the air cell.

Next the egg drops into the uterus or shell gland where moisture and other nutrients are absorbed through the inner and outer membranes to form the thin albumen and a highly mineralized

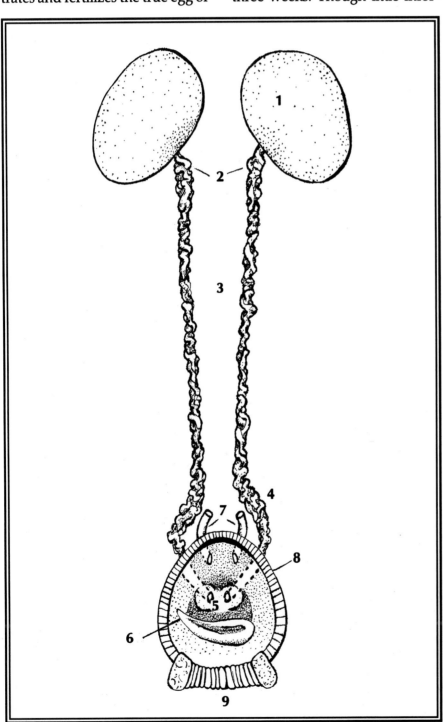

Figure 1. Reproductive tract of male ratite. 1: Testicle. 2: Epididymis. 3: Vas deferens. 4: Ampullae. 5: Genital papillae. 6: Phallus. 7: Ureters. 8: Cloaca. 9: Vent. (Illustration by Elizabeth Mitchell)

egg shell is deposited. The shell is composed primarily of calcium carbonate extracted from the blood stream where levels are under the control of biological enzymes or hormones.

Like many other birds, ratite eggs may have pigmented or colored egg shells. Ostrich eggshells are ivory or off-white, rhea eggs vary from a pale to almost lemon yellow, and emu eggs are normally a deep avocado green.

Shell pigments are porphyrins derived from the breakdown products of erythrocytes or red blood cells and carried from the liver to the uterus or shell gland by the blood stream.

Following deposition of the shell, a thin mucinous protein coat is laid down that dries immediately after the egg is laid to form a highly protective covering referred to as the cuticle. This process requires several hours in the uterus.

To more fully understand the anatomical arrangement and function of the female reproductive system the reader should carefully compare the schematic in Figure 3 with the natural ratite reproductive tract in Photo 11.

Once the formation of the egg is complete strong contractions of the uterus or shell gland, under profound influence of hormones, expel the egg into the vagina or terminal portion of the reproductive tract and subsequently though the vent, essentially bypassing the major portion of the cloaca. The active egg-laying process is correctly referred to as oviposition.

Since the cloaca serves as a terminal reservoir of the intestinal tract and the urinary system as well as the terminal reproductive tract, many observers believe that the egg passes through the same reservoir as fecal material. Actually, due to the location of the vaginal opening the egg really passes through the vent with little or no contact with the cloaca.

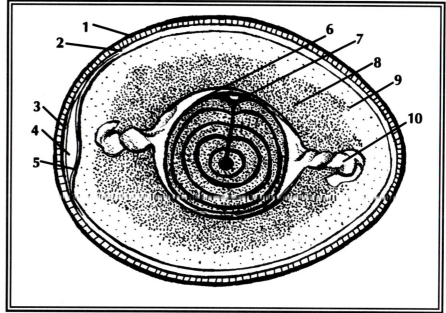

Figure 2. Essential structures of a bird's egg (ovule). 1: Cuticle. 2: Shell 3: Outer (shell) membrane. 4: Air cell (chamber). 5: Inner membrane. 6: Yolk (vitellus). 7: Germinal disk or blastoderm. 8: Dense albumen. 9: Fluid albumen. 10: Chalaza. (Illustration by Elizabeth Mitchell)

The shell gland or uterus of emus deposits an avocado-green pigmented shell. The traverse time of the egg in the reproductive tract of emus may be approximately 72 hours.

The interval between laying eggs varies, but in rheas it is about 48 hours. Rhea eggs are usually a modest lemon yellow.

Fertilization and egg development are essentially the same in all ratite species but oviposition in emus requires a 76-hour cycle while it may be only 48 hours in ostriches and rheas.

Stress and environmental and biological influences may elicit great variations in oviposition or egg-laying cycles in all species.

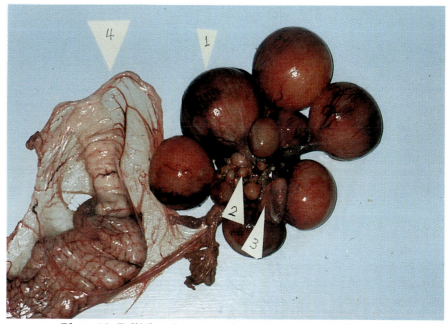

Photo 10. Follicles of varying sizes. Compare with Figure 3.

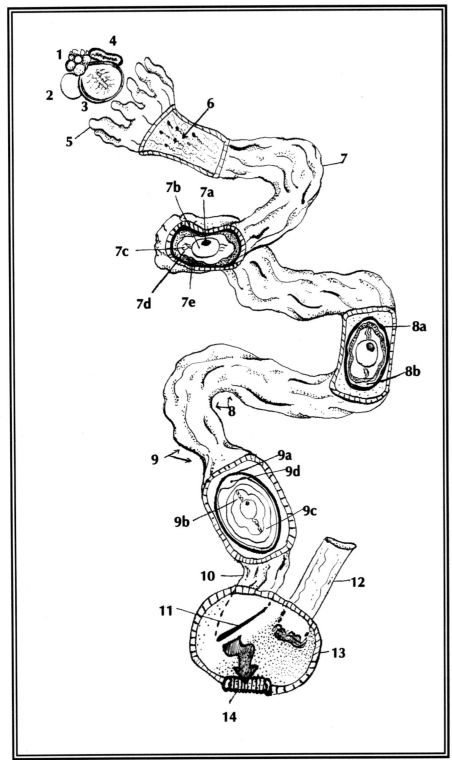

Figure 3. Reproductive tract of female ratite, with developing egg (ovule). Compare with Photos 10 and 11. 1-3: Ovarian follicles in various stages of development. 4: Post-ovulatory (residual) ovarian follicle. 5: Infundibulum. 6: Sperm in infundibulum. 7: Magnum. 7a: Germinal disk or blastoderm. 7b: Yolk or vitellus. 7c: Chalaza. 7d: Dense albumen. 7e: Endometrium of reproductive tract. 8: Isthmus. 8a: Shell membrane. 8b: Fluid albumen. 9: Uterus or shell gland. 9a: Egg shell. 9b: Chalaza. 9c: Dense albumen. 9d: Air cell. 10: Vagina. 11: Vaginal opening. 12: Intestine. 13: Cloaca. 14: Vent or common opening of intestinal tract, urinary tract (not shown), and reproductive tract. (Illustration by Elizabeth Mitchell)

Sudden, loud and unusual noises, unusual weather conditions, illness or even routine handling for treatment or vaccinations may cause a cessation of egg laying for an indeterminate amount of time, especially in young adult birds.

Ratites are considered to be indeterminate or continuous layers as opposed to determinate or discontinuous layers. Indeterminate layers will continue to lay eggs in the same nest if the eggs are removed from the nest. As a matter of fact, removal of the eggs as they are laid seem to stimulate continued laying.

BIOCHEMISTRY OF REPRODUCTION

The biochemistry of reproduction in ratites is a complicated, delicately balanced biological process controlled by endocrine glands that produce enzymes or hormones that affect specific organ and tissue targets and stimulate or suppress their functions (Figure 4).

In all animals hormones (enzymes) control most biological functions including growth, development, nutrition, energy utilization, and sexual activity and reproduction.

In most situations the hormones or enzymes of ratites and other birds are interrelated in a well-balanced feedback system similar to that found in mammals but different in some important aspects. The primary functions of some of the most important hormones are described below.

When discussing reproductive hormones it should be noted that no fully distinctive male and female hormones can be identified with specific functions that regulate the production of oocytes and sperm (gametogenesis), dimorphic anatomical features (secondary sex characteristics), or behavioral development.

All known reproductive hormones are present in both sexes and both male and female have hormone receptor mechanisms in target organs or tissue that are stimulated or suppressed by the same basic hormone.

For instance, in ostriches, features referred to as sexual dimorphism such as heavy bodied, black-feathered, red-skinned aggressive dominant male, and brown-feathered, submissive female are a result of the differences in cycles of glandular secretion of androgens, testosterone and estrogens in varying proportions.

Brown feathers, less aggressive attitude and ovarian development are under the control of significant amounts of estrogen and minuscule amounts of (testosterone) in young adult female ostriches.

In male ostriches the testes undergo very little growth in size or function until the bird reaches the sub-adult stage. The lack of estrogen and production of a limited amount of testosterone cause improved feather texture, sheen and distinct color.

The increased light of lengthening days signals the start of distinct but modest enlargement, but very important testicular tissue development. Longer hours of light perceived by the eye and other environmental influences stimulate a light-sensitive body, the pineal gland, attached to the meninges (covering) of the brain and large blood vessels of the brain deep within the invaginations of the brain stem and the cerebellum.

The pineal gland responds to light by the production of hormones (probably melatonin or 5-metaoxy-tryptophol), influencing the hypothalamus to produce and release another hormone called a gonadotropic releasing hormone (GnRH).

This hormone produced in and released by the hypothalamus has a direct effect upon the

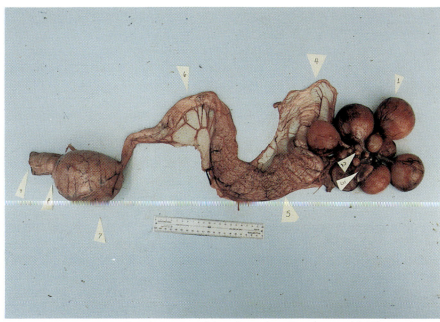

Photo 11. Reproductive tract of female ratite. Compare with Figure 3 and larger photo at beginning of chapter.

Figure 4. Schematic of biochemical or enzymatic influences on the reproductive process of female ratites. (Illustration by Elizabeth Mitchell)

anterior lobe of the pituitary gland by stimulating the production of two gonadotropic hormones.

Both gonadotropic hormones, luteinizing hormone (LH) and follicle stimulating hormone (FSH) have a major influence upon the development and function of the reproductive tract of both male and female ratites.

In females FSH is released into the blood stream and is carried to the ovarian follicle as one of its primary target organs. There in the theca cells of the ovary, FSH levels control the development and sequential motivation of the developing follicles.

LH is manufactured in and released from the anterior pituitary gland into the bloodstream, which subsequently determines the rupture of the ovarian follicle, releasing the oocyte and the associated vitellus or yolk.

The feedback of hormones and their level further influence the production of oxytocin, prostaglandins and other hormones that have an effect upon the final delivery of the egg from the uterus, vagina and cloaca.

In males, FSH and LH levels stimulate the maturation of the cells of Leydig within the testes, which in turn produce testosterone, initiating spermatogenesis.

Subsequently testosterone influences the secondary sexual characteristic such as feather nutrition and reddening of the beak, neck and skin of the legs. Though these changes may be gradual as roosters reach sexual maturity, they are dramatic and rapid with the onset of longer days and the breeding season in older birds.

The light-sensitive body adjacent to the optic chiasm in emus, though not fully understood, has the opposite response to the light of lengthening days. Cool nights and short days seem to stimulate the hypothalamus to produce GnRH, which then affects FSH, LH and subsequent androgen release in the same manner as increased levels of light affect ostriches and rheas. Toward the end of the breeding season for emus, with the lengthening of days and warmer nights result in a reduction in testosterone, and male emus are hormonally influenced to become *broody* in preparation for incubating eggs.

Broodiness is a common term used to describe the condition in birds when hormonal changes bring about an attitude that causes the individual to begin to incubate a clutch of eggs. In poultry this change occurs in females only, but in many other groups of birds it occurs in both sexes. In ratites, both male and female ostriches become broody, but in emus and rheas the male incubates the eggs and cares for the brood.

Though this broodiness does not occur in all males, many enter this phase in a sudden and dramatic way, sitting on a nest for long periods of time depriving themselves of feed and water until the weight loss may at times may be severe. Even in the most virile male this condition is considered to be normal.

Rhea males prepare a nest and defend it against all invaders, especially other males and predators. However, this seems to be a psychological condition, perhaps with high levels of testosterone that enhance virility and fecundity until one or more females lays a satisfactory clutch of eggs to be incubated. Rhea males also become broody. To this point the role of hormone levels during these periods is only speculative.

EGG FORMATION

Readers should closely follow the schematic display of the female ratite reproductive tract (Figure 3) as they read this section.

The earlier statement that yolk and oocyte formation in the functional left ovary of ratites is under the influence of hormones produced in the endocrine system begs further discussion related to the biology of egg formation in the reproductive tract and the basic functions of each feature as it relates to efficiency in reproduction.

Oocyte (true egg) development is seldom significantly influenced by nutritional influences because of the relative deference of other bodily functions to the importance of the reproductive process. However, there are a few bacterial and viral diseases that may have an depressive effect upon oocyte production.

EGG DEVELOPMENT AND FERTILIZATION

Normal yolk material concentrates antibodies from the female bloodstream that can be passed on to the developing embryo or the newly hatched chick. These antibodies play an important role in the protection against bacterial and viral diseases in birds. In addition the nutrient- and vitamin-rich yolk material is essential to the health and nutrition of chicks for the first few days of life.

Fertilization of the oocyte in the infundibulum of the reproductive tract is essential and will only take place in this portion of the reproductive tract within a very short time following ovulation or rupture of the mature follicle. The presence of a pale white ring around the germinal disc is evidence that the oocyte has been fertilized and has become a developing embryo or zygote.

The surrounding of the yolk and developing embryo with the thick albumen in the magnum of the reproductive tract is a metabolic function of the epithelial lining cells and secretory glands of this portion of the reproductive tract. In addition to being an important source of protein for the developing embryo the thick albumen is provided with a protein (enzyme) referred to as avidin.

Avidin is responsible for a very important protective adaptation of the egg to limit or prevent bacterial infection of the yolk and developing embryo. This product binds to, and thereby, prevents the utilization of biotin, an essential vitamin for bacterial growth.

At each pole of the vitellus or yolk are structures that develop in the magnum, the chalazae, delicate protein fiber-like strands (cordons) that stabilize the yolk and developing embryo within the thick albumen.

Though initially parallel in structure, the spiral descent of the developing albumen twists and effectively stabilizes the yolk within the enveloped structure.

The time element of the egg in the magnum varies in different species of birds. For example in the chicken it is known to be retained in the magnum for approximately three hours.

The developing egg then passes to the tortuous and relatively long isthmus where the inner and outer shell membranes that enclose the structure are formed. These two membranes are in close apposition in their entirety, except at the broad end of the egg where they separate to begin the formation of the air chamber (air cell).

The outer or shell membrane is thicker and stronger than the internal membrane. Both act as physical barriers of some significance, especially the prevention of bacterial penetration, but function primarily to control water loss, and gaseous exchange. The egg traverses the isthmus in a proportionally lesser amount of time (approximately one hour in chickens).

The shell gland or uterus forms the shell, which is made up primarily of calcium carbonate. Since the amount of calcium deposited in the egg shell by the uterus represents a significant amount of loss by the body it is important to give consideration to the origin of this essential metabolic mineral (Figure 4).

The calcium ions (ca++) in the bloodstream being carried to the uterus or shell gland are also under a complicated system of hormonal control. Falling calcium ion levels in the bloodstream stimulate the production of parathormone, an enzyme produced in the parathyroid gland that lies adjacent to the thyroid gland in the neck.

This gland also produces calcitonin, another hormone that increases ca++ blood levels.

Calcitonin decreases kidney calcium secretion and depletion of ca++ stores in the bone by transferring them to the bloodstream, which carries the mineral to the uterus or shell gland for eggshell deposition.

The shell may contain as many as 8,000 to 10,000 openings or pores of various sizes. These pores allow the passage of carbon dioxide from the developing embryo to outside air, and the intake of oxygen from the environment.

Unfortunately some pores are large enough to allow the penetration of bacteria that may destroy the developing embryo if they are able to bypass the other defense mechanism of the egg.

Since the uterus plays such an important role in the development of the shell, it is easy to understand that the quality, shape, structure, mineral content and appearance of the egg can be detrimentally affected by disease, nutritional and hormonal influences in the bird and especially in the uterus.

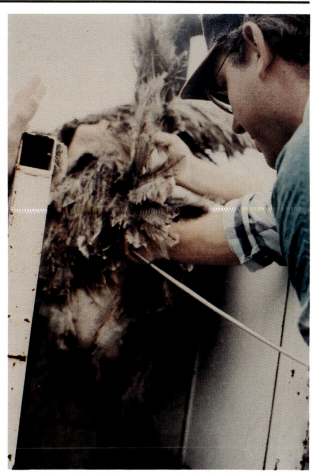

Photo 12. Taking a sample for testing of the female reproductive tract.

Last, the uterus and to some extent the vagina are responsible for the deposition of a thin protein-rich fluid that dries soon after the egg is laid, to become the cuticle. The amount of cuticle is often referred to as *bloom,* a term used to describe the amount of cuticle present on the shell.

The cuticle is the first line of defense of the egg against bacterial infection. However, as incubation progresses the cuticle dries and cracks, allowing for more freedom of penetration and free movement of gases through the shell to and from the developing embryo.

Thus it is essential that incubator sanitation becomes a primary concern to the operator. Incubation techniques should give careful consideration to the natural defense mechanisms that are discussed above.

DEFENSE MECHANISMS

It might be appropriate to conclude this section with a review of the egg's natural defense mechanisms against bacterial infections. The cuticle of the fully developed egg is the first line of defense to protect the contents of the egg and developing embryo from bacterial infection.

The pores in the mineralized shell allow the movement of gases into and out of the egg during the incubation process but do provide some physical barriers to infectious agents.

The inner and outer shell membrane prevent, to some degree, the penetration of bacteria but also provide for the movement of gases. The separation of these two membranes form the air cell (usually in the large end of the egg) that increases in size with storage or incubation and is a determining factor in grading of egg quality.

The viscosity of the albumen is also a factor in determining the quality of the egg, and is lessened during proper preincubation storage that enhances hatchability.

The enzyme avidin, contained in the albumen, serves as a vital protective mechanism against bacterial growth by binding biotin, an essential vitamin required by bacteria.

Finally, even though the yolk is a near-perfect medium for bacterial growth, the presence of protective passive antibodies in the yolk material is vital to the health of the embryo and young chick by serving as a protective mechanism against infectious agents, especially bacteria or viruses that would otherwise cause disease in the newly hatched chick.

REPRODUCTIVE DISEASE

Though many disease conditions may have an unfavorable effect upon reproduction in ratites, very little is known about diseases of the reproductive tract of these large flightless birds. However, for the purpose of discussion they are divided below into developmental, infectious, and mechanical or traumatic diseases of the reproductive tract.

Failure of normal development of reproductive organs and tissues play a major role in the reproductive processes of ratites. The gonads do not develop properly in some individuals.

Some males that may look normal from a physical standpoint may fail to breed or fail to be able to fertilize eggs from normal females. Some females may not develop ovaries capable of forming ova and/or yolk material or may have other reproductive organs that fail to function properly.

Though speculative in nature, a current theory holds that many of these maladies are thought to be the result of inbreeding depression or genetic weakness.

Hormonal mechanisms of reproduction can also be adversely affected by stress and environmental factors, to such an extent that otherwise normal ratites may have periods of reduced production or actually skip entire laying seasons.

Bacterial infections of the reproductive tract of females are usually the result of retrograde movement of bacteria in a fatigued reproductive system, and most frequently occur at the beginning or end of the laying season. Many different types of bacteria may cause reproductive infections but they usually arise from the intestinal tract of the hen.

COMMON INFECTIOUS AGENTS

In the most common bacterial infections, *Escherichia coli*, *Pseudomonas* spp., *Streptococci* or *Corynebacteria* are usually isolated.

Effective treatment depends upon isolation and identification of the infectious agent and determination of its antibiotic sensitivity profile.

Techniques are available for bacterial culture of the female reproductive tract (Photo 12) and it becomes a routine practice in many producer operations.

However, the routine culture of the reproductive tract of hens prior to the laying season, though advocated by some, may not be warranted unless there is a history or clinical indication of reproductive disease.

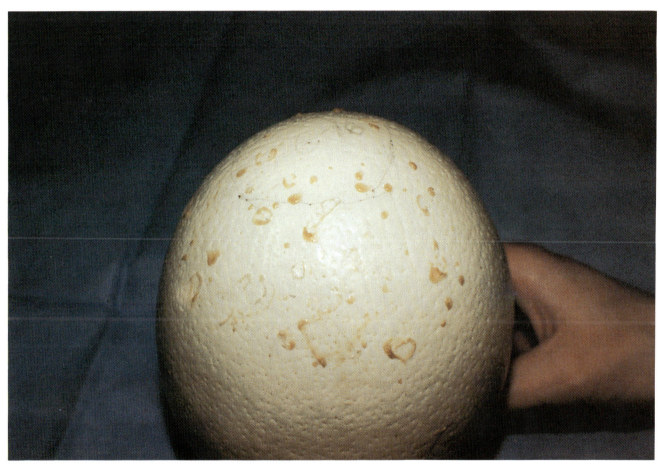
Bacterial contamination from within the shell has oozed out through the pores, giving it a speckled appearance. (Photo courtesy Dr. Brett Hopkins)

Eggs of emu (dark green), rhea, ostrich, and cassowary (light green).

THE RATITE EGG

D. C. Deeming, Ph.D., C.Biol., M.I.Biol.
Hangland Farm Ostriches Ltd.
Banbury, Oxfordshire, England

The egg plays a pivotal role in the development of ratite farming. The ability of the hen to produce a viable egg which we can incubate to produce top-quality chicks is a key feature in the expansion of captive ratite populations around the world.

Unfortunately, our understanding of the ratite egg is very poor in comparison with poultry eggs. As a consequence we are forced to use the egg of the domestic fowl as a model to describe ostrich, emu or rhea eggs, even though there are differences in size and composition between the different types.

Despite this reservation, fowl eggs can help us understand the ratite egg so long as we recognize these differences and understand the similarities.

The aim of this chapter is to describe the eggs of the three main ratites in domestication, ostriches (*Struthio camelus*), emus (*Dromaius novaehollandiae*) and rheas (*Rhea americana*). Where relevant, data for eggs of the Darwin's rhea (*Pterocnemia pennata*) and those of the cassowaries (*Casuarius* spp.) will be included for completeness.

The first part of the chapter will describe egg structure and composition with particular reference to the shell and its role during incubation. The second describes the embryology of the ratites and the process of hatching. Part three discusses egg quality and its role in hatchability.

EGG STRUCTURE

PHYSICAL DIMENSIONS

Weight

Ratites lay large eggs (photograph on facing page). The ostrich egg is the largest found in living birds, being 25 times the weight of an average 60 g domestic fowl egg. The eggs of emus, rheas and cassowaries are also larger than all other living birds, being 8 to 10 times larger than the fowl egg.

Although it is fitting that the largest bird should lay the largest egg, the ostrich egg is the smallest egg in terms of the body weight of the adult. It is only 1.5 per cent of adult body weight.

The weight of fresh ostrich eggs has been reported many times. On average it is around 1,500 grams, but ranges from below 1 kilogram to just over 2 kilograms, and weight of eggs within any batch is very variable.

Eggs collected from wild nests in Zimbabwe were on average 50 grams smaller than eggs from domestic hybrid ostriches, but there was a wide range of egg sizes in each sample, and the wild eggs may not have been fresh.

Weights of other ratite eggs are reported much lower. The emu egg averages 627 grams but can range between 570 and 680 grams, whereas cassowary eggs weigh around 600 ± 40 grams.

Rhea eggs are of similar size, weighing in at 590 ± 60 grams, with Darwin's rhea eggs weighing on average 621 grams.

The volume of 44 whole ostrich eggs averaging 1,517g in mass was 1,308 cubic centimeters (cm^3), with a density equal to 1.16 g per cm^3, whereas the internal volume of 19 eggs was 999 (± 149) cm^3.

Shape and dimensions

Ratite eggs are less pointed than a typical fowl egg, and it is often difficult to distinguish the pole of the egg with the air space without the aid of candling. Until the recent development of infrared and other candling methods which can penetrate the dark green shell, it was nearly impossible to candle emu eggs.

The ostrich egg averages maximum length of 15.3 cm (range 14-17 cm), an average maximum width of 12.3 cm (range 11-13 cm) and a degree of elongation (length divided by width) of 1.25 (range 1.18-1.25). The surface area of the eggshell is approximately 582 square centimeters (cm^2).

The eggs of emus, cassowaries and rheas are smaller in length than ostrich eggs. They average 13 cm in length, with an average breadth of 9 cm and a degree of elongation of 1.44. The volume is around 540 cm^3.

EGG STRUCTURE

Ostrich eggs take approximately 48 hours to form and are laid every two days on average. The mating required for fertilizing the egg, which occurs at the top of the oviduct, may have occurred some 7 days prior to oviposition.

Clutch size in wild nests varies from 10 to 15 eggs, but the number of eggs laid in a season can reach 100 if eggs are removed after oviposition.

The structure of a ratite egg (Figure 1) is very similar to that of the fowl egg (although it takes 45 minutes to hard-boil an ostrich egg). There is a central, spherical bright yellow yolk. The embryo (at this stage called the blastoderm) is a white spot 2-3 mm in diameter on the upper surface of the yolk. Although not easily seen, the yolk has a layered structure consisting of yellow and white yolk encased in an inert vitelline membrane (Figure 1).

These layers have different densities, which means that the top of the yolk immediately below the embryo has a lower density, ensuring the embryo is always found on top of the yolk whichever way the egg is turned.

The albumen is a composite structure with different layers surrounding the yolk (Figure 1), which were deposited during egg formation in the oviduct. The yolk is enclosed and suspended by the chalazae, twisted fibres of albumen proteins.

Immediately adjacent to the yolk is a layer of *thin* albumen. The bulk of the albumen is *thick* and is a solid gel. The different consistencies of these layers reflect their chemical composition. A further layer of thin albumen lies adjacent to the shell membranes. The albumen is enclosed by two shell membranes and the calcitic shell (see below).

CHEMICAL COMPOSITION

The contents of ostrich eggs constitute around 80-85 per cent of the egg mass (with a density of 1.04 g per cm^3) with the shell comprising the remaining 15-20 per cent. The yolk forms only 26 per cent of the whole egg mass (33 per cent of the egg contents) and weighs approximately 400 g (Table 1). The albumen makes up the rest of the mass (54 per cent of the initial egg mass) and weighs about 800 grams.

The contents of emu eggs weigh around 600 g and consist of a yolk weighing around 220 g and albumen weighing 380 g (Table 1).

The yolk is slightly larger a proportion of the contents of cassowary eggs (Table 1). By contrast, in the fowl egg the shell makes up only 12 per cent of the initial mass,

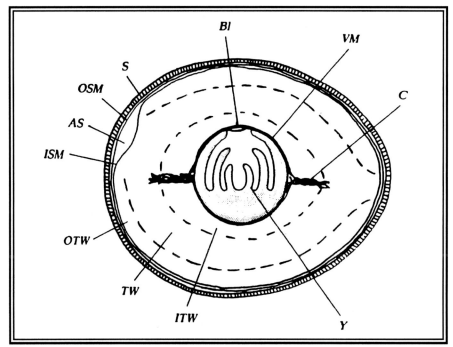

Figure 1. The structure of a ratite egg at oviposition, seen in section. Key: AS - air space; Bl - blastoderm; C - chalazae; ISM - inner shell membrane; ITW - inner thin albumen; OSM - outer shell membrane; OTW - outer thin albumen; S - shell; TW - thick albumen; VM - vitelline membrane; Y - yolk.

with the yolk 31 per cent and the albumen 57 per cent.

The chemical composition of the yolk and albumen of ratite eggs is poorly reported. Information is available only for ostrich and emu eggs, and composition is very similar to that of the fowl egg (Table 2).

However, there is considerable variation in the protein composition of the albumen between eggs from a variety of bird species (Table 3). Emu albumen has a low lysozyme content, while ostrich albumen contains relatively high levels of ovomucoid, but lacks avidin. At present, I am part of a team looking at the chemical composition of the fats and proteins of yolk, but results are not yet forthcoming.

THE EGGSHELL

Function and structure

The ostrich eggshell has all of the elements found in typical avian eggshells and is a composite structure typically 2 mm thick. However, shell thickness varies between eggs and can be as thin as 1.65 mm. As egg size increases the shell thickens and gets heavier. Smaller ratite eggs have shells ranging from 0.9 to 1.0 mm thick.

The functions of the eggshell are: to protect the contents from physical abuse; to act as a physical barrier which prevents microbial penetration into the egg contents; and to act as a mediating barrier determining the rate of movement of water, oxygen and carbon dioxide in and out of the egg. It has evolved to be tough and resilient to impact from outside, yet it is simple to break from inside, allowing easy escape for the chick.

Two fibrous shell membranes enclose the albumen; the outer membrane is thicker and has a more open mesh than the inner membrane (0.12 mm and 0.08 mm respectively in the ostrich). It is between these two membranes that the air space forms as water

TABLE 1. THE WEIGHT OF WHOLE RATITE EGGS AND CONTENTS, TOGETHER WITH COMPOSITION IN TERMS OF YOLK, ALBUMEN AND SHELL.

Species	Weight g	Content g	Yolk %	Albumen %	Shell %
Ostrich	1367	1096	32.0	68.0	19.8
	1400	1203	38.0	62.0	14.1
	1600	1280	33.0	67.0	20.0
Emu	710	619	35.0	52.2	12.8
	700	607	33.3	53.4	13.3
	710	619	40.0	60.0	12.8
Cassowary	644	562	42.0	58.0	12.7

TABLE 2. A COMPARISON OF THE NUTRIENTS IN OSTRICH AND FOWL EGGS (YOLK AND ALBUMEN COMBINED WITHOUT SHELLS). Data from Angel (1993).

Component	Unit	Ostrich	Emu	Fowl
Moisture	%	75.1	73.9	74.7
Nutrient (dry matter basis)				
Protein	%	47.1	42.9	47.4
Fat	%	43.7	48.1	45.4
Vitamin E	IU per g	0.062	0.045	0.12
Vitamin A	IU per g	19.29	13.1	20.5
Thiamin	ppm	5.85	2.43	3.55
Folic acid	ppm	1.93	0.511	1.18
Pantothenic acid	ppm	30.1	36.8	55.3
Riboflavin	ppm	9.72	11.87	12.6
Calcium	%	0.260	0.245	0.233
Phosphorus	%	0.798	0.817	0.810
Magnesium	ppm	559.0	510.0	490.0
Manganese	ppm	6.6	3.4	15.8
Selenium	ppm	1.57	1.18	0.60
Zinc	ppm	53.7	38.5	59.2
Iodine	ppm	3.2	3.05	2.8
Iron	ppm	101.3	98.3	90.9
Sodium	%	0.67	-	0.54
Potassium	%	0.4	-	0.50

TABLE 3. PERCENTAGE COMPOSITION OF THE PROTEINS OF EGG ALBUMEN
Units Given Are Percentage Of Total With The exception Of Avidin, Where It Is Units Per Gram.
Data From Osuga & Feeney (1968).

Protein	Ostrich	Emu	Rhea	Cassowary	Fowl
Dry weight (mg/ml)	113.0	101.0	110.0	114.0	121.0
Ovotransferrin	3.0	10.0	3.0	10.0	12.0
Ovomucoid	10.0	20.0	10.0	15.0	11.0
Ovoinhibitor	0.6	0.5	0.5	0.6	1.5
Lysozyme	0.45	0.05	2.00	0.5	3.4
Ovomacroglobulin	0.5	0.2	0.5	0.5	0.5
Sialic acid	2.1	3.1	1.4	2.3	0.29
Apoprotein	0.3	2.0	0.5	0.8	0.8
Flavoprotein	0.3	-	-	-	0.7
Ovomucin	2.8	-	4.6	2.4	2.9
Avidin	-	-	-	-	11.5

vapor is lost from the egg and is replaced by air (Figure 1).

A thick layer of calcium carbonate, as calcite crystals, is laid down on top of the outer shell membrane and forms the bulk of the shell's thickness. Ostrich shell has a higher magnesium carbonate content than that of the fowl. The calcitic layer is particularly dense, lacking numerous air-filled vesicles often seen in eggshells from other species. The distinct structural layers in the calcitic layer are shown in Figure 2.

Shell abnormalities recognized in ostrich eggs include: ridges and clefts in the shell which are often characteristic of a bird; *cauliflower* shells with a pebbled appearance due to a thickened calcitic layer; *pocky* shells which are generally thinner than normal, with cracks in the calcite layer and spherical protrusions of calcium carbonate; and *orange peel* shells which are very porous.

The seemingly impenetrable layer of calcite is actually permeated with numerous pores which allow the passage of respiratory gases and water vapour (Figure 2). The structure of these pores varies between different species of bird and is related to egg size. The domestic fowl has the simplest pore structure, a straight tube topped with a funnel-like opening on the outside.

However, as egg size increases, the eggshell gets thicker, the number of pores increases, and pore structure becomes more complex. This branching is seen in its simplest form in rhea eggshells and is at its most extensive in ostrich eggshells (Figure 3). The openings of these branched pores are located in pits which can be easily seen on the outer surface of any ostrich egg.

The degree of pore branching is variable, with some pores having a single pore canal. Emu and cassowary eggshells have pores which open into a network of holes underlying the surface of the shell, and which have separate openings to the outside air (Figure 3).

Porosity

Pore number and density varies between shells of ostrich eggs, ranging from 12 to 16 pores per cm^2 of shell. Pore density is higher at the poles of the egg, particularly in the shell over the air space. Pore numbers have not been recorded in other ratite eggs.

Eggshell porosity is usually measured as water vapour conductance (G_{H2O}), measured by determining weight loss under known humidity conditions. The value of G_{H2O} depends on both the number of pores and the thickness of the shell.

Values recorded for G_{H2O} of ostrich eggs vary between 785.7 and 1402.5 mg H_2O per day per kiloPascal (kPa, a unit of gas pressure), with the latter eggs having a functional pore area of 160 mm^2.

Values for G_{H2O} of emu eggshell vary from 343 to 388 mg H_2O per day per kPa whereas cassowary eggshells have water-vapor conductances of 638 mg H_2O per day per kPa. Rhea eggshells vary in water-vapor conductance from 583 to 656 mg H_2O per day per kPa, whereas the shells of Darwin's rhea eggs have a G_{H2O} value of 556 mg H_2O per day per kPa. By contrast, the eggshells of domestic fowl eggs have G_{H2O} values of only 108 mg H_2O per day per kPa.

While these absolute values give us some idea of the magnitude of shell porosity in ostrich eggs, it is important to remember

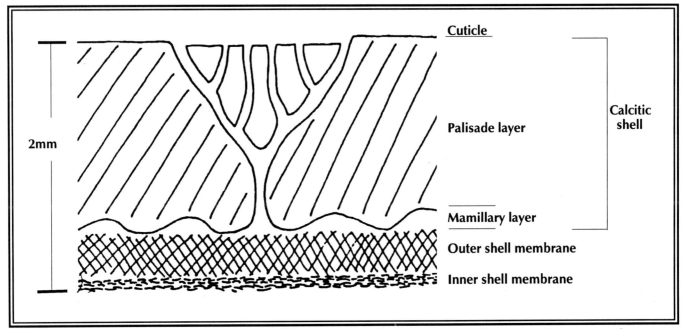

Figure 2. Radial section of a stylised ostrich shell, showing its ultrastructure and the branched structure of a pore.

that these values are only averages. There is great variation in the porosity of eggs observed within any batch of eggs, particularly if they are from different females.

A wide range of percentage weight losses (6-30 per cent around a mean of 11.38 per cent at 38 days) is normal for ostrich eggs incubated under the same humidity conditions (percentage of weight loss is proportional to porosity in this instance).

Comparative analysis of various incubation parameters (such as water vapour conductance, incubation period and egg weight) in many species of bird has shown that despite their size, ratite eggs are similar to other bird eggs in which shell characteristics are simply scaled for weight.

Color and the cuticle

Ostrich eggs vary in color from creamy-white to beige. This is unusual for ground-nesting birds which normally have shells with dark cryptic markings for camouflage. This color appears to be an adaptation to minimizing overheating of egg in the sun prior to incubation, despite the risks of increased predation.

Emu eggs are heavily pigmented with a dark green color produced by a methyl ester of biliverdin IXa. Cassowary eggs are also green, but are less heavily pigmented, and shadows can be seen using conventional candling lamps. Rhea eggs have pale yellow shells.

There has been a lot of unnecessary concern about the role of the cuticle on the surface of an ostrich eggshell. In terms of structure, it is a very thin layer of crystalline calcite. It is unlikely that it will be removed by washing. The idea that the *mucin coat* (which the cuticle is incorrectly called) cracks after 7-10 days of incubation appears to be unsubstantiated.

While it is likely to play a role in preventing bacterial invasion of the pores, it does not plug pore

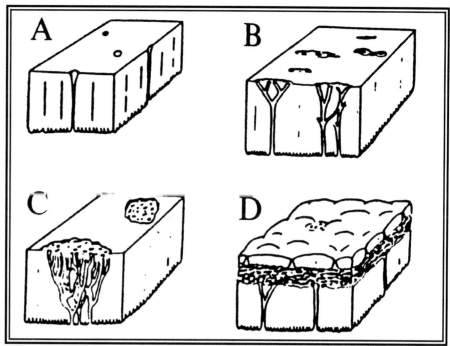

Figure 3. Radial sections of (A) domestic fowl, (B) rhea, (C) ostrich, and (D) emu and cassowary shells, showing pore structure (from Tullett, 1978).

openings, and bacterial and fungal spores can enter ratite eggs. The cuticle is not a significant barrier to gas movement across the shell. Its removal, if it could be achieved, is unlikely to affect the porosity of the eggshell, as is the case for other eggs like those of ducks.

EMBRYOLOGY

Ratite embryos

Very little is known about the embryology of any of the ratites. This paucity of information retards our understanding of the problems which face embryos during incubation, and will retard any attempts to solve such problems.

There are few reports dealing with ostrich embryo development, and these deal with specific organs. Even less is known about emu development. Again, reports deal with specific parts of the embryo's body. There are no detailed reports of embryogenesis in rheas or cassowaries.

This situation will almost certainly continue for the foreseeable future. Given the high value of fertile ratite eggs at present, the possibility of studying general development and growth of ostrich, emu or rhea embryos is very slight. Such research will have to wait until eggs are more plentiful and cheaper.

The only means by which embryonic development can be assessed without opening the egg is by candling. As we will see, this has inherent problems.

Embryonic development

It is useful to have an idea about the stages of development during incubation. The fowl embryo (incubation period of 21 days) is a useful model for ratites.

A short summary of embryonic development is presented here. Those seeking further understanding of the process should consult the photographs and table published by Tolhurst in Freeman & Vince, 1974.

There will almost certainly be slight differences in the pattern of development in the different ratites and the fowl, but it is helpful to have at least some idea of the development pattern rather than none at all.

Comparison of the timing of events in development are only estimates in the ostrich, rhea and emu, based on relative lengths of incubation at the normal incubation temperature.

In the birds so far studied, the zygote (the product of the fusion of the female ovum and the male sperm) begins its development during the formation of the egg in the oviduct and reaches gastrula stage (= blastoderm, 60,000 cells) at oviposition.

Embryonic development does not proceed beyond the gastrula stage if the egg is retained in the oviduct longer than usual. In effect, the embryo is in suspended animation until the egg is rewarmed at the start of incubation.

At oviposition, the ostrich blastoderm is only 2-3 mm in diameter. Despite the differences in egg size, this is only slightly larger than the fowl blastoderm. The blastoderm can be seen as a white spot on the top surface of the yolk in unincubated eggs (best seen in infertile fowl eggs). Considering that the ostrich chick can weigh over 900 g at hatch, ostrich embryos grow at a tremendous rate.

The embryo converts yolk and albumen into body tissues and organs and goes through two phases of development—differentiation and growth—to hatch as an independent chick. Differentiation involves the formation of the bodily organs and extends up to day 12 of incubation in the chick (probably day 24 in the ostrich and rhea or day 32 in the emu).

The brain, eye and other nervous tissues are the first organs to develop, with maturation starting at the head end of the embryo. The heart and blood vessels begin to form day 2-3 of incubation (day 4-6 in the ostrich, 5-8 in the emu).

The extra-embryonic membranes develop at this time and begin to grow out from the embryo (Figure 4). The body wall and viscera develop from day 3 in the fowl (day 6 in the ostrich, day 8 in the emu). The limbs appear on days 4 and 5 (days 8-10 in the ostrich, 10-13 in the emu).

As the mid-point of incubation approaches, the jaws and other facial structures have developed and the embryo begins to resemble a bird. At half-way through incubation, almost all of the organs and tissues found in the adult bird have formed but the embryo is small.

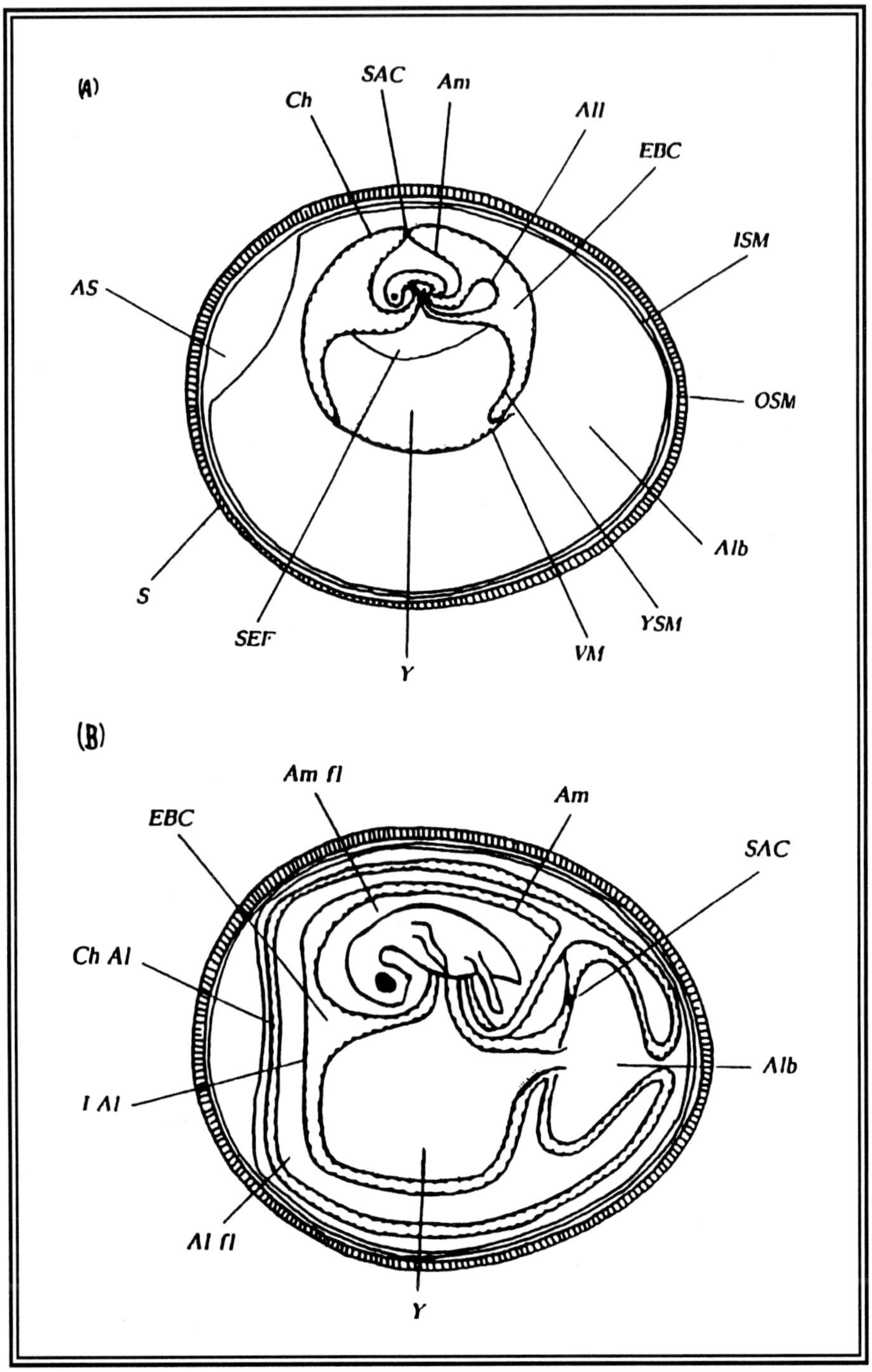

Figure 4. The pattern of development in a domestic fowl egg after (A) 5 and (B) 12 days of incubation. Key: Alb - albumen; All - allantois; Al fl - allantoic fluid; Am - amnion; Am fl - amniotic fluid; AS - air space; Ch - chorion; Ch al - chorio-allantois; EBC - extra-embryonic coelom; I Al - inner allantois; ISM - inner shell membrane; OSM - outer shell membrane; S - shell; SAC - sero-amniotic connection; SEF - subembryonic fluid; VM - vitelline membrane; Y - yolk; YSM - yolk sac membrane.

The extra-embryonic membranes are extensions of the embryo body and play important roles in development. The amnion grows out from the embryonic body wall and over the embryo, offering it physical protection. The yolk sac membrane grows out from the developing gut over the yolk so as to supply the embryo with nutrients from the yolk. In the first week of incubation this membrane also acts as a respiratory organ.

The allantois develops from the hind gut around day 5 in the fowl embryo (probably day 10 in the ostrich, day 13 in the emu) and acts as a bladder for the embryo. Additionally, in combination with the chorion (an extension of the amnion), it forms the chorio-allantoic membrane, which lines the inside of the shell and becomes the primary respiratory organ for the embryo. The arrangement of these membranes is shown on days 5 and 12 of incubation in the fowl egg in Figure 4.

The growth phase of development occurs during the second half of incubation, with the embryo increasing in size, its tissues maturing. The feathers develop during this period, and in the last few days the embryo begins to prepare for hatching by moving around to adopt the correct position within the shell.

The original contents of the egg are unrecognizable at hatching. The water and proteins in the albumen have been absorbed, converted into embryonic tissues with unused protein being stored in the residual yolk. The yolk has supplied nutrients and energy for the embryo but is far from being depleted, and is withdrawn into the body cavity prior to hatching.

In this way the yolk can support the hatchling in the first few days of life. In the ostrich it has been fully utilized by 8-9 days of age. The shell supplies calcium for bone formation as well as providing protection for the embryo.

Egg candling

Fertility of an unincubated egg can only be determined by opening it and examining the structure of the blastoderm using magnification. This task is not impossible, but it requires expertise in order to correctly assess the status of the embryonic tissue.

It is impossible to guarantee fertility of any unopened egg prior to incubation, but opening an egg almost certainly consigns the embryo it contains to death. However, when the egg is incubated, a viable embryo will develop and the fertility of the egg can be assessed by candling.

Of the ratites, eggs of the rhea are the most informative to candle. Some of the wonders of embryonic development can be observed, as the relatively thin yellow shell does not obscure the view.

By contrast, eggs of the emu are impossible to candle by conventional means. However, new systems using infrared lamps have now been developed with which the egg contents can be visualized. Ostrich eggs need a very bright light for effective candling, but even with a converted 150-Watt slide projector, the shell on ostrich eggs is too thick for any clarity.

Candling is important, though, as it can show you signs of embryonic development, signs of contamination, and the size of the air space.

A fresh ostrich egg will have no discernable dark structures and is translucent orange in color irrespective of which way the egg is candled. A faint shadow of the yolk may be seen deep within the egg, but this will freely move within the egg. This appearance will not change if the egg is infertile no matter how long the egg is left in the incubator.

If an "unincubated" egg does show uneven patches of light and dark, which do not move freely within the egg when it is rotated, then it is possible that the egg has been incubated previously or it is infected with microorganisms. In the former case, the embryo probably died either early in development or incubation may have been interrupted, causing the embryo to die. In all cases, although the egg is fertile, it is useless for hatching.

As normal development proceeds in the ostrich egg the size of the dark shadows increases, indicating that there is embryonic development within. The shadow is cast by the yolk-sac membrane which lies close to the shell. As the membrane grows it steadily increases the area of the shadow, but around halfway through incubation the shadow seems to stop growing. At this time the yolk sac membrane is growing under the yolk and away from the shell.

After a few days the chorio-allantois, which has been growing over the top of the yolk sac membrane, grows beyond the limit of the yolk sac membrane, and the shadow begins to increase again. With a very bright candling lamp and a thin-shelled egg, it is possible to see some of the chorio-allantois as it grows towards the pole of the egg away from the air space.

The egg proceeds to go completely dark and no changes will be seen until hatching begins and the air space moves around to the side of the egg. The first movement of hatching will be seen in the air space during candling.

Monitoring the size of the air space by candling can give an indication of the amount of water being lost from the egg. A record of the size of the air space should allow correlation with the weight loss from the egg and aid in future assessment of development in eggs. However, candling eggs solely to assess the size of the air space is not an alternative to weighing eggs on a regular basis.

Candling will also indicate cracks and other defects in the eggshell. In particular, if the air space is not fixed, but moves around within the egg as it is turned, such an egg will probably fail to develop.

What seems to happen is either that air is trapped in the oviduct and is enclosed by the shell membranes, or the air which enters the egg when water vapour is lost forms a bubble in the albumen and not between the shell membranes. As certain females consistently lay eggs with floating air spaces, it is likely that the former explanation applies.

Unfortunately, beyond these rather vague details of development, candling of ostrich eggs does not reveal much more. Therefore, when candling eggs, observations should be written down for comparison with previous observations for that egg.

If candling is done once a week, it is recommended that the egg be considered dead or infertile if no changes in the shadows occur after three successive candlings. In this way the risk of discarding living eggs is minimized.

When chicks hatch

The hatching process for ostrich chicks is often preceded by the embryos calling from the unpipped eggshell. It is unclear whether this calling is to inform the parents of the chick's imminent arrival or to help to synchronise hatching within the clutch, as has been observed for the common rhea.

However, a clutch of eggs can take 2 to 3 days to hatch; it seems unlikely that synchrony of hatch is important in ostriches.

The hatching process is first observed to begin in the ostrich when the air space which had formed a symmetrical position at one end of the egg begins to distort and move to one side of the egg. Prior to this change, however, the chick has rubbed away the shell membranes with its beak, making a hole which aids internal pipping. The shell membrane covering the air space is then pulled over the beak, allowing the bird its first access to air. In the emu this process appears to be the same, but further research is required in this species and other ratites.

External pipping, where the shell is first broken by the emerging chick, is usually seen as a large broken piece of shell which is often dislodged from the rest of the shell; the regular-shaped *pip hole* of the domestic fowl and other birds is not seen.

Hatching proceeds by the formation of a *window* in the side of the egg in which both the beak and the foot are visible. While ostrich chicks have a pronounced hatching muscle, the window is enlarged by the chick using its beak and kicking downwards while stretching its body. This eventually results with the shattering of the shell, or a crack extending around the middle of the egg, and the chick pushing itself out of the shell.

Hatching in the ostrich is unusual. Unlike domestic fowl, where the chick rotates $270°$ within the egg, the hatching ostrich rotates less than $90°$. In domestic fowl the beak stabs forward into the air space, but in ostriches the air space is pulled over the beak.

External pipping occurs in the ostrich when the head is thrown backwards to make the beak hit the shell. In addition, the ratite eggshell is shattered instead of being cut open and the foot plays a major role in the hatching process.

For these reasons malpositions in the ostrich vary considerably from that of the chicken. A chick with its head in the opposite end of the egg from the air space is the most common malposition in the ostrich, but chicks can also be malpositioned with their heads on their left sides and not the right. More observations are required in order to define the most common malpositions.

Hatching can take many hours to complete, and there are frequent calls and periods of rest. This time is the most stressful for the chick and its owner. Egg batches can hatch over a period of 4-6 days. In addition, hatching time is prolonged by storage time, low temperatures and large egg size.

When to help with hatching

Unfortunately, there have been too many instances of ostrich chicks being "helped" out of the egg. Usually, this assistance is based on ignorance of the hatching process. In most cases, help is premature. Holes are made in the shell to give the "suffocating" chick air, but it is not ready to hatch.

This practice is usually based on an assumed time for internal pipping as observed by candling. If you do help a chick to hatch before it has pipped, you will end up with a chick with a very poor growth rate if it has not died in the few days of life.

Hatching should be as natural as possible. The earlier the interference, the poorer the chick will be. Early interference usually leads to even more help being required.

Unlike some birds, the ostrich does not help its chick hatch. This is probably the best lesson an ostrich farmer can learn.

Assistance should only be given to hatching chicks as a last resort and then only under certain circumstances: cracking an unpipped eggshell should be avoided at all costs. It is best to wait and see if the chick can do this itself. If it cannot, helping it to hatch is almost always a waste of time and effort in trying to keep any chick produced alive.

If a chick has been able to make a large window in the shell but has not progressed in its attempts to break the shell for over 12 hours, there is a danger that the chick will be simply trapped in the shell even though it is still viable. These birds are commonly the stragglers of the hatch. If left to their own devices they may well die in the egg.

In this instance the physical restraint imposed by the shell should be removed by making a hairline crack all around the equator of the egg and linking the two sides of the *window*. The chick should be returned to the hatcher without removing any shell pieces or by widening the crack. If the chick is strong it will hatch at its next push against the shell.

This assistance simply removes the biggest barrier to hatching that the chick encounters, *i.e.* the intrinsic strength of the eggshell—an egg will withstand a load of 55 kg before breaking. If after this assistance the chick is unable to hatch, then it was never going to hatch and it is recommended that it be culled.

It is most important to resist the temptation to forcibly pull a chick from the egg—it may not survive the trauma of its premature birth. In this way time will not be wasted by keeping alive poor-quality birds which do not survive for long after hatching.

EGG QUALITY

Good egg quality is needed for high hatchability and chick survival. This is an ideal toward which all ostrich farmers should strive. A high-quality egg will be laid by a female in the best of health and condition, having been mated by a male in the same state. The nutritional status of the birds, particularly the female, will be properly catered for and matched to needs of reproduction. The hen should not be too fat through overfeeding, but should not be starving.

The egg will be of normal morphology and chemical composition, providing all of the components for normal embryonic development. Top-quality eggs are laid in a clean environment, collected promptly, and stored under the optimal conditions. In this way they will be free of microbial contamination.

Failure to hatch may be due to a number of reasons. Either sex may have been sterile, the diet may have been insufficient, or perhaps the egg was laid in a dirty pen where it lay in the full glare of the sun for 8 hours.

Infertility and microbial contamination automatically reduce hatchability, but careful management and good record keeping will help to reduce their influence on production.

It has to be stated that, even with the best of management, there will always be some fertile eggs which will die during incubation. There is a peak in mortality during the first and last weeks of development.

Factors affecting mortality include the above, as well as congenital defects, nutritional quality of the egg, and deaths caused by incorrect incubation parameters. Unfortunately it is often difficult to say for certain why an egg died.

The paucity of information about the normal composition of ostrich eggs hinders our understanding of what constitutes good egg quality in terms of composition. The similarity between fowl and ostrich eggs allows us to draw conclusions from the extensive work already done on other domestic species.

Further research into defining egg quality in ostriches, and how it affects embryonic development, is needed urgently.

Incubator circa early 1900s. (Photo courtesy Andy Weilbrenner)

INCUBATION & HATCHING

© *John Brake, Ph.D., PAS*
North Carolina State University
Raleigh, North Carolina

Bruce L. Rosseland
© *NatureForm, Inc.*
Jacksonville, Florida

Successful incubation and hatching result from the right combination of breeder management (including nutrition), egg storage, machine operation, and sanitation.

In the commercial poultry industry, many of these variables are sufficiently standard to allow us to make fairly definitive recommendations.

The emerging ratite industry has almost as many management scenarios as there are ranchers and producers. Additionally, the high value of eggs and chicks has made it difficult to sacrifice many eggs to determine essential information.

Therefore, we have had to use empirical field observations and field research, coupled with a basic working theory derived from chicken and turkey research, to develop this information. Recommended practices have been used successfully with ratites.

This chapter is intended to provide the reader with an overview of the basics of incubation and insight into how to troubleshoot their own unique situation and achieve positive results.

Within the egg shell is contained all of the essential ingredients to form a chick except oxygen. The mechanism by which the yolk, albumen, and blastoderm become a chick is truly intricately balanced and works with a very high degree of success in the wild.

We often find artificial incubation to be less successful, probably because our conditions do not achieve the often ideal environments provided by the natural habitat.

BASIC ANATOMY AND PHYSIOLOGY

The egg yolk, also called the ovum, is fertilized in the upper part of the reproductive tract of the hen and development of the embryo begins immediately. The embryo is at least 24 hours old and has over 2,000 cells when the egg is laid and collected. Therefore, incubation begins in the hen and continues through the hatcher. Only the rate of development changes with temperature and relative humidity.

The yolk is initially held in place in the center of the egg albumen (egg white) by the proteinaceous chalazae, which are attached to each end of the yolk, and the thick viscous nature of the albumen. This serves to keep the

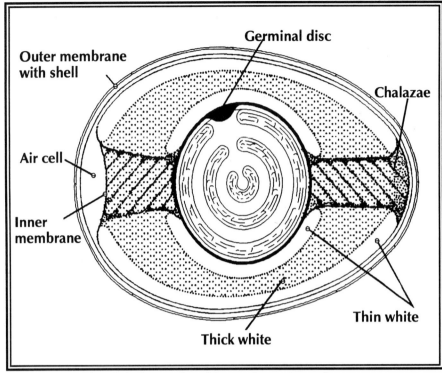

Figure 1. External and internal structure of an egg.

PREINCUBATIONAL DEVELOPMENT

Immediately after being laid the egg begins to undergo changes which prepare it for eventual incubation. It has often been stated in the chicken industry that eggs are at their greatest hatching potential the moment they are laid. Research has shown that this is not necessarily true.

When an egg is first laid, the albumen quality is such that it helps position the yolk and the embryo in the middle of the egg. This is a protective mechanism to prevent bacteria from reaching the embryo.

However, this means that if the egg is set fresh, oxygen exchange must occur across both the eggshell and the albumen. If the egg is allowed to sit for a few days, the albumen will degrade and the embryo (blastoderm) will rotate into the vicinity of the air cell if the egg is held in the vertical position (large end up). This creates a better incubation condition.

Many scientists have wondered how eggs that are laid under natural conditions, e.g. a 15-egg clutch laid over 45 days by an emu, can survive long-term storage at 70 degrees F and hatch at a similar time.

This timing mechanism has baffled many researchers. There are several theories about communication between the embryos as they develop.

While this may play a role, we believe the most likely explanation for most of the effect is that the albumen quality of eggs laid early in the clutch is much superior to that of eggs laid later in the clutch. Therefore, the eggs laid early in the clutch can withstand longer storage.

The hen probably accomplishes this by altering her intake and/or utilization of body stores of protein, which is the basic constituent of albumen.

developing embryo in the middle of the protective albumen. The albumen contains a number of specialized proteins which have antibacterial properties. The albumen also has a basic (alkaline) pH which is antibacterial.

The albumen breaks down quickly, which allows the developing embryo (blastoderm) to float up near the air cell. As albumen degradation proceeds the pH becomes much more basic, which causes the specialized proteins to lose their antibacterial properties.

However, during this time the cuticle has dried and sealed the pores so that further bacterial penetration does not occur unless the eggshell becomes wet.

The eggshell is composed of an inner shell membrane next to the albumen, and an outer shell membrane next to the shell, the shell proper, and the cuticle. Both the shell membranes and the cuticle are composed primarily of protein. The shell proper is composed primarily of calcium carbonate.

Eggshell pores pass through the shell proper, allowing the exchange of oxygen, carbon dioxide, and water. The pores are most numerous over the large end of the egg and this is why the air cell forms at the large end.

The air cell forms when air passes through the pores and fills the space between the inner and outer shell membranes when the liquid egg contents decrease in volume as the egg cools immediately after laying.

The eggshell appears wet as it is first laid. This appearance changes as the cuticle dries to form a relatively effective barrier to microbial penetration. Recent research has shown that the cuticle also helps the egg regulate water loss during storage and incubation. Knowledge of the role of the cuticle in water loss is essential to hatching egg management.

Germicides, when applied to the eggshell surface, may alter the components of the cuticle in such a way that water loss is altered during incubation and possibly storage. This may affect the optimum incubator conditions on a bird-by-bird basis.

The hen can do this simply by altering her appetite. Many wild birds exhibit anorexia during the egg-laying cycle, so that food intake decreases as the laying of the clutch proceeds.

After a few days pause at the end of the clutch, it is probable that the hen starts the incubation process with all the eggs at a relatively similar albumen quality.

We have observed that ratites eat voraciously at the beginning of the breeding season, only to exhibit a decrease in feed consumption later in the season.

We may obtain important hatchery management information by carefully monitoring individual hen feed intake and relating it to embryonic development.

EGG STORAGE

It is well known, in very young chickens which have thick eggshells and thick albumen, that incubation time is longer than would be expected for an egg of that size. The situation of ratites is less clear.

However, recent university studies indicate ostrich eggs stored more than three days produce better quality chicks, based upon subjective scoring and comparison.

This is consistent with chicken and turkey information that eggs stored for a few days before incubation produce better-quality chicks.

Field data on emus indicate eggs can be stored up to three weeks with minimal loss of hatchability in incubation. This is consistent with the length of the clutch in the wild, as the egg is formed with the ability to be stored for a long time.

Recent field data from southern Africa indicate wild ostrich eggs taken from the nest after a full clutch of 11 to 15 eggs (up to 30 days of storage) have been laid,

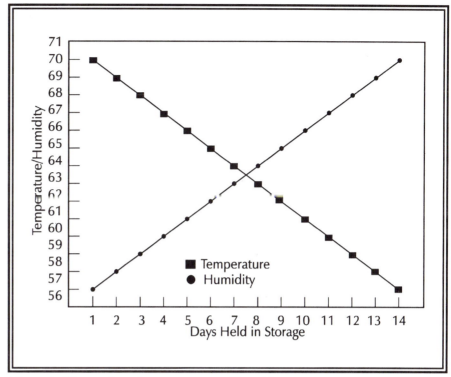

Figure 2. Illustration of temperature and humidity in storage conditions, plotted against the number of days the eggs are held in storage.

hatch better than domestic eggs laid in the same environment.

As the domestic eggs were set nearly fresh, this further suggests that ratite eggs are formed with and have the ability to be stored for a long time. Ratite eggs have not yet been stored long enough experimentally to determine if there can be a positive effect on chick quality with longer storage.

Storage conditions would typically be from 75 degrees down to 55 degrees F (23.8 to 12.7 C) for one to several days depending upon the situation. The following

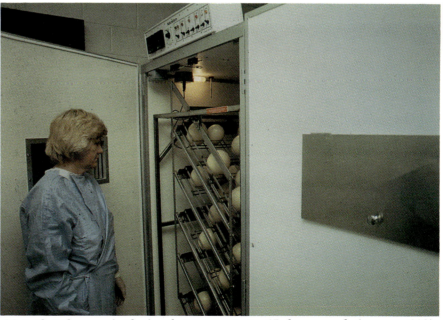

Note that the eggs in the incubator are set at a 45-degree angle (see page 110).

examples detail the options (see also Figure 2).

Average emu incubation settings are 96.8 degrees F (35.9 C) and 33 per cent RH. If eggs are not being set in batches (collecting eggs and setting them as they are laid), store eggs overnight at room temperature (70-75F)(21-24C). This will assist the albumen quality to break down a little faster than at a cooler temperature.

Incubating eggs at a slightly lower humidity than normal (-5 per cent) will also help overcome the problem of having fresh albumen. If eggs are being set in batches (storing eggs and setting once a week) the normal incubation humidity setting would be used as the albumen quality has declined during storage.

Daily setting of eggs may need to be combined with a slightly lower relative humidity and slightly higher storage temperature. For long-term storage, the opposite conditions would be expected to give the best results.

During the holding time the egg should probably be rotated (45 degrees either way from vertical) once or twice a day to help move the yolk toward the air cell.

Holding-room temperatures below 65 degrees F allow eggs to be held longer before setting. Eggs in holding-room temperatures above 70 degrees F need to be set more frequently.

We recommend a holding facility separate from the incubator room. It is suggested that the egg be held in the large-end-up position if at all possible. This can usually be determined by examining the density of pores on the eggshell and the shape of the egg and by candling with a pen light.

BASIC EMBRYOLOGY

Basic embryological development in the incubator and hatcher can be divided into three general parts. The first (early) third extends from placement in the incubator until the beak fully develops. This is an extremely important part of the total process, as the primary organ systems and all the basic membranes develop during this period.

As cell division is occurring, vital organs are being formed. If the dry-bulb temperature increases significantly during this time, the metabolism of the embryo will increase excessively, which can result in poorly developed organs. The embryo will most likely continue to develop, only to die toward the final stage of incubation. Short periods of low temperature are less of a concern during this time.

The embryonic chorionic and allantoic membranes begin to fuse with the eggshell to form the chorio-allantoic membrane (CAM). The CAM begins to become the respiratory organ, i.e. the lung, of the embryo during the latter half of this initial period.

Oxygen moves through the eggshell pores into the CAM blood and onto the embryo. Prior to this time the oxygen must also pass through the albumen in order to reach the embryo. Several days are required for the blood vessels to grow down the sides of the egg and completely cover the inner surface of the egg.

The second period (mid) extends until significant feathering develops on the body. This period generally has little mortality because the developed organ systems are simply growing without a great deal of complex cellular differentiation.

The CAM becomes completely developed. However, severe vitamin deficiencies and toxicities as well as severe incubation problems will cause an increase in mid-embryonic deaths. Increased mortality in other periods as well as malformities and malpositions are *not* reliable signs of a nutritional deficiency problem.

The third period (late) extends through hatching and includes the completion of feather growth, withdrawal of the yolk sac into the body, conversion from respiration via the CAM to respiration via the lungs, pipping, achievement of plateau (maximum) metabolic rate, and emergence from the shell.

Thus, many important sensitive developmental events are in progress and subject to easy disruption. Therefore, it is reasonable to understand why the two periods of high embryonic mortality occur early and late in development.

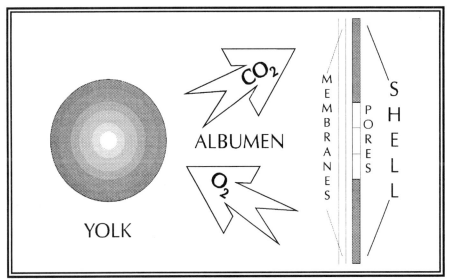

Figure 3. Gas exchange between the yolk and the outside air, through the shell and membranes.

EMBRYONIC RESPIRATION

The developing embryo produces carbon dioxide (CO_2) and water (H_2O) as by-products as it utilizes oxygen (O_2) to metabolize yolk lipids and consume albumen proteins. This process can be roughly monitored by weighing the egg.

The optimum weight loss for most species is believed to be between 12 and 14 per cent from the time the egg is laid until internal pipping occurs. However, successful hatching has been documented at weight losses from 5 to 25 per cent. Obtaining the correct weight loss alone will not ensure good hatchability. Each egg and chick has its own pattern of development and weight loss. A great deal of variability is to be expected.

Your eggs will provide you with the information needed to set the optimum humidity level for the average egg. Weighing the egg and keeping accurate records is recommended.

If problems are noted in hatchability, these records will provide the producer with a good reference of the performance of your incubator. Secondly, the eggs of some hens do not lose weight as readily as others while others lose weight quickly.

This information can be used to determine what action may be taken to compensate, e.g. raising or lowering humidity or increasing or decreasing the length of storage.

The weight loss of an egg is not constant during the incubation cycle. Higher weight loss is often noted at the beginning and end of the incubation cycle. This is because early in incubation more water must be lost from the albumen to provide space for oxygen diffusion to the blastoderm.

Late in incubation, water production (and loss) must increase as metabolic rate (water production) increases proportional to the larger embryo size. A low relative humidity must be maintained to allow this necessary water vapor loss to occur.

Daily alteration of incubator humidity to achieve a constant daily weight loss is not practical. Set the machine for the average and leave it alone.

The temperature of the incubator should in all cases be kept as stable as possible. High temperature can be detrimental to your hatch rate. Low temperature will delay your hatch.

Proper temperature controls have been designed to keep variations to an absolute minimum. Daily readings of your machine instruments should be made to ensure stability.

The dry-bulb temperature is directly proportional to the rate of embryonic development. The higher the temperature, the faster the rate of development.

The dry-bulb temperature also proportionally determines metabolic water production, oxygen demand, and water vapor pressure within the egg.

The humidity also contributes to the control of the rate of gas exchange of an egg during incubation. The higher the humidity, the lower the rate of gas exchange because high humidity slows the release of water from the egg.

Gas exchange is the process of oxygen entering the egg and carbon dioxide and water vapor leaving the egg. This is how the embryo breathes (Figure 3).

INCUBATION LENGTH

Incubation time varies, depending upon the interaction of temperature and humidity with the properties of each egg, from 39 to 44 days, with 42 days being about the average for the ostrich. There is also a considerable range in hatch time for the chicken.

Length of incubation is dependent upon temperature and humidity. Higher temperature produces shorter hatch times and lower incubation temperature produces longer hatch times.

Similarly, a high incubation humidity will delay hatch while low incubation humidity will tend to promote early hatch.

At present, it appears that optimum incubation conditions for ostriches are in the range of 96.0 to 98.3 degrees F dry-bulb temperature, with a relative humidity in the 15- to 28-per cent range in a high-air-flow (5-30 air turns per hour and rapid air movement) incubator. However, there is evidence that a lower humidity will work well and may be needed.

In low-air-flow (1-5 air turns per hour and low air movement) incubators, the humidity may also need to be much lower to compensate for the inability of the machine to remove water vapor fast enough.

The optimum temperature for emus is about 96.8 degrees F with about 33 per cent relative humidity in high-air-flow incubators.

The higher the dry-bulb temperature, the lower the relative humidity needs to be, because water production and embryo growth rate is faster.

As an example of the general principle for ostriches, at a dry-bulb temperature of 98.2 degrees F it is estimated that the relative humidity may need to be as low as 18 per cent.

However, at an incubation temperature of 96.8 degrees F the relative humidity may need to be as much as 28 per cent.

It should be remembered that the higher the incubation dry-bulb temperature, the more metabolic water that is produced, thus creating the need for a lower incubation humidity to remove this water from the eggs.

Individual hatchery incubation requirements will be dependent upon the lowest wet-bulb dewpoint temperature that can be maintained in the hatching room

TABLE 1: INCUBATION CONDITIONS

OSTRICH
- Humidity ranges may vary a little bit depending on storage time of the egg.
- Use the low end of the scale for short-term storage, approximately 15-18 per cent RH.
- Use the high end of the scale for longer-term storage, approximately 22-28 per cent RH.
- Temperature ranges used successfully for ostrich incubation are between 96.0 & 98.3 degrees F (35.5 & 36.8 C).

We consider 97.5 degrees F (36.3 C) to be an acceptable incubation temperature in most cases with an average internal pip around 39-40 days, and average hatch at 42-43 days.

We have seen isolated cases of ostriches hatching with a temperature as low as 92 degrees F (33.3 C). However 87 degrees F (30.5 C) does seem to be too low for successful embryonic development.

EMU
- Humidity ranges may vary a little bit depending on storage time of the egg.
- Use the low end of the scale for short-term storage, approximately 28-33 per cent RH.
- Use the middle of the scale for weekly storage, approximately 33-38 per cent RH.
- Use the high end of the scale for very-long-term storage, approximately 38-43 per cent RH.
- Temperature ranges used successfully for emu incubation are between 95.0 & 97.5 degrees F (34.9 & 36.3 C).

We consider 96.8 degrees F (35.9 C) to be an acceptable incubation temperature in most cases. 95 degrees F (34.9 C) incubation temperatures typically result in an average hatch time of 54-57 days, while 96.8 degrees F (35.9 C) typically result in an average hatch time of 49-52 days. Lower incubation temperatures require a considerably higher incubation humidity.

TABLE 2. PERCENTAGE RELATIVE HUMIDITY AT DIFFERENT WET- AND DRY-BULB TEMPERATURES

WET-BULB TEMPERATURE (F)	DRY-BULB TEMPERATURE (°F)				
	95	96	97	98	99
	% Relative Humidity				
66	20	17	15	14	13
67	21	19	18	16	15
68	22	21	20	18	17
69	24	23	22	20	18
70	26	25	24	22	20
71	28	27	26	24	22
72	31	29	29	26	25
73	34	32	30	28	27
74	36	34	32	30	29

when the right amount of fresh air is allowed to enter. This will determine the lowest operating humidity of the incubators.

If you cannot achieve low relative humidity, it may be necessary to incubate at a lower temperature for a longer time or invest in a dehumidification system.

There is no single limiting factor regarding incubation length. Some of the determining factors and effects are as follows:
- Thick albumen tends to slow down incubation.
- Thin albumen tends to speed up incubation.
- Thick egg shells tend to slow down incubation.
- Thin egg shells tend to speed up incubation.
- High temperature speeds up incubation.
- Low temperature slows down incubation.
- High humidity slows down incubation.
- Low humidity speeds up incubation.
- Small eggs with a thick egg shell slow down incubation.
- Large eggs with a low relative surface-to-volume ratio slow down incubation.

This explains to a large extent why there is so much variation in incubation time. With any given group of birds, the time for incubation from setting to hatch may vary as much as five to seven days. This is to be expected and somewhat characteristic for each hen.

PROPER MACHINE OPERATION

During evaluation of a hatchery, it is not uncommon to find machines that are not functioning properly. This is particularly true for wet-bulb temperature.

We recommend that *new* wicks be installed weekly and wet-bulb thermometer bulbs be cleaned as needed to keep them absolutely clean. Check the wick material to be sure each new roll sinks in a pan of water at the same rate as the previous roll.

We also recommend the use of distilled water in the wet-bulb thermometer reservoir.

The use of a reference psychrometer to check machine operation is highly recommended. A battery-powered motor-blower psychrometer is highly recommended for accuracy.

HATCHING

Hatching time is determined by hen age, egg weight, egg storage time, storage conditions, incubation temperatures and relative humidity.

Before transferring the eggs to the hatcher, allow internal pipping to occur. The embryo is said to be internally pipped when the beak is protruding into the air cell.

In emus a pipped chick will answer with one or two peeps when the shell is tapped. Do not be concerned if the occasional chick pips externally prior to transfer. In fact, some producers find this to give superior results.

From the time of internal pipping, it will be approximately 24 to 48 hours before the chick actually breaks the shell.

During this time period the CAM is closing down and the yolk sac is being internalized. This requires considerable oxygen. About 90 per cent of an embryo's energy is derived from metabolizing the yolk material. Retained yolk sacs are probably due to low oxygen consumption.

The embryo is also reaching plateau metabolism and beginning to produce a tremendous amount of embryonic heat and water at the end of incubation. The temperature should remain as constant as possible for the embryo during this time period. Again, high temperature is the most damaging.

It is often noted that the more internal pips prior to transfer, the higher the hatching percentage. This is due to the generally lower

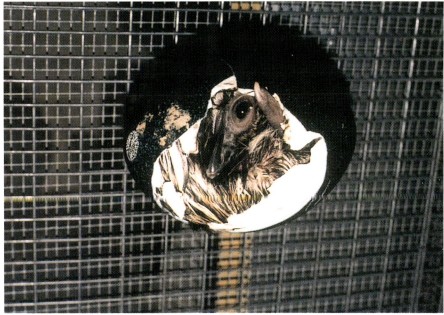

Normal hatching position for an emu chick incubated horizontally.

humidity of the incubator which provides more oxygen to the embryo by removing more water from the eggs.

Eggs are transferred to the hatcher for the purposes of sanitation and biosecurity but, for all intents and purposes, the hatcher is still an incubator and should be so operated.

The temperature at which to operate the hatcher has been controversial. The temperature of the hatcher should be adjusted according to its load.

If the hatcher is loaded to minimum capacity, raise the temperature 0.5 degrees F to compensate for the lack of metabolic heat from surrounding eggs. If the hatcher is loaded to half capacity, the temperature can be kept the same as the incubator. If the hatcher is loaded to full capacity,

Emu chicks in hatcher. Orange spot on one chick's head is iodine solution applied after microchip was placed in the pipping muscle.

the temperature can be lowered 0.5 degress F to offset the metabolic heat gain from the large number of surrounding embryos.

Typically in ratites, the best advice is to operate both the incubator and hatcher at the same temperature.

In many hatchers, the eggs are separated into single units so that there is minimal egg-to-egg contact. Since air is a good insulator, this has the effect of lowering the effective temperature. This is another good reason to raise the hatcher temperature a little.

The humidity at which to run hatchers has been a subject of at least as much controversy as the temperature. The hatcher is in fact a dual-humidity machine.

The humidity of the hatcher at transfer should be the same as the humidity of the incubator under normal circumstances. At transfer time the oxygen requirements of the embryo are near maximum. An increase in the relative humidity will reduce the rate of gas exchange and result in less oxygen reaching the chick.

Do not forget that the embryo is breathing air through the eggshell. We do not want to restrict this if at all possible.

As the chick pips externally, and can breathe without the eggshell, the shell membrane is exposed to the environment of the hatcher. As the membrane starts to dry, it may adhere to the chick, making it more difficult for the chick to hatch. If this occurs, the humidity may be raised 10% to keep the membrane moist. This results in less stress and energy depletion of the chick. If more than one egg is placed in the hatcher, the humidity may be raised after most of the chicks have externally pipped.

Large eggs have a lower surface area relative to volume than do smaller eggs. In fact, large embryos have less *lung* than do small eggs. Large eggs also have larger chicks and greater oxygen requirements.

At transfer this larger embryo is producing extra water which must be lost if oxygen is to enter the egg. To compensate for this, the hatcher can be run at a lower humidity at transfer to allow for an increased gas exchange rate. This will lead to an increased weight loss and help remove some of the excess moisture produced by the larger chick at hatch time.

This will reduce the incidence of *edema*, *drowned chicks*, and small air cells often observed in large eggs at the end of the laying cycle, as well as probably reduce the incidence of large retained yolk sacs and infection.

Typically in ratites, the best advice is to operate the hatcher at a relative humidity equal to, or lower than, that of the incubator at the time of transfer and raise the humidity if required *during* the hatch.

POSITIONING

There is evidence that setting eggs in the large-end-up position is probably best for most species, although there is conflicting data for the emu.

However, it is possible that this conflicting data for the emu arises from the difficulty of determining the large (air cell) end. Emu eggs seem to do best when incubated horizontally and rotated through a 90-degree plane (45 degrees either side of vertical) every three hours.

Several years of field research on this topic have led us to conclude that it is difficult and awkward to determine the air cell end of some emu eggs, therefore, the safest route to take is horizontal incubation. Most eggs throughout the course of incubation will tend to rise slightly at the air cell end of the egg and this should not be interfered with.

It has been suggested that an additional manual rotation of the egg through a 180-degree plane once a day, especially for the more torpedo-shaped eggs could be beneficial. This may be more true if eggs are firmly positioned in trays, preventing any movement except for the turning mechanism. Eggs that are allowed to move freely within the tray appear to adjust themselves just fine.

TURNING

Turning is another very important factor, especially in the early stages of embryonic development. The embryo lies on top of the yolk in the center of the egg. If the egg were allowed to remain stationary, the embryo would eventually float to the top of the egg and stick to the shell membrane. Therefore, the eggs should be rotated on a periodic basis through a 90-degree plane (45 degrees either side of vertical).

There are four basic reasons to turn an egg:
- The yolk is slightly more buoyant than the albumen; thus it has the capacity to float up to the shell membrane and dehydrate. Regular turning of the eggs will help prevent this from occurring during long-term storage.
- The embryo develops relative to gravity. If the egg is not turned, uneven development occurs, resulting in malformed chicks.
- The blood supply of the embryo normally grows over the upper surface of the yolk and down the sides of the egg between the albumen and shell membranes. Turning allows the albumen to pull away from the shell, providing space for the CAM to extend downward around the egg. Failure to turn often results in *blood-ring deads*.
- As the embryo is absorbing the nutrients, it is also producing waste. If the embryo is not moved by turning, it

can be poisoned by its own waste. Ratite eggs should be turned about every three hours during incubation.

Excessive turning during incubation has been reported to cause malformities. Turning every three hours during incubation appears to be acceptable.

VENTILATION

Often when we consider ventilation we look at the supply aspect and tend to overlook the removal element. Although supply of oxygen is vital, the extraction of foul air is equally important. The fundamentals of ventilation regarding incubation are as follows:

Provide oxygen O^2
Remove carbon dioxide CO^2
Remove water vapor H_2O
Remove heat BTU

These principles suggest that the removal of foul air from the incubator and out of the room is of equal, if not greater, importance than providing the correct amount of air. Incubation ventilation demands a supply of one item, but demands the *removal* of three important elements.

There is a general relationship between oxygen utilization for metabolism and carbon dioxide and water production. Dry-bulb temperature has the most pronounced affect on metabolism. Therefore, higher temperatures lead to increased oxygen demands as well as CO_2 and H_2O production.

The following information is for illustration comparison only and is based upon data presently available in the poultry industry, combined with recent field studies in the ratite industry.

Most of the calculations provided in this section are based upon 60,000 grams of egg weight

1,000 chicken eggs=60,000 grams
100 emu eggs=60,000 grams
40 ostrich eggs=60,000 grams

We should consider the fact that surface area (shell size) relative to volume (chick size) is less

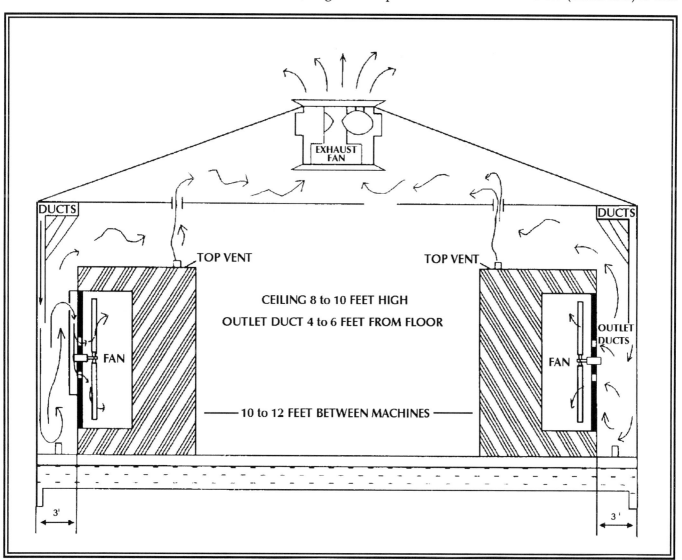

Figure 4. Diagram of an ideal hatching room, showing adequate spacing between machines and between walls, as well as an unobstructed flow of air from outside, through machines, and exhaust to outside.

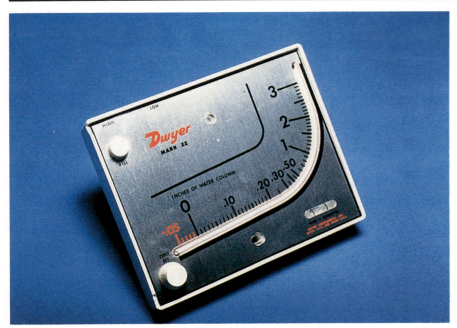
Wall-mounted manometer

for larger eggs. This suggests a slightly higher ventilation rate for larger eggs in order to reduce carbon dioxide to safe levels.

Machine requirements for *maximum* percentage room fresh air at the *maximum* machine capacity are *minimum* room requirements for percentage of fresh air. This is perhaps the most critical and overlooked element of incubation. It is typical throughout the ratite industry to partially meet these requirements. This is especially apparent at the beginning of the season while ambient temperature and humidity levels do not pose a problem. Machine loads have not reached maximum capacity and hatch rates are generally satisfactory.

It is when the machines are loaded at or near maximum capacity, combined with ambient temperatures and humidities beginning to rise, that we begin to see adverse effects on incubator humidity. When this occurs, it is generally incorrectly blamed on the ventilation system *bringing in too much moist air* from outside, and the amount of incoming fresh air is decreased to maintain desired humidity levels within the machines.

This is not good, as increasing incubator ventilation demands are then countered with decreased room ventilation rates.

Introducing fresh air close to intakes of machines effectively increases the percentage of fresh air by preventing dilution. If the minimum requirements for fresh air are met and the fresh air is delivered across the room from the incubator intake, the fresh air is thereby diluted with room air, resulting in less than minimal requirements by the time the fresh air reaches the machine.

During the first two thirds of incubation, water loss from the machine is the first limiting factor for removal of foul air. As we look at the contents of an egg during this period we can easily see the liquid mass is larger than the oxygen-consuming mass.

The ventilation required for removal of carbon dioxide during the last third of incubation is far greater than the removal of water vapor or the supply of oxygen. Therefore ventilation requirements should be calculated for the final third of incubation on the basis of carbon dioxide removal.

The total ventilation requirement to remove carbon dioxide and water vapor will depend upon the average egg age within the machine. Although ventilation rates can be adjusted to meet the various loads, it is advisable to calculate and set ventilation requirements based on maximum machine loads.

The *minimum* ventilation for 60,000 grams of eggs at maximum metabolic rate are as follows:
- to supply oxygen: 1.5 cubic feet per minute.

Alert ostrich chicks in hatcher.

- to remove carbon dioxide: 2.0 cubic feet per minute (CFM);

The requirement to remove carbon dioxide is greater because it is the larger and more slowly-moving molecule.

The machine fresh air CFM requirement is *ABSOLUTE*. The percentage of fresh air room requirement *VARIES* with machine ventilation rates. See Table 3 on the next page.

The correct percentage of fresh air delivered close to the machine and foul air removal are the factors limiting ventilation. The number of air turns in the room can be calculated afterwards.

The number of air turns within the room will vary depending upon egg requirements and machine flow. A 20% fresh air requirement in a 10' x 10' x 10' room would require 12 air turns per hour, while a 40% fresh air requirement would require 24 air turns per hour.

To move the rated amount of air, fans have to be at or near neutral static pressure. High pressure significantly reduces the efficiency of most fans. Optimum static pressure for incubator and hatcher rooms is .01 - .02 inches (water column) positive. The hatcher room should be slightly less than the incubator room.

Positive pressure is achieved by putting in more air than is going out, while a negative pressure is achieved by taking out more air than is coming in.

Hatchery air flow patterns should be set to go from clean to dirty. This is generally achieved by making the cleanest room the most positive pressure and the dirtiest room the most negative.

Manometers are useful devices for determining static pressures. Inexpensive models are available for easy mounting and installation that can be used to determine approximate static pressures in each of your rooms within the facility.

TABLE 3. ROOM FRESH AIR RULE OF THUMB

$$\% \text{ Room Fresh Air} = \frac{\text{CFM eggs require}}{\text{CFM machine flow}} \times 100$$

For example: A completely filled machine with 120 ostrich-egg capacity would call for 120/40 (60,000g EW) = 3 x 2 CFM per 40 eggs (60,000 g) = 6 CFM egg requirement.

If measurement of the exhaust vent indicated 18 CFM machine flow, the *minimum* room fresh air requirement would be 6/18 = 33% fresh air. It is often advisable to oversize by 50 per cent to provide a safety margin.

TABLE 4. CALCULATE CUBIC FEET PER MINUTE

To calculate volume (CFM), insert the velocity from the anemometer into the appropriate formula:

Rectangular ducts

$$\frac{\text{Length (in) X Width (in) X Velocity (fpm)}}{144} = \text{CFM}$$

Circular ducts

$$\frac{3.1416 \text{ X (radius)}^2 \text{(in)}^2 \text{ X Velocity(fpm)}}{144} = \text{CFM}$$

TABLE 5. CARBON DIOXIDE INCUBATION LEVELS
(Rule Of Thumb)

Safe levels   = 400-500 ppm = .04 - .05%
Suspect levels =   700+ ppm =   .07% +

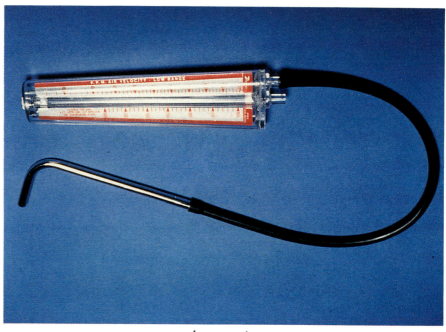

Anemometer

We know air moves just fine at zero ±.05 inches (water column) static pressure. Maintaining room static pressures somewhere in this range when fans are moving the correct amount of air should work adequately.

Initial indications within the ratite industry indicate that pressures of ±.3 inches (water column) or higher have adverse effects on hatch rates.

If the primary hatch failure is late mortalities/dead in shell with no apparent reason, and hatched chicks are having problems with retained yolks, especially once the machines begin operating at or near maximum capacity, it is possible that poor ventilation could be the problem.

It is always advisable to check wet-bulb and dry-bulb conditions in the machines with separate reliable thermometers. Psychrometers are a good secondary check as well.

Regardless, the temperature and humidity should be verified for accuracy. Once temperature and humidity levels are determined accurate and correct, the ventilation should be checked and monitored for the following:
- machine air flow,
- machine embryo load,
- required percentage fresh air,
- machine CO_2, and
- room percentage fresh air.

Tachometers should be available for checking fan speeds for proper settings. Fans should also be checked for proper rotation.

Inexpensive anemometers are a good means to estimate the amount of air movement through supply and exhaust ducts. Typical anemometers measure the speed or velocity of the air, which is generally expressed in feet per minute (FPM). See Table 4.

Measurement of gases can be accomplished in many ways. Our primary concern is the availability of oxygen (O_2) and presence of carbon dioxide (CO_2).

A low indication of carbon dioxide does not always mean proper ventilation. The facility could be oxygen deficient—therefore carbon dioxide production would not occur as a result of the oxygen deficiency. When in doubt, check for proper levels of each gas.

Oxygen detection devices are often cumbersome and awkward. Field data suggests that readings are generally around 20 to 21 per cent and have not been definitive enough to indicate inadequate ventilation; however, an indication close to this should exist.

Oxygen-deficient rooms are often detectible with your nose, as the room will feel and smell stuffy and not fresh.

Suspect carbon dioxide levels for ratites, on the other hand, are more easily defined. Initial field data suggest that a difference of as little as .02% CO_2 (200 ppm) could separate safe from suspect levels of carbon dioxide over the extended incubation periods of ratites, as compared to the short incubation periods of chickens.

Safe CO_2 levels for incubation are in the very low range. Detection devices are made for this low range, effectively resulting in increased accuracy of measurement compared to oxygen. See Table 5.

In instances where carbon dioxide levels higher than 700 ppm (parts per million) have been detected, ventilation rates have been increased, resulting in more favorable hatch results within a short time period.

It should be further noted that the possibility exists when significantly increasing ventilation rates (increased air flow) that egg weight loss could increase.

This increased gas exchange rate tends to speed the incubation time as well as the weight loss which can be offset by raising the humidity slightly. Weight loss should be closely monitored after making major ventilation adjustments.

BIOSECURITY

Hygiene is a very important factor for successful hatching. The traffic pattern of your facility should be set up to go from clean to dirty. When using disinfectants, care should be taken to follow the manufacturer's instructions closely. More is not better in this case.

When it comes right down to it, we have simply two options for a successful biosecurity program—keep the facility clean and dry, or overwhelm bacteria with chemicals.

The typical incubation temperatures and humidities used within the ratite industry are generally too low to support bacterial growth. Relative humidity levels below 50 per cent generally desiccate and kill bacteria. During incubation, bacterial numbers on the egg shell surface will be reduced to near zero. Keep your facility as clean and dry as possible.

An often mistaken impression about some disinfectants is they immediately kill bacteria. It could take up to thirty minutes from application to kill time. During this time, there can be an actual increase in bacterial numbers until the disinfected surface dries.

Disinfectants are not partial to what they attach themselves to. They will cling to a molecule of dirt just as quickly as they will to bacteria. Therefore the area being disinfected should be thoroughly cleaned prior to application of disinfectants. Applying the correct mixture of disinfects to *dirty* surfaces effectively dilutes the mixture by allowing dirt to attract the disinfectant away from bacteria.

Hygiene is a very important factor for successful hatching. Be aware of this need and keep your facilities as clean and dry as possible, and try to keep visitors inside the incubator room to a minimum.

It is generally not advisable to clean eggs unless absolutely necessary. Remember the wild bird.

In those cases where the eggs need cleaning, dry clean to the fullest extent possible.

Only in extreme situations wet the eggs during the cleaning process, since this will promote microbial growth and contamination. If eggs are to be wet there should be an individual towel for each egg which should not be reused.

The use of disinfectants in the cleaning solution can alter the eggshell cuticle and affect the rate of water loss during incubation, thus affecting chick quality and hatch time.

Foot baths are a good first defense against disease. Fogging your facility periodically after cleaning is also a good way to combat disease. Protective clothing may also be a good idea to further prevent infection.

Incubators should only need to be cleaned before and after each season. An exception to this would be oozing eggs, known bacterial infection, exploded eggs, etc. Hatchers should be cleaned after every hatch. The hatch residue is a perfect breeding ground for bacteria. If it is not cleaned, it could lead to an enormous buildup of pathogenic bacteria.

A good program to establish is the use of culture plates and swabs to routinely monitor the amount of bacteria in your facility. Be aware of the need for biosecurity. Remember, an ounce of prevention is worth a pound of cure.

POST HATCH

By the time the chick has emerged from the shell, it has done a fair amount of work and it is ready for a well-deserved rest. The chicks should be allowed to remain in the hatcher only for sufficient time to allow complete drying without dehydration. The chicks should be allowed to determine this length of time, so their activity should be monitored.

A chick that is up and moving about is ready to be removed from the machine. On average, this holding time after hatch should be about twelve hours. Chicks can be held quite successfully in the hatcher for a longer time if the temperature is reduced to 80°F. Contrary to popular opinion, raising relative humidity will not prevent dehydration at the high temperature of the hatcher, only reducing temperature will achieve this goal.

TYPICAL EMBRYO MORTALITY

The following are commonly seen embryonic deaths and a few of their causes.

Early dead in small eggs are often found at the beginning of the season. These can be caused by thick egg shells and/or thick albumen resulting in low water loss and low oxygen uptake. Increase storage time or lower humidity in the incubator.

However, egg weights should be monitored for excessive weight loss both in storage or early incubation, resulting in dehydration of the egg.

Early dead in large eggs are often found at the end of the season. These can be caused by thin egg shells, and/or thin albumen resulting in high water loss during early incubation. Decrease storage time or raise the humidity in the incubator.

Many very-early-dead embryos are misdiagnosed as infertile because the eggs are not opened early enough to clearly determine that the embryo died before blood was formed. This problem most often occurs early in the breeding season due to insufficient length of pre-incubation storage. For this reason, producers who ship part of their eggs often find higher *fertility* in those that are shipped and less fresh when set.

Mid-deads are rare unless there is an acute incubation problem, disease, or a severe nutritional deficiency such as a complete absence of vitamins or minerals or there is an oxygen deficiency.

Late dead in large eggs are often found at the end of the season. These are caused by a low surface-to-volume ratio, resulting in low water loss. Decrease humidity in the hatcher.

Late dead in smaller eggs can be caused by excess humidity during incubation.

Dead-in-shell chicks have pipped internally or externally but died before emerging from the egg shell. Many have small air cells and edema. Improper hatcher operation, excessive humidity, or insufficient ventilation can often be the cause.

The normal hatching position is head under the right wing with the legs drawn up and forward. Common malpositions are head turned left and head between thighs. The latter is probably not a true malposition as this is the normal position during much of incubation. It would appear that this is simply an embryo which has not progressed far enough to turn. This may be caused by lack of oxygen necessary for complete development.

Authors' note: Joint university-industry authorship does not imply endorsement by North Carolina State University of the products of the company, nor criticism of the similar products of other companies.

21-day-old emu embryo, window cut in shell to show development. (Photo courtesy Dr. Brett Hopkins)

EGG CANDLING

Lisa Kinder, M.S.
University of Arkansas
Fayetteville, Arkansas

Egg candling can be an important tool in the management practice of incubation. Candling can often detect problems within the egg shell that may not be visible from the outside.

Egg structure and incubation techniques have already been covered in previous chapters. This section will focus on the advantages of candling eggs and the possibility of learning patience, through understanding the embryological and hatching processes more completely.

Photographs of candling of ostrich and rhea eggs are readily available, so the pictures in this chapter will focus on emu eggs, which previously have been difficult to candle. This is not to show preference for the knowledge that can be obtained from candling a particular species of egg. It's merely new and exciting to those who have been frustrated with those dark green shells.

THE EGG

The avian egg consists mostly of yolk (mainly phospholipids), which is the main source of nutrients for the embryo. The yolk is surrounded by a see-through, non-cellular vitelline membrane. The membrane is surrounded by albumen (egg white) and the entire contents are contained within a multi-layered calcified shell. Two egg membranes separate the egg white and the hard shell. At the large end of the egg, between the two membranes, is the air sac. All of these components are secreted by the hen.

The embryo itself lies on the surface of the yolk, just under the vitelline membrane. The albumen surrounding the vitelline membrane is connected with the inner membrane by two glycoprotein threads called the chalazae. This allows the yolk to rotate so that the embryo always faces the top of the egg. Embryo position on the yolk is not determined by how the outer shell is handled or turned.

The structure of the egg is designed to allow gas exchange, to conserve water, and to prevent micro-organisms from coming into contact with the embryo. Nutrition and protection are also provided, as well as a uniquely complex environment in which the embryo can develop.

For example, the pH of the yolk is slightly acid, while the albumen pH is quite alkaline. During early stages of development, the edges of the single-cell thick embryo attach to the inner surface (yolk) of the vitelline membrane. This allows for as much as 3 pH units across a single cell.

Since most bacteria prefer an alkaline environment, this pH difference is a built-in barrier to prevent micro-organisms from passing from the egg white to the yolk. The albumen also contains

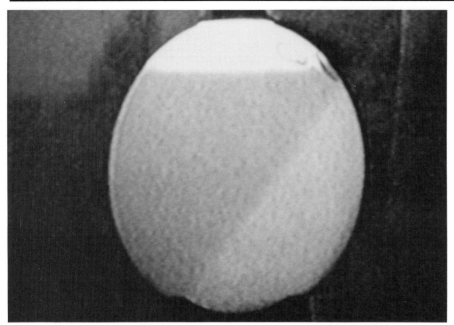

Photo 1. Infertile ostrich egg. Note clear appearance throughout the entire contents of the shell.

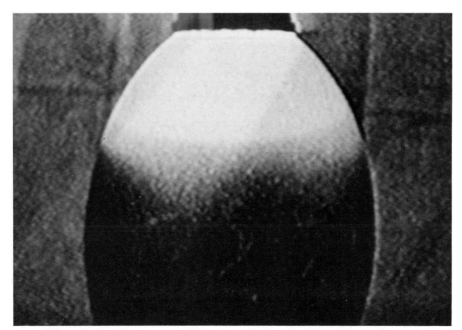

Photo 2. Fertile emu egg. Note dark shadowing throughout the shell. Dark lines separate the embryo appearance from albumen contents. Another line separates the albumen from the air cell.

the enzyme lysozyme, a bacteriostatic agent.

ADVANTAGES OF EGG CANDLING

An egg candler can be a tremendous asset when it comes to understanding the normal process of embryo development and interpreting the activity within the shell as the chick starts to hatch. Several insights may be obtained by the timely use of a candler throughout the entire embryo growth process. One of the key advantages is to determine signs of fertility (Photos 1 and 2).

Infertile eggs can be a tremendous expense to producers if they continue to occupy incubator space which may be needed for fertile eggs. As an operation grows, incubator space becomes very valuable. This is usually where producers first find they need to expand their facilities. The expense of an egg candler may be justified solely to avoid incubating infertile eggs.

Fertility should be determined for each egg and recorded for each male and female breeder bird in the production records. The use of candling records can be a useful tool in determining selection for quality breeder stock.

Bacterial contamination may also be detected by the use of a candler. Contaminated eggs may or may not produce an odor, depending upon the number and type of bacteria present. Needless to say, these eggs need to be removed immediately upon detection of a problem.

A tremendous amount of experience and practice with the candler may be needed to determine true contamination. Signs of dark shadowing caused by shell structure, internal membrane patterns, or a broken yolk may be misleading.

Isolation within the incubator or moving the egg to another incubator (designated specifically for suspect eggs) is recommended until true contamination can be determined. Isolation is important to reduce the risk of spreading bacteria to surrounding eggs. Contaminated eggs will often ooze albumen through the pores in the shell and sometimes even explode within the incubator.

Determining the position of the air cell and documenting its increase in size throughout incubation can be of significant help in understanding the weight-loss process of incubation management.

In going through the daily process of weighing eggs and recording the weight-loss percentage of each one, it is very easy for producers to think abstractly about the life process which is occurring within the shell. The use of an egg candler may help to clarify why the monotonous routine of weighing eggs is so important.

The air cell position may sometimes be determined even with freshly-laid eggs (Photo 3). In tests with several eggs, approximately half showed an air cell directly after the egg was collected from the breeder pen.

Other eggs did not have an air cell present until they had been stored and were ready to be placed in the incubator. Some did not clearly show an air cell until the incubation process had begun.

Consideration must be given to storage length and the environmental conditions in which the eggs were held. Higher humidity (above 50% relative humidity) will reduce weight loss during storage. Possible storage temperatures range from 50 to 65 degrees Fahrenheit.

Knowledge obtained from understanding the hatching phase of incubation and normal position changes (discussed later) that occur during hatching could be the most significant benefit of an egg candler. Learning to observe the internal and external pipping processes can help a producer become more patient during the hatching period.

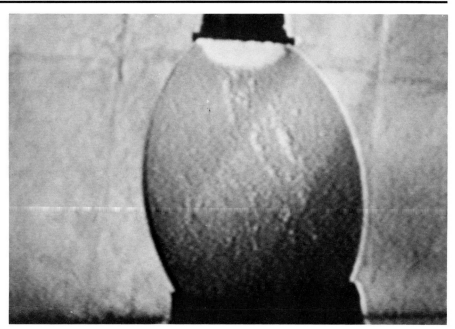

Photo 3. Air cell of freshly laid emu egg (light circle at top of egg).

As the chick progresses into the hatching phase, the air cell opens up as the vitelline membrane is pulled down the side wall of the shell. This process may begin to take place approximately 24 to 48 hours prior to internal pipping.

Once the chick has pipped internally, you may begin to hear a whistling noise coming from within the shell, especially when enticed. Many producers mistake this for a distress call and begin to interfere with the hatching process by opening a small air hole in the shell. This air hole may not be

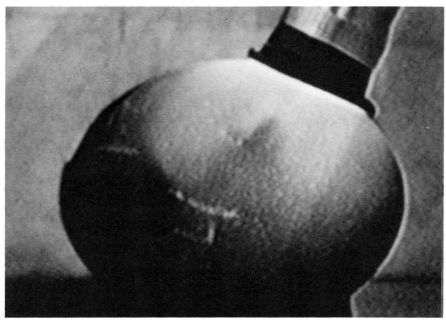

Photo 4. Internally pipped emu chick. Note opening of the beak as the chick respirates. This chick is not distressed and does not require assistance. Also note destruction of the straight membrane line, present in photo 2.

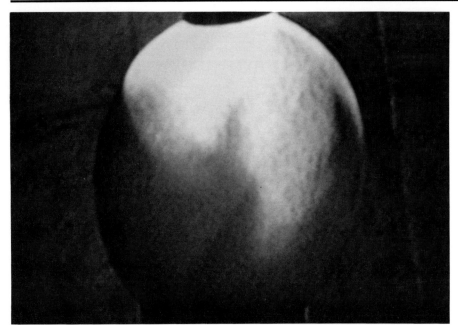

Photo 5. Internally pipped ostrich chick. Beak and toe may be seen moving as the egg is candled. Egg movement may stimulate the chick to move as the egg is being handled.

detrimental, but it does interfere with the physiological changes that are occurring within the chick.

As the chick pips internally (Photo 4), it must begin to utilize lung capacity as its source of oxygen, as opposed to relying on its circulating blood supply.

Once the oxygen is depleted from the air cell, the chick must pip through the shell to receive more air. The chick's need for more oxygen stimulates it to pip the shell externally.

If the air hole is already present, by some unnatural means, the chick lacks the incentive to start—and finish—breaking out of the shell, and may stay in the shell for a longer period of time.

This prolonged hatching process may lead to bacterial contamination of the yolk sac area through the release of fecal material within the shell. An otherwise healthy chick therefore becomes weak through the impatience of the producer, and will almost always cause problems later on.

Many producers open the egg shell on a certain day of incubation, regardless of the condition of the chick. With the use of an egg candler, the eggs may be moved to the hatcher according to the progress of the chick, usually within a few hours of external pipping. That time period must be determined by the hatchery manager based upon incubation parameters, hatcher space available, and inevitably, success.

The entire strategy must, however, take into account that the normal length of the hatching process, from internal pipping to hatch, may take as long as 3 to 5 days in all ratite species.

NORMAL CHICK POSITIONING

A tremendous amount of attention has been given to the normal versus abnormal positioning of hatching chicks and dead-in-the-shell embryos. Many people have developed theories as to what causes malpositions. However few have had much success determining how to prove it.

One must consider what is happening to the embryo as it develops and begins to move into hatching position.

We know proper weight loss is essential to the survival of the chick. If a chick loses too much weight, it will be dehydrated and weak when it hatches. Its legs may have the appearance of the skin sticking to the bones, and it will definitely want to lay around and sleep more than the other chicks. It may even take an extra day or two to begin eating and drinking.

What happens to those chicks from eggs that don't lose enough weight?

Let's look at the two major events which allow the chick to gain the room necessary to get into proper hatching position. First, as the yolk sac is absorbed, a large amount of room is freed up from around the stomach and tail area. Second, even more room is gained when the beak pierces the internal membrane.

The chick stretches its upper body, and twitches its feet to pierce the internal membrane and occupy the air space. But if the egg has not lost enough weight, the chick will be puffy with excess fluid, resulting in less room for movement. The chick will not be able to move into position as needed to successfully hatch.

Once the chick pierces the internal membrane, a transitional rest period occurs.

This rest period may last for as little as a few hours or as long as several days. This period of non-movement makes many producers very nervous.

The egg candler once again becomes a very important tool. You may observe the bird respirating and be assured that it is still alive.

As long as breathing or movement of any kind can be detected, one should have the peace of mind to leave the chick to progress on its own.

A terrifyingly large number of eggs achieve what we consider to be normal weight loss, but result in malpositioned embryos. The reasons for malpositions have been characterized for other avian species, but very little documentation has been recorded for any of the ratites. See Photos 6 & 7 and accompanying text.

One position needs particular attention from researchers. It has been found that many chicks die with their heads between their thighs, beaks pointing directly to the yolk sac.

It has been shown that this is a true normal position for all chicks and that these chicks merely did not or could not progress to the normal hatching position. These chicks apparently died approximately 10 percent short of their normal incubation length.

If while searching for the chick's beak you find it in this position, it should be assumed that the chick has not progressed far enough along in the hatching phase to find its correct position.

Therefore, it is not correct to assume in all cases that the failure of eggs to hatch is due to the position of the chick within the egg. Many of these malpositions may have been the result—rather than the cause—of embryonic death.

Several evaluations must be made if a producer is having a high incidence of malpositioned dead embryos. Temperature and humidity fluctuations in the incubator or hatcher are sure to cause stress upon the embryo. The chick may have had to constantly adjust to maintain body temperature.

Secondly, the adhesion of the allantois to the shell membrane is an important factor in restricting movement of the embryo and probably partially fixes hatching position.

Thirdly, eggs shifted during the middle third of incubation have a higher possibility of damaging the allantois, resulting in embryonic harm or mortality. Excessive handling and jarring may have occurred due to egg weighing or candling.

Photo 6. Ostrich chick, hatching in normal position.

Normal hatching position in ratites has been confused with the normal hatching position in chickens. However, ratites will pip the internal membrane from under the left wing—as opposed to the right wing in chickens.

The ratite chick will have the appearance of laying on his back and having his neck and head curled along the left side of the air cell if viewed from the externally pipped shell (Photos 6 & 7).

Photo 7. Emu chick, hatching in normal position.

And fourth, care should be taken, during the late stages of development, to place the egg back in the incubator or hatcher in the same position as it was removed. This will eliminate re-orientation of the embryo before hatching.

CONCLUSION

Several decisions must be made about purchasing equipment and supplies for a ratite operation. Expenses must be resonably figured into projected income to determine whether a piece of equipment is affordable.

There are producers who feel that an egg candler is just another expense which will reduce profits. However, another incubator purchase may be eliminated and the work load in the incubator room will be reduced by eliminating the weighing of infertile or dead-in-the-shell eggs.

Many producers have become very dependent upon egg candlers and have tremendously increased their knowledge of the embryo growth process.

As technology improves, and manufacturers have more competition for quality equipment, an emu egg candler will become a more affordable option for every operation.

THE FUTURE OF THE INDUSTRY

Featuring the Winners at the 1995 Houston Livestock Show & Rodeo

One of the most important things the ratite industry can do in coming years is to support local and statewide livestock shows. Make sure a class for ratites is offered at livestock shows in your area.

As you will see in the photos in the pages following, in some areas, ratite associations have started cooperative programs with the Future Farmers of America (FFA) and 4H Clubs for youngsters to raise and show ratites.

Contact your state or national association for information on how to implement a program in your area. Donate birds to FFA and 4H members and volunteer to help at the shows.

For the millions of people who attend livestock shows, state fairs, and county fairs, this will be their first chance to talk to ratite producers about the new *alternative livestock*.

FFA GRAND CHAMPION OSTRICH WINNERS
Danisha Thacker, Greenville, Texas FFA
and Rory Thacker, Celeste, Texas FFA.

FFA GRAND CHAMPION EMU WINNER
Dennis Browne, Magnolia, Texas, FFA
and Presenter/Sponsor Kent Robinson, Hockley, Texas

FFA Ostrich Winners: Rear, left to right: Darrell Ellisor & Cory Lazrine, 3rd place, Willis, TX, FFA; Grand Champions Danisha and Rory Thacker; Kimberly Laney & Alice Lipham, Reserve Grand Champions, Kingwood, TX, FFA; Jared Diehl & Melissa Oliver, 4th place, Magnolia, TX, FFA. Front, Paul Zylman & Eva Phelps, 5th place, Conroe FFA.

FFA Emu Winners, left to right: Katrina Black, 5th place, Tomball, TX, FFA; Brad Coker, 3rd place, Fairfield, TX, FFA; Grand Champion Dennis Browne; Reserve Grand Champion Lindsay Cartwright, Montgomery, TX, FFA; Teri Hill, 4th place, Conroe, TX, FFA; Nathan Bunting, 6th place, Bergman, AR, FFA; Kent Robinson, Presenter/Sponsor, Hockley, TX.

Commercial Grand Champion Ostrich Winners Carol & Bill Twyman, Hickory Hill Ostrich Ranch, Conroe, Texas. Left to right, Presenter/committee member Kay Tarkington, Carol Twyman, presenter/show coordinator Monte Bell, Bill Twyman.

Commercial Grand Champion Emu Winners Hank Ryder & Mike Hill, Fluff & Strut Emu Farm, Willis, Texas. Left to right, Kay Tarkington, Hank Ryder, Monte Bell, Mike Hill.

Commercial Grand Champion Rhea Winners Keith & Jannett Dennison, Rheal Enterprises, Katy, Texas

Note: There were no rhea entries in FFA competition.

A four-year-old blueneck male.
(Photo courtesy of Miller Studio, Stephenville, Texas)

OSTRICH BREEDER MANAGEMENT

Sharon Barron
Lucky W Farms
Lingleville, Texas

The ostrich is unique in the animal kingdom. The general consensus among researchers is that there is no other animal like it in the world.

The ostrich, which is a hindgut fermenter like a horse, is a grazer by nature and does well on good grazing pasture. It will probably be many years before everything will be known about the ostrich and its nutritional requirements. As with any livestock, we are still learning.

Managing breeders in the United States is relatively new in comparison to other domesticated animals. In Africa the birds have been raised in captivity for more than 160 years and are considered domesticated. But most of the ostriches in the US are descendants of wild-caught stock—the word *domesticated* may be somewhat optimistic. Still, ostriches, though quite different from the farm livestock we are used to, are relatively easy to handle.

As ostrich farming progresses into the commercial market there will be a need for managing the birds in larger areas and larger numbers.

However, at present the management method used most in the United States is *intensive breeding*. This is the practice of confining one pair—or a trio—of ostriches in a pen for the purposes of producing the maximum number of eggs.

In any endeavor, there are three keys to success: Keep an open mind, never quit learning, and temper learning with common sense.

BREEDER MANAGEMENT

CHOOSING YOUR BREEDERS

You should not choose young chicks as breeding stock based on the performance of the parent birds alone. This is not to say that heredity does not play a very large role in future performance.

However, we are dealing with an animal that reproduces in large numbers. In no way will every offspring of a top-quality pair of birds also be top quality.

When choosing future breeders for your farm, you must look at the overall survivability of the chicks that hatched, the number of chicks hatched versus the number of fertile eggs laid by the hen, and also the degree of difficulty involved in raising the chicks. For instance, were there a lot of yolk sac surgeries or other medical problems? These questions must be answered and records should be provided.

Conformation is another area much overlooked when choosing future breeders. A well-formed bird should be somewhat light in the chest and should carry itself in an upright position when walking in an alert manner. Don't be misled by the bird's natural tendency to slump forward when relaxed. However, the body carriage is determined by the overall conformation of the bird.

A bird should have more body mass from the center of the thigh to the tail than from the center of the thigh to the front of the chest. This allows the bird to stand more upright, and have a downward slope from the base of the neck to the tail. This is important in excreting body fluids which otherwise could be retained, allowing for a higher possibility of reproductive-tract infections.

Birds should look like everything matches—a bird with a long neck should also have long legs. Conditioning is another area that should be looked at closely. The appearance of the feathers is very important. They should be clean and fluffy, not brittle and matted.

Of course, this can be somewhat deceiving after a rain, when most birds look very rough. As desert animals, the ostrich's feathers are not capable of repelling water.

Pull a couple of feathers from a bird and check for stress lines. These are long, very distinct lines running through the feather that can indicate stress and/or illness.

If the eyes are the mirror of the soul, they can also be a mirror into how a bird feels. Eyes should be clear and alert.

Legs should be straight. Some birds will have their toes pointed out at a slight angle, but provided the angle is not severe and is equal on both feet, it is acceptable.

The overall look of the bird should be smooth sleek lines and an easy way of moving. A defect such as a crossed beak, crooked neck, or rolled, broken, or bent toes, is not acceptable. These defects *do not correct themselves*.

If you are not experienced with ostriches then take someone along with you who is. Take your time in choosing, be picky, know what you want, and accept nothing less.

BEHAVIOR

Females

For the most part female ostriches are very docile by nature. Though most do not want to be touched, they can be handled without much problem.

With proper nutrition and a good environment, about 50% of two-year-old hens will lay eggs. Many of these hens will lay only in small numbers as two-year-olds, but others will lay prolifically. Once again you are dealing with individuals where genetics, environment and nutrition play a great part in overall results.

Females in heat (ready to breed) will drop their wings all the way forward, often touching the ground, and shake them, sometimes making the joints sound as though they are popping. This action is referred to as *fluttering*. Usually at the same time a hen flutters she will drop her head to the ground and clap her beak. This is called *clucking*. The entire procedure is called *displaying*.

This type of behavior is brought about by the high levels of estrogen present in the hen's body, which is a sign that laying

A four-year-old redneck male
(Photo courtesy of Miller Studio, Stephenville, Texas)

should follow within 30 days or so. Hens that flutter for 60 to 90 days and do not lay an egg should be checked by a veterinarian to make sure that there are no problems.

In rare cases, fluttering behavior can be seen in female chicks at three months and up. This does not mean that the chicks are ready to breed, but rather that they are checking their bodily responses. When seen in young chicks this behavior is only momentary.

It isn't until a hen begins to flutter and cluck continuously that she is generally ready to accept a male for breeding.

The breeding season normally (there are exceptions to every rule) starts between January and April, depending on where you live and the weather. Once started, the breeding season can last anywhere from 30 to 180 days. This depends on the animal, and your geographical location.

Once a hen settles into her laying pattern she will lay an egg every other day. However, she may begin her cycle by laying one egg and waiting a week to lay another, or she may start by laying every three days. The patterns vary from hen to hen.

Other unusual things that may be encountered are:
- a hen may lay an egg with no shell near the beginning of her cycle, or
- she may lay an egg with bloody streaks on it, or
- she may lay an egg standing up and drop it to the ground, breaking it.

Oftentimes young hens are just not real sure what is going on with their bodies. Before they settle into a real cycle, many will start to lay before they have been bred, some will strain very hard, others will sit or stand many times before their eggs are laid.

Most of these problems are simply due to immaturity and will correct themselves within a week or so. Do not panic. This is mother nature at work.

The time to be concerned is when a hen consistently lays eggs with no shell or wrinkled shells, or if she does not establish a correct laying pattern of every other day. If this pattern continues for two weeks, contact a vet. There may be a problem.

Some hens will start to lay and continue in the every-other-day cycle until they are through.

Other hens will lay a clutch of ten to twenty eggs and take a break for a couple of weeks, then begin again and do this several times during the laying season.

The average number of eggs laid by one hen in a season is fifty. There are many reports of hundred-plus layers. However, at this point in our industry it is not known whether hens that lay large numbers will continue this pattern for life or whether this could cut their laying life-span in any way. Too little is known about these animals at this time to answer this question.

In general a good strong hen that will lay fifty eggs per year with a good hatchability and survivability rate in her chicks is far more profitable than one that lays a large number of eggs where hatchability and chick survival is a problem.

Males

The male ostrich is a majestic creature. During the non-breeding season he is quite docile for the most part, willing to take a bite of grass from your hand and in general allow you to come into his territory without much fuss. Of course a lot of this depends on how much time you spent with him as a youngster.

Males will begin to get their black feather plumage somewhere between the ages of eleven and eighteen months, depending on the maturity of the individual.

All birds are not created equal. Some males can and do fertilize eggs prior to two years of age, and some are three to four years old before they are considered prolific breeders.

The male's phallus can enlarge from 2-3 inches to 16-18 inches in length in a matter of weeks. The size of the phallus is directly related to the male's ability to breed and fertilize eggs.

At the onset of maturity the male will begin to fill his neck with air and make a very loud noise

Female displaying. Note dropped wings. (Photo courtesy of Dr. Brett Hopkins)

Phallus of a reproductively active male ostrich. Note the curve and twist to the left.
(Photo courtesy of Dr. Brett Hopkins)

Blue-neck ostrich cantling.

Red-neck ostrich booming. Note his neck, filled with air.

referred to as *booming*. This is both a mating call and a warning signal of something unfamiliar to him.

The male's displaying will consist of both booming and cantleing, which is a very interesting procedure whereby he gets down on his hocks (first joint of the leg above the ankle), and extends his wings while swaying back and forth and striking his head against his sides.

Cantleing is used to ward off intruders from his territory as well as to entice his female companions. A male will sometimes sway from side to side as many as sixty or seventy times in one sitting.

If he is cantleing for his mate and she is receptive, then he will get up and extend his wings well above his head, get up on his tip toes and stomp his feet in a very fast motion while bumping her on the tail. The willing female will then lay down and allow him to breed her.

The male will mount by placing one foot on the hen's back and the other foot on the ground near her side and insert his phallus while striking his head on his sides and swaying back and forth.

If copulation is achieved, the female will move her head back and forth with her neck extended and both birds will then vibrate their wings and make a loud moaning sound. As with most bird species of the world their mating ritual is unique and fascinating.

WORKING WITH YOUR BREEDERS

Male ostriches have, over the years, acquired a reputation for being mean.

This reputation is for the most part undeserved. Anyone who has had any dealings with animals in breeding situations is well aware of the fact that males of all species are more aggressive during the breeding season.

The ostrich is no different. He will warn you to stay away by flipping his wings over his back and hissing at you. Simply avoid contact with a breeding male by constructing your facilities so that you can collect eggs without antagonizing him. The breeding male is no more dangerous than a stallion or bull during breeding season, if common sense is used.

PAIRING YOUR BREEDERS

A pair of ostriches is just that: one male and one female making up a pair. For the most part pairing breeders is not a problem. If you are introducing birds that were not raised together, it is a good idea to put both into a new pen at the same time.

Avoid moving, pairing, or any other types of changes during the breeding season if at all possible. Try to pair birds and place them in their breeding pens at least sixty days prior to the beginning of breeding season.

Trios consist of one male and two females, which allows more production and less pen space. It is a good idea if you are going to use trios to place them in their pen as yearlings.

Most males can handle breeding more than one female. If you have a pair and he is breeding the hen five or six times or more a day then you may want to think about making a trio for the next breeding season.

Never introduce a new female to an established pair of breeders. More than likely one or the other or both will try to kill her and could succeed if you are not careful. Remember this is their territory and they do not like quick changes.

To introduce a new hen to an established pair of breeders, the wise thing to do is to place the hen from the pair and the new hen into a new pen together and give them plenty of time to get acquainted. Do this a couple of months before breeding season.

Usually after a couple of weeks they will hang around together, eat together and often sleep together. The pen will become the hens' territory and they will set the rules. Now you can introduce the male to the pen. This method is much safer and you will have fewer problems.

If a new or different pen isn't possible, put up a makeshift pen alongside the pair and leave the new hen in it until they make friends across the fence.

Be patient and you will be rewarded. Be careless and you will pay.

FACILITIES

PEN LOCATION

The ideal location for breeder pens is in a very secluded area away from traffic and the everyday workings of a ranch. Birds love trees. If possible give them at least one large tree in part of their pen and yet leave them plenty of room to bask in the sun during the winter months.

If a tree is out of the question in your area, then provide the birds with an artificial shade of some type, preferably an extended lean-to in front of their shelter, facing the south.

When building your facilities be aware of wind directions. Though many birds will not go inside during bad winter weather, most will seek a windbreak. Provide this for them.

PEN SIZE

This subject is a classic case of *more is better*, though some will argue this point. One should never consider a pen smaller than a half-acre per pair or trio.

Males and females do not always come into season at the same time. If you give the female plenty of room to run from an aggressive male, until she is ready to breed, you could save yourself the cost of replacing a dead hen.

If possible make all corners 45-degree angles, to prevent the male from cornering a hen and hurting her. When your hen's body tells her it is time to breed, she will. Allowing an overly-aggressive male to beat up on her is senseless.

Try to allow for a 14- to 20-foot wide alleyway between breeder pens, which can double as an extra pen for the purpose of holding an injured or sick bird, or just to separate your birds until both are ready to start breeding.

Closed alleyways also give the birds a safe haven against free-roaming predators, such as stray dogs or coyotes. The birds learn that the predators can't get close to them when they are against the alley fence. As a general rule they will run to this safety zone and will not run fences, which can lead to injury or even death.

SHELTERS/HOLDING PEN

Shelters need not be fancy or expensive. A simple two- or three-sided structure, approximately 12' x 12' to 16' x 20' will work nicely. Always feed your birds inside the shed. If you purchase a pair of birds and they refuse to go into the shed, train them. This is not hard to do. Simply place their feed in a tub outside of the shed or where they will eat. Feed them in this area until they readily come to eat. Move the feed pan two to four feet per day toward the shed.

If they get stubborn as you get too close to the shed, back off moving the feeder for a couple of days. Then proceed again—slowly—to move the feeder and before you know it they will go right in.

A must for your breeder pens is what is referred to as a bull pen or holding pen around your shelter. This should be made of the same fencing as the pen. A simple design of thirty feet in front and thirty feet to the side, with a gate leading to the main part of the pen will work. (See Figure 2).

This simple and relatively inexpensive addition to your pen can save you countless hours of frustration, time, not to speak of the safety.

Once you have trained your birds to go into the shed to eat, you simply close the gate to the main pen and proceed to gather your

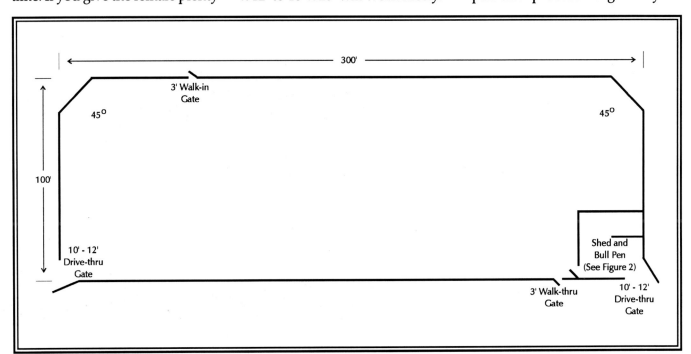

Figure 1. Layout of a roomy, easy-to-work pen. See Figure 2 for detail of shed area.

eggs in safety, mow the pens, clean water troughs, etc.

Should you need to catch your bird for one reason or another this is a perfect way to do so. Birds are much easier to handle in an enclosed area. There are so many advantages to having a holding pen that there is little or no excuse not to have one.

FENCING MATERIAL

There are several types of fencing material that are suitable for ostriches.

The best of the best is 9-gauge chain link (ordered with knuckle top and bottom) using 2.375" pipe for posts and top rail. However, this type of fencing is very expensive, unless you are a welder, in which case the cost is in line with any other type of fencing.

The next choice would be 2 x 4 no-climb horse wire. This type of fence does not require a top rail. However if birds hit this wire they will be more apt to lose feathers and cut themselves than with the chain link.

The next type most recommended would be Tight-Lock game fencing, eight feet high. This wire will give if hit by the birds but due to the height does not seem to cause problems.

The more room you give the birds the fewer fence problems you will have, and more room allows for less-expensive fencing. Always take fencing all the way to the ground. Leaving one or two feet at the bottom of a fence can cause injury should the birds lay down too close to the fence and get caught underneath. A space also allows predators to invade.

Use good sense when building fences. This is no place to cut corners. Make no safety concessions. You'll save money in the long run.

FOOD AND WATER

FEEDING

Feeding birds is very important, not only regarding nutritional quality, but the manner in which they are fed. Whether you feed once or twice a day, birds should have cleaned up all of their feed at least one to two hours before the next feeding.

If they have not cleaned up, they are being fed too much food, or they do not like it. Decrease the amount by 1/4 to 1/2 pound per day until your birds are cleaning up their feed.

The best situation possible is to have birds running to the shed to greet you at the feeder. This says that the bird's appetite is good and they like their feed.

Use caution here: DO NOT starve birds to the point of being ravenous at the sight of food. On the contrary, give breeders plenty of good-quality feed for best results. Feed breeders about 4.5 pounds of feed per bird per day.

Birds should not be fat, yet they should be ready and waiting for their feed every day. Just as with horses or any other animal, some ostriches are easy keepers and then there are those that are hard keepers. Get to know your birds and you will soon learn what is good for them.

It is always a good idea to top-dress feed with a couple of cups of corn when a severe winter storm is coming. Some prefer to use alfalfa—both will provide extra body heat and carbohydrates during the cold winter months.

Another important item to remember is to feed at approximately the same time every day. This too will make the birds ready and waiting.

Be consistent in your feeding, cleaning and other chores, such as mowing pens. The birds will soon become comfortable with having their handler around.

Another major reason for wanting birds to come running at dinner time is to see how everyone is feeling. A sick bird has little interest in eating. Monitoring eating habits to detect illness has saved many birds over the years.

Never allow a bird to miss more than one complete meal. If a bird doesn't come to the feeder a second time, it should be pulled up to a sick stall or taken to a vet.

Never wait for a bird to go down. By that time it will probably be too late.

Figure 2. Shed and pen allow easy access to feed birds and enough room to bring in a truck if necessary, but are small enough to corner and catch a bird.

If a sick stall is not available for the bird then pen it up in the holding area and do the following:
- Take the bird's temperature and record it.
- Palpate the belly for any signs of impaction.
- Use a stethoscope to listen to both sides of the chest for signs of cracking or rattling.
- Note the consistency of the stool in the pen.
- Check for any physical signs of injury, such as bruising or bleeding.

After doing all of these things call your ratite veterinarian and give him or her a complete list of all symptoms. Oftentimes these problems can be corrected with a little telephone help from a vet.

WATERERS

A thirteen- to fifteen-gallon plastic muck bucket works very well. They are inexpensive and can be purchased from any equine supply center.

One reason for this preference is the ease of cleaning. Dump the water and bleach the container at least once per week. Particularly in summer, algae and parasites are very common in water. They can cause problems with bacteria and internal parasites.

Many people prefer automatic waterers. However, the problem with the preface *auto* is that we become complacent and forget to check to see if in fact everything is working. Too often things can go wrong and are not discovered in a timely fashion.

Remember that cool clean water does make a difference in how much water the birds will drink. This is important.

Sand nests are a must. Not only do they help keep eggs clean, they also give the birds a place to take a sand bath.

LAYING SEASON

NEST SITE

Choosing a nest site can be tricky. The human rancher thinks Spot A would be great for a nest, but since she is not an ostrich, more often than not she picks the wrong spot.

The best way to choose the correct nesting spot is to place the birds in their pen and give them a couple of months to settle in and watch where they spend most of their day. Most of the time it will be under a tree on the fence line.

After establishing where their favorite spot is, have a load of sand brought in and dumped there. This will probably work.

Sand nests are a must. Not only do they help keep eggs clean, they also give the birds a place to take a sand bath. This is one of their favorite pastimes, and also helps them in removing external parasites.

EGG COLLECTION

If you have constructed pens as suggested, using the bull pen concept, then collecting eggs is as simple as feeding your breeders. While they are eating, push the gate to the bull pen closed and proceed to pick up the egg.

If you have an unruly male or do not have an area to lock up your birds, you should have a helper get the male's attention, on the opposite side of the pen from the egg, by offering him a treat such as lettuce, grapes, or even freshly-pulled grass, while you go in and retrieve the egg.

The less painful and traumatic you make this process the better for the birds and the collector. Going into a pen with a weapon to fight off a male is foolhardy and only antagonizes the animal.

There are many ways to collect eggs. Many people use rubber gloves. This works if you have only one pair to collect from, but if you are collecting from many hens, you could spread bacteria from one egg to another by using this method. You would need to change gloves for every egg retrieved—not very cost-effective.

We have found that keeping a roll of paper towels on hand works well. Simply tear off a sheet and use it to pick up the egg. Wrap the towel around it and place it in a container, such as a plastic tub with a lid. Go to the next egg and do the same. Colored stickers are effective in identifying eggs until you get to the preparation area.

In the preparation area, the eggs should be washed with a mild disinfectant solution and water at least 10 degrees warmer than the eggs. Allow them to air dry, and then mark each one.

My personal preference is colored stickers, with the egg numbers written on them. Each hen has her color assigned at the beginning of the season.

Some people like to use a lead pencil and make other notations on the eggs. You should never use a marker—the dye is very strong and could damage the embryo.

This is also the time to note in your records all relevant information—date laid, hen, weight of the egg, temperature, and weather conditions if other than normal.

Immediately place the eggs in storage. This can be anything from a chest-type cooler with a 2-liter bottle of frozen water to a modified freezer—anything that will hold a temperature of approximately 55 degrees until you are ready to set a batch of eggs in the incubator.

NEW ARRIVALS

Closed ranches are always best—the fewer incoming birds to your ranch the better off you will be. But this is not always possible, so the next best situation is to have a quarantine area located on the opposite side of your facility from your other birds. It should be as isolated as possible.

The quarantine area should be large enough for a bird to exercise, with a stall or shed area where it can be closed in and medicated or examined. This area need not be large or expensive—20' x 50' would be just fine. Make sure that runoff from this pen does not drain to any other bird pen.

Males

For male birds a complete CBC blood panel should be required. This blood work should be done before the bird is purchased. If the bird belongs to a potential client and is being shipped to your ranch, then the blood should be taken by a vet as soon as the bird is loaded in the trailer.

In case of a poor catch, where the bird is highly stressed, then it is best to wait until the bird has settled in for 48 to 72 hours before having blood work done. Stressed birds will show very high blood counts, which can mask or distort a possible medical problem.

Blood samples should be sent off to a lab that works with your vet, regardless of where the blood is being sent from. Results should be faxed to your vet.

Keep the bird in quarantine until blood results are complete. If medication is required, do it in the quarantine facility. Allow 30 to 60 days after medication before introducing a bird to your flock.

Females

Females should receive the same treatment as described for males, but they should also have a complete oviduct culture and ultrasound if the hen has had a laying season.

Make sure that you have these tests done on hens by ostrich-qualified reproduction experts. There are not many in the United States at this writing. If no expert is available to you then have blood work only done. This will give a baseline for any possible problem.

Non-reproducing birds can be handled in much the same way. All birds should be wormed and dusted for external parasites prior to being introduced to your flock.

PREVENTIVE MEDICAL EXAMS

An ounce of prevention *is* worth a pound of cure. Although nothing is ever foolproof, the best way of entering a breeding season is with a clean bill of health. Establish a working relationship with a veterinarian who is experienced in ostrich reproductive medicine. It is worth the time and money.

Whenever possible we make arrangements with neighboring farms to vet all birds at the same time, which is easier and less expensive. Place the birds in an enclosed horse or ostrich trailer for examination.

Do not be afraid to catch birds, just because you can't put a halter on them and walk them into a stall. If your facilities are correctly built, working birds is no more trouble than working any type of livestock.

If necessary, hire a professional handler until you get the hang of it. There are many very good haulers out there who will come help work birds.

Catch all females and have them ultrasounded. In an enclosed trailer a vet can read an ultrasound, draw blood for a full blood panel, take samples for cultures of the trachea and oviduct, administer Ivomec worming, read microchips, replace leg bands, and dust for external parasites.

All males should be caught and wormed, their microchips read, and they should be dusted for parasites. Blood should also be drawn for a full blood panel.

Medical checkups are usually done in October. This gives the vet plenty of time to get the results of blood work and cultures in time for any medications or corrective procedures to be done prior to the beginning of breeding season.

Nothing is 100% foolproof. However, taking all of the above precautions prior to breeding season can save a year's production.

There is no magic to breeder management, only good common sense and sound proven practices that are used in every type of agricultural farming and ranching. Healthy, happy, well-adjusted birds from good genetic backgrounds will be good producers.

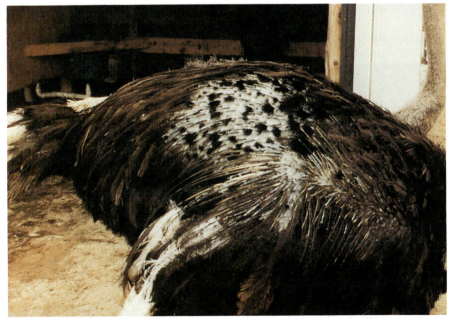

Male ostrich with severe feather loss, with some regrowth (dark black feathers). This was caused by his mate picking at his feathers. (Photo courtesy of Dr. Brett Hopkins)

Bob "Senior" Smith with a friend at the American Ostrich Company, Lytle, Texas. (Photo courtesy Bob Moreau, Perfection Photography, San Antonio, Texas)

OSTRICH CHICK REARING

Susan Dunn
Windwalker Exotics
Dilley, Texas

Ostrich chick rearing has been one of the most challenging and rewarding undertakings of my life. In the late 80s and early 90s the most-often-quoted phrase in the industry was "Ostrich chicks just wake up every morning looking for a place to die!" This was the attitude of many of the early pioneers of this industry.

I can tell you unequivocally these birds are extremely tenacious creatures. Only with a gross misunderstanding of their needs and poor management techniques will they finally succumb. On the other hand ostrich chicks can be very unforgiving of our ignorance.

It is my hope that in this chapter I can impart techniques found to be successful in the rearing of these chicks, making this experience more positive for future breeders than has been the case in the past.

STARTING OUT

Successful chick rearing begins when you purchase your breeders. The primary consideration is sound genetics. Although we are very early in the genetic history of our breeder birds, you will be far ahead of the game to research the records of birds you intend to purchase for your foundation flock.

Be cautious—accept only verifiable records. Errors at this stage are very costly in time and money. Rectifying mistakes can be a painful process.

There are many components that will determine the health and survivability of your chicks. It is extremely important that you fully understand everything possible about ostriches, hatching equipment, biosecurity, genetics, and breeder management, before you begin to hatch ostrich chicks.

The chapters in this book which cover those subjects should be read before you start looking, and they will also provide a background for this and other chapters.

HATCHING

NORMAL HATCHING

Ideally, 85% of your eggs should hatch on their own, or with only minor assistance. So please be patient and prudent before rushing in to assist where it's not needed.

Begin candling eggs on day 39 of incubation. When the drop of the air cell membrane begins, this is the first sign the chick is beginning to position itself to hatch.

At this stage, which will last approximately 24 to 48 hours, candling every 12 hours is adequate. If the desired weight loss has been achieved, and the eggs have been incubated properly, unassisted internal pipping is the rule.

As the chick positions itself you will see progressive movement at the air cell membrane, which exhibits itself as uneven protrusions of the usually smooth membrane.

This movement is the beak and feet pushing against the membrane. As you gain experience you will recognize correct, as opposed to incorrect, movement.

When internal pipping is confirmed through candling, you will observe a darkening of the air cell due to the chick entering the air space. At this time it is important to note the time of internal pip. As a rule of thumb 24 hours is the optimum time from internal to external pipping.

However, if movement continues to be vigorous without a significant change, the 24-hour window can be lengthened with careful observation.

As the chick rotates, it uses a muscle in its neck (appropriately termed the pipping muscle) to break the egg shell. The matrix of the cellular structure of the shell makes it easier to break from the inside than from the outside.

From the external pipping point to the completion of the hatching process, approximately 12 to 24 more hours should elapse.

ASSISTED HATCHING

With time and experience you will learn when a chick needs assistance or when to let nature take its course. It is a good rule of thumb not to allow a chick to remain in the air cell more than 24 hours without intervention.

Stress can cause many problems in a neonatal chick. The fact that a chick has internally pipped does not necessarily mean that he is in a position to continue the hatching process.

It must be stressed at this point that if more than 10% to 15% of eggs need assistance at hatching time, it may indicate a problem in the incubation process or with the reproductive health of the hen.

If you do need to assist, here is the procedure we use:
- Place the egg on a towel, on a well-lighted level surface. Turn the air cell end of the egg toward you, using the rule of thumb that the chick's beak should be located approximately at the 1 o'clock position.
- Using a blunt instrument such as a tack hammer, or other similar object, tap the egg until a small crack appears.
- Use a pair of tweezers to break *very* small pieces of shell away, until you have broken a hole about the size of a quarter in the egg.
- The chick is known to be in the air cell at this point. You should hear the bird chirp, or by placing your ear near the egg you can hear the chick breathing. Try at this point to see the bird's beak.

In some cases a chick may appear to be in the air cell when in fact the inner membrane has collapsed around the beak.

If this is the case,
- break away more of the shell in order to be able to reach into the egg and tear the membrane;
- using clean tweezers or small, sharp scissors (very carefully, avoiding blood vessels) pull the membrane away just enough to expose the beak.

Once you are sure that the nasal passage is clear and the chick is breathing, close the hatcher and leave the chick alone for at least two hours.

Slow and cautious are the key words here. If after two to three hours the chick has made no progress, slowly remove enough of the shell to extract the head and neck completely from the shell so that aspiration will not occur.

At this point you need a product called Nolvasan Suspension (manufactured by Ft. Dodge and packed in a hand-held syringe-type container).

Place the end of the syringe at the end of the chick's neck, between the chick and the membrane, and depress the plunger, dispensing half of the tube.

This will bathe the yolk sac in an antimicrobial solution prior to being absorbed into the body, and allow easy movement within the confines of the egg.

The chick's struggle to exit from the egg is an extremely important part of the hatching process. Any interference beyond this point will interrupt the internalizing of the yolk sac. Chicks hatched with exposed yolk sacs are predisposed to a high mortality rate.

ROUTINE POST-HATCH PROCEDURE

1. Bathe the umbilical area with 7% iodine, Nolvasan Suspension, or Betadine ointment. Cover with a gauze pad and secure with vet wrap for 24 to 48 hours (see photo). This allows for the drying of the navel but the chick can still move around.

Pink vest on new chick is made from vet wrap. Holes are cut for head and tail. The "vest" keeps the fresh umbilical area from becoming soiled.

Healthy, alert chicks.

2. Implant a microchip in the pipping muscle. I do this as soon after hatch as possible. The muscle is enlarged for approximately 24 hours after hatch.

3. Chicks who have problems trying to stand (edematous chicks are more prone to this problem) due to weak legs or legs that splay out to the sides should be hobbled, for a day or so, using a half-inch strip of vet wrap (see photo).

- Place the chick on its back to enable you to see the correct placement of the hobble.
- Wrap the strip around one ankle and press it to hold it in place. (Vet wrap adheres to itself.)
- Now pull the other leg in so that both legs are perpendicular to the body, wrap the strip around the other ankle and press it in place.

This will reduce problems that can develop from splaying.

Vet wrap is a good product due to its softness on the chicks' puffy legs, and its elasticity, which allows the chick to become mobile.

4. The next 36 hours are crucial to ostrich chicks. Thermal regulation should be the primary object.

Allow the chick to bring its body temperature to 102 degrees and stabilize there for approximately 6 to 8 hours. Do not let body temperature climb past 103.5 degrees. Chilling or heat stress will be an insult that can lead to yolk sac retention.

5. After the chick's temperature stabilizes, place it in an enclosure where temperature is controlled, allowing it a choice of temperature ranges from 75 to 92 degrees.

Let the chick make some choices, although this is a period where disorientation can lead to chilling or overheating if proper controls are not provided.

Overhead heat and floor heat may be used. Simple articles can be very appropriate, such as a play pen with a heating pad. Monitor conditions with well-placed thermometers.

6. Weigh the chick and attach a leg band, and now it is ready to face the real world.

7. Record all procedures performed during hatching, including assistance in hatching, weight, date, medications given, etc.

Sexing the chicks can be done in the hatcher, but we usually wait until the chicks are approximately three months of age. At that time their sex organs are large enough for a more positive identification. At that age, a 95% positive identification is possible.

INTRODUCING NEW HATCHES TO OTHER CHICKS

When the chick is ambulating well, after 24 to 48 hours, place it in the brooder pen area. Chicks should be provided with a clean indoor area where they can stay

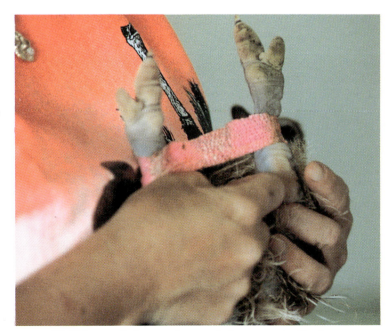
Hobbles made from vet wrap help prevent splaying, especially in edematous chicks.

warm and dry at night and still have the freedom to run and play during the daytime hours, weather permitting.

Studies have revealed that 224 sq. ft. per chick is required for brooding chicks to get the proper amount of exercise to allow them to utilize their yolk sacs properly.

The floor of the enclosed area should be concrete, covered by DriDek flooring (or a similar product which will allow night time elimination to be drained away so that the chick does not become wet or chilled during the night).

It is critically important that the enclosure and the exercise area be thoroughly cleaned daily.

At the same time that a chick is introduced to the brooder pen and other hatchlings, food and water should also be made available. As the yolk sac is absorbed the chick will become more interested in eating and drinking.

If placed with chicks that have mastered eating and drinking, the chick will copy them and weight gain will begin earlier. Eating and drinking does not affect yolk sac absorption whatsoever.

There are good commercial ostrich starter rations on the market. Feed three times a day allowing food to be eaten completely approximately one hour before the next feeding. This three-times-a-day feeding schedule should start as soon as eating has become normal (4 to 5 days).

Water is extremely important to the rearing of healthy chicks. Clean water is critical. If well water is the source of drinking water a chlorinator should be added. Water should be replaced with clean water every two to three hours throughout the daylight hours, and water containers should be bleached at least once every day.

Water supplies change due to environmental factors. They do not stay constant. Check your water supply frequently—at least every three months.

Water and food should be removed from the chick area during the night, until chicks are able to stay out at night. This would be dependent on the weather as well as the health and size of the chicks.

COMBINING BROODS

At three months of age we combine pens of birds who were raised in different breeder areas. Ostriches accept new pen mates at a young age very readily. As long as adequate feeding stations are available for the chicks which are lower in the pecking order, no problems should be encountered.

Regardless of age, we try to keep birds of the same size together to minimize injuries.

At one year of age chicks become more territorial and introducing one or two new birds into an already established group could provoke fights.

Placing new birds in an adjoining pen with a common fence line for a week or two is a way of minimizing these problems.

We change feed from starter to grower at three months, with grazing available from day one. I think this is one reason for our success. The birds can balance their own diets if given a choice.

Depending on the season, if night temperatures are sixty degrees or more, three-month-old chicks can stay out at night.

A shelter to keep feed dry, and to allow chicks the option of staying dry, is a prudent measure. This is only humane for animals of any species.

ENCLOSURES

A good rule of thumb: Build large pens whenever feasible. Large is relative, but at this point in the industry, grow-out pens smaller than one acre won't accommodate enough birds for a grow-out operation. In a one-acre pen, 60-70 birds could grow up. Again, larger is always better.

Stress is a factor in crowded pens at less than three months of age. They tolerate crowded grow-out facilities better the older they get—at least until sexual maturity. One reason is their immune system is functioning much better after three months.

We clean our outdoor pens of feces every day in the age groups under three months.

Chicks should begin drinking within 2 to 3 days of hatch.

Ostrich chicks love water on hot days. A sprinkler will also help them cool off.

CHICK CONDITION

SIGNS OF HEALTHY CHICKS

- Eager eaters that will run out of the barn in the morning, twisting and twirling and happy to be alive.
- Curious about their surroundings—chasing butterflies, pecking at rocks and weeds, sifting sand through their beaks.
- Except for several naps in the warm sun, ostrich chicks are busy all of the time.
- Hearty drinkers, to the point of drinking too much during the heat of the day.
- General posture is head up, alert, with a full-bodied appearance—full neck and stout full legs with no veins or tendons showing.

There is little else that need be said about healthy chicks. Just feed and water them and clean their pens and all should be well.

SIGNS OF SICK CHICKS

- The absence of spinning or twirling—chick trots out with the other chicks but does not participate in their playing.
- Posture—low neck carriage, hump-backed appearance.
- Skinny neck and legs.
- Staring blankly and not keeping up with pen mates or standing and sleeping while others are busy.
- Any chick that stands out from the others most likely has a problem.

A chick which has had surgery is more prone to impaction. Since the bird is not feeling normal it will tend to eat all the wrong things. Post-op chicks have about a 75% higher chance of becoming impacted than normal chicks.

COMMON PROBLEMS

Yolk-sac retention

Weighing chicks in the morning is a tool that can be useful in making decisions on yolk sac retention. Ostrich chicks should gain 1 to 2 ounces each day after day five. Losses are normal until this time.

If weight loss occurs two days in a row, suspect yolk sac retention. Fluids given (see the sidebar) at this time can help prevent dehydration, which can lead to lethargy and, ultimately, death.

Caloric intake can provide energy. High-fat-content foods are not recommended for this situation, since fat is not a digestible substance in a starvation situation.

The biggest threat to the ostrich chick at this time of life is to get into a weight deficit situation. They seldom recover.

If a chick does not respond to recommended treatment within 24 hours, yolk-sac retention should be considered.

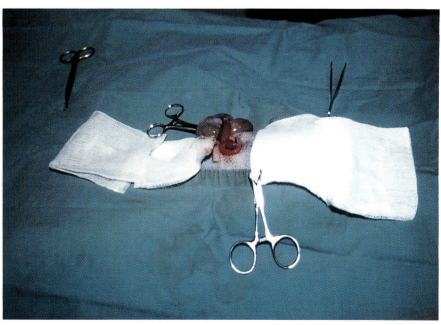

Surgical removal of a retained yolk sac.

Studies have shown that ostrich chicks come to food and water 600 times a day. A chick with a yolk-sac problem will come only 15% as often. So observation is extremely important.

The yolk sac should be absorbed by day 10 to 14. Therefore, this period is critical.

Yolk-sac retention is a problem that requires surgical intervention. Therefore, impeccable management techniques are vital.

Long before surgery or other medical treatment is necessary, you should have located a qualified ratite veterinarian, preferably one with surgical experience. Ask how many successful yolk sac surgeries he or she has accomplished. This is a very simple surgery.

If 10% mortality occurs, the surgery technique is faulty, the client has waited too long, or post-op care is inadequate.

To decrease the effects of stress prior to surgery, administer a pre-op dosage of Dexamethasone and Banamine. Call your avian vet for proper dosages.

Chicks who have had yolk sacs surgically removed usually grow up to be normal adult ostriches, healthy in every way. The first few times you will need to have your veterinarian do this, but it's a relatively simple procedure.

If your vet will teach you to do it yourself to keep cost down, there is no reason not to save retained-yolk-sac chicks.

After surgery, it is important to administer fluids—see the sidebar at the end of this chapter.

Impaction

Healthy birds will not impact on organic matter. Impaction is a problem that occurs secondary to stress, foreign object ingestion, parasitic infestation, or bacterial or fungal infection.

Signs and symptoms are poor appetite, chronic weight loss, firm or pelletized fecal balls or absence of feces, a firm proventriculus upon palpation, and lethargy.

Pens constructed so as to control the environment can save many birds which otherwise would be surgical candidates.

A 6'x10' inside run opening into a 10'x100' outside area with a covering of shadecloth, weedcloth, or something similar will allow you to control what your birds are ingesting. Keep feed and water in front of your birds at all times during the day.

- If sand impaction is suspected give the mixture containing Metamucil (sidebar).
- If it is a combination of grass and sand, give the mixture containing meat tenderizer. Meat tenderizer breaks down fibrous structure of grasses and hay.

Administer small amounts frequently, and you will not overload the bird's system.

Bacterial Problems. If bacterial infection is suspect, a tracheal culture should be obtained and sent to a laboratory.

If a single bird in a pen appears thin or lethargic, treat singly. If all the birds in a pen become lethargic, and their appetites are not what they have been, or there is weight loss across the board, one should suspect bacterial infection which will slow intentional movement dramatically, resulting in impaction.

Treatment for Impaction

When a culture is obtained, initiate antibiotic therapy after conferring with an avian veterinarian. In 24 hours the laboratory will have a preliminary report identifying the organism.

In 48 hours a final report should be available, with a sensitivity culture which will tell you if you are giving the correct antibiotic. If it's not, you should then change to the correct one.

Antibiotics are usually given twice a day for 10 to 14 days. You should also give the Sustain #3 replacement (sidebar) along with the medication.

Do not curtail antibiotic therapy when birds begin to improve. Administer all of the medication prescribed.

Treatment of impaction differs slightly depending on the etiology. Palpation is the first way in determining what is going on in the proventriculus.

Refer to the chapter on anatomy. You must know where the proventriculus is located. Then you must know what a normal proventriculus feels like as opposed to an abnormal one. It should feel soft early in the morning before feeding. This is the best time to palpate. The bird will normally begin to feel full as the day progresses.

Learning to palpate takes time and experience. At first you will not be able to tell what you are feeling, but with practice you will soon be able to ascertain whether you are feeling grass, sand, or a foreign object.

Things you could never believe they could swallow are removed on the operating table. Foreign objects—rock, plastic, metal—usually require surgery. They block the outlet from the proventriculus, and only fluids might be passing through or nothing at all. At times what appears to be diarrhea is actually fluid going around an impaction.

Post-op care is very important. Use the fluid recipe given in the sidebar. Be very conscientious. Get up once or twice during the night for a very dehydrated bird. During the daylight hours watch for the first voiding of urine after any procedure. This will be your monitor as to whether you are doing an adequate job of hydrating.

Very often after voiding, the bird will begin eating and drinking on its own, but you should continue with intermittent fluid replacement for a few days.

Never leave a bird with a vet after surgery. Bring the bird home as soon as it has fully awakened from anesthesia. Place the bird back in the pen with the same pen mates as before. After impaction surgery, give a broad spectrum antibiotic per your vet's instruction. Depending on the weather, be sure that the post-op bird stays warm. Remember hypothermia is a problem that is easily avoided with forethought.

Parasitic Infections

As our flocks grow and we stay in the same location for a few years, parasites can become a major problem. As with other animals, routine de-worming is a great adjunct to our management programs.

Taking stool samples is a good screening tool. However, many times parasites are present and the ova (egg) or the actual worm is not visible with a microscope. They just are not present in that particular stool sample. In the human hospital setting, stool specimens are collected at three different times to avoid obtaining false negatives.

A de-worming schedule that is adhered to throughout the year will minimize problems. Ivomec is a very safe drug and can be given subcutaneously or orally.

Begin worming chicks at thirty days, and follow up every three months from that time until one year of age. At this point parasites are still a problem, but due to the sheer size of animals twice-a-year worming should be sufficient unless you observe worms in the stool.

Ivomec does not kill all parasites so using an additional wormer is prudent. Talk with your veterinarian to see which one he or she prefers.

Fungal problems

Fungal problems should be avoided as they are highly detrimental to ostriches. If you live in a humid or wet climate, Nolvasan will be a great asset.

If you have had three days days of rain or more and the ground is saturated, use Nolvasan solution in the chicks' drinking water at a concentration of 5cc to 10cc per gallon.

The water will be blued in color and the chicks will be reluctant to drink but in a short time they will drink readily, actually enjoying the bubbles.

Use Nolvasan as a prophylactic measure. If a chlorinator is used, fungal problems will be kept to a minimum.

Viruses

Viruses are very contagious and devastating. When mortality in chicks reaches 90 to 100%, a virus is most likely the culprit.

Unfortunately viruses are very hard to isolate and diagnose and have been blamed for many high-mortality losses on certain ranches.

If you suspect a viral problem support your chicks with fluids, probiotics, and sometimes antibiotics for secondary infections.

Many universities are doing much-needed research in this area but vaccines are our only hope in controlling viruses. The poultry industry uses a few and I am sure we will too in the future.

Limb Deformities

A disheartening problem that will occur in a small percentage of chicks is leg deformities. With a proper diet and exercise they should be minimal.

These birds should never be allowed to breed, but if they are otherwise healthy and the deformity does not prevent them from getting around and feeding,

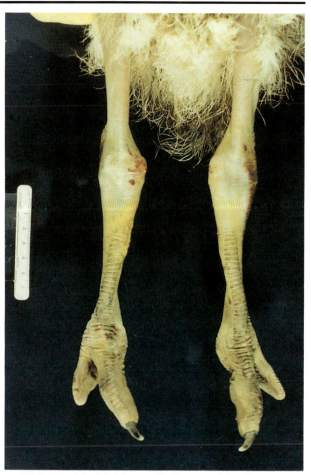

This ostrich chick has rolled toes, which is often related to riboflavin (Vitamin B$_2$) deficiency. (Photo courtesy Dr. Brett Hopkins)

they can be raised for leather, feathers, or meat.

Proper diagnosis is very important. Your vet should be consulted to determine what type of deformity your chick has.

If gait changes are noted, giving an anti-inflammatory for a few days may help. Chicks which have an injured leg compensate with the unaffected leg, which can cause additional problems. Easing pain will lessen stress to both legs.

Crowding and mixing birds of different sizes will increase the incidence of angular deformities. These occur when the epiphyscal plate (hock area) is subjected to injury from trauma—being run over by another bird or hitting an object such as a wall, post, or fence. The injured side of the epiphysis begins to produce increased amounts of calcium,

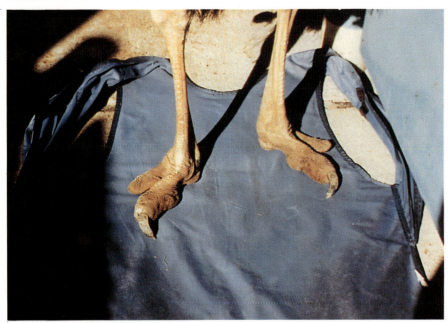

7-month-old ostrich chick with rolled toes, overgrown toenails, and long "flat" feet. In addition, this bird suffered from retarded growth, fungal pneumonia, and lead toxicity. The feet are classic examples of chronic B-complex vitamin deficiency, especially riboflavin. (Photo courtesy Dr. Brett Hopkins)

which begins angulation of the joint. These injuries occur predominately from 2-3 months of age. We do not know when the epiphysis is mature and closed in an ostrich. Your vet can perform a procedure called periosteal stripping, which will cause the unaffected side of the epiphysis to begin an overgrowth of calcium. This has been successful in straightening these deformities, and it is a minor surgical procedure at very low cost. If caught early enough 90% of these types of deformities can be arrested.

Prevention is the key. Proper nutrition, genetics, and good management will keep limb deformities to a minimum. If they occur in more than three to five percent of your birds, further investigation is warranted.

BIOSECURITY

Biosecurity is another area where prevention is the key. Dealing with organisms which are invisible to the naked eye is a constant battle with employees, visitors and ourselves. The poultry industry has very tight controls and their animals are only worth a fraction of what ours are worth—learning from them is very prudent.

Bacteria, viruses, fungi and parasites are all around us, on every surface inside our bodies and our ostriches' bodies. The immune system is able to protect us from all of these organisms as long as the system is not compromised.

When the immune system is compromised, an overgrowth of the organisms causes illness.

Keeping the environment as clean as possible is the defense. A closed farm would be a wonderful control, but we are still building our flocks and selling birds to other interested individuals. All we can do at this time is minimize the risks.

Visitors

When potential buyers call, ask them to come to your farm before any others that day. Ask if they own birds. If they do, ask them to wear shoes they have not worn in their pens. Provide a coverall and spray their shoes with disinfectant. Do not let them into your pens or incubating or hatching areas.

A video of your operation is nice to show if people are interested in your facilities. We should be as open and share as much as

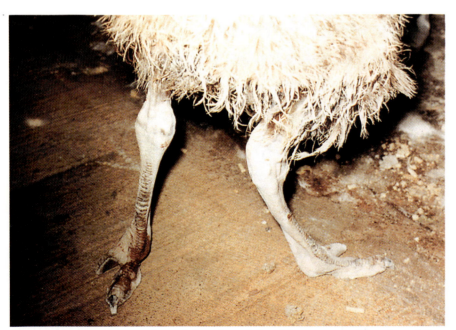

Outward rotation, or valgus deformity, of the tibio-tarsus and bowing of the metatarsal bone in an ostrich chick. A common condition unfortunately. Note also the flat feet. (Photo courtesy Dr. Brett Hopkins)

possible—without jeopardizing our chicks. Most people are impressed with these measures, and feel more secure buying birds from ranches that have good biosecurity protocols.

Employees

Employees who understand the dynamics of micro-organisms will follow biosecurity procedures more readily. All should receive training in these measures.

Provide step pans with a disinfectant, such as a phenol solution, which doesn't become inactivated by organic material, and change it every morning. To minimize tracking infectious material from pen to pen, place a pan in front of every chick pen. Demand that employees use them.

If an infection does occur, using a separate pair of boots for that pen only, in conjunction with step pans, is a measure that can help you contain your problem.

New Arrivals

Isolation pens are necessary for incoming birds. Incubation periods vary from ten days to two weeks. A thirty-day isolation period should minimize problems.

The stress of moving should bring any incipient problems to the forefront. CBCs and cultures should be obtained prior to moving. The tests take about 48 hours so plan ahead. Again, prevention will minimize contamination.

Isolation pens should be built so prevailing winds don't carry microorganisms into your flock. Winds and traffic flow should move from the youngest to oldest.

With these measures I hope you will have the success we have enjoyed in the past. As the industry matures we will refine our techniques and management protocols so managing larger numbers of birds will become easier and more efficient, an important aspect in becoming a competitive alternative livestock industry.

These recipes will help give sick chicks a new chance at life if used correctly. Read carefully and use according to the directions.

Keep all listed ingredients on hand. Purchase everything prior to the hatching season. It will save a lot of time and could save lives.

Many have heard me call these recipes "slime" due to their appearance, but we'll call them "Sustain" for propriety's sake.

Do not force fluids. If the chick cannot keep fluid down, use smaller doses with longer times between. Birds that are not feeling well will not eat, but giving these replacements will not stop birds from eating.

T = Tablespoon
C = Cup (8 ounces)

SUSTAIN #1
Indications for use:
- For rehydrating chicks under 10 pounds.
- Post-op yolk-sac surgery.
- Use as often as every thirty minutes provided chick can keep fluid down.
- Never give more than 15cc to this size chick.

Recipe
- 2 Tsp predigested bird food (for hand-feeding)
- 2 T amino acid
- 4 T warm water

Mix well to consistency of thin pudding.

SUSTAIN #2
Indications for use:
- For rehydrating chicks over 10 pounds.
- Poor eater or drinker.
- Any bird that looks like it has a problem, start right away.
- Give 15-30 cc minimum 3 times daily.

Recipe
- ½ can A/D Science Diet Prescription dog food
- ½ C Amino Acid or Pedialite, or ¼ C Gatorade
- 2 cups lukewarm water

Mix well to watery consistency. Refrigerate up to 2 days.

SUSTAIN #3
Indications for use:
- Impactions (will clear many without surgery).
- Post impaction surgery—a must.
- Constipation.
- Non-eating trauma victim.
- Birds on medication for infections, that are not eating well.
- Give 30-60cc for birds 10lbs+ 3 times per day, more often in severe cases.

Recipe
- 1 can A/D Science Diet prescription dog food
- 1 Tsp wheat bran
- 1 T olive oil
- 2 T Metamucil
- 1 Tsp probiotic (Probios, Ben-a-bac, etc.)
- 1/2 Tsp no-salt meat tenderizer (DO NOT use if bird has had surgery.)

Mix well with a wire whip to a consistency of semi-thin pudding. Refrigerate up to 2 days.

IN GENERAL

Administer replacement until bird is eating normally on its own, using a 12cc syringe for 12 or fewer cc's.

For larger amounts, use a red rubber catheter tube #12 (buy from your vet), cut about 5 to 6 inches long, and push it onto the end of syringe. For much larger amounts use a 60cc catheter-tip syringe #12. The catheter tube fits on the end of this syringe.

Ask your vet or an experienced ostrich farmer to show you how to do this the first time, to prevent injury to your birds.

Healthy ostrich chicks. (Photo courtesy James Sales)

OSTRICH CHICK REARING

William C. Sutton, M. D.
Chulagua Ranch
Camp Wood, Texas

There are many books, magazine articles, and pamphlets on the raising of ostrich chicks. One is tempted to list the subjects to be discussed and then follow in an orderly cookbook fashion. That approach is already available to anyone who is sufficiently interested to read this book.

I will depart from that approach by offering a discussion which is less structured, less didactic, and possibly is presented much as if we were sitting in the living room at our ranch.

One of the most often repeated phrases in the ratite vernacular is "Well, it works for me." That statement is little comfort to the new breeder for whom little or nothing is working. Where feasible, I have listed exact procedures, products, and advice. Where this is not feasible, I have suggested general approaches.

CHICK SURVIVAL

Any industry, including the ostrich industry, may be likened to a chain in which each link is vital to the integrity of the whole. Millions of dollars and billions of words have been exhausted upon such subjects as genetics, fences, pens, shelters, incubators, hatchers, trailers, feed, feed additives, drugs, importation, microchips, and on and on.

If each of the above facets of the whole picture is important, all is for naught if we cannot collectively raise sufficient numbers of chicks to support both breeder and production markets.

Toward the goal of total chick survival, the following is submitted based upon twelve years of hands-on experience in attempting to raise chicks from hatch to three months of age.

No matter whether the source of breeders is domestic or foreign; no matter how prolific the layers; no matter how fertile the males; no matter how successful the incubating and hatching processes—the survival of the chicks is imperative.

I think most ostrich breeders will agree that the most critical period for chick survival is the first four weeks of life, with the peak period of deaths being clustered about the 21st day.

A few deaths occur earlier and a few later, and most breeders also agree that by the age of three months, no chick should die except by accidental injury or by swallowing a dangerous object.

While every breeder may experience the mystery of the deaths of three-week-old chicks, insuffient study has been directed to this narrow window of time. In our experience, more than 95% of all ostrich deaths occur at three weeks.

WHY?

The most obvious answer seems to lie in the immune system of the young.

Without going into a very long subject, the young of most species either come equipped with an immune substance (egg yolk, transfer across a placenta) or are given immune substances by the mother (mother's milk, crop milk, etc.).

- Could baby ostriches have only enough immunity to last three weeks?
- Could they have no immunity until later and it takes three weeks for a viral or bacterial infection to kill them?

We obviously don't know, but the immunity theory seems to fit the three-week death window better than anything else on the horizon.

LEARN FROM FAILURE

The purpose of taking this much time and space at the beginning of this chapter is to urge every breeder to try to learn something from failure.

- Send your infertile eggs to a poultry expert. You may be amazed at how many eggs were actually fertilized but did not begin to develop.
- Find someone who may be a little more knowledgeable than you to examine any dead-in-the-shell birds.
- Do the same for dead chicks.

You may learn nothing. You may spend a little money on lab or vet fees.

You may actually be misled by a culture or finding which is reported to you but whatever you learn or even whatever you don't learn is better than throwing away your failed eggs or birds.

A *smart* man learns from his own mistakes. A *wise* man learns from the mistakes of others.

Now that I have completed the philosophy hour and have that off my chest, let's get down to helping these baby chicks survive.

THE ENVIRONMENT

First we must realize that we are dealing with a completely artificial environment for these chicks. Instead of being hatched and raised by their parents, the entire process—from the time that the egg is picked up by human hands—everything is ersatz.

We try to simulate many of the conditions that we hope to be natural, but the environment which we provide is not natural—not even close.

Of course in some ways the quality of our unnatural environment may far exceed the conditions in the natural state, and thus we feel deep down in our hearts that we should be able to raise all our hatched chicks. Why then can't we?

We will start with the newly hatched chicks and see if we can raise them to the age of three months. Since raising chicks can be such a fight, let's label it as such.

ROUND ONE

I shall identify the first period as the time from the internal pip until the chick is placed outside.

At our facility, we keep the eggs in a NatureForm incubator at a temperature of 96.5 degrees and a relative humidity of 18 per cent until the chick has obviously pipped the internal membrane and is moving a great deal.

The egg is then transferred to a NatureForm hatcher, maintaining the same temperature and humidity as in the incubator.

At this point a great deal of judgment is required to allow the chick to hatch naturally.

This is more fully covered in other sections of the book, but I will state categorically that the natural hatching process produces a much stronger and much more ready chick.

Once the chick is hatched, we transfer it to a second-stage hatcher. We use an older, glass-topped RCO hatcher which allows for careful observation of the chicks.

Care of the Navel

The first procedure performed upon the chick is care of the navel, because the blood vessels which connect the structures of the egg membrane to the internal structures of the chick can act as a wick along which viruses, bacteria, or fungi may travel. We treat the navel in the following manner:

1. Spray the area well with 7% iodine.

2. Place gentle traction on the dried wick and cut it with sterile scissors at skin level.

3. Cauterize the dimple with a silver nitrate stick.

4. Spray with 7% iodine a second time.

5. Place a very small dab of Betadine ointment on the navel.

6. Place a small (2" x 2") gauze pad on the navel.

7. Wrap the chick with a crosshatch, figure-eight bandage to hold the gauze against the navel. Use either vet wrap or masking tape.

8. Write on the wrap the chick's identification and place it back in the second-stage hatcher, also called a brooder.

Our chicks usually stay in the brooder for eight to twelve hours, until they are dry and they have become active.

The last procedure which occurs before the chicks are taken outside is the placement of a microchip. We place a microchip in the region of the hatching muscle, again using a spray of 7% iodine both before and after the chip is placed.

Skeptics may think that our method of treating the navel may be excessive and a great deal of trouble. I wish to argue that if ever there was an example of an ounce of prevention being worth a pound of cure, it is the care with which the navel is handled—or mishandled.

ROUND TWO

The second period of the chick's life is that time from the first outside exposure until it is placed down on the substrate and possibly mixed with older chicks. This period at our ranch usually begins at twelve to eighteen hours of age.

Once the chicks are dry, their bandages in place, their microchips implanted, and observation indicates that their general health is good, they go directly from the hatcher-brooder to a larger brooder in the chick barn.

The approximate dimensions of the brooder are 2' x 2' x 8' and the floor is covered by tightly-woven indoor/outdoor carpet. It is heated by thermostatically controlled coils and by movable heat lamps. The chicks usually remain in a brooder overnight and are ready to hit the ground the next morning.

Careful control of the temperature is an absolute must during this period of transition. Much has been made of possible chilling of baby chicks.

If one but thinks back, it is obvious that the temperature inside the egg was 96.5 degrees for about 25 days and then gradually increased to about 99.5 degrees.

When the organs of the embryo begin to function and the metabolism of the embryo occurs, the temperature within the egg is approximately 3 degrees hotter than the temperature setting of the incubator.

The temperature then drops from 99.5 to 96.5 when the egg shell is cracked, and to 95 degrees in our brooder.

We keep the outside brooder at 85 to 90 degrees for the first 36-48 hours. We try to keep the chick's temperature from fluctuating—certainly not below 85 degrees, because the chicks' ability to regulate body temperature is limited for the first few days.

How much regulation they can manage and for how long is not known, and rectal temps are not checked often due to stress on the chicks. Apparently a transition to temperatures of 75-95 is tolerated very well after 48 hours.

Our chicks are usually placed down on the ground by the second day because we think that early activity is extremely important and we don't wish them to become lazy, hot-house plants.

Chicks are not given feed or water until they are placed *down*. Much controversy has arisen over the subject of early feeding and the subject will be discussed in the next section.

ROUND THREE

For the breeder, the most critical decisions are those affecting the third round of the chick's life.
- What substrate?
- What feed & how much?
- Water?
- Grit?
- Additives?

There are a large number of extremely important decisions which must be made, each critical to the survival of the chicks.

Remember, you have substituted yourself for the natural parents. The chick has no choice but
- to walk in whatever area you provide;
- to eat whatever you provide for food;
- to drink whatever liquid that you provide for drink;
- to sleep wherever you provide for sleep;
- to adjust to whatever extremes of temperature that you provide.

In short, this fragile orphan is totally at your mercy.

It would be OK if we knew all of the details of raising chicks but when one couples helpless, dependent, complicated beings such as ostrich chicks with a beginning breeder, the stage is set for a very interesting time. Just never forget that the chick is your total responsibility. Its *only* choices are whether or not to eat, drink, or exercise. Every other aspect of its environment is dictated by you.

Let's try to break down that all-important first 28 days into special segments: temperature, shelter, ventilation, substrate, food, food additives, water, medical care, and defects.

Temperature

The chicks are not very smart at this age but they do recognize discomfort when they are too hot or too cold.

The inside of the barn must have some type of central heating so as to provide a fairly uniform temperature throughout. Additional heat should be provided in the form of portable heat lamps which can be placed around the pen to allow a few warmer areas.

Even when the air temperature is warm, the evaporation of urine, as with the evaporation of any liquid, produces a chilling effect. If the chicks are allowed to lie on carpet, astroturf, or concrete, the moisture from the evaporation of urine may produce a very cold tummy.

To avoid the cold, wet tummy, place a flat heating pad (pig blanket) on the floor and cover it with DriDek flooring. The finished inside sleeping area then offers a large volume of heated (and therefore drier) air, a warm and dry surface on which to sleep, and an infra-red heat lamp close by should the chicks still feel the need for more heat.

Leave plenty of room in the sleeping area for a chick to move away from the heat lamps, however. You do not want to come into the barn and find roasted chicks because there was no way to get away from the heat lamps.

A quick reminder here—don't put more than eight chicks together, because they tend to pile up and smother.

Chick barn. Note overhead heaters, exhaust fan, portable heat lamps, and DriDek flooring.

We provide, therefore:

1. Ceiling-mounted radiant gas-fired heaters. They come in natural gas and LP gas models with thermostats. The thermostat should be mounted 12 inches above the floor.

Remember that hot air rises and the chicks are very short—especially when they are lying down. The air can be very warm at your level and pretty cold near the floor.

Note thermostat mounted 12 inches above the floor.

2. Electric pig blankets provide excellent, uniform surfaces for heat but the surface is very slick. One must cover the pig blankets with DriDek flooring, not only for drainage but to prevent slipping and possible leg or hip injuries.

3. Infra-red heat lamps are available at any hardware store or poultry supply house. The only safeguards must be a strong, reliable clamp to prevent slippage and breakage. If a bulb breaks, the chicks will eat the broken glass.

Shelter

Temperature control can be very difficult on a cool or rainy morning. The chicks are awake, hungry, and ready to run. The inside pens are a mess and cleaning must begin soon. But where do the chicks go?

An excellent place is an extension of the barn, sheltered on each end and covered above. If this area is provided and a fence made to confine the chicks to this area, drop-type poultry heaters can provide warmth until later in the day when they can go out into natural or unheated areas.

Our "porches" are twelve feet deep and ten feet wide, each with its own heater. The chicks can be fed and watered early, can get exercise, and can stay warm until conditions improve. While breakfast is being served on the heated and sheltered porch, the nighttime mess can be cleaned up.

Fortunately, most ostrich chicks are spending their first month at a time when temperatures are favorable, but chicks can hatch as late as mid-October, and can face tremendous fluctuations in temperature.

For the first month, and preferably for the first three months, the temperature should be at least 72 degrees during the day and 80 to 85 degrees at night.

At 72 degrees during the day, the chicks can exercise and produce some heat of their own but sleeping temperatures should be a little warmer.

If you depend upon electricity to run all these heaters except the outside poultry heaters, you must consider a standby generator.

Our radiant heaters burn gas but the igniters, etc. are electric. The pig blankets and heat lamps are electric. Should the supply of electricity be interrupted, the chicks could suffer.

Standby generators should have an automatic transfer switch in case no one is at home at the critical moment.

Power outages are not always associated with bad weather. The longest outage that we ever experienced occurred on a bright sunny day with no wind, when some drunk ran his pickup into a power sub-station. Be prepared.

After three months, the birds need only to have shelter from very cool or cold weather, especially if it is wet. Wet is not too bad; cold is not too bad; wet *and* cold is very bad.

Ventilation

One often neglected aspect of chick rearing is adequate ventilation. In daytime it is not usually a problem, but ventilation becomes

Outside "porch." Note drop-type poultry heater.

or can become a real problem at night.

Why at night? There is a combination of problems that can turn lethal at night.

We have just gone to a great deal of time and expense to get our little chick-darlings all settled down for a comfy sleep—right? Right. But if that's all we've done, we have set the stage for disaster.

Remember that I mentioned DriDek flooring to let urine drain away? Great, but DriDek doesn't prevent the urine on the floor from giving off ammonia fumes.

Ammonia is a toxic substance whether in liquid or gas form. The ammonia gas not only is toxic to the eyes but also to the lining of the air sacs.

What is even worse, ammonia is heavier than air and tends to settle all around the chicks, who can unwittingly urinate themselves to death. Not only are ammonia fumes toxic, but the urine is more concentrated at night when the chicks are not drinking.

Often the chicks are put to bed at 6:00 PM and not let out until 8:00 AM, making the exposure time very long.

Temporary or permanent blindness and/or air sacculitis may occur, causing the loss of the birds. Incidentally, ostriches of all ages suffer the same results if exposed to ammonia fumes.

The answer to problems induced by ammonia lies in prevention, and prevention lies in proper ventilation.

It may be necessary to consult an expert in order to provide the proper airflow patterns, exhaust fans, multi-speed ceiling fans, and various shutters.

Stale air is not a precise scientific term, but stale air should be exhausted whether or not it contains ammonia fumes.

Another reminder—occasionally, get down to chick level and sniff the air. It may be vastly different from the air at human levels of five to seven feet.

Substrate

Several authors have estimated the numbers of hours or minutes in each day that an ostrich spends performing various functions. While differing times have been reported for eating, drinking, walking, running, etc., the largest portion of the time is spent in trying to eat something that will kill it.

Nothing that an ostrich eats will kill it faster than all that stuff that is put down for it to walk on.

Over the years we have used Bermuda grass, St. Augustine grass, Astroturf, indoor-outdoor carpeting, several different types of sand, gravel, concrete, DriDek flooring, and probably some others that we have forgotten, and with good reason.

The most important aspect of choosing a substrate is to remember that chicks are not very smart.

Shelter for older chicks.

You as the breeder have taken away their only role-models (the parents).

Certainly the chicks cannot learn from each other, so they eat everything that they can. The most available thing to eat is whatever they are walking on, and usually that is in great supply.

Whatever you decide to use in the beginning should be continued for the first three months because the chicks love security.

They love a stable environment. They love boredom.

Change is very upsetting; whenever there is change, they become upset, nervous, and insecure. Like many humans, when they become insecure, they find solace in eating and they will eat anything.

If a chick is started on grass, there is a good chance that the chick will take it for granted, will walk on it but not eat it. If you start with grass, stick with grass. If you start with sand, stick with sand. If you start on concrete, stick with concrete.

As the result of our twelve years of experience, we have built the last three chick barns in the following manner:

- Concrete on the inside (closed) portions of the barn.
- Concrete on the three-sided, covered outdoor porches.
- Concrete on the outside covered area, which is open on the sides.
- Runs covered with masonry sand.

Each of our barns has four complete sections for four separate groups of birds. Each inside shelter is 10' x 14'; each outside porch area (covered on 3 sides) is 10' x 12'; each outside area (roof only) is 10' x 44'; and each totally outside sand run is 10' x 100'.

Concrete constitutes the floor for all of the first three covered areas and the outside runs are dry masonry sand, which does not pack and does not readily produce impaction.

Bottom line on Substrate
- Do not give chicks anything foreign that they can eat.
- Start with something that you like and stay with it.
- Avoid anything that unravels or comes apart (carpeting, astroturf).
- Change and stress are open invitations to impaction.

Gravel and indoor/outdoor carpet fibers surgically removed from an impacted ostrich chick. (Photo courtesy Dr. Brett Hopkins)

Food

I'm spending the shortest time of all on food. Suffice it to say the following:
- We (collectively) do not yet fully understand the ostrich chick's nutritional requirements.
- All major feed companies make several starter feeds.
- Probably, all commercial feeds are far superior to the chick's wild or natural diet.
- Do not attempt to produce your own chick food. Experienced breeders have apparently developed successful formulas for older birds, but the feeding of chicks is no place to either experiment or economize.
- Choose a supplier who has sufficient business to insure that the food supply is fresh, and who is close enough to provide an uninterrupted supply.
- Do not buy large quantities of chick feed at any given time to avoid problems which relate to old feed, prolonged storage, improper storage, or excessive heat.
- Don't look for bargain feeds.
- Don't be misled by the claims that a feed that costs half as much as another is the same or is just as good.

Possibly the cheapest item in the breeder's budget is the cost of chick feed for the first three to six months of life. Just grin and bear it because that chick's first three months will tell it all.

We believe in free-feeding, that is, keeping food always available. If you think that your chicks are eating too much, as evidenced by excessive weight gain, give them their regular feed in the morning and in the evening and substitute alfalfa (rabbit) pellets during the middle of the day.

Rabbit pellets have a protein content of 14%-16% and both the taste of the alfalfa and the fiber content are pleasing to the chicks.

Food Additives

If, indeed, we are paying for and getting quality feed, why should we have to add to the feed?

At this point we are like the fellow who is not superstitious but thinks that it is silly to take chances, so he doesn't walk under ladders, doesn't let a black cat cross his path, and is careful not to spill salt at meals.

Most breeders feel safer if the feed is top-dressed with Clovite, and water-soluble vitamins are added to the drinking water.

Theoretically, it is possible to overdose on fat-soluble vitamins such as A, D, E, and K, because they can be stored not only in fat but in the liver.

While there are clearly-recognized syndromes of excessive A and D, I am not aware of any toxic effects of an oversupply of E or K.

Water-soluble vitamins such as the B complex and C must be obtained on a regular basis and since there is no recognized toxicity to excessive amounts, their addition to the drinking water is a sound policy.

Other trace vitamins and minerals are included in the multivitamin/mineral water-pack.

Beyond the use of the basic vitamins and minerals already listed, selective addition of such items as calcium, selenium, phosphorus, and pyridoxine should not be done except upon the advice of a real expert.

Much overmedication and overdosing of trace minerals have occurred as the result of some unsubstantiated anecdotal testimony, and much harm can be inflicted upon the chicks.

The word *trace* is used with good reason. Most trace minerals are a portion of, or are closely-related to, enzyme systems whose functions can be impaired, destroyed, or even reversed by a mass-action excess of minerals.

Never has it been more false to assume that if a little does a little good, a lot will do a lot of good.

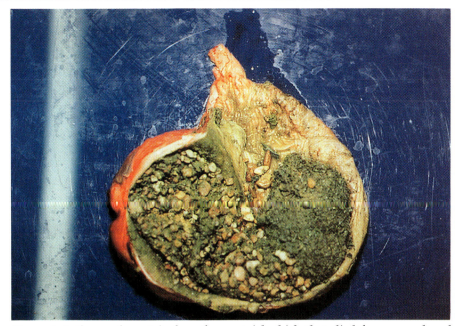

Proventriculus and ventriculus of an ostrich chick that died from gravel and carpet fiber overload. Most of the gravel is in the ventriculus; the green carpet fibers are in the proventriculus. (Photo courtesy Dr. Brett Hopkins)

Other so-called additives which we use at our ranch are green food coloring in the water and fresh-chopped spinach, supposedly as a treat.

A controlled study showed us that chicks are attracted to green water more than to clear water or water of other colors. They also prefer cool or even cold water so we use a lot of ice in the summer.

The spinach is a very poor nutritional item but it is a nice, safe source of fiber and it makes us feel good to offer them an item that they devour with such gusto.

Grit should not be necessary for the proper digestion of pellets

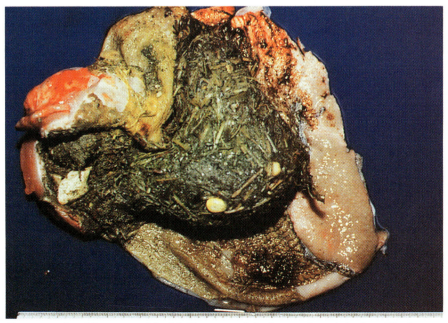

Grass overload in an ostrich chick's proventriculus and ventriculus. The brown areas at top and bottom are digested blood, due to hemorrhage from secondary clostridium perfringens infection. (Photo courtesy Dr. Brett Hopkins)

or starter crumbles. In the spirit of not taking chances, however, we offer small granite grit. The chicks may ingest grass stems, leaves, or other objects that could break down by a combination of grit and the muscular action of the ventriculus.

Do not use oyster shell grit because a great deal of the calcium can be absorbed, markedly elevating the serum calcium levels.

The final additive to consider is a method of establishing within the gastrointestinal tract of the chick a colony of friendly bacteria. Colonization of the intestinal tract occurs very quickly in all species because none of the food offered to humans or animals is sterile.

In the wild, chicks eat the droppings of the parents. Some commercial feeds have bacteria added. We have established a policy of giving chicks a preparation such as Benebac to start growth of bacteria known to help with fermentation of ingested food.

The administration of antibiotics destroys friendly bacteria easily—if antibiotics are used, the bacteria must be replaced.

Water

It appears obvious from the observation of ostrich chicks that the greater the amount of water consumed, the healthier the chick.

One exception to that observation can occur if a chick becomes very hot, drinks massive amounts of water, but *does not eat* and develops water intoxication. The condition is due to an excessive amount of water in proportion to serum electrolytes such as sodium, potassium, and chloride.

Either excessive drinking or a loss of electrolyte through diarrhea can cause the relatively low sodium and potassium to produce weakness, lack of coordination, dizziness and staggering, and can result in heart rhythm disturbances and death.

If a chick is observed to be having diarrhea or is drinking too much and develops the above signs, administration of a salt solution is mandatory to save it.

Fresh, cool, filtered and probably chlorinated water is essential to chicks' early survival. Later, older chicks will drink almost any kind of dirty water and show no signs of trouble—but not during the early months.

We add a small amount of green cake coloring, a multivitamin powder, and in the summer, some ice cubes to their water.

Medical Care

The success of any livestock operation is the production of naturally-healthy, strong offspring with high survival rates. There are obviously some animal species in which the offspring are few and far between. There are others in which thousands of live offspring or eggs must be produced in order for a very few to survive.

Humans require a gestation period of 266 days for the production of—usually—one offspring but all are expected to survive. Fish may lay thousands of eggs for each surviving fingerling because of the myriad of dangers standing between fertilization and the gaining of adulthood.

Oversimplification could cause one to assume that the fewer the eggs at the beginning, the higher the success rate is to be, and the more the eggs at the beginning, the lower the success rate is to be.

If one accepts this principle, another way to put it is the theory of the survival of the fittest.

Nowhere, perhaps, is that theory more applicable than in the raising of ostrich chicks. Whereas we do not advocate ceasing the treatment of sick chicks, working with minor deformities, and attempting in every way to increase the survival rate, the breeder must realize that there is a very sharp distinction between normal and abnormal chicks.

For a production market, it is feasible to raise a bird with one or more rolled toes. One can raise a production bird with a slightly deformed leg or beak, less-than-perfect body configuration, and maybe a black hen.

There are always a few borderline birds who will grow to production age but certainly should not—must not—be passed on as breeders.

Fortunately, most chicks with even moderate deformities do not survive and as their incapacity increases, must be destroyed. It is perfectly reasonable to apply splints to rolled toes, but it is far better to improve incubation errors which are thought to produce the problem.

The bottom line in a complete breeder to production chick industry is the establishment of sound, reproducible techniques of selection of breeders, feeding of breeders, collection of eggs, incubation of eggs, and hatching of eggs. If all these steps are proper, the percentage of good chicks should be very high, and of chicks with some type of problem very low.

We have spent a large fortune on veterinary treatment because we can't stand by and not try, but the answer is in the production of healthy birds, not the treatment of sick birds.

By now, every condition which we find ourselves treating and operating on should be preventable by better research, better education, and better management. That goes for omphalitis, yolk sac infection, impaction, crooked legs, and even the fading chick syndrome.

Once we master the elements of chick rearing—whether by genetics, vaccination, or by mastering the above list—the only times that we will have to call on our veterinarian is for treating injuries and carrying out health inspections when we sell the now-grown ostriches.

POST-SCRIPT

A final word on the rearing of chicks: At this point we in the industry are just as much beginners and babes as are the tiny chicks that we are trying to raise.

We, largely because of our higher intellects, have made some giant-leap assumptions that may possibly seem stupid in coming years.

Now, some of us look at these animals and think *big chicken* and try to apply chicken management procedures.

Some of us look at them and think *big turkey* and try to apply turkey management procedures.

We look at them and think *stupid*, so we treat them as stupid when if they were on their own they might survive better because they would not do the things that humans insist upon; would not eat the things that humans insist that they eat; they might pick different mates; and they might do a lot of things not only differently but maybe—just maybe—better.

We must continue research at all levels whether on mom-and-pop farms or at major universities. We must share with others our successes and our defeats.

In some instances we must forego the search for patentable products so that the industry can expand more quickly than it is doing right now.

Above all, we must be honest with ourselves and in our contacts both with other breeders and potential customers. We have a great deal to gain and nothing to lose if we can work together toward the goal of a real ostrich industry.

May all your eggs be fertile.

Sausage and a variety of processed ostrich meats. (Photo courtesy Texas A&M University)

OSTRICH MEAT

*Craig Morris, Ph. D.
Texas A & M University
College Station, Texas*

The most enjoyable part of the ostrich industry is the meat. Like no other food, meat provides valuable vitamins, minerals and protein to keep us healthy and strong, while at the same time is one of the most satisfying foods known.

What food provides more pleasure than a spicy sausage, a juicy roast, or a thick steak?

In this chapter we will cover the nutritional profile and consumer acceptance of ostrich meat, how the ostrich industry may enter the meat market, and recipes collected from ostrich enthusiasts over the past couple of years.

NUTRITIONAL PROFILE

Nutritionists and doctors have recommended decreasing consumption of many meats due to their high fat content. But in contrast to many other meat products, ostrich meat is extremely low in fat. There are only two or three grams of fat in a 100-gram serving (about three and a half ounces, or slightly larger than the size of a deck of cards). This is close to the recommended serving size of meat products.

Table 1 on the next page compares the fat content of cooked lean meat products. Obviously, ostrich ranks well among other lean meats. In addition to total fat, the percentage of saturated fat is very low in ostrich steak (similar to roasted skinless chicken breast).

Ostrich meat is also quite low in calories, with only about 120 to 130 calories in a 100-gram serving. Table 2 shows the caloric content of cooked lean meats. Once again, ostrich steak ranks well.

To compare ostrich steak with other foods on your shelf, a 52-gram serving of instant rice has 190 calories.

The list of nutritional benefits of ostrich meat goes on and on. It is high in iron (similar to beef, with about three milligrams in a 100-gram serving), and consistent with other lean meats with high protein (about 25 per cent).

Ostrich meat, like all animal products, has cholesterol, and it is somewhat typical in cholesterol levels with other lean meats.

Table 3 shows that ostrich is lower in cholesterol than chicken, but higher than beef. (Contrary to popular opinion, chicken—breast or thigh, skin off—is lower in fat and calories than lean beef, *but it is actually higher in cholesterol*.)

Ostrich meat has between 76 and 96 mg of cholesterol in a 100-gram cooked serving of ostrich steak. But what do these numbers mean to consumers?

There is a difference between dietary cholesterol (the cholesterol in your food) and blood cholesterol (the cholesterol circulating in your body).

Dietary cholesterol comes from animal products like meat, eggs, cheese and milk. The 1988 National Cholesterol Education Program recommended that everyone over two years of age consume fewer than 300 milligrams of cholesterol a day. This recommendation was in response to the widely-accepted assumption that dietary cholesterol may influence blood cholesterol levels. Elevated blood cholesterol has been associated with increased risk of heart disease.

There are actually different forms of blood cholesterol. The *good* cholesterol is high-density lipoprotein (HDL) and the *bad* cholesterol is low-density lipoprotein (LDL). Both of these are found in our blood, but they have different relationships to heart disease.

HDLs help protect against coronary heart disease. Exercise and weight loss may increase HDL levels. LDLs influence the cholesterol that is deposited on artery walls and are associated with an elevated risk for coronary heart disease. Smoking and obesity may increase LDL levels.

The 1988 National Cholesterol Education Program developed the table on the facing page for adults to classify their blood cholesterol levels (Table 4).

Recent research has indicated that for many people, dietary cholesterol may have little effect on blood cholesterol levels. Dr. Donald McNamara of the University of Arizona indicated that for every 100-milligram per day change in dietary cholesterol, blood cholesterol changed only 2.2 mg/dl, or just one per cent.

This change is not always a simple reduction of only the bad cholesterols. We may see dietary cholesterol reductions actually reducing the good cholesterol more than the bad cholesterol in the blood. This could place an individual at an even higher risk of coronary disease.

Dietary fat can also raise blood cholesterol levels. In general, saturated fats have been associated with elevated blood cholesterol levels, while monounsaturated and polyunsaturated fats have not. However, there isn't a simple relationship between the type of

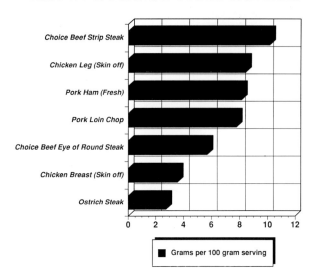

Table 1. Fat Content of Cooked Lean Meats

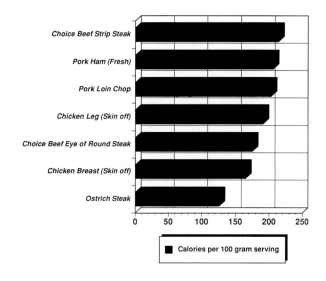

Table 2. Caloric Content of Cooked Lean Meats

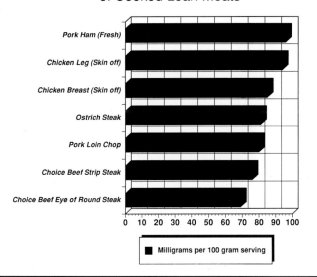

Table 3. Cholesterol Content of Cooked Lean Meats

TABLE 4: RECOMMENDED BLOOD CHOLESTEROL LEVELS

CATEGORY	TOTAL BLOOD CHOLESTEROL MG/DL	LDL CHOLESTEROL MG/DL
Desirable	<200	<130
Borderline High	200-239	130-159
High	>240	>160

fat consumed and your blood cholesterol level. Many other factors play into the blood cholesterol equation that the scientific community does not yet completely understand.

We know that genetics is a major reason individuals have elevated blood cholesterol levels. Unfortunately, due to genetics, some people are going to have high blood cholesterol levels regardless of changes in their diet.

All animals produce cholesterol in their bodies. It is a vital constituent of animal-cell membranes and is a required precursor of several sex hormones and vitamins. It is a necessary component of our systems, and even if dietary cholesterol was completely eliminated, we would still have cholesterol in our bodies—fortunately.

The best way to maintain reasonable cholesterol levels is to follow dietary guidelines, maintain ideal body weight, exercise, and avoid smoking.

Ostrich meat can easily fit into the dietary guidelines. Ostrich meat is very lean, with only 2 to 4 grams of fat and 120 to 130 calories in a 100-gram cooked serving.

As for your own blood cholesterol levels, have your doctor check them. If they are high, let your doctor prepare a treatment that fits your individual needs.

Research into the nutritional benefits of ostrich meat is not complete and more research into this area must be funded. Research must look into the role of diet on the nutritional profile of ostrich meat.

Who knows? With further research, ostrich meat may be found to be lower in cholesterol than we currently believe. However, until more research is completed, we will have to rely on the limited data we have to work with.

CONSUMER ACCEPTANCE

The nutritive value of ostrich meat will help its marketability, but by no means guarantees ostrich steaks on the plates of consumers world-wide. There are other variables to deal with, the most important of which are taste, price and consistency.

Contrary to popular perception, the reason chicken is everywhere today is not because it is low in fat and calories. Chicken is popular because it is cheap, tastes good, and always tastes the same. When was the last time you had chicken that tasted different or tougher than you expected? Probably never.

Beef, pork, and chicken retail for between $1 and $6 per pound. What is the current price for ostrich meat? Often much higher. Ostrich meat will not be widely accepted, or even tried by most consumers at an unreasonable price.

There are currently other variables that dictate the price of a live ostrich, but will the ostrich industry wait for the market value of the birds to drop before we begin marketing meat products? We should hope not. These are variables we must deal with in the ostrich industry.

The taste of ostrich meat is excellent. Those of us who have had the pleasure of eating it know how good it its. However, those of us who have cooked ostrich meat know that it presents some culinary challenges.

Remember that ostrich is very lean. Lean meats must be cooked differently. Do you cook a lean chicken breast the same way you cook a hamburger? Of course not. Why should you cook an ostrich steak the same way you cook a hamburger?

All lean meats will dry out at higher internal cooked temperatures. Ostrich is no different. If you overcook ostrich without adding sauces or marinades, it will be dry and unacceptable in flavor.

We need to work together as an industry to publish ostrich recipes that work well and are easy to prepare. You don't have to look any farther than your television to see that other meat industries are doing this.

Just as beef tenderloin eats differently and is more valuable than beef eye of round or top sirloin steaks, and chicken breast eats differently and is more valuable than chicken thigh or leg meat, not all ostrich muscles are the same. However, the ostrich industry as a whole is not yet marketing ostrich muscles separately.

When you do find ostrich meat in a restaurant, the chefs often have no idea what muscles they are preparing. Research shows that some ostrich muscles are significantly tougher than others, some are leaner, and some muscles are simply more acceptable to consumers.

Certain ostrich muscles from the thigh region, like *M. obturatorius medialis*, *M. iliotibialis cranialis*, and *M. iliofemoralis* are much more tender. And muscles from the lower leg, like *M. gastrocnemius* and *M. fibularis longus* are tougher,

Ostrich carcasses. Note the color. Diners who order ostrich dishes for the first time in restaurants are often surprised to find that ostriches are, like many wild fowl, red-meat birds. (Photo courtesy Texas A&M University)

and should be made into sausage or ground products, or at the least, slow cooked like a roast.

If the ostrich industry continues to allow ostrich meat to be marketed in this manner, first-time consumers of ostrich meat may have unacceptable eating experience. When this happens to one new consumer, we lose several potential consumers by word of mouth. These consumers are lost for no reason but our own lack of preparation.

Out of all of the non-tradional meat products trying to enter the market today, ostrich meat is the most promising. But if this industry waits too long, it will run out of time, and possibly its market potential will be lost.

The ostrich industry needs to form alliances with reputable restaurants and hotels, and work closely with them in the marketing and preparation of palatable meat products.

If consumers are not educated, and they prepare ostrich meat products incorrectly, they will not enjoy it. People who try ostrich for the first time and do not like it are unlikely ever to try it again.

If consumers have good eating experiences at restaurants, they will want a similar experience at home. Consumers will then try to prepare ostrich products at home the same way they were prepared when they dined out.

If consumers prepare ostrich products correctly, the ostrich meat industry will have arrived and it will have guaranteed its place on the plates of consumers.

Consumers demand good taste in their foods, and ostrich meat will have to be marketed as a great-tasting product and not just good for you. Unfortunately, there is currently little information available on ostrich-meat cookery methods, recipes, and consumer acceptability of these products.

COOKING METHODS

Lean meats are good for you, but typically they aren't as tasty to eat as meat which is higher in fat content. Fat keeps meat juicy and enhances the flavor when cooked, but when there is not that much fat to begin with, cooked meats often turn out dry and with an aftertaste.

Ostrich meat is no exception to this rule. It is a great tasting product, but it can be a challenge to prepare properly.

With lean meats, there are several options when it comes time to cook. Slicing the meat into thin strips and cooking them for a shorter period of time (as in wok cooking) works very well, as does cooking steaks and roasts to a lower degree of doneness.

A medium-rare degree of doneness (at or slightly above 145 degrees F) works the best. That is high enough to prevent any food-borne illnesses, but low enough to keep meat juicy.

Sauces or marinades that will keep meat juicy and cover aftertastes work well with ostrich meat.

Adding fat back to the meat in the form of oil or butter can guarantee a mouth-watering steak.

Any of these will work well when preparing ostrich steaks or roasts. What can't be done is to treat ostrich steak like a pork chop by cooking it on the grill until it is well done, and still expect it to taste good.

When I was at Texas A&M University, we conducted several consumer evaluations of different ostrich-meat products.

In one study, we compared ostrich steaks from four locations in the carcass, with a USDA-Choice beef strip steak. We cooked the steaks to a medium-rare degree of doneness and added no spices, seasonings or sauces.

The results indicate that there were no significant differences in acceptability between beef and ostrich, and one ostrich cut was not significantly different for flavor acceptability with beef steak.

Considering the nutritional advantages of the ostrich steaks over the beef steaks, these results are promising.

The results of this study have been published in the *Journal of Poultry Science* and are available by contacting Texas A&M University in College Station, Texas.

In a second study, we compared an ostrich and pork Polish sausage with an all-pork Polish sausage. The ostrich-pork sausage was prepared with 2/3 ostrich lean and 1/3 pork fat. The pork fat was added to keep the product moist and juicy at a high degree of doneness.

We then served the two products to consumers. Results indicate there were no significant differences in texture, tenderness, flavor intensity, flavor acceptability, or overall acceptability. This study has also been published in the *Journal of Animal Sciences*, and can be obtained by contacting Texas A&M University.

The results of the studies back my belief that processed ostrich meat items show great promise as products to be used in wide-scale ostrich-meat marketing programs.

Processed meat products have several advantages over whole muscle cuts. They are very consistent in flavor, have a longer shelf life, and are very easy to prepare. A product like our Polish sausage would work out well for the ostrich industry.

We know that whole-muscle ostrich cuts are somewhat inconsistent in flavor, have a short shelf life (like all fresh meats), and offer challenges to cook properly.

I believe that sausages, hams and other processed ostrich meat products will sell well in the market place and have the case life necessary to wait for interested consumers. And, unlike other processed-meat products, ostrich products are very healthy to eat.

The ostrich and pork sausage we prepared was less than 12 per cent fat, which compares very favorably with other sausage products that can contain as much as 30 per cent fat.

Two sausage recipes we used will be found on the next page.

THE MARKET FOR OSTRICH MEAT

We have established that ostrich meat is very nutritious and delicious, but ostrich is currently not available in most stores. To get ostrich meat into retail cases, there are many things the ostrich industry must do.

Reaching the grocer's meat case may be difficult simply because the ostrich industry is very segmented. This is in contrast to many other food industries where the companies who raise livestock are the same as those who process and sell the meat products.

Separation allows for small family farms to exist and for people to concentrate on the segments of the industry they enjoy. For most ostrich producers, this means raising ostriches and not worrying about other segments, like producing meat products.

The only problem with a segmented industry is that there is often a lack of communication between different segments of the industry and potential profits are often never realized.

In the beef industry, another segmented industry, a study entitled the National Beef Quality Audit showed that for every steer or heifer slaughtered, nearly $280 was lost.

There were a variety of reasons for the $280 loss, ranging from overproduction of fat to branding animals in the wrong location, but the take-home message was that the beef industry's worst enemy was itself.

The ostrich industry is in a unique situation in that it can learn from other established meat industries what mistakes have been made and not repeat them. The ostrich industry is young enough that alliances between different segments don't have to break down the status quo, but can become the industry norm from the outset.

With alliances, producers can come together and share management practices and bargain as one unit. Producers can then locate and work with meat lockers to provide the needed numbers of birds in the condition the meat processor desires. The meat processor can then guarantee consistent quality and quantity of products to their patrons.

The most-often-heard complaint from meat processors today

Preparing an ostrich carcass for study.
(Photo courtesy Texas A&M University.

isn't that ostrich meat won't sell, but that it is too expensive and there is no consistent supply available. When producers come together to form alliances, they can provide packers with a consistent supply. Once the meat locker has a consistent supply of ostrich meat and by-products, the packer can find restaurants and retail outlets to market the end products. Producer partnerships can then target their input expenses to meet the value of a live bird based on what meat lockers can pay for it.

With alliances between producers and retailers of ostrich meat made, the ostrich industry will be well on its way to guaranteeing itself a bright future.

PROCESSED OSTRICH MEAT RECIPES

These recipes would work well for your local meat locker to process your ostrich into a delicious boneless ham product or Polish sausage. They are the recipes that we used here at Texas A&M University for our sensory evaluations, and they were found to be very acceptable to consumers when compared to high-quality traditional all-pork products.

CURED OSTRICH HAM-STYLE PRODUCT

Cured ostrich ham-style product is produced by the following sequence. Approximately 50 lb of lean ostrich muscle pieces, trimmed free of connective tissue, are stored at 1°C and are injected with a cure to 110% of green weight to yield a content of 2.25% NaCl, 2.0% dextrose, 0.3% sodium tripolyphosphate, 550 ppm sodium erythorbate, and 200 ppm NaNO2.

Pumped pieces are ground through a 3.8 cm kidney-shaped plate. The lean meat is vacuum-tumbled for 40 minutes and vacuum-stuffed (Vemag, Verden, Germany) into 7.6 cm diameter fibrous, prestuck casings (Viskase, Chicago, IL).

Casings are then clipped (Tipper Tie, Apex, NC), hung on a smokehouse truck, and refrigerated at 1°C for 24 hours. Stuffed casings are then cooked, using a staged cooking cycle to an internal temperature of 71.1°C, and smoked with hickory sawdust (Bruner Ivory Handle Co., Hope, AR).

Cooked ham-style products then are chilled at 1°C for 12 hours, vacuum packaged, and stored at 1°C prior to slicing (3 mm thick).

POLISH-STYLE SAUSAGE

Cured ostrich and pork Polish sausages are made by the following sequence. Ostrich lean (66.6%) and pork trim (33.4%) about 20% fat are coarse-ground through a 1.27 cm plate, and paddle-mixed with a Polish Kielbassa sausage seasoning mixture of salt, dextrose, spices, MSG (4.55%), garlic powder, and sodium erythorbate (A. C. Legg Packing Co, Birmingham, Al), and 0.25% Prague(r) Powder (containing 93.75% sodium chloride and 6.25% sodium nitrite), and 3.0% ice.

After mixing for 5 minutes, the meat is reground through a .328 cm plate and held at 7.1°C for 2 hours to allow for cure color development. The product is then vacuum-stuffed (Vemag) into 30 mm clear cellulose (No-Jax) casings (Viskase), and cooked/smoked to a temperature of 68.3°C using a staged cooking cycle.

Sausages are chilled at 1 degree C for 12 hours, the casings removed, and the product vacuum packaged and stored at 1 degree C or frozen.

For the ostrich industry to sustain its development past the year 2000, it will have to become a permanent part of the meat industry. The meat and livestock industry is one of the largest, most competitive, and well-developed markets in the United States.

In fact, 35.6% of all receipts from farming come from the meat animal and poultry sector alone. Beef marketings brought in over $37.8 billion in the United States last year.

What few people outside the meat and livestock industry understand is that it is very difficult to make a profit raising livestock or producing meat. Most livestock and meat producers operate under low profit margins, and are continually challenged to incorporate new technology to increase efficiency.

However, the meat industry is currently in the midst of a major revolution. The food preferences of American consumers have changed in recent years, potentially opening a window for ostrich to establish itself as a meat of choice in the years to come.

Currently, Americans spend over $600 billion a year on food, which is more than 13% of disposable income. More than 17% of food dollars are spent on meats. This provides a large market share which we can capture.

The bad news is that, in the past fifteen years, Americans have decreased their beef consumption by 30%. Today we consume about 62.8 pounds of beef per person per year.

In response to this trend, different meat companies and industry promotion boards have greatly increased spending on development of new products and advertising to maintain market share.

Since ostrich meat will probably enter the market as a slightly-higher-priced product, we should concentrate our market development on the consumer patterns of upper-income Americans.

Unfortunately, in the past decade, the wealthy have had the most significant decrease in their red-meat consumption (down 31%), and consume less meat per capita than any other income group.

But the good news is that, even though wealthy Americans eat less meat, they still spend more total money per capita on meat than any other income group. This indicates that the wealthy prefer to purchase higher-priced cuts (like ostrich).

In addition, the wealthy had the most significant increase in their poultry and fish consumption (up 20%), indicating that they are more receptive to new and healthy products (also like ostrich).

Even though we have seen significant drops in beef consumption in the United States, per capita consumption of meat, poultry and fish is higher today than ever. In 1992 we consumed more than 189 pounds of meat, poultry and fish per person per year. That is a 6.6% increase over 1960 values.

The increase is due, in large part, to a total poultry production increase of 418% since 1960. We consume almost 46 pounds of chicken and 14 pounds of turkey per person per year. The significant strides the poultry industry has made in recent years should be an inspiration for our industry to follow.

Producing a market for ostrich meat will not be easy, but the opportunity is there. Consumers are currently changing their eating habits and looking for more healthy alternatives.

A recent survey showed that two out of three consumers believe their diet could be healthier and are concerned about the nutritional content of their foods.

More importantly, among nutritional attributes, 60% of consumers consider fat content the most significant factor influencing health. We in the ostrich industry know that ostrich meat is one of the lowest-fat meat products available.

But before the ostrich industry rushes to put ostrich into the meat case tomorrow, it must remember that taste is the most important factor influencing consumer purchasing decisions (ahead of nutrition). It must continue palatability research to guarantee the taste of ostrich meat that reaches consumers.

If the ostrich industry enters the meat market improperly and unprepared, it will do far more damage than good. Alliances made between producers and retailers are the key to the success of the industry.

Once the ostrich industry knows its consumers and products better, it will simply be a matter of connecting the dots to bring them together.

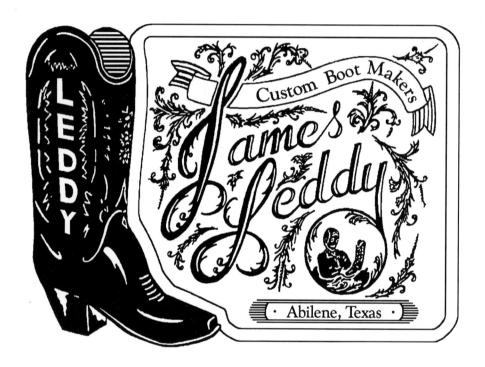

AN INTERVIEW WITH JAMES LEDDY

James Leddy Custom Boot Makers
Abilene, Texas

On December 27, 1994, publisher Charley Elrod and editor Claire Drenowatz drove to Abilene to talk with bootmaker James Leddy, about ostrich-skin boots and the boot business.

E: *Charley Elrod*
L: *James Leddy*
D: *Claire Drenowatz*

D: I suppose I should start by asking how you got into this business in the first place.

L: I grew up in it. My dad had a shop in Tulsa, where we were from. We moved from Tulsa to San Angelo in 1949.

The first year, when I was eleven years old, I started shining shoes. I started stitching boot tops the next year. It's all I knew.

E: You just went from there.

L: We moved down here in 1953, and my dad went partners with his brother. He was a saddle maker, and he wanted to start making boots.

Dad sold out to him in 57 and I kept working for him. I quit him once and went to Brownwood and worked for six months, came back. Quit again, went to San Angelo and worked for six months, came back. Then he moved out on First Street, and decided he wanted to retire.

So I bought the boot department from him, and I was back on Pine Street, for about five years, for myself, and then moved to El Paso and Cowtown Boots out there.

The old man that had Cowtown wanted me to come out there and make a real good handmade boot. We made a deal and the old man died the month before I moved out there.

D: When was that? Did you go anyway?

L: That was in '70. Yeah, I went. His boys, they were good boys. They went across the river, got six or seven of the best hands, got papers on them, and we built boots for about six or seven months, real good boots.

And they finally decided it just takes too long to make a real good boot, but they could still sell anything they could turn out. They got to making a thousand pairs a day, and I didn't want to stay for that.

So my contract was for a year, and at the end of the year I came back here, moved on this corner, that was in '71, been here ever since.

D: Have you been making ostrich boots all this time, or is that something new?

L: The ostrich started out in the fifties.

D: Have you always had a good supply of skins?

L: Yeah. We always have. Paid for it through the nose.

D: Uh huh. You did have a little grin when I asked if you had a good supply.

L: Well, John G. Mahler, over in Dallas, was the only importer in

James Leddy showing an ostrich hide to Jonelle and Todd Shelton Elrod.

the United States for years. And he handled soles and insoles and if you bought so much sole leather, well, he would let you have so many ostrich skins.

And it was a wooly bear, there in the late seventies, early eighties. I'd buy my soles from him, and sell them to a repair shop.

Mahler got to where he was sending me ten skins of ostrich a month. For a guy my size, I mean I took it, I wasn't about to tell him, no, John, I can't handle it, but I'd always sell off some.

And one time I had about $50,000 worth of ostrich skins out in my garage . . .

E: (whistle)

L: . . . and we had a fire here, in '84, and I knew I didn't have enough insurance, so I sold about $25,000 worth of skins to a guy in El Paso. You talk about catching hell, John let me know about it . . .

D: Mahler?

L: . . . I said "Hell John, I had to have some money, I didn't have no money but I had ostrich skins. I had to sell some." He wasn't happy, but he let it slide.

John died about three years ago, that's why you see ostrich everywhere now. But they still get good prices.

D: Because he doesn't control the market?

L: Because he doesn't control the market anymore.

D: Where do most of the skins come from?

L: South Africa.

D: Still?

L: Far as I know.

E: We were talking about that on the way up from San Antonio. All those restrictions about not trading with South Africa because of apartheid, how did they get around that? Do you have any idea?

L: All I know is that ostrich skins kept coming in.

D: Yeah, just like DeBeers and diamonds. If there's a market, someone will find a way.

E: Klein Karoo is the union, cooperative actually, that controls ostrich exports. John G. was the only importer here for a long time. There was one on the east coast for a while, but . . .

D: Do you have any idea how he got the control?

L: He'd been in the leather business for years and years. He'd sell some ostrich skins to Ken Davis, there in Dallas, and Davis would mark it up and sell it to the little boot makers.

But Mahler controlled it. He'd allow Justin so many skins, he'd allow Tony Lama so many skins, and he had it all sold before it came into the country.

D: Well, that makes perfectly good sense if you're trying to control a market.

L: And he'd just keep the price up.

D: When he died, did the prices change much?

L: No, they just kept going up and up and up. In the last five years I've paid as high as $52 a foot.

D: That's how they're measured? By the square foot?

L: Uh huh. The lowest I've paid recently is about $39 a square foot.

D: How do you measure something like an ostrich hide? I mean, they're not exactly regular in shape.

L: They just run them through a machine and everything is measured. This one here (showing a hide) is 17 square feet, thats $746.80 worth of ostrich hide.

D: Do you have a use for the whole hide? Isn't there a lot of waste?

L: Well, you cut the full quill, sometimes we cut the smooth part. We get $1250 a pair for the full quill, $750 for the smooth.

D: What do you do with all the little leftover stuff? On any of your hides?

L: We don't just throw it away. We make belts out of the necks, other stuff. Now, there for a long time I was cutting a lot of patchwork, for boot tops. I used a lot of scraps like that.

D: Oh, that sounds neat.

L: Like that pretty purse you've got.

D: Yeah, I was thinking along the lines of purses, but a pair of boots, I've never seen a pair of boots like that.

(Handling a hide) So this is the prime part, where the quills were. Well, that makes sense, otherwise it looks like just any other soft leather. I didn't realize how soft this stuff is. I guess I figured it for being a lot tougher.

L: It's soft, but it wears just fantastic.

E: I'd have every kind of boot made, but James said "Charley you can't afford as many kinds of boots as you'd like to have." Years ago, I wanted a pair of eel-skin boots, but James told me to go ahead and get another pair of ostrich, because they wear real well.

Over the years, James has made me elephant, lizard, horse hide, kangaroo, calf, hog hide, rough-out, and black patent leather to wear with my tux, but I've never had anything better than ostrich for the softness and the durability.

D: I saw a whole bunch of colors out there. How many do you get it in? Or can you get any color you want?

L: About twenty, I guess.

D: Is that something that changes, like other colors do, with the seasons and with the whims of the fashion industry? Or do boots stay pretty much the same?

L: It changes a little, but not much.

D: What sells best?

L: In ostrich, probably that brown Charley's got on there. Or black is a real big color.

D: What color is the hide naturally?

L: Kind of a grayish white, not much color at all. (Pulls out a skin.) Now here's an ostrich skin from a local boy lost his bird. He had it tanned here in the States, and the color isn't nearly as good, and it's stiffer.

E: James, from what I've heard in the industry, in other parts of the world they can use chromium-based tanning process, and EPA says we can't use that here. Is that the key, or is that just what I hear?

L: I've heard that, Charley, and I don't know of any leather that's tanned in the states using chrome. [Note: we later found that, while it's not prohibited, using a highly toxic heavy metal like chromium requires very expensive safety precautions, and few tanners in this country use it.]

D: Are you selling more ostrich boots now that people are raising them?

L: No. Since I got above $1,000 for a pair of ostrich boots, I'm not selling half the ostrich I was two years ago.

D: Is that because of the market, the recession and stuff?

L: Yeah, that, and people just say $1,000 is just too much. But this year, I've been selling ostrich again . . .

E: The economy's been a little better, James.

L: Yeah, that, and they wore some other boots, and they say, hell, the ostrich lasts better than two pairs of kangaroo boots . . .

D: Really! I would have thought the kangaroo'd be a tougher hide.

L: No. Kangaroo's about the only thing that's as soft as ostrich, but it scuffs up easier.

D: I see. So this is not necessarily particularly tough, it just doesn't scuff as bad. Is that because of the tanning or finish, or is it inherent?

L: I'd say it's inherent, because if it was in the tanning, they'd do it to the kangaroo too.

D: This ostrich skin here, has it been split, like a cowhide?

L: No, this is as it comes off the bird, the whole skin. And it's real fleshy. I think that's one reason it doesn't crack. Because there's a lot more fat in the skin than in other hides.

D: Earlier, you mentioned Jane Seymour. How did she learn about you? How does anyone hear about James Leddy, Boot Maker?

L: They were working up close to Anson, and she'd seen a cowboy boot I'd made, so while they were here they came by.

D: You've got autographed photos of a lot of famous people on the wall.

L: Well, I do a lot of boots for the older country and western folks. Mel Tillis, Faron Young . . .

D: The older ones?

L: Yeah. I've been doing boots for Mel Tillis for, oh, about eighteen years, nineteen years. Faron Young, back into the sixties. George Jones, Hank Snow, Jimmy Dean (chuckle), Buck Owens, lots of . . .

D: Why did you laugh about Jimmy Dean?

L: Oh, I got a picture of him out there, I started building boots

James Leddy with ostrich hides and boots.

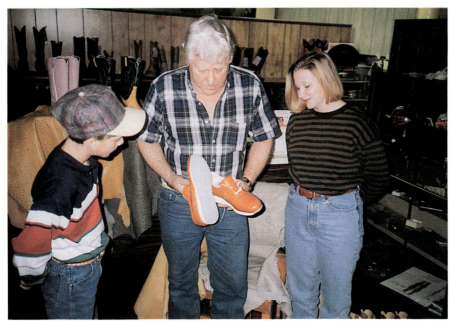
Showing the younger generation custom-made ostrich shoes.

for him when he was about Charley's age . . .

E: Twenty-six.

D: You said the *older* country and western stars. After looking at some of the photographs in your book with those wild designs, I should think some of the younger guys would really get into that.

L: Well, these younger guys, the big ones, Justin, Tony Lama will furnish their boots.

E: To get their endorsement.

D: I see. Just like everything else, you get rich and famous and everyone gives you things for free. I don't understand the logic there . . . 'scuse me, I'm poor, I'll endorse the heck out of your boots.

E: Doesn't have quite the same appeal, hunh?

L: Jimmy Dean brought us out to Reno, had us measure some folks for boots out there. I think that was the first time I'd ever been in a gambling casino, man I just couldn't believe my eyes, it was such a crowd.

D: Do you have many customers that you deal with for years, and just keep reordering?

L: Oh, yes. Many. Most of them, I guess. We do take new measurements once in a while, because people's feet change.

D: How long does a good pair of boots last?

L: Anywhere from a year to fifteen years. I've got some fellas who'll run through a pair in a year . . .

E: 'Cuz they never wear anything else.

L: They just put them on and hit those cow lots in them, and they get pretty beat up.

E: James made me my first pair when I was fifteen and he was on South First.

D: Eleven years ago.

E: Pretty close.

D: Right. And I've got a bridge . . .

L: I had one customer come in about three months ago, I've built boots for him for twenty-five years, maybe. His wife said he should get him a new pair of work boots, rough-out boots.

And he said, "I don't need none."

She said, "Yeah, you do, you got patches all over."

He asked me, "James, what do you get for a pair of rough-out calf?"

"Four and a half," I said.

And he asked, "How much stitching will you put on there for four and half?"

"Two rows," I told him.

He said, "Remember, now, I'm ninety years old."

I told him, "Hell, if you're ninety years old and want a pair of work boots, for $450 I'll put any damned thing you want on 'em, no charge."

D: I noticed the calendar and the books out front . . .

L: Yeah, I had a big writeup in Southern Living last month.

D: Is this something you try to keep doing, keep people coming in?

L: No, they just keep coming.

E: Claire, when you make the best boots, you get a lot of word-of-mouth publicity—and that's the best kind.

D: Well, of course, but even the top movie stars have publicity agents. Obviously James doesn't need one.

L: Actually, I've got some fantastic customers. They keep sending me their friends.

And I've got a few others . . . I've got one customer, I've had about ten years, I guess. He ranches near here, and man, he's a tough hombre. He was in here one day to get some ostrich boots and some work boots.

And he said, "James, I need another pair of work boots. Can't you build 'em and put my initials and stuff in there, and more stitching than two rows?"

And I told him, "Yeah, I can do that. For more money."

And he went on and on and told me what a good customer he was, and how he was such a good ole (expletive deleted) besides, and how I should make him a pair with his initials for no extra money.

And every time he came to town he'd drop in and tell me again.

So finally I made him a pair with his initials. Big as day. S-O-B. Boy did he howl. But he wore 'em.

E: You know, I bet he shows them to everyone he meets, too.

D: I notice you always say that you build a pair of boots.

L: Well, I guess that's just the way I've always thought of it. Because you start from the ground up, and every little piece is done by hand, and you're always adding on to what you built before. So it's more like a construction project than say, sewing a skirt.

D: I noticed some ostrich shoes in the other room. What are they, golf shoes? Is that new?

L: Yeah, one of my customers thought it might be a good idea. Just to have something a little different. So I gave it a try. And we're selling a few.

And tennis, well, I guess they call 'em running shoes now. Yeah, we're branching out a little.

D: What's next?

L: Heck, I gotta catch up with the orders I've got before I start anything new. But I'm open to suggestion.

D: Well, we'll just have to keep an eye on you and see what you come up with. Thanks for talking to us.

We learned later, from someone else, that in 1993, at the Boot and Saddlemakers Roundup in Brownwood, Texas, an annual gathering of about 600 of the best, James Leddy was voted Bootmaker of the Year.

- ce & cd

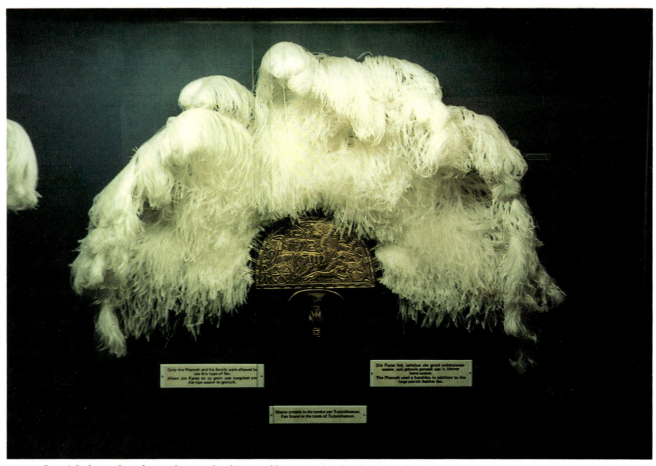
Ostrich fan taken from the tomb of Tutankhamun, in the C. P. Nel Museum, Oudtshoorn, South Africa. (Photo courtesy James Sales)

OSTRICH FEATHERS

James Sales, Ph. D.
University of Stellenbosch
Stellenbosch, South Africa

Although the ostrich feather was regarded by the ancient Egyptians as a symbol of justice, there is no evidence that ostrich plumes were worn as ornaments (De Mosenthal and Harting, 1879).

In their separate eras, the partiality of Elizabeth I of England and Marie Antoinette of France for ostrich feathers established them so firmly as a fashion must that their popularity lasted through the 19th century and into the early years of the 20th century (Holtzhausen and Kotze, 1990).

Although the demand for ostrich feathers nearly caused the extinction of the species, the same demand caused South African farmers to domesticate ostriches, thereby saving them from extinction (Wagner, 1986).

With proper care and management an ostrich will continue to give a feather crop without deterioration for about 35 years (Duerden, 1910a).The best feathers, however, are produced between the ages of 3 and 12 years (Wagner, 1986).

An adult ostrich can yield from 1 to 1.2 kg (2.2 to 2.6 lbs) of short feathers and 400 to 450 g (.9 to 1 lb) of plumes (Holtzhausen and Kotze, 1990).

Near the end of the 19th century De Mosenthal and Harting (1879) classified the qualities of feathers from wild ostriches from different parts of the world:
- Aleppo from the Syrian desert, most perfect in plumage, breadth, grace and color, very rare;
- Barbary from Tripoli;
- St. Louis from Senegal;
- Egypt, doesn't bleach well;
- Mogador from Morocco;
- Cape, similar in color to Aleppo but inferior quality;
- Yamani from Arabia, erroneously designated *Senegal*, most inferior in plumage, thin and poor.

The feather from the domesticated ostrich was much stiffer than the wild ostrich's, had not the natural graceful fall of the wild feather, and became stiff again after time, even when dressed and curled (De Mosenthal and Harting, 1879).

Because it seemed that domestication of the ostrich had led to a lower-quality feather, wild ostriches were imported from Barbary and Syria to South Africa between 1876 and 1903 in an attempt to improve feather quality of domesticated Cape birds by cross breeding (Smit, 1964).

According to Duerden (1910b) the feather of domesticated ostriches was so much improved by feeding strategies, management and breeding by around 1910 that it was of better quality than the wild feather from the time of De Mosenthal and Harting (1879). By 1911 the Cape feather was the best on the market.

The loose barbs of an ostrich feather, compared with the tightly-knit barbs of a white-wing dove.

Ostrich hen. Note how well her feathers blend into the background, perfect camouflage since predators see in black and white. (Photo courtesy C. P. Nel Museum, Oudtshoorn, SA)

Ostrich chick. Compare the loose, filamentary feathers to the downy feathers of a newly-hatched chicken.

Wild birds were again imported in 1912 from Barbary to South Africa and breeding experiments were again started in order to produce a feather of superior quality. This was due to potential stiff competition from American ostrich breeders. These experiments, however, ceased with the collapse of the ostrich feather market in 1914 (Smit, 1964).

PARTS OF THE FEATHER

The ostrich feather can be divided in the following parts (Duerden, 1909a):

(a) The *stem* or *scapus* is the strong middle axis of the feather, extending the whole length.

(b) The long upper part of the stem bears the *flue* and is known as the *shaft* or *rachis*.

(c) The *quill* or *calamus* is the lower, rounded, hollow, naked part of the stem that is embedded in the feather socket.

(d) The loose, soft, fluffy portion of the feather attached to each side of the shaft is called the *flue*. It corresponds with the web in ordinary compact feathers such as those of the fowl.

(e) The separate parts of the flue which are directly connected with the shaft are known as the *barbs*.

(f) The *barbules* are the short, fine, delicate parts of the flue which arise from each side of the barbs. They are split off from the barbs just as the barbs are split off from the shaft.

(g) The term *double floss*, or correctly *double flue*, is applied to the feathers where the barbs come off so closely from the shaft that they alternate with one another instead of being a single row down each side. This gives a double appearance to the flue.

(h) The *plume* is the part of the feather above the quill. The term *feather* includes the quill.

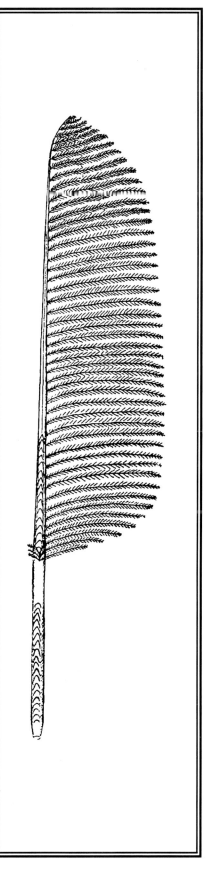

Diagram of a feather (the flue or vanes are shown on one side only). From Duerden, 1909a.

(i) The soft central part of a *green* feather in which blood flows is named the *pitch* or *medulla*.

(j) The small aperture on the inner side of the feather where the plume and quill meet is called the *superior* or *upper umbilicus*.

(k) The *inferior* or *lower umbilicus* is the circular opening at the tip of the fully ripe feather, through which the *pith* with the blood-vessels and nerves enter the feather from the skin.

(l) The thin, delicate *feather sheath* surrounds the growing feather before it opens out.

(m) The *feather socket* or *feather follicle* is the deep pit in the skin occupied by the lower part of the quill. The *feather germ* that gives rise to the new feather when feathers are plucked is situated at the bottom of the feather socket.

(n) The *follicle sheath* lines the socket.

(o) The tip of the feather is the end away from the quill, the butt is the end next to the quill.

KINDS OF FEATHERS

According to Duerden (1909a) the types of ostrich feathers can be classified as follows:

(a) Feathers are limited to definite areas, called the feather tracts or pterylae. These are separated by the featherless tracts (or apteria) over the lower part of each side of the body and on the entire leg of the adult bird.

(b) Small *contour* feathers, which are not of commercial value, occur over the body and wings. These feathers determine the general shape of the bird and overlap to protect the skin. They also help maintain the high temperature (103 F) of the bird. Farmers call these feathers body feathers.

(c) The *wing quills* or *remiges* are arranged in a single row and are the largest feathers in the wing. The *Whites* and *Bycocks* in the male and *Feminas* in the female are included in this group. The first wing quills (primaries) are attached to the bones of the wings (which correspond with the first two fingers and palm of the human hand), while the next (secondaries) are attached to the ulna (forearm).

(d) The first crop of wing quills grown by the chick are known as *spadonas*. These feathers taper toward the tip in a spear-like manner, hence the name spadona (Italian for a long, heavy sword).

(e) *Bycock* (or *fancies*) is the term used for the few parti-color wing quills towards each end of the row from the male bird.

(f) The upper *wing coverts* are arranged in rows above the wing quills. They are called *Blacks* in the male and *Drabs* in the female. These feathers are differentiated into major wing coverts (first row), median wing coverts (second row) and minor wing coverts (third row). The latter are never taken in plucking.

(g) The lower wing coverts, collectively known as *floss*, are the single row of light and fluffy feathers that cover the wing quills below. They are best seen when the wing is raised.

(h) The stumpy tail is covered by the *tail quills* or *rectrices*. These feathers are larger and differently colored from the body feathers, but smaller than the wing quills. They are known by the farmers as *tails*.

(i) The term *short stuff* is sometimes used to distinguish the wing coverts, floss, and tail quills from the *long stuff* (wing quills).

(j) On the skin around the wing quills and tail quills the small, hair-like *filoplumes* or *hair feathers* are found.

PLUMAGE

The entire covering of feathers on the bird is called the plumage. Due to differences between the bird's chick and adult condition, the covering is not the same at all periods. Four plumages can be distinguished in the ostrich's life cycle (Duerden, 1911).

NATAL OR BIRTH PLUMAGE

Feathers consist of small tufts of rather stiff rays or barbs, differing in length, starting from about the same level, no central shaft and no quill.

Feathers vary in color from light to dark brown or nearly black, giving a mottled appearance to the chick.

About a week or two after hatchng, the natal feathers begin to be pushed out of the feather sockets by the chick feathers growing below.

CHICK PLUMAGE.

Known as *spadona*, the chick plumage begins to appear soon after the chick is hatched and is complete at the age of about eight months. The chick feathers bear the natal down at the tip and are mottled in character because of the light brown upper and dark grey lower parts. Various kinds of feathers (body, neck, head, coverts, wing quills, and tail quills) start to show differences. No differences are found between sexes.

JUVENILE PLUMAGE

From four or five months of age the body feathers of the chick are pushed out gradually, one at a time, and are replaced by larger juvenal feathers. These feathers are of a uniformly dark grey or slate color with a rounded, not pointed, tip.

From eight or nine months of age the chick begin to lose its mottled appearance. All the juvenal feathers are fully ripe at the age of sixteen months, the last to ripen being the wing quills.

Slight sexual distinctions can be seen. Body feathers are darker in the female than in the male, ventral feathers are white in the female but change to black in the male. The wing quills of the male are pure white, while those of the female are tipped throughout with grey.

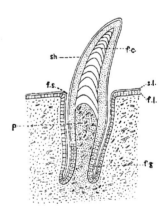

The illustrations here and on the next page are taken from Duerden, 1909a. They illustrate the stages of growth of feathers, from incubating chick to full plumage. In the first stage the feather germ (f.g.) is at first merely an upgrowth of the skin, consisting of the epidermis (ep) surrounding a similar projection of the dermis (dr). In the second stage the germ sinks down into the skin, the cavity which it occupies being the feather socket or follicle (fs). The portion of the dermis enclosed by the epidermis becomes the pith or medulla or pulp (p), which nourishes the growing feather. In a much later stage, the epidermis separates into the sheath layer (sl) and feather layer (fl). The cells of the feather layer above the germ cells become horny and change into feather material. The whole feather is enclosed in the sheath (sh) which also becomes horny. The pulp retreats from the upper part of the feather, which no longer needs nutrition.

ADULT PLUMAGE

Sex differences are most distinct in the adult plumage, reached when the birds are about two years old. The adult male plumage is characteristized by black body feathers and coverts, the female's by drab body feathers and coverts. The tail quills of the male are white below and yellowish brown above, while those of the female are a mottled light and dark grey.

GROWTH OF OSTRICH FEATHERS

The feather can be regarded as a highly specialized part of the skin. The skin of the ostrich, like that of other animals, consists of the epidermis or outer skin and the dermis or under skin. These two parts are closely joined together.

The epidermis consists of the horny or corneous layer (sheath layer) on the outside and the living active Malpighian layer (feather layer) on the inside. The epidermis is entirely devoid of blood vessels. Only extremely fine nerve branches pass into its lowermost part. The outer skin is thus incapable of any bleeding. The dermis, however, is richly supplied with both blood vessels and nerves.

Each feather is formed from the feather germ, a special group of cells, situated in the feather layer. New feathers are always formed below the old ones, each from a germ which is separate from the germ of the old feather.

The surface of the skin in a healthy ostrich is continually shedding the dead cells of the sheath layer. The feather layer continues to divide throughout the bird's lifetime, forming new cells which are gradually pushed outwards to replace those lost.

Long before hatching, the earliest state in the formation of feathers occurs. By the time the chick leaves the shell the down feathers, representing the natal or birth plumage, are already fully grown.

At an early stage the naked body of the developing embryo shows small cone-like projections (papillae) on its surface. These are the first rudiments or germs of the feather. At this stage the epidermis consists of a single layer of cells. The separation into outer sheath layer and inner feather layer has not taken place.

The next stage is where the feather germ begins to sink downwards into the skin. The germ is contained in a small rounded pit

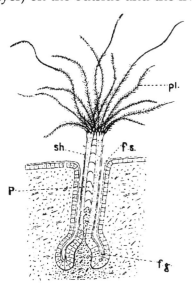
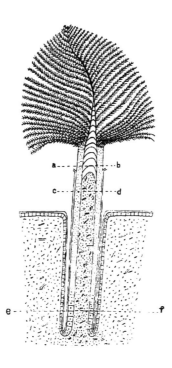
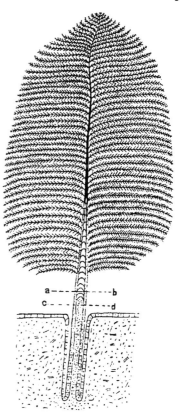

The fourth illustration shows the feather at the time the chick hatches. The sheath has broken away from the upper part of the feather and liberated the plumules (pl) of the natal feathers. The short thin quill is still partly within the socket (fs). The next feather, the spadona, is already forming below. Next, a partly-grown adult feather shows where the horny sheath has been preened away. The feather germ is still active. The pulp extends a bit beyond the mouth of the socket, but is cut off above by the feather cones. The line a-b shows where a cut would not bleed, c-d would cause bleeding, and e-f is where the feather would break due to accident. Finally, the fully grown feather in the last illustration shows the stage at which it is clipped. The quill is still growing below the skin. Again, if cut at line a-b, no bleeding would occur, and a cut at line c-d would cause bleeding. The feather sheath is omitted in this illustration for the sake of clarity. From Duerden, 1909a.

Garments and accessories from the heyday of the fashion craze for ostrich feathers. (Photo taken at C. P. Nel Museum, Oudtshoorn, South Africa.)

in the skin. This is the origin of the feather socket or follicle. The feather germ surrounds a plug of dermis which provides it with nourishment for growth. This may now be known as the pith or medulla or pulp of the feather.

By rapid multiplication and growth of the epidermal cells at the lower end, the germ sinks deeper within the socket and also grows further beyond the mouth of the socket.

The entire epidermis starts to show a separation into sheath layer and feather layer. Upper cells of young feathers start to convert into actual feather material. This material is arranged in definite wedges which give rise to the barbs and barbules.

The latest stage is when the growing feather, by continued multiplication of cells below, breaks through its delicate outer sheath. This is the feather stage at which the chick is hatched. The tip of the new feather, the spadona, begins to show through the mouth of the socket within a week or two after hatching.

The newly-hatched chick has just as many feathers as the adult bird, due to the fact that new feathers always come from the same sockets as the old ones.

The germ cells at the bottom of the socket are increasing in number and growing in size. This pushes the feather farther out of the socket.

Horny material, which ultimately forms the shaft, barbs, barbules and sheath, is formed from the feather and sheath cells beyond the soft cells of the germ. The feather is surrounded by the horny feather sheath for some distance beyond the lip of the socket. However, as this dries and cracks, the bird preens it away with its beak.

The part of the growing feather above the medulla is now fully-formed feather material. It no longer needs to be nourished with blood supply. This feather is ready for clipping. The quill, however, takes about two months to complete its growth.

The germ is still active at the bottom of the socket, and the added cells from it push the quill still further out of the socket. As the quill ripens it becomes narrowed and rounded off towards the tip, which is situated at the bottom of the socket. Below the ripened quill the new feather germ, which will give rise to the next plume, can be seen.

The walls of the socket collapse after the quill is drawn. The removal of a quill awakens the new germ to activity. In a few rare conditions, if the bird is not in good feather growing condition, the germ does not become active again and the socket remains empty, either temporarily or permanently. Such sockets are termed *blanks* (Duerden, 1913).

The rate of growth of ostrich feathers can be determined by tying at intervals a ring of fine thread around the growing feather at the mouth of the socket, and then measuring the distance of the ring or rings at intervals of a few days.

In the most vigorous birds with long plumes the wing feathers grow at least 1.75 inches a week. In weaker birds the growth may be scarcely half. Rate of growth varies in different ostriches, dependent upon the genetic strain of bird and its health. Under certain conditions, growth may cease altogether, or the appearance of new feathers may be long delayed (Duerden, 1907b).

FEATHER OPERATIONS

PLUCKING
The feather as a whole is taken from the socket by hand (Duerden, 1909a).

CLIPPING
Plumes and a short portion of the quills are clipped, leaving the remainder of the quill in the socket to ripen (Duerden, 1909a). Today this is often performed with pruning shears (Smit, 1964).

QUILLING OR STUMPING
Drawing of ripe quills or stumps from which the plumes have been previously clipped

(Duerden, 1909a). The quills are drawn today by pulling with pliers or pincers.

After quilling, the socket collapses and the hole partly closes. Usually the surface should be smeared with Vaseline or oil to protect the socket from exposure, to soften the skin and to stimulate the new growth (Duerden, 1913).

SORTING

Various kinds and qualities of feathers of each bird are separately sorted and tied in bundles (Duerden, 1909a). *Loose* feathers, for example from the bellies of slaughtered birds, are sold in bags. Feather markets buy the plucking which is further sorted into classes according to color, quality and length by the buyer or manufacturer (Smit, 1964).

Feathers that stay on the ostrich after they become *ripe* lose their lustre and become dull and worn (Smit, 1964). If plumage is not drawn artificially, as in the wild, quills are not all moulted at the same time and some will remain in their sockets. This will delay the plumage stage (Duerden, 1908a).

Only the wing-quills were seen as being of value before World War I. Today also the floss and short stuff are plucked (Smit, 1964).

PLUCK OR CLIP?

From the earliest times of the development of the ostrich feather industry, the procedures of removal of the feathers received attention. The question was whether the feathers should be plucked or clipped.

According to Douglass (1881) it was soon found that plucking before the feather was ripe caused successive growth to become shorter and the quill stiffer. Feathers of birds of five or six years were thus of little value. During Douglass's time, cutting of the feathers after six months growth became a universal practice.

It was also stated by Duerden (1908) that spadonas are ready for clipping when the chick is about six months old and that quills are therefore drawn at eight months of age. All the *first-after-chick*, or juvenile feathers, are usually ripe at fourteen months of age. The quills of these are thus drawn at the age of sixteen months.

Compared with the spadona quills it is not necessary for the juvenile or successive quills to be drawn immediately on attaining ripeness. The germs may all remain dormant for several months beyond sixteen months as long as the quills are left in position.

If birds, however, are not in a high nutritive condition, some feathers of the new crop will appear and may introduce irregularities. The regularity of the eight-month system can only be maintained under the most favorable conditions regarding weather and food supply.

On farms where climatic changes between winter and summer are great and food not plentiful during the winter, a yearly system was conducted. The continuous practice of the eight-month system eventually results in a deterioration of the feather produced, whereas this does not follow from a yearly system.

In all birds it is found that the plumage is at its highest degree of development at the beginning of the mating season. The quilling of the tail and covert feathers should be done at about two months in advance of that of the wings. The new growth thus will serve as a protection to the latter and also induce a rich blood supply to the wing as a whole (Duerden, 1908a).

Mimosa Lodge, one of the "feather palaces" from the turn of the century, in Oudtshoorn, South Africa.

SORTING FEATHERS

Douglass (1881) recommended the following regarding the sorting of feathers:

Keep the wings, tails, blacks and drabs of males and females apart during plucking. Sorting is done inside, on tables.

The male's quill feathers are first sorted, feather by feather, into heaps consisting of prime white, first whites, second whites, tipped whites, best fancy-colored and second fancy-colored. Each heap is then taken separately and each kind is sorted into six or more lengths.

The female's wings are sorted into heaps according to their shades of color, with a second quality heap for each shade, and then again sorted into lengths as for whites.

The female's tails are sorted into six heaps (whites; light-colored, colored; dark-colored; short; broken feathers), and the male's tails into seven heaps (three lengths of whites; three lengths of mixed tails; broken feathers).

Blacks and drabs should each be grouped in seven different lengths, with a bunch each of broken feathers and one each of floss. Chick feathers should be sorted into white, light-colored, colored, tails and dark.

COMMERCIAL CHARACTERISTICS

According to Duerden (1909) the most valuable characteristics in feathers are: a long and broad plume; dense, compact and even flue with crowded barbs and barbules; a strong and flexible shaft and barbs, barbs self-supporting; sides of the flue should be equal and margins parallel; whole plume should be lustrous and glossy to feel; free from barring and other defects.

This is in accordance with more recent (Swart et al., 1984) findings that the size (width and length), appearance (evenness and self support of the flue and feather shape), flue quality (softness and lustre) and defects were the dominant factors controlling the price of fashion feathers.

Swart et al. (1984) recommended that feather size and appearance should be accepted as a basis for classing and sorting of feathers, with further emphasis on quality deviation and color faults, thereafter.

FAULTS IN FEATHERS
Bars

This most common defect in feathers consists of an imperfect development of the barbules. Barbules in the region of the defects are shorter and do not project from the barb to the same degree as elsewhere. The flue is weak in these places.

This is caused by a wrinkled outer sheath, which in turn causes the soft developing feather to be indented.

Wrinkling is due to alternations in day and night growth because of differences in blood pressure. This causes rings of different density and greater variations in blood pressure in the medulla.

Partial collapse of the feather sheath at the weaker night rings thus occurs, and compressing and starving of the feather substance takes place.

By eliminating such factors as poor genetic matches, ailments and accidents, internal and external parasites, exposure to weather, and rapid changes in temperature, the blood supply to the feathers can be kept constant. Barring can thus be prevented (Duerden, 1909b; Osterhoff, 1979).

Exposure to inclement weather produces a contraction or shrinkage of the skin upon the soft growing feather, the latter being thereby constricted in a ring-like manner, which fails to re-expand after the feather leaves the socket.

The skin shrinkage does not affect quills, and ripe, or nearly ripe feathers, as the quill is too firm and hard to respond to the pressure. Bars are produced during the soft growing period of the feather. Some ostriches are responsive to the same unfavorable conditions while others are very resistant (Duerden, 1907a).

Unopened Feathers

Unopened feathers are caused by dry, scaly skin. This is associated with poor physical condition due to disease, parasites, malnutrition, old age and drought conditions (Duerden, 1908b; Osterhoff, 1979). According to Swart (1979) this condition can also be the result of inbreeding.

USES OF FEATHERS

The best tail and wing feathers are exported to make fashion items such as fans, fringes, feathers boas or hats. The rest go into feather dusters (Wagner, 1986).

Ostrich feathers are readily charged with static electricity when stroked, causing dust particles to adhere. They are thus eminently suitable for feather dusters (Holtzhausen and Kotze, 1990).

African Black ostriches.

Male and female emu strutting at Gray Feather Farms, Austin, Texas. (Photo courtesy Susan Gray)

EMU BREEDER MANAGEMENT

Vern E. Brackett
Creola Bird Ranch
Creola, Alabama

In this chapter, we will analyze male and female emus and their activities relating to reproduction from about sixteen months of age until the first egg is laid.

Emus breed and lay their eggs in the winter months. In the northern hemisphere, eggs begin appearing as early as late September and continue until late April, with most of the laying being done late October through mid-March.

Fifty days is the average incubation period, and hatching peaks between late February and mid-March. Emus breed during the time of year when days are short and nights are long. The daylight-dark cycle is the prime motivating factor causing the breeding season to begin and end.

After fifteen or sixteen months of age, ranchers refer to both birds as *coming-twos*. As these coming-twos approach their second birthday their sexual hormones begin to take action, causing most to breed and about 60% of the females to lay during their second winter.

One can expect about twenty to thirty eggs from a first-time-laying female with about fifteen to twenty chicks being produced. Infertility is usually the culprit in the unproductive eggs. With older breeders the number of surviving chicks should average thirty per season per hen if she is healthy, is eating a good feed, and has a mate in the same condition.

The emu egg is about the size of a large avocado, green in color, and weighs about 550 grams when laid. Because of its shell make-up it cannot be candled in the same manner as the eggs of other ratites when a bright light is placed behind it (see photo on next page).

In order to inspect its contents, the industry has developed techniques using infrared cameras with television monitors, and separately, infrared night-vision goggles or binoculars to see the images created as infrared light (invisible to the unaided human eye) is passed through the egg. This allows for the determination of fertility or infertility as early as ten to twelve days after laying.

Candling can also show cracked shells, bacterial contamination, early deaths, and even malpositioning of chicks, along with internal pipping (breaking of the air-cell membranes). This allows continuous examination of the chick's development during the incubation-hatching cycle.

PRE-PAIRING CONSIDERATIONS

SEXING

Because male and female emus look alike, sexing is not a simple visual task. Gender determination can be done at about sixteen months of age or older by

Normal sized (approximately 560 grams) emu egg on the right; a rare small emu egg on the left.

having someone hold the bird while another inserts a glove-covered finger into the vent to feel the developing phallus or its lack.

One way to do a visual examination is called the "three-man take-down," wherein two handlers grab a leg each and turn the bird upside-down, while the third person, using a gloved finger, inverts the vent, exposing the phallus or clitoris, thus visually confirming the sex of the bird.

These two methods work with hens and maturing males. An immature male's phallus looks and feels very similar to the female's clitoris.

If the maturing phallus is there and of sufficient size to allow proper determination, whether by feel or visually, then obviously, sex is determined. Otherwise, there may be questions as to the accuracy of vent examination.

The most accurate method of gender determination developed to date is done by extracting DNA from a couple of drops of blood. The method offers near-perfect accuracy and can be done at any age. See the Resources section for information on companies which perform this service.

DNA examination provides other information: parentage identification, genetic relatedness between birds, and permanent bird identification.

Another method of gender confirmation is done by a surgical invasion that allows for examination of the testes, a simple operation that can be done in most veterinary clinics.

SEXUAL MATURITY

Before pairing coming-twos, it is important to consider the birth months of the birds being considered as possible mates.

It is not uncommon for female emus to mature several months before males born in the same month. If a rancher pairs two from the same birth-month and the female begins laying before the male is mature enough sexually, infertile eggs may appear.

It is better to put an older, experienced, proven-breeder male with the coming-two female for obvious reasons. He may encourage her to proper breeding sooner.

HISTORY AND PREPARATIONS

Another wise practice before trying to pair emus is to examine the parental genealogy as far back as the records are available, since the goal of breeding includes the idea of producing as many healthy offspring as possible.

Check the numbers of eggs laid by their parents and even their grandparents. Look at the fertility rates and the ratio of chicks hatched versus those that survived. Larger numbers of eggs

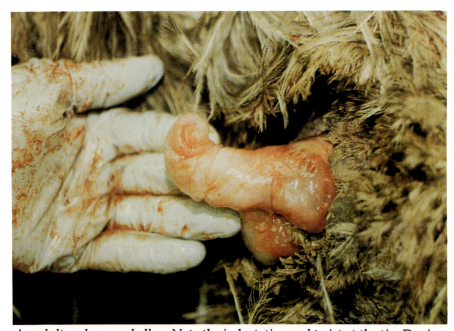
An adult male emu phallus. Note the indentation and twist at the tip. During breeding, the tissue at the base extends forward the full length of the phallus. (Photo courtesy Dr. Brett Hopkins)

laid, with more surviving chicks, indicate higher possibilities of success for your pair.

Before pairing it is smart to look at the individual bird's health records and then have an examination done. Check for past illnesses and injuries, and previous and current vaccinations and shots, particularly if you are unfamiliar with the bird.

Have your veterinarian give the bird a thorough examination, and give you a signed certificate of his or her findings.

Then you should examine the bird visually, familiarizing yourself with the points from the veterinarian's certificate, if any unusual ones have been noted.

If one or both of the birds of a pair are being relocated from a different ranch, isolate them for at least two weeks in a separate pen or pens, protecting them and your other birds from possible exposure to new bacteria or viruses.

Secondarily, you give the transported birds an opportunity to adjust to the new environment, and time to calm down from any moving stress.

FEEDING

Prior to pairing, be sure both birds are on the same brand and type of feed. When necessary, make a switch slowly, by substituting 10% per day of the new feed for the previously-used feed, until in ten days you have changed to 100% of the new feed. This slow change-over allows the bird's digestive system to adapt to the ingredients in the new feed, reducing the possibilities of diarrhea and intestinal problems.

There are many methods and variations within methods in the feeding of emus. Many work. The main concern of all methods of feeding is simple: getting enough proper nutrition into the birds to keep them growing and/or healthy.

A key point to remember when it comes to understanding emu feed includes the fact that emus are not herbivores. They are omnivores. In the wild, they eat small animals, a variety of vegetable substances, and insects.

Emus do not have the physical makeup to digest as much dietary fiber as do ostriches or rheas, due to the fact that the emu's cecum is relatively short—about 3.5 inches. Thus the percentage of fiber in their diet should be noted.

Protein levels should vary as the feed is changed in September to a breeder-type feed. An additional distinguishing point which designates the feeder to be "breeder-type" is the calcium-phosphorus ratio. These two minerals are very important for the egg-laying female.

It is suggested here that ranchers study emu nutrition as much as possible, and then make their own decisions after learning where the differences of opinion between ranchers and feed manufacturers lie.

PAIRING OPTIONS

COLONY PAIRING

Closely duplicating the birds' natural environment as it was for their ancestors in Australia is probably the easiest way to pair emus. Simply put them in a big pen and let them choose their own mates. Call this *colony pairing* or *community-pen pairing*.

Grouped emus will form some sort of pecking order, that is, in-line dominance. Left alone to establish this line of command, the most aggressive female will select her mate with each female down the line doing the same.

The details describing this process will be covered later. This method cuts down on the amount of fighting caused by forced matching, or, indeed, mis-matching.

However, this does not guarantee that all of the birds in a colony will pair. It may leave a few unpaired birds which will require further attention from the rancher in order to pair all for breeding.

Depending on the number of birds to be included, the suggested size of the colony pen varies from 100' x 100' for three pairs, to changes in these dimensions upward. The birds need the extra room to evade aggressors during the selection process.

If the colony is small, feeding and watering can be done on a daily basis. For larger colonies, water may come from a pond or lake, with feeding done weekly.

Some ranchers find it convenient to use this colony method of free-choice pairing to unite the birds, then move each bonded pair to a separate breeding pen for their permanent home.

INDUCED PAIRING

Another method used to pair the emus is done by simply putting the chosen male and female together in a breeder pen. One advantage of this method is that it takes much less room than colonies. A disadvantage is the greater possibility of a mismatch. Call this the *immediate introduction* method.

A suggested breeder pen size is 30' x 100' with some form of shelter to keep the feed dry and to give the birds a place to go in or under in inclement weather. Obviously, special care and special facilities are needed in colder climates where freezing temperatures are expected.

Feeding and watering can be done daily. However, many ranchers use automatically controlled waterers, and some use feeders containing more than one day's feed supply.

WHEN TO PAIR

SEXUAL MATURITY

Emus normally start showing signs of sexual maturity at about fourteen to sixteen months of age. The female will start making a sound that is called *drumming* or *booming*. It sounds like a soft-ended baton beating lightly on a small tom-tom or bongo drum, or maybe, bubbles softly gurgling through a plastic jug.

The sounds are made by first passing air through a slit in the trachea into a muscle void (called the air sac or air bag) located in the frontal lower neck, then forcing it back into the trachea.

The female may begin to strut with her head and neck cocked backwards and over her back, with her air sac showing profusely, at the same time sounding her sexuality.

Another sign of the female's approaching sexual maturity originates in her oviducts, when the green which gives the eggs their cover and color is first produced and some of it is passed through the vent with urates, giving this excretion a bright, vivid-green appearance.

Similarly, at fourteen to sixteen months of age the male emu enters sexual maturity, showing early signs by making a grunting sound, using his air sac as the source. His sound imitates that of a grunting hog.

He, too, may strut with his head and neck back, similar to the female. It is not uncommon for the male to attempt to pile grass or straw as if trying to build a nest.

Another way to determine sexual maturity is by the use of sonograms and X-rays, with the veterinarian looking at images of the testes of the male and the ovaries and oviduct of the female.

Additionally, sperm counts may be obtained through some veterinary clinics, when collection can be done through stimulation of the male.

BONDING

While the first signs of sexual maturity are the booming or drumming of the female and the grunting of the male, it is not uncommon for the female to chase the male and swat him on the rump, knocking out a small clump of feathers. The male may do the same to the female. Call this activity *feather fighting*.

Once this aggressive activity starts, it is wise to keep a constant watch for serious fighting. It is not uncommon for pairs that had previously bonded, bred, and produced chicks to fight. Daily observation and early detection is the best prevention tool.

OVERCOMING PROBLEMS

Serious fighting does not mean, necessarily, that a pair cannot be made to bond.

One method to try is to put the fighting pair into a small pen with a panel or fence separating them, but forcing them to be close. Place their feed and water so that they have to eat and drink next to each other for several days. They may change their minds.

A sign that they may be ready to accept each other would be their staying close to each other during the day, eating and drinking simultaneously, and sleeping adjacently. When that happens, they need to be reunited in the same pen, but you should keep a watchful eye for a day or two.

Another forced bonding technique is to put the disagreeing pair into a totally-dark enclosure such as a barn room or a stock trailer for several days and nights. It needs to be small enough to allow very little movement space, and allow very little or no light. This method includes a chance that they will fight immediately, but usually they don't.

THE PECKING ORDER

Probably, the colony-pen environment offers the best opportunity to observe the steps that the birds go through in their bonding process, because of the number of birds. Not all of them will go through all of the known steps.

Here's what to look for. Once two or three are put together, you will see that they establish some form of pecking order by hissing, pecking, extending their heads high in the air over the others, chasing each other, feather-fighting, sometimes claiming territory over part of the pen and keeping

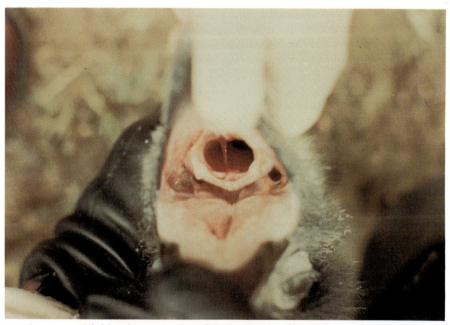

An emu with bloody mucous and irritation in the trachea. The mouth is being held open; the opening in the center is the trachea.
(Photo courtesy Dr. Brett Hopkins)

others out of it, and by sleeping every night in the same spot. The dominant females are, usually, the first in the group to show these characteristics.

When a new bird is added to the group, the pecking order is reestablished, causing some degree of stress among the birds. Sometimes it may take several days before calm returns.

It is not a good idea to add or remove birds once the first egg is found. In fact, many ranchers try not to rearrange birds at all after the first of October, or to change anything significant in the birds' environment.

Once a female has chosen her mate and he accepts, they can be seen walking, eating, selecting a specific spot in the pen to rest, sleeping feather-to-feather in that area of the pen, and generally, warding off others. The male may grunt excessively as he simulates nest building by stacking straw or grass.

Lastly, the surest sign that bonding has occurred is witnessing a pair breeding. But you may not be able, always, to witness the act. The most positive proof, of course, is a fertile egg.

BREEDING

Why emus evolved into winter breeders over the millions of years that they have been on earth is not known.

One theory derives from their behavior in the wild. The female breeds one male until he has a clutch of ten or twelve eggs (enough for his body size to adequately cover as he sits on them during incubation).

Only one female lays in each nest, and since the normal egg laying occurs every three days, it takes about thirty to thirty-six days to get enough eggs for his clutch. The winter months allow for the early-laid eggs to remain cool, delaying the incubation process until enough are laid for him to set.

Further, it is common for the female to seek another mate, leaving the first setting male behind. One female could have three or four mates per season, in the wild, depending on her laying continuously for five or six months.

September breeding is not uncommon, nor is it unusual to see birds breeding several times a day. Further research is needed to tell us just how long a single breeding lasts (implanted sperm life) and how many eggs (if more than one) can be impregnated in the hen's oviduct.

It is common for the hen to quit breeding and laying during the season for a week or two in order for her to rebuild body strength. This may be associated with her calcium and phosphorus levels. Research holds the answers on this question also.

When the hen wants to be bred, she will attract the male's attention by raising her tail feathers, signalling him to approach her as she squats on the ground and leans forward. The male approaches, squatting a foot or so behind; then he slides up to her with his legs outside hers, until his breastplate contacts her raised rump. He then signals with pecks on her back, neck, or head, followed by penetration. Once finished, he rises, and the hen rises as well.

Both birds may make noise during breeding. The male may remove small amounts of feathers from the hen's back by pecking. He may eventually make a bare spot. Additionally, the male's leaning against and over the hen's rump causes her tail feathers to crumple. The mating process may take as few as fifteen seconds for experienced, bonded mates, or up to a minute for beginners.

EGGS AND RELATED ACTIVITIES

In colony pens, the pairs tend to territorialize their spot around the perimeter fences. Therefore, where they sleep at night is where they can be expected to lay. Straw or hay can be used to make a sanitary bed for the laying hen. The birds may use the bedding material to cover the egg.

Emus tend to lay their eggs just at dark, after pacing back and forth along the fenceline. This predictability, once verified, makes egg gathering simple.

Since eggs are usually laid after dark, some ranchers, using a flashlight for guidance, walk or ride through the colony pen with a basket gathering eggs. The birds usually don't interfere, and, basically, could care less.

However, until all the possible layers have set their pattern, it is wise to criss-cross the pen checking for stray eggs, particularly when freezing temperatures are expected. This decreases the possibility of a frozen egg being found the next morning. Other ranchers, particularly in warmer climates, prefer to wait until morning to gather the eggs.

Easy egg-pair identification can be accomplished by placing the retrieved egg in a zipper bag, marked appropriately with a felt pen (mark the bag, not the egg).

With one pair per pen, egg gathering and identification is simpler. Look for eggs in the same spot as previously found.

Sometimes, dummy eggs are successfully used to motivate the hen to lay in a specific spot. Caution: If the male tries to set the dummy egg, remove it or he may stop breeding the hen.

If the birds are enclosed in a barn or shelter, as in cold northern climates, similar bird activities can be expected to occur inside, as compared to outside colony pens or breeder pens.

It is not uncommon for a female to lay intermittently before beginning a regular, three-day laying cycle. Further, coming-two hens may continue to lay on an irregular cycle their entire first laying season.

When gathering or handling eggs, always try to minimize bacterial contamination. Invert a zipper bag over your hand and pick up the egg with your bag-covered hand. Using your free hand, pull the bag back over the egg, enclosing it without touching it with your hands.

Then mark the bag with a felt pen, identifying the egg and making it ready for the first steps of the incubation process, which includes cleaning and preparing the eggs for your incubator.

MID-SEASON LAYOFF

It is common for the hen to take a recess at some time during the laying season. Some researchers feel this gives her time to rebuild the depletion in her body structure and minerals caused by the strain and stress of egg laying. This layoff cannot be predicted, time-wise or length-wise.

Some ranchers and feed manufacturers recommend supplementing the female's diet with additional calcium. One way to do this is to add calcium to the feed.

DAILY PEN AND BIRD CHECK

Checking the pens and birds every day is a must. Depending on the feeding methods used, feed may need to be checked daily, too.

Normally, birds can be expected to eat a pound and half to two pounds of feed daily, depending on the type of feed you provide. Fiber content is the primary influencing factor.

Once stabilized on a regular diet, birds will eat and drink enough to satisfy their need for water, minerals, fiber, and vitamins. If the percentage of fiber in the feed is increased significantly, it will take a greater volume of feed and water to get the proper nutrition into their systems.

Most laying pairs cut eating back considerably during the breeding season. Expect each bird to drink about half a gallon to a gallon of water per day. But supply them with water freely and abundantly. Water is more important to breeders than feed.

Every day, check the droppings for color, content, and fluidity. When they are passing urates, it will look like green diarrhea, with some white semi-solids in it. Normally, it will look greenish-brown, much like mush feed, if they are being fed commercially-manufactured feed.

Sometimes you will see grass in the stool. No problem—they have been grazing. If you see blood in the stool, talk to your veterinarian. Something's wrong.

Look the birds over carefully every day, checking for anything unusual, particularly prior to bonding, for signs of fighting.

Stress during laying season needs to be kept to a minimum. The pen environment should be kept unchanged and calm. Many ranchers keep strangers away from their breeders for this reason.

Check your shelters, fences, watering system, electricity, and gates daily, along with your security system, if you have one installed.

*The results of a successful breeder management program.
(Photo courtesy Susan Gray, Gray Feather Farms, Austin, Texas)*

Jeremy Potter and emu chicks. (Photo courtesy Lisa Kinder)

EMU CHICK REARING

Pat Jodoin
Jodoin's Emu Ranch
Whitney, Texas

Let's start with a look at chick facilities. Whether your first emu chicks come from your first pair of breeders or from another breeder, you need a place to raise them.

There are as many options in facilities as there are farmers, but a determining factor should be money available and the number of chicks you plan to house.

Your facilities can be very plain and inexpensive or very sophisticated. Both can work equally well for the chicks, but one may be more work-intensive in terms of farm management. You save money in the long run if you have a long-term plan for your farm, even though you may have to implement the plan in stages.

BROODERS

We keep chicks in a brooder their first few days of life, to observe them closely, control their heat, and withhold food for the first four days. However, some farmers with heated floors bypass this stage altogether.

Brooders can be made of metal with wire bottoms for droppings to go through and heat lamps hung above, or they may be totally enclosed with thermostatically-controlled heat.

An inexpensive option that works well is to have a brooder 2' x 2' x 8' made out of wood lined with metal flashing and a wire floor.

I found wire floors hard to keep sanitary so we put indoor\outdoor carpet (one that has minimal foam backing) on the bottom of our brooder. We change it daily, hosing down and sanitizing each soiled runner, leaving it in the sun to dry.

We do not use green carpeting since the chicks peck at green and try to pull out the fibers. Edges of carpeting should be taped or bound so as not to trap toes or give the chicks something to choke on.

We lay a small heat mat, set on low, under one end of the carpet and hang either infrared heat lamps or small radiant heaters at either end of the brooder to give chicks a choice of temperatures ranging from 75 to 90 degrees. It is important always to provide more than one source of heat.

We hang a small waterer at one end of the brooder and a small feeder on one side, keeping both scrupulously clean, and high enough off the floor to avoid contamination by droppings. Keep a generator and gasoline on hand in case of power failure (remember that even butane heaters require electricity to make them work).

OUTSIDE CHICK FACILITY

We prefer chick pens located so as to get early morning sun. The pens need to be well away from your breeders since chicks are very distracting to them and can even cause them to quit laying.

Chick enclosure. Note lower portion of fence made from corrugated metal.

The breeders should not be able to see the chicks (shade cloth can be used as a visual barrier). The runs should have good drainage and fencing with as many posts on the outside as possible.

The first chick facility I ever saw was an enclosed "box" with a heat lamp, opening into 2' x 20' runs made of hardware cloth. Our first was very similar to that.

Our second facility has five 10' x 10' enclosures with sand substrate, opening into runs that have two feet of corrugated metal topped by four feet of chain-link fencing (making the total fence 6' tall). I like corrugated metal for the sides not only because it serves as a wind break, but also because it doesn't damage chicks' feet or beaks as wire sometimes does.

Breeders in other climates have had great success using hardwood (not soft) shavings as a substrate, if it is available, especially in barns or greenhouses. Still others use Dri-Dek flooring or similar material.

The total size of each run, including the enclosure, is 10' x 100'. The first ten feet are enclosed and the second fifteen are under cover, so the chicks have protection in inclement weather and access to heat lamps in the enclosure at all times. The remaining 75' are open, but covered by game bird netting to protect chicks from predators, but allow maximum early morning sunlight.

We put 12 to 15 birds in each run. In previous years we put more birds in each, then used portable dividers to separate them at night to keep them from huddling and smothering a chick. But this caused both sanitation problems and stress for the chicks.

When growth demanded an additional facility we got somewhat more sophisticated. Our new facility is an all-metal building with a center aisle wide enough to accommodate a truck, and metal enclosures on both sides (photo this page).

The brushed concrete flooring can be hosed down into shallow troughs slanted to drain toward one end of the building, and then outside into large French drains.

This barn is well ventilated and has commercial radiant heaters that can be thermostatically controlled. We used Dutch doors in each pen, opening to outside runs that have 10' under cover, opening in turn into longer runs covered with netting.

This facility has 6-foot-wide runs with gates that can be closed to keep chicks totally in the outside area or open to give them access to the entire run. We put 10 to 15 chicks in each pen.

We call both our chick barns *all-in, all-out facilities*, since the chicks can stay in these runs, or be

Aerial view of chick facilities. Note that chicks can be moved through aisles to different grow-out pens without having to handle them, which greatly reduces stress.

herded into their adjacent grow-out pens through a system of gates.

Chick pens and runs should be cleaned on a regular basis by either raking or turning the dirt over. Lime can be used as a base under dirt to help in sanitation, but will burn the birds' feet if it is near the surface.

If you can smell ammonia in the chick facilities, imagine how it will affect a young chick on ground level. Keep pens clean and free of feces and ammonia build-up. These cause eye infections that can lead to serious respiratory infections, and also attract flies.

Make sure waterers are placed so the area around them doesn't stay wet, which encourages bacteria growth. I recommend placing large waterers in the sun to help keep the area around them dry. We clean our pens daily and sanitize pens and waterers weekly.

When building any emu pen or facility it is very important not to have any space or opening that can trap a bird's leg or head. If an emu gets trapped in any way it often goes into shock and dies.

Gates should close flush or can have hard rubber strips added to them to block the opening. They should be located in corners or be as wide as the run, making birds easier to herd, since they normally run down fence lines.

Emus rarely have impaction problems, so grass kept freshly mowed works well in pens. Since emus are fence-walkers and do not use the center of pens, it makes sense to have long, narrow pens so they can get their all-important exercise and sunlight.

GROW-OUT PENS

These larger pens can accommodate large numbers of chicks. In southern climates, many farmers use no shelters if they have shade trees. Otherwise farmers make some sort of shelters or windbreaks out or wood, metal, or even by stacking bales of hay.

Fencing material is usually chain-link or 6' non-climb fencing with posts on the outside. Gates should set be in corners, making it easier to move birds down fence lines.

You need to have at least one smaller pen off this grow-out pen—what I call a working pen—a place to herd birds for giving shots, sexing, checking microchips, banding, to use as a sick-bay, or to separate out birds you have sold, prior to loading them in a trailer.

We usually keep our feeder in the working pens, so birds are accustomed to going there regularly and are easy to close off in this smaller area so we can work with them.

These birds can be free-fed either in troughs, gravity feeders, or bulk feeders as long as the feed stays dry. Large galvanized automatic waterers may be used.

CLIMATE AND TEMPERATURE

Since hatchlings cannot regulate their own body temperatures, it is important that we as farmers give them access to varying degrees of temperature for them to be comfortable. At hatch a chick may need 80 to 90 degree temperature, whereas a one-week-old chick may tolerate from 60 to 80 degrees.

It is important not to *overmother*. If a chick is kept too warm he will not exercise properly. Usually chicks three weeks to one month of age can be let outside when temperatures are above 50 degrees.

Chicks tolerate cold weather or wet weather well. But they *do not* tolerate cold, wet weather and can easily develop respiratory problems. Heat is well tolerated as long as there is both shade and good ventilation.

GENERAL CHARACTERISTICS

Emu chicks usually start hatching in December and quit sometime in early June (a few stragglers may still be hatching in August), the heaviest hatch being in March and April. Generally they start earlier in the south and later in the north.

Emus are cute little chicks at hatch, having black-and-white stripes that look more like coarse dog hair than feathers.

They have tiny wings, holes in each side of the head which are their external ears, inner and outer eyelids, a beak with two nares or nostrils though which they breathe, and legs colored dark brown to grey-black.

If you open the mouth you can see a large hole at the bottom front, which is the windpipe, sometimes covered by a flap of flesh, the throat being behind this opening. They have three toes with large toenails which are scaly in texture.

At approximately six weeks of age chicks' head feathers start turning black, they start losing their stripes, and their feathers continue to turn brown down the body as they age. Three-month-old chicks will be nearly totally black and brown and are often called *blackheads* at this stage.

Young emus make a whistling sound. They especially whistle hello, if they are distressed, hurt, alarmed, or even lonely. They are social creatures, hate being alone, and can become very stressed if separated from their playmates.

Chicks huddle in corners when they sleep, often one on top of another, which can lead to smothering. This makes it important not to overcrowd brooders and pens.

Emus are very playful and will often jump straight up, twirl and run, causing other pens of emus to join suit. They are not going

Emu chicks love water.

THE FIRST THREE MONTHS

KEEP IT SIMPLE

After trying many ways of caring for our chicks at different ages and stages, we have simplified our farm-management practices into a system that requires minimum thought and effort.

We used to believe that we had to always be *doing something for the chicks* to raise quality stock.

Now we realize that quality starts with genetics, goes on to breeder feed, incubation precision, and overall good farm management, and what we're working with during the chick's life includes all of the above.

Care of the chick does NOT start when the chick does or doesn't hatch!

After spending hours chopping kale, feeding, and worrying, we have finally streamlined our operation and have learned how to keep it simple. I am writing for the purposes of this chapter from hatch to three months of age. These are the practices we followed last year, liked our results, and are therefore following this year—nearly a non-thinking process, believe it or not.

Day 1

1. Weigh chicks at hatch and replace them in the hatcher.

2. Put 7% iodine on the navels several times and either hobble the chicks' legs (photo this page) or provide non-slip flooring in the hatcher.

3. Band and microchip each chick. We place small leg bands above the hock, using electrical ties marked with laundry marking pens. We note the breeder or pen number and egg number. 9-26 would mean breeder pair in pen 9, egg number 26 from that pair.

4. Keep the chicks in the hatcher for 6 to 24 hours until they have dried out and and they are looking perky.

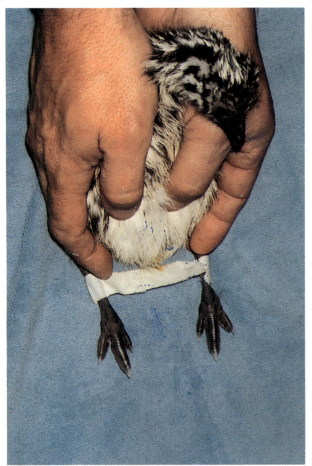
Hobble legs to prevent injury if you don't have non-slip matting in the hatcher. Chicks can be hobbled using vet wrap, elastic, or ¾-inch masking tape.

crazy—they are just having fun! They also love water and rain, playing in toy swimming pools with non-slip bottoms, or being showered with a hose.

Emus have one vent through which they defecate; their sex organs are located deeper inside this vent. Fecal matter is usually brown and often runny, depending on the fiber content of feed. This is norma. They don't have the *scours*, as some people think.

Chicks' bodies should be straight, with a gentle curve to the back. Legs and toes should be straight. The chicks should be bright-eyed and perky.

Hatchlings sleep a lot and often sleep on their sides instead of the sitting position of older birds.

Days 2-3

1. Give each chick a vitamin A/D shot and vitamin B-complex shot if you question the quality of your feed. Give one-tenth of a cc of each, subcutaneously. Also provide an oral probiotic.

2. Re-treat navel.

3. Move to brooder furnished with light and heat. Brooder has indoor\outdoor carpet with heating pad at one end and two heat lamps hung about three foot apart so the chicks can choose their own temperature. Brooder floor varies from 70 to 90 degrees.

4. Provide water to which poultry electrolytes and probiotics have been added.

5. Remove hobbles from leg.

Day 4

1. Keep providing water with electrolytes and a probiotic.

2. Introduce food. We use a 16-18 per cent ratite crumble, fed three times a day, all they can eat in one hour.

Days 5 thru 10

1. Move to outside small-chick facility—access to two heat lamps and/or small heating mat (during cold months). We have a 10 x 10 enclosure opening into 100-foot runs, partially covered.

If the chicks are microchipped, cut off leg bands or provide different-sized leg bands as the chicks grow.

2. Feed three times daily—all they can eat in one hour—16-18 per cent ratite crumble. Provide fresh water at all times, with vitamins, electrolytes, and probiotic in water.

3. Provide pigeon grit to give them something to peck at if they start eating dirt. (We no longer use oyster shells since vets say that could disturb the birds' calcium/phosphorous ratio).

Since we have many small rocks in our pens, we rarely provide grit. They do not need it to grind feed, only to help grind grass and other fibrous material.

1 to 2 Months

1. Slowly (switch 10 per cent per day over a ten-day period) change from ratite crumble to 18-21 per cent ratite grower pellets and feed 2 or 3 times daily, or free-feed, with fresh water available at all times. Add vitamins and electrolytes weekly.

2. Worm with Ivomec.

3. Sex birds. Check leg bands.

2 to 3 Months

1. Re-sex birds.

2. Move to large pen. Check leg bands.

3. Free feed 18-21 per cent ratite pellets and fresh water.

4. Add poultry vitamins and electrolytes weekly.

5. Worm with Ivomec.

6. Vaccinate for Eastern (EEE) or Western Equine Encephalitis (WEE) if mosquitoes are prevalent in your area.

DOs and DON'Ts

DO

1. Keep all brooder facilities and dishes clean and sanitary.

2. Always have more than one heat source available to give chicks temperature options, or in case one source fails.

3. Monitor chicks daily—look for straight legs, clear eyes, perky behavior, walking straight (neither with legs out or crossed), etc.

4. Whenever possible, encourage chicks to be in sunlight and to exercise daily.

5. Keep emergency supplies on hand.

6. Enjoy your chicks.

DON'T

1. Use water bowls or pails in which a chick could drown.

2. Allow any places in your pens or enclosures that could trap a chick's neck or break his toes, etc.

3. Put more than 10-15 chicks in a pen until you move chicks to a large grazing area, because they tend to huddle and can smother each other. Overcrowding also presents sanitation problems.

On occasion we have had success with 15 to 20 chicks of approximately the same size and weight in a pen when it was necessary; however, we don't recommend that number

4. Let the chicks become imprinted on you instead of on each other.

Emu chick with valgus or outward rotation of the tibia-tarsal bone of the right leg, often mistakenly called splay-leg. (Photo courtesy Dr. Brett Hopkins)

PROBLEMS

PREVENTION

As most of you know, it's a fact that emus are hardy and easy to raise, especially compared to other livestock. But emus are still livestock, and as such are subject to some problems.

Usually anything encountered in the first two weeks of life is due either to genetics, improper nutrition of the breeders, or improper incubation and hatching.

After two weeks, we're talking farm management of the chicks themselves—and that's 100% our responsibility. I can't stress enough the importance of good ventilation, sanitation and nutrition—and the serious detrimental effects of overcrowding.

Chicks at hatch are normally perky and bright-eyed, their legs are a dark gray color with fat little toes, and their navels have good tight closure (but may have a little pucker from having just absorbed the yolk sac). Chicks usually lose weight after hatch, but start gaining by day 6 or 7.

If a chick is swollen (edematous), has mottled-looking legs, or the navel is not tightly closed, chances are you have an incubation problem—usually too low temperature or too high humidity.

If the chick is dehydrated, or has a bloody or protruding navel, chances are your incubator temperature is too high or the humidity too low.

I have heard of farmers breaking into eggs, suturing navels, or tubing birds, but have found these practices are usually unnecessary if you have good breeding stock, breeder nutrition, and incubation and hatching practices.

I believe healthy, problem-free birds hatch completely on their own. If you have to help a bird hatch, chances are it will be less hardy and may develop problems later on. That can alert you to evaluate the breeder pair producing the problem eggs, as well as breeder nutrition.

Emu chicks will peck at a bird with an open wound. It's not because they're mean, but because of instinct—they peck at anything red.

Leave a cut to heal naturally unless it's bleeding. If bleeding doesn't stop, spray the wound with Bluekote or separate the injured bird from the group.

Parrot beak in an emu chick. This is a genetic deformity routinely seen in the offspring of certain emu pairs. (Photo courtesy Dr. Brett Hopkins)

Emus also peck at yellow or green, so do not use a yellow spray. If a chick develops a limp, give it time to heal naturally before trying other methods.

Remember that each time you confine or handle a bird, this creates stress, and stress is what emus tolerate least. Catch and handle birds in a slow, calm, considerate manner.

Keep similar-sized birds together. This prevents injury due to trauma or huddling while sleeping. An older bird may peck at a chick's eye, not to cause intentional harm, but simply because they peck at shiny objects.

Check chicks daily. Are they bright-eyed, straight legged, eating well (actually watch the food go in their mouth), breathing normally, and active?

Emus are masters of disguise, hiding illness or weight loss by fluffing out their feathers which, of course, protects them from predators in the wild.

This makes it even harder for the emu farmer to spot a sick bird. Since emus are very social birds, be very suspicious of illness if a bird separates itself from the group. Mark any unusual behavior in your records.

On the next page is a brief overview of problems concerning raising chicks, written only to increase your awareness. It is not written as a substitute for consulting your vet. You need to know that some of the possible solutions can be lethal if not administered properly and in correct dosages.

Many breeders no longer have these problems—they have learned prevention.

NUTRITION

We may not be able to manipulate the genetics of our breeder birds, but we can manipulate what they eat!

I cannot put too much emphasis on having a good feeding and

Emu Chick Rearing

vitamin and mineral supplement program. Genetics aside, "you are what you eat." Breeding birds can only put into the egg what is in their bodies—and what the breeders eat is the emu farmer's responsibility.

I will only list a few problems here caused by poor genetics, feed recipes, vitamin and mineral deficiencies: infertility, poor hatchability, soft-shell eggs, soft bones, slipped tendons, curling heads, crooked necks, curled toes.

In feed recipes the main things you hear about are crude protein percentage, crude fat percentage, and crude fiber percentage. It is generally agreed at this point in the emu industry that chick diets should include approximately 14-18 per cent protein, 3 per cent fat, 8-12 per cent fiber, and a 2-to-1 calcium-to-phosphorus ratio.

What is often not mentioned is the value of all the additional necessary vitamins and minerals and the source and purpose of each. To give you an idea of the importance of just a few:

VITAMIN A: Normal growth and development for bones and straight, strong legs.
VITAMIN D3: Deficiency causes rickets (soft bones); necessary for the absorption of calcium.
CALCIUM: Required for good skeletal structure.
PHOSPHORUS: Required for straight legs.
VITAMIN B-12: Deficiency causes retarded growth, decreased feed efficiency, and reduced hatchability.
MANGANESE: Deficiency causes slipped tendons.
IRON and COPPER: Deficiency causes depigmentation in feathers and anemia.
IODINE: Deficiency causes enlarged thyroids.
ZINC: Deficiencies cause hock joints to become enlarged, and leg problems develop. Long bones are shortened and thickened.
SELENIUM: Deficiency causes edema of skin, which causes it to

PREVENTABLE—OR TREATABLE—PROBLEMS

As noted in the text, the possible solutions below are not intended to be a substitute for consulting your vet. Some of the possible solutions can be lethal if not properly administered, in correct dosages.

Problem	Prevention or solution
Curled heads, sometimes swinging downward as if returning to fetal position (possible dehydration)	Injectable Vitamin E and selenium, Vitamin B complex or tubing with vitamin and electrolyte dissolved in water.
Rickets (feet crossing over when walking)	Lots of sunlight, vitamins A & D.
Curved, soft leg bones, soft beak	Additional calcium & phosphorous, sunlight, vitamins A & D, change feed.
Rolled toes	Splinting, riboflavin.
Slipped tendon on hock	Vet has great success in taping, adding manganese to water; prevent injury on hatcher flooring.
Impaction	Metamucil or similar product; drench with mineral oil.
Eating great quantities of sand or dirt (as in excavating)	Give small amount of fiber mixture weekly to keep them "cleaned out" (1/3 wheat bran, 2/3 crimped oats). Provide grit.
Prolapsed rectum	Put back in place—repeatedly if need be. Keep Kaopectate on hand. Take to vet for purse-string suture. Feed may be too high-energy.
Yoke sac infection	Treat hatchlings' navels multiple times with iodine. Keep antibiotic on hand. Maintain good hatcher sanitation.
Eye infection	Good sanitation. Keep eye drops and salve obtained from vet on hand.
Splayed legs	Hobble legs at birth or use non-slip matting to prevent injury in hatcher; do not overfeed, encourage exercise. Good nutrition (calcium/phosphorus ratio); leg brace as a last resort.
Weak immune system, bacterial infections	Good sanitation. Do not overcrowd pens. Use Solutracin 200 or similar product in water as prevention or give probiotic that encourages growth of "good bacteria" in the gut.
Worms causing staggering	Injectable Ivomec at 1 month, 2 months, and 3 months of age, etc.
Gnats, black fly infestation	Spray with Permectin or Avon Skin So Soft mixed with detergent and water.
Yolk sac retention	Do not feed until 4 days of age; plenty of exercise; vitamin supplement therapy in water may help.

bruise easily, and easily-damaged internal tissues.

VITAMIN E: Needed for good muscular development.

CHOLINE CHLORIDE: Prevention of fatty livers.

NIACIN: Lack causes swollen hocks and bowed legs.

PANTOTHENIC ACID: Deficiency causes high mortality.

RIBOFLAVIN: Deficiency causes curling of toes, and weak of legs.

FOLIC ACID: Deficiency causes excessive mortality, retarded growth, poor feather formation.

BIOTIN: Prevents perosis, and fatty liver and kidney syndrome.

VITAMIN K: Lack causes hemorrhagic anemia syndrome.

FIBER: Some spraddle-leg syndrome problems are exacerbated by too low a level of fiber.

Don't misunderstand—no one knows with 100% certainty what emus need—but we have a pretty good idea of what works. It just makes sense to use feeds that contain vitamin/mineral supplements.

The sources of the nutrients are also important. For instance, peanut hulls cannot compare to alfalfa as a quality source of fiber.

Some farmers chop up kale and boiled eggs to feed chicks, but I find that practice very work-intensive and unnecessary and rely on a good vitamin-fortified ratite feed instead.

FREE FEED?

There is always an argument over whether to "free-feed" or "hand-feed" with advantages and disadvantages to both.

While free-feeding is less work-intensive, the chicks can eat too much, compared to their ability to exercise. If they gain weight too rapidly for their bone growth and strength, it can cause splayed legs. And in free-feeding, a chick may not be eating and you would never know it.

Hand feeding, while more labor-intensive, allows farmers to monitor more closely their chicks' health and development.

Many emu farmers now hand feed 14-18 per cent crumble or niblets—all the chicks can eat in thirty minutes to one hour three times a day—until the chicks are six weeks to three months of age. They then change to free feeding.

Most add water-soluble poultry vitamins and electrolytes to the water on a daily basis, as well as a water-soluble probiotic powder (if it is not in their feed) for the first couple of weeks and thereafter on a weekly basis.

More is not necessarily better—over-dosing with vitamins can cause almost as many problems as deficiencies.

It is important to have fresh water in clean pans available at all times. Water should not be in deep buckets in which chicks could drown. Feed should be kept in such a way that mice or their droppings cannot cause contamination. The shelf-life of most ratite feeds is three months.

Feeding programs can be designed to accommodate various grow-out purposes—for birds to produce oil, meat, or leather, or to be raised as future breeders.

Ratite feed is available at most local feed stores. If you can order two tons or more, many feed companies will deliver to your farm.

There are many options on feeders from dog dishes to large rubber flat pails to automatic gravity feeders. The most important is to keep the feed and dish and the area around them clean and dry.

CATCHING AND HANDLING

Chicks can show amazing strength and quickness of movement for their size—facts to keep in mind when handling them. Usually it's best to handle chicks by holding their bodies firmly in one hand, with their legs held together tightly in the other hand, remembering how powerfully they can kick.

Alternatively, hold them firmly with their legs folded under them, tightly against their body. Often it may be convenient to wrap a chick in a towel to control its movements (this also protects you and your clothes from accidents).

Since chicks are fence walkers, it's easy to follow one down the fence line and trap it in a corner. Reach for its body, then immediately hold its legs together in your other hand. An emu always kicks forward, (not to injure you, but to get away) so keep your body to the back or side of the chick.

Handling does cause the chick to struggle, thereby creating stress, so minimal, well-planned handling that may serve more than purpose (such as sexing plus worming at the same time) makes for better chick management.

SEXING
DNA sexing

The advantage of DNA sexing is that it has a higher degree of accuracy than vent sexing. This is especially important to a breeder who guarantees sex and sells birds out-of-state.

There are two main methods of DNA sexing: from a blood sample or from feather quills (other methods are now being developed).

A vet can draw blood for the DNA sexing or the breeder can learn to do this himself. Often blood is drawn from the jugular vein or wing of an adult bird, but many find it easier to draw blood from the inside leg (between the ankle and elbow) of a chick.

This process is easiest when three people are involved—one holding the bird, one taking the blood sample, and one recording microchip number and other record keeping.

CHICKS: We vent-sex chicks at two months, and again at three months of age. It is possible to check them much earlier, but if you are not careful you can cause a prolapsed rectum.

By vent-sexing, I mean that someone holds the chick, and the organ is rolled out exposing the interior of the second fold of skin, and we visually determine if the chick is male or female.

At this age, the clitoris of the female is just a little *knot*. The phallus of the male is slightly more well-defined, with a pointed tip that has an opening (which is difficult to see), and it has a tiny spiral thread running from the lower right up about ⅔ around the protrusion to the point, similar to a corkscrew. The color may vary from crimson-red to gray.

If you have never sexed chicks before, you may have to sex several before you develop a discerning eye. An old timer in the business told us that if they all start looking alike to quit for the day and re-sex a week or two later. Most chicks are easy to sex at this age with great accuracy (though usually not 100%).

ADOLESCENTS: Emus go through various growth spurts, with their bodies sometimes growing faster than their sexual organs. Because of this, we rarely try to sex emus between six and thirteen months of age.

During this time, the bird would have to be flipped and vent-sexed, which is very difficult because of their size. It takes a couple of strong men to hold the bird down on its back, and another to vent sex the bird.

TRANSPORTING EMUS

Many emu farmers know how to transport their birds with a minimum of risk and stress and many make this service available to their buyers.

A common charge at this writing is $1 to $1.50 per mile, one way, if they haven't included the charge automatically in their selling price.

But, for many newcomers who choose to transport their own birds here are a few reminders:

Small birds can be transported in boxes or animal kennels large enough to hold the bird and tall enough for the bird to stretch its neck without hitting the top. Hay or a non-slip material should cover the floor.

Larger emus can be transported in an enclosed stock trailer with hay or non-slip flooring as for chicks. It is important that the stock trailer have adequate ventilation, yet have small-enough openings that the bird cannot get its head or feet injured or caught. Many people attach plywood, chicken wire, or other fencing to the trailer to make it suitable and safe for hauling emus.

This is doubly important since sometimes the first bird put in the trailer panics and thrashes around. This usually stops when you add a second bird—emus like company.

Our latest trailer specifically for emus has solid 48" sides, expanded metal covering any openings, and special compartments inside and we are very pleased with the results.

Since transporting is stressful to emus, it may be helpful to add vitamins and electrolytes to their water a week prior to as well as after transporting.

In the heat of the summer birds should be transported in the early morning or late evening to prevent heat stress. You can spray both birds and hay with water for added cooling.

Never tie an emu's legs together. We hear of several cases each year where people have done this and birds struggle to get free, panic, then go into shock.

After arriving at your destination (or more often if needed) give the birds water to which vitamins and electrolytes have been added. Feed the birds, but do not worry if a bird doesn't eat for a day or more—this often happens, especially when transporting older birds.

Some people load emus onto trailers using either ramps or having an incline dug out to back their trailer into so the emu can be guided directly into the trailer.

Since we're built nearly on solid rock, the latter doesn't work for us. We have a system of aisles that we can easily herd the birds down until they near the trailer, and then literally pick up the birds one by one and carry them into the trailer.

With one hand over the front chest of the emu, in front of the leg, the other hand in back of the opposite leg and under the bird's rump and up, it's easy to guide the emu into the trailer. The emu can kick forward, trying to get away, but is held securely.

PERMANENT IDENTIFICATION

While tattooing under the wing is an option, most emu farmers microchip their birds. A microchip is about ¼ to ½ inch long, very small in diameter, and has a permanent number that can be read electronically with a microchip scanner.

Microchips are usually implanted in the chick's pipping muscle using a microchip syringe made for this purpose. This is very easy to do, and does not hurt the chick or cause any bloodshed.

The injection is easily accomplished by one person holding the chick wrapped in a towel, while another person holds the chick's head steady and implants the microchip in the pipping muscle, following a path parallel to the spine in back of the ear.

We microchip to permanently record what chick is from what breeder pair, for our records in case a leg band slips and comes off, as well as for security purposes.

Ron Sandman and Charles Parsley demonstrate the use of an emu harness.

WORKING EMUS

Kent Robinson
Wildlife Ventures
Hockley, Texas

Emu handling, or working birds, as some emu ranchers call it, is necessary for many reasons. Here are some of the circumstances that may require it:
- Banding and microchipping
- Sexing
- Caring for sick or injured birds
- Moving birds from pen to pen
- Catching and loading for transportation
- Dividing a flock
- Separating fighting birds
- Physical exams
- Injections
- Showing birds

In this chapter we will look at handling techniques that can be utilized in the ranching of these wonderful creatures. Your main objective should be to minimize stress on your livestock and injury to the handler, workers, and birds. In handling these quick, fast creatures a certain amount of skill and training should be acquired beforehand.

If possible, assist in working emus at a neighboring ranch, or attend workshops and clinics that are held throughout the country. With practice and repetition your skills will improve—along with your confidence.

Strength is not a major requirement in handling emus. Proper techniques and tenacity are. Women can work emus as well as men.

BEFORE YOU BEGIN

Prior to handling them, it is important to be aware of the strengths and weaknesses of emus. Normally, emus are rather docile, cautious birds. But when you attempt to work them their quickness and speed become very evident.

You must respect their strong powerful legs, sharp claws and quick feet. Emus kick forward—always attempt to work from the side or from behind because of their ability to deliver powerful kicks to the front.

Here are some basic steps to follow prior to working emus.
- Survey your work site prior to handling. Check for hazards in your barn or pens.
- Gather and prepare any equipment or supplies that may be needed, such as microchipping equipment, medication, identification bands, markers and records.
- Check weather conditions.
- Find helpers, according to the size of the project.
- Assign worker responsibilities, according to their experience and knowledge.
- Utilize proper clothing such as chaps or brush pants for leg protection. Wear boots, gloves and long sleeve baggy shirts for protection from emu kicks or a worker's mistake.
- Work in the morning or late afternoon for cooler temperatures and calmer birds.

If handlers follow the above suggestions, handling errors or

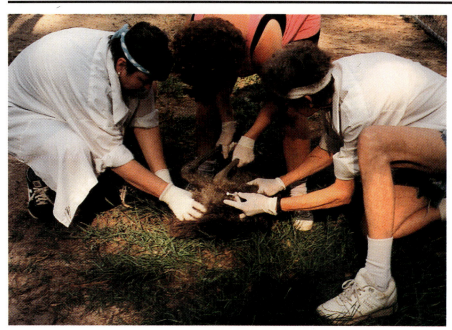
Vicki Robinson, Cheryl Platzer, and Carolyn Miller sexing and injecting three-month-old emu chick.

mistakes can be minimized and your job will be free of stress and injury.

HANDLING EMU CHICKS

When handling newly hatched emu chicks you can easily capture them by cupping your hand over the chick's sternum or breastbone to restrain its movement. You can then use your free hand to hold the chick's back, and then tuck its legs close to its abdomen. You can also restrain chicks with a scooping motion from the front, with your hand under the sternum.

Release young chicks by laying them on their sides, letting them get up by themselves. This will help prevent leg injuries.

Chicks of this size can easily be moved and restrained. Many ranchers utilize small carrying boxes to move chicks from one area to another. Always handle with care.

Picking Up Older Chicks

As chicks grow, the task of handling becomes slightly more challenging. It helps to work growing chicks in the barn facility when possible. This gives you the opportunity to capture them in a smaller area with relative ease. If growing chicks are to be worked outside, utilize narrow fencing runs or alleyways.

As the chicks move along the fence line or inside wall, place your hand in front and move with the bird, cupping your hand around the sternum. The motion slows the chick and enables you to secure it with your other hand. You can then grasp the chick's legs near the feet and tuck them up underneath. Using slight pressure around the sternum can assist in restraint. The chick can then be carried or moved.

Another technique that can be used for growing chicks is to grasp the chick's legs between the hock and feet after you have restrained the bird. Then slowly turn the chick upside down using your free hand to support its back and neck. When releasing the chick, lay it on its side and slowly release it, allowing it to get to its feet on its own.

Herding Chicks

When moving growing chicks from one area to another, herding becomes a real challenge. It seems that all it takes is for one chick to change its mind or direction and they all do the same.

Alleyways or fenced lanes work well when moving is needed. Use a portable fenced panel and walk the chicks down the lane to the new location.

When lanes are not available, it may become necessary to try luring your flock from one area to another. Feed works well but only if the birds are very hungry. Often

Picking up a newly-hatched emu chick with a scooping motion from the front.

Working Emus

Restraining an older chick. Note right hand on sternum.

Tim Cox (Conroe, Texas) carrying emu chick, legs tucked under body.

The author attempting to lure an emu to another pen with feed.

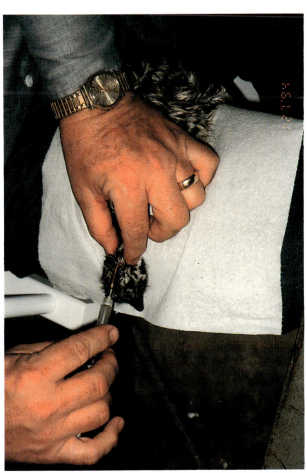

Microchipping a newly-hatched emu chick.

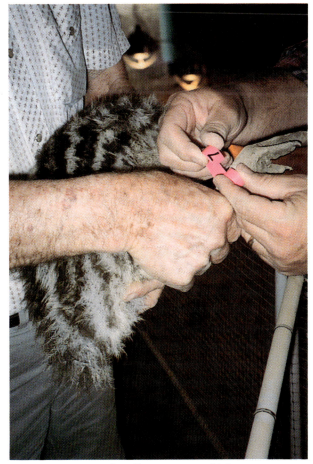

Leg-banding an emu chick.

The author restraining an adult emu using pressure on the sternum.

Charles Parsley (Magnolia, Texas) and the author walking a bird using the two-man wing-walk technique.

One-man wing-walking technique.

throwing a brightly colored cap on the ground can help attract the birds to another area.

YEARLINGS AND YOUNG ADULTS

Yearling is a rather vague term many ranchers use to describe an emu that is around one year of age. An emu that is not quite two years old is called *coming two*. Birds in this age group are rather frisky and spirited, and less docile than bonded adult breeders.

When handling birds in this age group it helps to have assistance. Once again, facilities play an important role. By working birds of this age in an alleyway or lane, you can capture birds in a more confined area.

Use the fence as your ally and slowly walk toward the emu. Try to walk the bird down the smooth side of the fence or corner of the area. You can then use your hand and arm to slow down the bird by cupping your hand over the sternum. After the bird has slowed down, move your other arm around its back and secure the wing with your hand.

By exerting gentle pressure on the sternum you can restrain the bird fairly easily. You can then *walk* it by walking behind the bird with one hand on each wing. Let the bird's own forward motion assist you to guide it the direction you want. This could be referred to as the *wing-walk* technique.

Because of its skeletal structure, rarely ever will an emu walk backward. However, when moving wild birds you can use the same restraining technique just mentioned but walk in reverse instead of forward.

Some spirited emus have a tendency to fall to the ground and kick their legs and feet up in the air. If a bird does have a tendency to do this, it may be necessary to lift and carry it. Restrain the bird, then put one arm behind one leg and place your other arm over the opposite leg. Lock your hands and lift the bird.

Adults

Adult emus can be handled using techniques similar to those for working yearlings and coming twos. Bonded-pair emus are usu-

Lifting a young adult.

The author has restrained the emu and is in position to flip the bird onto his (the handler's) thighs.

The emu rests on the handler's thighs and is being allowed to slide gently to the ground. Commonly called calf-roping technique.

The handler restrains the emu's legs, exerts pressure against the sternum, and immobilizes the bird's legs by placing his foot behind its hocks.

ally less active and more docile. In many instances, adult emus can be guided down alleyways or lanes with little difficulty. The wing-walking technique is also usually easier to use.

Calf-roping Technique

On occasion it is necessary to restrain an emu in a position that will keep the bird relatively immobile. The *calf-roping* technique enables the skilled handler to restrain a large emu and restrict its movement. With skill, one man can do it, but a helper may be needed.

After capturing the bird the handler places one hand firmly on the sternum, and with his other hand grasps the bird's thigh (or drumstick). The handler then slowly lifts the bird, allowing the bird to rest on and then slowly slide off the handler's thighs, with the bird ending up on its side on the ground.

The handler then grasps the bird's legs together between the hock and feet, and places his foot behind the emu's hock to prevent leg movement. The handler can then place slight pressure on the bird's sternum and subdue the bird. This technique is similar to one used by calf ropers on the rodeo circuit.

Flipping Technique

If you have a team of two or three skilled handlers, the *flipping* technique can be utilized. First, one restrains the emu. Then the second handler grasps both legs between the hock and foot. Slowly, he flips the bird over on its back while the one who is holding the bird lets it slowly slide to the ground (see photos next page).

It is important to have a firm grip on the legs. Remember the legs are the emu's power.

When releasing the emu lay the bird on its side and slowly release its legs. Help the bird get up in order to minimize the chance of

With the bird immobilized by the calf-roping technique, the handlers are able to sex the bird. Note the position of the foot behind the bird's hocks.

Charles Parsley grasps the emu's legs while the author restrains it, preparatory to flipping the bird.

Parsley has lifted the emu's legs out from under it, and both handlers will slowly lower it to the ground.

the bird cutting itself with its sharp claws.

The *stand-up* technique can be used for quick banding, sexing, or injections, using a two-person team. One handler restrains the emu as if using the one-man wing-walking technique—but doesn't walk. The other person then may perform whatever task is needed. Slowly release the bird after the job is completed.

SEXING EMUS

Mature adult emus have visual characteristics that can assist in determining the sex of the emu. For example, female emus usually have a pronounced air sac at the base of the throat. They also make a booming or drumming sound which the male emu does not make. The adult male emu makes a rather pig-like grunting sound and has no pronounced air sac.

Emu chicks and yearlings have no visual characteristics or differences, and vent sexing is necessary. The sex of emu chicks can usually be determined at an early age. After restraining the chick and laying it on its back hold both legs firmly. Then find the bird's vent, or cloaca. Gently roll back the cloaca until you find the sex organ.

The female organ or clitoris is a small appendage which is located at the top of the cloaca. It is usually smaller than the male organ or phallus and is light red in color. The male chick phallus is usually larger and has a corkscrew twist to it. Most of the time it appears to be a lighter color than the female clitoris.

Because the organs may have a rather peculiar shape, they are sometimes hard to identify and may require another look a month or so later.

The adult female emu has a small soft clitoris that at the top of the cloaca. After restraining the female utilizing one of the techniques outlined, gently roll back the vent or cloaca. The clitoris is not very long nor is it very thick, usually less than a half inch.

The adult male emu, vent sexed in a similar manner, should have a large cartilaginous-feeling phallus with a slight twist. The phallus is usually two to three inches long and about two inches wide at the base.

Sexing skills improve with practice and repetition. As you become more skilled, you will begin to get a feel for sexing birds, and confidence and accuracy will improve greatly. Be sure to use latex gloves to protect the bird and protect your skin from the odor and feces while sexing.

In summary, handling emus is a necessary function for any successful ranching operation. With proper knowledge, training, desire and experience, most emu ranchers can become quite adept at working their birds.

Ron Sandman (Cypress, Texas) and the author hold the bird's legs after it's been flipped to the ground, and Charles Parsley attaches a new leg band.

Clitoris of female chick.

Clitoris of yearling female.

Clitoris of adult female.

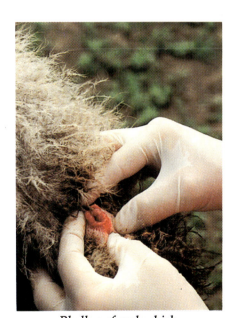
Phallus of male chick.

Phallus of yearling male.

Phallus of adult male.

This emu stir-fry exemplifies the heart-healthy value of emu-meat products. The combination of fresh vegetables and low-fat red meat in a non-fat recipe provides a delightful meal that contains fewer than 320 calories and 6 grams of fat per serving.
(Photo courtesy The Ostrich News)

EMU MEAT

Leslie Thompson, Ph. D.
Texas Tech University
Lubbock, Texas

The Australian Aborigines historically were nomadic hunter-gatherers relying on a variety of plant and animal species for food. One source of meat, or *kirra* as the Arunta say, was the emu (Spencer, 1927). The Aborigines were adept at hunting emus and used several resourceful techniques to capture and kill the birds.

Spencer describes how the Arunta took advantage of the bird's curious nature by digging a deep pit in the bird's normal feeding grounds. In the bottom of the pit they would secure a spear, sharp end up, surrounding it with loose brush and earth.

The emu would investigate this strange area, eventually step on the brush, and fall in the pit to be impaled by the spear.

Another inventive method involved placing a concoction prepared from the pituri plant in a small watering hole frequented by emus. The plant apparently had a narcotic-like effect on the birds, allowing hunters to spear them before they could escape.

Cooking was equally as inventive as hunting. Most accounts describe the Aborigines cooking the entire bird in a pit containing hot coals or in an earthen oven after the bird had been plucked and eviscerated.

Some Arunta stuffed the abdominal cavity with feathers and surrounded the bird with feathers before covering it with coals in a pit to cook.

On the Lower River Murray the Aborigines completely covered the bird, with only its head protruding from the pit. The proper doneness was achieved when steam emanated from its beak (Berndt and Berndt, 1964). Aborigines preferred their meat rare and thought the Europeans overcooked meat.

Oil for pharmaceuticals, cosmetics and industry; feathers for fashion; hide for fine leather; toe nails for jewelry; and the flesh for meat are the major products derived from the world's second largest bird, the emu.

Australian Aborigines were probably the first people to consume emu as a meat source. Their languages are replete with words for the emu—*waraguti*, *jundai*, and *gnooee* to list a few (Steele, 1983).

As well as being a food source, the emu was an important element in the Aboriginal culture as various totems, rock art and sacred ceremonies focused on the emu.

Today the emu, an Australian native, is raised commercially in Australia on government-licensed farms for its valuable products. The emu industry as it is known today started in 1987 from foundation stock originating from an Aboriginal farm in Western Australia (AQIS, 1993).

In 1994 it is estimated that about 6,500 emus were processed in Western Australia (Frapple, 1994). The meat is sold primarily

Emu carcasses. Unlike true poultry, emus are red-meat birds.

to restaurants in Australia and the remainder of the meat is exported to the United States and France.

The United States also has a rapidly-emerging emu industry. Ford (1994) has estimated that the emu population in the United States is approaching a half-a-million birds and that the birds are being raised in at least 43 states.

Numerous national, state and local emu associations exist and several cooperatives have been formed to represent and promote the growth of the industry.

The remainder of this chapter will be devoted to examining the current state of knowledge of one of the emu products, the meat.

SLAUGHTER

The exact age at which emus should be slaughtered to maximize returns, product yield, and the quality of various emu products is not known, although birds slaughtered in Australia for commercial purposes are about 12 months of age.

No full-scale slaughter operations exclusively devoted to the emu exist in the United States, but it has been suggested that optimal slaughter age will be between 12 and 18 months of age.

Many factors will dictate optimal economic slaughter age but three major factors include production costs, product quality and yield considerations, and end-product prices.

The slaughtering of emus involves the following nine steps: immobilization, exsanguination, defeathering, removal of feet, head and wings, hide removal, fat removal, evisceration, rinsing, and chilling.

Immobilization involves stunning the bird to render it unconscious prior to killing it by exsanguination. Stunning can be accomplished by several methods.

Commercial poultry are commonly stunned electrically by using wire leads or by immersion in an electrolyte solution that conducts a current.

This process renders the bird unconscious, thus reducing stress. It also relaxes the dermal muscles, increasing the ease of feather removal (Moreng and Avens, 1985).

In red-meat animals such as cattle and swine, stunning can also be accomplished electrically.

Other options for red-meat animals include using mechanical devices such as compressed-air concussion devices, captive-bolt stunners, firearms, or a chemical method involving the use of carbon dioxide gas (Forrest et al., 1975).

The Humane Slaughter Act of 1958 dictates that processors selling to federal agencies must comply with the Act and slaughter animals in a humane fashion, which includes stunning by one of the methods mentioned above.

The only penalty for non-compliance with the Humane Slaughter Act is removal of a plant from the list of plants eligible to sell to the federal government. Kosher-slaughtered animals are exempt from this act (Forrest et al., 1975).

Stunning must not kill the bird or animal according to the USDA, as the animal must die by bleeding. If stunning does kill poultry or red-meat animals, they are condemned by USDA as cadavers and may not then be processed for consumption by humans.

After stunning and hoisting the bird by one or both legs, it is killed by bleeding. This could be accomplished in several ways. The head can be removed, severing the jugular vein and carotid artery with a knife.

Another option could be to puncture the heart through the opening to the thoracic cavity at the base of the neck and/or to sever the major arteries and veins leaving the heart.

Feather removal can be accomplished simply by pulling the feathers out of the hide by hand. The feathers can be collected for further processing and use.

The poultry industry uses a scalding step prior to feather removal to loosen the feathers for subsequent mechanical feather removal using rubber picker fingers. Scalding of the emu, however, may have a deleterious effect on the hide and feather quality.

The head should be removed if it was not done as part of exsanguination. After exposing the esophagus and the trachea, they should be stripped from the neck and the esophagus tied off to prevent leaking of its contents.

Removal of the feet can be accomplished by cutting through the hock joint. The skin on the shanks can be removed either before or after separation of the feet and shanks from the carcass.

The vent should be excised, with care being taken not to rupture the cloaca or intestines, or contaminate the carcass with intestinal contents. After carefully severing the vent attachments, the vent should be withdrawn from the carcass, placed in a plastic bag and tied off.

Hide removal can be accomplished by carefully separating the hide from the external fat with a combination of a skinning knife and by inserting a hand or fist between the skin and the fat layer.

The use of the skinning knife should be kept to a minimum to avoid damaging the hide. Filtered compressed air may also be injected under the skin to aid in removal of the hide.

An incision along the middle of the sternum from the base of the neck, around the breast callous, to the vent area, and incisions along the front side of the drums will allow for removal of the hide from the carcass.

Care should be taken to avoid nicking or tearing the hide, as such defects will decrease its value. With the external fat now exposed, it can be easily trimmed from the carcass and collected for further processing.

The viscera can be removed by further opening the abdominal cavity with an incision from the vent area to the sternum. The viscera should be removed in such a manner as to avoid rupturing the gastrointestinal tract and contaminating the carcass with the contents.

After removal, the viscera, lungs and kidneys should all be examined for any signs of disease or abnormalities.

Emu muscle cuts.

A saw can be used to remove the breast plate by cutting between the sternum component of the ribs and the vertebral component, as well as severing the muscular attachment between the scapula and the vertebral component of the ribs.

The paired lungs and kidneys should be easily visible after removal of the sternum and should be removed from the carcass. The neck can be removed by a cut between the last cervical and first thoracic vertebra.

The carcass should be trimmed of any visible contamination and should be rinsed with potable water. Any microchip implants must be completely removed without question.

After a brief draining period the carcass should be placed in a cooler at or below 41 degrees F for chilling and aging.

To maximize tenderness of the meat the carcass should not be fabricated further or frozen until rigor mortis is completely resolved. It is expected that this would require up to a 24-hour aging period although the exact time required is not known at this time.

Inspection to assure wholesomeness, an important aspect of slaughter, has been neglected in this section thus far. As of April 1995, no federal regulations exist for the slaughter and processing of emus.

It is anticipated that the slaughter and processing of the birds will be regulated by the United States Department of Agriculture Food Safety Inspection Service (USDA/FSIS, personal communication).

The emu will most probably be classified as poultry, as will other ratites such as the ostrich, and regulated according to the Poultry Products Inspection Act, August 28, 1957 (Public Law 85-172, Statute 441). According to this law *poultry* is defined as any domesticated bird.

After the emu industry provided sufficient information to satisfy its requirements, USDA in October 1995 announced that it will grant voluntary inspections and approve acceptable facilities for emu slaughter.

Voluntary inspection can be converted to mandatory inspection for emus (or ratites) later. It is anticipated that promulgation of separate regulations for slaughtering ratites and processing the meat will occur.

TABLE 1: CARCASS DATA (LBS.) FROM DOMESTICATED AUSTRALIAN EMUS

TRAIT	AGE IN WEEKS		
	45	55	65
Live weight	67.46	76.50	91.10
Fat	7.78	11.99	22.58
Neck	1.92	2.14	2.23
Carcass	36.38	37.54	41.45
Fore quarter	2.05	2.16	2.42
Strip loin	.77	.77	1.04
Hind quarter	16.12	17.06	18.08
Drum	6.12	6.94	7.05
Mid drum	.92	1.21	1.15
Outside drum	.99	1.04	1.15
Inside drum	.99	1.04	1.15
Inner mid drum	.62	.68	.71
Inner outside drum	.71	.68	.75
Drum strap	.22	.22	.18
Bone	1.52	1.48	1.48
Thigh	9.83	10.12	11.02
Fore saddle	3.84	4.17	4.32
Fore rump	.64	.66	.70
Round	.82	.86	1.01
Oyster	.68	.68	.82
Flat fillet	.88	.84	.99
Hind saddle	3.99	4.39	4.56
Hind rump	.95	.99	1.08
Fan fillet	1.21	1.23	1.37
Flat rump	.46	.51	.53
Outside fillet	.70	.70	.86
Inside fillet	.42	.42	.53
Trim	.90	.92	.73
Bone	2.03	1.65	1.83

From Frapple, 1994

The USDA information categories that must be addressed by the emu industry before voluntary inspection can be granted include the following (list is not all-inclusive):
- humane slaughter (handling and stunning),
- ante-mortem (lotting, condemnation criteria, emergency slaughter),
- post-mortem (sanitary dressing and inspection),
- equipment, operating procedures (cooling and chilling requirements, maximum linespeed),
- diseases,
- further processing,
- industry data (slaughter classes, average live and dressed weight by class, estimate of slaughter numbers by class, byproducts, edible offal, expected markets),
- species physiological data and husbandry practices.

Several states have adopted regulations for emu or ratite slaughter.

The Texas Department of Health has promulgated such ratite slaughter guidelines in addition to the requirements under the Texas Meat and Poultry Inspection Act. The birds must undergo an antemortem inspection by a state official, during which the birds can be observed at rest and in motion to assure no abnormal conditions exist.

Additionally the producer must certify whether or not the birds have microchip implants or whether the birds have been treated with medications or vaccines. Any suspect birds may not be processed for human consumption.

Birds must also undergo a postmortem inspection. The carcass, head, trachea, esophagus, viscera, liver, heart, lungs and kidneys will be inspected for abnormalities such as swellings, abscesses, nodules, discolorations, inflammation, and exudates.

Any abnormalities can cause the carcass to be condemned. A passed carcass will be stamped with the approved *Texas Inspected and Passed* brand.

FABRICATION AND PACKAGING

A standardized description of emu fabrication and cuts has been developed by the Department of Agriculture, Western Australia in conjunction with the Emu Farmers' Association of Australia (Inc.) and the Australian Quarantine and Inspection Service (AQIS, 1993). The manual, entitled *Register of Approved Emu Cuts and Items*, is available through the Department of Agriculture, Western Australia.

According to the AQIS (1993), the carcass remaining after slaughter can be divided into two symmetrical halves by splitting the carcass along the vertebral column. Each half can be further divided into a fore quarter and a hind quarter by sawing at a right angle to the vertebral column through the juncture between the first free thoracic vertebra and the synsacrum (the fused vertebra).

The only cut derived from the fore quarter is the strip loin, weighing about .75 lbs in a yearling. No breast muscle is found on the emu.

The hind quarter, which contains most of the meat, can be divided into the thigh and the drum by cutting through the stifle or knee joint. These two portions can be further subdivided by separating the major muscles or muscle groups from each other and the bone.

The drum can be broken down into six major cuts: the inside drum, outside drum, mid drum, inner mid drum and the inner outside drum plus some trim.

The thigh can be divided in a variety of ways. A group of muscles found in the abdominal cavity attached to the pubis, ischium and the postacetabular ilium is the inside fillet. After removal of the inside fillet the thigh can be separated into the fore saddle and the hind saddle after removing the meat from the bone.

The fore saddle, which is basically the thigh muscles anterior to the femur, can be separated into the fore rump, round, flat fillet and oyster. The hind saddle is composed of the hind rump, flat rump, fan fillet and outside fillet.

As an alternative, rather than dividing the thigh into a fore and hind saddle, the most lateral and dorsal muscle, the full rump, can be removed as one large cut and then each of the previously listed cuts removed. The full rump is actually the fore and hind rump combined.

In addition to these major cuts a certain amount of trim will also be obtained. Presented in Table 1 are average weights of various cuts from yearling Australian birds (Frapple, 1994). All of the meat has a similar color, a deep purple similar to venison.

TABLE 2: COMPOSITIONAL DATA OF RAW EMU MEAT *

TRAIT	SOURCE		
	A[1]	B[2]	C[3]
Moisture %	73.60	66.18	74.05
Protein %	20.60	24.19	23.07
Fat %	1.7-4.0	8.38	1.89
Percentage of Fat			
Saturated		31.22	
Monounsaturated		49.03	
Polyunsaturated		19.75	
Cholesterol (mg/100g)	39.0-48.0	70.4	
Calories (kcal/100g)	113.0-127.0	174.0	116.0
Ash %		1.25	1.26
Na (mg/100g)		48.0	90.36
K (mg/100g)	314.0-317.0		317.0
Ca (mg/100g)	4.5-7.7		5.7
Fe (mg/100g)		3.0	5.53
Zn (mg/100g)			3.44
Mg (mg/100g)	28.7-31.0		
P (mg/100g)	480.0-490.0		

[1]Frapple, 1994
[2]ERI, 1994
[3]Thompson, et al, 1994

* Compare with Table 3

Vacuum packaging is the most common means of packaging the meat. Frapple (1994) found that refrigerated (36.5 degrees F) vacuum-packaged fan fillets had a shelf life of about nine weeks.

Many factors, however, affect the shelf life of a product: storage temperature, packaging materials and methods, and initial microbiological loads. During processing unavoidable contamination of the carcass occurs as microorganisms are transferred from feathers, hide, intestinal contents, equipment and people to the surface of the carcass.

Good processing plant sanitation and careful processing techniques can help minimize the contamination of the product thus extending the shelf life and increasing the safety of the product.

The meat can also be frozen and held below 0 degrees F just as other meat and poultry can. The meat will have a longer shelf life in the frozen state than refrigerated but deterioration does continue to occur during frozen storage.

Over prolonged frozen storage, freezer burn and oxidation can occur. Freezer burn results from surface dehydration and discoloration of the meat which can cause the meat to have a dry appearance and a lack of juiciness after cooking. Oxidation will result in the formation of off flavors and odors that are caused by the oxidative changes that occur in the fat.

Additionally, slow freezing can cause the formation of large ice crystals which disrupt muscle fibers, causing excessive drip losses upon thawing. Rapid freezing will reduce the muscle damage and the amount of drip.

Frapple (1994) found that raw meat frozen for 12 weeks had acceptable appearance and odor ratings as well as acceptable flavor characteristics. The effects of prolonged frozen storage on emu meat have not yet be ascertained.

MEAT COMPOSITION

The nutritional composition of raw emu meat from three sources is shown in Table 2. The meat is a good protein source, with values ranging from 20.60 to 24.19 per cent protein.

The meat has a variable fat content with reported values ranging from .63 to 8.83 per cent and about half of the fat in the meat is monounsaturated with oleic acid being the predominant fatty acid.

Other fatty acids found at significant levels are palmitic and linoleic, with stearic and palmitoleic constituting a small portion of the lipids. Comparisons of fatty acid profiles among emu, beef, pork and poultry can be found in Table 4.

The cholesterol content is somewhat variable between the two sources listed (Table 2). Frapple (1994) reported that Australian birds had cholesterol contents between 39 to 48 mg/100g, while forty birds raised and processed in the United States in 1994 by a marketing co-op had cholesterol content of about 70 mg/100g (ERI, 1994), which is intermediate to raw beef and poultry.

The content of selected minerals in emu meat is shown in Table 2. The mineral content of emu meat appears to be more similar to beef or venison than poultry or pork. The iron and phosphorus content of emu meat is higher than beef, pork or poultry. Emu

TABLE 3: NUTRITIONAL COMPARISON AMONG VARIOUS RAW MEATS

MEAT SOURCE	BEEF[1]	PORK[2]	CHICKEN[3]	DEER[4]
TRAIT				
Moisture %	70.27	72.23	75.99	73.57
Protein %	20.78	21.43	20.08	22.96
Fat %	6.82	5.66	4.31	2.24
Percentage of Fat				
Saturated	44.8	34.5	31.3	45.4
Monounsaturated	50.5	45.2	38.2	32.1
Polyunsaturated	4.7	20.3	30.5	22.5
Cholesterol (mg/100g)	59.0	59.0	80.0	85.0
Calories (kcal/100g)	150.0	143.0	124.0	120.0
Ash (%)	1.03	1.05	.94	1.16
Na (mg/100g)	63.0	52.0	85.0	51.0
K (mg/100g)	359.0	389.0	222.0	318.0
Ca (mg/100g)	6.0	17.0	12.0	5.0
Fe (mg/100g)	2.13	.84	1.03	3.4
Zn (mg/100g)	4.32	1.84	2.00	2.09
Mg (mg/100g)	22.0	23.0	23.0	23.0
P (mg/100g)	199.0	211.0	162.0	202.0

[1] Beef: composite of trimmed retail cuts, separable lean, USDA Choice Grade (USDA, 1990)
[2] Pork: fresh loin, separable lean (USDA, 1992)
[3] Broiler: dark meat, no skin (USDA, 1979)
[4] Deer: (USDA, 1989)

TABLE 4: FATTY ACID PROFILE OF FAT FROM EMU, BEEF, PORK AND CHICKEN

		(% OF TOTAL FAT)			
FATTY ACID	FORMULA	EMU[1]	BEEF[2]	PORK[3]	CHICKEN[4]
Palmitic	16:0	22.7	27.1	22.8	21.1
Stearic	18:0	7.1	14.2	10.8	8.3
Palmitoleic	16:1	3.9	4.4	3.2	5.7
Oleic	18:1	45.1	45.9	41.0	31.6
Linoleic	18:2	17.4	3.7	10.8	23.4
Linolenic	18:3	1.2	.35	8.7	1.4
Arachadonic	20:4	1.1	.53	1.2	2.9

[1] ERI, 1994
[2] USDA, 1990
[3] USDA, 1992
[4] USDA, 1979

meat, like any other red meat or poultry product can be a valuable source of protein and minerals.

The vitamin content of the meat has not yet been reported with the exception of vitamin A. A US study of forty birds reported an average vitamin A content of 19 IU/100g (ERI, 1994).

This indicates that a 3.5-ounce serving of emu meat would supply less than 2% of the RDA for vitamin A, thus would not be considered a significant source.

COOKERY AND PALATABILITY

Limited studies have been published on emu meat preparation and acceptability. Frapple (1994) offered fried emu meat to 165 Western Australian consumers to evaluate consumer perceptions of the meat. Approximately 85 per cent of the consumers agreed to sample the meat.

Ninety-one percent of the consumers said the meat was comparable to or better than steak they normally purchase for grilling and 44 per cent described the flavor as beef-like. Only three percent felt the meat had a gamey flavor.

In evaluating the tenderness 15 per cent rated the meat very tender, 47 per cent tender, 18 per cent slightly tender, 2 per cent tough and none of the consumers rated the meat very tough.

Fifty-one percent of consumers indicated that they would purchase emu twice a month or more, 28 per cent indicated that they would purchase the meat once a month and only 11 per cent said they would never purchase the meat.

It should be noted that Australians historically have had little regard for the feral emu, often perceiving the bird as a nuisance, especially to farmers. Additionally, until recently the Australians thought that the oil and leather were the only products of value from the bird, not even considering the meat as a marketable product (Minnaar and Minnaar, 1992).

In a recent study emu meat was evaluated for tenderness, juiciness, and meat-flavor intensity by trained panelists in the United States (Thompson et al., 1994; Table 5). Two cuts, the full rump and the inside drum, were broiled to one of three degrees of doneness—rare, medium rare and medium.

With the exception of the full rump cooked to medium doneness, the panelists rated the full rump and inside drum slightly to moderately tender and very to slightly juicy. The full rump cooked to medium doneness was considered slightly tough and dry.

Average shear values ranged from 4.6 kg for the rare meat up to 6.9 kg for the meat prepared to a medium doneness.

In a study conducted on beef steaks in a retail setting, restaurant consumers had a tenderness threshold between shear values of 5.4 kg and 6.0 kg (Huffman et al., 1994). Steaks with shear values below this range were considered slightly tender or even more tender. Steaks with shear values above this range were considered slightly tough or tougher.

TABLE 5: SENSORY EVALUATION OF FULL RUMP AND INSIDE DRUM COOKED TO THREE DEGREES OF DONENESS

TRAIT	DEGREE OF DONENESS		
	RARE	MEDIUM RARE	MEDIUM
Tenderness[1]	5.6	5.0	4.2
Juiciness[1]	6.4	5.4	4.4
Meat-flavor intensity[1]	6.3	6.2	6.2
Warner Bratzler shear values(kg)	4.6	5.5	6.9
Cooking losses (%)	27.9	30.9	40.8

[1] Tenderness, juiciness, meat-flavor intensity
1 = Extremely tough, dry, and bland
8 = Extremely tender, juicy, and intense

TABLE 6: TENDERNESS OF EMU MEAT AND BEEF RIBEYE BROILED TO A MEDIUM-RARE DEGREE OF DONENESS

	Subjective Tenderness[1]	Warner-Bratzler Shear (kg)
Emu Cuts		
Fan fillet	6.8	4.1
Flat fillet	6.3	3.6
Mid drum	5.9	3.9
Outside drum	5.2	4.8
Round	4.5	6.2
Beef ribeye	6.5	3.8

[1] 1 = extremely tough; 8 = extremely tender

The average shear values for the rare and medium rare emu meat would probably be considered tender to some degree but the meat cooked to medium doneness would probably be considered tough to some degree.

It should also be noted that as the degree of doneness increased the cooking losses increased, accounting for a loss of juiciness in the meat cooked to a medium degree of doneness.

In a second study Thompson and co-workers (1994) determined the palatability attributes of broiled (medium-rare) steaks from five different emu cuts and beef ribeye steak (Table 6).

Panelists found that emu meat had a meat-flavor intensity and juiciness similar to beef, or in the case of the flat fillet, the emu meat had a slightly more intense meat flavor.

Tenderness values and Warner-Bratzler shear values give an indication of the relative tenderness of the cuts tested. The fan fillet, flat fillet, mid drum, and outside drum of the emu had shear values similar to the beef steak.

Of the emu cuts examined, panelists found that the fan fillet was the most tender cut (very tender) and the round was the least tender (slightly tough). When cooked to a medium-rare doneness, all of the cuts averaged about a 30% cooking loss.

Emu meat quality and acceptability will depend on a variety of factors such as the degree of doneness, the method of preparation, the cut of meat, the age of the bird at slaughter, the nutritional status and ante-mortem condition of the bird, and processing and postmortem handling of the carcass and meat.

Studies indicated, however, that the meat has a fairly intense meat-like flavor, and can be prepared to have a tender texture and a juicy mouth-feel.

Since the meat is relatively lean, care should be taken to avoid overcooking which can cause the meat to be dry and tough.

Emu meat seems to be well suited to grilling, broiling, and pan frying, or any cookery method or recipe that would be used to prepare other lean red meats.

CONCLUSIONS

Limited research has been conducted on emu meat but studies indicate that emu meat is a relatively lean, flavorful, tender meat and certainly has marketing potential. The meat is high in protein and higher in iron than beef, pork or poultry.

The cholesterol content of emu meat is similar to that of other low-fat red meat and poultry products and could find a place in a sensible nutritious diet.

The expense of the meat will probably limit the sale of the meat to upscale restaurants or specialty markets, but the current bird population in the United States and lack of processing facilities probably could not support a larger target market, at least not at this time.

Further studies need to be conducted to examine the acceptability of the meat in US markets and possible marketing strategies.

Additionally the industry needs to address other processing, packaging, regulatory, food safety, nutritional, and cookery issues.

AN INTERVIEW WITH DOUG ATKINSON

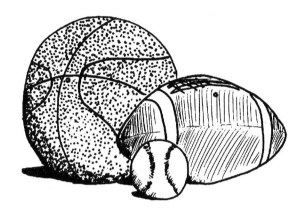

Trainer, NBA Dallas Mavericks
Atkinson Emu Ranch
Athens, Texas

On September 8, 1994, publisher Charley Elrod and editor Claire Drenowatz drove to Athens, Texas, to talk with Doug Atkinson about emu oil and the emu business.

E: Charley Elrod
A: Doug Atkinson
D: Claire Drenowatz

D: I was fascinated to read the chapter we got in from Australia. I didn't know anything about emu oil, so this is all new to me. How did you get involved with it?

A: When I first got into raising emus I heard about the properties of the emu oil. The people at Acres Away in Corsicana told me then that the Aborigines used it in Australia, to treat all their injuries, and they used it as a moisturizer.

D: This was after you were already into the emu business?

A: That was the first day that we checked into the emu business. But it took me two years before I actually got my hands on some emu oil and started using it.

D: Is it hard to find?

A: No, not now it's not. Well, it is. You can't buy it in a store.

D: That's what I meant.

A: There are about eight to ten companies that are marketing emu oil products now. Only about four of those companies are selling pure emu oil, which is what I use. The other companies are mixing it—making arthritic rubs, adding aspirin and alcohol, and camphor and eucalyptus, to make it like a topical analgesic.

But the pure oil is what I use, and what I've got everybody else using. And I don't think this can be compared to Ben-Gay, FlexAll 454, or other topical analgesics.

D: How do you mean it can't be compared to them? It's better or it's not as good?

A: It's better. First of all, the pure oil is an all-natural product. If you start adding things to it, now you're doing the same thing BenGay does, you've got the same product as they have. But this bottle here (held up a small bottle) doesn't have anything added to it.

D: And you just use it straight?

A: As is.

D: What do you use it for?

A: We use it for everything. Tendonitis, contusions, bursitis, ankle sprains, floor burns, open wounds, sunburns.

D: Do you get many sunburns at basketball games?

A: Not at the games, but our players do go out and lay outside, and they do get sunburned.

D: I'm sorry. I couldn't resist.

A: Oh, I understand, but really, I had several players come in this year after they'd been sitting by the pool.

I've used it myself for sunburn. After last season ended, I went fishing, and had on shorts and a short-sleeved shirt and got sunburned. My face got burned real bad. But within hours the emu oil took away the heat, and overnight the redness was gone.

The burn center at the Shriner's Hospital in Corsicana has been given emu oil, and last night I was told that the Shriner's Hospital is really enthusiastic about it.

D: Really! Have they done any research on it or have they just decided it works and they're not going to argue with it?

A: I think they decided it works and they're not gonna argue with it. There has been research done at Auburn University and Texas Tech, and Mississippi State and Purdue are doing research on it right now.

There have been some clinical studies, and they've found out that how emu oil works has to do with fatty acids. But as far as extensive clinical studies, it hasn't been done yet. I can tell you, I've seen it work.

D: I'm not arging with that. I'm just wondering whether anyone is going to the time and effort to find out why.

A: The way I understand it, is that the lipids, the active agents, are high in phosphorus. Skin is deficient in phosphorus, and so it absorbs emu oil readily, and the fatty acids go with it.

The fatty acids help cells to regenerate due to either age or an injury, to enhance healing is the way we have to say that. We can't make statements that emu oil is an anti-inflammatory, that, uh . . .

D: Because the FDA hasn't said you can.

A: Right. We can say it enhances or promotes healing, we cannot say that this is medicated. There are some brands of emu oil out that are labeled *medicated*, but they're very low in emu oil and very high in alcohol and aspirin. That's the reason they say it's medicated.

D: Aspirin? This is not . . . I'm unfamiliar with aspirin on the outside. This is not something you drink?

A: Oh, no, unh-uh. You rub it in.

D: You rub it in? You can do that with aspirin?

A: Yeah, but see, it's in a liquid form and the emu oil penetrates so much that it takes the aspirin in with it.

E: Acts as a driver.

D: I guess that sorta makes sense. So it's not really topical, it eventually gets to be internal.

A: Yeah. Pure emu oil is the same thing, it's like an aloe vera plant, or aloe vera juice. You don't have to have FDA approval for a completely natural product. What you have to have FDA approval for is what you claim it will do.

What I do, when I talk to the Texas state convention, local meetings, zone meetings, the national meeting of course, I say, "these are the results I have seen, adding emu oil to the other modalities that we use."

And then I give them the players' statements of what happens. There's no way that I am qualified to say "This stuff will do x."

D: What kind of injury do you see most? I know you're in basketball, but you've also been involved with football and baseball, haven't you?

A: Probably the injuries that I see the most and use emu oil on the most on are tendonitis, contusions, and sprains.

D: And it actually penetrates far enough to do some good on a deep joint problem, or a sprain?

A: Oh, yes. There's a player, Fat Lever, who had a deep joint injury in his knee. The articular cartilage was actually rubbed off, to where now he has an ulcer on the end of the bone. He missed two and a half years of playing basketball, and had operations on both knees.

When we got him from Denver, halfway through the season his knee went out. He had surgery on one knee one year, the next year on the other knee, and then he was out another full season, so he was out two and a half years.

When he came back, October of 93, we would only let him go through training camp with one practice a day, where everybody else practiced twice a day. And he had the freedom to take himself out of practice at any time if his knees were aching or sore.

From October until January we limited his time to twenty-four minutes a game. And if he played any more than that, we wouldn't let him practice or play the next day, because we wanted the longevity for the season.

D: He's good, huh?

A: He's very good. He's very active, he's a real wiry young man, he's a guard. He was having some discomfort and swelling that he was living with, that we controlled by therapy, from the beginning of training camp to January 20, when I started using emu oil.

I gave him some, and he was very open to it because he was already an emu owner. I know that it worked on me because I had tendonitis in my knees driving into Dallas.

I told him, "Fat, I can't say that this is gonna help you, but it won't hurt you."

He started applying it two to three times a day. Within three weeks, he told me, "I have no pain in my knees. And I cannot feel any swelling in my knees."

And he said, "I'd like to play more."

I told him, "If that's the case, we'll turn you loose and let you play."

We started adding minutes to his game time, and by the end of the season he was playing thirty-five minutes a game. With no swelling and no pain . . .

D: A professional game is what, forty-eight minutes?

A: Yeah, forty-eight minutes. He still uses emu oil, and he has no pain and no swelling in his knees. But he's not the only one. Tim Legler had a bad hip horner, a bad contusion from hitting the floor. It was a softball-size swelling.

We put emu oil on it, and our regular modalities—ultrasound, muscle stimulation, hot packs, cold packs, whirlpool—and it cut the treatment time in half.

D: Mmm-hmm.

A: Tim also had a bad contusion to his right biceps. We played back-to-back games in Phoenix and Denver. After the Phoenix game we flew to Denver, checked into the hotel, and gave the players the next morning off.

So at 5:30 that night we get on the bus to go play the Denver Nuggets. We get to the game and everybody suits up. Tim goes out and comes back to the locker room. Forty minutes before the game he told me, "I can't play."

I asked, "Why not, Tim?"

He answered, "Well, I didn't tell you this, but I caught a bad elbow in my biceps in last night's game, and it's so sore now that I can't fully extend my arm, and I can't control the basketball."

I said, "OK, well, let's don't give up, we got forty minutes here before game time."

So I go through the normal steps that I've done for twenty-four years of pro sports: muscle stimulation, ultrasound, hot packs, light massage. Except this time I added emu oil.

I soaked the muscle stimulator electrical pads in emu oil instead of water, which we usually use as a conductor for the electrical stim. I gave him ultrasound treatment, muscle stimulation, and hot packs for thirty minutes.

The team meeting goes on, and I asked Tim "What do you feel like? We got ten minutes before the game."

He told me, "Well, it feels better. I'm gonna go out, I'll give it a try."

And two minutes before the ballgame I ask him, "Tim, how are you feeling? Can you play?"

He says, "Yeah, I can play. It really feels a lot better." And he's extending his arm fully now. He didn't start the ballgame, but the coach put him in about four minutes into the ballgame, and he played all but those four minutes of the first half.

At halftime, we went back to the locker room, and I said, "Look, let's get some treatment on it."

Tim said, "I don't need any treatment, my arm feels fine."

I told him, "Well, rub in some more emu oil, we'll put a hot pack on it." (When I say hot pack, that's moist heat, hot moist heat.) Tim went to the team meeting, went back out, and played almost the entire second half.

We got on the plane to go back to Dallas, and Tim had ice on his arm, doing all the normal things for rehab.

The next morning at 10:00 I called him and asked him to come to the training room for treatment. He said, "Doug, I don't need to come to the training room."

I asked, "Why not? You couldn't play last night before the game."

He answered "Well, there is nothing wrong with my arm now, I have no pain in it, I have no stiffness, and I have no discoloration." He added, "I don't need treatment if there's nothing wrong with me."

I told him, "OK, Tim, it's your arm."

And he never bruised, never missed a game. And Tim credits it to emu oil, and I credit it to emu oil. Sean Rooks, Fat Lever, Tim Legler—all of them credit recovery due to emu oil—enhanced recovery, quicker than normal time.

D: You've been at this for a long time.

A: I've been in pro sports for twenty-four years.

D: How did you get into training? I mean, I've watched basketball games, but I'm not sure I even know what a trainer does.

A: My job is to make sure that the players are healthy and able to compete on the floor of a basketball game.

D: You're not a doctor?

A: No. that's not my job. I work very closely with two or three doctors. You would compare my qualifications to that of a physical therapist. I'm a certified and licensed athletic trainer. We do nutrition, strength conditioning programs, rehab, and we do preventive measures to enable the players to play.

D: Help them lose all that weight they gain between seasons?

A: Sure. Each player is on an independent program, according to what he needs—strength and conditioning, diet, flexibility. And if they're injured it's my job to do the therapy rehab to get them back on the floor.

D: Sounds like a lot of responsibility.

A: I've been with the California Angels, Los Angeles Dodgers, Chicago Bulls, and now the Dallas Mavericks. I've been with the Mavericks . . . this'll be the fifteenth year with the Mavericks.

So, I've been at it for a while, and I've never seen . . . I've used aloe vera in almost all forms, from gallon containers of pure juice—which we had been using on sunburns before I came to emu oil—or if we had a sprained ankle I'd submerge the ankle in pure aloe vera juice.

D: Really? I didn't know about that application. I've always thought of it as topical.

A: Well, you just let it soak in there. I've made aloe vera juice packs, I've used it in creams, and added it to cortisone creams. There's even aloe vera shampoo.

D: Oh, yeah, I use a lot of that.

A: Well now there's emu oil shampoo, which is even better than aloe vera. But emu oil is a hundred times better, therapeutically or enhancing healing, than aloe vera.

D: One of the things I keep reading about is that the industry is not to a slaughter market yet, you're still in a breeder market. Wouldn't that make the oil kind of expensive?

A: Well, but it lasts a long time. One bottle will last my player . . . let's say Fat Lever uses it on both knees three times a day. One bottle will last him about three weeks.

D: Mmm. I was wondering, how much emu oil is there in a bird?

A: Between 4.5 to 5 quarts from an adult bird, when it's rendered out. The emu bird has a layer of fat across its back, around its chest, and up the throat area.

Now, when the bird is slaughtered, first the hide comes off. And then the visceral fat and the body fat will just completely detach from the meat, the muscles of the bird. It's not like beef fat, where it's marbled and in the meat.

So the fat is in its own container in the body of the emu. Then it's hung in a heated area, and it drips, and then they start purifying it after it drips out.

D: So when you say rendering, you're not necessarily talking about sticking it in a pot and cooking it out.

A: Some of it is done that way. Puts it into a pure form.

D: Sort of like olive oil, first pressing and . . .

A: Sure. And there are three or four grades of oil, premium, commercial, industrial. The premium oil is the pure oil, it's the most unsaturated. You wouldn't use this pure oil for commercial or industrial use.

D: What commercial or industrial uses does the oil have?

A: Well, emu oil is being tested right now for high-tech lubrication, an additive to enhance lubrication of your car.

D: Really?

A: Sure, because it doesn't break down at high temperatures.

D: With the exception of whale oil, I didn't know of any other animal fat that was useable that way.

E: The viscosity does not break down.

A: This is so new. It's being tested for that right now.

E: See why we need this book?

D: So you've got commercial and industrial grades, and premium, and the premium is what you use on people.

A: Right. Right now we're using the very best oil. But it may be that the very best oil goes into . . . let's talk about the premium oil.

D: OK.

A: There'll probably three levels. Maybe the highest rendered best oil there is will go directly to the hospitals, to the burn units.

And the not-quite-so-good grade of premium oil will go into over-the-counter products. They'll put that into shampoos, conditioners, etc.

D: Sunburn remedies.

A: Sunburn remedies. Over-the-counter use. Into the retail market. But the biggest market I can see is going to be in the medical field right now.

D: Yeah, if Shriner is interested, I mean even mildly interested, if they can prove that it actually works, your market ought to take off. Are there enough birds?

A: Right now, there aren't enough birds in the United States for a sustained slaughter market. There is plenty of oil in storage, from Australia, to supply the market for emu oil in the United States.

D: How long does it keep?

A: They tell me up to two, two and a half years. There's enough oil over there right now in storage for us to have a market for the emu oil, big market, if it explodes here any time soon.

D: Do people actually import the byproducts from Australia? Other than the oil?

A: Oh yes. They import hides and meat.

D: Because the Australians have enough birds.

A: Yes. They have a slaughter market over there. See, you can't export a live bird or a fertile egg, from Australia right now. It has to be the products from a slaughtered bird.

D: Is that because of the market or is that protectionism?

A: That's protection because this is the national bird of Australia. And so the government there won't let you take a live bird or the fertile eggs out.

D: How did they get here?

A: From Europe, and there were also birds brought over before the government instituted this ban.

D: Reminds me of the Chinese and silkworms. I'm just wondering how many critters it takes to make a slaughter market.

I mean, Charley was telling me the other day that we slaughter a billion chickens in this country every year, and I thought, wait a minute, that's not a number I can relate to.

A: There's in the neighborhood of about 600,000 birds in the United States.

D: OK. You have one breeding pair. How many chicks will they produce each year.

A: Conservatively, when I talk to people about the emu market, to sell them emus, for them to either raise or for me to board and raise for them, I tell them between 20 and 25 live chicks a year.

D: And how many did you start with before you got 20 or 25 live chicks? I mean, is the mortality rate high or low or . . .

A: The mortality rate is very, very low. I know people . . . I had one pair of birds lay thirty-nine eggs last year. I know people that are getting 52 eggs and 47 of them are hatching. When I say 20 to 25 I'm trying to be conservative so I don't lead people down the garden path.

D: Where are you selling oil?

A: Well, in January of 1994 is when it broke into the sports world. Before that, emu ranchers were selling it to their neighbors, to elderly people to use on arthritic conditions, just by word of mouth.

D: What does it take to get it approved to sell in stores?

A: I don't think that you need FDA approval to sell it in stores, as long as what is printed on the bottle is legal.

To get into an major pharmacy chain, I don't know exactly what that will take.

D: Well, not only that, do you have the quantity to deal with something that large.

A: The quantity is available right now. There's a lady named Donna Karan who has a cosmetics line, who has it in Neiman Marcus, Saks, lots of the big . . .

D: Donna Karan is a name I recognize.

A: Well, she has a cosmetic line that has emu oil in it right now. It's already available in Saks and Neiman-Marcus and Macy's.

To get it into a major drugstore chain, we need an advertising campaign to sell it to the retail market. Like when the company that owns Flexall 454 wanted to make Flexall the number-one-selling topical analgesic in the United States.

D: I think I've seen it advertised on TV.

E: Joe Namath endorses it.

D: Joe Namath, yes.

A: All the pro sports trainers in the United States endorse it, from the four major sports. The first year they spent $8 million dollars on TV advertisements. So to get this over the counter nationwide . . . if I had the money, I'd do it.

E: And that's just the cost of the ads, not what they paid Joe Namath.

D: Or how much it took to make the stuff.

A: Yeah, they already had their own factory to build it, bottle it, everything. It's very expensive to add a new product line, or to create a new product line.

Now I'll be honest with you, the Flexall 454 people are . . . Chatham Corporation does have emu oil. And they are researching it to see what they want to do with it. There's a possibility they might put it right beside Flexall.

D: Something just occurred to me. Do you anticipate or have you run into any resistance because it's an animal product?

A: None so far. And the main reason for that is because we've only just started to develop a commercial slaughter market here in the United States.

Now when we do, I'm sure people will ask in what manner are we slaughtering the birds, is it humane, and all that kind of stuff.

When we do open a slaughter market, we will take and slaughter them in a humane manner so there's no pain to the animals. They'll be processed like other livestock.

D: I wasn't thinking of that so much as the fact that many people are against using animal products, period, no matter how they are processed.

A: As yet, I haven't encountered any of that. I do know some people that're against furs, everything.

D: I was just curious. If something occurs to me, I usually ask the question because I'm usually sorry later if I don't. Like, what got you into the bird business to start with? How did you get involved in all this?

A: I've been in pro sports for 24 years. I hope to retire when I'm 55, so I've got ten years to go. I've got 70 acres here that I'd like to be able to make a living on somehow. To do that at the present time I'd have to open a dairy, and run dairy cows.

I can't run beef cattle on 70 acres and make a living. I do run beef cattle right now and they pay for my taxes and insurance. So that's why I started looking at the ratite industry. I have 12 breeder pairs now. I'm going to go up to 45 breeder pairs.

I enjoy the breeder market right now and the price of these birds, but what I'm looking ahead to turn over a minimum of 600 yearlings a year to the slaughter market.

It's going to be very very comparable to cattle ranching. There's 3000 acres around my place, they run 600 mama cows, but it takes 3000 acres to do that.

I want to turn over 600 yearlings a year on 70 acres, buy several more tracts of land around here, be able to retire and have the lifestyle that I'm living right now and live in the country and make a living off my own property. And that's the reason I'm in the ratite business.

D: How long do you think it will be before you see a fairly serious slaughter market? Nationwide, how long is it going to be before you can buy emu oil products over the counter in any drugstore?

A: I think within two to three years you'll see emu oil products over the counter. I believe in five to seven years there will be a sustained slaughter market here in the United States. I believe it'll be about that long before it happens.

D: That would assume, it seems to me, that you have a market for all the products, because emu oil's not going to carry it. What's the market for the rest of the bird?

A: The emu oil will be the most dominant product, because of its properties, what you can use it for, what it enhances. Once it breaks through into the medical field, emu oil is going to sustain the market.

Emu meat, because of the health concerns of people in the United States, and the demand for food, worldwide, is going to be very, very productive.

D: Is there anything else I ought to know about emu oil that I haven't asked. Your basic dummy, here, remember, I'm the one who's writing for the folks who haven't got a clue what emu oil is about. Or sports training, or anything else?

E: Doug, one of the reasons this book is being published is to educate the consumer about the whole industry.

Somebody wants to buy a Ford, buy a Chevy, buy a Dodge, that's available. But if J Q Public doesn't know what a ratite is, and doesn't know what these birds are, we're sunk.

D: Let me tell you about the word *ratite*. A couple of times I haven't been able read a diskette one of the authors has sent, and I've asked Charley to fax the hard copy to me.

My fax is part of my computer, and the software has optical character reading capabilities. And the program keeps converting the word *ratite* into *rattle*.

And WordPerfect tried to do the same thing when I ran a chapter through the spell-checker program. At least until I told it *ratite* is a word. *Ratite* is not yet a household word.

E: Well, that's what we're working on. We have to get people to know that these birds are here, they're going to stay here, and they're going to see more and more of them, the meat, the hides. And the oil, at least for the emu.

A: That's really about it. Education is what's going to make this market work. And I don't really have anything else.

D: Well, I guess that's as good a place as any to end it. Thanks.

EMU OIL: A 40,000-YEAR-OLD THERAPY

Stephen Birkbeck
Mt Romance Pty Ltd
Denmark, Western Australia

The indigenous people of Australia thrived in one of the harshest climates in the world through living with the land and finding their means of survival in nature.

Traditional therapeutic qualities of emu oil are evident throughout Australia, although actual original discovery of the oil's qualities are locked in the oral history of the Aboriginal people, extending back thousands of years. Oral history indicates that emu oil was used by the Aborigines for the treatment of arthritic pain, inflamed joints, muscular aches, and burns.

This traditional use was adopted by European settlers in Australia in the nineteenth century, and ample written evidence is available in regard to this practice. It became limited, however, as natural products made way for twentieth-century "progress" and synthetic alternatives replaced the natural values of earlier centuries.

RE-DISCOVERY

The 1970s in Western Australia saw a return to natural products, as evidenced by Australian Federal Government directives toward investment in indigenous enterprises. As one outcome of the establishment of the pioneer emu farms in Australia, the wonderful properties of emu oil became more well known.

The Ngangganawili Community in Wiluna, Western Australia, began the first commercial work with emu oil in 1985. Early use of crude emu oil extracted from the farmed emus illustrated the commodity's commercial potential.

The early work was reinforced though Ngangganawili's association with Dromaius Enterprises (the first non-Aboriginal emu farm), and Orion Laboratories. Early work indicated good preservation qualities and cosmetic and therapeutic potential.

FROM BIRD TO PRODUCT

Emu oil is derived from separate areas of the emu, in subcutaneous and internal fat. In total, an emu will carry between four and fifteen kilos of fat, depending on age, sex and condition.

According to statistics accumulated since the 1980s, there is a clear age-to-fat ratio evident. The peak fat yield is at sixteen months of age.

The fat is actually a by-product of the main product lines derived from the emu—meat and leather. Fat can be easily separated from the meat through simple tasks during processing.

Through stabilization research done to date, it is clear that the fat will degenerate in a very short time, and immediate respect for the raw commodity must apply. Minimal ultraviolet light and immediate temperature reduction are essential for maximum-quality raw material.

An average of between 70 and 85 per cent ratio of oil to fat has been achieved, depending on the system and the quality of the fat.

CHEMICAL COMPOSITION

The diet of the birds will affect the fatty acids present in emu oil, and therefore chemical composition may vary. Emu oil is not a single chemical entity, but a mixture of trigycerides, of which most are fatty acids (Figure 1).

RESEARCH

CONTEMPORARY RESEARCH

Emu oil was first commercially released to the world in 1990, from farm-based stock in Western Australia. This market development was coupled with French and Australian research between 1990 and 1994.

Subsequent worldwide interest and attention has now been generated through this early work, and the USA and Europe appear to be at the forefront of medical discovery toward the end of this century.

PIONEERING RESEARCH

Dr. George Hobday

Through the pioneering efforts of Dr. George Hobday, General Medical Practitioner and founder of Dromaius Enterprises, the reputed qualities of emu oil were tried in his medical practice on more than 500 patients through a ten-year period.

This invaluable work has established clear trends that have led to many of the more sophisticated efforts made by specialist organizations.

See Dr. Hobday's article which is reproduced on the next page.

Hospital Research

Based at Sydney's North Shore Hospital Research Unit in New South Wales, Australia, research has since 1990 been undertaken into the active ingredients within emu oil, in relation to arthritis and the capacity to reduce inflammation and pain caused by arthritis.

The results of this work are confidential but on all accounts encouraging.

Mt Romance

Mt Romance was founded in 1988, and is Australia's market leader with emu products. The first commercial products using the oil were released in 1990. This early range was a comprehensive selection of body-care products.

In 1991, Mt Romance France was established in Europe. It was here that all of the founding pioneer research on the penetrative qualities, anti-inflammatory capacity, and cell-regenerative potential of emu oil was developed.

RESEARCH 1991/93

Through French government and private facilities in Australia and France, Mt Romance has established data on basic penetrative qualities of emu oil through free fatty acid compounds such as palmitoleic acid, and their relevance to the epidermis and joints (Figure 2).

ANTI-INFLAMMATION

Emu oil has qualities which will provide significant and immediate reaction in joint inflammation (Figure 3).

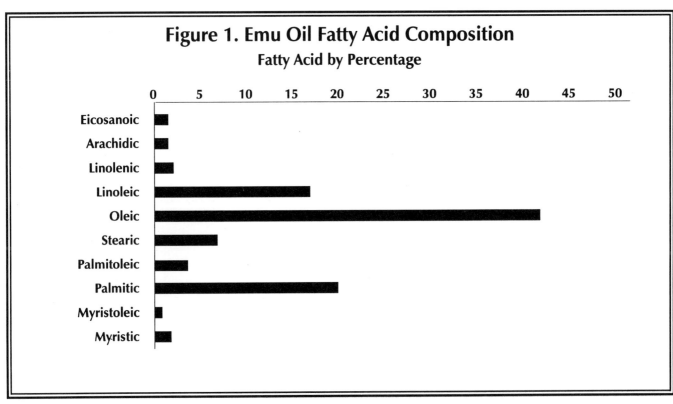

Extracts from Dr. George Hobday's article in *Australian Emu*, July/August 1994 (used with permission).

CLINICAL EXPERIENCES

I was initially introduced to emu oil by patients of mine . . . who advocated its use in treating their skin, painful joint, and muscle ailments. I was aware of the past reputation of emu oil, but it is satisfying for me to find that on no occasion over the past ten years, having exposed the oil to over 500 patients, using the oil over lengthy periods, it has been very rare for anyone to report that it had deteriorated or *gone off*.

Before recommending it, I had tests done to identify its content, which showed it contained a variety of fatty acids, but no hormones or steroids. I had the oil tested for bacterial content and found that in its pure state it grew no organisms.

In addition, when made into a moisturizer, which is a mixture of oil, emulsifier, and water, I had the cream challenged with four organisms (Staphylococcus aurius, E. coli, Pseudomonas, and Candida albicans) in increasing quantities, and compare with glycerol 10% in Sorbolene. The emu oil cream was found to withstand greater quantities of bacteria before growth took hold. Neither cream contained preservatives for this test.

From clinical experience with emu oil, it became obvious that its two major actions were its anti-inflammatory properties and its ability to penetrate the skin. It also appears to provide some solar protection. How these actions occur and to what extent remain to be discovered.

TEN YEARS OF CLINICAL USAGE

During this period, my experience with emu oil has been entirely confined to use on the skin. After advising patients of its experimental nature, I have prescribed emu oil for us in three main areas: dry skin problems, treatment of muscle aches and pains, and treatment of wounds which had epithelialised.

Eczema
Eczema sufferers often complain that the moisturizers on the market, such as glycerol 10% in Sorbolene, irritate their skin. I have found that emu oil, or creams made from emu oil, have often been of benefit and provide significant reduction of irritation and inflammation of the skin.

Emu oil does not appear to have sufficient anti-inflammatory properties for use against inflamed eczema. However, it is a very useful follow-up to steroid treatment.

Keloids
Massaging emu oil twice daily appears to significantly reduce recent keloid scarring, and have an anti-inflammatory action against the formation of keloid tissue. It does not seem to reduce oil keloid scarring.

Burns
The use of emu cream or oil immediately in early blistering appears to hold great promise. Although trials have been limited, it seems to promote faster healing with less pain and scarring.

Donor Sites in Skin Grafting
I have found that the donor site after skin grafting benefits from the application of the oil, which appears to reduce pain and promote a less-scarred heal.

Psoriasis
To date, use of emu oil on psoriasis has not been particularly effective, though some patients reported some benefit.

Joints
The benefits of emu oil on joints to reduce pain, swelling and stiffness is most evident where the joint is close to the skin surface, such as hands, feet, knees and elbows. Deep joints such as the hip do not appear to respond.

Stiff joints, particularly as seen in hands, is one area where massaging emu oil is of considerable benefit. Whether this is due to its anti-inflammatory (therefore pain-relieving) property or whether this is due to another facet of the oil remains to be determined by research.

The method used is to massage oil two or three times a day into the painful area, and the use of a compress of oil overnight. The best compress I have made is to use approximately eight thicknesses of ordinary paper tissues, folded to the size of the affected area, onto which the oil is poured and spread like butter. The compress is backed with a slightly smaller sheet of light plastic, and then bandaged over the painful area overnight.

I have found the oil not to deteriorate and the compress to be reusable for several days, with the addition of a little oil each day.

Growing Pains
This painful condition, usually experienced at 2:00 a.m. in the knees of six-year-old children, is caused, I believe, by the active growing child overstretching the ligaments and tendons around the knee. By day, the pump action of movement removes the reactive swelling of the area. At night, however, this swelling builds up, the child moves and cries from the pain in the joint, causing distress to parents and frequently a visit to the doctor where investigations for arthritis may be done.

To date, as a result of massaging emu oil into the joint prior to the child going to sleep, no parents have returned to say their child is suffering from growing pains.

Rheumatoid Arthritis
I have not found emu oil to be effective against active arthritis such as rheumatoid arthritis, although some colleagues have noticed benefit. This is an area that obviously requires further research.

Bruising and Muscle Pain
Emu oil appears to provide significant benefit to recent bruising and muscle pain, where the injury is relatively superficial. The treatment is the massage and compress combination previously described. Similarly, sports-related muscle strains have been significantly reduced with a post-exercise emu oil massage. Some trainers and masseurs are using this in preference to other oils, again indicating a superior anti-inflammatory action over commonly-use embrocations.

Recent Wounds
Emu oil applied to epithelialised wounds appears to reduce scar-tissue formation. Also, the anti-inflammatory action seems to soothe wounds after surgery. This has been very evident in coronary artery bypass graft operations, where the greatest discomfort often comes from the leg from which the vein has been removed. In my experience, massaging emu oil onto this area two or three times per day has significantly speeded up the healing process and reduced scarring.

As the emu oil is sterile, there is no concern with using it on any open area. I have encountered no ill effects from using emu oil on open areas such as a partially-healed wound or abrasion.

CONCLUSION

Used for centuries by the original inhabitants of Australia, emu oil has reached a point of usage where proper clinical studies need to be done to determine its true place in the medical armamentarium. To date, no true experimental work has been done. It is my hope that those skilled in research will take up this challenge and run with it as fast as the emu.

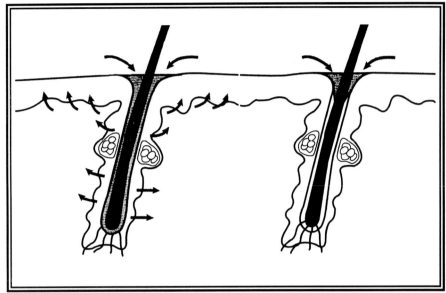

Figure 2. On the left, a representation of the depth of penetration of emu oil, as opposed to mineral oil on the right. Emu oil penetrates farther into the skin, allowing it to work deeper than the surface effects of mineral-oil based products.

CELLULAR REGENERATION

Under the experiments conducted by Mt Romance, cellular regeneration is achievable, but emu oil concentration must be specific to the base materials with which it is blended, and subtle changes to percentages may affect resultant cellular proliferation.

FUTURE RESEARCH

The future need of emu-oil marketing is clear. It is to take all existing work as a platform and try to get governments around the world to acknowledge the generic abilities of emu oil. To date, a number of brands, products and patents have been instigated for individual benefit. However, the viability of the international industry will rely on the generic emu oil having access to formal recognition.

CURRENT STATUS

Emu oil still has no internationally-recognized compendial standard. The Australian health authorities, under the direction of the Australian Therapeutic Goods Administration (TGA), has accepted the ingredient for use in topical therapeutic items. The inclusion of emu oil in the Australian Approved Names List was ratified in 1993.

There are now a number of products listed with TGA Australia. The challenge now is to have the substance gain international accreditation and be issued with acceptable standard references.

THE FUTURE

Emu oil has definite therapeutic qualities. However, the greatest challenge facing the industry is public reaction to animal-based compounds.

As such, the critical factor is not so much what emu oil can do for the consumer, but what the consumer's opinion will be of the exploitation of the Australian emu. For this reason, producers must exercise discipline in generic messages, and brand rivalry must be balanced with an overall image of the industry's environmental benefits.

Based upon Australian, American, and European productive capacity, the need to develop wide and varied markets is imperative. The penetrative qualities herein discussed, along with the oil's cosmetic and therapeutic qualities, must be documented. In addition to this, work is required on industrial applications and pharmaceutical potential.

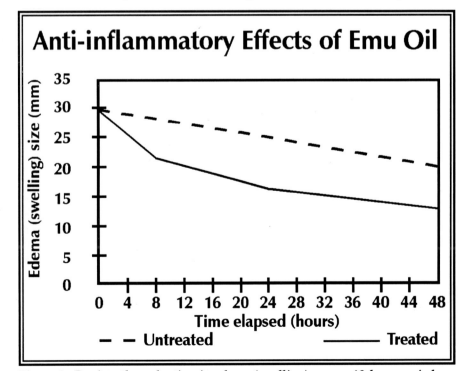

Figure 3. Depicts the reduction in edema (swelling) over a 48-hour period, on inflamed tissue left untreated (broken line) and treated with emu oil (solid line).

RAISING RHEAS

Mary Lee Stropes
Shad-ee Shack Farm
Booneville, Arkansas

Chris Ramsey
Little Creek Exotics
Utopia, Texas

The rhea is one of thousands of species of birds originating in South America, but it is one of only two ratites from that continent. The word *ratite* is derived from the Latin word *ratis*, meaning raft. The breast bone is shaped like a flat raft, lacking a keel.

With no large bone to which to attach wing muscles, the wings are not functional for flying. As they run they use their wings to balance when they change directions quickly.

Rheas are equipped with very powerful long legs to enable them to escape their predators. Rheas have three toes, each ending in a well-developed toe claw. The toes face forward, since rheas are not perching birds.

The feathers on the wings of rheas, as in all ratites, are loose and unbarbed, unlike the feathers of flying birds. Rheas lack the gland that produces an oil which other birds use to coat their feathers.

The two species of rheas, *Rhea americana* and *Pterocnemia pennata*, and subspecies from Brazil to the tip of South America, in general resemble the African ostrich in their habits.

Rheas are not as docile as ostriches and emus. Rheas can be difficult to handle and can not be maneuvered like the larger birds.

Studies of rheas have been limited primarily to the zoological field. Husbandry and medical management have only been studied and available to the public, university veterinary medicine departments, and poultry science departments in the United States in the last five years.

Rheas have not been studied in depth, and little knowledge of their lives in the wild is available. Raising rheas is a new entry in the field of alternative livestock for American farmers. We should remember that we have taken a magnificent, beautiful, fascinating bird from the wild out of its natural habitat into our fenced property.

Rhea farming or ranching in the United States has been based on the personal experience of people who have had rheas for many years. The success of raising rheas in captivity has, in many cases, integrated the knowledge of poultry raising, even granny's wisdom in setting and hatching back-yard chickens.

We raise our rheas very simply. We try to stay as close to nature as possible. We raise chicks and adults in two locations, the chicks in town in my big yard, and then they are moved to the farm at about 4 to 5 months, where they are allowed to roam freely. Once they are old enough to start breeding, the pairs or trios are kept in separate pens.

This has worked well for us, and we have extremely large, healthy birds. I have read a lot about what to do and what not to do, and it does not fit my program.

My chicks mostly raise themselves, with my feeding, watering, and making sure they are protected from the elements. That's what we learned from watching a male raise his clutch of chicks, and that's what we try to stay as close to as we can.

There are no secrets to raising rheas. Common sense, and relying on nature's way, will satisfy their needs. Let the chicks raise themselves. We certainly do not need to introduce them to unnatural things. Remember that they do not graze on grass in the wild. They thrive on leaves, bushes, flowers, and bugs.

- Mary Lee Stropes

FACILITIES

Before you purchase your rheas, you need a place to keep them. Your pens can be elaborate or they can be plain and simple. A good basic pen should be about 25' x 50'. Larger pens are OK, but I would not go much smaller.

The birds need room to exercise, and the ability to escape from one another if need be. Remember, you need to get into the pen if you are collecting eggs, so it should be kept to a size where you are able to go in and recover eggs quickly.

A fence height of at least five feet is recommended for breeders, as they can jump out of a shorter fence when cornered or excited. Fence material of 2" x 4" square welded non-climbable wire works well. The holes are not large enough for birds to get their feet or heads through, which minimizes self-inflicted injuries.

When you build a fence, use regular corner posts to stretch the fence, but use small or steel posts in between so the fence will have some give to it. When the birds are trying to get away from you or something else in the pen, they tend to hit the fence. So pull the fence tight but not rigid. As they hit the fence, it will give a trampoline fence. A very rigid fence could result in injured birds.

The birds need some form of shelter in their pens. Whether it is trees, or a man-made shelter, they need a place to get out of the sun and bad weather. Typically these birds do not use this shelter unless the weather is extreme (hot or cold) but it must be available.

The sheds most widely used are small three-sided 8' x 10' buildings about 8' tall in the front and 7' tall in the rear.

You should face the entrance side away from the prevailing direction of cold winter winds. You might also want to face the pens to the east since the summer sun is cooler in the mornings rather than to the west where you get hot afternoons.

How you position your sheds will depend on the area in which you live. A little common sense goes a long way in this business.

We use our shelters to keep the feed dry. By keeping the feed dry, especially in wet weather, you will have less waste.

Feed and water are important in your pens. You may decide to feed your birds daily, or use self feeders. The self feeders are nice because you do not have to feed every day. But this makes it easy for people to neglect their birds.

By feeding every day you will check your birds each day and may stop a potential hazard such as a bird hung up in the fence, or a wound that needs attention, as well as keeping your birds gentle and workable because they see you every day.

If you choose self-feeding, you need to ease your birds into it so they do not gorge themselves when you first start. You should not have trouble with adult birds overeating if you gradually increase the amount you feed until they are leaving some feed in the feeder when they are through.

Always have fresh water available for your birds. You can water your birds out of buckets, or use self-waterers. You must, however, periodically clean out the waterers, because they will build up scum, algae, and other potential disease-causing agents.

During breeding season you should give your birds vitamins in their water. Typically once a week is sufficient, but keep those waterers clean.

- Chris Ramsey

SELECTING YOUR BREEDERS

If you are getting birds three years old or older, find out their laying record from previous years. Any reputable bird breeder will keep records of what his or her birds have done in seasons past.

Total number of eggs is not as important as fertility. It is common, however, for some of the first eggs of the season to be infertile, as well as a few in the middle of the season, because storms and confusion may disrupt the breeding cycle.

If you are getting two-year-old birds, more than likely they would not have laid as yearlings, but you can get some idea of what to expect by what their parents have done in years past.

The birds you are acquiring should be big, straight, healthy birds. Rheas, which are the smallest of the domesticated ratites, should have long, big-boned legs. Visit several breeders—only after looking at several rheas can you get a good picture of what they should look like.

Stay away from stunted, dwarfed-looking birds. Some birds have heavy bones in the legs, but they are short from the ground to the hock. Typically the offspring will carry on this characteristic and it is not a good one to have.

Rheas should have straight legs, back and neck. The backs should form a straight line, without kinks.

You should stay away from birds that look like they are knock-kneed or cow-hocked. These characteristics could be from an injury. But most likely if both legs are crooked, it is hereditary or they had some deficiency when growing up. Either way, this may cause problems in rearing the offspring.

As you look at the birds, watch them as they walk in the pens. Look them over as they walk towards and away from you. From the rear, you can really see if the legs are straight.

The birds should be healthy. Birds are animals, and like most animals, if they feel good, they will act like they feel good. They should have slicked-off feathers, and they should be standing tall and walking around the pens.

Note the bird's eyes—see if they are clear of mucus and opened wide. A listless bird is a bird that is not feeling up to par.

If the birds pass these simple tests and you are ready to buy, it is a good idea to check the sexes of the birds. A reputable breeder should not have a problem with showing you the male's phallus and the absence of a phallus in the female. The female's clitoris is very small and sometimes difficult to see.

You can generally tell on mature birds which is the male and which is the female by their appearance. The male will have a black collar or *V-neck-sweater* look on his chest while the female's markings are somewhat lighter.

To sex the birds yourself is not difficult but it does take some practice. You should see this done by someone with experience before trying it yourself, as you may injure the bird in the process.

SEXING ADULT BIRDS

The best way that I have found to sex the adult birds is by catching the bird and feeling the organs. On adult birds you should not have to look at the organ to sex it, because you can actually feel the organ.

This is done by getting into the pen or stall with the bird, and as it passes you by on the left, reach out with your left arm and wrap it around the birds's chest. Let the bird keep on its path. As it passes you, keep your arm on its chest, rapidly slide your right arm between the legs, and grasp your left hand. In the same motion, lift the bird off its feet and plant its back to your chest.

Make sure you do not try to look around the bird, as when it is lifted, it will thrash its legs around for a short time. Their toenails are sharp and their legs have a lot of power. After the trashing stops you can slide your right arm down, through your left hand until you reach the vent.

Simply insert your fingers into the vent and you can feel for the organ. I use my middle and ring fingers. The male's phallus is a hard corkscrew-shaped cartilage that will be obvious to the touch. You can actually roll the phallus out of the vent if someone needs to see it for positive identification.

If the bird is a female, there will not be any cartilage and you can feel a small button which is a little smaller than a pea. Until you have done this several times it may be a little difficult to positively identify a bird as a female, since younger males do not have a large phallus, and your feel may not be experienced enough.

You can remedy this by *flipping* the bird and visually checking the organ. To flip a bird, use the same method of catching the bird, but you need to have two helpers.

After catching the bird and it has quit thrashing about, one helper on either side of you will grab a leg, gently but firmly, usually on a three count.

Each leg is grabbed with one hand above the hock and one below it. The legs are kept extended and the person holding the bird then lowers the bird's back to the ground—gently. The helpers, keeping the legs extended, should slightly lift the bird's rear end.

Be careful not to hurt the bird: again, firmly but gently. Keep in mind that these birds have a lot of power in their legs when pushing or kicking, but not much power pulling their legs back towards them. There is not a lot of stress on the birds with their legs extended, since they will not continue to try to push you away.

DON'T TRY sitting on the bird's legs when they are folded up. They are capable of pushing you off, or worse, breaking a leg trying to push you off.

You can now walk around to the bird's rear and physically roll out the phallus or clitoris. Insert your fingers, with your palm above the vent, and reach into the vent toward the bird's head. You can then feel the organ, and then simply roll it out for inspection.

Younger males have only a string-like phallus, like a small worm, that can be missed by palpation, but the female will have a clitoris and absence of cartilage.

When viewing is finished, the sexer should stand away and on a three-count the bird should be rolled over in a pre-determined direction. It should jump right up. Make sure to give the bird plenty of room to get up, because it will be a little disoriented and may stumble when trying to get up.

- *Chris Ramsey*

BREEDING SEASON

As spring gets closer, male rheas will start *booming*. They make a deep sound followed by a higher sound. It sounds like someone saying *uh-huh*.

The male will boom, attracting the female and put on a show for her. With his wings spread out to the side, the feathers on his neck and head will stand on end and he will walk 'round and 'round his mate.

This is a time to be cautious when entering the pen. The male is very possessive, and does not like intruders. The female, on the other hand, will stay docile all year long.

Females will start losing feathers on their backs and their necks. This is generally caused by the male biting during copulation. If a female's back get bloody or she starts getting torn up, you may decide to cut the hook off the male's beak.

Just let him bite a knife blade, sharp edge toward the front of the beak. Pull it quickly through the hook and it will trim off. We have never had this problem, but I have heard of people that have.

After the breeding season is completed, usually in the late summer, the males will start to gentle back down. I do have a couple of males that stay pumped up all year, but most of them calm down and become gentle.

There is nothing wrong with an aggressive male—this is normal. In my opinion, these males make better breeders.

- *Chris Ramsey*

BREEDER MANAGEMENT

Successfully raising rheas in captivity begins with healthy breeders. It is a fact that the genetics in this species are very tied, or set, due to the lack of new bloodlines. A proper method of breeding with records to correlate prevents an unacceptable flock of chicks.

There are no secrets to raising rhea chicks. The best study by far is to observe the male and duplicate to the best of our ability the way he raises his chicks.

Rheas usually start breeding in the second year. Some farmers have reported that their rheeas have started at 12-14 months, but this is not normal. Sexual maturity occurs at two to three years of age.

The season usually begins in March, depending on the climate. Longer, warmer days get the season started. Adult breeders should be put in their breeder pens at least six weeks before the season begins. Breeders can be divided in a variety of ways, pairs, trios, colony, or even free ranging.

As a rule, the program usually depends on the temperament of the male. If he can perform with several hens, it's best to allow him several for a productive season.

Breeders should be removed from the breeder pens when the season ends. If space is available, the adults should be allowed to run together in a large area. If not, they should be moved to alternate pens.

This will allow the ground in the breeding pens to rejuvenate until spring. Six to seven months of feces along the fence, mud holes, mold in the nest, and a lack of vegetation is an invitation for pestilence. The soil needs a chance to recover its health, and to grow new vegetation for next season.

The opportunity for interactions with others also appear to proved happier, healthy breeders. Nature provides the rheas the ability to survive the tests of dominance.

The acts of control subside when breeding season is over. This does not mean that the aggressiveness of some males will subside, especially to people.

THE MATING RITUAL

Mating sounds are in the air about two weeks before breeding begins. The male begins his ritual of pursuing prospective females. At this time the male can and usually will become very agressive. His neck will expand and his feathers will bristle out.

He will begin his vocal display of *fog horning*. Across the pasture you can hear what sounds like a ship approaching a light house. An aggressive male will vocalize year round in warm weather.

The male gathers his harem in an elegant manner. He spreads his wings out with the tips lightly touching the ground, with a spontaneous light fluttering. He will escort his ladies away from activity, other males, or onlookers.

Dominance is determined by beak locking, head and neck twisting, and occasional chest-bumping. In rare cases birds will kick. Usually, the less aggressive male will submit before any damage is done.

Mating occurs at different times of the day. The male approaches the hen with a grand display of flowing feathers. The hen usually sits down, and the male mounts and proceeds to breed.

The ritual at times appears violent. The male may peck the base of the hen's neck until it bleeds. Both birds engage in a ritual with both necks and heads forcefully slinging back and forth.

Usually, in two weeks you can expect an egg, especially if they are proven breeders. If you have more than one hen the male will breed each hen throughout the season.

Male rheas prepare the nesting site or sites. He will spend many hours working on the nest. Any material in the area will be used—leaves, sticks, straw, and feathers.

The male uses his beak and feet to dig the hole. Each male will dig a hole to his own specifications. In some cases the male will not prepare a nest at all, and the hen will lay out in the open.

On occasion you may notice the hen inspecting the site. At times she might be seen just sitting on it.

FATHER KNOWS BEST

Observing the male during the incubation period is a key to raising chicks. This is how we learned to raise rheas.

The male will usually be on the nest the day eggs are laid. He will sit on the nest for long inter-

White rhea displaying.

Male rhea showing signs breeding season is about to start. Wings will lightly touch the ground.

The male has covered his nest with his wings and body.

vals, getting off only to breed, eat a little, and drink a little water.

The hen approaches the nest and will have to tolerate aggressive behavior. The male will lunge and pop his beak at her, even thrust his body and head toward her. She will squat beside the nest and lay the egg. The male will then roll the egg into the nest with his beak.

If the ground is rocky, dry, and difficult to dig you can place hay in an area and the males will use the area for a nest. Rheas like to be private and produce more efficiently if a blind is available.

Hens usually lay every other day. A young first-year layer will skip several days. Production varies, but a proven layer can lay more than seventy eggs.

The normal laying in captivity is usually forty to fifty eggs. A hen will usually improve each year, with the peak at five years of age. The oldest hen I know that is still laying is fourteen years old.

The male rhea will determine the number of eggs he will incubate. When he decides he has enough he begins to incubate the eggs. He will on occasion stand up at the nest, and he will turn the eggs. He will also remove any rotten eggs. He incubates the eggs for thirty-five to forty days.

A male will move his nest if he perceives a problem. One of our males was observed rolling eggs to a brush pile across the pasture. He would attempt to pick them up with his beak and roll them to his new nest site. Males will also leave a nest if disturbed.

The male takes full responsibility for the eggs and later for the hatched chicks. The female will leave the area. This is the time to put the extra males to use. The hen will breed with another male.

When hatching begins you will notice excitement around the nest. If you listen you can hear the whistles coming from under the male.

Before long you will see the sweetest little thing in the world. A little head will pop up through the wing feathers. Before long others will appear. The male will remain on the nest until all the eggs hatch, waiting for several hours.

When the male does get up from the nest, he immediately heads out to feed. It has been a very long time since he has had a good meal. As he begins to walk the brood is right under foot. When he goes they go. The last-hatched chick is hardly able to stand up. He rolls, gets up and has to keep up.

The first thing the male does is peck at the ground. By imitation the chicks begin to peck. The chicks will pick up small rocks, bugs, and peck at leaves and weeds.

If a chick gets lost he voices his distress whistle. Papa hears this and begins to pop his beak. The reunion does not take very long. If the male notices the chicks wandering off, he will pop his beak loudly for them to return to him.

Rhea chicks can swim, but unlike water fowl they do not have a waterproof coating on their feathers, and must swim continuously or get soaked.

The male protects the chicks for two to three months. They gradually begin to wander off on their own. If it rains the chicks will protect themselves in the comfort of the male's feathers. The male also keeps the female from the chicks. She will peck at the chicks through the fence.

Watching the process of nature's way is a beautiful sight. It also suggests the best way to raise chicks. The main problem with

The white male is lunging and popping his beak at the gray female that has approached his nest.

papa wandering all over is the possibility of predators around a farm. Without good fencing, hawks, skunks and dogs will reduce the family size. With good fencing, however, the exercise produces good healthy chicks.

In commercial operations, the responsibility of egg hatching and chick rearing has been taken from the male rhea. We now gather eggs daily to prolong the laying season. The financial opportunity has turned the role of parenting over to surrogate parents—the rhea farmers of today.

- *Mary Lee Stropes*

RATITE FARMING

EGGS

To collect eggs for incubation, you will have to go into the pen to retrieve them. Typically, rheas lay every other day once they get going well, so you will need to have some sort of retrieval system.

What we have found that works best is to take a broomstick-sized stick, about 18 to 24 inches long, and hold it horizontally over the male rhea's head. He will bite it, and will not let it go.

We then enter the pen, still holding the stick, and pick up the egg. The rhea continues to follow, still biting the stick. After we are finished in the pen, we simply pull the stick from the bird's beak.

It sounds easy and it is, but that male can sure intimidate you.

There are other methods you can use, such as using a push pole. This is just a pole with a Y at the end, usually padded, and when the bird approaches you, just set the Y on his chest and keep him pushed back.

The problem with this is that he constantly keeps coming at you, making it necessary for two people to be there to collect eggs, one pushing the bird and one grabbing the egg.

Another method, also requiring two people, is for one person to get the bird's attention at the fence with a treat, while the other runs in and gets the egg.

This is the least desirable method because if the bird sees you in the pen, he will more than likely go after you. These birds will bite and the small hook on the ends of their beaks can really pinch you.

- *Chris Ramsey*

INCUBATION

Gathering the eggs will be a wasted task if they are not properly handled or prepared for incubation. Anyone can hatch a rhea egg, but the method definitely affects the ability to raise the chick.

Eggs should be collected as soon after being laid as possible. They can be picked up with gloves or bare hands, but this increases the risk of transferring bacteria from one egg to another. It's better to use one plastic bag per egg. Slip the bag over your hand, so you don't touch the egg, then pick up the egg and pull the bag around it.

The goal is not sterility, but the control of bacteria, contamination, and damage. Improper handling raises the possibility of damage to the shell, the coating on the egg, or even damage to the lining inside the shell.

The final coating on the egg, put on by the hen, is the main line of defense against infectious agents. A clean, dry egg is the optimum. The reality is usually a dirty, wet, mud- and feces-coated egg.

Dirty eggs are an invitation to problems. Extreme measures are sometimes used—dipping in antibiotic solutions, chemical misting, and even formaldehyde gas.

We prefer to use use the simple method of letting the eggshell dry and then brushing off debris with a soft brush. If the egg is heavily soiled, wiping gently with a paper towel and then patting it dry works well.

Remember, the coating on the eggshell should not be disturbed, and using harsh cleaning chemicals is not recommended.

EGG PREPARATION

Eggs can be stored for multiple *clutch* hatching or placed daily in the incubator.

Regardless of the procedure, remember that freshly-gathered eggs should not be put in the incubator immediately, nor stored immediately.

The egg needs a cooling-off time. Room temperature is satisfactory for a day.

If clutch storing is your choice, any ice chest can be used. They maintain the temperature, are easily cleaned, and require only a small storage area.

Eggs should be kept dry in the cooler and should be kept cool. The temperature should be maintained 60 degrees F or below. Eggs at 60 degrees are in dormant stage and do not need to be turned. The less the eggs are handled, the better the chances of successful hatching.

If eggs reach a temperature above 60 degrees F, the cells begin to develop. The process is crucial to the embryo's beginning, and the yo-yo effect of changing temperatures will reduce hatchability. The temperature must remain constant.

A simple milk jug, filled with water and frozen, and exchanged daily, will maintain the correct temperature. If you check closely the humidity will be at a safe level.

Despite the idea that stored eggs will hatch better if turned two to three times daily, they do not have to be turned at all. If you leave them alone they will hatch.

Stored eggs should be allowed to get to room temperature before setting them in the incubator. Putting cold eggs in a warm incubator produces a large amount of condensation. The dampness will increase the risk of bacteria invading the egg.

The moment an egg is laid bacteria begin to make a path to attack the embryo, but nature has provided a barrier in the form of a pH level which is not conducive to bacterial growth unless there are other contributing factors, such as a crack.

If the eggs are cared for properly, nature usually wins. If by chance bacteria win, the result is death. The chick may hatch and live for a short time but ultimately the result is the same.

The result of humidity too low for hatching.

RECORDS

Records are a critical tool in your operation. Every egg should be marked with a lead pencil (not markers, because they contain chemicals which could damage the egg) or with a stick-on label.

Records should be kept to assure the correct date to place the eggs in the incubator, the date they are due to hatch, designation of pens, and breeder stock.

The records will determine the less productive birds and the quality producers. Only top-quality birds should be used as breeder stock. Poor-quality breeders usually produce poor-quality offspring.

Records are vital in the breeder market. For breeding purposes unrelated birds should be used. As the slaughter market progresses, more emphasis on line breeding will be seen. The culling process will be standard procedure, as with other forms of livestock.

In order to assure unrelated chicks, place spiral color-coded bands on their legs when the chicks hatch. Use a specific color for each brooder pen, and microchip at the age of one month at the latest.

See the **Record-keeping and Management** chapter for some sample record-keeping forms.

INCUBATOR

In a large percentage of failing chicks, the problem is improper incubation practices. If the temperature is too low or too high, complications result in non-thriving chicks. They may live two weeks and then die. The temperature in the incubator should be 97.5 degrees with 45 per cent humidity.

The selection of an incubator is up to the producer, but you should have one that maintains the proper temperature, humidity, and ventilation which will allow the embryo to develop.

Placement of the incubator in a controlled environment enables you to control the temperature and humidity. Having a constant temperature in the room will help eliminate fluctuation of the elements within the unit itself. Any fluctuation has an adverse affect on the embryo.

In order to have a successful hatching rate the temperature and humidity must be maintained. An embryo has some control over its consumption of the water in the

One- and two-day-old rhea chicks.

egg, but it can not control the temperature.

HUMIDITY

Weighing the eggs helps determine the weight loss needed for chicks to hatch. See the charts in the back of the book, and the chapter on incubation and hatching, for a complete discussion of this process. A 15 per cent loss by the time the egg hatches is the normal amount.

You should have at least one thermometer, such as a mercury or alcohol thermometer, which is not part of your incubator or hatcher, to use as a cross-check. Most problems are created by malfunctioning thermometers. Hygrometers should also be calibrated by comparing them with wet-bulb readings.

An egg that does not hatch due to improper humidity is a questionable survivor. Too little moisture shrinks the egg contents. The embryo has difficulty utilizing the contents for growth. Its organs are unable to excrete waste, resulting in a sticky residue on the chick and in the shell.

This sticky albumen prevents the chick from getting into position to hatch. A misunderstanding of low humidity versus *wet chicks* prompts producers to lower the humidity in the incubator and hatcher, resulting in chicks dead in the shell.

VENTILATION

Incubators should be kept in a room isolated from the hatcher and brooder pens if at all possible. The temperature in the room should be below 80 degrees. One must remember that the air in the room serves as an exchange for the air flow in the incubator.

Good ventilation is crucial. Stale air should be exhausted outside the incubator room, to prevent it from being circulated back into the incubator. See the chapter on Incubation and Hatching for an illustration of an incubator and ventilation system, and recommendations on air exchange rates.

HATCHING

A duck is a duck, a ratite is a ratite. The usual incubation time for most ducks is 28 days, but Muscovy ducks take 35 days. Rheas require 35-40 days.

Rhea eggs should be taken from the incubator three days before they are due to hatch. Do not turn the eggs in the hatcher, as the chick is now positioning itself to prepare to hatch.

The chick will pip the internal membrane with its beak, and then the external membrane and the shell. Once it has broken through it will kick through and explode the shell. The next thing you will see will be a little chick sitting in the hatcher.

Eggs that do not hatch on their own usually are in trouble. If a clutch of eggs is placed in the incubator at the same time, they should hatch within hours of each other.

CANDLING

It is vital to candle eggs before putting them in the hatcher, mainly to discover which ones should be discarded, or set aside from the others to observe.

The progress of the embryo can be monitored by candling. Candling can be done at 7, 14, and 21 days.

An infertile egg is easy to determine—you can see completely through the egg. A rotten egg sloshes and appears to have a floating dark mass.

An egg with a chick forming will be dark throughout the smaller end of the egg. There will be a lighter area around the large end of the egg. This is the air cell. As the chick begins to prepare to hatch this area will get larger. The air cell serves as a chamber for breathing.

Anxiety about the fertility of eggs has created a problem for many beginners. Jerky movements in the excitement of seeing inside the egg have often caused a chick's death.

Careful handling is a must. The shell may be tough, but inside the egg are small blood vessels. An abrupt move can cause a vessel to rupture, resulting in the death of the chick. The less the eggs are handled, the better the chance of hatching.

At this period in the hatching process, if the beak is not present and the egg-chick outline is smooth, the chick is in trouble. It will require assistance.

Candling eggs on the 35th day of incubation will determine the status of the chick. From the 36th to 40th days the chick will get in position to hatch. If it does not hatch, then assist.

NORMAL VS. ASSISTED HATCH

If the chicks do not hatch on a given day, three options are available: keep it under observation through candling, discard it, or manually assist the chick to hatch.

Drilled or assisted hatching does not produce poor chicks. The majority survive and progress in a natural manner.

However, we should not spend a lot of time and effort on unhealthy chicks. Nature culls the unfit. Why doctor them to let them live for a month or two?

Improve your farming practices to ensure healthy chicks. Nature will provide the rest.

HATCHING

The eggs are in the hatcher. The chicks are as anxious to hatch as we are for them to appear. Movement can be seen in the shells, they will roll back and forth, and the chicks will whistle in the shell.

Chicks will also rest between attempts to break free of the shell. They also sleep. They have had a long process in preparing to arrive in this artificial world.

Humidity is as important in the hatcher as in the incubator. So many times the improper amount of humidity will cause chicks to have difficulty hatching.

These chicks are sometimes born severely dehydrated, a common cause of death in two- to six-week-old chicks.

Dehydration causes imbalances, thus preventing the chicks from thriving. Poor appetite follows—slow death.

When necropsies are done, with no apparent cause of death found, often the cause is the habits we have acquired in incubating and hatching.

MEDICATION

Betadine can be placed on the navel, only if it appears wet or slightly mushy. Otherwise no medication is used on the chicks. They do not need it. No vitamin or mineral supplements are needed to raise rhea chicks if they are receiving balanced commercial feed, and breeders are healthy.

Worming will depend on the area of habitat. Samples of droppings should be taken to your veterinarian twice a year for analysis. Usually rheas are free of parasites.

Correctible defects should be evaluated by the veterinarian. If chicks need medication, your vet should advise.

Chicks, like any animal, do get sick, but the vet should evaluate and prescribe treatment.

HATCHER TO BROODER

The time has come to remove the chicks from the warm comfort of their hatcher. This is their first step in gaining independence. This is also a crucial step in raising chicks in captivity. Papa bird is equipped with the know-how. We must try to duplicate it.

Chicks should be taken out of the hatcher as soon as their feathers dry and look fluffy. They require heat.

Our brooder is made of hardware cloth as a footing, raised several inches above the ground. Proper air circulation through the wire prevents moisture from building up. Urine and feces drop through openings in the wire, so the chicks neither walk in droppings nor eat them.

Chicks should be furnished a heat source if they desire, and an area at the other end of the box if they get too hot.

Our brooder boxes or pens are five feet long by three feet wide, and eighteen inches high. We enclose one side (which is the back side). The heat lamp (a 300-watt bulb) is placed to provide heat at one end of the pen.

INTRODUCTION TO FOOD

Contrary to popular opinion, the chicks need to eat. The chicks learn to eat by imitating the male. This is one of the first things he teaches them. Males have been observed expelling and pecking in a form of droppings, and the chicks follow suit. This is not the same as his regular droppings. He has not eaten for a while and this

Eggs pipping in hatcher. The hatcher temperature is 98 degrees F, and the relative humidity is 57 per cent.

is a different color and consistency.

Chicks should be fed immediately—crumbled boiled eggs, small pieces to encourage them to begin pecking. They will not eat a lot. When they begin pecking from the wire, place the egg on top of feed.

Newly-hatched chicks do not drink the first day. Offer them water on day two. Rhea chicks dip their beaks in water in a scooping effect, then throw their heads upward. They require a flat pan, not a chicken-watering pan. Within the first two days they try to walk and learn to eat and drink.

GOING OUTSIDE

Day two of their life of leisure has come to a halt. The first day of their life in the world of outside elements begins on the evening of the second day.

We place them in the yard to enjoy the savory bugs, nibble on grass and eat a few pebbles.

We provide a heated house with washed river sand for flooring. The house is an 8 x 10' metal, wood-framed structure. It has windows which are open to create proper ventilation, and heat lamps are on 24 hours a day.

During the day chicks are allowed access to the house, but at night they are all placed inside where they are warm and protected. If rain is likely, they are also placed inside—chicks need to be kept warm.

Introduction to the environment and elements will produce much healthier chicks. Ample room to run and exercise will utilize the remaining yolk sac and also help develop their legs.

Heat is essential for growth to young chicks. Chicks are unable to retain body heat until fat begins to accumulate on their bodies, usually at two to three months of age. Chicks that are chilled will hesitate to eat or drink, which can result in death.

Chicks should be sexed at one to two weeks of age, and new bands placed on their legs.

We place chicks outside in pens according to their size, not necessarily by age. We have three 12' x 50' pens, each with a house. All of the pens have weeds, flowers, leaves, and grass.

By the time the chicks are one month old, they have tripled in size. At one month, they are microchipped or wing tagged for permanent identification, and moved to the barn and the larger pens.

The barn is 20' x 70', divided into four grow-out pens with washed river sand flooring. Again chicks are separated by size, not necessarily age. Doors are opened daily for the chicks to run in the 15 x 150 pens.

The chicks are locked in at night until they are 4 to 5 months old. Even at that age, heat is available in the barn if they want it.

Several heat lamps are hung throughout the sections, and each division in the barn has a ceiling fan to circulate the air.

The barn also has cross-ventilation for fresh air. Multiple feeders and watering pans are provided in the pens.

We are fortunate in having a hillside location, with trees and rocks in grassy pastures. The adult birds find ample shelter. In other areas, artificial shelters would be necessary.

Because of predatory dogs in the area, the farm is surrounded by a six-foot perimeter fence, with additional fences around the pens.

FEEDING

All birds on my farm, from day one, are fed freely. Food is always available, 24 hours a day, from day one to adult breeders.

Newly-hatched chicks receive crumbled boiled egg immediately, water on the second day. Chicks are fed commercial chick starter until they wean themselves off.

At 3 to 4 months, additional pans are placed in the pens and a pelleted commercial feed is introduced, in addition to chick feed, allowing the chicks free choice.

Chicks are fed chick feed and maintenance feed for one year. At one year of age, the yearling birds are given the same feed as the adults.

Chicks need to be fed a balanced diet, including roughage. Fiber in their diet will assist in the digestion of the foods, vitamins,

Chicks require a heat source until they are two to three months old.

and minerals. Without fiber the foods are eaten and passed. Without the balance of the needed vitamins and minerals their systems will be out of balance, creating problems with deficiencies which can result in deformities and lack of proper growth.

In rheas, the ventriculus (gizzard or second stomach) performs the function of grinding the food. Chicks which eat only soft foods and no grit results in an under-developed grinding mechanism. This leads to grasses and other fiber packing into a mass which the bird is unable to pass—impaction.

We feed our adult birds from cattle feeders, the ones that turn when the wind blows. This helps to keep the feed dry.

PROBLEMS

Knowing your birds is the secret to raising healthy chicks and adults. Rheas of all ages do the same thing: they move all the time, eat, drink—and poop—a lot.

When you are working the pens, cleaning up and the like, keep an eye on your birds. They eat and drink frequently, and are constantly on the move. It doesn't take much time to spot one who isn't acting normally.

Chicks need exercise for rapid growth and complete absorption of their yolk sacs.

Signs of problems are a chick that is listless, or standing around with its head rolled toward its back, loss of appetite, diarrhea, constipation, dull eyes, standing with eyes half closed, or sitting around a lot away from the other chicks.

You must pick it up and place it in a warm pen. Watch to make sure the chick is eating and drinking. Sick chicks are usually light in weight. Any chick not feeling well should be isolated from the flock.

The first thing we do is warm it up. If a chick is chilled it begins a downhill slide. You can give supplemental foods, such as boiled eggs, a little apple, or lettuce.

We occasionally tube-feed with Ensure Plus, mainly to maintain sugar levels. Pedialyte is used because a sick chick likely has not been drinking and can easily become dehydrated. Tube-feeding is not difficult, but your vet should show you how, so that you don't inadvertently insert the tube into the chick's lungs.

The vet should be called for medical problems. Once you learn more, you can probably treat common problems with the vet's advice rather than a visit.

The cycle repeats itself. Healthy stock will assure the best chicks.

One more piece of advice: If you have a successful season in raising chicks, don't change your procedures!

- Mary Lee Stropes

Chicks are grouped according to size. Overcrowding causes stress.

Free-range rheas at a mineral trough.

FREE-RANGE RHEAS

©*Kathy Bader*
Lazy J Livestock
Brackettville, Texas

The old saying "You can't see the forest for the trees" may certainly apply to some parts of the ratite industry today. As ratite ranchers in general struggle through the growing pains of a breeders' market, a remote area of southwest Texas is a living example of where the industry may wish to be in the next five to ten years.

Exotics of several species have spread from game ranches in the Texas Hill Country to surrounding areas. Rheas are no exception.

On several ranches in Kinney County, Texas, rheas have migrated from ranch to ranch and pasture to pasture. In our case the birds appeared in a small grassy pasture approximately ten years ago. They now inhabit more than eight thousand acres.

My husband's family has been in the ranching business for five generations. Parts of the operation are cattle only, while my husband and I also run Angora goats and Rambouillet sheep. We operate a combination of owned and leased land.

In the beginning, we viewed the birds as a novelty and enjoyed observing them. We felt as long as they caused no problems, we would allow them to roam freely. Within five years the original ten to twenty young rheas multiplied over approximately five thousand acres and numbered in excess of five hundred birds.

It is remarkable that these animals have completely adapted to range conditions and that they did so with no help from us.

HABITAT

Our native range is very diverse. It is mostly brushland with a variety of thorny brush, cactus, sage, grasses, mesquite and more mesquite. Long draws break up the range. These draws are surrounded by stands of native pecan, live oak, hackberry, and more mesquite.

Water holes intermittently fill along the draws and a creek flows through the major portion of the ranch. Pastures range in size from three hundred to fifteen hundred acres.

We are also involved in the land-clearing business and much of the ranch has large strips of cleared areas in which native and improved grasses are planted. Like most ranchers, we have turned to hunting as a necessary source of income.

Conservation practices are important to increase the productivity of the range by providing cleared strips along the edges of pastures, mixed with heavy cover, and by the introduction of improved grasses. It also aids in gathering livestock by the traditional method of cowboys on horseback.

A flock of free-range rheas in typical Southwest Texas range land. Note that there are several different age groups represented.

Kinney County receives about twenty inches of rainfall annually. Most rains fall in May and September. Summers are long and hot. Winters are short and cold.

As previously mentioned, along with cattle, sheep, and Angora goats, there is a large variety of exotics, which like the rhea, have migrated onto the ranch from surrounding areas. These exotics include Barbados sheep, Blackbuck antelope, Aoudad sheep, a few Sika deer, and a few Axis deer.

Presently, the only hunting allowed on the ranch is Whitetail deer, although the necessity of hunting the exotics for maintenance purposes is a prospect in the near future.

Bobwhite quail and native turkey have steady populations and hatches vary from year to year along with other areas of the state.

RAISING CHICKS

We have attended seminars on raising ratites, conferences on exotics, and ranch diversification workshops designed to educate the ratite breeder. Very little of the information provided dealt with our particular situation in which the birds were allowed free range rather than being pen raised. Most of what we know about free-roaming rheas was learned through observing them over the past several years.

What we *do* know is that rheas are extremely adaptable. The birds do what they need to do to insure their survival. We have found that hatches closely follow those of native quail and turkey.

In good years with timely and adequate rains, they have good hatches with twenty-five to thirty-five chicks or more. In years with dry springs and little or no grass cover, the hatches are poor, with seven to twelve chicks.

The male collects and incubates the eggs from multiple hens. The hens start laying for the most dominant male in a group and continue laying eggs until he completes his nest.

He then releases the hens to the next dominant male who establishes his nest, and so on.

This makes for a very long breeding season. The first chicks begin to appear in late March or early April and new chicks have been seen in late August. It is our observation that several things can happen at this point. First, we have seen males with groups of chicks several months old combined with very tiny chicks only weeks old. In some cases this is a result of the death of the male parent, and another male simply adds the orphaned chicks to his group.

In other cases we've seen that the dominant male in a group simply collects all the chicks in the pasture and fosters them as though this was his right.

Single males and remaining hens then group as desired and lose interest in the chicks.

Second, extreme male aggression in the wild birds works to their advantage when protecting their chicks. This aggression toward anything they perceive as a predator is ferocious, even to the extent of attacking a helicopter when threatened.

In rheas, it is difficult to determine the cause of early chick loss because we do not see them for several days after they hatch. The male keeps the chicks close and in heavier brush. Hawks and other birds of prey do not bother the chicks once they reach a month or two of age.

According to one rhea breeder who has begun to allow her males to hatch collected eggs, males are also extremely aggressive in helping new chicks emerge from the shell. Often, they will rip the eggs apart and literally pull the chicks free—an interesting note for breeders.

Finally, because of the long breeding season there are some chicks that go into winter too young to survive. If the birds are in a pasture with heavy brush cover, they do better than chicks in more open areas.

We know of some losses due to sudden weather changes or when northers (cold, wet weather systems) persist. Older chicks fare very well. Even though we have never seen evidence of heavy losses in the pastures, we do find an occasional dead chick.

COMPATIBILITY WITH OTHER STOCK

We have introduced small groups of rheas into pastures where we lamb and kid our sheep and goats, with the idea that perhaps we could reduce predation.

In only two years we have increased our Angora kid crop by over twenty per cent and have experienced less than a three-percent death loss in our lambs. That loss is thought to be from avian predators such as caracaras, hawks, and vultures.

Free-roaming rheas appear to be very compatible with any combination of livestock and exotics.

Curiously, when they moved onto the ranch they chose to take up residence in pastures with only cattle, not into pastures with sheep and goats. Those pastures did contain herds of Blackbuck, Aoudad and Barbados.

The rheas quickly multiplied and we saw them traveling in groups intermixed with groups of exotics. We question whether their reluctance to enter pastures with domestic sheep or goats was due to competition for food or for space.

We are continuing to study this phenomenon because birds introduced into pastures with sheep or goats are also breeding successfully.

DIET

The rhea's diverse diet consists of plants and small animals. We believe that their diet closely follows that of the native turkey. They move from one food source to another as availability dictates.

Known foods are comprised of winter and summer weeds, the seed heads of native and improved grasses, and a large variety of berries, fruit and seeds from native brush.

These plants include the following:

- agarita, *Berberis trifoliolata*, an evergreen with holly-like leaves that puts on a small red berry in the spring (it is also highly prized by quail and turkey);
- native Texas persimmon, *Diospyros texana*, a small tree with a one-inch black berry and edible seeds;
- prickly pear, *Opuntia lindheimeri*, and the pear-apple fruit. Pear leaves are eaten year around, but are especially sought in the winter when we burn the spines off for the cattle. The rheas will help eat the plant to the ground;
- granjeno or desert hackberry, *Celtis pallida*, a thorny shrub that bears a reddish-orange edible fruit; and
- several varieties of wild grapes.

Of interest to ranchers, rheas do well on pastures that contain coyotillo (*Karwinski spp.*), which produces a berry very poisonous to sheep and goats.

Rheas graze in large groups across open areas, looking for insects. They eat grasshoppers, small lizards, and other small reptiles. We have been told they eat mice and snakes but have yet to confirm that. It is amusing to watch young rheas chase behind the shredder, catching bugs.

We have observed rheas browsing brush such as mesquite, guajillo (*Acacia berlandieri*), and huisache (*Acacia smallii*). All three of these acacias have large seed pods with edible seeds.

The mesquite bean is a highly nutritious food source for livestock and wildlife in South Texas. There are other less well known acacias that may serve as a source of food. This is another area we plan to study.

As a final note on the diet of wild rheas, we do not, nor have we ever, supplemented the birds in any consistent manner. These birds have existed and prospered entirely on their own. This exemplifies their hardiness and survivability. The only supplement these rheas have received has been within the daily operation of the ranch.

We feed protein cubes to the cattle on a regular basis during

Rheas browsing on native vegetation—or on critters inhabiting it.

certain times of the year. Rheas learn to listen for the truck and will pick up crumbs left by the cattle. They also like to nibble on corn scattered by deer hunters.

Most importantly, they have access to mineral supplement provided to the livestock. This is a ten-ten mineral and salt mix fed in both block and loose form.

We have had good results controlling internal parasites in our livestock by adding diatomaceous earth to the mineral mix in a one-to-four ratio.

Diatomaceous earth is ground, fresh-water fossil sold under many trade names and used in some garden products to control insects. It is environmentally safe and when fed with the mineral mix has reduced the number of treatments for internal parasites usually required by the livestock.

Rheas gather around the mineral feeders and consume the mix along with the cattle, sheep, and goats. We believe it helps the wildlife and exotics who would not otherwise benefit from any type of parasite control.

ROUNDUP TIME

THE FIRST RHEA ROUNDUP

We know that these birds, through natural selection, have developed into a vigorous and genetically healthy colony.

We also believe these rheas have done well because they have been incorporated into our existing, diversified ranching system. Here they have benefitted from a total plan of good management and maintenance. The key, as in all livestock operations, is in keeping the proper balance.

By 1992 we realized the birds were out of balance and decided to remove some from the pastures. Through contact with an experienced exotic handler and transporter, we contracted the sale of two hundred rheas to the Castleberrys in Lampasas, Texas.

The birds were gathered by helicopter—a new experience for all involved. Existing livestock pens were utilized for the roundup. Water lots, alleys, and catch pens were lined with black shade-cloth to reduce injury and direct the birds' path through the pens.

The helicopter, a Hughes 500, slowly pushed the rheas through the pasture into the water lot where the ground crew then pushed the birds into smaller pens.

There they were carefully caught by hand, wormed, examined and loaded directly into a compartmentalized haul trailer and transported as quickly as possible to reduce stress.

Overall, the operation was very successful. From the total gathered we lost five in the roundup and none that we know of in the transport.

Of the five rheas lost, two were killed by colliding with each other, one broke a leg, one was caught in a fence, and one large male became overexcited when accidentally separated from his chicks. He simply stood in the middle of the pen and died from the loss of his chicks.

Unfortunately, because the birds were sold to one buyer and then resold, we do not know how they fared upon reaching final destination. The birds sold were strong and healthy with few if any internal or external parasites.

Just a quick mention of some of the problems we experienced. We used trial and error to learn the safest way to capture and transport wild rheas.

The worst problem was that it was early July and it was hot. This restricted our working time to early morning and late evening and affected the general stress on the birds. There was also the unknown of how the birds would travel.

THE SECOND ROUNDUP

The second roundup in 1994 was as successful with a few major changes. We worked in January to reduce heat stress and allow us to work throughout the day. We used the same pens but also added temporary catch pens along pasture fences. By placing large nets between the fence and nearby trees, birds could be captured in the pasture farther from the permanent pens and thereby reduce the length of the drives. This worked well and reduced the amount of flying time.

A local helicopter pilot flying a Robinson R22 was used on the second roundup. As the birds were brought in they were again caught by hand, microchipped, wormed, given vitamin E and a tranquilizer to reduce stress, loaded and transported to individual buyers.

We sold approximately one hundred rheas this time with less than a three-per-cent death loss. This was a very smooth operation and again we learned a great deal.

ADAPTABILITY

The most important factor in selling wild rheas is that the buyer must understand that these *are* wild rheas and must be released into a large enough area for the birds to be freed without harm. They cannot be released into pens. Small pastures or traps will work. The birds will run for cover and must be allowed to do so.

As stated, rhea are very adaptable. They can be moved from larger to smaller pastures or traps and this works well for handling the birds.

The orphaned chicks of the irate male from the first roundup were given to a friend who was having disappointing results trying to breed pen-raised rheas on his ranch. He eventually released the wild chicks into a twenty-acre trap adjacent to a larger pasture.

The rheas are now reproducing in this trap and he has sold his pen-raised birds.

These young birds have become as docile as the pen-raised birds while retaining all the vigor and productivity of their parents. A barrel-type ratite feeder is used to supplement the birds' feed as needed and to entice them into a smaller pen when they must be caught. Banging a rock on the side of the feeder brings the birds running from the back of the pasture. The feeder is then moved into progressively smaller pens until the birds are captured.

FOR THE FUTURE

Knowing these rheas can successfully be raised under range conditions is only half of the equation. There are many questions still to be answered, not only about their unique survivability, but also their place in the future of the ratite industry.

In our case, we must look to how we can utilize our existing facilities to more economically capture and transport rheas to market. The concept of placing feeders in water lots and traps to capture birds is one promising idea.

Selling large numbers of rheas to a breeders' market allowed the use of a helicopter to move birds for long distances through large pastures.

During the roundup in 1994, a helicopter was used for a total of thirty-seven hours in the capture of eighty-six rheas. Half of the time was used in scouting and preparation and half in the actual capture. The actual capture averaged five birds per hour or forty dollars per bird. The cost did not include ground crew, medication, or transportation.

But without a strong breeders' market, alternative methods of gathering and marketing will have to be developed. The end products—hide, meat, oil and feathers—have all the possibilities of the other ratites.

We hope to be working closely with Texas A&M University and interested ratite organizations to address some of these and other questions:

- At what time of the year do the birds best utilize their natural food sources?
- At what time of the year would they most benefit from supplemental feeding?
- Do wild rheas need supplementation before slaughter?
- How does the carcass quality compare between wild rheas and pen-raised rheas ready for slaughter?
- Are mobile slaughter facilities feasible?
- With which animals, both domestic and wildlife, do they compete?
- What is a good balanced population per acre?
- Are there any long term detrimental effects on native quail or turkey?
- How will government regulations affect our ability to market wild birds?

CONCLUSIONS

We do not suggest that everyone should release their breeders and let nature take its course. However, we do suggest to breeders and potential breeders, as well as ranchers or farmers looking to increase income through diversification, that range-raised rheas are extremely adaptable and are a viable livestock alternative.

Processing plants and market outlets, while still in the development stage in 1995, need a steady supply of birds to support a viable industry.

Processing facilities must be willing and able to accept ratites; fair government inspection and regulation must be established; restaurants must be willing to include ratite meat on their menus; and the consumer must be educated about the meat's quality and taste if we are to be accepted as a legitimate and economically-sound addition to the agricultural industry.

White rheas at Shad-ee Shack Farm, Booneville, Arkansas. (Photo courtesy Mary Lee Stropes)

RHEA OIL

Donna Fezler
Grand Cypress Ranch
Jacksonville, Illinois

Just a short time ago, rheas had no commercial value whatsoever. Now the meat and hides are being sold, and the next major product will be rhea oil.

Rhea oil, with its perceived therapeutic qualities, is destined to become as important to the value of rheas as emu oil is to the value of emus.

There are presently five potential uses for the oil:
- nutritional supplements,
- machining cutting fluid,
- leather conditioning and penetrating oil,
- cosmetics, and
- anti-inflammatory, analgesic products.

Each product will require a different grade of oil, specifically refined for the intended purpose. No fat should be discarded—all of it should have a commercial application.

WHAT IS RHEA OIL?

Rhea oil is simply the rendered and refined adipose tissue of *Rhea americana*, or common rhea. On the bird, the fat is deposited mainly around the stomach and intestines, across the rump, and on both sides of the bowl-like sternum or breast bone. Small quantities can be found adjacent to most muscles.

Rhea hatchlings have about 3 cc of fat distributed over the sternum, stomach, and rump. Typically, with present nutrition programs, males do not begin to build fat stores until 12 months of age, and there is a marked increase in fat after sexual maturity.

Harvested fat ranges from three to fifteen pounds per yearling male, usually about ten per cent of body weight.

REFINING

To be able to sell the oil in the commercial market, standards must be set for each grade of oil, appropriate for its particular application. The tighter the standards which are set, the more impurities must be removed, with less oil being recovered for sale.

Refining costs are increased, and value of the more refined product is obviously much higher than the simpler product. Cost of refining can range from pennies a pound for edible grade to as high as $10 per pound for small batches (500 pounds) of highly-refined pharmaceutical grade.

The rhea industry will want to consider four grades of oil, each with its own refining and performance standards. The standards will define the minimum level for color, clarity, specific gravity, viscosity, refractive index, cloud test, peroxide value, melt point, fatty acids, and iodine value, to name several of the tests routinely done on oil.

Without standards, customers cannot be asured of consistent product quality and performance. Setting and defining standards will require a significant financial investment before we can consider a commercial market.

THE GRADES

The oil will go through several increasingly-stringent refining stages to produce at least four grades. Each grade will have detailed specifications listing its physical and chemical properties.

TABLE 1: PROPOSED GRADES FOR RHEA OIL

GRADES	POTENTIAL USES
Non-food	Cutting fluid, leather conditioner
Food	Nutritional supplementation
Cosmetic	Skin preparations
Pharmaceutical	Burn and post-operative creams; analgesic creams, parenteral medications.

The higher the grade, the more stringent and difficult to meet the specifications and the more costly to refine.

A commercial buyer has specifications that must be met to ensure the quality of their final product; buyers routinely reject out-of-specification raw materials. The refined rhea oil now available would be classified as non-food grade (Table 1).

PROCESSING THE OIL

Processing the oil for home use is best done by rendering the fat in the microwave, filtering it through a coffee filter to remove any organic matter which would support microbial growth, and storing it in the freezer. This will produce a white, nearly odorless product. Rendering the product in a crockpot will overcook it, producing a yellow oxidized oil which is actually in the beginning stages of rancidity.

Home-rendered oil should never be rendered for sale. The product will have met no quality-control parameters or testing standards. Contaminated or poor-quality oil could do great damage to the industry.

To fully refine the oil, specialized equipment is needed to filter it quickly and thoroughly. The processes will include bleaching to remove color bodies, deodorizing to remove all odor, distillation to produce the highest quality pharmaceutical grades, and tempering to prevent or control crystal growth.

It will take some time before these properties are defined, and even then they will be proprietary, so the producer will not participate in the refining of the oil.

For rendered oil, the recovery rate is about 89 per cent of fat; non-food grade refining will be close at about 86 per cent. Cosmetic grade may drop to 65 per cent, and there are no estimates for pharmaceutical grade. The price of the oil will reflect the reduced recovery rates and increased purity of the product.

PROPERTIES OF RHEA OIL

FATTY-ACID PROFILE

In our research, sixteen samples of rendered rhea oil were analyzed by gas chromatography. The samples were from home and commercially-slaughtered and rendered birds from various areas of the country.

Initially, there was such a great variation in the fatty-acid profiles of the samples that no standard could be published with confidence. Of the adult birds that died from accidental causes, it became apparent that there were actually two general profiles that could be called standards for the rhea.

One type of profile had 14 to 18 different fatty acids in similar proportions. The other had as few as 8 fatty acids, with no long-chain fatty acids at all.

Interviews with the farmers revealed that the birds with the low numbers of fatty acids were the only birds fed one particular brand of feed. The three samples from birds fed that brand of feed are not included in the standard (Figure 1).

Figure 1. Analysis of fatty acids in rhea and emu oil by gas chromatography.

It was felt that the diet of these birds may have been deficient, causing a change in their lipogenesis, the formation of body fat.

A POSSIBLE DIAGNOSTIC TOOL

Juvenile animals typically have different fatty-acid profiles than adults. The rhea is no different, but what was interesting was where the changes, or enhancements, occurred.

In another test, the adipose tissue from three malpositioned chicks from the same hen, one at the start of the season, one at the middle, and one at the end of the season was analyzed. The hen was fed a 7% fat diet and it should be noted that there was no reduction in chick survivability through this hen's last egg of the season.

The later-hatched chicks showed decreasing ratios of long-chain (C20-C24) fatty acids in their adipose tissue. These long-chain fatty acids are the precursors of powerful, important hormone-like substances called eicosanoids. See Table 2 and Figure 2.

In chickens, reductions in the levels of certain yolk lipids have been identified with metabolic disorders and embryo survivability. Although chicken hens have large essential-fatty-acid reserves, when these reserves are depleted, the surviving chicks will show impaired viability and growth even when fed adequate diets.

Since later-hatched chicks are historically more difficult to raise, further study of the fat of rhea hens, hatchlings and chicks may yield some answers.

Further unusual discrepancies were noted in fatty-acid profiles of chicks with abnormal bone development, hemorrhaging and/or aneurysms, rotated legs, stunting, abnormal gait, abnormal feathering, and abnormal leg scale and beak development. They may reflect a major problem in the metabolic process of adipose tissue formation when compared with a normal rhea.

TABLE 2. LONG-CHAIN FATTY ACIDS IN RELATION TO EGG NUMBER

	% OF C20-24 FATS	RATIO OF CHICK C20-24 TO ADULT
Adult Rhea	0.43	Standard
Chick #1, Egg #5	1.75	4.1 : 1
Chick #2, Egg #23	1.49	3.5 : 1
Chick #3, Egg #52	1.12	2.6 : 1

FDA APPROVAL

The process of planning to get FDA approval of rhea oil as an active ingredient has begun. It will be expensive and time-consuming but it is an absolute necessity.

What happens if we don't get approval? The worst-case scenario would have a pharmaceutical company developing a formulation using rhea oil, obtaining the patent and FDA approval, and paying the producer two pennies per pound of rhea fat.

This is a very real possibility unless the industry commits resources to a placebo study at a university to ascertain that rhea oil does have pain-relieving qualities.

This will not stop anyone from patenting their own formula. It will simply allow us to hold claim to rhea oil's unusual properties—claims that cannot be made at this time—and ensure that producers get paid for them.

Only by working together as members of a growing industry can we hope to fund such a project. We have everything to gain. The value of the oil to the producer will depend on FDA approval as an active ingredient, minimizing refining costs and maximizing marketing efforts.

USES FOR RHEA OIL

LEATHER CONDITIONING OIL

A formulation for leather conditioning is currently being tested in Oklahoma. Produced from a

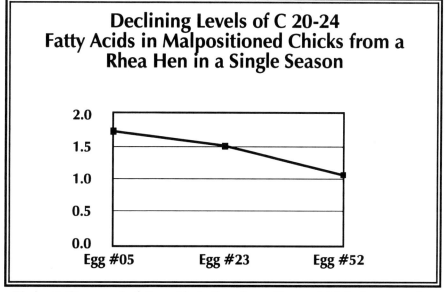

Figure 2. Decrease in fatty acids in the adipose tissue of chicks from one rhea hen, from early to late in the hatching season.

combination of neat's-foot oil and the dregs of rhea oil, it is an excellent use for poor-quality oil. The maker states that it penetrates better and keeps leather supple longer, increasing intervals between leather conditioning.

Sometimes laziness can be a great motivator: since oiling leather was not one of his favorite tasks, the leather-oil maker requested some unusable rhea oil to see if he could restore riding tack and increase time between applications. He is thrilled with the product's abilities to reduce his chores. Another leather oil manufacturer in Texas is testing rhea oil for his formulation.

CUTTING FLUID

The North American Rhea Association recently contracted with the Institute for Advanced Manufacturing Sciences to test rhea oil as a possible component of a metal cutting fluid. After much deliberation, it was decided to test a drilling operation, one of several processes that can be used to shape a piece of metal into a useful object.

Rhea oil performed equally as well as the conventional oil in the drilling operations, although it was recommended the study be repeated for other metal-working procedures.

The surprise came when, in a blind test, oil was sent to an ordinary machine shop for practical experimentation. It was found to be as good as conventional cutting fluids for stainless steel, with one major difference—the machinists loved using it.

Conventional fluids have sulphur and phosphorus additives which, according to the machinists, are brutal to the skin. The machinists were thrilled that this product not only got the job done, but the cutting fluid wasn't hazardous to their health, and it was biodegradable.

The metal products are still being tested, and will be examined microscopically over a period of time to determine if pursuing this use for our non-food-grade oil is advantageous.

NUTRITIONAL SUPPLEMENT

Research on lipid nutrition over the last thirty years has shown that certain types of fats are vital to health. Deficiencies of essential fatty acids can result in a wide variety of symptoms including growth retardation, depressed immune systems, sterility, kidney damage, bleeding tendency, skin problems, impaired vision, and central nervous system function.

In rapidly growing infants, especially pre-term infants, a deficiency of essential fatty acids can have serious consequences. Baby formulas have typically not addressed the essential fatty acid problem.

Rhea oil closely approximates the fatty-acid content of human breast milk, with the nutritionally-critical fatty acids listed as polyunsaturated fatty acids. See Figures 3 and 4 for a comparison of the content of fatty acids in rhea oil and human milk.

This aspect of rhea oil has exciting and far-reaching implications, but developing this product will require extensive work and communication with researchers in the field.

It is not feasible simply to call up baby-formula makers and tell them we have the perfect solution to the problem. Much more research needs to be done at the university level before we have an actual marketable product.

The value of the oil to the producer will depend on scientific data to back up this theory. This will be expensive but it is necessary if we are to be able to sell rhea oil as a nutritional supplement.

ANTI-INFLAMMATORY AND PAIN-RELIEVING ACTIONS

Rhea oil is beginning to earn recognition for its analgesic, therapeutic and cosmetic potential. The oil is being informally tested by various people around the country, and testimonials to its effectiveness are as glowing and positive as the results that have been seen with emu oil.

How the oil works is not known, but many people find it to be helpful. Rhea oil has been shown to have dramatic anti-inflammatory action in rhea chicks.

The many uses of rhea oil are so far mostly supported by anecdotal evidence. Much research is needed in many fields to prove that the oil does what people say it does.

Review of the data available for chick mortality, comparing it to the purported activity in humans, seems to suggest the fat is a prostaglandin-leukotriene inhibitor.

Prostaglandins and leukotrienes are the pro-inflammatory chemicals the body makes that produce many intense changes such as redness, swelling, blood-vessel dilation and constriction, pain and heat.

They are involved in many more reactions, but these are among the most visible and uncomfortable to us. Drugs such as aspirin and acetaminophen are used to reduce their effects. Many of the testimonials can be explained by applying known principles of prostaglandin and leukotriene actitivity.

Obviously, many people are using rhea oil for a wide variety of conditions and feeling that it is effective. It is thrilling to hear this, but it will take distribution efforts by each producer to gain widespread acceptance of rhea oil.

HOW DID THE FAT EVOLVE?

One must wonder why rheas have evolved such a unique fat.
- What is the evolutionary advantage of having an anti-inflammatory agent as part of a ready energy source?
- How does it help rheas survive in the wild?

- Can we control the pharmacological activity through dietary changes?
- Are we overlooking this unique feature when we look at the nutritional requirements of rheas?

DEVELOPING THE MARKET

Each producer needs to take an active role in promoting the product. If you produced one hundred birds this year, consider that the products of those hundred birds need to be used or sold.

We have no distribution channels yet, so consider this an opportunity to sell the product that you produce.

- One producer leaves samples at nursing homes, returns in a few weeks, and sells oil at a reasonable cost.
- A health-food store is selling rhea oil on consignment.
- Chiropractors and physical therapists are logical choices in the health field.
- Fitness clubs and high school and college athletes are natural choices.
- Give samples to people who tour your farm.

CONCLUSION

To make end markets a reality, each rhea producer must be willing to help create the market, to sell the product.

Producers often do not recognize that the intrinsic value of their birds depends on a unified marketing effort.

The products do not sell themselves—they must be actively promoted by each and every producer through personal use and personal efforts.

Use this wonderful product and offer it to other people. Your industry depends on it.

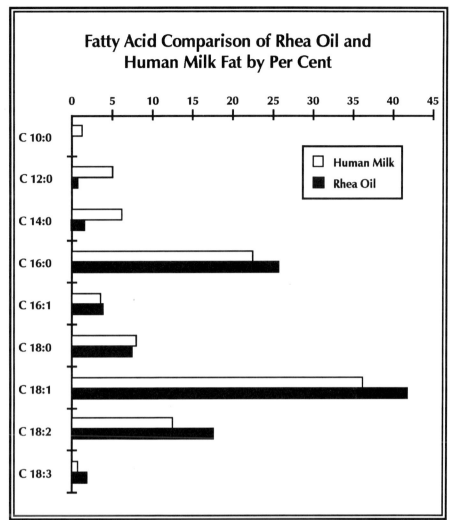

Figure 3. Graphical representation of fatty acids found in rhea oil and human milk, in relatively large amounts. See Figure 4 for comparison in lower ranges.

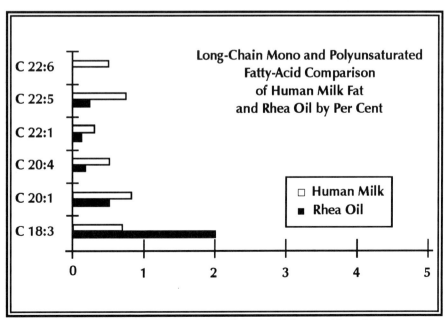

Figure 4. Comparison of the nutritionally-critical fatty acids, which appear in smaller quantities than those in Figure 3. C18:3 is repeated in both charts for a comparison of scales.

An attractive hors d'oeuvre arrangement by Chef Hubert Schmieder, featuring ostrich meats. (Photo by Doris Linemann, courtesy Department of Restaurant, Hotel, Institutional and Tourism Management, Purdue University)

RATITE MEAT

*Chef Hubert Schmieder, W. J. Stadelman, Ph. D.,
R. L. Adams, Ph. D, and R. F. Ghiselli, Ph. D.
Purdue University
West Lafayette, Indiana*

*K. W. McMillin, Ph. D.
Louisiana State University Agricultural Center
Baton Rouge, Louisiana*

*Joe Berry, Ph. D.
Oklahoma State University
Stillwater, Oklahoma*

Ratite meat is a relatively new product in the U. S. market. Presently the meat is in short supply—therefore, it is expensive.

With continuing emphasis on low-fat foods, ratite meat could become the low-fat red meat of choice. The fat content of the total carcass is about 10 per cent of the live weight, but the major muscles contain a paltry 2 per cent of fat.

As supplies increase and prices decrease, ratite meat may become the red meat of the twenty-first century.

Ratite meat is obtained almost exclusively from ostriches, emus and rheas. All major muscles are found in all species; however, differences exist in muscle texture among the three species.

All of the major muscles are found in the leg and thigh. There is no hand-separable breast meat on a ratite.

Since the muscles have been poorly identified, there is currently a need for a standardization of ratite muscle identification. Both scientific and common names are needed. While ratite muscles are similar in appearance to very-low-fat beef muscles, they more closely resemble poultry muscles in number and location in the leg.

In poultry, muscles of the drum and thigh have been identified and given scientific names (Bradley & Grahame, 1950). Thirty-five individual muscles of the hind limb of the chicken were identified, but because of the small size of the chicken and the relative uniformity in texture of the muscles of both the thigh and drum, only the anatomical parts were used for common names.

Scientific names of some ratite muscles, as listed by TOPS (Tops Ostrich Products and Services), were reported by Morris (1994) and by Harris et al. (1994). However, the same names were not listed by Bradley and Grahame.

Ratite muscle names, as used in the TOPS chart, were somewhat similar to those given by Getty (1975) for the blue grouse; however, not all scientific names were identical.

The TOPS chart shows only eight muscles from the thighs, indicating that these are marketable, while suggesting that all other muscles be used as ground meat.

The differences among authors for the listing of scientific names must be rectified and both scientific names and common names assigned to the muscles.

A note on the musculature of the proximal part of the pelvic link of the ostrich (*Stuthio camelus*) was published by F. D. Mellett in 1994.

TABLE 1. CORRELATION OF MUSCLE NOMENCLATURE WITH MARKET-CUT NAMES

SOURCE (SEE REFERENCES)

BRADLEY & GRAHAME	MARKET CUT	MORRIS	HARRIS ET AL.
Striploin	Striploin		
Inside drum	Heel **		Gastrocnemius
Outside drum	Broil **		
Mid drum			
Drum strap	Scallops **		
Inner mid drum	Medallions **		
Inner outside drum	Leg		
Full rump	Biceps **	Outside round	Biceps femoris
Inside fillet	Kalahari steak*	Inside strip	
Round	Heartland roast	Inside round	
Flat fillet	Tenderloin	Tenderloin	
Oyster fillet	Ostrich tip*	Ostrich tip	
Flat rump	Eye **	Inside roast	Semitendinosus
Fan fillet	Ostrich strip*	Ostrich strip	
Outside fillet	Top loin	Top loin	
A small fillet not listed before	Heartland tip		

** Nomenclature from McMillin, K. W. (See References)
 * Appropriate modification for emu and rhea meats

Fifteen emu muscles were named by the Western Australian Register of Approved Emu Cuts and Items (1993). A descriptive chart was included, but exact determination of each muscle identity was not possible from the chart. Also, names used were not appropriate for use in merchandising the meat.

In order to merchandise ratite meat successfully, muscles must have common names that are meaningful to producers, processors, purveyors, purchases, preparers and consumers. Several muscles of the thigh and of the drum portions might be combined and given common names for merchandising purposes.

However, more information on the textural and other sensory characteristics of each muscle is needed before making these decisions. All common names might not be the same for all species, as more muscles might be combined, especially for the smaller rhea, for merchandising.

An attempt to correlate names from the several charts is given in Table 1. Market names for the various muscles are included there as well.

MAJOR MUSCLES

The proposed names in Table 1 will be used in the following discussion of the major muscles. Differences in names of several thigh muscles among species, with reference to the Kalahari steak, ostrich tip, and ostrich strip will have to be adjusted for emu and rhea meat.

For example, these three muscles might be called the Nullebar steak and Pampas steak, emu tip and rhea tip, and emu strip and rhea strip for the emu and rhea respectively. It has been suggested that rhea meat might be marketed without separation of individual muscles (Fezler, 1994).

The largest muscle in the ostrich is the ostrich strip. It represents about 3.7 per cent of the live weight of the 12- to 16-month-old male bird (Blue X Black cross, with an average weight of 240 pounds).

Yields of all individual muscles for the three species are not yet available. With rheas, the total yield is about 38 per cent of live weight (Fezler, 1994). Of this, about 60 per cent of the meat can be marketed as steak and 40 per cent as ground meat.

Yield of emu meat is about the same. Because of the emu's larger size, as compared to the rhea, a slightly greater percentage of the meat is suitable for steaks or roasts.

The Australian emu charts include six muscles from the drum, eight from the thigh, and one from the back. Of these, the scallops and strip loin (Table 1) are small and generally would not be sold as separate, intact muscles.

Ostrich muscles are sufficiently large that leg and thigh muscles can be separated and advantageously merchandised. The

TABLE 2. WEIGHT PERCENTAGE, SUBJECTIVE AND OBJECTIVE TENDERNESS, AND COLOR VALUES OF OSTRICH MUSCLES

Muscle name	Weight[a] %	Sensory[b] Tend	W-B[c] Tend	L value[d]	a value[d]	b value[d]
M. ileotibialis cranialis	2.5-3.5	3.7	2.43w	25-29	10-13	4-6
M. ileofemoralis externus	2.0-3.5	3.2	3.03wx	20-26	9-10	3-5
M. iliotibialis lateralis	6.5-9.0	1.2	13.73xyz	18-28	7-12	3-5
M. flexor cruris lateralis	2.0-3.0	3.8	3.86xyz	24-27	11-13	3-6
M. obturatorius medialis/lateralis	1.5-3.0	2.0	3.03wx	17-26	6-12	2-6
M. Iliofibularis	6.0-8.0	4.6	2.81wx	21-27	9-11	4-5
M. femorotibialis medius	3.0-4.0	2.6	3.45wxy	23-25	9-11	2-5
M. gastrocnemius	6.0-7.5	2.8	3.33wxy	19-25	6-12	2-6
M. fibularis longus	3.0-4.0	2.5	3.92xyz	19-28	8-12	2-5
M. pectineus	1.0-3.0	2.5	4.18yz	22-24	8-12	3-5
M. flexor cruris medialis	0.5-1.0	2.8	2.87wx	19-23	6-11	3-4
M. ambiens	1.0-3.0	3.2	3.42wxy	20-24	9-10	3-4
M. obturatorius medialis	1.0-3.0	2.3	3.24wxy	25-28	10-12	4-6
M. iliotrochantericus caudalis	0.5-1.5	1.9	2.98wx	21-25	8-10	4-5
Femur trim	1.0-5.0					
Leg trim	1.0-7.5					
Bone	20.0-30.0					
Breast	13.5-15.0					

[a] percentage of carcass weight
[b] scale of 0 = very tough, 6 = very tender
[c] kg force/½-inch diameter core
[d] L (0 = darkness, 100 = lightness)
  a (+50 = more red, -50 = more green)
  b (+50 = more yellow, -50 = more blue)
[wxyz] Means with the same superscript letter are not different (P<0.05)

skinned, eviscerated carcass of the ostrich, without giblets (heart, liver, and gizzard), represents more than 60 per cent of live weight. The necks of all species represent about 2 per cent of live weight.

Major thigh muscles of the ostrich represent about 17 per cent of live weight and drum muscles about 7.5 per cent. Lesser muscles of the drum and thigh yield about 5 per cent of the live weight.

SENSORY QUALITY

The marketing of high-quality meat is essential to providing the greatest return to the producer and processor, as well as maximum satisfaction to the buyer.

Knowledge of the texture and tenderness of each muscle cut is essential. Some muscles should be marketed individually, whereas several muscles of similar textural characteristics (having different scientific names) might be marketed under a single market name.

The aging of meat, prior to separation of the muscle from the skeleton, is required for most animals. Electrical stimulation of the carcass immediately post-slaughter speeds the development of tenderness. Appropriate procedures for such stimulation are required for each species of animal.

If processing is done without electrical stimulation, aging time is needed. Beef and poultry processing plants use time to achieve acceptably tender meat. For gourmet-quality aging, the time may be extended. Limited data suggests that ostrich meat may be unique, in that aging time has very little effect on meat tenderness.

Muscles vary in their degree of tenderness. The TOPS chart rates four muscles, possibly five, as suitable for steaks, one or two for roasts, and one for curing. All others are designated as suitable only for ground meat.

According to the chart, only the Kalahari steak, ostrich strip, tenderloin, and top loin should be used for medallions or steaks. The eye of the loin was proposed as suitable for steak or roast, and the ostrich tip suitable only for roasting. The biceps and the eye were recommended for curing.

A report by Harris, et al. (1994) indicated a difference among four muscles in tenderness, as determined by a sensory panel and Warner-Bratzler shear values. The muscles were given scientific names as they relate to beef carcass muscles rather than to poultry muscles.

Chef Hubert Schmieder with hors d'oeuvre platter prepared for a banquet. (Photo courtesy Department of Restaurant, Hotel, Institutional and Tourism Management, Purdue University)

McMillin (1994) selected six muscles as suitably tender for steaks, five for roasts, and five for processing, either by curing or grinding. Obviously, the more muscles that can be kept intact, the greater will be the return.

Some of the less-tender muscles might be utilized as a jerky-type product, some may be marinated for tenderization, some cured for ham-like products, and some cut into strips or pieces for stir-fry cooking after marination. A summary of his work, as reported, is given in Table 2.

Federal inspection is a necessity if ratite meat is to attain a significant place in the meat industry. In order for the USDA Food Safety Inspection Service personnel to inspect meat for wholesomeness during processing, ratites must be classified as livestock or poultry. It is imperative that they *not* be classified as exotics.

The ratite processor can offer a wide variety of products. These can include, but are not limited to, fresh or frozen muscles, cured meat in intact muscle form, a variety of sausages and frankfurters, jerky, and ground meat. Only time will determine the degree of success of any specific product.

A significant amount of muscle tissue remains with the bones after the ratites have been processed at the slaughter plant. This meat might be recovered by mechanical deboning equipment such as that using in poultry-processing plants.

The meat can be utilized in emulsion-type products. The successful marketing of emulsion-meat products from ratites will dictate when a recovery system becomes economically feasible.

PREPARATION

Poultry meat is generally cooked to temperatures in excess of 170 degrees F. If ostrich meat is cooked to an internal temperature of 170 degrees F, the meat will remain pink in color, similar to that of medium-rare roast beef. If cooked to an internal temperature of 185 degrees F, the color changes to a light brown shade.

Harris et al. cooked ostrich meat to 63 degrees C (145 F) for their studies on meat cookery, chemical composition, and consumer acceptance. At this low temperature, the fluids in ostrich meat flow freely and the meat is raw in appearance.

Ratite meat may be cooked by the following methods: dry heat, moist heat, frying, or by a combination of these methods. Choosing the appropriate method depends on the tenderness of the muscle or cut.

Of particular concern is the type of connective tissue in the muscle. With red meats, the location of the muscle is the primary determinant when selecting a cooking method. The age or maturity of the animal is also an important factor.

Regardless of product, the choice of cooking method should contribute to the tenderness of the product, and enhance its flavor.

DRY-HEAT METHODS
Roasting and Baking

Even though the terms are sometimes used interchangeably, roasting usually refers to the application of dry, hot air to meat products, and baking to breads, cakes, and other bakery products.

Although there are some variations, such as spit-roasting, generally, roasted meat products are cooked uncovered in an oven so that the steam can escape.

Lower temperatures are advised to reduce shrinkage and allow more even doneness from outside to inside. Lower roasting temperatures range from 200 to 325 degrees F.

Sometimes a piece of meat is wrapped in thin sheets of fat to provide continuous basting during cooking. This procedure, called barding, helps prevent the product from drying out, and may be used with products that have little to no external fat covering.

Carryover cooking is a factor that should be considered when determining doneness. Although no exact amounts can be specified, the larger the food, the greater the amount of heat it will retain and the more the product will continue to cook after it is removed from the oven. As a result, roasts should be removed before they reach the desired degree of doneness as determined by temperature. The meat used in roasting should be reasonably tender.

Broiling, Pan Broiling, Grilling

All three methods apply high heat to cook meat relatively quickly. Broiling uses heat from above, grilling uses heat from below, and pan broiling requires that the pan be kept very hot and be able to retain its heat.

The object of these methods is to develop a flavorful crust on the outside while cooking the inside to the desired degree of doneness. Cooking times vary with the thickness of the meat; thick cuts may have to be finished in an oven to prevent the crust from burning.

Generally, these methods are used for the more tender cuts of meat. Mechanical pounding and/or mechanical tenderizing, using rows of thin sharp blades to pierce tough tissue, can be used to help break down the connective tissue prior to cooking.

MOIST-HEAT METHODS
Steaming

Food is cooked by surrounding with steam (not frequently used in the United States.)

Poaching and Simmering

In this method, the product is completely submerged in a liquid, and the liquid's temperature kept close to the boiling point.

This method of cookery is generally used for less-tender cuts of meat, where the moist heat and low temperatures are used to dissolve the connective tissue. An acid is often added to the cooking liquid to help tenderize as well.

The meat is done when it is fork tender. Meat cooked this way is frequently served with a separate sauce.

A variety of ratite cold cuts. (Photo courtesy Department of Restaurant, Hotel, Institutional and Tourism Management, Purdue University)

FRYING
Sautéing and stir frying

Both methods use small amounts of hot fat to cook foods quickly. Typically, small slices or strips are cut *julienne*, and seared *and* cooked over high heat. Because of the short cooking time, the meat must be naturally tender.

Pan Frying and Deep Frying

Like sautéing, these methods use fat as the cooking medium. In both cases, more fat is used, and the meat is battered or breaded.

In pan frying, the product is partially submerged in the fat and must be turned after it browns on one side. In deep-fat frying, the product is completely submerged in fat and usually cooked until it is golden brown.

The goal of both methods is to seal the juices inside the coating. The meat should be tender, since the heat is rather high and the cooking time relatively short.

COMBINATION METHODS
Braising and Stewing

Combination methods are so named because more than one method is applied. The usual procedure is to sear (brown) the meat product in a small amount of oil to develop flavor, then simmer in a seasoned liquid until done. Meat that is not properly cooked will lack eye appeal.

Larger pieces of meat are used in braising, and the liquid comes part way up the meat. In stewing, meat is cut into bite-size pieces and submerged in the liquid. Both methods use the liquid to make a sauce that is served with the meat.

These methods are usually used with less-tender cuts, or meat from older animals. More tender cuts can be used if adjustments are made in cooking time.

In addition to choosing the appropriate cooking method, the tenderness of any meat is greatly influenced by whether it is cut across the muscle fibers or with them.

With several of the ratite muscles, the fibers do not lay all in the same direction. To obtain uniformity in tenderness of such muscles, the carver must be alert to changes in direction of the muscle fibers.

For best results, ratite meat should not be cooked to the well-done stage. Medium is probably the optimum stage.

A partial aerial view of Texas Longneck Ranch. Note the wagon-wheel design of the emu pens. (Photo courtesy Holmes Photography, Lubbock, Texas)

RANCH LAYOUT

Scotty Flowers and Rollo Gurss
Texas Longneck Ranch, Inc.
Lubbock, Texas

We would like to thank the publisher for inviting us to contribute a chapter for this book. Since we formed Texas Longneck Ranch in 1992, we have been asked for assistance in designing other ranches, and it is nice to put those ideas in print.

We must point out that the solutions that work for us are not the only solutions available and others may work for you. We offer the following only as a guide to building your ranch, from land purchase to commercial production.

We will consider facilities of two sizes: small ranches (fewer than ten breeder pairs) and large ranches (more than ten breeder pairs).

Whether you plan a small or large breeding operation, you should think your entire project through before starting anything. In particular, make sure you have a goal in mind. Are you going to be happy with one breeder pair? Or do you plan to have 200 breeder pairs? Remember, it is very hard to remodel your facility after your birds are on site.

SITE SELECTION

In selecting a site, look for:
- Good access on paved roads for employees, visitors, customers, suppliers, and shipping.
- Abundant water, fertile soil, and drainage. Birds love grass and alfalfa. The more fresh grass and alfalfa you can grow, the cheaper your feed costs will be. Good drainage will diminish the chance of disease spreading in muddy pens. You must be able to feed and gather eggs in the worst weather.
- Protection from wild animals, domestic animals, noise, and theft.
- Room to lay out a good, efficient working ranch. There should be a good area for incubation and hatching, brooding and retailing.
- Sufficient room for the number of birds you want to raise. Also consider how many birds it would take for a given site to make money.

Most small ranches (fewer than ten breeder pairs) we have seen were adapted from existing facilities. This is the easiest and least expensive way to start, but a small facility must have all the elements that a large one does. The only difference is scale.

CLIMATE

What climate is best for raising birds? Ostriches seem to do best in warm, dry climates. However, we know ranchers who do very well in colder areas. They have designed their facilities to allow them to work around the weather.

Emus seem to do well in all climates from northern Canada to Mexico. *Your* facility must make adjustments for *your* weather. The best place for you to raise ratites is where you feel comfortable living.

SELECTING A DESIGNER AND CONTRACTOR

First and foremost, hire people who have good knowledge of the task you wish performed. You don't hire a plumber to wire your house. Remember that cheapest is

Texas Longneck Ranch, Lubbock, Texas

not always best—sometimes you save a dime and it costs a dollar.

We advise asking people in the business for help. They usually have crossed similar problems and will give you their options on who is good and who is not.

Your facility is highly specialized. You are spending large sums of money—don't settle for sub-par design, construction, materials, or workmanship. Your future product depends on it.

SITE DESIGN AND MATERIALS

When laying out the design for your ranch, your prime considerations are cleanliness, access, moving and working birds, outdoor pens, feed storage, barns, fencing, and your hatching, brooding, and office facilities.

Cleanliness

You should design so that you can work from clean to dirty and from healthy to sick. Design so you can feed chicks, then older birds. Treat healthy birds, then sick birds.

It should be easy to be able to wash your boots, hands, clothing, and even vehicles after working sick birds. It is best to design an isolation area for sick birds and a quarantine area for new arrivals.

Most people prefer to have their hatching and brooder facility at the highest point on their property. This allows less water contamination to enter the building.

Access

Your design should allow controlled access for employees, ranch management, retail sales, and suppliers. Parking should be provided for these functions.

Do not allow people who have been on other ranches access to your birds. Most ranchers have foot baths to disinfect their shoes. On our ranch, no one has access to incubation, hatching or brooding areas except hatching employees.

MOVING AND WORKING BIRDS

You will have to move birds from time to time and you will probably buy and sell birds over your ranch's life. There should be alleys between pens so you do not have to handle birds in order to move them. Holding areas for birds that are being shipped should have easy trailer access.

OUTDOOR PENS

We have pens of different sizes and shapes for birds of different ages.

Chick Pens

Chicks aged three months to a year or more are in pens 100' x 250', with a holding pen 20' x 40' and a barn 12' x 20' which opens to the holding area.

We installed an 8' gate from the holding area to the large pen

Note visitor controls: Appointment only and check in at office.

Ranch Layout

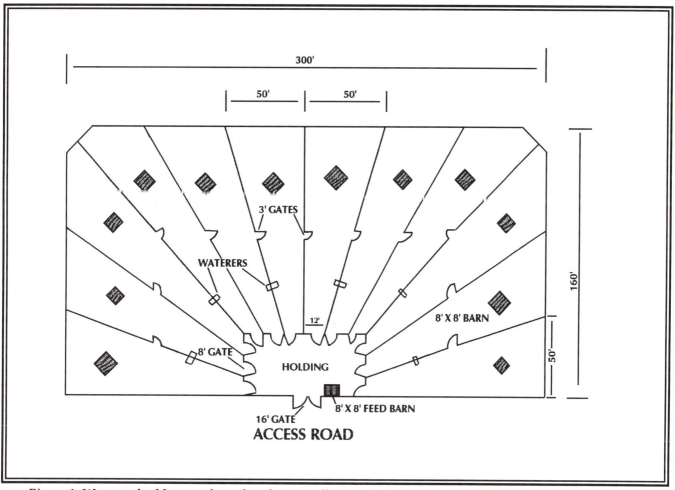

Figure 1. Wagon-wheel layout of emu breeder pens allow quick feeding and watering. The sheds in each pen are situated to provide shelter from the prevailing winds. The central holding area allows access as well as a place to isolate birds from any one of the pens.

Emu pens. Note heated waterers between pens, 8' x 8' metal barns, T-post with chain-link fence. White pipe is water mister for cooling birds.

to enable us to pen the birds when necessary. We can also place heat lamps in the barn if the weather is too cold. We run anywhere from ten to thirty birds in each one of these pens, thinning birds every other month as they grow.

Grow-out Pens

Grow-out pens (one to two years, emu and ostrich) and off-season pens can be as large as your property allows. Many breeders use one to ten acres with multiple shelters. Trees, grass, ponds, and alfalfa are common in grow-out pens. Your adult birds will do very well in this environment.

A holding area of 40' x 40' is a good idea in these pens to enable you to catch your birds. Get them used to being in this holding area

3' gate allows easy access to collect eggs. Note chain-link fence with no top rail.

Ostrich in holding area of breeder pen.

by providing them food and water there.

Emu Breeder Pens

We run twelve breeder pairs per acre on our ranch. Our emu breeder pens are designed in a one-half wagon-wheel design, with a holding area at the center and an 8' x 8' feed-storage barn. Our pens are 12 feet wide in the front (an 8' gate and 4' feeding area) and 50 feet across the back; the shortest depth is 150 feet. See Figure 1.

Twelve pairs can be fed from the holding area in ten minutes or less. This becomes important as the size of the ranch increases and if your winters are very cold. We prefer to feed our birds twice a day, so protecting feed from bad weather is not a large concern.

We share heated waterers between pens and have a 3' gate to allow easy walking for egg collection. Remember, most of your egg collection will be done at night.

We provide shelter with trees and 8' x 8' metal barns. We face our barns to the south-east because in our area the least amount of bad weather comes from that direction.

We place our barns in the center of the pens to allow birds to escape from each other. They can also rest in the shade without going in the barn. In general, most emus will not spend much time in the barn.

Another design that is used in warmer climates is community breeder pens. They can be similar in size and design as the grow-out pens. It is not recommended in cold climates because it is easy to miss collection of eggs at night and freezing will ruin the egg.

A drawback to this method is that you cannot identify eggs and parents when using this type of pen.

In a breeder market, you must be able to give the buyer the history of the parents, and this method of breeding will not allow

Ranch Layout

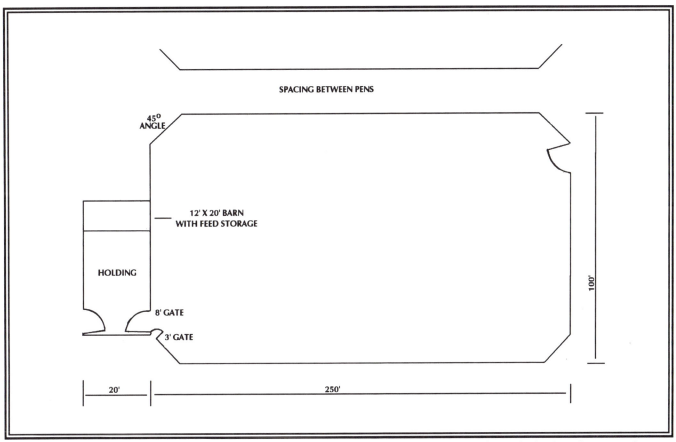

Figure 2. Ostrich breeder pen. The separate holding area, with a gate between, allows the birds to be trapped, either to collect eggs or to isolate them for examinations or treatment.

100% accuracy. We think you will see more of this type of pen as the commercial market continues to develop.

Ostrich Breeder Pens

We have our breeders in 250' x 100' pens with a holding area of 40' x 40'. There is an 8' gate from the large area to the holding area to enable us to trap the birds away from the eggs when collecting.

Adjacent to the holding area is a 12' x 20' barn in which we feed and water. This gets the ostrich used to going into the barn daily. You will appreciate that fact when you have to work your birds.

We also use a 45-degree corner on these pens, to enable the female to escape the male during breeding season. Trees or hay

8' x 8' metal feed storage barn in holding area at center of wagon-wheel pens. See Figure 1 and aerial photo at beginning of chapter for better view of layout.

Looking at breeder pens from inside holding area of wagon wheel.

Note ease of feeding 12 breeder pens from holding area without entering pens. Handle on feed trough allows it to be emptied and cleaned easily.

bales are a good idea during breeding season as well.

Feed Storage

This is an item for which many people fail to plan. You must be able to deliver feed to your storage facility and it should be easy to feed your birds. We built 8' x 8' metal barns with concrete floors and two metal doors for each breeder compound (twelve breeder pens).

The feed storage area should be dry and not too hot, to retain maximum vitamin strength. We feed different feeds for different-aged birds. As herd size increases, you may want to switch feed storage to bulk types to save time and feed cost.

Barns

On our farm we have two sizes of small barns. This gives us flexibility if we need to move them around or expand. We build barns on the rear of the property, away from our birds, and set them when needed.

Our breeder barns are 8' x 8' x 8' tall, open on one side, and the roof slopes 6" to the rear.

Our chick barns are 12' x 20' x 8' tall. They have an 8' opening to the holding pen and some have doors so that the young birds can be closed up at night.

All of our barns are metal frame and metal siding and are anchored to a concrete footing with piers in the corners. We get very high winds in this part of the county and do not want to take a chance of barns blowing over on our birds.

Many farms we have visited use wood framing with plywood siding and it works very well. This is a less expensive construction method, but will require more maintenance.

Fencing

We prefer 6' chain link, 11-gauge, double-knuckle fabric. We place two-inch-diameter posts in concrete every 50' and T-posts every 10'. We do not use a top rail, as this allows the fences to flex and will not let a running bird hurt his neck on the top rail.

We also have a perimeter fence around our property to secure it from animals and protect from theft. It also serves as a holding area for your birds if they escape from their pens. Believe us, they will get out.

BUILDINGS

Small farmers often use existing facilities which are adapted from other uses. These should use the same principle as a scaled-down large farm.

Many people incubate and hatch in garages, barns, extra bedrooms, laundry rooms, or even their living room.

These seem to work reasonably well if they don't have too large a volume—the more product you have, the more contamination you have.

We incubated, hatched, and brooded in an old barn for two seasons with some success. However, we increased our hatch percentage and had fewer neck and leg problems in the new facility. The most important thing is to use common sense: work from clean to dirty and keep your facility as clean as possible.

Large farms provide a chance to design a facility from scratch. Here are some ideas to consider before starting construction.

OFFICES

It is very handy to have an office area which includes reception space, work office, restroom, and sales area. There will be many people who want to see how your operation works, so remember this while designing.

It is a good idea to have windows from your office area into your incubation, hatching, and brooding area. This allows you to

Ranch manager Allen Hagens and secretary Cindy Gurss in the office. The window looking into incubation room allows visitors to see the facility but does not allow contamination to be brought into this critical area.

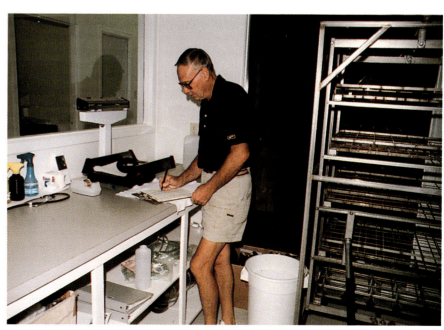

Ranch manager Allen Hagens in hatcher room. Note glass to outside office area.

Rollo Gurss weighs eggs in the egg storage room adjacent to the incubation room.

give tours without contaminating your facility. Potential buyers want to know how you run your hatching, and this type of design allows them to get a good look without carrying in dirt or disease they may have picked up at other facilities.

INCUBATION

In our opinion, this is the most critical room in your operation. You should condition the room so your incubators can do their job most efficiently.

We prefer separate heat, vent, and air conditioner systems for incubation, hatching, and brooding rooms. Air should not be mixed from either of these areas. We also recommend installing HEPA filters and UV lights in our duct system to purify the air.

Adequate ventilation is crucial. You should exhaust approximately 20% of your old air every 24 hours. You should exhaust carbon monoxide from your incubation units to the outside.

You may also want to make accommodations in this room (or an adjacent room) to store eggs. This will enable you to set eggs once or twice a week and hatch on the same schedule. Make sure you design your room (or rooms) to enable yourself to expand if that is your goal.

HATCHING

This room or rooms should be next to your incubation area.

We prefer two hatching rooms. This enables us to hatch for two weeks in one room, then rotate to the other. We clean the dirty hatcher and room thoroughly before we rotate back.

These rooms get very dirty and contaminated, so floor drains, work tables, and sinks are a good idea.

BROODER

Your brooder barn can be connected or separate from your incubation/hatching facility.

Brooder room. Note ceiling fans, remote control for door, overhead doors for easy outside access to chick runs. The room is air conditioned and heated.

It is important that people not walk from your brooder barn to your incubation and hatching area without first washing up. We have provided sink, boot bath, and if needed, shower to clean up before re-entering our incubation area from our brooder area.

We clean our pens twice a day so ease of cleaning is a must. Cleanable surfaces that are not slick when wet are preferred. As in the incubation and hatching rooms, washable walls work very well.

It is also important to heat and cool your brooder barn. We have an HVAC (heat, vent, air conditioner) unit and hot water pipes in our concrete floor. You can also purchase heating pads and/or heat lamps to do the same job. However, they are less efficient except when adapting an existing facility.

We provide access to the outside when weather permits. Birds need as much area as possible to exercise. We allow chicks to run outside after they are three days old. Our outside pens are a minimum of 10' wide and 150' long to 300' x 150'. We have a shaded area 25' feet deep for protection.

Chick runs from brooder room. Note overhead doors.

Inside pens are 3' to 8' wide by 40' long and 18" tall. Your chicks must be kept in a clean, well-protected area to ensure your chances of raising a healthy crop.

These areas are basically the same for ostrich, emu, and rhea. We suggest consulting a qualified designer before constructing an incubation, hatching, and brooding facility. Good planning makes your job easier to perform.

CONCLUSION

We hope that this general information will give you a good basis to construct your facility. As we stated before, the weather in your particular area will dictate your final design solution. Cold climates require very different facilities than warm areas.

Lyle Hague with a hooded ostrich.

TRANSPORTATION & HANDLING

Lyle Hague
Vision Exotix Express
Vision Exotix Ostrich Ranch
Lexington, Oklahoma

When transporting ratites via air or ground, every effort must be made to ensure that the birds are transported safely and with a minimum amount of stress.

Proper handling, combined with the proper equipment, will enable you to transport birds successfully while dramatically reducing the chance of injury or death.

HANDLING RATITES

To raise any form of livestock successfully it is imperative to know how to handle them properly. Ratites are no exception. With the proper knowledge, confidence, and equipment you should have no problem mastering the art of handling ratites.

The first priority when handling birds is safety, both of the birds and of the people handling them. Always exercise caution, good judgment, and common sense.

Most birds will react to handling in a similar manner; however, individual birds have their own unique temperaments, making it impossible to predict exactly how they will react.

Some birds can be restrained or moved with little or no resistance. This is certainly the exception, not the rule. Other birds are difficult to handle, which can make the process dangerous for the handler as well as for the bird.

There is no reason to fear a ratite, but remember that it is a wild animal which should be respected for just that fact.

The procedures discussed below are guidelines. Determine which will be most effective for a specific situation and use the technique or method in which you are most proficient and comfortable.

HANDLING CHICKS

Chicks of all ages, particularly those from hatch to three months of age, must be handled with extra care.

At this age their fragile bodies are developing rapidly, and the stress brought on by improper handling can lead to injury or even death.

OSTRICH CHICKS

To pick up an ostrich chick, place one hand at the base of the neck and one hand under the rear end, being careful not to squeeze or choke the chick.

To move an older chick that is too large to carry, place your hands in the same position and carefully restrain or guide the chick to its destination.

Never pick up an ostrich chick by the legs or neck. Finally, ensure that chicks are set down gently.

EMU AND RHEA CHICKS

To pick up an emu or rhea chick, place one hand at the base of the neck, in front of the sternum, and one hand under the rear end, being careful not to squeeze or choke the chick.

If the chick begins kicking when you pick it up, grab both legs at the ankle with one hand and fold them up tightly under the body. Next, either place your other arm over the center of bird's back or wrap it around its body and cradle it.

Depending on size, a chick may also be turned upside down once you have cradled it and tucked its legs up tightly. Chicks tend to put up less of a struggle in this position. Again, ensure that all chicks are set down gently.

HANDLING ADULTS

When handling birds of any age it is important to remain calm and be patient, and try to minimize the stress on the birds.

To catch a bird it is best to corral it into a small holding pen. The holding pen must be sturdy and void of any gaps or holes in the fencing where the bird might get its head, toe, or foot caught.

This procedure not only expedites the catching process but minimizes the chance of a bird running full speed into a fence and injuring itself.

OSTRICHES

Ostriches are powerful creatures that can reach speeds of up to 45 miles per hour in seconds and kick to the front with enormous force and velocity. But there are ways of getting around their speed and power in order to work them.

Using a Hood I

If you have to move or restrain an ostrich approximately six months of age or older, a hood can be an invaluable tool.

The hood is nothing more than a tubular piece of material with a large opening at one end for the head and a small elastic opening at the opposite end to fit snugly over a closed bill.

Once hooded, birds tend to relax and become much easier to work with. There are birds that will not require a hood and can easily be handled. However, to capture and handle the average bird the following methods and techniques are recommended.

If the bird is curious, somewhat friendly, and routinely comes to the edge of the fence to peck at an outstretched hand, you have an excellent opportunity to hood and capture it.

Slip the hood over your wrist, large opening toward your fingers. When the bird pecks at your fingers, quickly grab its bill with that hand.

Once you have a firm hold on the bird's closed bill, use your other hand to slide the hood quickly over the bird's head, ensuring that its vision is totally obstructed. Release the bill, allowing the head and neck to move freely.

Now immediately move to either side of the bird and grab a wing, while a helper grabs the opposite wing. The bird can now be restrained or moved.

When moving an ostrich, another helper may assist by pushing from the rear, although this is not always necessary.

In some cases a bird will be more willing to be walked backward. This procedure is fine. However do not attempt to do this with young chicks, as their developing legs are extremely fragile and could easily be injured.

Using a Hood II

Depending on a bird's nature and comfort level around humans, the above method may not be feasible.

Here's another method to try, if you have advance notice that a bird is to be captured.

First, withhold feed for several hours prior to capture. When ready, put out feed as you usually do, and place the hood on your wrist as explained above.

When the bird goes to the feeder, it should be hungry enough to take feed directly from the palm of your hand. When the bird takes the feed, quickly grab its bill with your hooded hand, and follow the instructions above.

Using a Hood III

If these methods prove unsuccessful, enter the holding pen and slowly maneuver the bird into a corner. Once cornered, quickly reach for the back of the neck with one hand and gently pull its head down. Quickly grab the bill with the other hand and hood the bird.

If a holding pen is not available and one is forced to capture a bird in a large open pen, first try to slowly maneuver the bird into a corner and repeat the hooding procedure explained above.

Using a Hook

If the bird becomes overly excited and begins running uncontrollably into the fence, it may be necessary to utilize a hook designed specifically for catching ostriches.

They vary in length and are usually constructed of aluminum. A hook can be dangerous to the bird and to the handler if improperly used, so use it only as a last resort.

The successful and safe hooking of a speeding ostrich requires quick and precise execution that comes only with experience. Never get in a hurry. If the bird becomes extremely excited allow it some time to calm down.

Then enter the pen and stand just beyond the path in which the bird is running.

Firmly grasp the hook with both hands and hold it to the ground directly in the bird's path, with the open end of the hook facing the bird.

Transportation & Handling

Lyle Hague demonstrates his technique for hooding an ostrich.
1. Entice the bird with a bit of food, or rely on its curious nature as you reach toward it.
2. Firmly but gently grasp its beak.
3. Slip the hood over the bird's head.

Lyle Hague with a hooked ostrich.

Lyle and Frank Hague with a hooded ostrich, ready to be moved or loaded.

Just before the bird passes by you, quickly raise the hook to approximately mid-neck level. When the hook makes contact, the bird will be caught off balance, and in some cases will whip around due to its momentum.

At this point, a helper must grab the bird's bill and slip the hood over its head. You may need two helpers, one on each side, since it's hard to tell to which side the bird will turn its head. Once the hood is on, remove the hook from around the neck.

EMUS

Although much smaller than ostriches, emus are quick and powerful for their size. They should never be underestimated. They are able to jump fairly high, thrash from side to side, and violently kick high to the front and to the sides.

When emus kick, it is not the force of the blow that can cause injury, but the extremely sharp toenails that can inflict damage on the downward motion. For this reason you should always wear protective clothing when handling emus.

To handle an emu you must first catch it. Once you've moved the bird into the holding pen, there are three basic options:

- slowly maneuver the bird to the fence line and pin it between yourself and the fence, or
- maneuver it into a corner and trap it, or
- try to grab the bird when it runs by.

Emus will almost always struggle when handled. Stay clear of the legs at all times, as they will vigorously jump and kick in an attempt to escape.

Once you've cornered an emu, you've got three more options.

1. Approach the bird from the rear and quickly take firm hold of both wings. The wings are small and often difficult to grasp firmly.

With a secure hold on the wings, hold the bird close to your body to maintain control. The bird can now be restrained or moved.

Many birds will move or load into a trailer more easily by walking them backward. This technique is by far the most common and preferred when handling emus, if for no other reason that it keeps the handler away from the emu's feet.

2. Another technique is to approach the bird from the rear and wrap one arm under the breast. Then place the other arm over the front portion of the back.

To do this you must straddle the bird, and this technique does not afford as much control over a bird as does the wing technique.

There is also a greater risk of personal injury because the handler's face and body are much closer to the kicking legs.

However, in cases such as handling a bird with an injured wing, it can be an effective alternative.

3. A third method is to approach from behind and to the side. Firmly place one arm underneath the bird's midsection and immediately bring your other arm between the legs from the rear and securely clasp your hands.

With both arms wrapped firmly around the bird, you can now pick it up and carry it. Once picked up emus usually cease kicking and become quite docile.

This technique is useful if a bird has to be moved a short distance or loaded into a trailer, but it requires some strength, and should only be used by those who possess the physical ability.

There are devices such as slings and harnesses that offer alternative ways to handle emus. They can be a safe and effective way to restrain and move birds. However, not all birds take well to them, and if used improperly, they can lead to injury.

RHEAS

Like emus, rheas are quick and powerful for their size, and should never be underestimated. They are capable of the same ability to jump, thrash, and kick violently to the front and sides.

As with emus, when rheas kick, it is not the actual force of the blow that can cause injury, it is the extremely sharp toenails that can inflict damage on the downward motion. Again, wear protective clothing when handling rheas.

Generally, rheas are handled in the same fashion as emus. The wings of rheas are much larger than those of emus, making them much easier to grasp.

At the present, there are no devices available that are designed specifically for handling rheas.

TRANSPORTING RATITE EGGS

Eggs must be carefully packaged to prevent breakage. The egg container must be of heavy duty construction for strength, and it should be sanitized prior to the introduction of the eggs.

Each egg must be wrapped in foam or similar protection to avoid breakage. After the eggs have been carefully packaged, they should be transported immediately to their destination, utilizing the quickest and safest means available, whether it be by air or by ground transportation.

TRANSPORTING RATITES

EQUIPMENT

Use of a properly-designed trailer is of paramount importance to the successful and safe transportation of ratites of all ages.

While it is a common practice to use a converted horse or cattle trailer, this is acceptable only if the trailer meets minimum standards for safely transporting ratites. The trailer must be fully enclosed—*never transport a bird in an open trailer*.

Trailers must have no gaps in which in which a bird could catch a foot or neck, have no sharp edges, and have excellent ventilation and air flow.

However, these are basic requirements, adequate only for short-distance hauls in moderate temperatures.

When transporting birds in extreme temperature conditions, over short as well as long distances, heating and air conditioning are critical to prevent heat- or cold-related problems which could possibly lead to death.

A non-skid loading ramp is essential, as it makes loading and off-loading easier and safer, and eliminates leg injuries often associated with step-up trailers without a ramp.

A darkened interior is also beneficial, as it simulates night and encourages birds to bed down during the move.

When transporting ostriches, provide as much headroom in the trailer as possible to avoid possible head injury.

Finally, after every use, thoroughly clean and disinfect the trailer. This procedure will greatly reduce the chance of cross-contamination from facility to facility.

LOADING

There are only general guidelines for loading and unloading ratites. It is best to load during the day; however, if absolutely necessary birds can be loaded at night.

More important than technique is the handler's attitude. Never rush the loading and unloading process. Slowly and gently load birds into the trailer one at a time.

Chicks are usually carried on board while older birds are normally walked directly into the trailer. Some birds will easily load by backing them into the trailer.

When loading ensure that each bird is allowed ample room to stand and sit. Never overcrowd, as it will result in birds injuring themselves or other birds.

TRANSPORTING

As soon as the birds have been loaded into the trailer, depart immediately. Once the trailer begins moving, birds will usually sit down. When it comes to a stop, some birds immediately stand up.

Therefore, any sudden starts or stops could cause birds to fall and injure themselves or other birds. *Always start and stop slowly and smoothly.*

During the move, periodically stop and visually inspect the birds to ensure that they are doing well.

Depending on the distance that the birds will be transported it may be necessary to stop and offer the birds water and feed. Only a small percentage will drink or eat, primarily due to stress, but it is important that the birds who will drink or eat be able to do so.

Younger birds are more inclined to eat and drink than are older birds.

Ratites may be tranquilized for transportation. However, this is an uncommon practice and it is no substitute for proper handling and the use of an adequate trailer.

If you are considering this option, consult a veterinarian for information on the possible effects and administration procedures.

Avoid transporting breeding ratites during their laying season. The sudden stress brought on by the move may adversely affect birds, and they may cease laying activity completely.

UNLOADING

Prior to unloading, ensure that the birds are given ample time to get on their feet and establish their bearings before they are slowly and gently escorted off the trailer. Because of the physical stress during transportation, ratites generally become very easy to handle during unloading.

If it is necessary to unload at night, see that extra precautions are taken to ensure that the birds will not run into anything when exiting the trailer. If possible illuminate the area in which the birds will exit. Once the birds are unloaded, assist them in locating feed and water.

Unloading in darkness has no lasting harmful effects on ratites. The effects of keeping them confined unnecessarily in a trailer is much more detrimental to them, and dramatically increases the likelihood of a bird succumbing to stress or injuring itself or another bird.

AIR TRANSPORTATION

Ratites may be transported via air depending on their age and/or size. They can be transported as young as one day old in some cases.

Chicks from one to thirty days old are normally placed in air carriers while older birds are sometimes placed in individual compartments. Air transportation is a viable alternative to ground transportation when eggs or birds have to be moved rapidly within a specific time frame.

MICROCHIP IDENTIFICATION

John R. Wade, DVM, and Jean Anne Mayhall
Microchip Identification Systems
Mandeville, Louisiana

A tiny injectable transponder, or microchip, has revolutionized animal identification around the world. Never before has a single technology had such an impact on improving man's ability to learn more about the animal kingdom.

Microchips help us do a better job of researching, raising, tracking, locating and just enjoying creatures of all species:
- a research doctor can monitor hundreds of laboratory mice as he seeks a cure for cancer,
- a university scientist studies tiny gecko lizards,
- an Arizona field team develops safer travel patterns for desert land tortoises,
- a midwestern dairyman monitors milk production,
- a lost dog is returned to its family and, yes,
- an ostrich farmer carefully documents the hatching of hundreds of chicks.

What do these people have in common? They all use microchips to accomplish their tasks. The animals they work with all carry tiny numbered chips n their bodies.

Increasingly, the world has turned to the safe permanent microchip as a means of reliable identification. The ratite industry is no exception—it is one of the largest users of microchips today.

This reliance upon the tiny identification chip began in the mid-1980s when the new American ostrich industry was faced with a dilemma. Thousands of chicks were hatching and, typical of the species, they had almost identical physical characteristics, making it impossible to distinguish one from the other.

Farmers tried every traditional method of marking their birds. Hot brands were too painful and destructive, freeze brands faded, external tags and legbands could be removed, and tattoos were impractical. The timely emergence of a new electronic identification system—the injectable microchip—provided a safe, simple and final solution.

Ostrich farmers and their veterinarians set an example for other livestock industries by adopting this progressive technique as a standard. When the emu and rhea farming industries began to emerge, they, too, took advantage of microchip identification.

As the ratite industries grew, so did the usefulness of implanted microchips. For the first time in history, animals carried permanent unalterable identification.

HOW IT WORKS

Microchip identification systems consist generally of two parts—the microchip and the microchip reader. The chip, as it has been nicknamed, is actually a

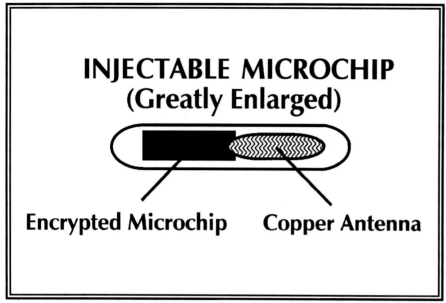

Figure 1. Simplified diagram of the working parts of an injectable microchip.

small transponder made up of two main components, a numbered microchip and an attached copper antenna coil.

These components are enclosed in a strong, bio-compatible glass capsule and sealed by laser. The entire device is about the size of a grain of rice, so it can be injected into the animal with a 12-gauge needle syringe.

The chip remains inert until activated by a radiowave signal from the reader. When the antenna in the microchip receives a clear signal, it transmits a specific number back to the reader where it is displayed for viewing on a screen.

This reading process takes place in milliseconds. Microchip numbers are unalterable and one-of-a-kind, never to be duplicated.

The implantation of the chip is a quick and easy procedure that causes only minimal, if any, discomfort, yet establishes lifelong identification for the animal.

The microchip is embedded in muscle and is therefore almost impossible to remove without surgery. Even with the proper equipment and anesthesia, these tiny chips are extremely difficult to locate within the body tissue. The animal carries his own "social security" number and the farmer is provided with identification on demand.

THE USES FOR CHIPS

FARM MANAGEMENT

It is fortuitous that microchip technology developed at the same time ostrich farming began to intensify in the United States. The two were made for each other. Many of the unique management challenges encountered in ostrich ranching have been addressed through the use of microchips.

Standard chick management techniques in the United States utilize the all-in, all-out system for chick rearing.

This system requires that all chicks hatched within one week's time be placed together in the same pen immediately after leaving the hatcher. In other words, they are grouped according to age and size as opposed to relatedness.

This means that although the majority of farms in America have multiple hens producing chicks, those chicks are not grouped according to the hen that laid the eggs from which they were hatched, but according to *when* they were hatched. For management purposes, however, it is important that accurate records be kept regarding family histories.

Therefore, although birds from different hens are mixed as they are being raised, and it is very necessary to be able to distinguish them from each other, it is impossible to do this visually.

Unfortunately, all of the conventional means of external identification have drawbacks with these fast-growing chicks. Leg bands are routinely lost, heat brands are too severe for young tender ostrich skin, and freeze brands or tattoos may damage hide and will fade with time. It is easy to see why the ostrich farmers found an ally in microchip identification.

All ratite farms are dynamic entities, assured of constant change in bird population with the general trend of growth. As his flock population fluctuates, the farmer must keep track of breeder birds, chicks hatched, birds sold, birds bought, birds that die, and other vital changes.

As a farm increases in size, the use of records becomes essential in tracking the disposition of birds or to document sales and purchases. Microchips provide a standard and consistent method for bird identification.

Because microchip numbers are permanent, unique and unalterable, and because they work well with all of the available farm computer programs, they are an ideal tool for improved farm management.

CONTRACTS AND SALES

When a private sale of birds takes place between two parties, the seller will generally guarantee one or more things such as gender, health, age and conformation. For this reason, ratite farmers are very diligent in documenting microchip numbers on bills of sale. In the event that a bird is returned, the chip number can be verified, thus providing absolute proof that the bird being returned is the same one that was originally sold.

Young ratites grow and change very rapidly during the first year of life. As is often the case, a buyer will choose chicks from a flock when they are a certain age and not take delivery until the chicks are several weeks or months older. Again the microchip plays a valuable role in verifying that the chicks being delivered are in fact the original chosen birds.

Similarly, when older birds are purchased both buyer and seller can rest assured that the transport of those birds is intact when microchips are read both before and at the end of the journey.

Microchip companies register the chips they sell to the farmers and veterinarians who purchase them. In other words, if an ostrich farmer purchases one hundred chips, all of those chip numbers are registered via computer to that farmer.

Should that farmer have a theft problem, he reports the particular stolen numbers to the authorities and the numbers are then made available to the public on printed hot sheets.

Therefore, when a new buyer prepares to purchase birds, he can ask that they be scanned for any stolen numbers, he can check the hot sheets and he can call the microchip company for the latest list of birds reported stolen.

A TOOL FOR VETERINARIANS

Veterinarians in all types of practices benefit greatly from microchip technology, but the reliable chip is particularly important to the ostrich or ratite practitioner. Microchips are used so extensively in the various ratite industries that virtually all veterinarians working with these species possess readers and microchips to be used as needed.

Medical records, health certificates, physical examinations, pre-purchase examinations, gender determination, and insurance examinations are only some of the situations in which veterinarians crucially depend upon the implanted microchip for positive identification.

Microchips provide the consistent and accurate identification so necessary for various medical records such as the basic individual health record that veterinarians chart on all patients.

Depending upon the computer capabilities of a particular practice, it is also possible for the veterinarian to pull up medical charts on individual birds by entering a microchip number into his computer.

Veterinarians are held accountable for certain procedures

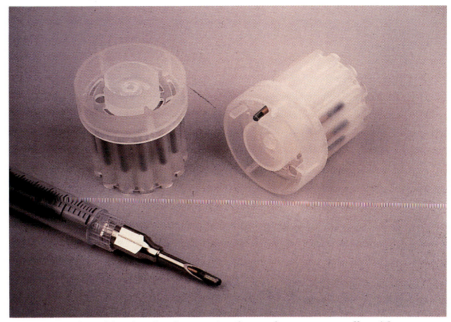

Microchips in plastic cases, and a twelve-gauge needle with a microchip, ready for implantation.

John Wade enticing an ostrich to hold still long enough to read its microchip with the reader.

such as health and physical conformation guarantees as well as gender determinations.

Should there be a discrepancy or dispute concerning one of these medical decisions or gender assessments by the veterinarian, this identification method assures that the bird whose condition is questioned is actually the one that was originally examined.

The animal health departments in certain states require that any ostrich, emu or rhea residing in or traveling into or out of that state be microchipped.

Documents such as health certificates, specific laboratory tests, and insurance exams rely upon microchips, and therefore often require that they be the form of identification for the referenced animal.

It is the veterinarian who performs these tests and signs her name to the required documents. It is the microchip that, by its mere presence, supports or denies the work of the veterinarian.

In similar circumstances, the research veterinarian depends upon microchips to document his findings. Many universities have ratite research grants in which feed, reproduction, disease and genetics are studied. Microchips offer the consistent, permanent identification needed for studying great numbers of birds.

SUPPORT FOR INSURANCE

Microchip identification technology found its way into the insurance community soon after its arrival in the ratite industry. Permanent, accurate and unalterable identification is of the utmost importance when issuing mortality insurance policies, some of which exceeded $50,000 per bird.

Today's livestock insurers require that a bird be microchipped and that a veterinarian verify that fact and sign a veterinary certificate before an insurance policy is issued.

If a claim is made, the insurance company will require a veterinarian to read the chip before the claim is paid.

Very simply, permanent microchips have given livestock insurers a perfect solution to the age-old problem of insurance fraud.

An additional benefit to these companies is that they can quickly and easily determine whether or not a bird is stolen before it is insured.

THEFT DETERRENCE

During the early 1990s, several million dollars worth of birds were stolen in the state of Texas alone. Other states reported theft and fraud, too, at alarming rates.

This threat was perhaps the single biggest motivator behind the almost mass movement of the ratite industry toward the use of microchip identification. The fear of having livestock and livelihood stolen in the night impelled farmers to give their animals the simple injection that would prove ownership.

As law enforcement agencies became aware of the small, injectable serial number, they were able to move more quickly. The existence of the microchip gave them the substance and probable cause they needed to initiate searches. Repeatedly, thieves were caught and sent to jail for having in their possession microchipped birds that had been reported stolen.

In 1993 alone, more than two million dollars worth of stolen birds were confiscated and returned to rightful owners after microchips confirmed identification.

It was this success in retrieving stolen birds that encouraged other livestock industries to utilize microchips for the same reasons.

THE FUTURE

Tiny electronic microchips have played a vital role in the development of the ratite industry. Their usage has been the basis for establishing guidelines for fair trade, progressive farm management and veterinary procedures.

The problem of theft was greatly curtailed when thieves realized that the big birds were chipped for protection.

Fraudulent deals also waned as buyers requested that the microchip be read before any money changed hands.

Ratite ranchers in other countries witnessed the success of America's new animal tracking system and began to implement the same technology.

In England, Australia, South Africa, Namibia, France, Canada and other countries, people have followed the lead of ranchers in the United States, and today implant millions of chips a year into livestock animals, particularly ostriches.

DISEASES OF RATITES

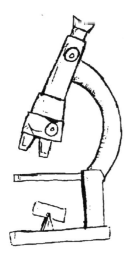

Amy M. Raines, DVM
Boondocks Ratite Hospital
Oklahoma City, Oklahoma

Disease: any deviation from or interruption of the normal structure or function of any part, organ, or system (or combination thereof) of the body that is manifested by a characteristic set of symptoms and signs and whose etiology, pathology, and prognosis may be known or unknown
- *Dorland's Illustrated Medical Dictionary, 1981.*

Diseases can be broken down into two categories, infectious and non-infectious. Infectious disease is caused by such organisms as bacteria, viruses, fungal organisms, mycoplasms, chlamydia, and parasites.

Non-infectious diseases include metabolic diseases such as gout and diabetes, nutritional disease caused by deficiencies or excesses, toxicities caused by toxic plants or contaminated feeds, and possibly behavioral problems that would lead to failure to breed or reproduce.

This chapter will discuss each area of disease in ratites, some of the clinical signs, pathology, and what to do when a disease problem occurs.

INFECTIOUS DISEASE

BACTERIAL

Bacterial infections in ratites are often secondary to some underlying cause—chronic stress, improper management, or some primary viral infection. These primary causes often lead to secondary bacterial infections by such organisms as *E. coli*, *Klebsiella* spp., *pseudomonas* spp, and other ubiquitous organisms.

Bacteria can be broken down into two categories: gram-positive bacteria and gram-negative bacteria. This classification is based on the staining properties of the bacteria. We can then break them down into aerobic (oxygen-dependent) and anaerobic bacteria (CO_2-dependent).

Salmonella

There are more than 2100 serotypes of salmonella. Only a few are considered to be significant. *S. Pullorum*, *S. Typhoid*, and *S. Arizonae* are important pathogens in poultry. *S. Pullorum* and *S. Typhoid* are reportable diseases.

Salmonella weltevreden was isolated from an emu in India and is an important serotype in humans (Shah, 1987).

Most salmonella-positive cultures in the United States are not serotyped unless the submitting veterinarian requests this procedure.

In the author's experience, it is more common to isolate salmonella from emus than the other ratite species. Some emus will show no clinical signs, while others tend to experience reproductive and hatching problems.

Recently the author cultured *S. Arizonae* from a cloacal swab of an emu hen. *S. Arizonae* is highly pathogenic in poultry, with egg transmission also occurring (Nagaraja, 1991).

Clostridium

Clostridium is an anaerobic organism which has been isolated from all three ratite species. Young ostriches less than one month of age will experience a bloody diarrhea and die within 24 to 48 hours. There has usually been an underlying management problem such as overheating the chicks. Once this problem is corrected the clostridium stops causing mortality.

Adult ostriches and emus have been known to develop clostridial infections following severe muscle trauma (Lublin, 1993). Many producers are vaccinating emus against the clostridial organisms at 3 months of age with a booster at 4 months. Cattle and sheep vaccines are currently being used with some success.

Tuberculosis

Mycobacterium avium (avian tuberculosis) has been isolated in ostriches and emus in the United States and Canada. There appears

Ostrich chick with fungal dermatitis.

to be two syndromes: a systemic form and a localized one.

In the systemic form of the disease, there appears to be a chronic wasting of the birds. The mycobacterium can be isolated from the stool.

The localized form tends to appear in one or both of the eyes and occasionally in the joints. Histologically, granulomatous inflammation with acid-fast bacteria will be seen. Treatment with Isoniazid has had some success with the localized form in ostriches. A guarded prognosis should be given and euthanasia of the affected animal or animals should be considered. *Mycobacterium avium* is not egg-transmitted in poultry (Nagaraja, 1991), and appears to act the same in ratites.

Chlamydia

Chlamydia spp. have been isolated from both ostriches and rheas. One ostrich hen was culture-positive from a cloacal swab. The clinical sign was infertility.

Rheas appear to develop a respiratory infection with sudden death as the most common presenting sign. Fibrinous airsacculitis, enlarged livers, peritonitis, and congested lungs were seen grossly (Grimes, 1994).

Chlamydia is usually treated with tetracycline or quinalone antibiotics (Dorrestein, 1993).

FUNGI

Fungal dermatitis has been diagnosed in ostriches and is usually associated with immunocompromised animals.

Diagnosis is made by skin biopsy and culture of the fungus.

Avian tuberculosis in conjunctiva of the left eye.

Treatment is with antifungal drugs such as griseofulvin for 30 days.

Aspergillas is commonly diagnosed as a respiratory disease in the winter. Chicks housed in buildings with poor ventilation on sand are at high risk for aspergillas infection.

Diagnosis is made at necropsy or by tracheal culture. Treatment is with itraconazole for 6 weeks.

When aspergillas is isolated, management should also be evaluated, and the infected birds given a guarded prognosis.

VIRUSES

According to Shavaprasad (1994), viruses which have been isolated in ratites include:
- Avian influenza
- Myxovirus-like
- Newcastle disease (Paramyxovirus-1)
- Paramyxovirus-2
- Corona virus
- Adenovirus
- Picornavirus
- Birnavirus
- Western equine encephalitis
- Eastern equine encephalitis
- Reovirus
- Astrovirus
- Poxvirus
- 35-40 nm virus
- 15-18 nm virus
- Paramyxovirus-3
- Borna disease
- Crimean-Congo hemorrhagic fever virus
- Wesselsbron virus
- Spongiform encephalopathy

Few of these viruses have been proven under controlled conditions to be pathogenic. Some may be secondary invaders or incidental findings. More research is needed to determine their pathogenicity in avian species.

Viruses should be suspected when bacterial infections are treated with the appropriate antibiotic and there is no improvement in the clinical sign, or chick mortality continues.

Adenovirus

Adenovirus in ostriches caused losses estimated at $7.5 million in the state of Oklahoma in 1992 (Raines, 1993).

Since then, the virus has been isolated in Texas, Ohio, Nebraska, Michigan, and North Carolina. As in other avians, adenovirus in ostriches is transmitted in eggs as well as orally and in stool.

A study has been completed at Oklahoma State University to determine pathogenicity of adenovirus in ostrich chicks. Test chicks were inoculated orally with adenovirus at three days of age.

All test chicks were dead before they reached 21 days of age. The virus has been isolated from these chicks (Raines, unpublished).

Clinical signs include high chick mortality (80-100 per cent), fading chicks with yolk-sac retention, secondary bacterial infections, hepatitis, and impactions. The virus will not grow on chicken embryos, and to date has only been grown on primary chicken-liver cell culture.

Encephalitis

Eastern (EEE) and Western Equine Encephalitis (WEE) are found to be significant in emus.

EEE causes acute to peracute disease with sudden death and/or bloody diarrhea. Death occurs within within 24 hours.

WEE is a more vague disease. Clinical signs are lethargy, anorexia, green stool, and birds will have high titers on serology. Birds do not recover from EEE once

7-day old chick after challenge with adenovirus. Typical "sick chick" appearance.

they show clinical signs. Some birds can recover from WEE, but will likely have chronic neurological signs.

Most emu producers are vaccinating with the equine products available. According to Tully (1993), serology tests show only about a 70 per cent response to vaccination in emus.

Mosquito control and elimination of standing water should also be part of management of emu farms.

Ostriches have been challenged with encephalitis virus and found to be refractory to infection (Craig, 1993; Tully, 1993).

PARASITES

To date, it is the author's experience that parasites are not a major problem in ratites. External parasites include feather mites and feather lice.

Feather mites can be seen in the shaft of the long white wing feathers of ostriches and rheas. Closer examination of this area under a dissecting microscope will give a positive diagnosis.

Mites cause problems with feather quality and cause puritis and folliculitis, leading to self-mutilation by the bird (Hoover, 1988). Treament is with Ivermectin, keeping loose feathers picked up.

Feather lice feed on feather dust, and are not bloodsucking lice. They are transmitted by other birds. Treatment is with topical insecticides.

Treatment should be repeated every two weeks for either of these parasites, unless the parasite is eliminated.

Houttuynia struthionis (tapeworm) has been reported in the ostrich (Craig, 1993; Fokema, 1985; Gruss, 1988). It has been the author's experience that tapeworms are seen primarily in chicks imported from Africa.

The tapeworm segments can be seen in stool, and are treated with fenbendazol and resorantel (Fokema, 1985; Gruss, 1988).

Other parasites are well described by Craig (1993). This author recommends routine fecal exams with treatment only on an as-needed basis.

Emus seem to be very susceptible to verminous encephalitis (Blue McClendon, 1992; Kwiecien, 1993; Tully, 1993). *Baylisascaris* spp. and *chandlerella quiscali* have been reported to cause neurological signs in emus. Chandlerella has been reported in Texas and Louisiana. Baylisascaris has been diagnosed in Texas, Oregon, North Dakota, and Canada.

Chandlerella is carried by grackles, which live mostly in the south, whereas baylisascaris is carried by raccoons, and thus is the more widespread disease. Control of grackles and raccoons aid in preventing contamination of feeding areas by these carriers.

In high-risk areas for chandlerella, emu chicks are given Ivermectin as a preventive, once a month until they reach six to eight months of age.

Once birds start to show clinical signs, treatment is unsuccessful. Signs include staggering, seizures, recumbency, and death. Torticollis or crooked necks and backs can also occur with chandlerella infection.

NON-INFECTIOUS DISEASES

Non-infectious diseases are those not caused by another living organism. These include metabolic diseases such as gout, behavioral problems, nutritional diseases, and toxicities. Nutrition is covered in another chapter.

GOUT

Gout is a metabolic disease caused by failure of the kidneys to excrete uric acid. The urates are deposited in the body (Harrison & Harrison, 1986).

Visceral gout occurs when the urates are deposited in body organs, the peritoneal cavity, and the pericardial sac. Synovial gout occurs when the urates are deposited in the joints.

Clinical signs can include ileus, dehydration, painful swellings in the joints with lameness, and elevated uric acids. Treatment with allopurinol has had limited success in ostriches.

The cause of gout can vary from long-term high-fat diets with obesity, chronic dehydration, or any primary disease that could lead to kidney problems (Ritchie, 1994).

BEHAVIORIAL PROBLEMS

Behavioral problems in ratites tend to be caused by boredom, overcrowding of birds, or incompatibility problems.

Feather-picking is usually started by bored or overcrowded birds. Once the habit has started it can be hard to break. Diversion techniques such as hubcaps in the pens, or other toys, seem to help. Separating the birds or providing more space can also be a benefit.

Stargazing is a condition seen in birds kept in confinement for long periods of time. This behavior seems to be most common in northern climates, during winter months when chicks are locked inside. Simply letting chicks outside will stop the behavior.

Aggression by the male or female is normal territorial behavior. Ostrich males are protective of their territory, especially during the breeding season.

Simply separating breeder pens from each other, and making them large enough for the hen to get out of the male's way, can prevent injuries.

Emu hens tend to be the aggressor of the species. Again, allowing birds to choose their own mates, separating breeders, and providing plenty of space in the breeder pens can prevent behavior problems.

WORKING WITH YOUR VETERINARIAN

©*Teresa Coble, DVM*
Uvalde Veterinary Clinic
& Ratite Health Center
Uvalde, Texas

A veterinarian can be of service to you only if she (or he) has an accurate picture of the facility and management procedures involved. The first and foremost thing that you must absolutely do is establish a *true* client-patient relationship with your veterinarian.

It is also extremely important that your veterinarian be experienced in treating ratites. Unfortunately, until the industry grows to a point where it is able to support ratite specialists, these will continue to be few and far between.

I consider it mandatory to visit each facility at least once a year. Frequently owners perceive things far differently than an outsider looking in. They can get into a *can't see the forest for the trees* mentality.

Conditions can change on a day-to-day basis, and serious problems which are developing may go unnoticed by managers because changes occur so slowly.

Post-breeding-season checkup time is an excellent opportunity for the veterinarian to look around and take stock. At that time, deficiencies can be noted and a plan of action laid out for the coming year. An ounce of prevention at this time of year can save an entire breeding season.

Once you have established a working relationship with your veterinarian, the next step is usually to stock an emergency cabinet. A list of suggested equipment and drugs will be found in Table 1.

The drugs should come only from your regular veterinarian (not discount drug houses) because different brands of drugs have different concentrations, different efficacies, and may be formulated for different routes of administration.

Improperly used drugs—or the wrong drugs for a particular case—can seriously harm or even cause the death of your animals.

Request specific dosages and instructions for usage for each drug in your possession.

Follow directions explicitly. If you have a question, ASK, don't guess!

Your veterinarian must have absolute faith that the drugs sent to you will be used only as intended.

Don't ever use your medications to treat another person's animals. If it works, you have set a precedent and it will be expected as routine in the future.

This can lead to misdiagnosis and treatment failure. If your treatment fails, you "killed their animal," even if it would have died anyway.

In addition, your veterinarian could incur indirect liability through any misuse of drugs assigned to you. No professional can afford the risk of dispensing drugs into the hands of a client who cannot be trusted.

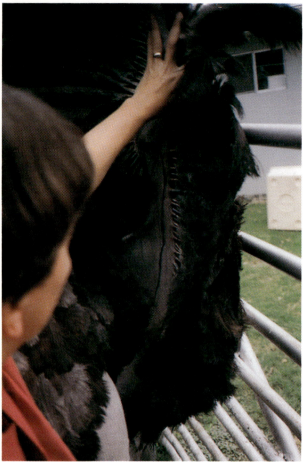

Black line drawn with felt pen denotes the wing vein of an ostrich.

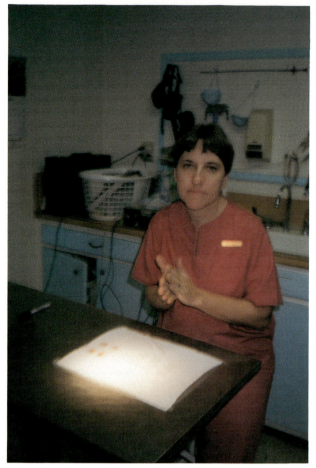

Dr. Coble rolling tube between fingers to mix anti-coagulant.

While insurance companies will of necessity always require a veterinarian to draw their laboratory samples, a properly-trained client can expedite routine procedures by obtaining the proper sample and taking it to their veterinarian in a timely manner for submission to the laboratory.

Ask your veterinarian to instruct you in the proper procedures, and practice under her supervision until you become proficient.

BASIC PROCEDURES

BLOOD SAMPLES

The value of lab results is only as high as the quality of the sample sent to the lab. Animals from which you are going to obtain a blood sample should be captured with a minimum of disturbance and held with the minimum restraint necessary for safety.

Stress causes numerous changes in the blood picture. They can be *read around* to a certain extent, but these changes can occasionally mask other significant findings.

The site of collection of blood samples varies with the age of the animal and the species. We usually collect blood from all emus from the median matatarsal vein, which runs up the inside of the leg. Ostrich chicks are sampled in the same manner.

Adult ostriches and rheas are easiest to bleed from the wing vein. Ideally, three milliliters of blood should be collected for each vial.

Once drawn, blood must immediately be placed in the appropriate tube for the laboratory tests required.

Serology is performed from the liquid portion of clotted blood (serum), so blood for such tests as avian influenza or pullorum go into a red-top tube. Bird chemistries are run off either serum or plasma from a green-top tube, depending on the lab.

Allow the blood to flow from the syringe into the tube. It is important not to force the blood, or you will break blood cells. Gently roll the tube between your fingers to mix the anticoagulant (already inside the tube) into the sample. Refrigerate (but do not freeze) at once.

For a white cell count and the examination of cell morphology, a thin film blood smear should be made within thirty minutes for optimum results. Blood cells begin to deteriorate very rapidly after that time and can cause normal cells to appear toxic.

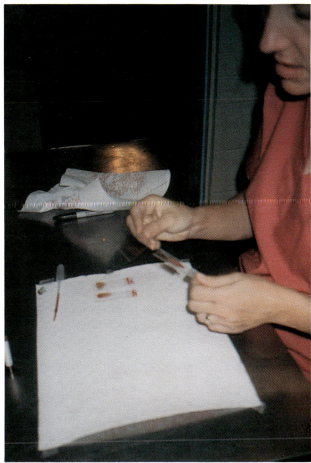
Dr. Coble preparing slides. Note the thin film of blood on the slides on the towel.

To make your smear, gently invert your green-top tube several times to completely mix the blood. Take a new 22-gauge needle on a 3cc-syringe or a micropipette and withdraw a drop of blood from the vial. On a precleaned microscope slide, center the drop of blood ½" from the left end.

While holding that slide in your left hand, take a second slide. At at a 45-degree angle, lower the second slide until its bottom edge just touches the bare inner edge of the drop of blood on the first slide.

Wait until the blood spreads along the edge of the second slide. In a rapid, smooth motion pull the second slide across the surface of the first slide to the right. This should result in a thin film with a fine feathered edge. (This edge is what the technician analyzes when doing the differential count on the white blood cells.)

Allow the slides to completely air-dry before packaging. Always send two good slides because occasionally a laboratory or shipping accident will damage one.

Lots of practice is required to be able to make an adequate slide, but submission of an inferior slide is a waste of both time and money. Refrigerate the remaining blood for any chemistries that you might want to run.

Blood submitted for chemistries and complete blood counts (CBCs) must be forwarded to the lab as fast as possible. If samples are allowed to sit around, certain test values will become invalid or misleading.

We always use an overnight express delivery service. Include a gel-pack (reusable cold packs sold for campers and picnickers) to keep the samples cold.

If a CBC is not necessary and only a chemistry panel is needed, you may collect the blood in a red-top tube, allow the sample to clot at room temperature for 30 minutes, centrifuge the sample, and separate the serum off the top into a new red-top tube.

Be sure either to use a needle and syringe to transfer the serum or to vent the tube with a needle so the increased pressure inside does not cause the top to pop off during shipping.

Cultures are also a very valuable tool, but in order for a culture to be of any benefit, certain criteria must be met.

First and foremost, it must be collected from a source that is compatible with the symptoms being seen.

It must be collected in a manner where outside contamination does not take place.

It must be placed into an appropriate transfer medium at once.

It must reach the lab in a timely manner accompanied by properly-completed paperwork, including a history.

NECROPSY

An animal which has just died can give invaluable information in a disease outbreak. Sometimes it is even advisable to sacrifice a single animal for necropsy when the entire flock may be at risk from a disease outbreak.

The longer the animal is dead, the more post-mortem changes and bacterial contamination in the tissues that will have to be dealt with when interpreting the histopath and culture results.

As soon as possible after the animal's death, the body should be thoroughly wet down with disinfectant to speed cooling and retard postmortem deterioration. Refrigerate the carcass at once. If it is too large for a refrigerator, lay bags of ice over the body and cover it with a tarp.

When doing necropsies, always wear gloves. Pathogenic bacteria can cause infection in humans as well as animals. Have culture swabs, formalin containers, plastic bags, etc. on hand and ready before you start.

Always do all necropsies in the exact same position and in the exact same pattern each time. This reduces the likelihood of accidentally missing a significant lesion.

Either have someone available to take notes for you or use a tape recorder to document your findings.

Gross examination.

Are there feathers missing from the top of the head? This indicates stress and that there may have been something going on for a while.

Look at the eyes. Is there any indication of any discharge? Are they swollen? Are there ulcers?

Is the head shape symmetrical? Does the head shape look normal?

Look inside the mouth. What color are the mucous membranes? Brick red may indicate toxicity. Pale or white may indicate anemia or shock. Is the tracheal opening clean, full of froth, or full of food material?

Examine the rest of the body. Look for bruises, fractures, or swollen areas.

Spray the carcass again with disinfectant. Place the body on its left side, with its head to your right, and the legs pointing towards you. Pluck away all feathers from the level of the midline (or just below) all of the way up to he top of the back.

Make an incision underneath the uppermost leg and lay back the leg over the body. Make an incision from the vent toward the sternum, continuing up along the base of the rib cage to the backbone.

Great care must be taken not to puncture the intestinal tract. Gross spillage into the abdominal cavity makes later cultures almost useless.

Note the position and the general appearance of all visible organs. Is there any fluid present in the cavity? What color is it? How much is there?

Using sterile instruments, snip and remove a small piece of liver. Take a culture swab from the cut surface. Place the swab back in its holder and crush the ampule of transport media to coat the end of the swab. Drop the piece of liver into a formalin container. Be sure that all samples are labeled as you go.

If the bird is less than three months old, next look for the yolk sac site. While a lump of necrotic tissue the size of a marble may not seem like much, remember that this would be like a mass the size of a baseball in you.

If there is a yolk sac present, it should be cultured. Soft, liquid contents can be aspirated out with a large-gauge sterile needle and syringe. Hard masses can be cut in half with a sterile blade and swabbed from the cut surface.

The appearance of the intestine on either side of the attachment frequently can shed some light on the status of the sac. Severe inflammation for six inches on either side of the attachment is a very strong indicator of a problem. If it is normal, it is less likely to have played an important role in the animal's demise.

Take a look at the rest of intestinal tract. Evidence of diarrhea? Are the contents of the tract hard or dry? Is there a large amount of gas present? Collect samples from several sites for routine cultures.

If there is a lot of gas, an anaerobic culture is prudent. These require a special transport vial. Collect multiple samples of intestine, with special attention to areas that do not look normal and place them in the formalin container.

In addition, make a composite of fecal samples from several levels of the intestinal tract for examination for internal parasites.

Next examine the proventriculus. Are there any signs of punctures? Open it up. How much fluid is present? What does it smell like? Carefully go through the contents. Look for masses of grass, pointed sticks, large rocks, pointed rocks, beetles, weed seeds, etc. Is the opening between the proventriculus open or is it blocked by a rock or mass?

Change gloves, take a pair of sterile poultry shears, and cut away the ribs over the chest. What do the air sacs look like? They should be clear. If they are cloudy, take a culture sample. Is there fluid in the sac around the heart?

What does the heart look like? If there is any suspicion of a systemic bacterial infection, take a sterile needle and syringe and draw a heart-blood sample for culture. Place this immediately into a blood-culture transport vial. A positive heart-blood sample taken very soon after death is highly significant.

What do the lungs look like? They should be light pink. If they are bloody looking, you may be dealing with a pneumonia. Take a culture.

Open the trachea and look for foreign material.

When doing a necropsy, it is prudent to save a mixed pool of fresh tissues and freeze it just in case a viral isolation attempt becomes necessary at a later date. These store very well in a zippered plastic bag placed inside a plastic container and then frozen.

Label the bag with a permanent marker as to the date, bird ID, and species. You can keep samples like this for several months.

A thorough and complete necropsy is always essential any time an animal dies. Even if the exact cause of death is obvious, you need to take a look. Sometimes early problems can be picked up before they become obvious in the live animal and handled in the rest of the flock before a serious situation arises.

You must know what is normal in order to recognize what is abnormal. This makes it essential to look at everything, every time that an animal dies, regardless of the cause.

RECORD-KEEPING

There are three rules in animal husbandry that absolutely must never be violated. They are:
- keep detailed records,
- if it dies, necropsy it, and
- *idiot-proof* anything you can.

Detailed records are of paramount importance. Write down *everything* that goes on: feed deliveries, new equipment, equipment repairs, storms, weather changes, power fluctuations, visitors, low-flying airplanes. These records are all too often the only clue you have as to what started a particular problem.

CASE HISTORY

Let's go over a case history as an example. A viral outbreak was suspected in emu chicks two weeks old and younger. At first glance it appeared to be random encephalitis. Some chicks acted drunk, had swollen livers, and died. Some chicks were perfectly normal. Affected chicks came from several hens.

The frantic client found me at a dog show and I agreed to see what I could figure out. She brought me her daily log (very detailed), her individual chick sheets (very detailed), a fresh dead chick, and three live chicks that were symptomatic.

On examination, the live chicks were normal in size and body weight and had normal temperatures. They were unable to maintain themselves in an upright position. When I palpated the abdomens, they literally screamed. I then necropsied the dead chick. Grossly, all tissues were normal except the liver, which was three times the normal size.

No tissues were sent off for histopath since it was the weekend and I was away from my office in a hotel room with nothing except my dog emergency kit.

I next went to her daily log. All of the affected chicks were hatched in a new hatcher. There were no problems in the chicks hatched in the old hatcher.

The first four eggs put into the new hatcher were very active at the time of transfer, but died in their shells. Because the owner was gone, no necropsy was done on the eggs—a major violation of Rule Number Two.

On further review of the chick records, I found that any chick that pipped and hatched in the new hatcher in fewer than 48 hours was fine. Any chick that spent more than 48 hours from pip in the new hatcher was affected.

All eggs were removed from the new hatcher and put back in the older unit, now designated exclusively for ostrich. No more sick chicks.

In the log, a very strong chemical odor was noted in the hatcher even though it had been installed eleven days earlier and run empty the whole time. The hatcher was properly vented to the outside. Box fans were brought in and aimed into the hatcher through the open door until all the odor was gone.

A minimal number of eggs were introduced into the hatcher. They suffered no ill effects so the hatcher was put back into full use. No more chicks were lost.

Close adherence to Rule Number One saved most of this client's hatch. However, she probably would have lost very few chicks if Rule Number Two had been followed and the first four dead-in-shell chicks been necropsied. Enlarged livers would have been noted and questions asked.

MURPHY'S LAW

Murphy is alive and well in the industry. Never forget that anything can and will happen if given the opportunity to do so. Carefully think through any and all possible scenarios for anything that you do and idiot-proof anything that you can.

Lock up all hazardous materials and limit employee access to potentially harmful products or dangerous combinations. I have a client who learned this the hard way.

A concentrated chlorine was purchased for disinfecting the chick building. Mixing directions for a stock solution were to add *one scoop* (provided with the product) to one gallon of water.

TABLE 1. EMERGENCY EQUIPMENT AND DRUGS TO KEEP ON HAND

Banamine	50 mg/ml
Dexasone	2 mg/ml
Lasix	50 mg/ml
Epinephrine	1/120 grain
Soludelta Cortef	200 mg and 500 mg
Centrine	.5 mg/ml
Reglan	5 mg/ml

Benadryl elixir
DMSO, sterile, medical grade
Nolvasan solution, unscented, not generic!

Syringes
  TB
  3cc
  12cc
  35cc
  35cc catheter-tip
  60cc catheter-tip
Needles
  27ga
  22ga
  20ga
3cc green-top vacutainers
3cc red-top vacutainers

precleaned microscope slides
culturette tubes
latex exam gloves
formalin containers
plastic baggies
necropsy knife
kitchen shears
scalpel blade with handle
spray disinfectant
oral electrolytes
A/D critical care diet (Hill's)
amino acid concentrate
red rubber feeding tubes
  of various sizes

Two cups of this *solution* was to be mixed with five gallons of fresh water and scrubbed onto exposed surfaces, allowed to set for thirty minutes, then rinsed.

An employee decided if a little is good, a lot is better. *Two cups* of the *concentrate* were added to the five gallons of water. The surfaces were washed and allowed to air dry—they were not rinsed. This occurred twice over a two-day period.

The chicks were out during the day but brought in at night and the building closed up. On day three, I saw a large group of dehydrated, very depressed chicks that were reluctant to eat or drink.

When I walked into the barn I was almost overcome by the chlorine fumes. I do happen to be extremely chlorine sensitive, but birds are also extremely sensitive to any inhalants due to the way that their respiratory system is made.

So, even though enough of the chlorine had evaporated to the point where the owner and assistants did not notice it, there was still a high-enough level to poison the birds.

When a pressure washer was brought in and the surfaces were hosed down, the water turned white from the residue.

We flushed the chicks with massive volumes of oral electrolytes, kept them outside in fresh air, force-exercised them to attempt to blow off any accumulated fumes from their air sacs, encouraged them to eat copious amounts of fresh kale, and gave them K/M (a botanical potassium supplement).

Within twelve hours all of the birds, including two that I expected to die, had rallied. Within 48 hours all appeared normal and by 72 hours weight gains had resumed.

IDIOT-PROOFING

I am very uncomfortable giving most hourly employees free access to hazardous chemicals of any kind. They must be fully instructed in the use of all compounds to which they have access.

In the case above, a wiser approach would have been for the owner to prepare the stock solution for the employee, keeping the concentrate under lock and key.

Carefully label all cleansers and disinfectants and write warnings that they are not to be mixed with other chemicals.

You would be surprised how many people don't know that mixing chlorine (Clorox) with ammonia (Mr. Clean) produces a very poisonous gas.

Write the warnings and instructions in the language that the employee can read. If your employee speaks primarily Spanish, *write it in Spanish*.

Provide a detailed written protocol for *all* routine day-in, day-out procedures, even something as simple as mowing the grass. Write it simply, in step-by-step fashion. *Do not* tolerate deviations from the protocol without prior clearance from you.

Make rules and enforce them. What do you think would happen if an employee mowed a grassy area next to a group of chicks on concrete and didn't use the grass catcher because he was in hurry?

Put in place as many automatic safety devices as possible. They don't all have to be sophisticated or expensive.

- A simple spring closure on a gate could well prevent a pen of birds from taking a walking tour if someone fails to lock a gate.
- A temperature alarm could keep you from cooking a barn full of chicks on days where we don't seem to be able to make up our minds if we need heat or an air conditioner.
- A smoke detector could prevent the loss of your barn from a fire due to a broken or malfunctioning heat lamp.
- What happens if a sparrow builds a nest in the exhaust pipe to your incubator? How much does a piece of hail screen cost?

Take a few minutes and look around your facility. Often very simple and inexpensive precautions can save you much heartache and hundreds of thousands of dollars.

Take a notepad with you and make notes as you go. It is easy to forget one item as you find something else that at the time seems more important. You have no way of knowing what might be the little thing that could get you.

Don't take chances. Fix what you can. There is enough that can go wrong in a season that we can do nothing about, without inviting trouble by ignoring something we can fix.

You can save both yourself and your veterinarian a lot of grief with just a few precautions.

BASIC NUTRITION FOR RATITES

Dennis H. Sigler, Ph. D.
Nutritionist, Muenster Milling Company
Muenster, Texas

Commercial ratite production is relatively new to the United States, although ratite farming in other parts of the world dates back a hundred years or more. But even after many years of experience, relatively little is known about specific feeding requirements of ostriches, emus, and rheas.

In the absence of more complete research data on which exact nutritional recommendations can be made, feeding methods have been developed based on a variety of factors.

Normal feeding and grazing habits, digestive anatomy and physiology, on-farm feeding trials, published research on other species, and limited ratite research are all considered in developing nutritional programs for ratites.

Since the ratite industry is in its infancy, there is still an immense amount of research needed to develop optimum feeding programs to meet the needs of both breeding-stock producers and commercial growers of ratites.

Commercial feed manufacturers, in cooperation with various ratite associations and individual producers, have made great strides in assuring the nutritional adequacy of birds, in spite of the great void in university research data. These improvements have already made significant progress in areas such as egg production, chick survivability, growth rates and feed efficiency.

Many challenges remain, however, for ratite producers, feed-industry professionals, and research scientists, to continue to improve and refine feeding methods in order to attain the level of production and performance which will sustain a viable commercial ratite industry.

BASIC NUTRIENT NEEDS

Ostriches, emus, and rheas do have physiological differences in their digestive systems. They also have certain differences and similarities to other avian species. Classes of nutrients needed for maintenance, production, growth and finishing are basically the same for all species. Therefore, before specific feeding practices are discussed, a basic understanding of nutrients needed by birds in general would be helpful.

WATER

Water is the most essential nutrient. It comprises over 50% of the body mass. It is essential as a substrate for many of the chemical reactions in the body, as well as a solvent for the transport of chemical compounds and nutrients. Water also plays important roles in the lubrication of joint surfaces and in the cerebrospinal fluid.

All the specific roles of water are simply too numerous to mention. Animals can survive without food for long periods, but will last only a few days without water.

Intake of water depends on numerous factors including environmental temperature and humidity, type and amount of food consumed, stage of production, rate of production or growth, and water quality.

A general rule of thumb for producers is that water consumption should be roughly equivalent to twice the amount of dry feed consumed on a weight basis.

Although this may serve as a reference point, in practice birds should have unlimited access to fresh, clean water for optimum production and growth.

Water quality, especially in water drawn from farm wells, is a very important consideration in meeting the needs of ratites. Water should be checked on a regular basis for total dissolved solids (TDS) and for nitrates, sulfates, total coliform bacteria, and other harmful substances.

Table 1 shows guidelines for TDS in water for poultry. These should serve as helpful references for ratite producers as well. Water filters or softeners may be indicated in some cases to bring water quality up to standard.

PROTEIN

As major components of all living cells, proteins are essential to all plant and animal life. Plants are the original source of proteins and have the luxury of being able to synthesize proteins from simple compounds such as carbon dioxide, water, nitrates and sulphates.

Animals, on the other hand, are not able to synthesize required proteins from elements or simple compounds. They depend on plant material or tissue from prey animals tissue as their sources of dietary proteins.

In animals, proteins are the primary constituents of organs and soft tissue such as muscle. Proteins are principal structural components of bone and other skeletal tissue.

They also play essential roles in the body in the form of blood components, immune antibodies, genetic material, enzymes, hormones, and other metabolites.

Simple-stomached animals such as avian species do not have merely a protein requirement, but have specific amino acid needs.

These amino acids (the building blocks of proteins) are required in certain ratios and in proper amounts in the daily diet in order to support optimum growth and reproduction.

The significance of protein quality is that when one or more essential amino acids are in short supply, synthesis of specific body proteins cannot occur. Depressed growth, production or hatchability will result.

There are 22 amino acids that make up proteins in the body. Twelve of these are considered essential in the diet, because they cannot be synthesized by avians.

Five of these twelve are referred to as *critical amino acids* because not only are they essential, they are also likely to be in short supply in normal feeds such as cereal grains. The critical amino acids are methionine, cystine, lysine, tryptophan, and arginine.

Total protein in feed, often referred to as *crude protein*, is only a laboratory measurement of the total nitrogen content of the feed. The term *crude protein* gives no indication of the amino-acid levels or the amino-acid balance of the feed. Amino-acid balance varies considerably from one feedstuff to another, as do levels of specific critical amino acids.

For example, most grains are deficient in lysine, while soybean meal is high in lysine, but low in methionine. Fish meal has one of the most complete amino-acid profiles of any high-protein source, but, unfortunately, it is also very expensive. By using a variety of feedstuffs with complimentary amino-acid profiles, protein quality is greatly improved over one or two sources.

Feed tags give guarantees in percent of protein. However, protein and amino acid requirements are in absolute amounts per day, not in percentages. Protein percentage is relative only to total daily intake of feed.

For example, if the daily protein requirement for a given bird is 300 grams of protein, this requirement could be met either by 3 pounds of 22%-protein feed or four pounds of 17%-protein feed. Therefore, daily intake must always be considered when discussing dietary needs.

Protein requirements also must be considered relative to dietary energy intake, especially for

TABLE 1: GUIDELINES FOR POULTRY FOR THE SUITABILITY OF WATER, WITH DIFFERENT CONCENTRATIONS OF TOTAL DISSOLVED SOLIDS (TDS)

TDS (ppm)	COMMENTS
Fewer than 1,000	Should present no serious burden to any class of poultry.
1,000-2,999	Satisfactory to all classes of poultry. They may cause watery droppings (especially at higher levels) but should not affect health or performance.
3,000-4,999	Poor waters for poultry, often causing watery droppings, increased mortality, and decreased growth (especially in turkeys).
5,000-6,999	Not acceptable waters for poultry, and almost always cause some type of problem, especially at the upper limits, where decreased growth and production or increased mortality probably will occur.
7,000-10,000	Unfit for poultry but may be suitable for other livestock.
10,000 +	Should not be used for any livestock or poultry.

growing birds. Since many avian species eat to meet their energy needs, total intake—and therefore protein intake—are affected by energy density in the diet.

Even though some research has been completed, the exact protein or amino acid requirements for maintenance, growth, or reproduction of ratites have not been determined.

However, practical observations of feeding ratites, field studies, and extrapolation of research data from other species have provided useful information in formulating balanced diets for growing and breeding ratites. Commercial diets for ratites typically range from 15% to 23% crude protein.

ENERGY

All bodily functions require energy, which is provided by carbohydrates, fats and proteins in the diet. Energy needs for avian species are expressed in terms of metabolizable energy (ME) per pound of feed. ME is the portion of the energy taken in by the bird that is actually digested and absorbed.

Since actual ME values have not been determined for ratites, most nutritionists use poultry ME values when determining energy levels in the diet. Ratite rations usually range from 900 Kcal up to 1200 Kcal ME per pound of feed.

Fats, of course, provide the highest concentration of energy of all sources. However, fats are probably not digested very well by very young birds. Fats are also more expensive as a source of energy than carbohydrates.

Carbohydrates from grains are the most common source of energy in the diet. Low-fiber feedstuffs such as corn contain much higher energy levels because of the soluble carbohydrates they contain, as compared to high-fiber feeds such as oats.

Limited research with ostriches indicates that growing chicks need in the neighborhood of 1050 to 1100 Kcal ME per pound of feed for good growth rates.

Avian species generally eat to meet their energy needs. All other nutrients, therefore, must be formulated in the right proportion to the energy level in the diet.

As an example, protein-to-calorie ratio is more important than actual levels of either energy or protein in the diet. Protein-to-calorie ratios may even be altered to affect such things as growth rates and fat deposition.

If protein levels are low in relationship to energy levels, with free-choice feeding, fat deposition is increased. With higher protein levels and the same energy, less fat is deposited.

MINERALS

Minerals are essential inorganic chemical elements with numerous structural and metabolic functions. There are many complex interactions between minerals that can lead to deficiencies or imbalances if specific minerals are provided in the ration or in supplements at high levels.

For example, high calcium levels in the diet interfere with the absorption of some trace minerals such as zinc. High levels of zinc can reduce copper utilization.

TABLE 2: CRUDE PROTEIN AND POULTRY ME VALUES FOR SELECTED FEEDSTUFFS (AS-FED)

INGREDIENTS	CRUDE PROTEIN	ME (Kcal PER POUND)
Alfalfa, dehydrated	17.5	545
Barley	11.5	1,200
Corn	8.5	1,525
Oats	11.5	1,160
Fish meal	60.5	1,280
Soybean meal	48.0	1,110
Fat	0.0	3,730

Adapted from *National Research Council, Nutrient Requirements of Poultry, 1994*, National Academy of Sciences.

Table 2 shows the poultry ME values for several common feedstuffs. Notice that high-protein feeds are not necessarily higher in energy. This is a common misconception. Note also that straight alfalfa would probably fall far short of meeting the daily energy needs of fast-growing or heavy-producing birds.

Producers, therefore, should be cautious about supplementing diets with additional mineral sources without considering the changes they are making to the total mineral balance in the diet.

In discussing mineral nutrition, it is important not only to consider the level of minerals in the diet, but also the source. Animals are more able to utilize some sources than others.

For example, iron from ferrous sulfate is easily assimilated, while the iron from iron oxide is almost totally unavailable. Chelated or complexed forms of trace minerals are even more available than the traditional inorganic forms.

Major Minerals

Calcium (Ca) is important for bone and egg formation, muscle contraction, and several body functions. Shortages or imbalances of calcium may lead to leg disorders in growing or adult birds, and reduced laying rates. Calcium is required in the largest amount in the ration of all minerals, especially for laying hens.

Phosphorus (P) is critical for bones, energy metabolism, and electrolyte balance. Imbalances lead to the same problems associated with calcium shortage or imbalance. Phosphorus absorption is closely related to calcium and Vitamin D levels in the diet. Phosphorus from plants is not utilized very well; therefore, some source of inorganic phosphorus must be included in the diet.

Sodium (Na), a major constituent of extracellular fluid, is important for electrolyte balance and muscle contractions. Sodium is normally provided in the salt portion of the ration. Deficiency signs include reduced growth, lesions of the eye, and early reproductive problems in hens.

Chlorine (Cl), an important electrolyte, functions in acid-base balance and helps form hydrochloric acid for digestion. The most common sign of deficiency is poor growth rate.

Magnesium (Mg) is important for bone formation, and is also important in the activation of several enzyme systems in energy metabolism. Common signs of deficiency are hyperirritability, loss of equilibrium and trembling, eventually leading to muscle tetany (a pathological state marked by severe intermittent muscle contractions and pain) and death.

Potassium (K) is a major electrolyte in intracellular fluid and plays a critical role in muscle activity. Signs of shortage include diarrhea, lethargic condition with distended abdomen, and a general unthrifty appearance. A severe shortage of potassium can lead to coma and death.

Sulfur (S) is important in the syntheses of sulfur-containing amino acids and in the formation of biotin and thiamin by the bacteria of the hind gut.

A deficiency of sulfur leads to reduced growth due to amino-acid imbalance.

Trace Minerals

Iron (Fe) functions as an important component of hemoglobin. Deficiency leads to anemia due to shortage of red blood cells. Iron requirements are normally increased during laying periods.

Copper (Cu) is a cofactor in several enzyme systems in the body, functions in hemoglobin synthesis and bone formation, and is responsible for hair and feather pigmentation. Signs of copper deficiency include lameness, swelling of joints and other leg disorders, anemia, or nervous symptoms.

Zinc (Zn), also a cofactor in enzyme systems, is needed for bone and feather development. Poor hair or feather development and/or rough and thickened skin can be signs of deficiency.

Manganese (Mn) functions as an important activator of several enzyme systems. It is also essential for bone formation, growth and reproduction.

Shortages will lead to poor growth, leg disorders, slipped tendons (perosis) in poultry, and an impaired reproductive rate in both males and females.

Cobalt (Co) is a component of vitamin B12. Shortages lead to B12 deficiency in ruminant animals, and to reduced hatchability in poultry.

Selenium (Se) is closely related to vitamin E absorption and utilization. If vitamin E is also deficient mortality, exudative diathesis (edema of subcutaneous tissue), white muscle disease, poor egg production, low hatch rate, and anemia can result.

Selenium is also toxic at fairly low levels (above 5 ppm), and toxicity causes reduced growth rates, poor hatchability, and increased embryonic malformations.

Iodine (I) is involved in thyroxin formation. Deficiencies lead to goiter, stillbirths in animals, and reduced hatchability in poultry.

Molybdenum (Mo) is involved in the metabolism of certain nitrogenous compounds.

Deficiencies of molybdenum in normal feedstuffs are very unlikely, but excess molybdenum interferes with copper metabolism and leads to induced copper deficiency symptoms.

Fluorine (F), which protects humans against tooth decay, is required in very minute quantities; excesses are more common than shortages, due to atmospheric contamination. Toxic levels lead to soft, porous bone, and development of hard, bony tissue in joint surfaces.

VITAMINS

Vitamins are organic compounds that are generally not synthesized by body cells but are necessary for maintenance of body functions, growth, and egg production.

Most vitamins are required in fairly minute quantities. When they are deficient in the diet, specific manifestations result.

Discussed below are specific vitamins, their importance, and deficiency symptoms.

Since most of the research in the area of vitamin nutrition has been conducted with poultry and not ratites, it is assumed here that some inferences can be made to ostriches, emus, and rheas.

Fat-soluble Vitamins

True *Vitamin A* is found only in animal tissue; however, a precursor, carotene, is found in green, leafy plants and in corn. Carotene is converted to vitamin A in the body.

Young chicks, however, are not very efficient at converting carotene to vitamin A, and supplementation with vitamin A acetate is necessary.

Vitamin A is required for normal vision, growth, egg production, and reproduction.

Signs of deficiency in poultry include absence of liquid in tear ducts, blindness, retarded growth, weakness, skeletal disorders, ruffled feathers, impaired egg production, and poor hatchability.

Vitamin D has two forms, but only D3 (cholecalciferol) can be utilized effectively by poultry. Under natural, unfiltered sunlight, ultraviolet rays absorbed into the skin allow animals to produce their own vitamin D.

Since vitamin D plays such an important role in calcium and phosphorous absorption as well as bone formation and growth, it should be added to the ration.

Signs of vitamin D deficiency are very pronounced, and include general unthriftiness, rickets, soft pliable bones and beaks, soft-shelled eggs, lowered egg production, and poor hatchability.

Vitamin E is a natural antioxidant in the body and is required for adequate productivity of cells, especially in blood and muscle. Recent research also shows that higher levels of vitamin E may improve immune response and stress resistance in animals.

Symptoms of Vitamin E deficiency include encephalomalacia (twisted neck, prostration, curled toes), early embryonic mortality, muscle dystrophy, and reproductive failure.

Vitamin K is responsible for the blood-clotting mechanism. Signs of vitamin K shortage include spontaneous hemorrhages and increased blood-clotting time. Vitamin K should be added to all poultry and ratite rations.

Water-soluble Vitamins (B Vitamins)

Almost all B vitamins function as a coenzyme for functions such as digestion, energy and protein metabolism, and numerous other metabolic processes. Many B vitamins are contained in ordinary feedstuffs, but are added to most commercial diets to guard against uncertain levels in some ingredients.

B-vitamin deficiencies are uncommon when a good commercially-prepared ration is fed. Specific signs of deficiencies for each one will be discussed below.

Thiamin shortages lead to poor appetite, polyneuritis and convulsions (head retraction over the back), anorexia, cardiovascular problems, and emaciation.

Fortunately, thiamin is relatively abundant in cereal grains and most common feedstuffs.

Riboflavin is added to the ration because most normal feedstuffs do not contain adequate amounts. Curled-toe paralysis, reduced growth rates, diarrhea, and poor hatchability are common signs of riboflavin deficiency.

Pantothenic acid is present in many feedstuffs, but is also added to most rations as calcium pantothenate.

Signs of pantothenic acid deficiency include poor growth, ruffled feathers in chicks, lesions around the eyes and mouth, dermatitis over toes, reduced egg production, and hatchability.

Niacin shortages, if severe, cause dermatitis, poor feed consumption, diarrhea, reduced growth, swollen hocks, and inflamed tongue and mouth (black tongue).

Pyridoxine deficiencies are extremely uncommon because it is abundant in most feedstuffs.

Purified experimental diets low in pyroxidine cause reduced growth, convulsions, nervous disorders, and eventually death.

Biotin is also common in most feeds, but is not always totally available to the bird. Signs of biotin deficiency include scaly dermatitis, mild perosis (slipped tendon), retarded growth, and reduced hatchability.

Folic acid deficiencies are seldom found. Signs of deficiency are reduced growth, anemia, poor feathering, feathers lacking proper pigmentation, and increased embryonic mortality.

Vitamin B12 is normally contained only in feedstuffs of animal and fish origin. It is low in plant products; therefore, B12 is usually added to most rations. Shortages lead to depressed growth, anemia, poor hatchability, and excess fat deposition in the liver, heart, and kidneys.

Choline, found in the lecithin of many plants, should be added to the diet because a growing chick has high demand for it. Deficiency signs include perosis, fatty liver, and retarded growth.

USE OF SUPPLEMENTS

Poor nutrition can manifest itself in many ways, and can sometimes be devastating to a flock or herd if not corrected immediately upon diagnosis. However, producers should be cautioned against adding large quantities of supplements to an already balanced diet simply as a preventive measure. This may lead to gross vitamin or mineral imbalances and interactions with nutrients, which can cause problems in themselves.

Before supplements are used, consider the diet already being fed and if a vitamin or mineral supplement is deemed necessary, follow directions carefully to avoid over-supplementation.

THE DIGESTIVE PROCESS

All avian species are simple-stomached animals. The gastrointestinal tracts of ratites do have certain functional similarities to chickens and turkeys, but also have important differences.

Unlike poultry, ratites do not have a crop for temporary storage of ingested material. As the ingesta moves down the esophagus, it enters the proventriculus (glandular stomach). In ostriches and emus, the large physical capacity of the proventriculus takes the place of some of the storage capacity of the absent crop.

In the proventriculus, gastric juices containing hydrochloric acid and the enzyme pepsin are secreted to begin to break proteins down into digestible fractions. Ingesta moves through the proventriculus rapidly, so very little actual digestion occurs until the food passes into the gizzard (muscular stomach). It is here, with the help of grit and the strong contractions of the muscular gizzard wall, that food particles are crushed and broken down into fine particles so they can pass into the small intestine. The gizzard also helps mix and blend ingesta so that particles are further exposed to gastric juices.

Even though grit (small gravel or stone) is not essential to break down commercial pelleted ration, it is recommended to provide grit on a regular basis, to help break down leaves, stems, grass and other material typically picked up by the birds every day.

The small intestine is where true digestion of most nutrients begins. As food is presented to the intestine, enzymes such as trypsin, lipase and amylase are secreted by the pancreas into the intestine. These enzymes and others secreted by the intestinal wall help break down proteins, fats and carbohydrates into smaller, more digestible compounds.

A large portion of the amino acids, fats, soluble carbohydrates (sugars), fat-soluble vitamins, and most minerals are absorbed through the small intestine. The more fibrous, insoluble material passes on to the hindgut. The hindgut (ceca and large intestine) is relatively short in emus and rheas. The large intestine of ostriches is, however, about three times as long as the small intestine.

This difference in hindgut capacity is one of the main distinctions between the ratite species. Because of the large, functional hindgut, ostriches are able to make more efficient use of fibrous material in the diet.

Microbes (bacteria and protozoa) in the hindgut of ostriches have essentially the same function as those found in the rumen of cattle. They facilitate the breakdown of insoluble carbohydrates (cellulose) into volatile fatty acids, which the animal can then use as energy sources.

The physical length of the large intestine and the slower passage rate (39 to 48 hours) of ostriches, compared to emus (5 to 6 hours), indicates the use of higher-fiber rations for ostriches. Even though emus have a much shorter hindgut, they apparently do have considerable microbial fermentation. Their ability to digest dietary fiber greatly exceeds that of chickens or turkeys. Rheas appear to have more hindgut fermentation than emus, but less than ostriches.

Water is absorbed from the large intestine, and along with it, B vitamins. With proper microbial fermentation in the hindgut, it is likely but has not been proven that many of the B vitamins are synthesized by the bacteria and then may be available to the bird.

The cloaca is the common opening into which the digestive, urinary and reproductive tracts empty, and has no functional role in the digestion of nutrients.

NUTRIENT NEEDS

MAINTENANCE

The nutrients needed to maintain normal physiological body processes and meet the needs of daily activity are referred to as maintenance requirements. Breeder birds during the off season are at maintenance, or even below, in the case of overweight birds that need to lose weight. Protein, energy, vitamin and mineral needs are much lower than that needed for growth or production. Replacement breeders during the late development state would have requirements only slightly above maintenance.

GROWTH

Growing birds have the most precise requirements in terms of nutritional balance and ration quality. Amino-acid balance, zinc, calcium, phosphorous, magnesium, manganese copper, and vitamin requirements are important for optimum soft-tissue and skeletal development. Most ratite feeding programs are designed to start chicks on moderate-protein, high-quality rations, to promote moderate growth and optimum health at an early age.

The starter ration is then followed by a grower diet designed to promote slightly faster growth than the starter. Even in the grower stage, amino-acid balance, minerals and vitamins are critical to prevent skeletal misdevelopment in rapidly growing birds.

Protein vs. energy ratios and mineral balance are especially important in this stage, as birds tend to eat to meet their energy needs.

Table 3 shows the National Research Council (NRC) minimum recommendations for turkeys. Since this type of information has not been published for ratites, these values might serve as comparisons in selecting or developing ratite diets.

However, because of the anatomical and physiological differences between ratites and poultry, one cannot assume all values will apply to ratites. Most commercial ratite diets contain substantially higher vitamin and mineral levels, and lower energy levels, than those recommended for poultry.

Producers should be careful about mixing straight grains or other high-energy feedstuffs to the diets without proper supplementation, as the critical nutrient/calorie ratios may be changed, resulting in growth disorders.

FINISHING

Research on feedlot diets for ratites and feeding recommendations for slaughter birds is limited. The economic importance of specific end products such as meat, oil, hide and feathers will have to be considered in developing specific feedlot rations for the different species of birds.

Limited data from initial feedlot trials indicate that quality, well-balanced, feeding programs give the most efficient growth. The bottom line on feeding slaughter birds will always be the least cost to produce a pound of quality end product.

BREEDERS

A producing hen requires a higher nutrient density in the diet compared to growing or maintenance, to maintain her own body functions as well as produce fertile eggs. The feeding of the hen is the most critical stage of production on any ratite farm.

When the cost of maintaining breeder birds and the management costs of raising chicks are considered, the greatest opportunity for increasing profits for both the breeding-stock raiser or the commercial producer is in increasing the number of live chicks hatched per hen.

Genetics and management play a major role in determining the number of eggs produced per hen. Research on poultry indicates that nutrition can also affect production rates of laying hens.

Table 3 shows the minumum nutrient recommendations set for turkeys by the National Research Council. Obviously, ratites are not turkeys, but some of these values can be used as references in evaluating ratite breeder diets.

The most critical nutrients are protein, calcium, phosphorous and vitamins A and D.

Other nutrients which can affect egg production are zinc, iron, copper, vitamin E, riboflavin, pantothenic acid, and pyridoxine.

As more intense genetic selection is practiced on ratite farms, specific feeding programs for different species, genetic strains, management systems, and expected production levels can be developed.

Until then, most feed manufacturers have formulated feeds for breeding birds based on average or slightly-above-average producers. This may be a slight economic loss to the farmer with below-average producers, and may be somewhat limiting to farmers with exceptionally high productivity.

However, until more carefully controlled nutrition research is conducted with breeding birds, it will be difficult to pinpoint the exact nutritional needs of breeding ratites.

FEEDING MANAGEMENT

Regardless of how well formulated a commercial diet might be, the feeding program will only be as good as the total management of the birds. Producers should strive to incorporate good animal-husbandry techniques into their feeding practices.

Discussed below are some common-sense guidelines that should be considered by all ratite farmers.

REDUCE STRESS

Ratites are very prone to adverse reactions to any type of stress. Stress affects general health, appetite, digestive processes, growth, and breeding.

Stress factors—such as moving birds, changing pens, new birds, new employees or visitors, outside activity, weather, and other environmental factors which your birds perceive as different—should be avoided.

TABLE 3: NUTRIENT REQUIREMENTS OF TURKEYS (AS-FED BASIS)

NUTRIENT	GROWING TURKEYS 12-16 WKS	GROWING TURKEYS 16-20 WKS	LAYING HENS
Metabolizable Energy, Kcal/Kg	3,100.0	3,200.0	2,900.0
Crude Protein %	19.0	16.5	14.00
Methionine %	0.35	0.25	0.20
Methionine & cystine %	0.65	0.55	0.40
Lysine %	1.0	0.80	0.60
Calcium %	0.75	0.63	2.25
Available phosphorus %	0.38	0.32	0.35
Potassium %	0.5	0.40	0.60
Magnesium %	0.05	0.05	0.05
Manganese, mg/Kg	60.0	60.0	60.0
Zinc, mg/Kg	40.0	40.0	65.0
Iron, mg/Kg	60.0	50.0	60.0
Copper, mg/Kg	6.0	6.0	8.0
Iodine, mg/Kg	0.4	0.4	0.4
Selenium, mg/Kg	0.2	0.2	0.2
Vitamin A, Iu/Kg	5,000.00	5,000.0	5,000.0
Vitamin D, Iu/Kg	1,100.00	1,100.0	1,100.0
Vitamin E, Iu/Kg	10.0	10.0	25.0
Vitamin K, Iu/Kg	0.75	0.75	1.0
B_{12}, mg/Kg	0.003	0.003	0.003
Biotin, mg/Kg	0.125	0.10	0.20
Choline, mg/Kg	1,100.0	950.0	1,000.0
Folic acid, mg/Kg	0.8	0.7	1.0
Niacin, mg/Kg	50.0	40.0	40.0
Pantothenic acid, mg/Kg	9.0	9.0	16.0
Pyroxidine, mg/Kg	3.5	3.0	4.0
Riboflavin, mg/Kg	3.0	2.5	4.0
Thiamin, mg/Kg	2.0	2.0	2.0

Source: *National Research Council Nutrient Requirements of Poultry, 1994*, National Academy of Sciences

Ratite raisers should do everything possible to reduce stress factors, from proper facility design to restricting activity around the farm. Stress appears to be a key factor in early chick mortality.

EXERCISE

Providing plenty of free, or if necessary, forced exercise is a key factor in raising healthy chicks. Chicks should be put outside as soon as weather permits and provided adequate pen space to allow for unlimited exercise. This is important to stimulate appetite and skeletal development.

Exercise is important in the general well-being of breeder birds as well. Breeder pens should be designed to provide as much free activity as possible and still allow ease of feeding, egg gathering, and catching of birds.

FREE-CHOICE WATER

Plenty of fresh clean water at all times is a key to good feeding management. Water should be maintained at the proper temperature to encourage intake in summer or winter. This may mean changing water several times a day. There is nothing on the farm as important as a consistent supply of clean water (Table 1).

PROVIDE GRIT

Grit is not needed to digest most commercial rations, but since ratites will pick up other material such as sticks, leaves, grass, and insects, grit is recommended unless the birds are housed on ground which contains gravel or small stones.

Even for young chicks, small grit should be provided by the time they are a few weeks old to enhance gizzard development. Select the size of grit according to the size of the bird. It is not critical to have grit available at all times as long as it is provided two or three times a week.

Oyster shell or crushed limestone should not be used, as they are sources of soluble calcium, which can upset the calcium-phosphorous balance in the diet.

LIMITING FEED INTAKE

Many ratites can successfully be fed free choice. However, when breeding birds are over-conditioned, or when young birds appear to gain too much weight, feed intake should be limited.

Most birds will consume about 2 to 3 per cent of their body weight in dry feed daily. Growing birds will eat about 3 per cent or more, while adult birds at maintenance may need only 1 to 1.5 per cent.

A good rule of thumb is to feed birds three or four times a day, an amount which they will clean up in fifteen to thirty minutes. This practice also allows the manager to observe the appetite of all birds, which could be an early warning sign of stress or illness.

Unless obesity is a problem, most breeders in full production should be allowed free access to properly-formulated feed.

FEEDER MAINTENANCE

Feeders should be inspected daily for feed intakes, presence of foreign material, needed repairs, and cleanliness.

Plenty of clean feeders which are at the right level to encourage good intake are important. With large groups of birds it is important to provide plenty of feeder stations so timid birds aren't crowded out.

PROPER FEED STORAGE

Feed should be stored in the coolest, driest environment possible. Store feed in rodent- and insect-resistant containers. Do not use feed that appears damp, moldy, or has an off odor. Farmers should try to coordinate their needs with their feed dealers so that feed is as fresh as possible. Although properly stored feed is good for several months, it is recommended that it be used within 45 to 60 days of manufacture.

OVER-SUPPLEMENTATION

If properly formulated feeds are used for their intended purpose, supplements are seldom needed. Over-supplementation of certain nutrients can cause imbalances in the diet, which may be harmful to birds.

If supplements are required for specific reasons, such as low feed intakes or for extremely high-producing hens, directions should be followed carefully to avoid overfeeding.

Producers who utilize good-quality pasture or forage for part of their feeding program should select supplements which will complement and enhance the forage, and make up for deficiencies.

Before adding any supplement to the diet, producers should know precisely what it does and whether it will improve the production of their birds.

CONCLUSION

Common sense, experience, and the limited practical research data available continue to help producers achieve their goals. Many questions have yet to be answered or even addressed by scientific research. Opportunities for future research programs include:

- improved egg production through lighting and feed management programs;
- optimum diets for raising chicks under different types of management;
- diets for feeding slaughter birds to maximize valuable end products; and
- utilizing forage for growing and breeding ratites.

Nutritional research can be expensive, but without it ratite producers will not be equipped to make the necessary sound management decisions which will enable ratite ranchers to reach the level of production necessary to sustain strong commercial and breeder markets.

BIOSECURITY

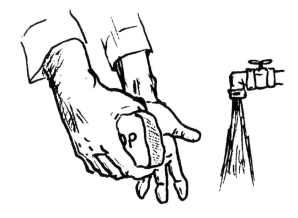

Rocky Terry, DVM
Terry Veterinary Clinic
Glen Rose, Texas

Biosecurity is a process of planning daily management functions to prevent the introduction and spread of diseases which could interrupt the profitability and functions of your ratite farm.

In planning your biosecurity program, you must consider that bacterial or viral diseases can be transferred from bird to bird or flock to flock in many ways:
- airborne,
- egg transmission,
- introduction of healthy birds which are carriers of disease, organisms,
- improper disposal of dead birds,
- poor water drainage,
- contact with inanimate objects—equipment, transport trailers—containing disease organisms,
- rodents or free-flying birds,
- shoes and clothing of people who move from flock to flock, and
- contamination of the ground by disease-causing organisms.

For many years, the commercial poultry industry has utilized a set of biosecurity principles which have been proven highly effective in preventing or eliminating diseases in very large flocks. The following recommendations are adapted from these tried and true methods of disease control.

ISOLATION AND QUARANTINE

Isolation means that the farm should be isolated from people and equipment that have been around other ratites. This includes visitors, potential buyers, and live-haul equipment.

If it is necessary to permit visitors and/or equipment on the farm and around your flocks, it is important to furnish footwear and disposable coveralls.

All equipment, live-haul trailers, and trucks should be cleaned and disinfected before they enter the premises.

Newly purchased ratites should be placed in a quarantine area for four weeks of isolation from the rest of your flock before they are added to the group. This will prevent the introduction of diseases such as Newcastle, influenza, or chlamidosis.

Depending upon the size of your operation and the risk to the rest of your birds, I would recommend blood tests for antibodies to determine carrier or exposure status to known diseases before purchasing new stock.

If Salmonella is a concern in your area, fecal samples from the new acquisitions should be examined before purchase. If Salmonella is identified, the serotype should be determined.

The reason for the four weeks of isolation is to identify birds that could be incubating disease but not showing clinical signs at the time of purchase.

When isolating a new group, the ratites should be kept at least 400 yards away from and downwind of the main groups. There should be no direct movement of people or equipment from the new group to the main flocks without cleaning and disinfecting.

Always go to the isolated group last, and then shower and change clothing and footwear before going back to the main group. Even better would be to place the new birds on a different premises under the care of someone who is not going between the different groups.

KEEPING IT CLEAN

MOVING BETWEEN GROUPS

Direct traffic from the youngest to the oldest age groups.

Direct traffic from the resident group to the isolated group.

Use a different pair of boots or foot covers and coveralls between flocks. Disinfect the boots before entering the facility with a footbath of fresh disinfectant.

Wash your hands before and after handling birds in isolation or different age groups.

DISINFECTION OF EQUIPMENT

Disinfection means to destroy disease-causing bacteria, fungi, or viruses. The first step in disinfecting is to physically remove all visible dirt and feathers. When the surface of the equipment is clean almost any disinfectant will work.

Most quaternary, iodine, and chlorine disinfectants are immediately rendered useless in the presence of organic material such as dirt, blood, or feathers. These products will work against almost any disease-causing organisms only if the surfaces are cleaned and free of organic material.

The synthetic phenol disinfectants will be more effective if the surfaces are not as clean as needed for chlorine, iodine, or the quaternary disinfectants.

DISINFECTION OF PENS

Disinfectants will not sterilize dirt. To use any type of disinfectant on the surface of dirt is futile. Pens can be made safer only with time between flocks, sunlight, and dryness.

PREVENTING EGG-BORNE DISEASES

Very little is known about the transmission of salmonellas, *E. Coli* bacteria, and viruses either inside or on the surface of ratite eggs. It is known that in poultry these disease-causing organisms can be transmitted by the ovaries to the yolk and then to the chick. Disease organisms may also be spread to the surface of the egg by contaminated fecal material.

In poultry, the mycloplasmas such as *M. gallasepticum* and *M. synoviae* and salmonellas such as *S. pullorum* and fowl typhoid can be transmitted through the egg.

It has not been shown that these organisms can be transmitted through ratites in this manner, but we may find other disease organisms that can.

Potentially pathogenic bacteria can be transmitted on the surface of the eggs and just inside of the eggs in the inner and outer shell membranes. Bacteria can penetrate small openings in the shell (the pores) and move into the two shell membranes that are just under the shell where the bacteria would be protected from disinfectants and fumigants.

HATCHER CONTAMINATION

It is known that there is an increase in bacteria in the air of the hatcher at the time of hatching. This increase comes from bacteria that were trapped in the shell membranes and from the waste products of the chick. The bacteria are sources of contamination of the navel areas of newly-hatched chicks.

While it is not possible to produce bacteria-free eggs, it is possible to produce good-quality chicks by keeping bacterial contamination low on the surface of the eggs; inside of the eggs by maintaining hen health; and inside the hatchers by cleaning and disinfecting.

PRODUCING CLEAN EGGS

The goal of any egg producer is to produce eggs that require a minimum of surface cleaning. To achieve this goal the producer should design the pen so that water is either drained away or will penetrate the ground rapidly so the egg does not stand in water.

Another aid in producing clean eggs is to train the hens to lay under a shed.

Care should be taken to prevent condensation on the surface caused by taking cold eggs into a warm room, and eggs should be warmed gradually before they are placed in the incubator. Moisture on the surface of the egg helps bacteria such as *Pseudomonas*, *E. coli*, and the *Salmonellas* to penetrate the egg shell.

As the warm egg cools and shrinks, a pressure gradient is formed whereby air and moisture from the outside are sucked in through the pores, inviting contamination by bacteria which are then protected inside the shell and can multiply.

There have been many recommendations on washing ratite hatching eggs. These recommendations were based on procedures used by the poultry industry, but there has always been controversy in the poultry industry over the washing of chicken and turkey eggs.

Clean eggs should not be washed because there is a much greater risk of causing bacterial problems because of improper washing techniques.

I have had personal experience in hatching clean versus dirty eggs by the millions, and *in my opinion dirty eggs should be discarded*.

The odds are high that they will be contaminated, and the risk of spreading that contamination to the rest of your incubating eggs makes it unwise to try to hatch *risk eggs*.

The real payoff is in making changes in management practices to produce clean eggs. Current market prices have given the producer a real incentive not to cheat on quality anyway.

If you do decide to clean an egg, I recommend using an abrasive pad rather than any liquid to knock off dirt and fecal material. Whatever you do, do not use a damp cloth with cold water to wash the egg.

REDUCING HATCHER BACTERIA

When the hatching process starts, there will be a natural increase in the numbers of bacteria in the air of the hatchers. This increase cannot be prevented but it can be controlled.

The first step in controlling this increase is to set one batch of eggs weekly. It has been common practice for less-knowledgeable producers to place the egg in the incubator as soon as it is laid.

This practice causes chicks to be hatching on a daily basis, which produces a constant high number of bacteria. It also prevents thorough periodic disinfecting of equipment, since it is always occupied.

By setting one batch a week, the bacterial numbers will increase as the chicks hatch and decrease each time the hatcher is cleaned. As soon as the chicks are removed from the hatcher, the feces, down and dander can be removed. Then the hatcher can be disinfected to kill remaining bacteria. The hatching process is then started again with a low bacterial count.

If chicks are hatching on a daily basis, the numbers of bacteria will always remain high and active.

The fact that the bacteria numbers are elevated does not necessarily mean that the chicks will be sick, but it does mean that there is an increased chance of being infected with a bacteria capable of making the chick sick.

CONCLUSION

As the ratite industry transitions from breeder to slaughter market, many small breeders are deciding to get out, while others are buying quality ratites to take advantage of prices and improve their economy-of-scale numbers.

The ratite producers will have to produce larger numbers of eggs or birds in order to stay competitive because there will be less potential profit per unit. Therefore, it is imperative for the producer to follow proven management practices for biosecurity, nutrition, incubation, and growing.

By starting a good monitoring program, the producer may not eliminate all diseases, but there will be far fewer problems, and those that do occur will be easier to control.

RECORD KEEPING & MANAGEMENT

Charley Elrod
Co-author, Ratite Record Book

In traditional agriculture, farm and ranch management methods change slowly. But the ratite industry is in the early stages of development, and management practices are changing quickly.

Because of the learning curve, producers are now in a trial-and-error situation to find out the most economical and efficient ways to raise these birds for slaughter. The data for working out solutions to management problems are rapidly evolving. Research conducted at universities and colleges throughout the United States, along with private industry (equipment suppliers, for instance), producers and veterinarians is continually providing answers for the industry.

The collection and analysis of production and financial data need efficient organization to help interpret what will work at present and what will hold true in future years of the industry. As the ratite industry matures, it will follow other animal-industry-related paths.

Good management is essential in any business. The ratite industry is no exception. Questions that often arise are:
- Why do some producers make more money?
- Why do some operations hatch more eggs?
- Why do some producers have higher chick-survival rates?

The answer to these and other questions is *management skills*.

A manager's job must include a continuing process of evaluating how the business is structured. The evaluation must include new information that applies to markets and production, and often means old decisions must be reconsidered or abandoned.

Once again: An industry in its infancy, such as the ratite industry, will experience more management challenges than traditional agriculture.

The old saying, "plan your work, and work your plan," has merit.

Let's look at some of the fundamentals of management.

PLANNING

The most important step in management is a business plan. Very little will happen without a precise course of action.

DEVELOP A PLAN
Write down everything you want to accomplish, what resources you need to accomplish your plan, how much it will cost, and the time frame needed to get the work done.

IMPLEMENTATION
Once your plan is developed it should identify all resources and

materials necessary to put it into effect. You are ready to begin your ratite business by overseeing or staffing your plan of action.

CONTROL

This is the process of overseeing the project, monitoring the results, and keeping records to provide information and warning signs at different stages, to see if goals are being met or if adjustments must be made.

SETTING GOALS

A large part of every manager's job is to establish specific goals for the business. Without specific goals there is no way to measure the results of decisions or practices. Always keep the following suggestions at the forefront of goal making.

GOALS MUST BE WRITTEN

By writing down and evaluating them, everyone involved can agree on the specific goals. The goals must be reviewed periodically using the records you have kept.

GOALS MUST BE SPECIFIC

"To make a profit in three years" is not a specific goal. Examples of specific goals might be:
- to make a profit of $30,000 in three years, or
- to produce thirty breeding pairs in three years.

These goals must be accompanied by detailing the steps you will take to achieve them, and the time frames in which the steps must be accomplished.

GOALS MUST BE MEASURABLE

$30,000 per year is a measurable goal. Thirty breeding pairs is a measurable goal. By setting specific goals and steps within specific time frames, you can measure if and how much of the goal is being met, or whether changes are needed to accomplish it.

Because family agriculture operations are different from other businesses, personal and family satisfaction should be considered along with financial rewards when establishing goals.

Please remember that no business will survive long without making a profit. The determination of whether your operation is a business or hobby is not merely a personal choice—the Internal Revenue Service has very specific tests to make that determination.

MANAGEMENT RECORDS

MEASURING PERFORMANCE

The records you keep will help you measure the financial success of your business. The records will also establish whether the manager is doing the job he or she was hired to perform.

If the owners are the managers, it is imperative that they face the reality that it is their responsibility to accomplish the goals that have been set. If the manager is an employee, it should be obvious that his job will not last long if the goals are not met.

With accurate production and financial records, it is easy to analyze whether you are on track. An accounting program or system must be incorporated into your management practices from the start. Choose a system that will furnish the data needed and one that you can understand. It must provide the information needed to produce the "report card" of success or failure.

Please refer to the chapter **Tax Considerations for the Ratite Farmer** for information on other basic considerations.

ENVIRONMENT

Because all ratites have different anatomical and physical characteristics, you must work a management plan within the reasonable and practical limits of each species. For instance:

- within a reasonable range, a female will lay only a certain number of eggs per year, and,
- regardless of how much we feed young birds, the feed conversion ratio is a certain percentage until time of slaughter.

You must be realistic in planning what can be accomplished. These and other limitations are important considerations in the business and animal environments in which our decision-making process takes place.

RECORD-KEEPING SYSTEMS

There are essentially two types of record-keeping systems, manual and computer. Both begin with data entered onto standardized forms. In a manual system the data are then entered into journals and ledgers. You do all the calculations and analyses yourself.

In a computerized system data from the forms are entered into one of many available software programs that will automatically do the rest for you. As the size of your operation increases, so does the number of data input and calculations.

Record keeping with computer assistance is recommended. Having the ability to output information needed for management decisions lends itself very well to computerized record keeping.

The availability of accounting software, databases, spread sheets—several designed specifically for ratite producers—gives you fingertip ability to chart the growth of your business, calculate your profitability, keep track of your production, expenses, and income, as well as forecast future trends both for your ranch and for the industry.

If you are not computer literate you can still obtain this data from your manual set of books—just not as quickly. Design your own forms or utilize those

Record Keeping & Management

THE PURPOSE AND USE OF RECORDS

1. Measure profitability and assess financial condition:
   A. Profitability is measured by an income and expense (profit or loss) statement.
   B. Financial condition is shown on a balance sheet.

2. Provide data for a complete business analysis. This will reflect whether your business is really profitable. It will reflect the results of past decisions and help in making current and future decisions.

3. Assist in obtaining loans:
   A. Lenders will require good records. They will greatly increase your chances of receiving a loan, and will help show that your ratite enterprise is a business, not a hobby.
   B. Statistics on where the industry has been, what trends and prices are now, and what is predicted for the future.

4. Separate the ratite operation from others:
   A. Break down the ratite enterprise specifically. Many farms and ranches have other operations such as cattle, wheat, or hogs. You must keep separate records for each one in order to be able to determine if each is successful.
   B. Business or income outside the farm, or overall ranch income, cannot support your ratite business indefinitely.

5. Assist in decision-making about new needs for expenditures. Records can and will be an excellent source to help determine the need for an additional incubator, new pens and sheds, repairs, etc.

6. Selection and replacement of breeder stock. Production records will assist in selection and replacement of breeder stock and will aid in growth of the operation.

7. Establish a hatching or grow-out operation. Use expense records to determine the expenses of boarding and hatching birds, to show what percentage of profits comes from boarder birds versus your own, and what additional income your hatching operation brings.

8. The relationship of marketing expenses and individual time requirements invested for the sale of birds. Sales and marketing records give a realistic overview of how much time and money was spent to sell birds, after-sale support, hauling, any printing or advertising costs, etc. This allows the owners to determine what changes need to be made if any.

9. Tax benefits and tax reporting. Good records will increase income tax benefits and can reduce taxes. In case of an audit they are invaluable.

---

already designed specifically for the industry.

Check out the various software programs available. Decide what information you want from your program to help you find the one best suited to your needs. A simple-to-use system will allow you to spend more time working and enjoying your ranch than working at the computer. However you look at it, the simple fact is that this industry is record intensive. And for the effort to be worth anything, of course, accurate recording is essential.

FINANCIAL RECORDS

In a cost-effective management system financial records must be presented so an evaluation can be assessed on expenditures of all facets of the business. Only by evaluating expenses from every aspect of your operation can you project and analyze where expenses may be cut and what expenses will stay constant.

Financial records consist of checks, invoices, bills, sales tickets, cash receipts, charge tickets, contribution receipts, rent and boarding receipts, and any other records with which you can document the sources of your income and where your expenditures have been made.

A manual record keeping system using a cash basis and single entry accounting may provide all the record keeping necessary for your business. Examples of a cash journal (expenses) and sales journal (income) are shown in Figures 1, 2, and 3.

Monthly Expense Total Sheet

August Expenses 19 ___   Page 1

FEED	Date	Llbs.	Cost	Date	Llbs.	Cost	Date	Llbs.	Cost	Date	Llbs.	Cost	Monthly Total	Year to Date
Breeder/ Layer														
Grower														
Starter														
Vitamin/Mineral Supplement														
Seed														
Fertilizer														
Vet. Supplies	Memo		Cost	Memo		Cost	Memo		Cost	Memo		Cost		
Vaccines														
Worming Medications														
Antibiotics														
Egg Disenfectant														
Vet Expenses	Memo		Cost	Memo		Cost	Memo		Cost	Memo		Cost		
Health Certificates														
Bloodwork														
Surgery														
Bird Sexing														
Fecal Exam														

TOTAL Expense this page ■■■ A
TOTAL Expense Year To Date ■■

RR © 1993 Rev. 1995

Figure 1

Monthly Expense Total Sheet

August Expenses 19 ___   Page 2

Identification Equipment	MEMO	Ttl. Cost	Balance year to date	Ratite Equipment & Exp.	MEMO	Ttl. Cost	Balance year to date
Transponder				Incubator/Hatcher			
Microchips				Oxygen Analyzer			
Identification Bands				Scales			
				Thermometer			
				Egg Candler			
Ranch & Build. Materials							
Pen & Barn Materials							
Feeders/Water Troughs				**Office / Business Expenses**			
Plumbing Equipment				Phone & Fax			
Trailer & Related Expenses				Office Supplies			
Labor Costs				Business Forms			
				Postage			
				Labor			
Bird Purchases				Insurance			
				Marketing & Advertising			
				Accounting Fees			
Hauling & Transportation				Legal Fees			
Educational Material & Exp				Brokerage and/or Commision Fee			
Dues & Membership Fees				Security			
Seminars							
Travel							
Exp. Hotel, Food, Etc.							
Books, Video, Trade Mags							

TOTAL Expense this page ■■ B ■■■■■■■■■■■■■■■■ C

August Total Expenses   A $_____ + B $_____ + C $_____ = $_____

RR ©1993 Rev. 1994

Figure 2

Sales and Cash Received Journal

Month(s) _____ Year __   Page _____

Date	Ref. No.	Sale Description and Information	Charges	Amount Received	Balance Due	Analysis By Item Sold				Fees		Other and/or Industry products	
						Egg	Chick	Adult Birds	Incub/Hatch	Board	Description	

TOTALS FOR THIS SHEET

RR© 1993 to reorder call (210) 822-1280

Figure 3

PRODUCTION RECORDS

There are many reasons for keeping production records in the ratite industry:
- You must keep records just to produce live chicks in the incubation and hatching process;
- They will assist you in evaluating flock health performance; and
- Breeding records on your birds will help you decide which you will keep for breeding stock and which birds should be sold for slaughter (Figure 4).

The charts on the following pages are some of the production records required for raising ratites. You may want to incorporate all of them, or skip some, or you may want to add more.

Remember, the more records you keep, the easier it will be to choose your replacement stock. Good records will also greatly assist in pinpointing flock health problems (disease investigations) when they appear.

Incubation and Hatching

The Incubation and Hatching Information chart (Figure 5) will take you from where the egg was laid to the hatched chick.

Just as poor shell quality was a factor in pollution-caused crashes of peregrine falcon, pelican and other wild bird populations decades ago, and has long been recognized by the poultry industry, eggshell thickness may play a role in hatchability of ratite chicks.

Eggshell thickness can easily be measured using a micrometer See the photos on the next page.

Egg sizes for domestic ratites fall within the following ranges (weights in grams):

Ostrich	small	800-1200
	medium	1200-1600
	large	1600-2000
	ex large	2000-2400
Emu	small	370-440
	medium	440-570
	large	570-700
	extra large	700-850
Rhea	small	345-425
	medium	425-540
	large	540-660
	extra large	660-825

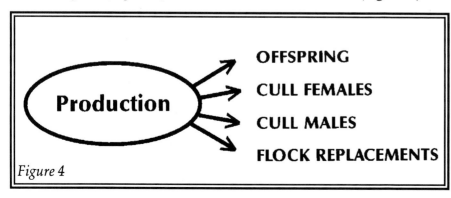

Figure 4

Figure 5

Incubation and Hatching Information Year _____ Page _____

Egg #1 | Egg # 1

Pen Number		Weight	Date	Grams	% Loss
Male ID		Weight			
Species/Age (yr/mo)		Weight			
Female ID		Weight			
Species/Age (yr/mo)		Weight			
Egg ID No.		% Weight Loss (total)			
Date Laid		Candling	Fertile Yes ❑ No ❑		
Egg Size	Small ❑ Medium ❑ Large ❑ Ex. Large ❑		Date	Growth Rate Satisfactory/ Non	
Stored Egg	Hours __ Days __	Candling	Yes ❑ No ❑		
Batched	Yes ❑ No ❑	Candling	Yes ❑ No ❑		
Storage Temp.		Candling	Yes ❑ No ❑		
Storage Humidity		Candling	Yes ❑ No ❑		
Egg Washed	Yes ❑ No ❑	Candling	Yes ❑ No ❑		
Set Date (Egg in Incubator)	Date	Candling	Yes ❑ No ❑		
Move To Hatcher	Projected Date	Candling	Yes ❑ No ❑		
Projected Hatch Date		Total Days in Incubator			
Incubator #		Egg to Hatcher	Date Moved		
Egg Location in Incubator	Tray / Row / Slot	Hatcher #			
Incubator Temp.		Temp.			
Humidity Level		Humidity			
Possible Risk Egg	Yes ❑ No ❑	Location in Hatcher	TRAY # ____		
Isolated	Yes ❑ No ❑	Hatch Date			
Weather Conditions	Hot ❑ Cold ❑ Warm ❑ Rain ❑ Sunny ❑ Cloudy ❑	Assist in Hatching	Yes ❑ No ❑		
Approximate Temp.	Day __ Night __	External Yolk Sac	Yes ❑ No ❑		
Sterilization Lamps	Yes ❑ No ❑	Chick Weight			
Set Weight	Date / Grams / % Loss	Shell Thickness			
Weight		Live Condition	Good ❑ Fair ❑ Poor ❑		
Weight		Did Not Hatch* See did not hatch page	Yes ❑		

RR © 1995

HATCHING FAILURES

If eggs do not hatch you must keep a record for hen production analysis (Figure 6). These records will also assist in your replacement breeding stock decisions, determining the fertility of your roosters, help analyze incubation and hatching procedures, and track health problems or potential problems.

Open and examine eggs that did not hatch, and if needed, send them to a qualified university or laboratory for help in determining the cause.

YEARLY SUMMARY

Now that you have recorded the incubation and hatching records—including the eggs that did not hatch—a yearly summary of all the information can be calculated. See Figure 7, next page.

It is important to realize hatchability has two formulas:
- the number of chicks hatched as a percentage of all eggs set;
- the number of chicks hatched as a percentage of all fertile eggs set (North & Bell, 1990).

The yearly summary chart helps evaluate egg production by hen or pair.

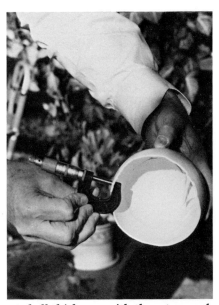

Measuring eggshell thickness with three types of micrometers.

Did Not Hatch

Reason Key
1. Infertile
2. Bacterial infection
3. Incubator Temp.
4. Humidity Incubator
5. Risk Egg
6. Mal Positioned
7. Edemateus - Wet
8. Dry
9. Other

Explanation Key
1. Embryo development
   A. Early Dead - embryo may appear as coagulated blood on the surface of the yolk to an embryo in which you can readily identify its' body parts.
   B. Mid Dead - Embryo fully developed & about half the size of a normal live chick. Beginning/up to complete feather development.
   C. Late Dead - The embryo occupies almost the entire area within the shell. May have an external yolk sac.
2. Photo taken (date) Be sure and note date and egg number on photo
3. If sent for research note where and results.
4. All other pertinent information

Day/mo/yr	Egg No.	Reasons no(s)	Explanation (See Key)

RR© 1993 Rev. 5/94

Figure 6

Yearly Summary Chart

Evaluation of Egg Production by Hen or Pair

Did Not Hatch Incubation and Hatching Information

Pen Number						
Female ID #						
Female Info.		**Age ___ yr ___ mo. Species ______**				
Male ID #						
Male Info.		**Age ___ yr ___ mo. Species ______**				
Total Eggs Produced		**Total**	**Sm.**	**Med.**	**Lg.**	**XLg.**
Fertile	QTY					
	%	%	%	%	%	%
Hatched	QTY					
	%	%	%	%	%	%
Average Shell Thickness						
First Egg Laid		Date				
Last Egg Laid		Date				
Total Days in Production						
Chick Condition at Birth		Good	Fair	Poor		
	QTY					
	%	%	%	%		

Did Not Hatch	QTY	%
Infertile	QTY	%
Early Dead	QTY	%
Mid Dead	QTY	%
Late Dead	QTY	%
Malpositioned in shell	QTY	%
Other	QTY	%

RR ©1995

Figure 7

INDIVIDUAL BIRD PRODUCTION RECORDS

Health Records

It is always necessary to keep flock health records on your birds, to assist in determining health problems that may arise and help assess the overall profile of expenses for tax purposes and business profitability. See the chart in Figure 8 (next page) for one way to keep track.

Early Egg Producers

It is absolutely necessary for cost effectiveness to maintain and acquire birds that have a history of early egg production. Always record the age when your hens first start laying. Early layers should be your replacement breeder stock. Genetics, nutrition and management all play a part in early egg production. Reference the yearly summary chart (Figure 7) for egg production by hen or pair.

Chick Survivability

It will be necessary to record which breeder birds produce chicks with higher survivability (Figure 9). This will also be important in knowing which birds you want to select for replacement stock. Genetics, nutrition and management all play a role in survivability.

Egg Production

The cost of maintaining a bird with low egg production is the same as for one with high egg production. This is obviously another important selection trait for breeder replacement stock. Refer to the Yearly Summary Chart Evaluation (Figure 7) of egg production by the hen or pair for yearly total egg information.

Mortality/death Information

Keeping death records may show a pattern in your flock's health, and will assist your veterinarian or consultant in evaluating problems or potential problems. See Figure 10.

Individual Bird Health Records

VACCINATION	DATE	DATE	DATE	DATE	DATE

PROCEDURE	DATE	DATE	DATE	DATE	DATE
De-Worming					
Blood Work					
Fecal Exam					

SURGERY DATE	DESCRIBE

STRESS EFFECT	CAUSE

Sickness,Lameness, Parasites, etc.	Length of Recovery	Medications Used	Weather Conditions	Recently Transported	Change Eating Habits	Date	Other

RR © 1995

Figure 8

Chick Survivability by Hen or Pair

Year: _____ Total Hatch: _____
Hen ID _____ Total Died: _____
Rooster ID _____ % Survived: _____
Total Chick Death by Month: Jan. ___ Feb. ___ Mar. ___ Apr. ___ May ___
June ___ July ___ Aug ___ Sept ___ Oct. ___
Nov. ___ Dec ___

Dead Bird ID	Month	Week 1	Week2	Week3	Week4	Month 2	Month3	3-6 Mo.	6Mo-2yr

RR © 1995

Figure 9

Record Keeping & Management

Mortality / Death Information
Age : Yr ____ Mo. ____ Day ____
Date of Death: Yr. ____ Mo. ____ Day ____
❑ Slaughter
Cause: ❑ Accident ❑ Stress
❑ Impaction ❑ Disease
❑ Other: _____
_____
_____
Necropsy Information: _____
_____
_____

RR © 1995

Figure 10

Flock Purchase Record
Date of Purchase: _____
Purchased From: _____
Phone # ( ) _____ Fax # ( ) _____
Address: _____
County _____ City _____ State ____
Farm/Ranch Location: _____
Broker: _____ Phone # ( ) _____
Auction: _____ Phone # ( ) _____
Bird ID Number: _____
Sex: ___ Age ___ Yr. ___ Month ___ DOB ___
Breed: OSTRICH- ❑ Red ❑ Blue ❑ Black ❑ Cross
         EMU ❑   RHEA ❑ White ❑ Grey ❑ Cross
Health Certificate: ❑ Yes ❑ No Date: _____
DNA Tested: ❑ Yes ❑ No Date: _____
Production Records of Parents Supplied: Yes ❑ No ❑
Date Delivered: _____
RR © 1995

Figure 11

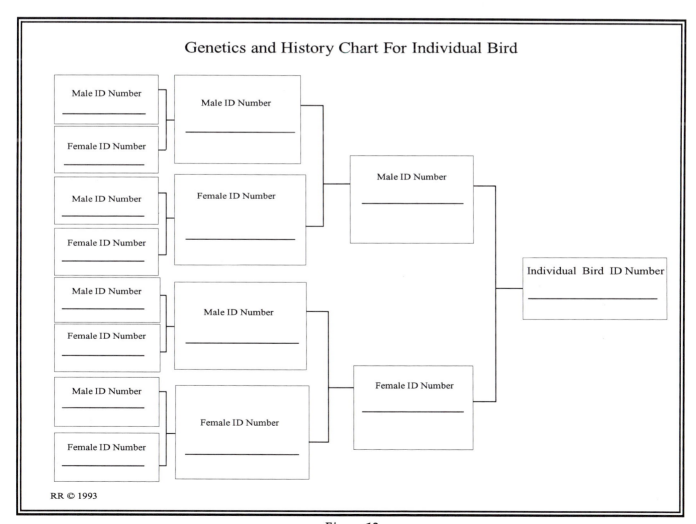

Figure 12

Incubator/ Hatcher Room Worksheet

Incubator#	Hatcher#	Date	Time	Temp. Wet/Dry	Humidity	# of eggs	Counter #	Times Turned Daily	Change Wick	Water (+ -)	How Much

Attire	1st Visit	2nd Visit	3rd Visit	4th Visit
Gloves	Yes ❑ No ❑	Yes ❑ No ❑	Yes ❑ No ❑	Yes ❑ No ❑
Hands Clean/	Yes ❑ No ❑	Yes ❑ No ❑	Yes ❑ No ❑	Yes ❑ No ❑
Disinfected	Yes ❑ No ❑	Yes ❑ No ❑	Yes ❑ No ❑	Yes ❑ No ❑
Foot Bath	Yes ❑ No ❑	Yes ❑ No ❑	Yes ❑ No ❑	Yes ❑ No ❑
Shoe Spray	Yes ❑ No ❑	Yes ❑ No ❑	Yes ❑ No ❑	Yes ❑ No ❑
Protective Clothing	Yes ❑ No ❑	Yes ❑ No ❑	Yes ❑ No ❑	Yes ❑ No ❑
By: (Initials)				

Room Temperture ________

Room Humidity ________

#Chicks Removed From Hatcher____

#Chicks Microchipped ________

Egg ID #	Microchip #

Biosecurity		Product Used
Floors Cleaned	Yes ❑ No ❑	
Foot Bath Cleaned	Yes ❑ No ❑	
Hatcher Cleaned	Yes ❑ No ❑	
Rooms Fogged	Yes ❑ No ❑	

Note Repairs made or Changes Here:
Changed Products Used:
Yes ❑ No ❑ Reason: __________

____

New Product:: ____________

New Equipment: ____________

____

Eggs Moved to Hatcher ________

Egg ID #

Figure 13

Weather

Weather affects all animals in some aspect. It may or may not have an adverse effect during breeding season, but it is always a good idea to note weather conditions if birds stop laying. Refer to the Daily Field Sheet (Pen Check List) (Figure 14) for weather conditions.

Flock Purchase History

Flock purchase history (Figure 11) will assist in genetic tracking, date of purchase, and reference should disease transfer occur. These records should be included with Individual Bird Records for reference purposes.

Genetic And History Lineage Chart

Following your birds back a few generations will be beneficial in assessing the productivity of a specific line of selected breeder birds (Figure 12).

OTHER HELPFUL RECORDS

If you are just getting started in the ratite industry, helpful reminders of things to look for can give you a big advantage.

If you have employees it is important that they use—and you review—daily or weekly summaries or check lists. This will benefit in standardizing daily performance and possibly in trouble-shooting problems.

Two sample checklists are the Incubator and Hatcher Room worksheet and the Daily Field Sheet (Figures 13 and 14).

The Incubator and Hatcher Room worksheet will help remind you or your employees to:

- check temperature and humidity of the incubator and hatcher,
- see if your automatic turner in the incubator is working,
- add water to the incubator if needed, and
- follow biosecurity procedures.

If chicks have been moved to the brooder area, note microchipped chicks and the microchip numbers.

The Daily Field Sheet (pen check list) is a daily check list for egg collection, feeding, cleaning, daily weather conditions, and notes of jobs or tasks that need to be done.

STANDARDIZED RECORDS

As stated earlier, the ratite industry will follow the same historical path as other animal agriculture industries.

Historically, beef, dairy and poultry producer associations, working within each product specialization, record and evaluate all aspects of their industry, utilizing large databases for different segments of each specialty. Working together with producers, industry associations make evaluations by species and products.

The producers of individual species within the ratite industry must provide a standard number and type of specific records to be kept for scientific performance evaluation purposes.

If records for genetic selection for different species and for different products of the industry are not compiled in databases, ***no real evaluation for breeding characteristics or by-products can be made. Records on a local and national level must be compiled in*** *databases to calculate breeding values.*

This will not mean every producer will use the same software or the same manual record-keeping system. It just means obtaining and using information on breeding and production records that are standardized so an accurate, continuing evaluation of the industry can be initiated and the growth of the industry can occur.

BASIC RATITE MANAGEMENT

The ratite industry is still learning what management practices are the most effective for production of a healthy flock. As research and experience continue, efficiency and production will increase. Here are a few management practices to consider in your ratite operation.

HEALTH MANAGEMENT
Space Density

The pen size or space density (the area of space in which the chicks or birds are raised) is critical in ratites. Plenty of room for exercise is necessary. In pen sizes for both chicks and adult birds, usually bigger is better. Overcrowding, especially with chicks, can lead to diseases, trauma, and undue stress.

Stress

Ratites seem to be especially sensitive to stress. Some of the causes may be chilling, overheating, loud noises, unusual surroundings, changing feed, and hauling. Limiting stress-causing situations will increase overall flock performance.

Ventilation

Correct air flow, with an air purification system, in the incubator and hatcher rooms will decrease or prevent contamination. Good air circulation will assist in both the incubation and hatching processes.

Proper ventilation in chick barns is an absolute must. Poor ventilation will increase respiratory infections. Exhaust fans will help control temperature and will exhaust the deadly ammonia fumes from urine and feces which the birds expel during the night. While good ventilation is critical, however, there should not be a draft on the chicks in brooder barns during the night or in cold weather.

Water

Good-quality water is a must for all animals. If you use well water, a periodic check for coliform bacteria should be performed. Twice yearly would be a good rule of thumb. These tests can usually be performed by your city or county water departments.

Cool water will help reduce body temperature in summer. Warm water will help increase body temperatures in winter. Not only is the quality of water important but also the availability for consumption and for proper sanitation purposes.

Behavior

Learning the behavioral patterns of your birds is critical. What is normal and abnormal will require some time to learn if you are just entering the business. A good

Figure 14

time for visual examinations and observation is while they are at rest, eating, or at play, rather than during activities which may excite the birds. Observe them both close-up and from a distance.

Look for everything from pen activity to eating habits. You will be able to identify sick birds early before serious damage can arise and note if birds are reacting adversely to weather, predators or management changes. Many times behavior changes are very subtle. Take the time to study your birds.

Traffic Flow

Traffic flow by visitors and labor should be from clean areas to dirty areas. Start with incubation and hatching area, to chick pens, to grower pens, to breeder pens, to quarantine pens.

Pen Areas

Pens should be kept free of any debris. Ostriches especially are notorious for swallowing anything.

Chick pens should be cleaned daily. Solid surfaces should be washed daily. Periodic washing should include a disinfectant. Sand or dirt floors should be scooped out daily.

Observation has shown that in the first year or two in production, ratite ranchers will have fewer problems with sickness in their flocks. Bacterial build-up from fecal deposits in the pens have been shown to cause increasing health problems throughout the industry.

My recommendation is to rotate small pens and grow-out pens every other year or to use portable pens. Chick runs should have a minimum of 30 days rest before reuse. Sunlight and time are the best methods to kill bacteria.

Internal Parasites

Fecal examination may be necessary for suspect birds. Lab work can be done by your veterinarian. Depending on conditions in your area, a regular de-worming program may be advisable.

External Parasites

Feather mites and feather lice can be dusted with proper insecticides. Check feather shafts for feather mites.

Drainage and Prevailing Winds

Proper drainage from brooder barns and pen areas will diffuse disease problems and benefit flock health. Prevailing winds must be considered in ranch design for odor and contamination, especially from quarantine areas.

All-in All-out Production

This system has several advantages.
- Start with the egg storage facility. Setting eggs once weekly (or batched hatching) allows thorough cleaning of storage units before starting the next cycle.
- Eggs incubated in a batched cycle will allow time for the hatcher to be cleaned and disinfected between hatching cycles. The hatcher will always be the most contaminated equipment in the incubation and hatching area.
- As the chicks progress in the brooder area and chick barns, cleaning and disinfecting will be simplified.
- By keeping birds of the same age together, stress will be limited when moving them from pen to pen, because the pecking order will already have been established. Continually mixing birds of different ages forces them to re-establish the pecking order, creating undue stress and fighting.

NUTRITION

Feed costs traditionally constitute the greatest expense in raising animals to the desired slaughter weight. This will continue to be true in the feeding of ratites. A proper feed ration must be provided for birds to attain their genetic potential.

Exact nutritional requirements are still uncertain for ratites. It is understood we should feed different age groups different feed rations. The categories for feed types are starter, grower, maintenance and breeder.

Clean feed is essential. Make sure no mold or other contaminants are present in feed. Do not use old feed.

Brand-name feed formulated specifically for ratites is recommended. Always monitor consumption. If a decrease occurs, investigate immediately.

High bird prices in the past have affected all aspects of the industry, including feed. The need for less expensive and more efficient feed is part of the growing pains the industry is experiencing.

Many feed companies and nutritionists are now researching more exact formulas for all ages of birds. Clinical tests are ongoing by the research community for feed conversion ratios and exact rations needed.

The two factors to examine in your feeding/nutrition program are *conversion of feed to weight gain* and *feed to egg production*. Cheap feed will not necessarily save you money. The question should not be cost per pound of feed, but rather "How much body weight gain is produced from each pound of feed consumed?"

The productivity and profits of your operation are not based on feed price alone. The same will be true for egg production. Considering, calculating and analyzing all information is necessary to show true gains in production by nutrition.

Grazing

Grazing may be one source of reduced feed costs. If land is available, here are some points to consider if grazing will be a part of your feeding program.

Remember that all grazing animals are selective foragers. In the wild, ratites eat grass, true, but they also eat shoots, weeds, flowers, the tips of growing shrubs, insects, and even small animals.

As noted in the chapter on **Free-Range Rheas**, birds from chick to full grown mingle with other livestock, eating mesquite and other vegetation, helping keep undesirable plants in check. Ostriches have been reported to eat pigweed and careless weed.

While supplemental feeding may be necessary in some areas, we may find that combining ostriches and other ratites with livestock may maximize pasture utilization, without competition for the same forages or browse.

This is just one more asset to combining traditional agriculture with production of ratites for maximum production and income.

Another grazing option for ostriches and possibly emus and rheas will be wheat, oat and milo stubble, utilizing crops for additional income in the farming and ranching business.

Protein and energy sources vary for each forage and browse species. If you are not knowledgeable about native forages and browse in your area, consult your soil conservation service or county agent to obtain a list with percentages of protein and mineral content. This will help in establishing what percentages of protein and minerals may need to be added for supplemental feeding along with grazing.

If you intend to plant a specific forage (annual or perennial), first have the soil analyzed for fertility for optimal production. The laboratory can recommend fertilizers to maximize yield.

The selection of forage will depend on the adaptive characteristics of your area. Soil type, temperature and moisture are key factors in selecting the right forage for your geographical location.

For supplemental feed rations contact a university researcher or nutritionist in your area who is knowledgeable about ratites. With knowledge of the types of forage and browse available, soil analysis, and fertilization recommendations, you can ask your feed supplier for a supplemental feed which will make up for nutrients missing in the forage and browse.

For instance, many consider alfalfa to be an excellent forage and hay crop. But in the **Nutrition** chapter, you'll find that it has some serious deficiencies which would require a supplement. Ostriches grazed on alfalfa reportedly just strip the leaves and leave the stem, therefore damaging the alfalfa field (A. Raines, personal communication, September 1995).

During the non-breeding season, it may be most economical to cut costs by grazing breeders, turning them out into large pastures or pens, along with providing supplemental feed. A combination of grazing and supplemental feed may produce a high-quality slaughter bird at reduced feed costs, even if the time to produce maximum slaughter weight takes a little longer.

For cost effictivness of production, I would encourage producers to experiment with forages and browse. Only with experimentation can the industry learn what will work best in different geographical locations.

Egg Candling

The cost effectiveness of utilizing an egg candler will far outweigh the initial expense. The incubator space occupied by infertile eggs is a cost you cannot afford. As your operation grows the cost of additional incubators can be significant.

Identifying and understanding chick development in the egg will help in understanding the internal and external pipping process. In turn, this knowlege will help you decide when to assist in the hatching process.

Recording the fertility of eggs will assist in assessing possible breeding problems, especially early in the season, and help in determining replacement stock.

MARKETING

Equally as important as raising healthy birds is marketing your product. You are in business to make a profit.

There are several meat processors in the ratite industry and more coming on line every month. They are currently buying birds for processing meat and by-products. This is one source for selling your birds.

MARKETING TO THE PUBLIC

Spread the word. In a young industry, education and exposure to the general public should be part of your marketing plan:

- Advertise outside the industry publications.
- Establish a speakers' group in each local ratite organization. Local service clubs always need speakers.
- Provide products to show. Let people feel the oil, touch the leather, and taste the meat if possible.
- Provide a handout list of all local producers so that the audience can contact them if they have questions about the industry, or about purchasing industry products.

There is no need to talk about selling birds—these are product *consumers*. The more knowledge they have, the more the opportunity for industry products to be consumed.

There are two types of people you should focus on in marketing your birds. Ratites have been called the alternative livestock. Today, many people in the ratite industry in the United States have come from a non-agricultural background, looking for an alternative way of life to provide a good income and a healthy, wholesome lifestyle.

The untapped market, and at this point in the industry probably the main focus, should be people already in the business of raising animals—traditional agricultural families.

Available land, some facilities and a basic understanding of animal husbandry is a good start for your presentation. Traditional agriculture operates on a low profit. Most people will listen if you present your industry carefully.

Remember change comes with difficulty for most people. Do not try to argue ratites versus other animals—especially the ones they are raising. They will be more knowledgeable about different types of livestock than many ratite producers.

Explain the future potential of the industry. Present examples of what has happened to other animal products and eating trends in the past. One example is the turkey industry.

- Approximately 295 million turkeys are produced annually in the United States.
- The American consumer eats 18.3 pounds of turkey over the course of a year.
- 72% of the turkey will be consumed as turkey sausage, sandwiches or some other form of processed meat.
- Only 28% will be consumed at Thanksgiving, Christmas and Easter.

It wasn't too many years ago the only time turkey was eaten was at Thanksgiving and Christmas. Now, it is a regular part of the American diet.

Ask logical and reasonable questions, for instance:

- What is their net profit per animal unit?
- How much land do they need per animal unit?
- How much do they know about the ratite species you are marketing?
- Do they have land available to start a ratite operation if they thought they could increase their income over the next three to five years?

Generally people know very little or nothing about ratites. Don't intimidate them—remember you are probably just planting a seed. Let it grow.

Be Prepared

Carry literature and products with you everywhere you go. Most of all, stay informed about the industry. *No hype—just facts.* Knowledge of traditional ranching will help you the most. Do some homework.

The ratite industry should not set itself up as competition for traditional agriculture. A combination of both is starting to appear on many farms and ranches and many more will follow in a few years.

Livestock Shows

One of the most important things the industry can do is support local and statewide livestock shows. Make sure a class for ratites is offered at livestock shows in your area.

In some areas, ratite organizations are cooperating with the Future Farmers of America (FFA) and 4H Clubs in programs for youngsters to raise and show ratites.

Contact your state or national association for information on how to implement a program in your area. Donate birds to FFA and 4H members and volunteer to help at the shows.

For many people this will be their first chance to really examine ratites and have an opportunity to talk to people about the new *alternative livestock.*

The gate attendence at the Houston Livestock Show in 1995 was 1,810,007 people. How many saw the ostriches, emus and rheas at the show I don't know, but even a small percentage of 1,810,007 is a lot of people.

Educate yourself, believe in the future of the industry, promote the products and tell everyone you talk to about this new alternative livestock. This is your industry and your responsibility.

INEVITABLY, THE INTERNET

Marketing on the Internet can reach a tremendous number of people—people who are looking to get into the business as well as people already in the business. The Internet web page address is

http://www.yournet.com/cgi-bin/ssis/-~ektor/emuhome.html.

There is a fairly extensive web site for ratite enthusiasts already in place on the Internet. Among other things, you'll find a list of veterinarians—worldwide—who practice ratite medicine, and people engaged in research on ratites. There are lists of breeders and other general information.

Unfortunately, there is also a fair amount of misinformation, but if the various ratite associations were to establish a presence, much of this could be countered by people and associations who have established their credibility.

At present, if you find information which is not factual, all that can be done is to contact those who have put it forward and explain that we do more harm than good to the industry by spreading misinformation.

I strongly recommend that all of the national associations—and even state and local groups—establish their own home pages and keep the information current.

Some possibilities for the types of information to post would be recipes, local association contacts, information on industry-sponsored research, even local association newsletters. The use of the Internet as a powerful marketing tool will continue to grow, and industry associations should be getting involved.

Potential consumers of ratite products and potential new ratite farmers—Web browsers and Internet surfers all—are interested in learning about ratites. The various associations can provide that knowledge by getting good information out where it can be seen.

GOOD GENETICS vs. GOOD MANAGEMENT

BREEDING FOR SPECIFIC TRAITS

A good replacement stock program is essential for a good breeding program. The relationship between good genetics and good management must find a balance to enhance the overall flock breeding program.

These are some of the traits and qualities you will need to consider:
- docility vs. aggressiveness,
- egg hatchability,
- egg size,
- shell thickness,
- pore size,
- fertility,
- egg production,
- chick livability,
- early breeders,
- body conformation,
- body weight,
- feed efficiency,
- growth rate,
- hide production,
- quill patterns in ostriches,
- feather density,
- feather production,
- fat production in emus and rheas,
- diameter of the metatarsus in emus and rheas.

These and other heritability percentages must be studied and analyzed in ratites.

Some hereditary traits occur in higher percentages than others, but to my knowledge the industry has established no percentages for ratites at present. We have only the percentages of poultry traits for guidelines today.

IMPORTANCE OF MANAGEMENT

North & Bell (1990) state that, in poultry, the difference between the heritability percentages and 100% is due to management. For example, 10% of hatchability of fertile eggs is due to genetics, while 90% is attributable to management. Similarly, they estimate that age at sexual maturity is 25% heredity and 75% management, and adult body weight is 55% heredity and 45% management.

To gauge your performance you will need to look at the performance of the entire flock as well as individual birds. A summary of all aspects of production must be considered in your selection plan. This will be the road map for your selection of breeding stock. *Birds that have not been bred for a specific purpose to improve the desirable traits of the next generation will decrease in value as time progresses.*

It is necessary for the growth and survival of the ratite industry for producers to start selective breeding programs at this point in the history of the industry.

It may be time in your operation to seriously consider culling from your flock breeders and offspring that have not proven to have genetic qualities that will enhance your operation or the growth of the industry.

By culling inferior birds, you will improve the productivity and efficiency of your operation by good genetic selection and reduced feed costs. It will also prevent birds that are not top breeder quality from passing into the marketplace.

It is a hard decision to slaughter these animals, but a few hard decisions now will reap large rewards in the future.

You should not attempt to try to breed for too many different traits at the start of your selective breeding program. In time, you will want to import genetic traits from other producers to enhance the breeding program you have decided on.

Once again you must set goals. Make a list of traits you want to breed for. Then put your plan into action and keep records.

In the near future, the industry will breed and genetically match birds that will have high fertility, good feather quality, weight needed for slaughter, early production, high fat content to produce oil, etc., making each generation of birds more cost-efficient to produce.

COST-EFFICIENT MANAGEMENT

The ratite industry, like other meat and livestock industries, must find ways to increase production in the most efficient manner to maximize good economic returns.

Let's take just one example, from the cattle industry, of what good management can accomplish. An evaluation for one ranch demonstrated that by changing the calving season to match forage availability (in this case about 30 days to grazeable forage), profits were increased significantly.

Changing the calving season alone was estimated to increase the ranch's carrying capacity by 30 to 40 per cent in terms of animal units (Taylor, 1992).

High bird prices in the past have compensated for poor management or the need to consider good management. Bird prices are declining as the slaughter market develops, and may continue to decline. In some instances, as markets are developed for products we may see price increases.

Wherever the market prices stabilize, good management will play a large role in a successful ratite operation.

EGG PRODUCTION

Egg production will become of paramount importance in increasing profits over the life of your operation.

Consider hens that lay 40 eggs in ostrich production and 25 eggs in emu production. Increasing egg production by ten eggs per hen will have a significant difference in the profitability of your ranch:
- If you have five breeder pairs you theoretically would increase productivity by 50 chicks per year.
- Ten breeder pairs will give you 100 more chicks.
- Ten trios will produce 200 more each year.

Never base projected income on the fertility of all eggs or survival of all chicks. Calculate a percentage of loss for infertile eggs and losses due to death after hatching (see Table 1). As research continues survival rates will increase and the percentage of loss will decrease.

Remember that first-year layer production will usually be substantially lower than in succeeding years. Also remember: An ostrich hen that consistently lays 80 eggs or an emu hen that consistently lays 50 eggs with *low hatchability and chick survival rates* will not profit your operation.

Likewise, your feeding costs are the same whether a bird produces 40 eggs or 25.

TRIOS AND COLONIES

By breeding trios instead of pairs, the cost efficiency of feeding only one rooster, and the lower infrastructure cost of one pen for two hens, will reduce your capital investment considerably.

With reduced internal costs and increased production your net profits increase considerably over a one hen-one rooster breeding program. In a colony breeding situation your costs are reduced again. Net profit percentage may double.

The possible increased expense of an additional incubator and/or hatcher should be offset by lower pen and infrastructure costs. You should analyze the capital investment costs over a seven-year period. Labor and feed should stay constant or increase only slightly.

Use your spreadsheet software (with realistic costs and conservative sales estimates) to evaluate increased hen production versus capital expense increases, for net profits over a seven-year period.

There are many factors to consider in a good management plan. In Table I we've provided examples of the kinds of information you can generate.

By beginning with the data from good records and projecting forward, using history and analyzing trends, you can get a clear picture of the potential of your operation.

EARLY BREEDERS

If your goal is maximum profit, it will not be feasible to feed and carry birds that do not start laying at an early age. For this discussion to make sense, you must understand that ratites start breeding *when breeding season starts*, not because they've reached sexual maturity. This is a particular problem with birds that hatch late in the season.

For example, ostriches are expected to start breeding when they are three years old; i.e., a bird which hatches in the spring of 1991 should be ready to breed in the spring of 1994. But late hatchers quite likely will not be sexually mature until several months later, and may not breed until the start of the 1995 season. Meanwhile, you have the cost of feeding, maintaining, and housing the birds for an extra year.

The First Year

When possible, always use older males with hens in the first year of breeding. Males seem to mature later than hens most of the time. First-year production is usually lower than subsequent years, and using older males should help increase first-year production.

If the cost of feed* is $150 per year per bird, twenty late breeders could cost you $3,000 in feed bills alone. You must also consider, however, the loss of income from the sales of chicks not produced during this non-laying year.

If ostrich yearlings are selling at $400* each, and an average hatch per ostrich hen is fifty eggs, theroetically you will have missed $20,000 in sales *per non-producing ostrich hen.* (*Feed cost and yearling prices are for example only, and may not reflect true prices.)

These are just two examples of an approach to good management. There are others which are equally important.

TABLE 1. EXAMPLES OF THE EFFECT OF INCREASED EGG PRODUCTION ON PROFITS

```
$    400      Yearling Sale Price *
   x 80       Additional Chicks Due To Increased
                Production (20% Loss)
$ 32,000      Additional Sales


$    400      Yearling Sale Price *
    X 95      Additional Chicks Due To Increased
                Production (5% Loss)
$ 38,000      Additional Sales
```

* Prices are for example only and may not reflect market prices.

PLAN YOUR OPERATION

You may need to replan your bird operation, or if you are just entering the industry, give serious consideration to what type of ratite operation you wish to have. We live in an age of specialization.

SPECIALTY OPERATIONS

These are some of the specialty operations which will develop as the industry matures into a slaughter market.

Breeder Stock: Highly genetically-selected birds bred for specific qualities and traits will provide breeder stock for commercial growers.

- *Commercial Growers*: Raising quality birds for the slaughter market.
- *Feed Lots*: As in cattle operations, many birds will be kept on special feeds for growth and weight gain. This could be accomplished by contract for weight per pounds of gain or by outright purchase of birds.
- *Hatching Operations*: Custom hatching to a predetermined age may become a specialized operation for fellow ranchers.
- *All-inclusive Operations*: The industry is sure to see the growth of large enterprises which includes all facets of ranching from incubation and hatching to grow-out for slaughter, and may or may not include breeder stock operations.

By deciding early on the direction you want to take, you may avoid investing in unnecessary equipment and facilities, greatly increasing your likelihood of success. The cost effectiveness of planning will reap large rewards.

ENTERING THE RATITE INDUSTRY

In assessing different facets the industry has to offer, you may want to consider the following:

- Starting small and growing into the industry has merit. It just takes longer for financial returns.
- A large capital investment will mean quicker returns, but it requires more initial planning.
- Joint venture or partnerships increase available capital and labor, but you must have a specific agreement for duties and responsibilities of each partner.

When the decision is made to purchase birds a pre-purchase exam by a qualified ratite veterinarian is recommended. This investment cost is small but could mean the difference of your success or failure in the industry.

Always research records to the best of your ability on the parents of birds, require records of parents as part of the sale. The records will be the basis to start your own record keeping system for production purposes.

If you are interested enough to read this book it is important to remember that these are only some examples and opinions in raising ratites. As the industry matures husbandry practices will change to increase efficiency and productivity.

CONCLUSION

The industry is young and there will be many opportunities for people who enter the business in the next few years.

As mentioned at the beginning of the **Genetics** chapter, this new alternative livestock comes along at a great time in the history of agriculture. With current DNA technology, the ratite industry can progress much faster than meat industries in the past.

Good ratite production business practices do not mean new facilities, white board fences around your ranch, expensive pens, or brooder barns. It does mean practical, cost-efficient, low-maintenance and labor-effective management practices.

Pretty is nice, but profitable is admirable. We often hear in conversations, "He's been lucky in the ratite business." But remember, the harder we work, the luckier we get.

NOTES

INSURANCE AND THE OSTRICH INDUSTRY

Alex Fairly
HRH Insurance of Amarillo
Amarillo, Texas

As the ostrich industry in the United States has rapidly grown and evolved over the last seven to ten years, it could be argued that the insurance industry's role has had as large an impact on the growth of the ostrich industry as any other single influence.

While the insurance industry's evolution has had many obstacles to clear, the breeding market in the United States has, in large part, been supported by the investors' ability to insure their investment. Without the option to protect this investment, many investors would not have ventured into the US ostrich arena.

As the American industry continues to mature, insurers will have to move and evolve with it, creating products that address the needs of the ostrich producer. During this process, the insurance industry's participation will remain very important.

HISTORY

When insurers first began insuring ostriches, they, like many ostrich farmers, knew relatively little about what they were getting into. Understandably, this led to mistakes that ultimately resulted in insurers losing money much faster than they made it.

In the beginning, all birds were insured in foreign insurance markets (usually London) and the overseas insurers were not aware of specific causes of loss. Thus, rates were set and anyone who would pay the premium could be insured.

Even as late as 1993, a common complaint was "Why do I pay the same rate as my neighbor down the road who has a history of losing so many birds?"

Generally, no attention was paid to loss experience or the methods and facilities used in farm management. The insurance industry was experiencing growing pains along with the American ostrich farmer.

Another major factor of influence in the early years was fraud. Insurers did not require formal identification and, unfortunately, insurers paid many claims on birds they could not be sure were the birds they originally insured.

Insurers began to require identification in birds, usually using the microchip as we know it today. While this greatly decreased the existence of fraudulent claims, many breeders continued to find ways of letting insurance companies pay for their mistakes.

Another major factor in the generally unsuccessful attempts by insurers to make a profit in this business was their decision to insure three-month-old birds. Losses in this age group were horrendous and some insurers were driven out of business because of this serious error.

Usually, when an agent creates an agreement with an insurer, an annual contract (that comes in different forms) is agreed upon by both parties. When London began insuring three-month-old birds, it did not take a full year for them to realize the incredibly expensive mistake they had made.

However, because of annual contracts, they were not always able to stop agents from insuring three-month-old birds. By the time the agreements had expired, many insurers had literally lost their shirts, some of them taking such a tremendous loss that they were forced out of the insurance business entirely.

As you can see by now, insurers, not unlike all American ostrich pioneers, have had much to learn about this industry. As insurers suffered during the learning curve, rates climbed.

Yet the breeder market's demand and opportunity for profit drove the insurance industry forward, and many continued to insure birds. Although by 1993 the cost to insure birds was at an all-time high, the profit potential still usually outweighed the cost of insurance.

To an extent, the insurance industry had paid for a large part of the American ostrich farmer's learning curve. Insurers had been in and out of the market and there was little stability. In insurance markets around the world, insuring these birds profitably was considered very risky business.

It is important to understand how insurance was (and in most cases, still is) purchased. Ostrich producers called their American agents and, when they received their policies, they were written, more often than not, on "American paper." This means the insurance company named on the front cover of the policy was an American insurance company.

Most ostrich producers did not (and still do not) understand that these companies were usually what insurance people refer to as *front* companies, meaning a company licensed to do business in America, state by state, but who did not actually take on all of the risk of insuring these birds.

Some of these companies took on none of the risk—they merely fronted for the real insurers, known as reinsurers, usually an European insurance entity such as Lloyds of London.

Even those that did assume some of the risk usually never assumed all of it, often taking on as little as five to ten per cent. The rest was passed on to the foreign reinsurers.

This process is normal and common in the insurance world, especially when insuring things that are considered very risky. The important point is that all the strings were usually controlled by European insurers.

To make the process a little more complicated, the local agent usually had an agent between him and the American front company. Additionally, there was usually a broker between the front company and the foreign reinsurer.

Because of this, most agents and brokers had little or no flexibility in negotiating insurance programs on a farm-by-farm basis.

This is not unusual in the insurance world, but it kept the ostrich insurance industry from progressing at a faster rate in creating programs that not only served the American ostrich producer, but also rewarded producers who had learned to be more successful in keeping birds alive.

EMUS AND RHEAS

Most of the insurance industry's growing pains and learning curve occurred with ostriches, as it was the first of the ratites to gain prominence. By the time the emu and rhea industries had a need for insurance of any volume, many of the bugs (microchipping, vet certificates, etc.) had been worked out.

Thus, the process of insuring the three species is almost identical. Most agents who insure ostriches also insure emus and rheas, and require identical paperwork.

The only significant difference is that emus are considered by insurers to be of slightly lower risk and rates (usually about 2 percentage points less) reflect this feeling.

Conversely, rheas are considered to be of slightly higher risk than ostriches, and rates for rheas have been about 2 to 3 percentage points higher.

Other than a little different rating structure, insurance for the three ratite species is almost identical.

COVERAGES

Let's take a look at the kinds of coverages available for insuring ostriches, emus and rheas. The rates for the three have been and still are different, but the coverage is essentially the same.

NAMED PERILS

This cover is aptly named, as it is an insurance agreement that *names* the perils (or causes of loss) that it covers. It is generally the least expensive and offers the least coverage.

Obviously, if all the perils it covers can be named in writing, there is not an overabundance of them. It is probably the least popular insurance product available. As you will see, the perils listed in this policy are usually not what kill birds. Generally speaking, the perils are *acts of God* and *theft*.

As is the case with all types of insurance, these discussions about coverage are general. Specific policies could have small differences in them, as each insurer may do things a little differently. But usually the coverages found in the different bird-mortality policies are amazingly similar.

In this case, we will simply list the perils that a named-peril policy covers:
- fire
- lightning
- explosion
- smoke resulting from fire, lightning and/or explosion
- collision, derailment or overturning of rail transportation
- sinking, burning or collision of water-borne vessels
- windstorm (including tornados and hurricanes)
- hail
- earthquake
- flood
- objects falling from an aircraft, and
- theft.

As you can tell, a few of these would almost never apply to an ostrich, emu or rhea. Generally speaking, if your birds were killed because of a weather-related accident, they would be covered.

Accidents like birds running into fences, getting necks and legs caught in fencing, injury by other birds, and any kind of loss to disease or impaction (or any other physical ailment) are not covered by this kind of insurance. For obvious reasons, this type of insurance has never been very popular with the American ostrich farmer.

FULL MORTALITY

This is the most complete cover you are currently able to purchase. It is what insurance people refer to as *all-risk* coverage, meaning that instead of listing the perils that are covered, this policy lists the perils that *are not* covered (exclusions) because almost everything is covered by this policy.

With this in mind, we will list common exclusions that are found in this coverage. As we go through them, we will attempt to explain the insurers' motives.

Intentional Slaughter

The policy will usually go on to list exceptions to this exclusion, usually stating the obvious: If a bird is sick, injured and/or in pain, and a qualified veterinarian deems it necessary, the bird may be put down. Usually most insurers require that they be informed **before** this occurs.

Death From War, Invasion, Etc.

This is the usual war exclusion that is found in most insurance policies of any kind. The assumption is that if war or civil commotion breaks out, ostriches may not be able to be protected in a reasonable manner. (If war breaks out, it may not or may not matter who owns an ostrich.)

Death By Surgery or Medical Treatment, If Not Done By Qualified Veterinarian

This one is obvious. Insurers do not want just anyone cutting into a bird for who knows what reason. Most insurers want to be informed when surgery takes place. They are also usually understanding if they are not able to be reached and the bird's life is in jeopardy.

Death From Willful Injury

If you decide to harm your birds, insurers will probably not be willing to pay for them.

Death caused by poison

This one is in there because of the difficulty in determining if birds were intentionally killed by the insured. Look ahead to the discussion on moral hazards to help explain the insurers' thoughts on this exclusion.

Death from transit

Almost all full-mortality policies exclude transit. See the discussion which follows.

> *The intent of these exclusions is not to find a way out, but to protect the underwriter from fraud in the case of a market disaster.*

This is not an all-inclusive list. Policies differ on some exclusions and their wording. It is always best for you to read the wording in your policy and talk to your agent if you need an explanation.

THE MORAL HAZARD

Some of these exclusions deal with what insurers call the *moral hazard*—that is, the possibility of an insured harming birds to collect on an insurance policy in a market that may be deemed risky.

This issue is of heightened importance in underwriters' minds. The worry is that if the ostrich market collapses and bird values decrease dramatically over a short period of time, the moral hazard would rise.

Unfortunately they are aware of this only because all insurers pay out millions of dollars every year because of fraud. If the market drops in any industry, insureds are often tempted to cause an insurance claim to cut losses.

This is the reason for exclusions such as poison and willful or malicious injury. If the market dropped quickly, poison would be an easy way to kill birds and collect on insurance policies.

You will probably find, however, that most companies would pay for a bird dying from a bad batch of feed if the insurer could be sure it was an accident that is unlikely to recur.

The intent of these exclusions is not to find a way out, but to protect the underwriter from fraud in the case of a market disaster. It is unfortunate that underwriters have to worry about such matters, but the fact is that some insureds do take advantage of situations such as these.

MARKET VALUE

Before we get into transportation insurance, another very important concept that goes along with this discussion is what will actually be paid for birds in the case of a drastic market drop. In most insurance policies, the wording starts something like this:

The underwriters agree . . in the event of the death of such animal . . . to indemnify the assured in respect of the actual value of such animal at the time of the accident up to but not exceeding the limit of the underwriters' liability specified in the schedule.

In more readable terms, the insurer promises to pay what the bird is worth at time of death, up to the value for which it was insured. This is frustrating to many who buy insurance. Let's look at the idea behind the wording.

The bottom line is that, in case of a drastic market drop which causes birds to be worth pennies on the dollar, the insurer protects itself from people who would allow or cause the death of birds to collect the insurance money.

It is important to note here that insurers are not insuring against the stability of the market, only the health and life of the birds. The fundamental concept of insurance is that the insurer agrees to indemnify the insured.

To indemnify means to put the insured back in the same position he was in at the time the insurance was purchased in reference to the insured object—in this case, birds.

For example, if you insured an ostrich for $10,000 and the market dropped, making the bird worth only $4,000, the insurer would pay $4,000 if the bird died. If insurers agreed to pay $10,000 for all birds that were now worth $4,000 many birds would die mysteriously.

If the insurer paid $4,000, you would probably be refunded the difference in premium between $10,000 and $4,000. With the $4,000 you received from the insurer, you would be able to replace that bird in the depressed market and thus be indemnified.

This concept is not new. It applies to almost all insurance where an object is insured (whether birds or buildings) that could be replaced for pennies on the dollar in case of a market drop.

Let me explain that this concept should not be feared by those who have birds insured. As is almost guaranteed to happen, the value of ostriches will continue on a downward trend as we near the slaughter market.

There are many theories on how this will occur and when, but as bird values have slowly come down in recent months, this should not affect what would be paid for your bird in case of a loss.

The progression of our industry will inevitably bring lower bird values and the insurer expects and welcomes these market trends. The application of this insurance concept would most likely affect insurers only if the market were to produce a situation where fraud was running rampant.

In all cases, in the event of a lost bird, you should be confident of your ability to replace the dead bird with the insurance money you receive, as it will always reflect the market value of that bird.

TRANSIT INSURANCE

Transit insurance has taken several turns over the years. Let us first examine the two types.

NAMED-PERILS TRANSIT

This transit covers crash or collision on the road, whether caused by the insured or not, and theft. It does not cover any death due to loading, unloading, stress or any accident with the birds while on the road that does not include a crash or collision.

This cover could be purchased for almost any distance. Since stress and anything that may go wrong inside the trailer during transit is covered, the distance is usually not a concern.

FULL-MORTALITY TRANSIT

This transit has similar exclusions to the annual full-mortality insurance, and includes loading, unloading and accident while in the trailer—and of course, crash, collision and theft. Because this coverage is so far-reaching, distance travelled is a consideration. Rates usually go up with distance.

At one time, named-perils transit was included with the annual named-perils policy. This ceased when insurers began to experience extensive losses.

The named-perils policy also included bodily harm done to the birds while in the trailer. As underwriters learned about the ratite business, they quickly learned that transit was a risky business.

While there are those who would dispute the risk level of hauling birds, the fact is that many birds have been paid for by insurers due to the perils of moving.

While there is no *tail* (meaning that the insurer's risk is completely over once the trip is completed) in this type of coverage, transit coverage has never been profitable for insurers.

For this reason it can only be purchased with an annual policy. In case of a loss, the insurers' loss is at least minimally offset by a year's worth of premium.

This issue will have to be addressed as the industry moves closer to a slaughter market. Some day, when thousands of birds are loaded every year into tractor-trailers and taken to market, haulers and producers will have to be able to purchase insurance for these animals to protect from disaster during transit.

The fact that the birds will be worth far less will help, but methods of transporting birds safely will need much improvement before insurers will be interested in this class of business.

Another issue that has affected transit insurance methods and rates was fraud.

The most common worry was when a bird was either uninsured during transit or insured only for crash and collision. If a bird died in transit from other causes, the insured could simply drag it into a pen, call the agent, and claim it had an accident after being unloaded.

One answer to this has been for insurers to require an examination by a veterinarian after bird(s) have been transported. Unfortunately, insurers learned this lesson the hard way.

TODAY'S PRODUCT

As the American ostrich industry progressed, so did some insurers' programs. In 1993 HRH Insurance of Amarillo began to address some of the problems plaguing the ostrich insurance industry. Some trends began to emerge.

One was the fact that many losses are caused by management mistakes. While some loss is due to the nature of the birds, HRH began to notice that many losses involved bird management and facility quality.

The second trend that HRH noticed was that, while almost everyone in the bird business has experienced loss, some farms continued to have substantial losses year after year.

This should not have been a surprise to insurers, as the concept is common in almost all lines of insurance. Generally, those who had losses continue to have losses.

The final obvious trend was that the more experience farmers had, the lower their losses generally were.

HRH, however, was not ahead of its time. Ostrich farmers had been telling insurers this for some time when they asked, as noted earlier, "Why do I pay the same rate as my neighbor down the road, the one who has a history of losing so many birds?"

The obvious answer was to address the trends in a careful manner. With help from board members of the American Ostrich Association, a program was put

Figure 1. Typical bird insurance application. (Courtesy HRH Insurance of Amarillo)

into place with written conditions for insuring birds.

Simple things (like having pens large enough to lessen the risk of a bird hitting them, requiring shelter when the region's weather called for it, and prohibiting gaps in fences or gates) were codified and sent to interested insurers. People with a history of good loss ratios were rewarded, as well as those with experience.

The result was predictable. Common-sense methods of farm management are actually bringing insurance rates down.

Let us now look at what is required when insuring birds.

An application (Figure 1). This can take many forms. Usually it describes the farm, fencing and other facilities. It also usually asks for a description of the birds, including sex, age, laying record, purchase price, insured value, and verified microchip number. This form is signed by the insured.

Veterinary certificate (Figure 2). To be filled out by the attending veterinarian, this is a brief evaluation of the bird's overall health.

Blood work. Some agents require blood work to be done on all insured birds, at least once. The requirements here are a question for your agent. This topic has been debated for some time as to validity and consistency. Some veterinarians are hesitant about the procedure, and most bird owners do not want blood drawn during breeding season.

Some insurers may also require things such as a history of losses, pictures of the farm, drawings of the farm's layout, and detailed descriptions of the farm.

CONCLUSION

The future of the American ostrich industry holds great promise. As it matures, insurers will need to respond with new products that address the needs of a production market. The nature of the birds that will be insured will change, as well as the insured's purpose in insuring the flock.

We hope that the future will find insurers listening to the industry's needs and being ready to respond with innovative, affordable products.

Name of owner:

VETERINARIAN'S EXAMINATION
(NOT REQUIRED FOR NAMED PERILS INSURANCE)

Microchip # Required — *I have examined the following bird(s) and have seen them in motion:*

A) ________ Sex ____ B) ________ Sex ____ C) ________ Sex ____ D) ________ Sex ____

To the best of your knowledge answer all questions, explain any adverse answers and give bird number.

Birds alert & active? ____ Any eye problems? ____ Cataracts? ____ Conjunctivitis? ____ Ocular Discharge____ Corneal Ulcer ____

Eye Bruising? ____ History of GI problems? ____ Any beak abnormalities? ____ Any feather abnormalities ____

Lice or mites? ____ Wounds? ____ Moulting?____ Is appetite normal?____ Any signs of anorexia?____

Any weight problems? ____ Any lameness? ____ Leg pointed out?____ Rolled toe? ____ Curled toe? ____

Splay leg? ____ Bowed tarsometatarsus? ____ Old fractures? ____ Tibiotarsal rotation? ____ Rickets? ____

Joint swelling? ____ Slipped tendons? ____ Twisted neck? ____ Feces normal? ____ Any signs of diarrhea? ____

Urine normal? ____ Polyuria? ____ Urate color normal? ____ Any sign of blood in urates? ____ Is abdomen normal? ____

Temperature – Normal ____ Y/N ____ F Proventricularis: ❑ Normal; Palpated ❑ Yes ❑ No Conformation: ❑ Good ❑ Average ❑ Poor

Any egg retention problems? ____ Any history of being egg bound? ____ Any abnormal shelled eggs? ____ Yolk sac retention? ____

Impaction? ____ Abdominal swelling? ____ Any abnormal heart sounds? ____ Any respiratory system problems ____ Cyanosis? ____

If female, is she actively laying? ____ # of fertile eggs? ____ If male, is he mating and fertile? ____ Male Fertility percentage ____

Any vices or objectionable habits? ____ Any contagious/infectious diseases on the premises? ____ Any blood work or lab test been performed? ____

If yes, show results ____ Note any recent illness, recent medication, dietary problems ____

In your opinion, do these birds need: Shelter? ____ Heat? ____

Comments and explanations to abnormalities; negative answers or previous surgeries: ____

Note any bird that in your opinion is in poor health ____

Please rate on a scale of 1 to 5, 5 being the best, the following: protection from dogs, ____, dryness ____, warmth ____, objects that can injure birds ____, and ventilation ____

In your opinion or to your knowledge are there any medical facts that should be brought to the attention of the company or affect insurability of birds? ____

Additional Comments: ____

Date ____ Signature of Veterinarian ____

Address ____

Office Phone#____ State License # ____

VETERINARY CERTIFICATES ARE NOT ACCEPTABLE UNLESS COMPLETED WITHIN 15 DAYS PRIOR TO BEING RECEIVED

Figure 2. Typical veterinarian's examination certificate. (Courtesy HRH Insurance of Amarillo).

TAX CONSIDERATIONS FOR RATITE RANCHERS

Walter G. Miller, CPA
Dennis L. Sisson, CPA
©Miller and Schroeder, CPAs, Ltd.
Fayetteville, Arkansas

This chapter will discuss the important income-tax considerations related to ratite ranching.

The chapter is divided into three sections: definitions and qualifications; an example of tax planning for an unincorporated ratite rancher; and an example of tax planning for a more advanced S-corporation ratite rancher.

WHO IS A RANCHER?

Qualifying as a rancher, or farmer, for federal income tax purposes, is not always simple.

No meaningful discussion of farm income tax planning can begin without a clear understanding of the governing rules and characteristics required of taxpayers who claims to be operating a *for profit* farming operation.

Farmers must participate in the growing process and bear the risk of loss.

ACCOUNTING METHODS

Farmers may use the cash method of accounting, or the accrual method for tax purposes, and either method for lenders.

Farming corporations must use the accrual method of accounting unless they are S corporation or a family-controlled corporation with gross receipts of $25 million or less.

A cash/accrual *hybrid accounting method* may be used when inventories (animals purchased for resale) are a significant operating factor. The choice of accounting method is very basic and important to the ratite farmer. It should be selected only after careful consultation with a qualified tax professional.

REPORTING OF INVENTORY

The *cost* method to value inventory (animals purchased for resale) is common for accrual method farmers wherein mature animals purchased are valued at cost, and immature animals purchased are valued at cost plus additional expenditures, such as feed, until maturity.

Cash-method farmers cannot expense the cost of inventory held for resale until the year in which the sale occurs.

REPORTING BREEDING STOCK

Sales of livestock held primarily for sale (whether they are purchased or raised) are reported as ordinary income on Schedule F of the farmer's income tax return. All gains are subject to self-employment tax, with acquisition costs reported as a deduction in the year of the sale.

Sales of livestock held primarily for breeding purposes are reported as unearned income on Form 4797 when sold, instead of Schedule F. These gains on sales are not subject to self-employment tax.

Raised breeding stock, held over one year (two years for horses and cattle) and sold, are reported as capital gain under Internal Revenue Code (IRC) Section 1231, limiting the federal taxation rate to 28%.

The intended use of the animal, at the acquisition date, determines whether the sale is reported on Schedule F or Form 4797. Substantial self-employment taxes can hinge on this intent. I recommend my clients keep a detailed journal that identifies the particular animal, records the acquisition date and purchase price, and clearly discloses the intended use for the animal.

BOARDING FACILITIES

Unincorporated landlords, who *materially* participate in the activity of raising animals, are farmers under the federal income tax rules and should report all income received in the ordinary course of farming on Schedule F, subject to self-employment tax.

Rents received by *non-participating* landlords are not *earned* income and should be reported on Schedule E as rental income, not subjecting it to self-employment taxes.

Investors who buy interests in animals, but do not regularly participate in the activity, may be classified as either *passive* farmers or investors. Landlords who are selling these investment interests must be careful not to violate state and/or federal securities laws. Legal counsel, experienced in securities matters, should be consulted whenever a farmer considers bringing in operating capital from other equity sources.

FARM EXPENSE DEDUCTIONS

If expenditures are for both business and personal purposes, the unincorporated farmer must allocate all common expenditures between each purpose and reduce farm business deductions accordingly.

Typical allocable expenditure items include:
- the personal consumption of raised products,
- interest expense on both the residence and the farm,
- real estate taxes on the residence and the farm,
- insurance premiums on the residence and the farm,
- utilities on the residence and the farm, and
- professional fees, including legal, tax and accounting.

Vehicle deductions should be supported by a mileage log to establish the business-use percentage, whether the *actual expense* method or the *standard mileage rate* (29 cents per mile in 1994) is used to determine the deduction.

Farmers may select the 75% business-use *safe harbor* and eliminate substantiation requirements.

Contrary to the general income tax prohibition against cash-basis taxpayers taking current deductions for payment of future expenses, cash-basis farmers may deduct certain (i.e. feed) prepaid expenses, subject to 50% statutory prepaid-deduction limitations.

SECTION 179 DEDUCTION

Up to $17,500 of the cost of IRC Section 1245, tangible property such as mature breeding stock and equipment may be expensed in the year it is first placed into service, subject to trade or business income limitations. Actively conducted rental activity results (profits or losses) are also included within the income limitation computation.

DEPRECIATION

Generally, farmers are limited to the *150% declining balance* depreciation method on personal property, and to the *straight-line* method on real property.

Although *mid-quarter* or *short-tax-year* considerations may limit the regular depreciation deduction, the Sec. 179 deduction is not prorated.

Certain leases must also be depreciated and are treated as sales contracts (asset purchases) instead of rentals. These are classified as *capital* leases under the tax rules, instead of operating leases.

Ostriches, emus, and rheas belong to the 7-year class life and recovery period for depreciation purposes.

PASSIVE ACTIVITY LOSSES

A passive activity is any trade or business in which the taxpayer does not materially participate, or any rental activity.

Passive activity losses (PALs) are generally deductible only against income from passive activities. They may also be carried over indefinitely and used to offset gain realized upon disposition.

Rental real estate activities, for actively participating owners, have a $25,000 loss exemption from limitations.

Material participation is regular, continuous and substantial involvement in the activity. The landlord in a crop-share arrangement is not conducting a rental activity for PAL purposes according to IRS regulations. Form 4835 instructions, however, state that a crop-share is a rental activity. The Form 4835 instructions are generally more beneficial to a taxpayer and would allow loss deductions up to $25,000.

Non-material participating, absentee bird owners may not qualify as *farmers*. Instead, their investment will probably be considered a *capital* investment, like any other risky venture (i.e. buying and selling publicly-traded corporate stock). Investment deduction treatment and limitations could apply to these ratite owners.

BASIS AND AT-RISK LOSS

Generally, early-year loss deductions from farming activities will be limited to the sum of cash contributions, basis in non-cash contributions, and loans borrowed by the taxpayer for use in the activity. Suspended losses (just like PALs) may be carried over indefinitely and may be used to offset gain on disposition.

LIVESTOCK INSTALLMENT SALES

With the exception of depreciation recapture, brood animal sales can be reported using the *installment* method for tax purposes. The sale of inventory animals under deferred payment terms, however, is considerably more complex. Income recognition determination is subject to numerous variables. Consult your tax professional on this matter.

FIRST-TIME FARMERS

You are not in the animal-breeding and offspring-sale farming business until you have mature animals.

If you start a ratite farm with chicks you are planning to raise only for breeding, you cannot begin deducting any of your farm expenses until those immature birds are old enough to be placed into service as breeding stock. It is our firm's position that this period of time is what the IRS refers to as the *preparatory period* discussed within Reg § 1.162.12(b)(3).

All the expenses (i.e. feed, medicines, etc.) directly related to raising those birds must be capitalized, added to the birds' original costs, and depreciated over the depreciable life of the birds, after they reach maturity.

No other expenses, such as depreciation, IRC Section 179 deductions, labor, utilities, etc. can be deducted until the breeding chicks reach maturity and the farming operation actually begins (for income tax purposes—IRC Section 162).

You are not in the animal-breeding and offspring-sale farming business until you have mature animals.

Depreciation on equipment, buildings and other depreciable assets starts when the business begins (the birds start breeding).

All other costs during the preparatory period are considered *start-up* costs and must be capitalized or amortized over 60 months, beginning in the month that birds start breeding and the farming operation officially commences.

A livestock-breeding operation starting with at least some birds purchased as inventory for resale will avoid the preparatory-period suspension of certain operating deductions.

If a farm is started in mid-year, depreciation is limited to that pro-rata portion of the year. The end of the preparatory period and the commencement of a farming activity (or *development* period) commonly cause a *short tax year*.

The amortization of start-up costs cannot begin until the month that business begins and must be elected in writing on the current year tax return (IRC Section 195).

OWNERS OF EXISTING FARMS

An existing farm can buy chicks to be raised for breeding and deduct all normal farming expenses currently. It still must capitalize the actual cost of birds purchased for breeding, until they mature and are put into service.

Since the taxpayer is already in the business of farming (presumably), the farmer does not have to wait until the birds reach maturity to deduct operating expenses (other than depreciation on the immature birds).

HOBBY-LOSS ISSUE

It is not uncommon for the IRS to contend that a business that is showing repeated losses over a period of years is a *hobby* instead of a business. As a hobby, no losses are deductible.

There are 9 factors listed in code IRC Section 183 that are used to make the hobby vs. business determination:

- manner in which the taxpayer carries on the activity,
- the expertise of the taxpayer and his advisors,
- the time and effort expended by the taxpayer in carrying on the activity,
- expectation that assets used in the activity may appreciate in value,
- the success of the taxpayer in carrying on other similar or dissimilar activities,
- the taxpayer's history of income or losses with respect to the activity,
- the amount of occasional profits, if any, which are earned,
- the financial status of the taxpayer,
- elements of personal pleasure or recreation.

Nothing in the law states that you must make a profit in any business. The law states that in order to deduct losses from an activity you must have a *profit motive* and act accordingly (Edward and Kathleen Holbrook v. Commissioner, TC Memo 1993-383, 66 TCM 484, Filed August 24, 1993).

IRC Section 183 allows an election by the taxpayer to have a *safe harbor* apply. This safe harbor states that, if the business makes a profit in three out of five years, the business is automatically deemed *for profit*. The five-year period begins with the first year you are in business.

The easiest way to prevent your farm losses from being disallowed is to be sure that you are running the farm in a business-like manner, with good records and sensible expenditures.

If the IRS does challenge your losses, you can make the election under IRC Section 183 to have the safe-harbor apply.

If you do this, the returns for the first five years of your farming will be audited at the end of the five-year period. This election is generally made during the audit or appeals process.

COMPARISON OF ADVANTAGES AND DISADVANTAGES OF COMMON BUSINESS ENTITIES

ADVANTAGES	DISADVANTAGES
SOLE PROPRIETORSHIP	
Simplicity	Personal liability
Economical formation	Lack of continuity
Control	No fringe benefits to proprietor
Family wages and fringe benefits	Self-employment tax
Non-taxable dissolution (generally)	Title ambiguities
PARTNERSHIP	
Less complex than incorporation (generally)	Partner authority
Multiple ownership	Joint liability with partners
Partner authority	No fringe benefits to partners
Inside basis step-up	Self-employment tax
Non-taxable dissolution (generally)	Additional tax return
Limited partnerships	
Special allocations of income and deductions	
S CORPORATION	
Limited liability	Formation costs
Ownership transferability	Limited asset access
Indefinite life	Dissolution complexities
No self-employment taxes	No fringe benefits to 2% shareholders
Loss pass-through	Taxable dissolution
Single dissolution tax	Income pass-through
Income shifting	
C CORPORATION	
Limited Liability	Formation costs
Ownership transferability	Limited asset access
Indefinite life	Dissolution complexities
Fringe benefits	Double taxation of dividends and at dissolution
Lower tax rates	
LIMITED LIABILITY COMPANY	
Limited liability	Formation costs
Multiple ownership	Not available in all states
Inside basis step-up	New governing laws
Special allocations of income and deductions	Potential self-employment tax
Member authority	Governing instrument construction complexities

The election can also be made by filing a statement with your tax return. (This is not advised by our firm.)

Even if you do not make profits after making the election, you can still use the nine factors to determine the deductibility of losses.

CHOICE OF ENTITY

Farming business entity alternatives include:
- sole proprietorship,
- partnership,
- S corporation,
- C corporation, and
- limited liability company.

See the accompanying table for the advantages and disadvantages of each of these entities.

TAX PLANNING

Before presenting an example of tax planning for an unincorporated ratite rancher, we must first examine some of the considerations which have a bearing in this type of situation.

COMMODITY WAGES

Wages to farm employees, in the form of non-cash commodities, are exempt from social security, federal withholding, and unemployment taxes.

There should be an employment agreement, issuance of Form W-2 at year-end reflecting the fair market value of the commodity, and documentation of the commodity title transfer to the employee before the sale of the commodity by the employee.

Attention to detail is extremely important to defend against an IRS employment tax attack.

SPOUSAL WAGES AND BENEFITS

Bona fide wages paid to the farmer's spouse can reduce danger of an IRS family partnership assertion, provide support for the deduction of spouse's business travel expenses, and allow a 100%

deduction for tax-free medical insurance and reimbursement fringe benefits provided to the spousal employee, with extended coverage to include spousal employer.

PAYMENT OF RENT TO SPOUSE

Bona-fide rent payments made to an unincorporated farmer's spouse for the spouse's interest in the jointly-owned property can save substantial self-employment taxes. There should exist:
- a written lease,
- reasonable rentals, with checks actually paid to the spouse by the tenant,
- spouse's deductions for spouse's share of interest, taxes, etc. on the spouse's Schedule E and actually paid by spouse to the creditors, and
- IRS Form 1099 for rents paid to the spouse issued by the tenant at year-end.

MEALS AND LODGING

Farmers can provide tax-free meals and lodging to employees, if the fringe benefits are necessary for the farming business. Such qualified expenses are deductible by the farmer and excludable from gross income by the employee.

MORE ON PAYROLL-TAX-FREE COMMODITY WAGES

One of the issues addressed earlier in this writing was the concept of paying farm workers in non-cash commodity wages instead of cash. The primary advantage is the fact that the Internal Revenue Code specifically states that non-cash wages paid for agricultural labor are exempt from all withholding and social security taxes.

The exemption from social security is an automatic savings in payroll costs of 15.3% of wages. Commodity wages include payments made in the form of raised farm products such as grain, milk, and livestock.

EXAMPLE

Self-employed farmer Jones pays his/her spouse $12,000 in commodity wages (not subject to payroll taxes), later sold by the spousal employee at a $10 capital gain, and claims a Schedule F employee benefit deduction for spouse's family health insurance of $3,000 with another $2,000 for reimbursed out-of-pocket medical expenses.

In addition, the farmer pays his/her spouse $6,000 annual rent for the spouse's 50% ownership interest in the assets used in the farming operation. The farmer also hires his/her fifteen-year-old dependent child and pays the child $3,500, in social-security-exempt wages (even if paid in cash), for work actually performed. Farm profits before the described deductions are $60,000.

1993	OPTION #1	OPTION #2
Spousal Wage	0	$ 12,000
Schedule F	$ 60,000	60,000
Less: Spousal wage	0	(12,000)
Spousal rent	0	(6,000)
Health Insurance	0	(3,000)
Medical reimbursements	0	(2,000)
Dependent's wages	0	(3,500)
Schedule D(comm. sale)	0	10
Schedule E (rents)	0	6,000
25% health insurance	(750)	0
IRA (spouse)	0	(2,000)
50% SE tax	(4,239)	(2,367)
Standard deduction	(6,200)	(6,200)
Exemptions	(7,050)	(7,050)
Taxable income	$ 41,761	$ 33,893
Tax	$ 6,900	$ 5,081
SE tax	8,478	4,733
Total tax	$ 15,378	$ 9,814
Annual Tax Savings		$ 5,564

One beneficial use of this tax-saving provision in the law is the payment of wages to a spousal employee. If you have an unincorporated farming operation, such wages can create significant savings in self-employment tax.

Commodity wages should consist only of farm products which you have raised. Because of this, you will have no *tax basis* in the commodity.

When the commodity is paid as a wage, your farm must recognize income and deduct labor expense in the same amounts as the wage reported to the employee on form W-2 at year-end. There are two disadvantages to this tax saving strategy, however.

The first is the fact that the employee does not receive credit for social security paid in on the commodity wages. The second is the fact that it is considered to be an aggressive position to take on your income tax return.

Our research indicates that the IRS has been challenging the social security exemption for commodity wages wherever possible, even though the Internal Revenue Code clearly states that they are legal.

The primary focus of the IRS attack appears to be the factual determination as to the economic substance of the transaction.

The IRS can target any transaction which does not follow the strict form of transferring title in the commodity to the employee prior to its sale. It is very important that the employee assume title and the related risk of loss before the commodity sale takes place.

There are a number of IRS national office rulings which have disallowed commodity wage social security exemptions where risk of loss was never truly transferred to the employee, or where the sale took place on the same day as the transfer of the commodity to the employee.

However, there have also been rulings where the exemption is allowed. The deciding factor in these cases is generally whether title and risk of loss in connection with the commodity are passed to the employee prior to the time that he/she sells it.

The IRS District Director in Indiana issued a statement in March 1992 indicating that that office will challenge the social security exemption for commodity wages. The statement goes on to say that the IRS interprets the social security exemption to apply only to nominal non-cash payments, and that the title and risk of loss issues are irrelevant in determining whether commodity payments are the equivalent of cash. Cash wages are subject to all employment taxes.

At this point, no official challenge has been made, and the director of one IRS district does not

PROCEDURES FOR USE WHEN WAGES ARE PAID IN COMMODITIES

1. Prepare a written employment contract between yourself (the employer) and your employee, setting out all aspects of your agreement, including the fact that you will pay commodity wages from time to time. Our research has indicated that the commodity wages paid, which are for farm work, are exempt from all withholding, employer's share of social security and medicare, and federal unemployment taxes. However, there are two exceptions where unemployment taxes are required. The first is if cash agricultural wages of $20,000 or more are paid during any calendar quarter. Payment of commodity wages should eliminate any concern about this exception. The second is if you have 10 or more workers employed on the farm.

2. It is very important that certain procedures be followed when paying commodity wages.
- The employment contract should clearly state the type and quantity of the commodity to be paid each year. The contract should state that the employee has complete control and risk of loss with respect to the care, marketing and sale of the commodity after it is transferred from the employer to the employee as wages. As a result of this risk, the ultimate sale of the commodity should not be delayed unreasonably.
- Title in the commodity should be transferred some period of time prior to the sale of the commodity by the employee. In other words, the perception that the transaction is nothing more than a payment with something that is immediately converted to cash should be avoided.
- To accomplish this, the employee should find his/her own buyer for the commodity, and should do so after the transfer from the employer to the employee has occurred. Under no circumstances, should the employer find the buyer and handle the sales transaction. It should be clear, both in writing and perception to both the buyer and seller, that the buyer is dealing with the employee and not the employer.
- Title in the commodity should be transferred by way of a bill of sale or other documentation, in both the commodity wage payment and the subsequent sale to the unrelated buyer.
- During the time between the transfer of the commodity and its sale by the employee, the employee should reimburse the employer for the expense of caring for the commodity within the employer's facilities. This should also be evidenced by a written contract in which a stated reimbursement is established. The reimbursement should be paid by the employee writing a check to the employer in accordance with the understandings within a written contract.

3. Records of all commodities paid to employees should show date of transfer, the specific commodities transferred, the fair market value of the commodities, and the method of determining fair market value.

4. It is a good idea to have only a portion of the employee's wages paid in commodities to avoid the appearance that the only reason for paying commodity wages is to avoid taxes.

5. We also believe it would be wise to include a statement in the employment agreement which makes it very clear to the employee that no social security taxes will be paid on the commodity wages and that this could, in turn, reduce the amount of social security benefits the employee is entitled to receive in the future. These wages do, however, make the employee eligible to contribute to a deductible IRA.

speak for the entire organization. However, care should be taken when considering this tax strategy, and you should consult with your tax specialist before paying commodity wages.

CORPORATE FARMERS

If you are an employee/shareholder in a farming corporation, you should consider another point when deciding whether or not to pay commodity wages to yourself. Generally speaking, most people incorporate their businesses in order to protect themselves, personally, from business liabilities.

If one of the liabilities you are concerned about is the potential for lawsuits over the sale of livestock, receiving commodity wages consisting of livestock could, once again, expose you to that liability.

If, after considering the risks, you decide to receive a commodity wage of this type, it may be a good idea to structure your wage in a way that limits your exposure to liability as much as possible.

This could be accomplished either by receiving a large number of low-value animals, therefore reducing the amount of each sale that may be contested later, or receiving a few higher-value animals and selling them to a buyer with whom you feel secure.

The decision concerning which of these methods is right for you should be made only after your situation has been thoroughly reviewed. The type of livestock you raise can also be a significant factor. If you raise livestock with sales prone to litigation, receiving them as commodity wages from your corporation would probably be unwise.

If shareholder/employees are being paid in commodities, it is advisable to pay other, unrelated employees, a portion of their wages in commodities as well in order to help establish that the transaction is not solely for the purpose of avoiding taxes on shareholders.

Finally, it is important to remember that paying commodity wages should only be undertaken after careful consultation with your tax professional.

RENT PAYMENTS TO SPOUSE

Now that we have more carefully addressed the strategy of reducing self-employment tax and/or payroll tax expense by paying wages in the form of commodities rather than in the form of cash, I would like to discuss the strategy of deducting rental payments made to a spouse for your business use of the spouse's half of jointly owned property.

This strategy, first given approval by the IRS in 1974, has been reinforced in 1993 by a decision in Tax Court. As with the payment of commodity wages, it is important that this strategy only be used on your tax return if you have followed all the procedures suggested and only after discussing the strategy (as it applies to your particular situation) with your tax professional.

TAX COURT RULINGS
Facts

There are two taxpayers, husband and wife, who jointly own a piece of farm business property. It is assumed to be real estate. The husband operates a ratite-farming sole proprietorship which uses the jointly-owned property for farming-business purposes.

Question

Can the husband deduct rent payments made to his wife for his business use of her 50% share of the jointly-owned property as an expense on his Schedule F, and thereby avoid paying self-employment tax on that amount of income?

Findings

In 1974, the IRS issued Revenue Ruling 74-209, which allowed a husband to deduct rental payments he made to his wife for his business use of her share of jointly-owned property as an expense on his Schedule C. In this ruling, the husband paid a fair rental value to his wife and they reported their incomes on separately filed income-tax returns. No mention is made in the ruling as to whether the determination would have been different if a joint return had been filed.

In Technical Advice Memorandum 9206008, the IRS ruled that, where the same situation existed (except that all the expenses related to the real property, such as taxes, interest, etc., were deducted on the husband's Schedule C rather than being allocated in part to the wife's Schedule E as rental expenses), the arrangement lacked an arms-length landlord-tenant relationship, and did not qualify for the deduction of the rental payments as Schedule C expenses.

These rulings by the IRS are based upon the long-standing position of the IRS that income from property held in joint tenancy is taxable to the tenants in proportion to their respective interests in the property.

In T.C. Memo 1993-326, July 22, 1993, the Tax Court ruled that a taxpayer could deduct, as a business expense against self-employment income, payments made for one-half of the fair rental value of property owned jointly by him and his spouse. The court ruled that the husband could deduct the rental payments to his spouse because they represented payment for his use of her ownership interest in the property. The taxpayers in this case did file a joint tax return.

Analysis

These rulings indicate that the IRS will accept rental payments to a spouse for business use of jointly-held property, if the transaction is structured in the form of an arms-length, landlord-tenant relationship.

For those who are not familiar with tax terminology, the term *arms-length* is used to describe a situation where two or more related parties enter into a transaction with the transaction being essentially the same as it would have been with an unrelated party.

Whenever the IRS sees a transaction between parties who are related or for some reason have financial interests which would indicate they might tend to give each other favorable financial treatment, it takes a much closer look at the transaction to determine if it has the economic substance which would be present in the same transaction between unrelated parties.

If the IRS finds that a transaction is not at arms-length (i.e. lacks the economic substance of a transaction between unrelated parties), it may disallow any favorable tax treatment the transaction has created. In the example we are using, the IRS would disallow the deduction of rental payments to one's spouse and increase self-employment tax on the return (along with interest and possibly penalties).

Recommendations

In order to use the strategy of paying rent to your spouse for your farming business use of jointly-owned property, thereby reducing self-employment tax, we advise that certain procedures be strictly adhered to.

This strategy is only suitable for taxpayers who use the sole proprietorship (unincorporated) form of doing business. The following procedures are suggested:

- A fair rental should be determined, an amount which the property would likely bring if rented to an unrelated party. The rent must be paid by check at least annually, and the payee spouse must have total control of the funds after payment. The funds should not be deposited into an account over which the payor has control or signature authority.
- Title to the real estate must include the name of the receiving spouse. Having property solely in the name of the receiving spouse is acceptable, and could allow for higher rent payments.
- A written lease agreement should be prepared.
- Payment of the spouse's portion of principal and interest on real estate debt should be the responsibility of the payee spouse, with the interest deducted on the spouse's Schedule E.
- The spouse's portion of real estate taxes also should be paid and deducted by the landlord-spouse (unless the lease term provides for a *net lease* arrangement where the rent is reduced by the amount of any expenses).
- A Form 1099-MISC should be issued by the tenant-spouse to the landlord-spouse (with a copy to the IRS) reflecting the amount of rent paid each year.
- The rental income must be reported on a Schedule E by the landlord-spouse.

For a better understanding of how this strategy works, see the example in the box below.

Assume you have a net farm profit of $50,000 and no other income. This entire $50,000 would be subject to the self-employment tax of 15.3% (due to the calculation used in determining self-employment income, the actual rate of the self-employment tax is 92.35% of the 15.3% rate, or 14.13%). Also assume that you use real estate in the farming operation which is jointly owned by you and your spouse and has a total fair-rental value of $20,000 per year.

As a part of the strategy, you will need to report one-half of the expenses related to the property, such as taxes and interest, to the Schedule E of your spouse. For this example, we will assume that total expenses are $2,000.

	NO RENT PAID	RENT PAID
Net Farm Profit	$ 50,000	$ 50,000
Payment of Rent to Spouse (1/2 of $20,000 Fair Rental)	0	(10,000)
Allocation of Expenses (1/2 of $2,000 total expenses)*	0	1,000
Self-Employment Income	$ 50,000	$ 41,000
Self-Employment Tax Rate	X 14.13%	X 14.13%
Self-Employment Tax	$ 7,065	$ 5,793
Self-Employment Tax Savings		$ 1,272

* The expenses allocable to the spouse's share of the property must be deducted on the spouse's Schedule E. As a result, that portion is not allowed as a farm expense and must be added back to farm income. Since this strategy has no effect on income taxes, the Schedule E has not been shown to illustrate the rental income and expenses it would reflect.

Because the retention of this deduction, during an IRS examination, will depend upon proper procedures and legal documentation, do not attempt this without proper professional guidance.

Now that we have completed our discussion of some of the tax saving opportunities available to the unincorporated ratite farmer, in the following pages we will turn our attention to other tax benefits available to the S corporation ratite-farming operation.

S CORP TAX SAVINGS

The public accounting profession is working with an ever-increasing number of farming S corporations. Along with this increase, we are also seeing more and more farmers who do not understand how to take full advantage of the tax benefits of an S corporation, nor how to prevent some of the major pitfalls which can occur if certain precautions are not taken. As a result of this, my remaining comments in this writing will deal exclusively with S corporations.

Following the *benefits* discussion section is an example which illustrates how, with proper planning, a farming S corporation can save nearly $14,000 in federal taxes per year when compared to a farm proprietorship, each making a $100,000 profit (before owner compensation).

BENEFITS OF S CORPORATIONS

Although the *corporate veil* (limiting liability to the shareholder/owners) can be a very compelling reason for forming a corporation, there are additional tax benefits available to an S corporation which can often be reasons enough to form the entity. These benefits include income shifting, reducing payroll/self-employment taxes, and favorable tax treatment during liquidation.

Income Shifting

Income shifting is accomplished by making a transfer (gift) of a portion of the stock of an S corporation to other family members (usually children), who are in lower tax brackets. Since S corporation profits are taxed at the shareholder level, such a transfer can effectively lower the amount of tax paid on the income related to the gifted portion of the stock.

This is a popular strategy for parents with college-age (or high school) children who require significant amounts of money for the students' upkeep and tuition. (Watch out for the 50% support dependency test, however.)

The end result is that all taxes saved serve as a federal *subsidy* or *grant* of money available to help pay for the children's education.

There is one potential drawback to this strategy, however. In order to shift the income to the children, you must make an unrestricted gift of the stock to the children and the corporation must make proportionate dividend (or liquidating) distributions to them, henceforth.

If this is not done, the IRS may assert that the corporation has more than one class of stock (by the appearance of preference to certain shareholders) and terminate the S election.

The best way we have found for the *majority* shareholders (parents) to protect themselves when making gifts of stock in their closely-held farming corporations to their children, is to have all stock in the corporation subject to a shareholder agreement which provides for optional redemption of any of the corporation's stock under certain conditions. Shareholder agreements are discussed in more detail later in this chapter.

Reducing Payroll and Self Employment Taxes

Unlike sole proprietorships and general partnerships, whose profits are also taxed at the individual's level, S corporation profits are not subject to the 15.3% self-employment tax.

However, Internal Revenue Code Section 3121(d)(1) provides that an officer of a corporation, who provides services to the corporation as an officer, is an employee of the corporation, and, accordingly, must receive *reasonable* compensation.

Since S corporation profits are not subject to self-employment tax, but wages are subject to social security (unless they are non-cash commodity wages), we, unfortunately, often see S corporations with substantial profits, but no wages paid to participating shareholders in an effort to avoid payroll taxes altogether.

If this comes to the attention of the IRS, the reviewing revenue agent may assert that all distributions to the shareholders are disguised wages, resulting in the assessment of social security taxes, interest, and potential penalties.

An easy way to avoid this (and still save self-employment taxes) is to pay yourself (as a shareholder/employee) a *reasonable* salary. If your corporation has other employees and/or capital assets, that help to generate the income of the farm (leveraging), it can be argued successfully that the distributions of the remaining profits from the corporation are non-taxable dividend distributions rather than wages.

A *reasonable* wage is defined as the wage which one would expect to pay a person with similar skills to perform a similar job. We normally suggest that shareholders and employees clip help-wanted ads from local newspapers to provide evidence of what other farmers are paying employees for similar work. The goal is to pay the smallest reasonable wage to the shareholder/employee in order to minimize payroll taxes.

By doing this, it is possible to have a substantial portion of your S corporation profits avoid the additional 15.3% social security tax (or self-employment tax normally due from unincorporated farming operations).

Of course, this savings is reduced to only 2.9% if the shareholder's salary is required to be greater than the 1994 social security cap of $60,600.

Liquidation

One of the lesser-known parts of the Tax Reform Act of 1986 was the repeal of the General Utilities Doctrine. This doctrine had provided that, when a corporation's assets were transferred to shareholders in exchange for their stock, the exchange was considered as payment for the stock and did not create a taxable event at the corporate level. With the repeal of this doctrine, when a regular C corporation exchanges assets for outstanding stock, there are two taxable transactions.

First, the corporation is deemed to have sold the assets to a third party for fair market value, which will often create a taxable gain at the corporate level.

Second, the shareholders are deemed to have been paid the fair market value of the assets in exchange for their stock. This can also result in a taxable gain at the shareholder level.

Here is where S corporations are preferable. A liquidating distribution does require that the assets be considered *sold*, with the resulting gain or loss passed through to the shareholder(s) on the K-1.

But because S corporation shareholders can withdraw their entire investment and accumulated profits from the corporation without it being taxed a second time, the repeal of the General Utilities Doctrine has no effect.

Although this may not seem to be very important, we see many corporate farm clients who, for one reason or another, would like to make either a partial or total distribution of assets to shareholders. If they are not S corporations, the tax cost of these transactions can be substantial. If they are S corporations, the tax effect is often greatly reduced.

The table on this page shows the savings which can be generated by an S corporation.

Note: In this example, the taxpayer could not afford to fund IRAs for himself/herself, a spousal IRA, or IRAs for the children (prior to the tax savings illustrated) because of the $27,276 of taxes due with the return.

The savings shown allow full funding of all four deductible IRA accounts, which can grow tax-deferred until retirement.

In addition, prior to using the S corporation strategy, the taxpayer would have been allowed a maximum IRA contribution of only $2,250 (taxpayer and non-working spouse).

$5,263 in social security taxes have been saved by paying all wages in payroll-tax-free commodity wages.

EXAMPLE OF S-CORPORATION TAX SAVINGS

Assume that you have a ratite ranch, which has 1993 profits of $100,000, and no other income. In this activity, you (or you and your spouse) are the majority shareholder(s) and you perform all management duties on the ranch.

A substantial part of the work, which brings in money from your customers, is also done by employees who are not shareholders, and/or you have made substantial contributions of revenue-generating assets to the corporation.

You also have two children in college who require a constant flow of money. Your children also work summers on the ranch. All of the family wages are paid in non-cash commodities. You believe in IRAs more than you do in Social Security.

1993	PROPRIETORSHIP	S CORP
Annual Profits	$ 100,000	$ 100,000
Commodity Wages to You	0	(25,000)
Commodity Wages to Spouse	0	(2,000)
Commodity Wages to Children	0	(7,400)
Business Profit	$ 100,000	$ 65,600
20% Profits Shifted to Children	0	(13,120)
Salary from above	0	27,000
1/2 of S.E. Tax	(4,910)	0
IRA Deductions	0	(4,000)
Adjusted Gross Income	$ 95,090	$ 75,480
Standard Deduction	(6,200)	(6,200)
4 Exemptions (FUTA omitted)	(9,400)	(9,400)
Taxable Income	$ 79,490	$ 59,880
Income Tax	17,456	11,968
Self-Employment Tax	9,820	0
Tax on Children's Income		
$ 7,400 W-2 Income		
13,120 20% of Profits		
(4,000) IRAs		
(7,400) Standard Deduction		
9,120 Taxable Income		
X 15% Tax Bracket		
$ 1,368 Tax	0	1,368
Totals	$ 27,276	$ 13,336
Annual Tax Savings		$ 13,940

ELECTING S STATUS

In order to elect S status, a corporation must file Form 2553 with the IRS within 2.5 months of the beginning of the tax year for which the election is made. To be a valid election, the Form 2553 must be signed and dated by each of the shareholders indicating his/her consent to the election, and also signed and dated by an officer (generally the president) of the corporation, to request the election.

One of the common errors we have observed with invalid S elections for new corporations is the execution of the Form 2553 before the articles of incorporation are perfected at the Secretary of State's office and/or before there are actual shareholders.

A valid S election cannot be made before the beginning of the new corporation's first tax year. A new corporation's first tax year cannot begin before it becomes a legal entity. After *perfection* of the corporate articles, the beginning of the first tax year of a corporation is the earliest of the following:
- the first date the corporation has shareholders,
- the first date the corporation has assets, or
- the date the corporation begins operations.

All of the discussion to this point has focused on the federal requirements for electing S status. Do not forget, however, that many states require that a separate S election be filed with the state taxing authority.

Some states also tax S corporations just like regular corporations. For example, the new Texas Corporate Franchise Tax levies a 4.5% tax on all corporate profits, including S corporation profits.

TAX-FREE INCORPORATION

Internal Revenue Code Section 351 requires that, when a corporation exchanges its stock for property, and the new shareholders own at least 80% of the outstanding stock of the corporation immediately after the transfer, no taxable gain will be recognized by the shareholder in regard to the transfer.

The Regulations require that a disclosure be made on the returns of the shareholders and the corporation for the year of the transfer, which provides detailed information concerning the fair market value and *tax bases* of the assets and liabilities transferred in the exchange.

The goal in most corporate formations is to qualify the transaction as a non-taxable exchange. Therefore, the requirements of IRC Sec. 351 must be known and met by the incorporators. Failure to meet the requirements of this code section could subject the incorporators to substantial income taxes.

Although the non-recognition of gain on qualified transfers is generally mandatory, there are some situations where it is advantageous to fail the requirements intentionally, in order to recognize gain on the transfer of the assets. The following are the most notable of those situations:

- *When appreciated real property is about to be developed.* In this situation, the recognition of gain before the development begins could provide significant tax savings by making the gain a capital gain on investment property rather than ordinary income on developed property.
- *When the shareholder has expiring net operating losses or tax credits and needs to gain some tax benefit from them now rather than lose them forever.* While developing a strategy to make the *realized* gain taxable, care should be taken to insure that the transaction is not challenged by the IRS as being either a disguised sale or thin capitalization.

Internal Revenue Code Section 357(c) requires that income be recognized by the shareholder in an IRC Sec. 351 transfer whenever there are transferred debts greater than the tax bases in the transferred assets. The amount of the gain is the difference between the tax bases in the assets and the larger debt balances in aggregate.

Watch for this carefully. If you transfer a building with an undepreciated tax basis of $50,000, along with a related mortgage of $100,000 (because the building is now worth $150,000) you must recognize and pay tax on a $50,000 gain! Proper professional guidance is essential to the avoidance of this often overlooked tax trap.

MAKING CORPORATE FAILURES FULLY DEDUCTIBLE TO THE SHAREHOLDERS

Although the vast majority of people starting a new corporation believe that their businesses will never fail, the sad fact is that the majority of new small businesses do fail. The general rule for the deductibility of losses on stock limits the deduction to a net capital loss of $3,000 per tax year.

Therefore, if a corporation in which you have invested $75,000 (in exchange for stock) fails, you can generally only deduct $3,000 of the loss per year (carrying forward the unused loss).

Internal Revenue Code Section 1244 provides limited relief for taxpayers in this situation. This investment incentive is designed to *subsidize* the stockholder for certain investment losses with larger immediate tax savings.

If stock is purchased by an individual either for cash or property, and the stock was purchased as an original issuance of stock by the corporation, the taxpayer can deduct his/her basis, up to $100,000 on a joint return and $50,000 on other filing statuses, as an ordinary deduction in the year in which the stock is disposed of or becomes worthless.

This rule applies only to stock in a corporation which has no more than $1,000,000 in capital stock, contributions to capital, and paid-in surplus.

Historically, it has been common for small C corporations to have only a minimal amount of capital and reflect the remainder as loans from shareholders. It was generally done to avoid the dividend double taxation on cash distributions to the investors. This strategy is generally not applicable to S corporations.

Such *thin incorporations* have a significant negative side to them, however. In this situation, only the amount shown as contributions for capital stock would be deductible under IRC Sec. 1244. The IRS would probably assert that the loans from shareholders not only would not qualify for the IRC Sec. 1244 ordinary deduction, but would, in fact, be either non-business bad debts or additional paid-in capital which does not qualify for IRC Sec. 1244 treatment. Both of these treatments could result in capital loss deductions limited to $3,000 per year.

Since IRC Sec. 1244 treatment is limited to issuances of stock, any additional contributions of capital after the start of the corporation, which do not involve the issuance of additional shares of stock, are not eligible.

In addition to the qualification limitations for IRC Sec. 1244 treatment, there are also specific requirements for disclosures which must be made on the individual return when the deduction is taken. The courts have consistently ruled that any deviation from these disclosure requirements is grounds for disallowance of the IRC Sec. 1244 deduction.

WE RECOMMEND

Whenever clients are considering starting a new corporation, we generally encourage them to make sure they are careful to protect themselves and their investments. The following are some of the things we recommend:

1. Consider electing S status. As we have shown, the tax benefits can be substantial.

2. Carefully consider the requirements of a *tax-free* incorporation under IRC Sec. 351. Watch out for the *excess debt* tax trap under IRC Sec. 357(c). Perhaps leasing some assets to the corporation (e.g. farm land and buildings) would be wiser than *contributing* them (create a written lease).

3. Consider placing or retaining valuable assets within whichever entity which has the least business-liability exposure. All business decisions must weigh the tax implications and the legal ramifications.

4. Unless there is only one shareholder, we strongly recommend that a shareholder agreement be in place which sets out specific situations wherein shareholders can be forced to offer and sell their stock to either the corporation or other shareholders.

It should include formulas to determine the amount of the sales price. This arrangement is very useful in a situation where stock has been gifted to a child.

The agreement can state that no person can be a shareholder if he/she is not an employee of the corporation. Then, if the child refuses to work or in some way loses favor with the rest of the family, the family can remove the child from the corporation's employment and then reacquire the child's stock at a pre-set price in order to *preserve and protect* the company.

S CORP REQUIREMENTS

An important element which must be addressed in any discussion of this choice of entity is the types of corporations which are eligible to elect S status. S corporations must:

1. be a domestic corporation;

2. have no more than 35 shareholders;

3. have as shareholders only:
   A. individuals who are citizens or residents of the U.S.,
   B. estates, or
   C. trusts included in
      i. a voting trust,
      ii. a trust under which all income and corpus is treated as owned by a person who is a US citizen or resident, or
      iii. a trust continuing in existence following the death of the deemed owner, but limited to the 60-day period following the date of death (limited to a two-year period if the entire corpus of the trust is includable in the gross estate of the deemed owner);

4. have only one class of stock (differences in voting rights among shares are allowed, but not differences in distribution and liquidation rights).

5. *not* be a financial institution, insurance company, corporation electing to use possessions tax credit, domestic international sales corporation, or member of an affiliated group.

Corporations which revoke S status cannot re-elect for five years.

5. Employment contracts are an important part of reinforcing a position that a shareholder's wages should be limited to some amount which is less than the total cash distributions to the shareholder. They are also important to have in a situation where payroll-tax free commodity wages are paid from a farming corporation.

6. Always make a proper disclosure of the details of an IRC Sec. 351 transfer within the tax returns and the corporate meeting minutes. This will provide evidence supporting the identification of assets that were actually contributed to your corporation. We also recommend creating a bill of sale for these assets showing their transfer to the corporation.

7. For new corporations, be sure to mail all S elections before the 15th day of the 3rd month after the beginning of the tax year of the election. **Never** date or mail an S election before the date that the corporation is actually incorporated (the articles are *file-marked*) and has shareholders. An election which is mailed or dated before either of these dates is invalid and can cost a taxpayer substantial, unexpected tax should the IRS become aware of the election's defect.

8. **Always** remember to look at the disclosure of IRC Sec. 1244 information on your return for the year in which the loss is claimed, and be certain it complies with the information required in the Regulations.

CONCLUSION

If structured properly, ratite-ranch S corporations can provide ranching taxpayers with significant tax and reduced liability exposure benefits.

Please remember that this writing is very general in nature and may not be appropriate to your particular situation. Professional advice should be sought before any of the above strategies are implemented.

NOTES

LEGAL ASPECTS OF RATITE RANCHING

Jack W. Ledbetter
Ledbetter & Benjamin
Attorneys and Counselors at Law
Austin, Texas

The laws governing the conduct of ratite ranchers and the business of ratite ranching are basically the same as those governing other areas of farming and ranching in the United States.

In turn, the laws governing farming and ranching are basically the same as those relating to other businesses, with certain exceptions arising because of the unique nature of ranching and farming.

Farmers and ranchers deal with live and growing products that are created from virtual nothingness, and which grow in value without the necessity of human additions and modifications. Also, since farmers and ranchers deal with living animals and products, they are subject to the frailties of life; that is, death, disease, injury and destruction of their crops and animals.

These matters are additionally complicated by problems which seem to be more pronounced in the ratite than many other species; that is, the difficulties of sex and pedigree determination under the current state of technology.

Into this world comes the ratite rancher and asks, *What special rules and laws do I need to watch out for? What should I be doing to improve my chances of having a fair opportunity in the market place? How can I protect myself, my family and my business from those who would take advantage of me?*

We will address these and other questions in this chapter.

SCOPE

Because of the broad reach of the law in our lives, it was necessary to limit the scope of this chapter to general discussions of those subject matters which were considered to be of greatest interest and usefulness to ratite ranchers in the United States.

The primary areas selected were a general overview, the selection of the appropriate business entity, legal aspects of buying and selling birds, and legal aspects of boarding and managing birds with or for others.

Other areas, such as tax aspects, financial and estate planning, torts, and many more, have either been totally omitted or only briefly mentioned, where necessary to clarify a point in other topics under discussion.

No attempt has been made to give any legal advice in any given situation, and nothing stated in these pages should be relied upon other than as general information in the area represented.

Although I have attempted to be as accurate as possible in addressing the topics, the reader is cautioned to secure the advice and assistance of a qualified attorney licensed to practice in the jurisdiction where the advice is to be applied.

The attorney should also be fully informed of the factual conditions and the nature of the matter presented for consideration.

BASIC PRINCIPLES

STATE VS. FEDERAL LAW

Despite the common belief of many, the greatest body of law governing our conduct in the United States is *state law*, derived primarily from the common law of England and the civil laws of France and Spain. Although most states developed from common ancestry, there are a number of differing principles which distinguish each from the other.

For example, southern and western states have a stronger agricultural heritage. Therefore they generally give greater protection to agricultural pursuits than do the more industrial northern and eastern states. Laws to protect livestock, to regulate slaughters, and to punish improper conduct affecting land and agriculture are traditionally more favorable to the rancher-farmer in the agricultural states than in the industrial states.

Additionally, since the agricultural states derive a greater portion of their revenues from the furtherance of agricultural businesses, there is a tendency for the state legislatures and courts in the so-called agricultural states to be more tolerant of the activities of farmers and ranchers than in some other states.

Because the United States has traditionally been known as having a strong agricultural economy, and the farmer is recognized as an essential player in the underlying strength and support of the country, the federal government has also developed a number of special rules for the benefit of farmers and ranchers, most notably in the federal tax and subsidy laws.

Despite all of this, however, the basic source of law for farmers in everyday agribusiness endeavors is the law of the states in which his ranch is located and where he does business. If he elects to buy, sell, transport or otherwise do business across state lines, the ratite rancher must be prepared to deal not only with the federal and state laws on his operations, but also the state laws governing the other part of his transaction; that is, where the buyer or seller is located, where the birds are to be delivered, or where the birds are to be picked up.

CIVIL VS. CRIMINAL LAW

Again, contrary to common belief, the vast body of law governing our conduct is *civil* law, and only a very small part is *criminal* law.

Since we read so much about the activities of criminal elements today, it is easy to get the impression that most problems and disputes are criminally related and are governed by some form of criminal law. Nothing could be farther from the truth.

Only a very small part of our legal conflicts involve criminal activities, and the law enforcement agencies, the police, the sheriff, and the district attorneys, have neither the time nor the resources with which to provide much assistance to those involved in the common business civil dispute.

We cannot expect any of the law enforcement professionals or agencies to solve our disputes for us. We must use the civil laws and the resolution of disputes through negotiation, mediation and civil law suits.

ORGANIZATION

People commencing business endeavors often do not appreciate the many legal and tax aspects, nor the personal legal exposure they may be creating for themselves.

And, certainly, they rarely expect and plan for the extensive administrative delays and expenses that seem to arise every day from their business activities. Many of these issues relate to the form of business entity the parties select for their business activities.

Before we begin our consideration of the various forms of business entities, the reader's attention is invited to the fact that the purpose of this section of the presentation is only to highlight general rules and principles of law relating to business organizations.

Anyone having specific questions concerning a legal matter, including the appropriate form of legal entity for their business, should seek the professional advice of one knowledgeable not only in the laws of the state in which they are located, but also the particular circumstances of their business and goals.

Having said this, let us begin our discussion with the characteristics of a few of the more common types of business entities.

THE SOLE PROPRIETORSHIP

The simplest form of business entity is the *sole proprietorship*. This is a business conducted by a single person (or by a husband and wife). The owner, or sole proprietor, is both owner and manager, and has control over all aspects of the business.

The sole proprietor owns and manages the business and its assets and is personally liable for any legal injuries caused by himself, the business, and its employees and agents.

The duration of the business is measured by the life of the sole proprietor. Most ratite ranch operations in the United States are conducted by family sole proprietorships.

THE PARTNERSHIP

The next level of business form is the *partnership*. There are several types of business partnerships, but all share the concept of two or more persons or entities joining together to conduct one or more on-going business activities.

Following is a discussion of some of the advantages and disadvantages of the various types of partnerships.

The General Partnership

This is the classic or traditional entity formed by two or more persons or entities to carry on a business endeavor for profit. The partners may enter into a formal written agreement, an informal written agreement (such as with a memo or letter), a verbal agreement, or an understanding or handshake.

The difficulty with the more informal arrangements is that if a question arises among the partners concerning their duties or responsibilities, the law looks to the *intent* of the parties as evidenced by documentation and conduct. The more formal the documentation, the less chance there will be for misunderstandings and differences of opinion.

Unless the partnership agreement provides otherwise, the partnership membership is limited to the initial partners, and new partners can be admitted only with the unanimous consent of all partners.

Each partner is deemed by the law to be the agent for the partnership in all matters related to the business of the partnership, and all partners are fully liable for all obligations of the partnership, regardless of the partnership interest owned.

Thus, a 5% partner may have 100% liability for a partnership debt incurred to a third party by the 95% partner without the knowledge of the 5% partner; and vice-versa, the 95% partner can have full liability for the actions of the 5% partner.

It is this legal feature that makes the partnership form of doing business risky, particularly for the partner with financial holdings outside the partnership.

The partnership agreement can provide for contribution and indemnities among the partners, but such internal agreements are not binding upon third parties.

The Joint Venture

The joint venture is merely a partnership formed for a specific project or for a limited time period. An illustration might be two emu ranchers pooling their money and efforts to make a one-time purchase of some yearlings from a third party.

In most aspects the joint venture is treated the same as the partnership, except that the scope of authority of each joint venturer to bind the venture and the other venturers is generally more limited than among the general partnership since the scope of the entity's activities are more limited.

The Limited Partnership

The limited partnership is a partnership in which one or more of the partners, designated as the *general partner* or *general partners*, have authority to manage the partnership, with personal liability for his or their actions.

The remaining partner or partners, called the *limited partners*, have only limited authority (primarily in organizational but not operational matters) and have no personal liability beyond the amount contributed to join the partnership or otherwise personally committed for.

A limited partnership requires certain formalities of formation and must be filed with the Secretary of State or other appropriate state agency if the limited partners wish to avoid personal liability.

The Registered Limited Liability Partnership

This is a newly-recognized legal entity, and is not yet authorized in all states. It attempts to permit full participation in management of the entity by all partners, while limiting each partner's individual liability through insurance and legal provisions.

This, too, is a statutory entity and requires filing with the appropriate agency, most commonly the Secretary of State. Also, the limita-

> *... a 5% partner may have 100% liability for a partnership debt incurred to a third party by the 95% partner without the knowledge of the 5% partner ...*

tions from liability are not absolute and do not equal the protection afforded by corporations.

THE CORPORATION

The last of the traditional business entities is the *business corporation*, or *corporation*. This entity differs from all of the others in several particulars.

First is separation of ownership and management. Unlike the sole proprietorship and the partnership where the owners and managers are customarily the same persons, in the corporation ownership is held by the shareholders while management is conducted by the officers and board of directors.

In some smaller corporations the shareholders also serve as the officers and directors, thereby creating a combination of ownership and management. In this case, however, the role of each person in each capacity is clearly identified and recognized.

Second is protection against personal liability. Unlike sole proprietorships and partnerships, neither the officers, directors nor stockholders are personally liable for obligations of the corporation in the absence of special circumstances, nor for their own acts if performed within the scope of their employment duties.

Third is continuity of life or perpetual duration. Since corporations are artificial entities, under the laws of most states they enjoy the right of perpetual existence, independently of the lives of their stockholders. Sole proprietorships and partnerships are limited by the lives of their participants.

This distinction is probably less important today, since under most modern partnership laws, the partners may provide for a continuation of the partnership by admission of new partners.

Fourth is ease of transferability of interests. Since ownership in a corporation is evidenced by stock and is separate from management, changes in ownership or management can be made easily and without a corresponding change in the other aspect. This, of course, is not possible in the sole proprietorship and is not normally feasible in the partnership.

The *S Corporation*, a business corporation with special federal income tax privileges, will be discussed below.

OTHER ORGANIZATIONS
The Limited Liability Company

A newly-developing form of business organization, now authorized in many states and growing in popularity, is the *limited liability company*, or LLC. This entity has characteristics of both the S Corporation (described below) and the limited partnership, but is more flexible than either.

The LLC is formed like a corporation and in most states is liable for state franchise taxes imposed upon corporations. However, it is treated as a partnership for federal income tax purposes if it is properly formed. It is managed by the owners, called *members*, but they still have limited liability, like corporate shareholders. The exact status of the LLC is unclear due to its newness and limited acceptance at this time.

Other Forms of Business Entities

There are several other types of business and trade organizations recognized in the law. Normally these are special-purpose organizations, and are not formed for traditional business purposes, although they may have business aspects. For example, the *non-profit*, or *not-for-profit* corporation is a corporation formed under special statutes for various social, political, philanthropic and other purposes. The trade or marketing association, which may be either a corporation, a non-profit corporation, or a cooperative or association, is another illustration.

The American Ostrich Association and the American Emu Association are both examples of trade associations. Emu Ranchers, Inc. and Emu Marketing Unlimited are illustrations of marketing cooperatives formed as not-for-profit corporations.

TAX CONSIDERATIONS

No discussion of legal entities would be complete without at least some consideration of the tax aspects of each. The tax considerations in any business decision are extremely varied and complex. They encompass such aspects as federal and state income taxes, federal and state estate and inheritance taxes, and state sales and franchise taxes.

Although the general subject of taxation is beyond the scope of this presentation, the following comments on some of the more common federal tax aspects may be helpful in making the decision whether to use one or another business entity. My comments will be limited to the federal income tax and federal estate and gift tax laws, and no comment is made concerning state tax laws.

Under federal income tax laws, the sole proprietorship and partnership are taxed at the individual level. That is, the entity itself is not subject to a tax separate from its owner/participants.

Thus, the sole proprietor includes his income from his various business activities in his personal income tax report, and the partnership *passes through* its income to its partners so that they may report and pay federal income taxes at their respective tax rates on their portion of the partnership's income.

The partnership itself is treated as a non-entity for federal income tax purposes. This is also true for the limited partnership and the limited liability partnership, and may be true for the limited liability company depending upon how it was formed.

The corporation, on the other hand is treated as a separate taxpaying entity by the federal income tax laws, and it is subject to an income tax on its net income independently of the tax which may be owed by its stockholders. This can result in double taxation if net income in the corporation is distributed to shareholders in the form of dividends.

The federal tax laws do permit a small corporation meeting certain requirements to elect to be taxed as a partnership by making an appropriate filing with the IRS under Subchapter S of the Internal Revenue Code. A corporation making this election, called a *Subchapter S election*, is known as an *S Corp* or *S Corporation*.

The only difference between the S Corp and other corporations is the right to have the net income pass through to the stockholders for federal income tax purposes.

The S Corporation also must satisfy a number of special qualifications, including restrictions on the types of stockholders it may have, and a corporation's status as an S Corporation may be lost if these requirements do not continue to be met at all times.

As far as federal estate and gift taxes are concerned, there is no distinction between the entities. Federal estate and gift taxes are based upon asset transfers, not upon income. Therefore they apply to the specific asset owned by the donor or decedent at the time of transfer or death.

For the sole proprietorship, the assets are the assets of the business itself; for the partner in a partnership, the asset is the partner's interest in the partnership; and for the corporation, the asset is the stock owned by the stockholder.

The foregoing is a very simple overview of this complex area. The independent counsel and advice of an competent legal and tax advisor should be secured before attempting to apply any of the generalized comments here to a specific situation.

BUYING & SELLING

The subject of *buying and selling* is somewhat difficult to explain and comprehend because it actually involves two distinct legal concepts.

The first element is the *contract* of purchase and sale itself. This is the part of the transaction where the parties enter into their *agreement* for the transfer of ownership of the birds.

The birds may be in existence at the time of the contract, or the contract may be for purchase and sale of birds to be acquired or hatched in the future.

The second element is the *performance* or *carrying out* of the transaction; ie, the actual transfer of ownership and transfer of risk of loss. (Normally, this also involves a transfer of possession, but not always; for example, a combination sale and boarding arrangement.) This part of the transaction involves a number of different issues and creates its own set of problems for the buyer and seller.

In order to fully understand the overall legal aspects of the buy-and-sell transaction, one needs to be able to distinguish each of the above elements and analyze the impact of each upon the overall transaction.

GENERAL LEGAL PRINCIPLES

The contract for purchase and sale of ratites must include all of the basic requirements for contracts generally. That is, the contract must reflect or include:

A Perceived Meeting of the Minds

This requires that there be a clear *offer* and *acceptance*, an identification of the parties, an identification of the *goods* (in our case, the ratites), and the general terms of the transaction (these will be discussed later in more detail).

Consideration

This means that both parties must commit to provide something of benefit to the other, *and* each such commitment must be in return for the commitment by the other.

In the simplest agreement, the buyer promises to pay money for the seller's birds, and the seller promises to deliver his birds to the buyer for the buyer's money. Note that the value of each party's promise need *not* be the same as the other party's promise; but each must have offered something of benefit to the other.

Legal Capacity

The parties to a contract must have legal capacity to understand the intent and meaning of the agreement. This is normally not a factor in business contracts, but it can become a problem if one is dealing with a minor or a person of limited mental faculties.

Lawful purpose

To be a legally enforceable contract, the agreement must be for a lawful purpose. This means that the courts will not enforce a contract between two parties to steal a pair of emus, or a contract to defraud another. This is not normally a factor in business contracts, although it can arise if the parties become overly zealous and lose sight of the legal limits on their activities.

In addition to these four conditions, the law also imposes other requirements in certain circumstances. For example, a contract for the sale of goods having a value of $500 or more must be in writing or evidenced by a written memorandum signed by the party to be charged.

The term *goods* as used in the Uniform Commercial Code, in use in every state except Louisiana, refers to all tangible objects other than money and negotiable instruments standing for money. Ratites are *goods* for this purpose, and any contract for the sale of ostriches, emu or rheas for a total price of $500 or more must be in writing or have a written memorandum sufficient to be enforceable by a court. (The states vary on what writing is sufficient as a *memorandum* to make the contract enforceable.)

Note that the law does not require that the item contracted to be purchased and sold be in existence at the time the contract is created. In fact, it is quite common for a seller to contract for goods to be manufactured or to be purchased from others; or, in the case of farm products, to be raised, born or hatched.

One of the primary values of a contract is to provide resale terms and a willing buyer so that the seller can make the necessary commitments to purchase or acquire products knowing that he has the means of resale when the products are acquired.

WHEN DO YOU NEED A WRITTEN CONTRACT?

Under the laws of most states, there are several statutes which require written contracts or written memoranda of intent in certain contractual situations if the agreement is to be enforceable in the courts.

The most common of these in the ratite sale transaction is the Uniform Commercial Code requirement, described above.

These statutes, however, are normally not the determining factor in deciding when an agreement should be in writing. As a matter of fact, very few legal problems arise solely upon the presence or absence of a written agreement.

The vast majority of contract related disputes arise because of problems of determining and proving the true intent of the parties and the specific terms of the agreement itself. The lack of the written agreement makes the proof doubly difficult.

The reason, then, why a written contract is important is not that a statute requires it, but because it is only with a carefully-thought-out and written agreement that the specific intent of the parties can be expressed; and the rights, duties and responsibilities of each party can be spelled out.

COMMON PROVISIONS

Unfortunately, recognizing that a written arrangement is desirable is only half the battle.

If an agreement is to be effective, it must not only satisfy the legal requirements for a binding contract, but it must also contain sufficient terms and details so that all parties know where they stand and what their respective rights and duties are.

Let us look at the general principles in greater detail and consider the words, clauses and provisions which make them up.

Identification of the Birds

If the contract is to be fully enforceable, the items to be bought and sold should be fully and completely identified. This is relatively easy if the birds are in existence and in the possession of the seller.

With microchipping commonplace today, the contract needs only to identify the birds by reference to the microchip identification number, with perhaps the leg band identification and the bird's name for back-up reference.

Be careful, however, that you do not inadvertently create ambiguity by identifying a bird by both a leg band and a microchip, and requiring that both be in place. In that situation, if the leg band is lost or placed on another bird, there is confusion as to which applies.

It is better practice to use the microchip as the primary identification with the others being used for non-binding corroboration and convenience only.

In the future, it is anticipated that DNA or other scientific identification techniques will be developed to a degree where even more precise identification may become the standard.

The identification problem becomes more complex where the contract is for the purchase and sale of birds to be acquired by the seller from a third party or to be hatched at some future time.

In this situation, unless the seller provides otherwise, if the seller promises to deliver birds without reference to the source or any limitations or conditions of his obligation, he will be deemed to have made no conditions and will be obligated to deliver the birds contracted for regardless of the circumstances.

Thus, if a seller promises to sell emu chicks from the 1995 hatching season, without limiting his offer to his own flock, he will be expected to get the contracted birds from whatever source possible to satisfy the sale commitment. If he wants to limit his obligation only to those birds which are available from his own breeding birds, he must say so in the agreement.

Similarly, if the seller is planning to purchase birds or has a contract to purchase birds from a third party which he plans to resell to the buyer in this contract, he must be certain to limit his obligation to sell only those birds which he is able to acquire from the contact he has with another.

Note, however, that if the seller becomes too vague or indefinite in his obligations, this may render the entire contract unenforceable because of a failure of the first basic requirement discussed above, the *meeting of the minds* requirement.

In other words, if the seller's commitment is so indefinite as to be nothing more than an *attempt to provide birds*, the buyer may be able to avoid his responsibility by claiming there was never any real contract in the first place.

The key here is clear and precise language setting out the specific obligations of each party, and specific limitations; i.e., lack of birds, bad hatch season, failure of a third party to deliver, unexpected defects or deaths, etc. The key element is to see to it that when the contract is read, each person knows where he stands.

Identification of the Parties

The contract should carefully identify the parties.
- Is either a corporation? If so, use the proper name and authorized officers.
- Is there to be an individual guarantor?
- If the buyer or seller is not a corporation, is it a husband and wife, or just one spouse?
- Is either party a partnership? If so, who are the partners?

These seem like simple matters, but we frequently find that the parties fail to complete even the simple provisions, leaving the contract difficult to enforce for lack of clearly identifiable parties.

Terms of Sale and Delivery of Possession

This is an area filled with danger. For some reason, ostrich, emu and rhea ranchers will go to great lengths to specify some of the details in a contract, then leave out some of the most obvious and critical provisions.

For example:
- How much down payment is required?
- When and in what amount is the balance due?
- Is payment due on delivery?

- Is the balance to be paid in installments?
- Is there financing by a third party?
- Must payments be by cashier check, or is a personal check satisfactory?
- When is possession to be transferred?
- What are the requirements for health, transportation, inspections, etc?

See the section on *Boarding and Management Agreements* for discussions of common provisions in contracts. Many of the provisions discussed there have application, with modifications, to purchase and sale transactions as well.

Again, the key is clarity and simplicity. Spell out the circumstances under which the birds are to be delivered and the money or other consideration is to be paid, and 90% of the potential disputes will be avoided.

If the agreement is for the sale of birds to be acquired, spell out in the contract that delivery will be made *not more than 30 days after acquisition of the birds*, or *delivery shall be made on or before x date, subject to availability of the birds at that time*, or, if you are the buyer, *seller agrees to deliver the birds and consummate the sale on or before x date, without grace* (meaning without a *grace* or delay period).

In other words, the contract can and should contain all material provisions and conditions, on both sides. In this manner, the parties know their duties, as well as their rights.

Details of Delivery and Performance Defaults

The place of performance is very critical in the sale of goods agreements, particularly where the goods are to cross state lines.

As in the previous discussion, there are many details of performance which should be spelled out clearly:
- Where and when is payment to be made?
- Where are the birds to be picked up, where delivered?
- Who has the responsibility for loading the birds if transport is required?
- Who has the responsibility of providing the transport?
- Who has the unloading responsibility?
- Who has the duty of satisfying the various state health conditions? Who pays for it?
- Is insurance required? Who pays?

All of these terms need to be set forth in a well-drafted sales contract. With this, each party knows exactly where his obligations begin and end, and he can protect himself through personal attention, engagement of professional licensed and bonded personal, and insurance coverage.

A common series of problems that can develop in this area are those relating to performance defaults. For example:
- What if ten pairs are contracted for, but only five pairs are available?
- What if none are available?
- What if three birds are the wrong sex?
- What if two birds have splayed legs?
- What if the buyer fails to pay the balance when due or makes unreasonable demands?

If nothing is said in the contract about performance variances, the law generally requires *full* performance as agreed. If performance is impossible, such as where chicks are not available to satisfy the contract, the seller will normally be held legally obligated either to secure comparable birds from elsewhere or to deliver the equivalent value as of the date of the court judgment plus interest and attorney's fees.

If the court finds that the conduct of the seller was such as to constitute a *deceptive trade practice*, the seller may be subject to additional damages (treble in Texas) as a penalty. All of this can be avoided simply by spelling out the conditions of the contract and the specific rights and duties of each party.

I recognize that as a practical matter it is sometimes difficult for a buyer or seller to be too specific. It may drive the other party away, or raise questions that are difficult to answer.

In this case, the disclosing party must make a decision. Does he spell out the rights and duties, and run a risk of some business problem? Or does he operate on a hand-shake or skimpy non-enforceable purported contract?

I cannot answer the dilemma except to say that a carefully-thought-out and worded agreement frequently provides a personal feeling of confidence and satisfaction that makes the entire transaction better for all involved.

Mediation and Arbitration

Because of the rising costs and delays of litigation, there are now developing throughout the United States a series of procedures for resolution of disputes without litigation. These procedures are generally called *alternate dispute resolution* or ADR.

The principal techniques are *mediation* (where the parties attempt to resolve their disputed in controlled settlement discussions with one or more neutral mediators working to assist the parties to reach a settlement) and *arbitration* (where a neutral third-party arbitrator hears all of the details of the dispute, in an semi-formal setting without the complexities of the court room, and decides the case for the parties).

Both techniques are voluntary, and it is becoming common for business contracts to contain a provision agreeing to the use of one or another form of Alternate Dispute Resolution in the event a dispute develops in the course of the contract.

PASSAGE OF TITLE AND RISK OF LOSS

Once there is a legally enforceable contract, we become concerned with the second phase of the legal equation; i.e., the sale transaction itself. Here we have the issues of *passage of title* and *risk of loss*.

Normally, risk of loss follows the transfer of possession and title to the goods, and we say that the person with the title or ownership of an object must suffer the risk of any injury or loss of that object or item. When, then, does title and risk of loss pass from the seller to the buyer in a purchase and sale transaction?

The first rule of law is that neither passage of title nor transfer of risk of loss can occur until the goods are in existence and *identified to the contract*. In other words, if there is a contract to sell chicks to be hatched, title to those chicks cannot pass until the birds are actually hatched.

Further, if there is a contract for the purchase of five pairs of chicks from a hatch, no title can pass to those chicks until five *specific* chick pairs are set aside and specifically *identified* as the chicks for that contract.

Once the goods (chicks, yearlings, etc.) are in existence and specifically allocated and identified to the contract, the law states that the title and risk of loss will pass when the parties agree, if they specify in their agreement. If the parties fail to specify when they wish title and risk to pass, the law establishes some presumptions, which become the rule if not proven otherwise.

The first presumption is that if the goods are to be delivered directly by the seller to the buyer, title and risk passes from seller to buyer when possession of the goods is tendered or delivered.

In the absence of an agreement, title to goods passes to the buyer at the time and place where the seller performs physical delivery of the goods. In a contract, the delivery arrangements should specify when this occurs.

- If the seller is to ship, then delivery of the birds to a mutually acceptable carrier or a common carrier is *delivery*, and title passes to the buyer at that time.
- If the seller is to deliver the birds to the buyer, title does not pass until the seller satisfies the condition and delivers the birds to the agreed location.
- If the buyer is to pick up the birds, title passes when the birds are specifically identified to the contract and the buyer is notified that the birds are ready for pickup.

In this case, however, if the seller is a *merchant* (defined as one engaged in the business of dealing in the goods involved in the transaction) risk of loss remains with the seller until the buyer actually takes possession of the birds. Mere notice that the birds are ready for pickup does not relieve the seller of his responsibilities.

Where the seller fails to deliver the goods as contracted, or delivers defective goods, or delivers different goods or different quantities than contracted for, the buyer has a variety of remedies:

- He may accept those delivered and demand damages;
- he may allege fraud or deceptive trade practices and demand additional damages; or
- he may claim a breach of warranty and seek recovery of his money paid plus damages.

The mere presence of this clause will sometimes act as a deterrent for disputes between the parties, particularly if the clause contains agreed penalties for the one found to be at fault.

The various remedies for a buyer are beyond the scope of this presentation, but suffice it to say that if the contract contains no qualifications or limitations on the seller's obligations, he may be subject to severe legal exposure.

Conversely, if the seller tenders the goods and the buyer defaults, regardless of the reason (other than a breach of the contract by the seller), the seller also has remedies, including suit for breach of contract.

It is likely that the remedies for the seller are not as strong as those available to the buyer because the seller still has the goods and presumably he can resell them to minimize his losses; but if the buyer defaults at the time when there is a decline in the market value of the product, the seller would be able to recover the full amount of his contracted profits from the buyer.

THE SEX PROBLEM

One unique area of concern and legal exposure for buyers and sellers of ratites arises from the inability of the parties to determine with absolute certainty the sex of birds at the time of the purchase and sale transaction.

Although great strides have been made in the recent years in the development of techniques which will establish sex without question, such techniques have so far failed to give sufficient assurances. Also, because of the time it takes for the necessary tests to be conducted and analyzed, the sale transactions are frequently complicated and extended.

The only means for handling this problem in the current state of the law and scientific technology is for each party to recognize the nature and scope of the problem, and for the contract to spell out clearly where the risk is going to be if it does turn out, in fact, that a bird is not of the expected sex.

Commonly, in these situations a time period is provided to

permit the buyer to have the birds re-examined by the buyer's own experts or by an acceptable testing system, after which the buyer loses any rights to have the situation corrected.

Until scientific tests reach sufficient levels of accuracy, with corresponding speed of results, this will continue to be a problem, and the careful buyer and seller will be sure that they have covered the possibilities in their contracts.

PURCHASE AND SALE TO BOARD

Where a purchase and sale transaction involves not only a transfer of ownership of birds but a contemporaneous boarding arrangement, the contract becomes more complex.

Indeed, many attorneys, when confronted with this situation, elect to handle the transaction as two separate transactions; a purchase and sale agreement, and a boarding agreement. This has the advantage of simplifying each contract, but creates some redundancy since each document must be able to stand alone.

Whether one uses the one- or two-contract approach, both parties must be careful to specify clearly when title and risk of loss pass from seller to buyer, and perhaps back to seller as a bailee (custodian) under the boarding agreement.

BOARDING OR MANAGEMENT AGREEMENTS

The *boarding agreement*, sometimes called a *maintenance agreement* or a *management agreement*, contemplates that one party, the owner or manager of a ratite ranch (called the *manager*) agrees to maintain, care for, and board certain ratites belonging to another (called the *owner*).

The manager may merely provide boarding services; or he may provide hatching and grow-out services; or he may provide full-scale services, including purchasing the birds, maintaining them, hatching and caring for their offspring, selling the birds and their progeny, and delivering the net proceeds after costs and commission to the owner.

The simple term *boarding agreement*, or other such terms, give little indication as to the true nature of the arrangement. Since there is no standard arrangement and each boarding agreement is different in scope and terms, it is imperative that each party know all of the terms of the specific boarding or maintenance document being considered. Do not assume that it is like any other you may have seen previously.

This leads to the next question then, *What should be included in a boarding or management contract?*

BASIC LEGAL REQUIREMENTS

As with the contracts for purchase and sale, every boarding contractual agreement should contain four basic elements:
- a perceived meeting of the minds,
- consideration,
- legal capacity, and
- lawful purpose.

See the discussion of these elements above, under the heading *Buying & Selling*. The same principals apply in all contracts.

COMMON PROVISIONS

Turning to the agreements, *What items should be addressed if we are to arrive at a good legal relationship and contract?*

Some of the more important considerations are as follows.

Identity of the Subject Matter

Obviously, the subject matter (goods or services) which forms the basis for the agreement should be clearly identified. If it is an emu hen or a pair of ostriches, it or they should be identified by microchip number, sex, band number, and date of birth. If there are any special characteristics or markings, these should also be specified.

Identification of the Parties

The contract should carefully identify the parties.
- Is either a corporation? If so, use the proper name and authorized officers.
- Is there to be an individual guarantor?
- If the buyer or seller is not a corporation, is it a husband and wife, or just one spouse?
- Is either party a partnership? If so, who are the partners?

These seem like simple matters, but we frequently find that the parties fail to complete even the simple provisions, leaving the contract difficult to enforce for lack of clearly identifiable parties.

Health and Condition of the Birds

One of the most important areas of coverage in a properly-drafted contract are the provisions relating to the health and physical condition of the birds before, during and upon expiration of the boarding arrangement.

The parties should clearly agree, prior to entering into the contract or as a part of the contract, exactly what is the physical condition of each bird being brought under contract. The contract may specify or require that there be a veterinary examination of each bird or that the birds have a certified record of vaccination, worming, etc.

Certainly the contract should provide that no bird can be taken under contract that is not personally examined and accepted by the manager-rancher.

Other health-related provisions should address the continued health and well-being of birds during the course of the boarding. For example:

- If a bird becomes ill, diseased or injured, does the manager have the right to kill the bird at that time, or terminate the agreement and require that it be removed by the owner?
- What is the manager's obligation with respect to maintenance of the health of a bird if it becomes ill, diseased, or injured?
- Who pays for medications and veterinary services?
- Who decides what medications are given and when?
- If a bird is not laying, does the manager have the right to withhold food or provide a hormone injection, or must the manager obtain approval from the owner?
- And, if a bird dies, who is responsible for examination and disposal of the carcass?

As we can see, there are a variety of circumstances which may reasonably be expected to occur that relate solely to the health and well-being of birds maintained in a boarding environment.

Because of the value of these birds, it is important for both the owner and the manager that there be a clear delineation of rights and duties with respect to the preservation, health and well-being of birds in the custody of the manager, as well as delegation of authority in the event of adverse circumstances.

Other Bird Management Matters

Although not directly or specifically related to the health of the birds being boarded, there may be a number of bird related questions that should also be considered in appropriate situations.

For example, what if the represented sex of one bird in a breeder pair is subsequently discovered to be incorrect? Is this sufficiently serious and probable to be addressed in the contract, or is it too remote to be worth specific consideration?

Other similar items for consideration, and possible inclusion in the contract, are provisions relating to compatibility of the owner's birds with other birds.

- Should there be a provision permitting the manager to reject a bird or terminate a boarding arrangement if the owner's bird fights with its mate or is disruptive to the flock or another bird?
- Or is this an area to to be omitted in the contract and left to be worked out if a problem develops?
- Does a manager have the right to change bird mates without the owner's consent if the birds are not laying or the eggs are infertile?

The answer to these and many other questions frequently depend upon the relationship between the manager and the owner and the nature of the over-all agreement.

Incubation and Hatching

A critical area of concern in breeder boarding agreements relate to the duties and responsibilities of the manager in handling incubation and hatching of eggs, and care and maintenance of hatchlings. A well-drafted agreement should include provisions for all of these circumstances. For example:

- What standards, if any, are to be imposed upon the manager?
- Is there any warranty, guarantee or assurance that the manager gives the owner with respect to the number of eggs to be hatched from a given pair, the percentage required to be fertile, etc.
- Or, conversely, is the manager disclaiming all warranties of activities or results?

In either event, the document should clearly specify the obligations and limitations.

A common provision in this regard is for the manager to agree only that he will exercise the same degree of care and responsibility for the handling, incubation and hatching of eggs from the owner's birds and eggs as he exercises with respect to his own eggs and birds, and expressly disclaims all other warranties or guaranties as to production.

Although this is a simply-stated standard, it is well recognized in the courts and can be used by the owner if the manager is favoring his own birds to the detriment of the owner's birds, or by the manager if the owner is being unreasonable or unrealistic with his expectations.

Hatchlings

The agreement should provide a clear procedure for care and maintenance of the hatchlings from the owner's birds.

- How long are they to remain under the care and custody of the manager?
- What responsibility does the manager have for the health of each chick?
- What authority does the manager have in the case of illness, injury or death of a chick?
- What additional fees, if any, are owed by the owner?
- Who is responsible for microchipping, and when?

Compensation

There are several possible provisions relating to compensation to be paid the manager for boarding and maintenance services.

Depending upon what it is that the manager is obligated to do, a common form of compensation for breeder-pair boarding is for the manager to retain a percentage of the hatchlings from the breeder pair.

This creates a number of circumstances under which disputes can arise, and the proposed terms should be carefully discussed and understood by all parties prior to signing the agreement. The percentage to be withheld by the manager and the circumstances under which it occurs should be carefully specified.

Special provisions may be included whereby the percentage allocated to the manager increases or decreases depending upon the number of eggs, the percentage of fertility, or other standard.

Almost any variety of arrangements can be agreed by the parties as long as the terms are carefully spelled out in the agreement.

Once the percentage allocations are determined, the contract should specify how the hatchlings are to be divided; i.e., by date of hatch, by sex, by lot, or by a combination of factors. Also, who makes the division or allocation—the manager, the owner, or the manager and owner together?

A common provision is for the birds to be divided automatically, by some formula, either by sex or date of birth or by a combination of both hatch date and sex.

Another provision might be to combine the chicks from the owner's birds with other chicks from other birds belonging to the manager or other owners under boarding arrangements to provide a broader mix for division.

Provisions should also be made for illness, death or injury of hatchlings, both prior to and subsequent to the division but prior to the removal of the chicks by the owner.

Cost Allocations

Another area of importance in is the allocation of costs between owner and manager.
- If the contract relates to breeding pairs, and the manager is going to receive a percentage of the chicks hatched, what maintenance costs will be borne by the owner?
- Is the owner going to pay for microchipping, or is this a service provided by the manager?
- Similarly, are such items as medications, feed, worming, veterinary charges, etc., part of the service provided by the manager, or are they cost items to be borne by the owner?

A common allocation is for the manager to have responsibility for all routine or day-to-day maintenance costs, such as feed and water; and for all special costs, such as medical treatment, medications and veterinary costs, to be paid or reimbursed by the owner.

Between these two cost items, however, a number of questionable items can arise, such as periodic vaccinations, worming and microchipping; which can be the subject of differences of opinion if not allocated in the agreement.

Another common area of confusion relates to costs during the non-laying season where the agreement is for year-round boarding or maintenance of breeder pairs. In this situation, the manager may agree to maintain the breeder pair at no charge during the off-season, or he may establish a monthly maintenance fee for feed and water during that period, in addition to his allocated percentage of the hatch during the laying season.

Similarly, questions may arise concerning the imposition of a monthly maintenance charge for chicks immediately after hatch and prior to the removal by the owner. If this is contemplated, it should be addressed in advance to avoid later misunderstandings. If there is to be no charge, this should also be stated.

The manager may wish to require the payment of a cash deposit as an advance against monthly maintenance charges and other cost items. This may be especially important in boarding agreements not involving some form of breeding, incubation and hatching services, in situations where the owner is from another state or area, or where collection of costs from the owner could be expected to be more burdensome.

Additionally, the parties may wish to further spell out in the agreement the terms and conditions for payment of the periodic maintenance fees and the procedures for enforcement and penalties for default or delays.

Bankruptcy, Business Defaults and Other External Factors

Areas frequently overlooked in contracts are provisions respecting adverse external events which impact upon the parties and interfere with their ability to carry out the terms of the agreement.

Examples of items which may occur in this area are bankruptcies, lawsuits, claims brought against either party by outside parties, and business failures.

Although there may be no specific event directly relating to the boarding contract, the impact of the external event may be sufficiently great as to cause actual or potential damage to one or the other of the parties through no fault of his own.

For example, if the manager defaults on his bank loan, he may be unable to purchase feed on credit, and his assets may be subject to foreclosure proceedings. This obviously could have serious adverse impact upon the owner, and there should be provisions in the contract to provide as much protection as possible.

Similarly, an owner may suffer financial reverses, which will interfere with his ability to maintain his portion of the maintenance costs, or a creditor may attempt to levy on the owner's breeder birds on the manager's property in the midst of the laying season.

A few well-chosen sentences in the contract can minimize the inconvenience upon the innocent party in either situation.

Standards of Care

Another important area for consideration in a boarding contract are the standards of care required of the manager, and the remedies for a failure to meet those standards. Both the owner and the manager are concerned about the manager's responsibilities for care of the owner's birds.

The owner wishes to be certain that the manager is held to an adequate standard and that the manager will be responsible for negligence as well as intentional disregard of his responsibilities.

The manager, on the other hand, is concerned that he not be held to an artificial standard that is unreasonable and beyond his capacity to meet. Both are concerned about the enforcement procedures and wish to avoid costly litigation if possible.

This is where well-drawn provisions setting forth the standards of care and the specific duties and responsibilities of the manager can provide a measure of comfort to both parties, as well as guidelines to which each may look in the event something not specifically addressed happens during the term of the contract.

Transportation

Provision should be made for transport of the birds to and from the boarding location. This would include an agreement between the parties as to which of them is responsible for arranging and paying for the cost of delivery of the birds to the manager and the delivery of chicks and/or breeder pairs back to the owner during or on termination of the agreement.

Acts of God and Risk of Loss

No matter how detailed and careful we are, there are always circumstances that can cause economic or other damage to one or the other of the parties. These are commonly called *acts of God* and include such unpredictable events as fires, storms and floods.

They may, however, include other events as agreed by the parties. In these cases, neither party is *at fault*, and in the absence of agreement between the parties, the law must decide who has the *risk of loss*.

In many cases the risk is minimized by insurance, but insurance rarely covers all of the damages, and there remains a residual loss to one or the other of the parties.

Sometimes a few sentences inserted at the appropriate place can allocate the loss in a way that is more in keeping with the desires of the parties than the law would without such directions. These provisions should also extend to the responsibility and risk of loss for accidental injury and death of the hatchlings from a breeder boarding agreement.

Insurance

Provisions should be inserted covering the insurance expectations of the parties. This includes not only insurance covering death or injury to the birds, but also fire and casualty insurance covering the ranch and its facilities. Other insurance may be added to cover death of the manager and business interruption, depending upon circumstances.

Expiration of the Contract and Prior Termination

The contract should contain provisions relating to the term of the agreement and activities responsibilities of the parties upon its expiration. Additional provisions should also be considered if a right to demand an early termination is desired by either party.

For example, the manager may wish to have the right to terminate the entire agreement at any time for cause; or without cause if he determines that continuation of the boarding arrangement is not in his best interests or the interest of his other birds or boarders.

Similarly, he may want to have the right to cancel the agreement as to some of the owner's birds if continuation is deemed detrimental to other birds or to the flock.

In the same vein, the owner may wish to reserve the right to withdraw his birds for cause; or without cause if he determines that the manager is not maintaining the birds properly or is not carrying out the terms of the agreement in a manner satisfactory to the owner.

In any of these situations, however, the wording of these provisions need to be carefully considered. If either party has too much liberty in terminating the contract at any time without any reason or cause, a court could find the entire contract to be too vague and uncertain to be enforceable by either party.

Record Keeping, Reports, Visits, and Communication

Record-keeping requirements and procedures for written and oral communications between manager and owner should be covered in the agreement.

As the boarding business grows, there will be larger numbers of investors placing their birds with ranchers for boarding purposes. Unless reasonable standards for record keeping, communications, reports and visitation are agreed, ill feelings, and even disputes, can arise based on differences in expectations.

This can easily be avoided by the insertion of a few simple provisions setting forth the records to be maintained and the terms under which periodic or specific reports will be given to the owner by the manager.

These provisions may also state when owners may contact the ranch and visit with the employees and their birds.

Again, this is a balancing of interests, and the purpose of the agreement is not to require unnecessary reporting or record keeping, or to prevent visits or communications, but rather simply to delineate further the respective rights and responsibilities of the owner and the manager.

Marketing and Sale of Birds

An area which should be considered for inclusion in a boarding agreement is a provision for marketing of birds.

If the owner is purchasing his birds from the manager, or if the arrangement contemplates hatchlings, the owner may also wish the manager to arrange for advertising and sale of the owner's birds or hatchlings along with his own.

This can be covered with proper power of attorney or selling agency provisions which set forth the duties and authority of the manager, how the advertising and other costs are to be shared, the price at which the manager/agent is authorized or required to sell, and the commission or other compensation to be paid.

Enforcement

There should be provisions governing the procedures for legal enforcement of the agreement in the event of a default.

The contract should grant to the manager a contractual lien on the owner's birds to secure the manager in the payment of all sums due him. Provisions should be included for collection of damages and costs of enforcement favoring the owner for improper conduct or failure to perform on the part of the manager.

Indemnities, Guarantees and Warranties

There may be circumstances where one or the other party will be called upon to guaranty or warrant a given result or to indemnify the other party under certain circumstances.

Conversely, there may be situations where a party expressly wants to *disclaim* or limit his responsibilities. In either event, the agreement should address these events and include the language that will clearly express the intent of the parties.

Mediation and Arbitration

A good provision to consider for insertion is one providing for mediation or arbitration in the event of dispute. These are gaining in popularity throughout the business world and are being well received. See the discussion under this same topic in the section *Buying and Selling* for further explanation of these provisions.

Special Provisions

Almost every legal undertaking has some special terms or conditions that the parties wish to include. Perhaps these relate to some interim event or some incentive compensation, or the like. Such special conditions are frequently the cause of disputes because the parties take them for granted and fail to carefully set forth the details.

Venue, Jurisdiction, Attorney Fees, Etc

If the parties are unable to resolve a dispute arising out of the boarding relationship, and one or the other feels the need to seek relief under the judicial system through a law suit or other legal remedy, it is important that the contract have language covering the important enforcement areas, such as jurisdiction, venue, types of remedies, and most importantly in some states, allocation of attorney fees and court costs.

This is particularly important where the owner and the manager reside in different states.

USE OF STANDARD FORMS

Although there is much to be said for the use of standard agreement forms, there is also some danger. The use of a standard form, with its so-called *fine-print boilerplate*, frequently leads to a sense of complacency or carelessness, which can defeat one of the basic reasons for having the written agreement in the first place—the development of a clear understanding of rights and responsibilities by all parties.

For the manager, however, the standard form does have a particular benefit in that it encourages development of standardized procedures and policies for all boarding arrangements, which are more cost effective and have less chance for inadvertent violation.

Rather than a pre-printed generic form, however, I recommend a form drawn up by the manager's attorney, who is familiar with the manager's needs.

LOCAL LAWS AND CUSTOMS

Before closing I must again remind the reader that the discussions here are based upon the author's general knowledge of the law of contracts as it exists in the United States. It does not purport to reflect the specific laws of any particular state. Nor does it purport to cover any specific fact or contract situation.

Each state has its own body of law and its own judicial interpretations, and a contract must satisfy the laws of the local state if it is to be enforced.

Likewise, there are numerous special factual conditions and circumstances which may exist and which may substantially alter the manner and language required to accomplish a given legal result.

Each agreement, therefore, must stand upon its own and must be carefully crafted by one who is knowledgeable not only in the law of the jurisdiction where the contract is to be performed, but also the facts and intentions of the parties creating the agreement.

NOTES

GLOSSARY

Charley Elrod

Randall W. Sullivan, DVM
Crossroads Veterinary Hospital
Seguin, Texas

The glossary on the following pages is as complete as we could make it. It includes terms which may be familiar to readers who are already in the livestock business, but not to those new to the industry.

Most of the terms on anatomy, genetics, and medicine are included because they're used in the text. Some won't be found in this book, but they are included because they are used throughout the industry and in other publications.

We've included extra space on each page for you to add terms we've not included, or your own notes on the ones we have.

NOTES

AAV	Association of Avian Veterinarians.	
Abscess	Localized collection of WBC in cavity formed by disintegration of tissues; often caused by bacteria.	
Acid shock	The surge of acid into aquatic systems produced by the melting of winter-long accumulations of acid-bearing snow.	
Active immunity	Immunity or resistance to disease that has been acquired by host response to a antigen. It can be acquired by recovering from a disease or by vaccination.	
Acute	A disease which has a short and relatively severe course.	
Adipose	Fat cells or fat tissue.	
AEA	American Emu Association: A national organization promoting the emu industry, education, research, etc.	
AFA	American Federation of Aviculturists.	
African black ostrich	See ostrich	
ASCS	Agricultural Stabilization and Conservation Service: An agency of the US Department of Agriculture that administers farm production control, price stabilization, and conservation programs.	
Airsacculitis	Inflammation of air sacs.	
AI	Abbreviation for artificial insemination.	
AI	Abbreviation for Avian Influenza.	
Albumen	The white of an egg consisting primarily of protein.	
Allantois	The membrane that acts as the lungs and kidneys of the developing chick in the egg while the definitive organs are forming. It arises as an out-growth of the hind gut, so acts as a depository for waste products as well.	
Allergy	A severe reaction or sensitivity which occurs in some individuals following the introduction of certain antigens into their bodies.	
Amino acid	An organic acid in which one or more of the hydrogen atoms has been replaced by the amino group ($-NH_2$). Amino acids are the building blocks in the formation of protein.	
Anatomy	Science of animal body structure and the relation of the body parts; the branch of biological science dealing with the structure and form of living organisms.	

Glossary

Anemia	A condition in which the blood is deficient in quantity or quality (lack of hemoglobin content or in number of red blood cells), characterized by paleness of skin and mucus membranes and loss of energy.
Animal behavior	The reaction of the whole organism to certain stimuli, or the manner in which it reacts to its environment.
Animal environment	All the conditions, circumstances and influences surrounding and affecting the growth, development and production of animals.
AOA	American Ostrich Association: A national organization promoting the ostrich industry, education, research, etc.
Anomaly	Deviation from normal structure, behavior, or appearance; as in congenital or hereditary defects.
Ante mortem	Before death.
Anterior	Situated in front of or toward the front part of a point of reference; toward the head of an animal.
Antibiotic	(1) A chemical substance produced by molds, bacteria or chemical synthetics, which has the ability to inhibit the growth of, or to destroy, other microorganisms; used in treatment of infectious disease. (2) A product of living organisms, such as yeast, which destroys or inhibits the growth of other microorganisms, especially bacteria.
Antibody	A specific protein molecule that is produced in response to a foreign protein (antigen) that has been introduced into the body. (2) A substance that opposes the action of another substance.
Antigen	A foreign substance that, when introduced into the blood or tissues, causes the formation of antibodies. Antigens may be toxins, usually a foreign protein or polysaccharide.
Antiseptic	A chemical agent used on living tissue to control the growth and development of microorganisms.
Antiserum	A serum containing a specific antibody used to treat a specific disease.
Antitoxin	A specific kind of antibody that will neutralize toxin.
APHIS	Animal and Plant Health Inspection Service: An agency of the US Department of Agriculture.
Archaeopteryx	An early bird, evolved from the subclass *Archosauria* approximately 180 million years ago.

NOTES

NOTES

Artificial vagina	A device used to collect semen from a male when he mounts in a normal manner to copulate. The male ejaculates into the device, which simulates the vagina of the female in pressure, temperature and sensation to the penis or phallus.
Ascites	Accumulation of serous fluid in the spaces between tissues and organs in the cavity of the abdomen.
Aspergillosis	A mycotic (fungal) disease that occasionally causes respiratory disease in ratites; organism is found everywhere and is associated with contaminated food and housing.
Assimilation	The process of transforming food into living tissue.
Assisted hatch	Intervention when a chick is overdue to hatch. Requires making a small hole in the egg shell so the chick can acquire needed oxygen, and then the chick will proceed with the natural hatching process.
Atrophy	Wasting away or diminution in size.
Autopsy	A postmortem examination in which the body is dissected to determine the cause of death.
Aves	Class of true birds.
Avian	Refers to birds, including poultry.
Bred	Female has been mated to the male.
Breed	Animals of common origin and having characteristics that distinguish them from other groups within the same species.
Breeder feed	A specially-formulated ration for birds or animals during the breeding or mating season, to meet increased nutritional and energy requirements.
Breeder market	A market where there is a demand for adult mating birds which produce offspring.
Breeding value	A genetic measure for one trait of an animal, calculated by combining into one number several performance values that have been accumulated on the animal and the animal's relatives.
Brooder	A heated structure used in raising young fowl during the first week of life.
Brooder box	A small box, usually heated or temperature controlled, for chicks that have just hatched.
Brooder room	Brooder houses or barns specially designed and constructed in which to rear chicks.

Brooder pens	Pens specially designed to raise young chicks to a certain age.
By-product	A product of considerably less value than the major product. For example, in meat animals in the United States, meat is the major product, and the hide, pelt and offal are by-products.
Calamus	Root of feather.
Callosity	A hard or thickened part of the skin.
Candling	The shining of a bright light through an egg to see if it contains a live embryo. In case of emu eggs an infrared light is used.
Carcass	The major portion of a meat animal remaining after slaughter.
Carcass merit	The value of a carcass for consumption.
Carcass weight	The weight of the carcass once the hide and internal organs have been removed.
Carrier	An apparently healthy animal that harbors disease organisms and is capable of transmitting them to susceptible animals.
Carrying capacity	The maximum population an environment can sustain without causing damage such as overbrowsing/overgrazing. Measured in terms of biomass or number of animals per species per unit area.
Catabolism	Destructive metabolism; the breaking down of living organisms of more complex substances into simpler ones with the release of energy.
Catarrhal	Describes an inflammatory condition of the mucous membranes characterized by an increased flow of mucous.
Caudal	Of, at, near or toward the tail end of the body.
CBC	Complete blood count.
CCC	Commodity Credit Corporation: An entity controlled by the US Department of Agriculture which buys and sells surplus commodities and provides loans for certain government farm programs.
Chalaza	A spiral band of thickened albumen which serves to maintain the yolk in its position.
Chick density	The number of chicks in a pen area. High chick density can cause many adverse effects, such as disease, trauma, and stress.

NOTES

NOTES

Chill factor	Wind-chill index: A measure of cold stress that combines temperature and wind velocity. For example, at 16 km/hr and $0°C$, the chill factor is the equivalent of $-8°C$.
Chorion	The membrane formed coincidently with the amnion. After formation it fuses with the developing allantois.
Chromosomal defects	Inversion, translocation, triploidy; a deviation from the normal.
Chronic	A disease of long duration.
Clitoris	The ventral part of the vulva of the female reproductive tract that is homologous to the penis or phallus in the male. It is highly sensory.
Cloaca	Portion of the lower end of the avian digestive tract that provides a passageway for products of the urinary, digestive and reproductive tracts often called the vent.
Clutch	Eggs laid by a hen on consecutive days in a single nesting attempt.
Clutches	Time pattern in which hens lay eggs.
Colace (docusate sodium)	Used as a stool softener
Conception	Fertilization of the ovum (egg).
Conformation	The structure or shape of an animal or its carcass.
Congestion	Excessive accumulation of blood or other body fluids, such as lymph or mucus, in a body part or area.
Conservation tillage	An all-encompassing term for minimum tillage, no tillage, zero tillage, and other kinds of farming practices that eliminate or reduce plowing. Newly-planted croplands are protected by at least thirty per cent cover formed by residue from the previous crop. Besides enhancing soil and water conditions, conservation tillage improves habitat, especially cover, for several species of wildlife.
Contagious	An infectious disease that may be transmitted readily from one individual to another.
Contagious Disease	Infectious disease; a disease that is transmitted from one animal to another.
Copulation	The act between male and female to bring about the union of a spermatozoa and an ovum; fertilization.

Cost of gain	The total cost divided by the total pound gain; usually expressed on a per pound basis.
Crooked neck	A condition due to infection, trauma, or genetics causing a deviation from the normal alignment of the neck.
Crossbreeding	Mating animals from genetically diverse groups (i.e., breeds) within a species.
Culling	Removal of the least productive part of the flock or herd, to prevent retrogression.
Culture	The propagation of microorganisms, or of living tissue cells, in special media conducive to their growth, e.g. incubation.
Custom hatching	A person or hatchery that hatches eggs for a ranch or a producer for a fee.
Cutability	The proportion of trimmed retail cuts a carcass may yield.
Dead in shell	(DIS) Death anytime prior to hatch occurring in either first, second or third trimester.
Debilitating	Weakening; loss of strength.
Density-dependent factor	A factor that acts in proportion to the density of animals. Some diseases are density-dependent because a higher percentage of the population becomes infected as density increases. Natality and mortality often fluctuate with changes in density.
Dimorphism	The occurrence of two forms distinct in structure among animals of the same species; e.g. the physical differences associated with sex.
Disease	Any deviation from a normal state of health.
Disinfect	To kill or render ineffective harmful microorganisms and parasites.
Disinfectant	A chemical that destroys disease-producing microorganisms or parasites.
Distal	Away from the point of origin or attachment, as of a limb or bone.
DNA	Deoxyribonucleic acid: A complex molecule consisting of deoxyribose (a sugar), phosphoric acid and four nitrogen bases. A gene is a piece of DNA.
DNA sexing	Determination of the sex of an organism by DNA testing of tissues or blood.
Dorsal	Of, pertaining to, or situated on, the back.

NOTES

NOTES

Dressing percent	Carcass weight divided by live weight and multiplied by 100. Usually the cold carcass weight is used.
Drumming	The sound made by female emus that are approaching or have reached sexual maturity; observed mainly during breeding season.
Dry bulb	The normal temperature at which an incubator is set.
Early dead	Death in the first trimester. The appearance of the ranges from coagulated blood on the surface of the yolk to an embryo in which you can readily identify body parts.
Ectoderm	The outermost of the three layers of the primitive embryo.
Ectoparasite	Parasites found on the body of a host.
Edema, edematous	Abnormal fluid accumulation in the intercellular tissue spaces of the body.
Egg identification number	A label or marking of an egg stating date laid, and oftentimes parent identification. Used for incubation purposes to establish approximate date of hatch and to track production of the hen.
Egg peritonitis	Inflammation of the abdomen of a hen due to complications in egg laying; also called egg bound.
Egg production	Eggs laid by hens producing at a high rate are more fertile and possess higher hatchability than eggs laid by low producers.
Egg turning	Refers to the turning of incubating eggs from side to side.
Egg weight loss	The weight loss an egg experiences during incubation, from the time it is laid until it hatches.
Egg yolk	The yellow part of the egg, containing stored nutrients.
Electrolytes	Substance that dissociates into ions when in solution; e.g. Na+, K+, Cl.
Emaciation	A severe loss of weight or wasted condition.
Embryo	Very early stage of individual development within the uterus in mammals, within the eggshell in birds.
Embryologic studies	The study of the development of the chick embryo.
Embryonic deaths	Embryo of the eggs die at some stage during the incubation period, usually divided into first, second, and third trimesters.

Emu oil	Oil processed or rendered from the fat of an emu; currently being used for topical medicinal purposes.
Encephalitis vaccine	A vaccine used to inoculate against encephalitis virus (EEE, triple E, Eastern and Western encephalitis).
Endocrine gland	Any of various glands, as the thyroid, adrenal, or pituitary glands, that secrete certain substances or hormones directly into the blood or lymph; ductless gland.
Endocrine system	Composed of a number of glands that produce, store, and secrete hormones.
Endogenous	Growing or proceeding from within; originating within.
Exocrine gland	Any of several glands, as the salivary glands, that excrete externally through a duct.
Endoparasite	Parasites that live within the body of a host.
Enteritis	An inflammation of the intestinal tract.
Enterococcus	Gram-positive bacteria of the streptococcus genus of the intestines.
Environment	The sum total of all external conditions that affect the well-being and performance of an animal.
Enzootic	A disease confined to a certain locality. A disease present at all times in a certain locality, but occurring in small numbers.
Epizootic	An outbreak of disease. Large number of animals die in a short period in a given region.
Estrogen	Any hormone (including estradiol and estrone) that causes the female to come physiologically into heat and to be receptive to the male. In birds, estrogens are produced by the follicle of the ovary.
Estrous	Of or pertaining to estrus.
Estrus	The period of heat or rut; the period of maximum sexual receptivity of the female.
Ethology	Study of animal behavior.
Etiology	Study of the cause of disease.
Eviscerate	The removal of the internal organs during the slaughtering process, disembowelment.
Excreta	Excreted material; waste matter from the body.
Exogenous	Having external origins; derived externally.

NOTES

NOTES

Exsanguination	Draining of blood in the slaughter process.	
External pip	In the process of hatching, when the chick first breaks the egg shell.	
Extirpation	The elimination of a species from one or more specific areas, but not from all areas. (2) Complete removal of an organ or tissue.	
Exudate	A leakage from blood vessels consisting of fluid, cells, and cellular debris into or on tissues.	
Fading chick syndrome	A condition upon hatching in which a chick deteriorates over a period of time; often associated with disease, nutrition, or environment, usually resulting in death.	
FADR	Foreign Animal Disease Report: An agency of the US Department of Agriculture.	
Farm management	The process of making decisions about the allocation of scarce resources in agricultural production for the purpose of meeting certain management goals.	
Fat	Adipose tissue.	
Feather	The external covering (plumage) of avian species, extending from follicles in the skin, used as protection, temperature control, sexual attraction, and camouflage.	
Fecal culture	The incubation of a fecal swab sample to determine normal flora (bacteria) verses pathogenic bacteria.	
Fecal exam	Usually the technique used in determining the presence of intestinal parasites, e.g. worms.	
Feces	The product of bowel movements; excrement from the intestinal tract; stool.	
Fecundity	The inherent capacity of an organism to reproduce rapidly.	
Feed conversion	The amount of feed needed for an amount of weight gain. Grower is paid on specific rates based on feed conversion.	
Feral	Existing in a wild state; not domesticated, or that which was once domesticated and has now become wild.	
Fertility	The capacity to initiate, sustain and support reproduction. With reference to poultry, the term typically refers to the percentage of eggs that, when incubated, show some degree of embryonic development.	

Fertilization	The process in which a sperm unites with an egg to produce a zygote.
FFSTF	Farm Financial Standards Task Force: A committee of agricultural financial experts that developed a set of guidelines for uniform financial reporting and analysis of farm businesses.
FHA	Farmers Home Administration: An agency of the US Department of Agriculture that provides credit to beginning farmers and other operators who are unable to obtain it from conventional sources.
FMIA	Federal Meat Inspection Act: An agency of the US Department of Agriculture.
Follicle	A blisterlike, fluid-filled structure in the ovary that contains the egg. Also a sac or pouch-like structure, e.g. hair follicle.
Formaldehyde gas	Used in fumigation of incubators to destroy salmonella organisms, or bacteria in general, on shell surfaces if used as soon as possible after the eggs are laid.
Free choice feeding	Feed always available. (2) Refers to individual feeds being available to animals so they can choose the proportion of each they prefer.
FSIS	Food Safety Inspection Service: An agency of the US Department of Agriculture.
Fungi	Certain vegetable organisms such as molds, mushrooms or toadstools.
Gametes	Male and female reproductive cells. The sperm and the egg.
Gametogenesis	The process by which sperm and eggs are produced.
Gastrulation	The process by which cell division proceeds. The blastoderm spreads out over the yolk and becomes differentiated into layers of cells: ectoderm, mesoderm, and endoderm.
Gene	A small piece of chromosome (DNA) that codes for a trait and determines how a trait will develop; a biological unit of heredity.
Genetics	Study of heredity.
Gestation	The time from breeding or conception of a female unit until she gives birth to her young.
Gizzard	The muscular stomach of birds that grinds food, usually with the aid of grit. Gizzards serve as the functional equivalent of teeth in mammals; referred to as the ventriculus in ratites.

NOTES

NOTES

Glomerulus	A tuft of convoluted capillaries in a nephron, that filters certain substances from the blood and passes a protein-free filtrate into the associated tube.
Gram-negative bacteria	Bacterial species which are decolorized by acetone or alcohol.
Gram-positive bacteria	Bacterial species which retain crystal-violet colors even when exposed to alcohol or acetone.
Gram's method	A method of distinguishing bacteria, in which a bacterial smear is stained with crystal violet, treated with Gram's solution (iodine, potassium iodide and water), decolorized with alcohol, counterstained with safranine, and washed with water.
Grit	Added to ration to supply additional surface for grinding within the gizzard; also serves to break down ingested feathers and litter. Limestone is sometimes used for grit, as well as gravel and pebbles.
Gross	A change in tissue which can be seen with the naked eye.
Grower feed	A ration specially developed for birds after the chick stage of life and before breeding stage.
Grow-out pen	Pen design, usually a large area, where a group of birds (usually several months old) are placed to grow to breeding age.
Hatchability	Percentage of fertile eggs which hatch under artificial incubation.
Hatcher	A device similar to an incubator in offering heat and humidity but in which no turning occurs. Trays are flat and offer egg separation for the hatching process.
Hematocrit	Concentration of red blood cells in a given amount of blood. Also referred to as packed cell volume (PCV).
Hemorrhage	Escape of blood from vessels; bleeding.
Heritability	The degree to which heredity influences a particular trait.
Heritability percentages	A composite average; e.g. chick livability, adult livability, age at sexual maturity, egg production, egg shell quality, fertility, hatchability of fertile eggs.
Heterosis (hybrid vigor)	Performance of offspring that is greater than the average of the parents. Usually referred to as the amount of superiority of the crossbreed over the average of the parental breeds.

Heterozygous	Having dissimilar pairs of genes for any given hereditary characteristic; an individual whose genes for a particular trait are different.
Hides	Skin from animals such as cattle, horses, pigs, and ratites.
Homoiotherm	Also homeotherm: A warm-blooded animal. An animal that maintains its characteristic body temperature even though environmental temperature varies.
Homozygous	Having identical pairs of genes for any given pair of hereditary characteristics; an individual whose genes for a particular trait are alike.
Hormone	A chemical substance secreted by a ductless gland, usually carried by the bloodstream to other places in the body where it has its specific effect on another organ.
Hybrid vigor	See Heterosis.
Hyper sensitivity	A state in which the body reacts to a foreign agent more strongly than normal.
Hyper vitaminosis	A condition in which one ingests too much of one or more vitamins.
Hypoxia	A condition resulting from deficient oxygenation of the blood.
Ilium	The broad, upper bone which with the ischium and pubis, form the pelvis.
Identification bands	Bands usually applied to the legs of birds to identify one from another.
Immune	Resistant to a particular disease.
Immunity	The ability of an animal to resist or overcome an infection.
Impaction	A blockage of the intestinal tract with foreign material, occurring at any point of the intestinal tract, but most commonly in the proventriculus and gizzard. Can also occur due to abnormal amounts, texture, or size of feed stuff.
Imprinting	Learning associated with maturational readiness; learning process along with social attachment; socialization.
Inspissated yolk sac	A hardened or dried yolk sac.

NOTES

NOTES

Inbreeding	The mating of individuals who are more closely related than the average individuals in a population. Inbreeding increases homozygosity in the population, but it does not change gene frequency.
Incross breeding	The mating of closely related individuals for several successive generations.
Incubation	The act of bringing an egg to hatching.
Incubation period	The time that elapses from when an egg is placed into an incubator until the young is hatched. Time varies for different species.
Incubator	A device in which eggs are incubated artificially, under conditions of controlled temperature, humidity, and ventilation.
Infection	Invasion of the tissue by pathogenic organisms resulting in a disease state.
Infectious	A disease produced by living organisms. Most infectious diseases of poultry are contagious; however, a few such as aspergillosis are not caused by infection.
Infertile	The failure of the male and female gametes to unite, or in the male the lack of productive sperm. An infertile egg will have a complete yellow yolk.
Inflammation	Response of tissues to an injury or other irritant.
Influenza	A virus disease characterized by inflammation of the respiratory tract, high fever, and muscular pain.
Infundibulum	Where the egg is fertilized. (2) Oviduct, the section of the reproductive tract closest to the ovaries.
Ingestion	The taking in of anything into the stomach.
Inheritance	The transmission of genes from parents to offspring.
Initial weight	Egg: The weight of the egg before being placed in the incubator to calculate the weight loss during incubation process; usually weighed just after being laid. Chick: The weight of the chick just born, used to determine health and growth rate in first 10 to 30 days of the chick.
Integument	The outer protection of the body; skin, or in birds, formed by the skin and feathers.
Internal pip	A process of hatching when the chick breaks or penetrates the air cell membrane for oxygen.
Intradermal	Into, or between, the layers of skin.
Intramuscular	Within the substance of a muscle.

Glossary

Intrauterine	Within the uterus.
Intravenous	Within the vein or veins.
In vivo	Occurring in the living body.
Ischium	The lower bone which forms the floor of the pelvis.
Isofluorane	A gas used in anesthesia of birds; an inhalant anesthetic.
-itis	Suffix denoting an inflammatory state, such as enteritis, an inflammation of the intestines.
Ivermectin	A deworming medication supplied as an injectible or topical application.
Late dead	Death in the last trimester. The embryo occupies almost the entire area within the shell. It may have an external or partially internal yolk sac.
Legume	Any plant of the family *Leguminosae*, such as pea, bean, alfalfa and clover.
Lesion	Visible change in size, shape, color or structure of an organ, may be pathological or traumatic.
Lessee	An operator who leases property from the owner; same as tenant.
Lessor	An owner who leases property to a lessee.
Lethargic, lethargy	Drowsiness, loss of will power, trance-like.
Leukocytes	White blood cells.
Line breeding	A mild form of inbreeding that maintains a high genetic relationship to an outstanding ancestor, e.g. father to daughter or mother to son.
Line crossing	The crossing of inbred lines.
Lipid	Any of a group of organic compounds comprising fats, waxes and similar substances that are greasy, insoluble in water and soluble in alcohol.
Listless	Indifferent to surroundings, somewhat unresponsive, depressed, weak.
Livestock share lease	A lease agreement in which both the owner and operator contribute capital and share the production of crops and livestock.
Locus	The place on a chromosome where a gene is located.
Lumen	The canal, duct, or cavity of a tubular organ.

NOTES

Macroclimate	The large, general climate in which an animal exists.
Macromineral	A mineral that is needed in the diet in relatively large amounts.
Maintenance	A condition in which the body is maintained without an increase or decrease in body weight and with no production or work being done.
Malposition	Abnormal positioning of a chick within the shell at hatching.
Marek's disease	Fowl paralysis; occurs in poultry flocks throughout the world. Usually affects younger birds (two to five months), involving the larger peripheral nerves.
Meat	The tissues of the animal body that are used for food.
Medium spectrum antibiotic	An antibiotic which attacks a limited number of Gram-positive and Gram-negative bacteria.
Mendelism	The essence of Mendelism is that inheritance is by particles or units (called genes); that these genes are present in pairs (one number of each pair having come from each parent) and that each gene maintains its identity generation after generation.
Mesentery	The membrane that surrounds the intestines, attaching them to the posterior wall of the abdomen, maintaining them in position and supplying blood vessels, nerves, and lymphatics.
Metabolism	The changes which take place in nutrients after they are absorbed from the digestive tract, including the building-up processes in which the absorbed nutrients are used in the formation or repair of body tissue, and the breaking-down processes in which nutrients are oxidized for the production of heat and work.
Microchip identification number	Small electronic device inserted into the body, containing a discrete number which can be read or displayed by a transponder.
Microclimate	A small, special climate within a macroclimate, created by the use of such devices as shelter, heat lamps and bedding.
Micromineral	A mineral that is needed in the diet in relatively small amounts. The quantity needed is so small that such a mineral is often called a trace mineral.
Microorganism	Any organism of microscopic size, applied especially to bacteria and protozoa.
Microscopic	Invisible to the naked eye. Visible only by the aid of a microscope.

NOTES

Glossary

Mid-dead	Death occurring in the second trimester. The embryo is fully developed and about half the size of a normal live check. The chick has either started feather development or has completed feathering.
Morbidity	Percentage of deaths from any specific disease, determined by dividing the number of deaths by the total number of those contracting the disease.
Mortality rate	Death rate; relative frequency of death, as in a district, community, or population.
Moving air incubator	An incubator that forces its own air flow.
Mycro-plasm(a)	Highly pleomorphic, aerobic to anaerobic, Gram-negative microorganism; smallest known free-living organism.
Myositis	Inflammation of muscle.
NARA	North American Rhea Association: A national organization promoting the rhea industry, education, and research.
Narrow spectrum antibiotic	An antibiotic whose activity is restricted to either Gram-negative or Gram-positive bacteria. For example, penicillin is active primarily against Gram-positive organisms, whereas streptomycin attacks only Gram-negative organisms.
Natality	Birth rate. Expressed in several ways, but often as the number of offspring per female per year or per 100 females per year.
Necropsy	The examination of bird or body after death; autopsy.
Necrosis	Death or dying of local tissue; cell death and degradation.
Neoplasm	Abnormal growth such as a tumor.
Nephron	A functional structure of a kidney.
Net energy	The energy of a feed that is available to the animal for growth, production, or work after digestion and metabolism.
Nicking	The way in which certain lines, strains, or breeds perform when mated together. When outstanding offspring result, the parents are said to have nicked well.
Nictitating membrane	A semitransparent flap of skin that acts like a second eyelid, closes upward and protects the eye while allowing the ostrich to see. Also refered to as the third eyelid.

NOTES

NOTES

NPIP	National Poultry Improvement Plan: An agency of the US Department of Agriculture.
NTIS	National Technical Information Service: An agency of the US Department of Commerce.
Nutrition	The sum of events involved in taking in nutrients, assimilating and utilizing them.
Oral	Given or taken in by mouth.
Orbit	The bony cavity of the skull which contains the eye; eye socket.
Ornithology	The branch of zoology which deals with birds.
Osmo-regulation	The mechanism that controls the rate at which fluids pass through a membrane or porous partition.
Ostrich	Largest bird in the world. Red-necked North African: *Struthio camelus camelus* Red-necked East African: *Struthio camelus massaicus* Red-necked Syrian: *Struthio camelus syriacus* (extinct) Blue-necked Somali: *Struthio camelus molybdophanes* Blue-necked South African: *Struthio camelus australis* African Black Domestic: *Struthio camelus var. domesticus*
Ova	Plural of ovum, meaning eggs.
Ovary	The female reproductive gland in which the eggs are formed, and in which progesterone and estrogenic hormones are produced.
Oviduct	A duct leading from the ovary to the horn of the uterus; in birds referred to as the infundibulum. It opens into the vent.
Oviposition	The act of laying an egg.
Oxygen analyzer	An instrument that measures oxygen content in gaseous mixtures, or oxygen dissolved in liquids, or saturation of blood with oxygen.
Palatability	Result of the following factors sensed by the bird in locating and consuming feed: appearance, odor, taste, texture and temperature.
Palpation	A massaging or stroking of animal tissues, used in diagnosis.
Papilla	Any small, nipple-like projection; one of certain small protruberances concerned with the senses of touch, taste, and smell.
Parasite	An animal form that lives on or within a bird to its detriment.

Glossary

Parenteral	In drug or vaccine administration, to inject subcutaneously, intramuscularly.
Parthogenesis	The development of unfertilized eggs. A modified form of sexual reproduction whereby a gamete is produced without sexual fertilization.
Pathogen	A disease-causing agent; includes bacteria, viruses and parasites.
Pathogenic	Disease producing.
Pathology	The study of disease
Pathological	Diseased, or due to disease; referring to pathology.
Pecking order, peck order	Social order; the tendency of animals to behave in an order of social dominance.
Peristalsis	The coordinated contraction and relaxation of a tubular muscle system, especially the alimentary system, creating a unidirectional movement which pushes the contents through the digestive tract.
Perosis	Slipped tendons due to manganese deficiency in chicks; also bone deformities associated with certain dietary deficiencies.
Phalanges	Plural of phalanx; any of the bones of the fingers or toes.
Phallus	Sexual organ of male ratites, analagous but not identical to the penis in mammals.
Pharynx	The structure which controls the passage of air and feed. The throat.
Physiology	The science that pertains to the functions of organs, organ systems, or the entire animal. The functions of living organisms and their parts, involving both chemical and physical factors and processes.
Pneumatic	Containing air or air cavities.
Postmortem	After death, especially examination after death.
PPIA	Poultry Products Inspection Act. An agency of the US Department of Agriculture.
Predispose	To confer a tendency toward disease.
Preening	A process in which birds pull their feathers through their beaks for cleaning; in birds other than ratites, also to spread body oil over the feathers.
Pre-sold birds	Birds sold under contract, usually from an upcoming hatch.

NOTES

NOTES

Prolapse	The falling down, inversion, or displacement of a part or viscera.
Prolific	Having a tendency to produce many offspring.
Prophylaxis	Preventive treatment against disease.
Protein	A substance made up of amino acids that contain approximately 16% nitrogen (based on molecular weight).
Proventriculus	The glandular prestomach of birds, located between the esophagus and gizzard, where chemical digestion softens food.
Pseudomonas	A pyogenic bacteria resulting in pus of a bluish or greenish color; Gram-negative microorganism responsible for diseases such as pneumonia, encephalitis, and endocarditis.
Pygostyle	The bone at the posterior end of the spinal column in birds, formed by the fusion of several caudal vertebrae.
Quill	The hollow, main shaft of a feather.
Rachis	Quill or shaft of feather. Also can refer to the vertebral column.
Rate of growth	Fast gains are efficient gains; when birds grow at maximum rates, they require fewer nutrients and fewer pounds of feed per pound of grain.
Rate of lay	Time interval in which a particular species of bird lays its eggs.
Ration	The quantity of feed fed to an animal over a given period of time.
Ratitae	Superorder of the subclass Neornithis, a division encompassing the more primitive birds, such as ostriches, emus rheas, moas, cassowaries, and tinamous.
Ratite	Having a flat, unkeeled, raftlike sternum (breastbone), e.g. ostriches, emus, and rheas.
Recessive	The tendency for a gene to be overshadowed, in its influence on traits, by its partner, after conception occurs and genes exist in pairs.
Renal failure	A condition in which the kidneys fail to function correctly, due to trauma, disease, or toxins; can be acute or chronic.
Reproduction efficiency	The tendency to produce large numbers of offspring in a given span of time.

Renest	A new clutch of eggs laid in the same breeding season after an earlier clutch.
Retained yolk sac	A condition in newly hatched chicks resulting in the failure to uptake and utilize the yolk sac contents.
Rhea oil	Oil that is processed or rendered from the fat of an rhea, currently being used for topical medicinal purposes.
Risk egg	An egg that is cracked or is contaminated. May or may not produce a live chick. Often set in separate incubator, to eliminate possible contamination to other eggs.
Rolled toe	A condition where a toe rolls onto its side, resulting in lameness and decreased locomotion.
Rostral	Beaklike; toward the beak.
Salmonella	Gram-negative, rod-shaped bacteria that cause various disease such as food poisoning in animals; presents a human health concern.
Scale	(1) Size. (2) Equipment on which an animal is weighed.
SCS	Soil Conservation Service: An agency of the US Department of Agriculture that provides technical and financial assistance for carrying out soil and water conservation practices.
Secondary sexual characteristics	Characteristics of animals which differ between the sexes, such as color and size, but excluding reproductive organs and their associated ducts and glands.
Selection	Differentially reproducing what one wants in a herd or flock.
Serum, blood	The clear portion of blood, separated from its more solid elements once it has been allowed to clot.
Sesamoid bone	Shaped like a sesame seed, as certain small nodular bones and cartilage.
Set date	The date eggs are placed in an incubator.
Sexing	Determination of the sex of chicks by DNA examination of sex-linked genes (feather or color sexing), surgical identification (e.g. laparscopic examination), or visual examination of the male and female organs.
Sexual maturity	Age at which birds are ready to reproduce.

NOTES

NOTES

Shell quality	The quality of the shell is related to hatchability. The amount of calcium and vitamin D in the ration affects the shell. Thickness and number of pores present are indicative of quality.
Sign	Discernable evidence of disease; symptoms or lesions.
Slipped heel tendon	A condition where the tendon has luxated off the heel (or ankle); can result from trauma or abnormal conformation.
Slipped hock tendon	A condition where the tendon has luxated off the hock, usually laterally; can result from trauma or abnormal conformation.
Social order	The tendency of animals to behave in an order of social dominance; pecking order.
SPF	Specific Pathogen Free.
SPF Program	A combination of breeding, testing, sanitation and management practices designed to establish and maintain breeder flocks free of specific known infectious diseases.
Sporadic	A disease outbreak occurring here and there; not widely diffused.
Spore	Bacteria or fungi capable of resisting unfavorable environmental conditions. A refractile body, regarded to be in a resting state.
Staphylococcus	Gram-positive microorganisms, occasionally pathogenic to man and animals, widespread in nature.
Starter feed	A ration developed for birds at the early chick stage of life.
Sterilization lamps	Germicidal lamps: low-pressure mercury-vapor tubes that artificially produce invisible ultraviolet energy (called UV-C or short-wave ultraviolet) with each wave measuring 253.7 angstroms in length, and lethal to all types of microorganisms. The correct application of these lamps depends greatly on the type of lamp and the type of germicidal fixture in which they are installed. The most recent new application of germicidal lamps and fixtures has been in the ratite industry for the entire incubation, hatching and chick brooding process, which has proven a successful type of biosecurity.
Still-air incubator	Incubators not designed to move their own air, requiring venting and manual air exchange.

Stress	An unusual or abnormal influence causing a change in an animal's function, structure or behavior. Factors tending to lower resistance of an animal to disease, such as chilling, moving, etc. Physical or psychological tension or strain.
Stress factors	Predisposing causes of disease such as weather, handling, hauling, etc.
Subcutaneous	Under the skin.
Substrates	The surface on which an animal or organism lives or grows.
Supportive treatment	Treatment of individual symptoms of a disease where diagnosis is obscure, or where a specific treatment has not been established.
Symptoms	Detectable signs of disease.
TDN	Total digestible nutrients; includes the total amounts of digestible protein, nitrogen-free extract, fiber and fat (multiplied by 2.25) all summed together.
Territorialism	The tendency for animals to inhabit and protect a specific geographical region or domain.
Therapy	Treating disease; rehabilitation.
Top producers	Usually referring to breeder birds with the higher rates of egg laying, fertility, hatchability, and survivability.
Toxemia	A condition produced by the presence of poisons (toxins) in the blood.
Toxin	Poison produced by microorganisms, plants and some animals.
Tremulous air cells	The shaking or quivering of the air cell found vertical to the trachea in the neck region, used in drumming and booming.
Trilling	A tremulous sound or fluttering made by certain birds, such as ratites.
Turned legs	A condition in which a leg rotates around its long axis, usually involving the long bones; related to nutrition, trauma, exercise, environment, and genetics.
Unabsorbed yolk sac	See retained yolk sac.
Uncinate	Hooked, bent at the end like a hook.

NOTES

NOTES

Uncinate process	A curved, bony projection on certain ribs of birds that projects backward and overlaps the succeeding rib, serving to strengthen the thorax.
USAHA	United States Animal Health Association.
Vaccination	The injection of an agent such as a vaccine into an animal for the purpose of preventing disease. The act of administering a vaccine or antigen.
Vaccine	(1) Suspension of attenuated or killed microbes or toxins administered to induce active immunity. (2) A suspension of live microorganisms (bacteria or virus) or microorganisms that have had their pathogenic properties removed but their antigens retained.
Vaginal culture	Testing for microorganisms which may affect reproductive capability or the health of eggs or chicks.
Vent sexing	The physical sexing of birds by everting the cloaca and looking for a phallus or clitoris.
Ventral	Situated on the abdominal side of the body; of, pertaining to, or situated on the lower side or surface, as an organ or part.
Veterinary health certificate	A certificate of health issued by a veterinarian upon examination of an animal.
Virulence	As applied to microscopic organisms, refers to its ability to overcome the body defenses of the host.
Virus	(1) Ultra-microscopic bundle of genetic material capable of multiplying only in living cells. Viruses cause a wide range of disease in plants, animals and humans, such as rabies and measles. (2) The smallest living microorganism, not visible under an ordinary microscope, which lives parasitically upon plants and animals, and sometimes causes disease.
Viscera	The organs in the cavities of the body, especially in the abdominal cavity.
Vitamin	An organic catalyst, or component thereof, that facilitates specific and necessary functions.
Vitelline membrane	The very thin membrane, or skin, surrounding the yolk.
Waltzing	The dancing display of ratites; also called twirling.
WBC	White blood count.
Weight-loss graph	A chart used as an aid to estimate weight loss in incubation, following initial weighing of the egg.

Wet bulb	Hygrometer reading: achieved by placing a wick in a small bottle of water in the incubator and the other end of the wick over a thermometer; compared to the dry bulb, determines relative humidity.
Wet chicks	Chicks born with generalized edema and wet feathers, associated with infection or inadequate weight loss.
Worming	Oral, injectable, or topical products used to rid an animal of internal parasites.
Yield	The percentage of the live animal weight that becomes the carcass weight at slaughter, determined by dividing the carcass weight by the live weight, then multiplying by 100. Also called dressing percentage.
Yolk	The yellow part of the egg; stored nutrients of the egg.
Yolk sac	Layer of tissue encompassing the yolk of an egg. Enveloping the yolk, this membrane secretes an enzyme that changes the yolk contents into a soluble form so that the food material may be absorbed and carried to the developing embryo. The yolk sac and its remaining contents are drawn into the body cavity just prior to hatching to serve as a temporary source of food material.
Zygote	The cell formed by the union of a male gamete (spermatozoa) and a female gamete (ova); fertilization.

NOTES

NOTES

CHARTS

The charts on the following pages are included to help you determine hatching dates, convert common weights and measures, and learn more about common problems with hatching, incubation, and diseases of ratites.

The charts dealing with medical and other problems are intended as a quick reference, not as a substitute for qualified medical advice.

For the veterinarian who is not completely familiar with ratites, they may provide a start in diagnosing or treating common problems, but again, they are not intended as a substitute for consultation with university or other experts.

CONTENTS

Ostrich Hatching Chart	378
Ostrich Egg Weight Loss Chart	379
Emu Hatching Chart	383
Emu Egg Weight Loss Chart	384
Rhea Hatching Chart	387
Rhea Egg Weight Loss Chart	388
Egg Weight Loss Graph	390
Incubation Trouble-shooting Chart	391
Conversion Tables (Weights & Measures)	393
Charts & Discussion by Brett A. Hopkins, DVM	
Pre-purchase Examination Guidelines	404
Blood Count & Serum Chemistry Analysis	409
Reproduction Quick Reference	412
Diseases & Disorders	414
Save the Skin	428

OSTRICH HATCHING CHART

The date on the left is the date the egg is placed into the incubator. The date on the right is the approximate date of hatch, based on an incubation period of 42 days.   * Subtract a day in leap years.

Jan 01 . Feb 12	Mar 03 . Apr 14	May 03 . Jun 14	Jul 03 Aug 14	Sep 02. Oct 14	Nov 02. Dec 14
02 13	04 15	04 15	04 15	03 15	03 15
03 14	05 16	05 16	05 16	04 16	04 16
04 15	06 17	06 17	06 17	05 17	05 17
05 16	07 18	07 18	07 18	06 18	06 18
06 17	08 19	08 19	08 19	07 19	07 19
07 18	09 20	09 20	09 20	08 20	08 20
08 19	10 21	10 21	10 21	09 21	09 21
09 20	11 22	11 22	11 22	10 22	10 22
10 21	12 23	12 23	12 23	11 23	11 23
11 22	13 24	13 24	13 24	12 24	12 24
12 23	14 25	14 25	14 25	13 25	13 25
13 24	15 26	15 26	15 26	14 26	14 26
14 25	16 27	16 27	16 27	15 27	15 27
15 26	17 28	17 28	17 28	16 28	16 28
16 27	18 29	18 29	18 29	17 29	17 29
17 28	19 30	19 30	19 30	18 30	18 30
18 Mar *01	20 May 01	20 . Jul 01	20 31	19 31	19 31
19 .... *02	21 02	21 02	21 . Sep 01	20. Nov 01	20 .. Jan 01
20 .... *03	22 03	22 03	22 02	21 02	21 02
21 .... *04	23 04	23 04	23 03	22 03	22 03
22 .... *05	24 05	24 05	24 04	23 04	23 04
23 .... *06	25 06	25 06	25 05	24 05	24 05
24 .... *07	26 07	26 07	26 06	25 06	25 06
25 .... *08	27 08	27 08	27 07	26 07	26 07
26 .... *09	28 09	28 09	28 08	27 08	27 28
27 .... *10	29 10	29 10	29 09	28 09	28 09
28 .... *11	30 11	30 11	30 10	29 10	29 10
29 .... *12	31 12	31 12	31 11	30 11	30 11
30 .... *13	Apr 01 13	Jun 01 13	Aug 01 12	Oct 01 12	Dec 01 12
31 .... *14	02 14	02 14	02 13	02 13	02 13
Feb 01 .... *15	03 15	03 15	03 14	03 14	03 14
02 .... *16	04 16	04 16	04 15	04 15	04 15
03 .... *17	05 17	05 17	05 16	05 16	05 16
04 .... *18	06 18	06 18	06 17	06 17	06 17
05 .... *19	07 19	07 19	07 18	07 18	07 18
06 .... *20	08 20	08 20	08 19	08 19	08 19
07 .... *21	09 21	09 21	09 20	09 20	09 20
08 .... *22	10 22	10 22	10 21	10 21	10 21
09 .... *23	11 23	11 23	11 22	11 22	11 22
10 .... *24	12 24	12 24	12 23	12 23	12 23
11 .... *25	13 25	13 25	13 24	13 24	13 24
12 .... *26	14 26	14 26	14 25	14 25	14 25
13 .... *27	15 27	15 27	15 26	15 26	15 26
14 .... *28	16 28	16 28	16 27	16 27	16 27
15 .... *29	17 29	17 29	17 28	17 28	17 28
16 .... *30	18 30	18 30	18 29	18 29	18 29
17 .... *31	19 31	19 31	19 30	19 30	19 30
18 Apr *01	20 . Jun 01	20 Aug 01	20 Oct 01	20. Dec 01	20 31
19 .... *02	21 02	21 02	21 02	21 02	21 . Feb 01
20 .... *03	22 03	22 03	22 03	22 03	22 02
21 .... *04	23 04	23 04	23 04	23 04	23 03
22 .... *05	24 05	24 05	24 05	24 05	24 04
23 .... *06	25 06	25 06	25 06	25 06	25 05
24 .... *07	26 07	26 07	26 07	26 07	26 06
25 08	27 08	27 08	27 08	27 08	27 07
26 .... *09	28 09	28 09	28 09	28 09	28 08
27 .... *10	29 10	29 10	29 10	29 10	29 09
28 .... *11	30 11	30 11	30 11	30 11	30 10
Mar 01 12	May 01 12	Jul 01 12	31 12	31 12	31 11
02 13	02 13	02 13	Sep 01 13	Nov 01 13	

OSTRICH EGG WEIGHT LOSS CHART (42-Day Hatch Period)

TARGET LOSS	12%		13%		14%		15%	
INITIAL WEIGHT	DAILY LOSS	TARGET WEIGHT	DAILY LOSS	TARGET WEIGHT	DAILY LOSS	TARGET WEIGHT	DAILY LOSS	TARGET WEIGHT
900	2.57	792	2.78	783	3.00	774	3.21	765
905	2.58	797	2.80	788	3.01	778	3.23	769
910	2.59	801	2.81	792	3.03	783	3.25	774
915	2.61	805	2.83	796	3.05	787	3.27	778
920	2.62	810	2.84	801	3.06	791	3.28	782
925	2.64	814	2.86	805	3.08	796	3.30	786
930	2.65	819	2.87	809	3.10	800	3.32	791
935	2.66	823	2.89	814	3.11	804	3.34	795
940	2.68	827	2.90	818	3.13	809	3.36	799
945	2.69	832	2.92	822	3.15	813	3.37	803
950	2.71	836	2.94	827	3.16	817	3.39	808
955	2.72	841	2.95	831	3.18	821	3.41	812
960	2.74	845	2.97	835	3.20	826	3.43	816
965	2.75	849	2.98	840	3.21	830	3.45	820
970	2.76	854	3.00	844	3.23	834	3.46	825
975	2.78	858	3.01	848	3.25	839	3.48	829
980	2.79	863	3.03	853	3.26	843	3.50	833
985	2.81	867	3.04	857	3.28	847	3.52	837
990	2.82	871	3.06	862	3.30	852	3.53	842
995	2.84	876	3.07	866	3.31	856	3.55	846
1000	2.85	880	3.09	870	3.33	860	3.57	850
1005	2.86	885	3.11	875	3.35	864	3.59	854
1010	2.88	889	3.12	879	3.36	869	3.61	859
1015	2.89	894	3.14	883	3.38	873	3.62	863
1020	2.91	898	3.15	888	3.40	877	3.64	867
1025	2.92	902	3.17	892	3.41	882	3.66	871
1030	2.94	907	3.18	896	3.43	886	3.68	876
1035	2.95	911	3.20	901	3.45	890	3.69	880
1040	2.96	916	3.21	905	3.46	895	3.71	884
1045	2.98	920	3.23	909	3.48	899	3.73	888
1050	2.99	924	3.24	914	3.50	903	3.75	893
1055	3.01	929	3.26	918	3.51	907	3.77	897

INSTRUCTIONS FOR USING THE WEIGHT LOSS CHARTS

1. Weigh the egg carefully (using an accurate gram scale) the day you place it in the incubator and record the weight. Weigh it a couple days later, and again a couple days later, each time noting the weight. Divide the amount of weight lost by the number of days to find the loss per day. (Refer to the weight-loss graph for calculations if necessary.)
2. Find the initial weight in the chart.
3. Read across to the "daily loss" figure closest to the figure you've calculated. Then read the "target weight" figure next to it. Read up to the top of the column to the percentage of weight loss. Generally a weight loss of 15% is recommended. If it is much lower, refer to the instructions for your incubator to adjust temperature and/or humidity.
4. Weigh the egg periodically and repeat the procedure to be sure it remains within the target loss.
5. Remember that not all eggs hatch on the day you expect them to. Toward the end of the hatching period, use a candler to help determine the status of the egg.

OSTRICH EGG WEIGHT LOSS CHART, Cont'd. (42-Day Hatch Period)

TARGET LOSS	12%		13%		14%		15%	
INITIAL WEIGHT	DAILY LOSS	TARGET WEIGHT	DAILY LOSS	TARGET WEIGHT	DAILY LOSS	TARGET WEIGHT	DAILY LOSS	TARGET WEIGHT
1060	3.02	933	3.28	922	3.53	912	3.78	901
1065	3.04	938	3.29	927	3.55	916	3.80	905
1070	3.05	942	3.31	931	3.56	920	3.82	910
1075	3.06	946	3.32	935	3.58	925	3.84	914
1080	3.08	951	3.34	940	3.60	929	3.86	918
1085	3.09	955	3.35	944	3.61	933	3.87	922
1090	3.11	960	3.37	949	3.63	938	3.89	927
1095	3.12	964	3.38	953	3.65	942	3.91	931
1100	3.14	968	3.40	957	3.66	946	3.93	935
1105	3.15	973	3.41	962	3.68	950	3.94	939
1110	3.16	977	3.43	966	3.70	955	3.96	944
1115	3.18	982	3.45	970	3.71	959	3.98	948
1120	3.19	986	3.46	975	3.73	963	4.00	952
1125	3.21	990	3.48	979	3.75	968	4.02	956
1130	3.22	995	3.49	983	3.76	972	4.03	961
1135	3.23	999	3.51	988	3.78	976	4.05	965
1140	3.25	1004	3.52	992	3.80	981	4.07	969
1145	3.26	1008	3.54	996	3.81	985	4.09	973
1150	3.28	1012	3.55	1001	3.83	989	4.11	978
1155	3.29	1017	3.57	1005	3.85	993	4.12	982
1160	3.31	1021	3.58	1009	3.86	998	4.14	986
1165	3.32	1026	3.60	1014	3.88	1002	4.16	990
1170	3.33	1030	3.62	1018	3.90	1006	4.18	995
1175	3.35	1034	3.63	1023	3.91	1011	4.19	999
1180	3.36	1039	3.65	1027	3.93	1015	4.21	1003
1185	3.38	1043	3.66	1031	3.95	1019	4.23	1007
1190	3.39	1048	3.68	1036	3.96	1024	4.25	1012
1195	3.41	1052	3.69	1040	3.98	1028	4.27	1016
1200	3.42	1056	3.71	1044	4.00	1032	4.28	1020
1205	3.43	1061	3.72	1049	4.01	1036	4.30	1024
1210	3.45	1065	3.74	1053	4.03	1041	4.32	1029
1215	3.46	1070	3.75	1057	4.05	1045	4.34	1033
1220	3.48	1074	3.77	1062	4.06	1049	4.36	1037
1225	3.49	1078	3.79	1066	4.08	1054	4.37	1041
1230	3.51	1083	3.80	1070	4.10	1058	4.39	1046
1235	3.52	1087	3.82	1075	4.11	1062	4.41	1050
1240	3.53	1092	3.83	1079	4.13	1067	4.43	1054
1245	3.55	1096	3.85	1083	4.15	1071	4.44	1058
1250	3.56	1100	3.86	1088	4.16	1075	4.46	1063
1255	3.58	1105	3.88	1092	4.18	1079	4.48	1067
1260	3.59	1109	3.89	1096	4.20	1084	4.50	1071
1265	3.61	1114	3.91	1101	4.21	1088	4.52	1075
1270	3.62	1118	3.92	1105	4.23	1092	4.53	1080

OSTRICH EGG WEIGHT LOSS CHART, Cont'd (42-Day Hatch Period)

TARGET LOSS	12%		13%		14%		15%	
INITIAL WEIGHT	DAILY LOSS	TARGET WEIGHT	DAILY LOSS	TARGET WEIGHT	DAILY LOSS	TARGET WEIGHT	DAILY LOSS	TARGET WEIGHT
1275	3.63	1122	3.94	1110	4.25	1097	4.55	1084
1280	3.65	1127	3.96	1114	4.26	1101	4.57	1088
1285	3.66	1131	3.97	1118	4.28	1105	4.59	1092
1290	3.68	1136	3.99	1123	4.30	1110	4.61	1097
1295	3.69	1140	4.00	1127	4.31	1114	4.62	1101
1300	3.71	1144	4.02	1131	4.33	1118	4.64	1105
1305	3.72	1149	4.03	1136	4.35	1122	4.66	1109
1310	3.73	1153	4.05	1140	4.36	1127	4.68	1114
1315	3.75	1158	4.06	1144	4.38	1131	4.69	1118
1320	3.76	1162	4.08	1149	4.40	1135	4.71	1122
1325	3.78	1166	4.09	1153	4.41	1140	4.73	1126
1330	3.79	1171	4.11	1157	4.43	1144	4.75	1131
1335	3.80	1175	4.13	1162	4.45	1148	4.77	1135
1340	3.82	1180	4.14	1166	4.46	1153	4.78	1139
1345	3.83	1184	4.16	1170	4.48	1157	4.80	1143
1350	3.85	1188	4.17	1175	4.50	1161	4.82	1148
1355	3.86	1193	4.19	1179	4.51	1165	4.84	1152
1360	3.88	1197	4.20	1183	4.53	1170	4.86	1156
1365	3.89	1202	4.22	1188	4.55	1174	4.87	1160
1370	3.90	1206	4.23	1192	4.56	1178	4.89	1165
1375	3.92	1210	4.25	1197	4.58	1183	4.91	1169
1380	3.93	1215	4.26	1201	4.60	1187	4.93	1173
1385	3.95	1219	4.28	1205	4.61	1191	4.94	1177
1390	3.96	1224	4.30	1210	4.63	1196	4.96	1182
1395	3.98	1228	4.31	1214	4.65	1200	4.98	1186
1400	3.99	1232	4.33	1218	4.66	1204	5.00	1190
1405	4.00	1237	4.34	1223	4.68	1208	5.02	1194
1410	4.02	1241	4.36	1227	4.70	1213	5.03	1199
1415	4.03	1246	4.37	1231	4.71	1217	5.05	1203
1420	4.05	1250	4.39	1236	4.73	1221	5.07	1207
1425	4.06	1254	4.40	1240	4.75	1226	5.09	1211
1430	4.08	1259	4.42	1244	4.76	1230	5.11	1216
1435	4.09	1263	4.43	1249	4.78	1234	5.12	1220
1440	4.10	1268	4.45	1253	4.80	1239	5.14	1224
1445	4.12	1272	4.47	1257	4.81	1243	5.16	1228
1450	4.13	1276	4.48	1262	4.83	1247	5.18	1233
1455	4.15	1281	4.50	1266	4.85	1252	5.19	1237
1460	4.16	1285	4.51	1271	4.86	1256	5.21	1241
1465	4.18	1290	4.53	1275	4.88	1260	5.23	1245
1470	4.19	1294	4.54	1279	4.90	1264	5.25	1250
1475	4.20	1298	4.56	1284	4.91	1269	5.27	1254
1480	4.22	1303	4.57	1288	4.93	1273	5.28	1258
1485	4.23	1307	4.59	1292	4.95	1277	5.30	1262

OSTRICH EGG WEIGHT LOSS CHART, Cont'd (42-Day Hatch Period)

TARGET LOSS	12%		13%		14%		15%	
INITIAL WEIGHT	DAILY LOSS	TARGET WEIGHT	DAILY LOSS	TARGET WEIGHT	DAILY LOSS	TARGET WEIGHT	DAILY LOSS	TARGET WEIGHT
1490	4.25	1312	4.60	1297	4.96	1282	5.32	1267
1495	4.26	1316	4.62	1301	4.98	1286	5.34	1271
1500	4.28	1320	4.64	1305	5.00	1290	5.36	1275
1505	4.29	1325	4.65	1310	5.01	1295	5.37	1279
1510	4.30	1329	4.67	1314	5.03	1299	5.39	1284
1515	4.32	1334	4.68	1318	5.04	1303	5.41	1288
1520	4.33	1338	4.70	1323	5.06	1307	5.43	1292
1525	4.35	1342	4.71	1327	5.08	1312	5.44	1296
1530	4.36	1347	4.73	1331	5.09	1316	5.46	1301
1535	4.37	1351	4.74	1336	5.11	1320	5.48	1305
1540	4.39	1356	4.76	1340	5.13	1325	5.50	1309
1545	4.40	1360	4.77	1344	5.14	1329	5.52	1313
1550	4.42	1364	4.79	1349	5.16	1333	5.53	1318
1555	4.43	1369	4.80	1353	5.18	1338	5.55	1322
1560	4.45	1373	4.82	1358	5.19	1342	5.57	1326
1565	4.46	1378	4.84	1362	5.21	1346	5.59	1330
1570	4.47	1382	4.85	1366	5.23	1350	5.60	1335
1575	4.49	1386	4.87	1371	5.24	1355	5.62	1339
1580	4.50	1391	4.88	1375	5.26	1359	5.64	1343
1585	4.52	1395	4.90	1379	5.28	1363	5.66	1347
1590	4.53	1400	4.91	1384	5.29	1368	5.68	1352
1595	4.55	1404	4.93	1388	5.31	1372	5.69	1356
1600	4.56	1408	4.94	1392	5.33	1376	5.71	1360
1605	4.57	1413	4.96	1397	5.34	1381	5.73	1364
1610	4.59	1417	4.97	1401	5.36	1385	5.75	1369
1615	4.60	1422	4.99	1405	5.38	1389	5.77	1373
1620	4.62	1426	5.01	1410	5.39	1393	5.78	1377
1625	4.63	1430	5.02	1414	5.41	1398	5.80	1381
1630	4.65	1435	5.04	1418	5.43	1402	5.82	1386
1635	4.66	1439	5.05	1423	5.44	1406	5.84	1390
1640	4.67	1444	5.07	1427	5.46	1411	5.85	1394
1645	4.69	1448	5.08	1432	5.48	1415	5.87	1398
1650	4.70	1452	5.10	1436	5.49	1419	5.89	1403
1655	4.72	1457	5.11	1440	5.51	1424	5.91	1407
1660	4.73	1461	5.13	1445	5.53	1428	5.93	1411
1665	4.75	1466	5.14	1449	5.54	1432	5.94	1415
1670	4.76	1470	5.16	1453	5.56	1436	5.96	1420
1675	4.77	1475	5.18	1458	5.58	1441	5.98	1424
1680	4.79	1479	5.19	1462	5.59	1445	6.00	1428
1685	4.80	1483	5.21	1466	5.61	1449	6.02	1432
1690	4.82	1488	5.22	1471	5.63	1454	6.03	1437
1695	4.83	1492	5.24	1475	5.64	1458	6.05	1441
1700	4.85	1497	5.25	1479	5.66	1462	6.07	1445

EMU HATCHING CHART

The date on the left is the date the egg is placed into the incubator. The date on the right is the approximate date of hatch, based on an incubation period of 52 days.   * Subtract a day in leap years.

Oct 01 Nov 22	Dec 01 .. Jan 22	Jan 31 Mar *24	Apr 02 May 24	Jun 02 .. Jul 24	Aug 02 . Sep 23
02 23	02. 23	Feb 01 .... *25	03 25	03 25	03 24
03 24	03. 24	02 .... *26	04 26	04 26	04 25
04 25	04. 25	03 .... *27	05 27	05 27	05 26
05 26	05. 26	04 .... *28	06 28	06 28	06 27
06 27	06. 27	05 .... *29	07 29	07 29	07 28
07 28	07. 28	06 .... *30	08 30	08 30	08 29
08 29	08. 29	07 .... *31	09 31	09 31	09 30
09 30	09. 30	08 Apr *01	10 . Jun 01	10 . Aug 01	10 . Oct 01
10 Dec 01	10. 31	09 .... *02	11 02	11 02	11 02
11 02	11. Feb 01	10 .... *03	12 03	12 03	12 03
12 03	12. 02	11 .... *04	13 04	13 04	13 04
13 04	13. 03	12 .... *05	14 05	14 05	14 05
14 05	14. 04	13 .... *06	15 06	15 06	15 06
15 06	15. 05	14 .... *07	16 07	16 07	16 07
16 07	16. 06	15 .... *08	17 08	17 08	17 08
17 08	17. 07	16 .... *09	18 09	18 09	18 09
18 09	18. 08	17 .... *10	19 10	19 10	19 10
19 10	19. 09	18 .... *11	20 11	20 11	20 11
20 11	20. 10	19 .... *12	21 12	21 12	21 12
21 12	21. 11	20 .... *13	22 13	22 13	22 13
22 13	22. 12	21 .... *14	23 14	23 14	23 14
23 14	23. 13	22 .... *15	24 15	24 15	24 15
24 15	24. 14	23 .... *16	25 16	25 16	25 16
25 16	25. 15	24 .... *17	26 17	26 17	26 17
26 17	26. 16	25 .... *18	27 18	27 18	27 18
27 18	27. 17	26 .... *19	28 19	28 19	28 19
28 19	28. 18	27 .... *20	29 20	29 20	29 20
29 20	29. 19	28 .... *21	30 21	30 21	30 21
30 21	30. 20	Mar 01 22	May 01 22	Jul 01 22	31 22
31 22	31. 21	02 23	02 23	02 23	Sep 01 23
Nov 01 23	Jan 01. 22	03 24	03 24	03 24	02 24
02 24	02. 23	04 25	04 25	04 25	03 25
03 25	03. 24	05 26	05 26	05 26	04 26
04 26	04. 25	06 27	06 27	06 27	05 27
05 27	05. 26	07 28	07 28	07 28	06 28
06 28	06. 27	08 29	08 29	08 29	07 29
07 29	07. 28	09 30	09 30	09 30	08 30
08 30	08 Mar *01	10 . May 01	10 .. Jul 01	10 31	09 31
09 31	09. .... *02	11 02	11 02	11 . Sep 01	10 Nov 01
10 . Jan 01	10. .... *03	12 03	12 03	12 02	11 02
11 02	11. .... *04	13 04	13 04	13 03	12 03
12 03	12. .... *05	14 05	14 05	14 04	13 04
13 04	13. .... *06	15 06	15 06	15 05	14 05
14 05	14. .... *07	16 07	16 07	16 06	15 06
15 06	15. .... *08	17 08	17 08	17 07	16 07
16 07	16. .... *09	18 09	18 09	18 08	17 08
17 08	17. .... *10	19 10	19 10	19 09	18 09
18 09	18. .... *11	20 11	20 11	20 10	19 10
19 10	19. .... *12	21 12	21 12	21 11	20 11
20 11	20. .... *13	22 13	22 13	22 12	21 12
21 12	21. .... *14	23 14	23 14	23 13	22 13
22 13	22. .... *15	24 15	24 15	24 14	23 14
23 14	23. .... *16	25 16	25 16	25 15	24 15
24 15	24. .... *17	26 17	26 17	26 16	25 16
25 16	25. .... *18	27 18	27 18	27 17	26 17
26 17	26. .... *19	28 19	28 19	28 18	27 18
27 18	27. .... *20	29 20	29 20	29 19	28 19
28 19	28. .... *21	30 21	30 21	30 20	29 20
29 20	29. .... *22	31 22	31 22	31 21	30 21
30 21	30. .... *23	Apr 01 23	Jun 01 23	Aug 01 22	

EMU EGG WEIGHT LOSS CHART (50-Day Hatch Period)

TARGET LOSS	12%		13%		14%		15%	
INITIAL WEIGHT	DAILY LOSS	TARGET WEIGHT	DAILY LOSS	TARGET WEIGHT	DAILY LOSS	TARGET WEIGHT	DAILY LOSS	TARGET WEIGHT
370	0.89	326	0.96	322	1.04	318	1.11	315
375	0.90	330	0.98	326	1.05	323	1.13	319
380	0.91	334	0.99	331	1.06	327	1.14	323
385	0.92	339	1.00	335	1.08	331	1.16	327
390	0.94	343	1.01	339	1.09	335	1.17	332
395	0.95	348	1.03	344	1.11	340	1.19	336
400	0.96	352	1.04	348	1.12	344	1.20	340
405	0.97	356	1.05	352	1.13	348	1.22	344
410	0.98	361	1.07	357	1.15	353	1.23	349
415	1.00	365	1.08	361	1.16	357	1.25	353
420	1.01	370	1.09	365	1.18	361	1.26	357
425	1.02	374	1.11	370	1.19	366	1.28	361
430	1.03	378	1.12	374	1.20	370	1.29	366
435	1.04	383	1.13	378	1.22	374	1.31	370
440	1.06	387	1.14	383	1.23	378	1.32	374
445	1.07	392	1.16	387	1.25	383	1.34	378
450	1.08	396	1.17	392	1.26	387	1.35	383
455	1.09	400	1.18	396	1.27	391	1.37	387
460	1.10	405	1.20	400	1.29	396	1.38	391
465	1.12	409	1.21	405	1.30	400	1.40	395
470	1.13	414	1.22	409	1.32	404	1.41	400
475	1.14	418	1.24	413	1.33	409	1.43	404
480	1.15	422	1.25	418	1.34	413	1.44	408
485	1.16	427	1.26	422	1.36	417	1.46	412
490	1.18	431	1.27	426	1.37	421	1.47	417
495	1.19	436	1.29	431	1.39	426	1.49	421
500	1.20	440	1.30	435	1.40	430	1.50	425
505	1.21	444	1.31	439	1.41	434	1.52	429
510	1.22	449	1.33	444	1.43	439	1.53	434
515	1.24	453	1.34	448	1.44	443	1.55	438
520	1.25	458	1.35	452	1.46	447	1.56	442
525	1.26	462	1.37	457	1.47	452	1.58	446

INSTRUCTIONS FOR USING THE WEIGHT LOSS CHART

1. Weigh the egg carefully (using an accurate gram scale) the day you place it in the incubator and record the weight. Weigh it a couple days later, and again a couple days later, each time noting the weight. Divide the amount of weight lost by the number of days to find the loss per day. (Refer to the weight-loss graph for calculations if necessary.)

2. Find the initial weight in the chart.

3. Read across to the "daily loss" figure closest to the figure you've calculated. Then read the "target weight" figure next to it. Read up to the top of the column to the percentage of weight loss. Generally a weight loss of 15% is recommended. If it is much lower, refer to the instructions for your incubator to adjust temperature and/or humidity.

4. Weigh the egg periodically and repeat the procedure to be sure it remains within the target loss.

5. Remember that not all eggs hatch on the day you expect them to. Toward the end of the hatching period, use a candler to help determine the status of the egg.

EMU EGG WEIGHT LOSS CHART, Cont'd (50-Day Hatch Period)

TARGET LOSS	12%		13%		14%		15%	
INITIAL WEIGHT	DAILY LOSS	TARGET WEIGHT	DAILY LOSS	TARGET WEIGHT	DAILY LOSS	TARGET WEIGHT	DAILY LOSS	TARGET WEIGHT
530	1.27	466	1.38	461	1.48	456	1.59	451
535	1.28	471	1.39	465	1.50	460	1.61	455
540	1.30	475	1.40	470	1.51	464	1.62	459
545	1.31	480	1.42	474	1.53	469	1.64	463
550	1.32	484	1.43	479	1.54	473	1.65	468
555	1.33	488	1.44	483	1.55	477	1.67	472
560	1.34	493	1.46	487	1.57	482	1.68	476
565	1.36	497	1.47	492	1.58	486	1.70	480
570	1.37	502	1.48	496	1.60	490	1.71	485
575	1.38	506	1.50	500	1.61	495	1.73	489
580	1.39	510	1.51	505	1.62	499	1.74	493
585	1.40	515	1.52	509	1.64	503	1.76	497
590	1.42	519	1.53	513	1.65	507	1.77	502
595	1.43	524	1.55	518	1.67	512	1.79	506
600	1.44	528	1.56	522	1.68	516	1.80	510
605	1.45	532	1.57	526	1.69	520	1.82	514
610	1.46	537	1.59	531	1.71	525	1.83	519
615	1.48	541	1.60	535	1.72	529	1.85	523
620	1.49	546	1.61	539	1.74	533	1.86	527
625	1.50	550	1.63	544	1.75	538	1.88	531
630	1.51	554	1.64	548	1.76	542	1.89	536
635	1.52	559	1.65	552	1.78	546	1.91	540
640	1.54	563	1.66	557	1.79	550	1.92	544
645	1.55	568	1.68	561	1.81	555	1.94	548
650	1.56	572	1.69	566	1.82	559	1.95	553
655	1.57	576	1.70	570	1.83	563	1.97	557
660	1.58	581	1.72	574	1.85	568	1.98	561
665	1.60	585	1.73	579	1.86	572	2.00	565
670	1.61	590	1.74	583	1.88	576	2.01	570
675	1.62	594	1.76	587	1.89	581	2.03	574
680	1.63	598	1.77	592	1.90	585	2.04	578
685	1.64	603	1.78	596	1.92	589	2.06	582
690	1.66	607	1.79	600	1.93	593	2.07	587
695	1.67	612	1.81	605	1.95	598	2.09	591
700	1.68	616	1.82	609	1.96	602	2.10	595
705	1.69	620	1.83	613	1.97	606	2.12	599
710	1.70	625	1.85	618	1.99	611	2.13	604
715	1.72	629	1.86	622	2.00	615	2.15	608
720	1.73	634	1.87	626	2.02	619	2.16	612
725	1.74	638	1.89	631	2.03	624	2.18	616
730	1.75	642	1.90	635	2.04	628	2.19	621
735	1.76	647	1.91	639	2.06	632	2.21	625
740	1.78	651	1.92	644	2.07	636	2.22	629

EMU EGG WEIGHT LOSS CHART, Cont'd (50-Day Hatch Period)

TARGET LOSS	12%		13%		14%		15%	
INITIAL WEIGHT	DAILY LOSS	TARGET WEIGHT	DAILY LOSS	TARGET WEIGHT	DAILY LOSS	TARGET WEIGHT	DAILY LOSS	TARGET WEIGHT
745	1.79	656	1.94	648	2.09	641	2.24	633
750	1.80	660	1.95	653	2.10	645	2.25	638
755	1.81	664	1.96	657	2.11	649	2.27	642
760	1.82	669	1.98	661	2.13	654	2.28	646
765	1.84	673	1.99	666	2.14	658	2.30	650
770	1.85	678	2.00	670	2.16	662	2.31	655
775	1.86	682	2.02	674	2.17	667	2.33	659
780	1.87	686	2.03	679	2.18	671	2.34	663
785	1.88	691	2.04	683	2.20	675	2.36	667
790	1.90	695	2.05	687	2.21	679	2.37	672
795	1.91	700	2.07	692	2.23	684	2.39	676
800	1.92	704	2.08	696	2.24	688	2.40	680
805	1.93	708	2.09	700	2.25	692	2.42	684
810	1.94	713	2.11	705	2.27	697	2.43	689
815	1.96	717	2.12	709	2.28	701	2.45	693
820	1.97	722	2.13	713	2.30	705	2.46	697
825	1.98	726	2.15	718	2.31	710	2.48	701
830	1.99	730	2.16	722	2.32	714	2.49	706
835	2.00	735	2.17	726	2.34	718	2.51	710
840	2.02	739	2.18	731	2.35	722	2.52	714
845	2.03	744	2.20	735	2.37	727	2.54	718
850	2.04	748	2.21	740	2.38	731	2.55	723

RHEA HATCHING CHART

The date on the left is the date the egg is placed into the hatcher. The date on the right is the approximate date of hatch, based on an incubation period of 37 days.   * Subtract a day in leap years.

Set	Hatch	Set	Hatch	Set	Hatch	Set	Hatch	Set	Hatch	Set	Hatch
Apr 01	*08	Jun 01	Jul 08	Aug 01	Sep 07	Oct 01	Jan 07	Dec 01	Jan 07	Jan 31	Mar *09
02	*09	02	09	02	08	02	08	02	08	Feb 01	*10
03	*10	03	10	03	09	03	09	03	09	02	*11
04	*11	04	11	04	10	04	10	04	10	03	*12
05	*12	05	12	05	11	05	11	05	11	04	*13
06	*13	06	13	06	12	06	12	06	12	05	*14
07	14	07	14	07	13	07	13	07	13	06	*15
08	15	08	15	08	14	08	14	08	14	07	*16
09	16	09	16	09	15	09	15	09	15	08	*17
10	17	10	17	10	16	10	16	10	16	09	*18
11	18	11	18	11	17	11	17	11	17	10	*19
12	19	12	19	12	18	12	18	12	18	11	*20
13	20	13	20	13	19	13	19	13	19	12	*21
14	21	14	21	14	20	14	20	14	20	13	*22
15	22	15	22	15	21	15	21	15	21	14	*23
16	23	16	23	16	22	16	22	16	22	15	*24
17	24	17	24	17	23	17	23	17	23	16	*25
18	25	18	25	18	24	18	24	18	24	17	*26
19	26	19	26	19	25	19	25	19	25	18	*27
20	27	20	27	20	26	20	26	20	26	19	*28
21	28	21	28	21	27	21	27	21	27	20	*29
22	29	22	29	22	28	22	28	22	28	21	*30
23	30	23	30	23	29	23	29	23	29	22	*31
24	31	24	31	24	30	24	30	24	30	23	Apr *01
25	Jun 01	25	Aug 01	25	Oct 01	25	Dec 01	25	31	24	*02
26	02	26	02	26	02	26	02	26	Feb 01	25	*03
27	03	27	03	27	03	27	03	27	02	26	*04
28	04	28	04	28	04	28	04	28	03	27	*05
29	05	29	05	29	05	29	05	29	04	28	*06
30	06	30	06	30	06	30	06	30	05	Mar 01	07
May 01	07	Jul 01	07	31	07	31	07	31	06	02	08
02	08	02	08	Sep 01	08	Nov 01	08	Jan 01	07	03	09
03	09	03	09	02	09	02	09	02	08	04	10
04	10	04	10	03	10	03	10	03	09	05	11
05	11	05	11	04	11	04	11	04	10	06	12
06	12	06	12	05	12	05	12	05	11	07	13
07	13	07	13	06	13	06	13	06	12	08	14
08	14	08	14	07	14	07	14	07	13	09	15
09	15	09	15	08	15	08	15	08	14	10	16
10	16	10	16	09	16	09	16	09	15	11	17
11	17	11	17	10	17	10	17	10	16	12	18
12	18	12	18	11	18	11	18	11	17	13	19
13	19	13	19	12	19	12	19	12	18	14	20
14	20	14	20	13	20	13	20	13	19	15	21
15	21	15	21	14	21	14	21	14	20	16	22
16	22	16	22	15	22	15	22	15	21	17	23
17	23	17	23	16	23	16	23	16	22	18	24
18	24	18	24	17	24	17	24	17	23	19	25
19	25	19	25	18	25	18	25	18	24	20	26
20	26	20	26	19	26	19	26	19	25	21	27
21	27	21	27	20	27	20	27	20	26	22	28
22	28	22	28	21	28	21	28	21	27	23	29
23	29	23	29	22	29	22	29	22	28	24	30
24	30	24	30	23	30	23	30	23	Mar *01	25	May 01
25	Jul 01	25	31	24	31	24	31	24	*02	26	02
26	02	26	Sep 01	25	Nov 01	25	Jan 01	25	*03	27	03
27	03	27	02	26	02	26	02	26	*04	28	04
28	04	28	03	27	03	27	03	27	*05	29	05
29	05	29	04	28	04	28	04	28	*06	30	06
30	06	30	05	29	05	29	05	29	*07	31	07
31	07	31	06	30	06	30	06	30	*08		

RHEA EGG WEIGHT LOSS CHART (35-Day Hatch Period)

TARGET LOSS	12%		13%		14%		15%	
INITIAL WEIGHT	DAILY LOSS	TARGET WEIGHT	DAILY LOSS	TARGET WEIGHT	DAILY LOSS	TARGET WEIGHT	DAILY LOSS	TARGET WEIGHT
370	1.26	326	1.37	322	1.48	318	1.59	314
375	1.28	330	1.39	326	1.50	323	1.61	319
380	1.29	335	1.41	331	1.52	327	1.63	323
385	1.31	339	1.43	335	1.54	331	1.65	327
390	1.33	344	1.45	339	1.56	335	1.67	331
395	1.34	348	1.47	344	1.58	340	1.69	336
400	1.36	352	1.48	348	1.60	344	1.72	340
405	1.38	357	1.50	352	1.62	348	1.74	344
410	1.39	361	1.52	357	1.64	353	1.76	348
415	1.41	366	1.54	361	1.66	357	1.78	353
420	1.43	370	1.56	365	1.68	361	1.80	357
425	1.45	374	1.58	370	1.70	366	1.82	361
430	1.46	379	1.60	374	1.72	370	1.84	365
435	1.48	383	1.61	379	1.74	374	1.87	370
440	1.50	388	1.63	383	1.76	378	1.89	374
445	1.51	392	1.65	387	1.78	383	1.91	378
450	1.53	396	1.67	392	1.80	387	1.93	382
455	1.55	401	1.69	396	1.82	391	1.95	387
460	1.56	405	1.71	400	1.84	396	1.97	391
465	1.58	410	1.73	405	1.86	400	1.99	395
470	1.60	414	1.74	409	1.88	404	2.02	399
475	1.62	418	1.76	413	1.90	409	2.04	404
480	1.63	423	1.78	418	1.92	413	2.06	408
485	1.65	427	1.80	422	1.94	417	2.08	412
490	1.67	432	1.82	426	1.96	421	2.10	416
495	1.68	436	1.84	431	1.98	426	2.12	421
500	1.70	441	1.86	435	2.00	430	2.15	425
505	1.72	445	1.87	439	2.02	434	2.17	429
510	1.73	449	1.89	444	2.04	439	2.19	433
515	1.75	454	1.91	448	2.06	443	2.21	438
520	1.77	458	1.93	452	2.08	447	2.23	442
525	1.79	463	1.95	457	2.10	452	2.25	446
530	1.80	467	1.97	461	2.12	456	2.27	450

INSTRUCTIONS FOR USING THE WEIGHT LOSS CHART

1. Weigh the egg carefully (using an accurate gram scale) the day you place it in the incubator and record the weight. Weigh it a couple days later, and again a couple days later, each time noting the weight. Divide the amount of weight lost by the number of days to find the loss per day. (Refer to the weight-loss graph for calculations if necessary.)

2. Find the initial weight in the chart.

3. Read across to the "daily loss" figure closest to the figure you've calculated. Then read the "target weight" figure next to it. Read up to the top of the column to the percentage of weight loss. Generally a weight loss of 15% is recommended. If it is much lower, refer to the instructions for your incubator to adjust temperature and/or humidity.

4. Weigh the egg periodically and repeat the procedure to be sure it remains within the target loss.

5. Remember that not all eggs hatch on the day you expect them to. Toward the end of the hatching period, use a candler to help determine the status of the egg.

RHEA EGG WEIGHT LOSS CHART, Cont'd (35-Day Hatch Period)

INITIAL WEIGHT	12% DAILY LOSS	12% TARGET WEIGHT	13% DAILY LOSS	13% TARGET WEIGHT	14% DAILY LOSS	14% TARGET WEIGHT	15% DAILY LOSS	15% TARGET WEIGHT
535	1.82	471	1.98	466	2.14	460	2.30	455
540	1.84	476	2.00	470	2.16	464	2.32	459
545	1.85	480	2.02	474	2.18	469	2.34	463
550	1.87	485	2.04	479	2.20	473	2.36	467
555	1.89	489	2.06	483	2.22	477	2.38	472
560	1.90	493	2.08	487	2.24	482	2.40	476
565	1.92	498	2.10	492	2.26	486	2.42	480
570	1.94	502	2.11	496	2.28	490	2.45	484
575	1.96	507	2.13	500	2.30	495	2.47	489
580	1.97	511	2.15	505	2.32	499	2.49	493
585	1.99	515	2.17	509	2.34	503	2.51	497
590	2.01	520	2.19	513	2.36	507	2.53	501
595	2.02	524	2.21	518	2.38	512	2.55	506
600	2.04	529	2.23	522	2.40	516	2.57	510
605	2.06	533	2.24	526	2.42	520	2.60	514
610	2.07	537	2.26	531	2.44	525	2.62	518
615	2.09	542	2.28	535	2.46	529	2.64	523
620	2.11	546	2.30	539	2.48	533	2.66	527
625	2.13	551	2.32	544	2.50	538	2.68	531
630	2.14	555	2.34	548	2.52	542	2.70	535
635	2.16	559	2.36	553	2.54	546	2.72	540
640	2.18	564	2.37	557	2.56	550	2.75	544
645	2.19	568	2.39	561	2.58	555	2.77	548
650	2.21	573	2.41	566	2.60	559	2.79	552
655	2.23	577	2.43	570	2.62	563	2.81	557
660	2.24	581	2.45	574	2.64	568	2.83	561
665	2.26	586	2.47	579	2.66	572	2.85	565
670	2.28	590	2.49	583	2.68	576	2.87	569
675	2.30	595	2.50	587	2.70	581	2.90	574
680	2.31	599	2.52	592	2.72	585	2.92	578
685	2.33	603	2.54	596	2.74	589	2.94	582
690	2.35	608	2.56	600	2.76	593	2.96	586
695	2.36	612	2.58	605	2.78	598	2.98	591
700	2.38	617	2.60	609	2.80	602	3.00	595
705	2.40	621	2.62	613	2.82	606	3.02	599
710	2.41	626	2.63	618	2.84	611	3.05	603
715	2.43	630	2.65	622	2.86	615	3.07	608
720	2.45	634	2.67	627	2.88	619	3.09	612
725	2.47	639	2.69	631	2.90	624	3.11	616
730	2.48	643	2.71	635	2.92	628	3.13	620
735	2.50	648	2.73	640	2.94	632	3.15	625
740	2.52	652	2.75	644	2.96	636	3.17	629
745	2.53	656	2.76	648	2.98	641	3.20	633

EGG WEIGHT LOSS GRAPH

EGG NUMBER _____   INCUBATION PERIOD _____   SPECIES _____

DATE LAID _____   INCUBATOR # _____   PEN # _____

DATE SET _____   HEN ID# _____

DATE TO HATCHER _____   ROOSTER ID# _____

DAY #	DATE	TARGET WEIGHT	ACTUAL WEIGHT
2			
4			
6			
8			
10			
12			
14			
16			
18			
20			
22			
24			
26			
28			
30			
32			
34			
36			
38			
40			
42			
44			
46			
48			
50			
52			
54			

THE HEAVY LINE BELOW REPRESENTS THE TARGET WEIGHT. PLOT THE ACTUAL WEIGHT AGAINST IT. EACH LIGHT LINE REPRESENTS A ONE-GRAM DIFFERENCE IN WEIGHT.

IF WEIGHT IS HIGHER THAN EXPECTED, RECORD ON THIS SIDE.

IF WEIGHT IS LOWER THAN EXPECTED, RECORD ON THIS SIDE.

TO CALCULATE WEIGHT LOSS, USE THE APPROPRIATE CHART, OR CALCULATE:

INITIAL WEIGHT x % WEIGHT LOSS = TARGET LOSS ÷ DAYS TO HATCH = DAILY LOSS x 2 = 2-DAY LOSS
(Example) 580 g   x   .15   =   87 g   ÷   52   =   1.67g   x 2 =   3.34 g

GENERAL INDICATIONS FOR THE RESULTS OF YOUR PLOT
If weight varies significantly, refer to the chapter on Incubation and Hatching,
and consult the instructions for your incubator to make adjustments.

INCUBATION TROUBLE SHOOTING

SYMPTOMS	PROBABLE CAUSES	SUGGESTIONS
Many clear eggs. No blood. (Determined by candling, then broken out appearance.)	1. Infertility. Two few males, too many males, males too old, inactive, or frozen combs and wattles. 2. Embryo died early 1-2 days.	1. Use young, vigorous males. 2. Do not hold eggs longer than 14 days. Keep at temperatures of 50 to 55 degrees, in moist atmosphere. Gather often.
Slight blood rings.	3. A. Improper temperature. B. Fumigation. 4. Improper care of eggs before setting.	3. A. Check thermometer, thermostat, heating element, current. Check temperature against instructions. B. Do not fumigate at high concentrations during the first 5 days of age. 4. See suggestion 2 above.
Many dead germs.	5. Temperature too high or too low. 6. Improper turning of eggs. 7. Improper feeding of flock. 8. Breeding (low hatchability, inherited). 9. Improper ventilation, insufficient oxygen.	5. See suggestion 3 above. 6. Turn two times daily, same time morning and evening. 7. Check vitamin and mineral content of breeder mash. 8. Avoid close inbreeding. 9. Increase ventilation of incubator and incubator room, avoid drafts.
Pipped eggs not hatching. Hatch non-uniform. Hatching too early. Hatching too late. Sticky hatch.	10. Insufficient moisture. 11. Too high temperature. Most frequent cause of poor hatches. 12. Too low temperature. 13. Probably too high temperature.	10. Increase humidity during incubation (wet bulb 82-86 degrees), add second water pan last 3 days (wet bulb 90-92 degrees) during hatching. 11. See 3 above. 12. See 3 above. 13. See 3 above.
Cripples and malpositions.	14. Temperature too high. 15. Too low moisture. 16. Improper turning or setting. 17. Hatching trays too smooth.	14. See 3 above. 15. See 10 above. 16. See 6 above. Set eggs large end up. 17. Use wire-bottom trays or crinoline.
Very large, soft-bodied, weak chicks. Mushy chicks. Dead on trays, bad odor.	18. Low average temperature. 19. Poor ventilation. 20. Navel infection in incubator.	18. See 3 above. 19. See 9 above. 20. Careful cleaning and fumigation of incubator between hatches.
Rough navels.	21. High temperature or wide temperature variations. 22. Low moisture.	21. See 3 above. 22. See 10 above.

INCUBATION TROUBLE SHOOTING (Cont'd)

SYMPTOMS	PROBABLE CAUSES	SUGGESTIONS
Temperature reading not constant.	23. Incubator in unheated room or barn where temperature varies. *24. Thermostat damaged or with pinpoint leak in water. *25. Improper adjustment of thermostat (can be caused by someone tampering or playing with adjusting screw).	23. Keep incubator in room with uniform temperature and where temperature is never below 50 degrees. *24. Replace wafer (part #3007). 25. Readjust thermostats. Make slight adjustments with adjusting screw and wait 15 minutes for temperature to stabilize.
Temperature has gone to $102°$.	*26. Failure of front thermostat switch.	*26. Replace front thermostat switch at once (part #3009). Do not attempt to use a switch that has failed even though it may appear to operate all right. Once a switch has failed it will fail again. Check temperature often.
Temperature has gone above $102°$.	*27. Failure of both front and back thermostat switches.	*27. Replace both front and back thermostat switches. (See #26 above.) Open door to cool eggs. If temperature above $110°$ replace thermostat wafers (part #3007).
Incubator fails to heat.	28. Improper setting of thermostat. 29. Power failure, incubator unplugged, or poor plug connection. 30. Loose wire connection.	*28. Turn adjusting screw to "increase" heat until pilot light comes on. 29. If fan not running, electricity not getting to incubator. Check fuses and plug connections. *30. Remove back of incubator and check for loose wires.
Fan rattles.	*31. Blade hitting metal shroud. *32. Blade bent. *33. End play in motor shaft.	*31. Bend metal away from blade. *32. Remove and straighten blade or replace with new blade. *33. Place block under back legs of incubator.
Hygrometer reading above 94 degrees.	*34. Dry wick on hygrometer.	*34. Wash calcium deposits from wick or replace with new wick.

* Denotes instructions specific to GQF incubators. Courtesy of GQF Manufacturing Co., Savannah, GA.

CONVERSION TABLES

INCHES TO MILLIMETERS

1/8	3.2
1/4	6.4
3/8	9.5
1/2	12.7
5/8	15.9
3/4	19.0
7/8	22.2
1	25.4
2	50.8
3	76.2
4	101.6
5	127.0
6	152.4
7	177.8
8	203.2
9	228.6
10	254.0
11	279.4
12	304.8
13	330.2
14	355.6
15	381.0

EXACT CONVERSIONS
1 in = 25.40 mm
1 mm = 0.0394 in

MILLIMETERS TO INCHES

1	0.04
2	0.08
3	0.12
4	0.16
5	0.20
6	0.24
7	0.28
8	0.31
9	0.35
10	0.39
11	0.43
12	0.47
13	0.51
14	0.55
15	0.59
16	0.63
17	0.67
18	0.71
19	0.75
20	0.79
25	0.98
50	1.97
75	2.95
100	3.94

EXACT CONVERSIONS
1 in = 25.40 mm
1 mm = 0.0394 in

INCHES TO CENTIMETERS

1/8	0.3
1/4	0.6
3/8	1.0
1/2	1.3
5/8	1.6
3/4	1.9
7/8	2.2
1	2.5
2	5.1
3	7.6
4	10.2
5	12.7
6	15.2
7	17.8
8	20.3
9	22.9
10	25.4
11	27.9
12	30.5
13	33.0
14	35.6
15	38.1
16	40.6
17	43.2
18	45.7
19	48.3
20	50.8
30	76.2
40	101.6
50	127.0
60	152.4
70	177.8
80	203.2
90	228.6
100	254.0

EXACT CONVERSIONS
1 inch = 2.540 cm
1 cm = 0.3937 in

CONVERSION TABLES

CENTIMETERS TO INCHES

1	0.39
2	0.79
3	1.18
4	1.57
5	1.97
6	2.36
7	2.76
8	3.15
9	3.54
10	3.94
11	4.33
12	4.72
13	5.12
14	5.51
15	5.91
16	6.30
17	6.69
18	7.09
19	7.48
20	7.87
30	11.81
40	15.75
50	19.69
60	23.62
70	27.56
80	31.50
90	35.43
100	39.37

EXACT CONVERSIONS
1 in = 2.540 cm
1 cm = 0.3937 in

FEET TO METERS

1	0.3
2	0.6
3	0.9
4	1.2
5	1.5
6	1.8
7	2.1
8	2.4
9	2.7
10	3.0
20	6.1
30	9.1
40	12.2
50	15.2
75	22.9
100	30.5

EXACT CONVERSIONS
1 ft = 0.3048 m
1 m = 3.2808 ft

METERS TO FEET

1	3.3
2	6.6
3	9.8
4	13.1
5	16.4
6	19.7
7	23.0
8	26.2
9	29.5
10	32.8
20	65.5
30	98.4
40	131.2
50	164.0
75	246.1
100	328.1

EXACT CONVERSIONS
1 ft = 0.3048 m
1 m = 3.2808 ft

YARDS TO METERS

1	0.9
2	1.8
3	2.7
4	3.7
5	4.6
6	5.5
7	6.4
8	7.3
9	8.2
10	9.1
15	13.7
20	18.3
30	27.4
40	36.6
50	45.7
75	68.6
100	91.4

EXACT CONVERSIONS
1 yd = 0.9144 m
1 m = 1.0936 yd

METERS TO YARDS

1	1.1
2	2.2
3	3.3
4	4.4
5	5.5
6	6.6
7	7.7
8	8.7
9	9.8
10	10.9
15	16.4
20	21.9
30	32.8
40	43.7
50	54.7
75	82.0
100	109.4

EXACT CONVERSIONS
1 yd = 0.9144 m
1 m = 1.0936 yd

CONVERSION TABLES

MILES TO KILOMETERS

1	1.6
2	3.2
3	4.8
4	6.4
5	8.0
6	9.7
7	11.3
8	12.9
9	14.5
10	16.1
15	24.1
20	32.2
30	48.3
40	64.4
50	80.5
60	96.6
70	112.7
80	128.7
90	144.8
100	160.9

KILOMETERS TO MILES

1	0.6
2	1.2
3	1.9
4	2.5
5	3.1
6	3.7
7	4.3
8	5.0
9	5.6
10	6.2
15	9.3
20	12.4
30	18.6
40	24.9
50	31.1
60	37.3
70	43.5
80	49.7
90	55.9
100	62.1

EXACT CONVERSIONS
1 mi = 1.6093 km
1 km = 0.6214 mi

SQ. INS TO SQ. CMS.

1	6.45
2	12.90
3	19.35
4	25.81
5	32.26
6	38.71
7	45.16
8	51.61
9	58.06
10	64.52
20	129.03
25	161.29
50	322.58
75	483.87
100	645.16
125	806.45
150	967.74

EXACT CONVERSIONS
1 in^2 = 6.4516 cm^2
1 cm^2 = 0.155 in^2

SQ. FEET TO SQ. METERS

1	0.09
2	0.19
3	0.28
4	0.37
5	0.46
6	0.56
7	0.65
8	0.74
9	0.84
10	0.93
20	1.86
25	2.32
50	4.65
75	6.97
100	9.29
250	23.23
500	46.45
750	69.68
1000	92.90

EXACT CONVERSIONS
1 ft^2 = 0.929 m^2
1 m^2 = 10.7639 ft^2

SQ. CMS. TO SQ. INS.

1	0.16
2	0.31
3	0.47
4	0.62
5	0.78
6	0.93
7	1.09
8	1.24
9	1.40
10	1.55
20	3.10
25	3.88
50	7.75
75	11.63
100	15.50
125	19.38
150	23.25

EXACT CONVERSIONS
1 in^2 = 6.4516 cm^2
1 cm^2 = 0.155 in^2

SQ. METERS TO SQ. FEET

1	10.8
2	21.5
3	32.3
4	43.1
5	53.8
6	64.6
7	75.3
8	86.1
9	96.9
10	107.6
20	215.3
25	269.1
50	538.2
75	807.3
100	1076.4
250	2691.0
500	5382.0
750	8072.9
1000	10763.9

EXACT CONVERSIONS
1 ft^2 = 0.929 m^2
1 m^2 = 10.7639 ft^2

CONVERSION TABLES

ACRES TO HECTARES

1	0.40
2	0.81
3	1.21
4	1.62
5	2.02
6	2.43
7	2.83
8	3.24
9	3.64
10	4.05
20	8.09
25	10.12
50	20.23
75	30.35
100	40.47
250	101.17
500	202.34
750	303.51
1000	404.69
1500	607.03

HECTARES TO ACRES

1	2.5
2	4.9
3	7.4
4	9.9
5	12.4
6	14.8
7	17.3
8	19.8
9	22.2
10	24.7
20	49.4
25	61.8
50	123.6
75	185.3
100	247.1
250	617.8
500	1235.5
750	1853.3
1000	2471.1
1500	3706.6

EXACT CONVERSIONS
1 acre = 0.4047 hectares
1 hectare = 2.471 acres

CU. INS. TO CU. CMS.

1	16.39
2	32.77
3	49.16
4	65.55
5	81.93
6	93.32
7	114.71
8	131.10
9	147.48
10	163.87
11	180.26
12	196.64
13	213.03
14	229.42
15	245.81
20	327.74
50	819.35
100	1638.71

EXACT CONVERSIONS
$1 \text{ in}^3 = 16.3871 \text{ cm}^3$
$1 \text{ cm}^3 = 0.0610 \text{ in}^3$

CU. FT. TO CU. M.

1	0.03
2	0.06
3	0.08
4	0.11
5	0.14
6	0.17
7	0.20
8	0.23
9	0.25
10	0.28
11	0.31
12	0.34
13	0.37
14	0.40
15	0.42
20	0.57
50	1.41
100	2.83

EXACT CONVERSIONS
$1 \text{ ft}^3 = 0.0283 \text{ m}^3$
$1 \text{ m}^3 = 35.3147 \text{ ft}^3$

CU. CMS. TO CU. INS.

1	0.61
2	1.22
3	1.83
4	2.44
5	3.05
6	3.66
7	4.27
8	4.88
9	5.49
10	6.10
11	6.71
12	7.32
13	7.93
14	8.54
15	9.15
20	12.20
50	30.50
100	61.00

EXACT CONVERSIONS
$1 \text{ in}^3 = 16.3871 \text{ cm}^3$
$1 \text{ cm}^3 = 0.0610 \text{ in}^3$

CU. M TO CU. FT.

1	35.3
2	70.6
3	105.9
4	141.3
5	176.6
6	211.9
7	247.2
8	282.5
9	317.8
10	353.1
11	388.5
12	423.8
13	459.1
14	494.4
15	529.7
20	706.3
50	1765.7
100	3531.5

EXACT CONVERSIONS
$1 \text{ ft}^3 = 0.0283 \text{ m}^3$
$1 \text{ m}^3 = 35.3147 \text{ ft}^3$

CONVERSION TABLES

CU. YDS. TO CU. M.

1	0.76
2	1.53
3	2.29
4	3.06
5	3.82
6	4.59
7	5.35
8	6.12
9	6.88
10	7.65
11	8.41
12	9.17
13	9.94
14	10.70
15	11.47
20	15.29
50	38.23
100	76.46

EXACT CONVERSIONS
1 yd^3 = 0.7646 m^3
1 m^3 = 1.3080 yd^3

CU. M. TO CU. YDS.

1	1.31
2	2.62
3	3.92
4	5.23
5	6.54
6	7.85
7	9.16
8	10.46
9	11.77
10	13.08
11	14.39
12	15.70
13	17.00
14	18.31
15	19.62
20	26.16
50	65.40
100	130.80

EXACT CONVERSIONS
1 yd^3 = 0.7646 m^3
1 m^3 = 1.3080 yd^3

AVOIRDUPOIS OUNCES TO GRAMS

1	28.3
2	56.7
3	85.0
4	113.4
5	141.7
6	170.1
7	190.4
8	226.8
9	255.1
10	283.5
11	311.7
12	340.2
13	368.5
14	396.9
15	425.2
16	453.6

GRAMS TO AV. OZ.

1	0.04
2	0.07
3	0.11
4	0.14
5	0.18
6	0.21
7	0.25
8	0.28
9	0.32
10	0.35
20	0.71
30	1.06
40	1.41
50	1.76
60	2.12
70	2.47
80	2.82
90	3.18
100	3.53
250	8.83
500	17.65
750	26.48
1000	35.30
1250	44.13
1500	52.95

EXACT CONVERSIONS
1 av. oz. = 28.3495 grams
1 gram = 0.0353 av. oz.

POUNDS TO KILOGRAMS

1	.45
2	.91
3	1.36
4	1.81
5	2.27
6	2.72
7	3.18
8	3.63
9	4.08
10	4.54
20	9.07
30	13.61
40	18.14
50	22.68
60	27.24
70	31.78
80	36.32
90	40.86
100	45.36

EXACT CONVERSIONS
1 lb = 0.454 kg
1 kg = 2.205 lb

KILOGRAMS TO POUNDS

1	2.2
2	4.4
3	6.6
4	8.8
5	11.0
6	13.2
7	15.4
8	17.6
9	19.8
10	22.0
20	44.1
30	66.1
40	88.2
50	110.2
60	132.3
70	154.4
80	176.4
90	198.5
100	220.5

EXACT CONVERSIONS
1 lb = 0.454 kg
1 kg = 2.205 lb

CONVERSION TABLES

FLUID OUNCES TO LITERS

US OZ.	LITER	UK OZ.	LITER
1	0.0296	1	0.0284
2	0.0592	2	0.0568
3	0.0888	3	0.0852
4	0.118	4	0.114
5	0.148	5	0.142
6	0.178	6	0.170
7	0.207	7	0.199
8	0.237	8	0.227
9	0.266	9	0.256
10	0.296	10	0.284
11	0.326	11	0.312
12	0.355	12	0.341
13	0.385	13	0.369
14	0.414	14	0.397
15	0.444	15	0.426
20	0.592	20	0.568
50	1.48	50	1.42
100	2.96	100	2.84

LITERS TO FLUID OUNCES

LITER	US OZ.	UK OZ.
1	33.8	35.2
2	67.6	70.4
3	101.4	105.6
4	135.3	140.8
5	169.1	176.0
6	209.2	211.2
7	236.7	246.4
8	270.5	281.6
9	304.3	316.8
10	338.1	352.0
11	372.0	387.2
12	405.8	422.4
13	439.6	457.5
14	473.4	492.7
15	507.2	527.9
20	676.3	703.9
50	1690.7	1759.8
100	3381.5	3519.6

EXACT CONVERSIONS

US
1 fl oz = 0.0296 liter
1 liter = 33.814 fl oz

UK
1 fl oz = 0.0284 liter
1 liter = 35.1961 oz

CONVERSION TABLES

PINTS TO LITERS

US PINTS	LITERS	UK PINTS	LITERS
1	0.47	1	0.57
2	0.95	2	1.14
3	1.42	3	1.70
4	1.89	4	2.27
5	2.37	5	2.84
6	2.84	6	3.41
7	3.31	7	3.98
8	3.78	8	4.55
9	4.26	9	5.11
10	4.73	10	5.68
11	5.20	11	6.25
12	5.68	12	6.82
13	6.15	13	7.38
14	6.62	14	7.95
15	7.10	15	8.52
20	9.46	20	11.36
50	23.66	50	28.41
100	47.32	100	56.82

LITERS TO PINTS

LITER	US PINT	UK PINT
1	2.11	1.76
2	4.23	3.52
3	6.34	5.28
4	8.45	7.04
5	10.57	8.80
6	12.68	10.56
7	14.79	12.32
8	16.91	14.08
9	19.02	15.84
10	21.13	17.60
11	23.25	19.36
12	25.36	21.12
13	27.47	22.88
14	29.59	24.64
15	31.70	26.40
20	42.27	35.20
50	105.67	87.99
100	211.34	175.98

EXACT CONVERSIONS
1 US pint = 0.83 UK pint
1 UK pint = 1.20 US pint

US
1 pint = 0.4732 liter
1 liter = 2.1134 pint

UK
1 pint = 0.5682 liter
1 liter = 1.7598 pint

CONVERSION TABLES

QUARTS TO LITERS

US QUART	LITER
1	0.95
2	1.89
3	2.84
4	3.78
5	4.73
10	9.46

UK QUART	LITER
1	1.14
2	2.27
3	3.41
4	4.55
5	5.68
10	11.36

EXACT CONVERSIONS
US
1 quart = 0.9463 liter
1 liter = 1.0567 quarts
UK
1 quart = 1.1365 liter
1 liter = 0.8799 quarts

GALLONS TO LITERS

US GAL	LITER	UK GAL	LITER
1	3.78	1	4.55
2	7.57	2	9.09
3	11.36	3	13.64
4	15.14	4	18.18
5	18.93	5	22.73
6	22.71	6	27.28
7	26.50	7	31.82
8	30.28	8	36.37
9	34.07	9	40.91
10	37.85	10	45.46
11	41.64	11	50.01
12	45.42	12	54.55
13	49.21	13	59.10
14	52.99	14	63.64
15	56.78	15	68.19
16	60.57	16	72.74
17	64.35	17	77.28
18	68.14	18	81.83
19	71.92	19	86.37
20	75.71	20	90.92
21	79.49	21	95.47
22	83.28	22	100.01
23	87.06	23	104.56
24	90.85	24	109.10
25	94.63	25	113.65
50	189.27	50	227.30
75	283.90	75	340.96
100	378.54	100	454.61

EXACT CONVERSIONS
US
1 gallon = 3.785 liter
1 liter = 0.264 gallon
UK
1 gallon = 4.546 liter
1 liter = 0.220 gallon

LITERS TO QUARTS

LITERS	US QUART	UK QUART
1	1.06	0.88
2	2.11	1.76
3	3.17	2.64
4	4.23	3.52
5	5.28	4.40
10	10.57	8.80

EXACT CONVERSIONS
US
1 quart = 0.9463 liter
1 liter = 1.0567 quarts
UK
1 quart = 1.1365 liter
1 liter = 0.8799 quarts

CONVERSION TABLES

LITERS TO GALLONS

LITER	U.S.GAL	U.K.GAL
1	0.26	0.22
2	0.53	0.44
3	0.79	0.66
4	1.06	0.88
5	1.32	1.10
6	1.58	1.32
7	1.85	1.54
8	2.11	1.76
9	2.38	1.98
10	2.64	2.20
11	2.91	2.42
12	3.17	2.64
13	3.43	2.86
14	3.70	3.08
15	3.96	3.30
16	4.23	3.52
17	4.49	3.74
18	4.76	3.96
19	5.02	4.18
20	5.28	4.40
21	5.55	4.62
22	5.81	4.84
23	6.08	5.06
24	6.34	5.28
25	6.60	5.50
50	13.20	11.00
75	19.81	16.50
100	26.42	22.00

EXACT CONVERSIONS

US
1 gallon = 3.785 liter
1 litre = 0.264 gallon

UK
1 gallon = 4.546 liter
1 liter = 0.220 gallon

CONVERSION TABLES
FAHRENHEIT TO CELCIUS (CENTIGRADE)

°F	°C	°F	°C	°F	°C	°F	°C
1	-17.2	56	13.3	111	43.9	166	74.4
2	-16.7	57	13.9	112	44.4	167	75.0
3	-16.1	58	14.4	113	45.0	168	75.5
4	-15.5	59	15.0	114	45.5	169	76.1
5	-15.0	60	15.5	115	46.1	170	76.7
6	-14.4	61	16.1	116	46.7	171	77.2
7	-13.9	62	16.7	117	47.2	172	77.8
8	-13.3	63	17.2	118	47.8	173	78.3
9	-12.8	64	17.8	119	48.3	174	78.9
10	-12.2	65	18.3	120	48.9	175	79.4
11	-11.6	66	18.9	121	49.4	176	80.0
12	-11.1	67	19.4	122	50.0	177	80.5
13	-10.5	68	20.0	123	50.5	178	81.1
14	-10.0	69	20.5	124	51.1	179	81.7
15	-9.4	70	21.1	125	51.7	180	82.2
16	-8.9	71	21.7	126	52.2	181	82.8
17	-8.3	72	22.2	127	52.8	182	83.3
18	-7.8	73	22.8	128	53.3	183	83.9
19	-7.2	74	23.3	129	53.9	184	84.4
20	-6.7	75	23.9	130	54.4	185	85.0
21	-6.1	76	24.4	131	55.0	186	85.5
22	-5.5	77	25.0	132	55.5	187	86.1
23	-5.0	78	25.5	133	56.1	188	86.7
24	-4.4	79	26.1	134	56.7	189	87.2
25	-3.9	80	26.7	135	57.2	190	87.8
26	-3.3	81	27.2	136	57.8	191	88.3
27	-2.8	82	27.8	137	58.3	192	88.8
28	-2.2	83	28.3	138	58.9	193	89.4
29	-1.7	84	28.9	139	59.4	194	90.0
30	-1.1	85	29.4	140	60.0	195	90.5
31	-0.5	86	30.0	141	60.5	196	91.1
32	0.0	87	30.5	142	61.1	197	91.7
33	0.5	88	31.1	143	61.7	198	92.2
34	1.1	89	31.7	144	62.2	199	92.8
35	1.7	90	32.2	145	62.8	200	93.3
36	2.2	91	32.8	146	63.3	201	93.9
37	2.8	92	33.3	147	63.9	202	94.4
38	3.3	93	33.9	148	64.4	203	95.0
39	3.9	94	34.4	149	65.0	204	95.5
40	4.4	95	35.0	150	65.5	205	96.1
41	5.0	96	35.5	151	66.1	206	96.7
42	5.5	97	36.1	152	66.7	207	97.2
43	6.1	98	36.7	153	67.2	208	97.8
44	6.7	99	37.2	154	67.8	209	98.3
45	7.2	100	37.8	155	68.3	210	98.9
46	7.8	101	38.3	156	68.9	211	99.4
47	8.3	102	38.9	157	69.4	212	100.0
48	8.9	103	39.4	158	70.0		
49	9.4	104	40.0	159	70.5		
50	10.0	105	40.5	160	71.1		
51	10.5	106	41.1	161	71.7		
52	11.1	107	41.7	162	72.2		
53	11.7	108	42.2	163	72.8		
54	12.2	109	42.8	164	73.3		
55	12.8	110	43.3	165	73.9		

EXACT CONVERSIONS

Fahrenheit to Celcius
$n - 32 \times 5 \div 9$

Celcius to Fahrenheit
$n \times 9 \div 5 + 32$

CONVERSION TABLES

CELCIUS TO FAHRENHEIT

C	F		C	F
1	33.8		54	129.2
2	35.6		55	131.0
3	37.4		56	132.8
4	39.2		57	134.6
5	41.0		58	136.4
6	42.8		59	138.2
7	44.6		60	140.0
8	46.4		61	141.8
9	48.2		62	143.6
10	50.0		63	145.4
11	51.8		64	147.2
12	53.6		65	149.0
13	55.4		66	150.8
14	57.2		67	152.6
15	59.0		68	154.4
16	60.8		69	156.2
17	62.6		70	158.0
18	64.4		71	159.8
19	66.2		72	161.6
20	68.0		73	163.4
21	69.8		74	165.2
22	71.6		75	167.0
23	73.4		76	168.8
24	75.2		77	170.6
25	77.0		78	172.4
26	78.8		79	174.2
27	80.6		80	176.0
28	82.4		81	177.8
29	84.2		82	179.6
30	86.0		83	181.4
31	87.8		84	183.2
32	89.6		85	185.0
33	91.4		86	186.8
34	93.2		87	188.6
35	95.0		88	190.4
36	96.8		89	192.2
37	98.6		90	194.0
38	100.4		91	195.8
39	102.2		92	197.6
40	104.0		93	199.4
41	105.8		94	201.2
42	107.6		95	203.0
43	109.4		96	204.8
44	111.2		97	206.6
45	113.0		98	208.4
46	114.8		99	210.2
47	116.6		100	212.0
48	118.4			
49	120.2			
50	122.0			
51	123.8			
52	125.6			
53	127.4			

EXACT CONVERSIONS
Fahrenheit to Celcius
$n - 32 \times 5 \div 9$
Celcius to Fahrenheit
$n \times 9 \div 5 + 32$

COMMON ELEMENTS

Al	aluminum
Ar	argon
As	arsenic
Au	gold
B	boron
Ba	barium
Br	bromine
C	carbon
Ca	calcium
Cl	chlorine
Co	cobalt
Cr	chromium
Cs	cesium
Cu	copper
F	fluorine
Fe	iron
Ga	gallium
H	hydrogen
He	helium
Hg	mercury
I	iodine
In	indium
K	potassium
Li	lithium
Mg	magnesium
Mn	manganese
Mo	molybdenum
N	nitrogen
Na	sodium
Nb	niobium
Nd	neodymium
Ni	nickel
O	oxygen
P	phosphorus
Pb	lead
Pd	palladium
Po	polonium
Pt	platinum
Rh	rhodium
Rn	radon
S	sulphur/sulfur
Sb	antimony
Sc	scandium
Se	selenium
Si	silicon
Sn	tin
Zn	zinc

PRE-PURCHASE EXAMINATION FOR RATITES

A pre-purchase exam is defined as an examination of a bird prior to purchase, with the intent of identifying conformational anomalies and existing diseases, and perhaps gender, estimation of age, and sexual maturity.

An unplanned, poorly performed examination can only cost the buyer money and time. However, a well-planned examination, performed properly, by an experienced, informed veterinarian who understands ratites in terms of husbandry, physiology, nutrition, disease and pathology, will be the best investment a buyer can make.

Many diseases and pathology seem to go unnoticed by producers and veterinarians. This is due to their lack of knowledge of common and uncommon disorders, how to perform a physical exam properly, what samples to collect, and how to collect them for ancillary tests.

The current trend in the ratite industry is to take the seller's word that birds are healthy. Some ratite owners will often have post-purchase examinations performed to make sure birds are healthy. They often reveal anomalies and/or disease, but it is too late because the birds have already been purchased.

I strongly recommend pre-purchase examinations. If an anomaly is found, a replacement bird can be selected or the price reduced prior to finalizing the purchase.

CAUTIONS

A thorough pre-purchase examination can prevent buying poor-quality or diseased birds, but it is not fool-proof. There are two other major factors to remember.

Incubation Period

The first is that there is a given time frame from exposure to a disease agent where it is *not* detectable by any means. This is called the incubation period. If a bird harboring a disease is examined during this incubation time (which varies in length for different diseases), it will not be detected. The bird will be considered healthy, although in a couple of days it may become ill.

Stress

The second point is that birds under stress are often more susceptible to an illness and the stress will often shorten the incubation time. It is common for birds to become stressed during shipments, causing them to break with an illness 1 to 5 days after arrival on the new farm. The cause of the illness may have been a combination of exposure to a disease agent on the seller's farm and the stress of shipping by the buyer.

Both exposure to potential pathogens and transportation stress must be reduced to insure that healthy birds arrive at their new home.

A pre-purchase examination can be expected to provide only as much information about a bird as the examination plan outlines. The examination plan is the decision of the buyer and the attending veterinarian regarding exactly what is to be looked for.

The bird's age, gender, species, geographic location and the season of the year should be considered when developing a plan. The outline is derived from a set of guidelines.

The guidelines are a reference of common, known disorders and diseases and the routine methods for detection. They provide a useful tool in selecting what should be included in a pre-purchase examination. *Obviously, not every item in the guidelines will be included for every bird purchased.*

The three species of domestic ratites have different diseases, pathology and husbandry, although some are common to all three species. This creates the need for a different set of guidelines for each ratite group. The guideline provided here is generic, covering diseases and disorders of ratites, regardless of age, sex, species, or geographic location.

- Brett A. Hopkins, DVM

We would like to thank Dr. Brett Hopkins for supplying the discussions and charts on pages 404 through 427. It is hoped that they will be of assistance in identifying common nutritional, management, and disease-vector problems. Dr. Hopkins would be the first, however, to caution producers that the charts are not intended as a substitute for expert veterinary care.

- ce & cd

EXAMINATION GUIDELINES FOR RATITES

TO BE EVALUATED	DISEASE or DISORDER	POSSIBLE ETIOLOGIES	EVALUATION METHOD
GASTRO-INTESTINAL	Impaction, partial impaction, constipation	Grass, rocks, hay, plastic, carpet, sand, metal, leaves, sticks, feed, dehydration, etc.	Palpation of proventriculus, ventriculus, intestines, radiography, stool quality, endoscopy, serum chemistries, history, ultrasound, visual
	Foreign body, hardware disease	Nails, sticks, wire, bolts, miscellaneous metal, lead weights, etc.	Palpation of proventriculus, ventriculus, intestines, abdomen; radiography, endoscopy, history
	Yolk sac retention, volvulus, intussusception	Infection, parasites, foreign body ingestion	Palpation, ultrasound, radiographs, serum chemistries, history, chicks with infected yolk sac often have a foul odor
	Bacterial	*Salmonella spp.*	Feces, selective media culture
		Serpulina hyodysentariae	Feces, selective media culture, Victoria blue or Warthin Starry, stain of fecal smear
		Campylobacter spp.	Feces selective media culture
		Pseudomonas spp.	Feces culture
		Shigella spp.	Feces culture
		Clostridium spp.	Feces anaerobic culture
		Mycobacterium spp.	Feces, centrifugation with acid, fast stain of pellet smear
		Chlamydia spp.	Feces or cloacal swab, Kodak Sure-Cell ELISA kit
	Viral	Avian influenza	Cloacal swab, viral culture
		Other viral organisms	Feces, viral culture or electron microscopy
	Internal Parasites	Coccidia, strongyles	Fecal float and direct smear
		Tapeworm, *Giardia* spp., other protozoa, etc	
MUSCULO-SKELETAL Legs	Bowing, widened proximal metaphysis, rotation, fractures, abrasions, lumps, growths, etc.	Rickets, trauma	Visual, palpation, radiographs, culture, ultrasound tendons and joints, history, serum chemistries, serum analysis for certain vitamins and minerals are available

EXAMINATION GUIDELINES (Cont'd)

TO BE EVALUATED	DISEASE or DISORDER	POSSIBLE ETIOLOGIES	EVALUATION METHOD
MUSCULO-SKELETAL, Cont'd			
Feet	Lacerations, swelling, hyperkeratosis, discoloration, etc.	Trauma, vitamin/mineral imbalance	
Toes	Lacerations, swelling, hyperkeratosis, fractures, rotation, missing, etc.	Trauma, vitamin/mineral imbalance	
Spine	Scoliosis, lordosis, fracture, infection, etc.	Trauma, parasite migration, infection, congenital, malposition in egg	
Skull	Fracture, hematoma, malformation, etc.	Mineral imbalance, trauma, congenital, rickets	
Beak	Fracture, malalignment, brachygnathism, parrot beak, ulcers, soft, pliable, hyperkeratosis, etc.	Congenital, vitamin deficiency	
Wings	Fracture, missing, paralysis, laceration, contusions	Trauma, congenital	
Ribs	Fracture, beading, bowing, etc.	Trauma, rickets	
Joints	Ligament rupture, meniscus tear, arthritis, swelling, infection, malalignment, gout, penetrating wounds, luxation, subluxation	Trauma, rickets, metabolic, bacterial infection, tendon contraction	
Toenails	Rotation, fracture, overgrowth, missing, infection, growths	Mineral imbalance, soft surfaces, trauma, infection, vitamin deficiency	
Tendons	Rupture, contracted, stretched, infection, swelling, subluxation, luxation	Vitamin imbalance, mineral imbalance, trauma, bacterial infection	
INTEGUMENT			
Skin	Bruising, laceration, scars, incision sites, abrasions, dry skin, lumps, growths, etc.	Parasites: ticks, flies, maggots, trauma, tumors, infection	Visual, palpation, history, biopsy
Feathers	Missing, discolored, fractured, fragments, ruffled, bleeding, retained feather sheaths, not molting, odor	Parasites: lice, possibly mites, feather picking, infection, nutritional, trauma, mating, psychogenic	Visual, palpation, history, biopsy of feather shaft, microscopic examination
OCULAR	Blindness, detached retina, missing globe, corneal edema, ruptured globe, glaucoma, keratitis, cataract, foreign body, hyperkeratosis of eyelids	Congenital, trauma, physiologic disorders, ammonia gas, dust, sand, grass, sticks, feathers, etc., vitamin deficiency, penmate picking, fence rubbing, or other trauma	Visual, culture, biopsy, palpation

EXAMINATION GUIDELINES, Cont'd

TO BE EVALUATED	DISEASE or DISORDER	POSSIBLE ETIOLOGIES	EVALUATION METHOD
OCULAR, Cont'd	Infection Bacterial, fungal, parasitic, viral	*Chlamydia* spp, *Mycoplasma* spp, *Pseudomonas* spp, *Mycobacterium* spp, *Aspergillus* spp, *Filaria*(parasite, etc.), Newcastle's disease virus, avian influenza	
	Congenital anomalies	Microphthalmia, dermal cyst, inflammation, blepharitis, conjunctivitis, ophthalmitis, uveitis	
RESPIRATORY Nasal sinuses	Clogged with dirt or mucous, infection, inflammation	Bacteria, fungi, virus, as above	Visual, culture, palpation, endoscopy, auscultation, microscopic examination of mucous
Trachea	Infection, trauma, foreign body, inhalation	*Cyanthostoma var.*	
Lungs	Aspiration, infection, fungi, bacterial	Gram-negative bacteria	
Air sacs	Aspiration, infection, fungi, bacterial	*Aspergillus* spp, etc.	
REPRODUCTIVE Cloaca	Conformation, prolapse, infection	Gram negative bacteria, *Clostridium* spp, oviduct fluid, egg bound, constipated, diarrhea, GI, foreign body, etc.	Visual, palpation, endoscopy, culture, biopsy
Ovary	Inactive, active	Maturity, hormones, stress, disease, etc.	Ultrasound, blood test
Oviduct	Presence, infection, egg bound	Gram negative bacteria, large egg, etc.	Ultrasound, radiographs, CBC, biopsy, endoscopy, culture
Phallus	Conformation, bacterial infection, fertility, presence	Gram-negative bacteria, *Mycobacterium* spp	Visual, biopsy, palpation, ejaculation with spermatozoa examination, culture
PHYSIO-LOGICAL	Vitamin deficiency	B-complex, E, D_3, A, etc.	History, clinical signs, blood test
	Mineral toxins	Zinc, lead, iron, selenium, etc.	Blood test
	Mineral deficiency	Iron, copper, selenium, etc.	Blood test
	Electrolyte imbalances	Diarrhea, renal impairment, high electrolyte content water, volvulus, GI disease, etc.	Serum chemistry analysis
	Organ dysfunction	Congenital, infections, physiologic disorders	Serum chemistry analysis

EXAMINATION GUIDELINES, Cont'd

TO BE EVALUATED	DISEASE or DISORDER	POSSIBLE ETIOLOGIES	EVALUATION METHOD
PHYSIO-LOGICAL, Continued	Anemia	Chronic disease, malnutrition, iron deficiency, vitamin deficiency, trauma, etc.	CBC, visual exam of oral mucosa and eyelids
	Dehydration	Illness, lack of access to water, etc	Clinical signs, palpation, CBC, serum chemistry analysis
	Gout	Dehydration, renal impairment, etc	Serum chemistry
	Rickets	Malabsorption, Ca/P imbalance, Vitamin D_3 deficiency, etc	Clinical signs, palpation, serum chemistry
IMPORTANT INFECTIONS	Gastrointestinal	*Serpulina hyodysentariae*	Fecal culture or stained fecal smear, Victoria blue or Warthin Starry
	GI or septicemia	*Salmonella* spp	Fecal culture
	Respiratory or septicemia	*Chlamydia* spp	Conjunctival, trachea, or cloacal swab culture
	Respiratory/trachea	Tracheal worm, *Cyanthostoma variegatum*	Visual, microscopic examination of tracheal mucous, fecal float, history, clinical signs
	Respiratory	Avian influenza	Serology, trachea, choanal, or cloacal swab
	Neurologic or general viremia	EEE/WEE	Serology
	Skin, visceral	*Mycobacterium* spp	Biopsy external lesion, acid fast tissue stain, fecal centrifugation with acid fast stain of fecal pellet, possibly serology, and tuberculin skin test

BLOOD COUNT AND SERUM CHEMISTRY ANALYSIS

Serum chemistries and complete blood-count results by themselves will rarely provide you with an etiologic diagnosis. However, they are extremely useful for defining a disorder and providing clinical data to support or discount a presumptive diagnosis. Reference ranges are slightly different between ratite species and ages within a species. A list of values for ostriches is provided

At the University of Missouri our serum chemistries are performed using a Kodak Ektachem 500. Complete blood counts are done manually using EDTA or lithium heparin samples. Avian RBC's are nucleated, therefore coulter counters are routinely not used as most cannot differentiate between RBC and WBC nuclei.

Serum chemistries are performed using serum or plasma from lithium heparin. Ostrich RBCs hemolyze easily in EDTA; however, this is not a problem with emu or rhea blood.

If sample analysis will be delayed for a few hours, it is best to use lithium heparin instead of EDTA to prevent hemolysis. It is best to make blood smears at the time the blood is drawn and send the slide with the samples to the lab. The chemistry analysis can be performed with either plasma (from lithium heparin, but not sodium heparin or EDTA) or serum. It is best to harvest the plasma or serum as soon as possible after draw for the most reliable results.

In summary, for mail-in blood samples for CBC and chemistry analysis, send a good feathered edged blood smear, harvested serum or plasma and an EDTA tube for rhea and emus only or lithium heparin for any species. It has been observed that WBC clumping may occur with lithium heparin vs. EDTA.

Total WBC counts vary tremendously between birds and between samples of the same individual. This makes it difficult to accurately assess a value if it is near the high or low range of normal.

RBC counts are much lower than mammals, as are total protein, albumin and cholesterol. LDH and glucose are normally much higher than seen in mammals. Other values are similar.

The GGT is routinely higher in emus vs. ostriches, probably due to the presence of a gallbladder in the emu, which is absent in the ostrich.

The calcium/phosphorous levels should be near 2:1 ratio or 1.5:1 in young chicks. If the ratio is much greater than 2:1, rickets should be suspected.

Young chicks usually have higher values for alkaline phosphatase, phosphorous, total protein and albumin. A hen near the start of laying or that is in lay should normally have increased calcium and alkaline phosphatase values.

Liver disease is often associated with increased AST, LDH, bile acids and GGT values. Birds with impactions, muscle damage, or wasting often have increased AST and LDH values as well, but the AST rise is lower and the LDH:AST ratio is higher in the case of impactions, muscle damage, or wasting compared to the ratio associated with liver disease.

Below is an outline of conditions associated with abnormal values.

- Brett A. Hopkins, DVM

A. **Leukocytosis**
   1. Increased lymphocytes
      a. fungal infection
      b. chronic diseases of air sac, joint, bone, gizzard, muscle, meninges, spinal cord, brain etc.
   2. Increased heterophils
      a. bacterial infection: trachea, liver, lungs intestines, abdomen, oviduct, wounds, etc.
      b. stress
      c. iatrogenic steroid use
      d. excitement causing epinephrine release
   3. Increased eosinophils
      a. parasites
      b. hypersensitivity

Note: It is common to see increased WBC count after a "rodeo round-up" prior to collecting blood. DO NOT confuse this with an acute infection. Glucose levels may also be high due to excitement prior to blood draw.

B. **Hyperproteinemia**
   1. Dehydration
   2. Inflammation
      a. pneumonia
      b. salpingitis
      c. acute hepatitis
      d. acute enteritis, etc
   3. Hen during egg production

C. **Hypoproteinemia**
   1. Hepatopathy
   2. Pancreatopathy
   3. Malabsorption, enteropathy
   4. Chronic disease, cachexia
   5. Malnutrition, maldigestion, starvation, anorexia
      a. cold weather
      b. rock, grass, sand, etc. overload
      c. poor quality feed
   6. Hemorrhage
   7. Overhydration with IV fluids
   8. Unabsorbed yolk sac in chick 2 weeks of age

D. **Leukopenia**
   1. Severe infection - pneumonia, peritonitis, septicemia, salpingitis, etc
   2. Immunosuppression

E. **Hyperglycemia**
   1. Iatrogenic steroid use
   2. Excitement
   3. Stress, cachexia
   4. Post-pyrandial
   5. Too high dextrose levels in IV fluids
   6. Pancreatic fibrosis, chronic zinc toxicosis
   7. Idiopathic diabetes (decreased insulin utilization or secretion)

BLOOD COUNT AND SERUM CHEMISTRY ANALYSIS (Cont'd)

F. **Hypoglycemia:** very common in chicks and must be *quickly* corrected
   1. Grass, sand, rocks, etc. overload: common in birds that are thin to emaciated.
   2. Malnutrition
   3. Cold environment
   4. Septicemia
   5. Liver disease
   6. Anorexia
   7. *Downer* birds
   8. RBC's metabolism due to delayed harvest of serum, plasma
   9. Over-hydration with IV fluids, lacking dextrose, eg. especially NaCl
   10. Malabsorption of nutrients
   11. Enteropathy
   12. Insulin overdose

G. **Anemia:** Low Hgb, low PCV, low RBC count
   1. Liver rupture
   2. Hepatopathy
   3. Proventriculus or ventricular ulcers
   4. Hemorrhagic enteritis
   5. Hemorrhagic typhlitis
   6. Hemorrhagic colitis
   7. Hemorrhagic tracheitis
   8. Chronic disease
   9. Vitamin deficiency
   10. Long term use of Tribrissen or phenylbutazone
   11. Emaciation
   12. Iron deficiency
   13. Bone marrow suppression, eg. *Pseudomonas* spp, septicemia
   14. Commonly seen with stunted bird syndrome
   15. Unknown, etc.

H. **Hypernatremia**
   1. Dehydration due to several causes
   2. Inappropriate IV fluids with excess Na

I. **Hyponatremia**
   1. Diarrhea
   2. Lipidemia
   3. Use of 5% dextrose in H_2O for IV fluids
   4. Associated with peripheral SQ edema
   5. Volvulus and/or intussusception of the small intestines
   6. Chronic hepatopathy (cirrhosis)
   7. Glomerulopathy (rarely documented)
   8. Polydypsia

J. **Hyperkalemia**
   1. Severe leukocytosis
   2. Hemolysis in vivo or in vitro
   3. Severe tissue necrosis (trauma, Blackleg, etc)
   4. Possible acidemia
   5. High K in diet or IV fluids
   6. Severe dehydration

K. **Hypokalemia**
   1. Diarrhea
   2. IV fluids low in K
   3. Use of Lasix
   4. Possible alkalosis
   5. Prolonged anorexia i.e. chronic impaction, starvation
   6. May see with hyperglycemia as insulin moves K into intra-cellular spaces: common with high concentration of dextrose in IV fluids
   7. Possible renal disease, rarely seen

L. **Hyperchloremia**
   1. High NaCl in IV fluids
   2. Possible acidosis or increased dietary intake of NaCl
   3. Dehydration

M. **Hypochloremia**
   1. **Diarrhea**
   2. Chronic hepatopathy (cirrhosis)
   3. Glomerulopathy (rarely documented)
   4. Possible alkalosis
   5. Low level Cl in IV fluids
   6. Volvulus and/or intussusception of the small intestine
   7. Polydypsia

N. **High Uric Acid**
   1. Dehydration
   2. Decreased renal clearance
   3. Gout
   4. Increased metabolic production

Note: In theory, if the diet is high in protein and the bird becomes dehydrated, the uric acid levels in the plasma will be greater than if the bird was on a low protein diet.

O. **Low Uric Acid**
   1. Normal
   2. Polyuria/polydypsia: seen with iatrogenic overdose of glucocorticoids and renal tubular necrosis, eg. ketoconazole toxicity
   3. Secondary to osmotic diuresis, eg. hyperglycemia

P. **Hyperphosphoremia**
   1. Normal growing chick
   2. Hemolysis of sample
   3. Delayed harvest of serum, plasma away from RBC's
   4. Possible renal disease
   5. Imbalance in diet
   6. Low parathyroid hormone

Q. **Hypophosphoremia**
   1. Rickets
   2. Low dietary calcium
   3. Increased parathyroid hormone with increased excretion by kidney
   4. Decreased intake: deficient diet or anorexia
   5. Increased Vitamin D3 intake
   6. Increased tissue catabolism

BLOOD COUNT AND SERUM CHEMISTRY ANALYSIS (Cont'd)

R. **Hypercalcemia**
1. Increased parathyroid hormone activity
2. Low Ca in diet or lowered Ca:P ratio in diet
3. Hen in lay or becoming ready for lay

S. **Hypocalcemia**
1. Decreased absorption of calcium
2. Decreased Vitamin D3 intake
3. Decreased parathyroid hormone activity with increased phosphorus
4. Hypoproteinemia

T. **Hypermagnesemia**
1. High levels in diet
2. Ingestion of Epsom Salts ($MgSO_4$)

U. **Hypomagnesemia**
1. Anorexia/decreased dietary intake
2. Deficiency in diet
3. Inhibited absorption by another mineral component of an imbalanced diet
4. Imbalanced IV fluids
5. Overhydration

V. **Increased AST**
1. Liver damage (from fungal infection, aflatoxins, EEE, WEE, bacterial septicemia, etc.) Values are higher than seen with skeletal muscle damage. See W1 below
2. Skeletal muscle damage
3. Cachexia
4. Possible cardiac muscle damage
5. Lipidemia
6. Hemolysis of sample
7. Delayed harvest of serum plasma from RBCs

W. **Increased LDH**
1. Skeletal muscle damage:
   a. myositis
   b. capture myopathy
   c. impaction, foreign bodies in ventriculus
   d. ventricular ulcers
   e. downer birds
   f. blackleg
   g. cachexia
2. Liver damage: less dramatic rise than with skeletal muscle damage (See V1 above)
3. Hemolysis of sample
4. Lipidemia

X. **Increased Alkaline Phosphatase**
1. Growing chick
2. Hen close to lay or in lay
3. Bone repair, remodelling
4. Biliary or liver disease (see V1 above)
5. Occasionally enteropathy

Y. **Increased GGT**
1. Biliary or liver disease (see above) Note: Values slow to increase in ostrich and damage is usually severe if a significant increase is seen
2. Hemolysis of sample
3. Lipidemia

The rule-outs for abnormal values that have been discussed in this outline have been seen in actual cases, except alkalosis and acidosis have not been clinically diagnosed. Primary renal disease has been very uncommon in the ratites I have examined, although iatrogenic drug toxicities that have caused renal tubular necrosis have occasionally been seen.

CBC

WBC	<12,000
RBC	1.1×10^6 (1.5-2.5 million)
Hgb	14-16 (=anemic)
PCV	35-50
Platelets	10,000-40,000 (not evaluated in birds due to erroneous values)
Heterophils	78-92% (increases with bacterial infections and stress)
Lymphocytes	5-10%
Monocytes	1-3%
Eosinophils	<1%
Basophils	<1%

With stress you will see an increase in cortisol as well as an increased number and percentage of heterophils.

BLOOD VALUES FOR OSTRICHES

Glucose (mg/dl)	200 - 275
Na (mmol/L)	139 - 145
K (mmol/L)	3.5 - 5
Cl (mmol/L)	98 - 112
Albumen (g/dl)	1.5 - 2.5
Total protein (g/dl)	3.4 - 5.5
Ca (mg/dl)	9.8 - 11.3
P (mg/dl)	3.5 - 5.5
Cholesterol (mg/dl)	<80
ALP (U/L)	1 - 10
AST (U/L)	300 - 400
LDH (U/L)	2000 - 2500
Mg (mmol/L0	1.9 - 2.3
Uric acid (mg/dl)	<12

QUICK REFERENCE - RATITE REPRODUCTION

RATITE	LAYING SEASON	# EGGS IN CLUTCH	INCUBATION PERIOD	EGG COLOR	EGG WEIGHT
Ostrich	Jan - Oct, lay every other day	18 - 24 2 - 4 clutches per year	42 days	Cream	1200-2300 gm
Emu	Nov - April, lay every third day	10 - 40	49 - 55 days	Avocado	500 - 700 gm
Rhea	May - Aug, lay every 2-4 days occasionally lay year-round	18 - 30 2 - 3 clutches per year	35 - 39 days	Light yellow with tinge of green	400 - 700 gm

Sexual maturity occurs between 2 and three years of age. Some ostrich hens begin to lay as young as 17 months of age, while others may be as old as 48 months. Until the onset of sexual maturity, ratite chicks are monomophic. The males of the three ratite species are very active in nest preparation and incubation of the eggs. The ostrich males prepare the nest and, in the wild, incubate the eggs at night. Emu males prepare the nest, incubate the eggs, and rear the chicks in the wild. Rhea males dig a large nest, and incubate the eggs in the wild. Domestic commercial operations gather the eggs soon after they are laid, therefore, the males do not have a role in incubation, but they still prepare and protect the nest.

ADULT OSTRICHES
Females have grey feathers.
Males have black feathers with white wing-tip feathers. During breeding season, the beak and the scales over the metatarsal bones become bright pink to red in the male. In the breed called red neck, the skin on the neck and legs also becomes red in color. The booming sound is created by inflating the esophagus. Aggressive behavior is common during breeding season.

ADULT EMUS
Both sexes are the same color (dark grey to charcoal with darker feather tips). Females are usually larger in body size. In addition, the females make a booming or drumming sound during their reproductive season. This sound originates from the tracheal diverticulum, which can be seen externally as a pendulous pouch just cranial to the thoracic inlet. The males also have tracheal diverticulum that is not as easily seen, but is used to make a gurgling, grunting sound. Male emus are usually very docile during breeding season.

ADULT RHEAS
Both sexes can be white or grey, with the males being larger than the females. During the reproductive season, aggressive males often raise the feathers on their necks. The male booms by inflating the esophagus.

ADULT BODY WEIGHT (IN POUNDS)

	FEMALE	MALE
Ostrich	200 - 350	250 - 400
Emu	90 - 150	80 - 125
Rhea	30 - 65	45 - 80

ADULT HEIGHT (IN FEET)

	OVER COXOFEMORAL JOINT	HEAD HEIGHT WITH NECK EXTENDED
Ostrich	4.5 - 5 (male & female)	7.5 - 9'
Emu	3.5 (male & female)	6'
Rhea	2.5 (female) 3 (male)	4 - 5' 4 - 5.5

COMMON TECHNIQUES AND REPRODUCTIVE DISORDERS OF FEMALE RATITES

A: Indications a hen is preparing for egg production
1) Serum calcium levels increase
2) Follicle development detected by ultrasound. Probe placement on left inguinal region
3) Rise in serum/plasma total protein, increased alkaline phospatase activity
4) Personality changes, flutters

QUICK REFERENCE - RATITE REPRODUCTION (Cont'd)

B: Detection of egg binding
1) Ultrasound, using a 3.0 or 3.5 mHz sector or linear scan in the ostrich or 3.5 or 5.0 mHz in the emu or rhea. Probe placment is on the left lateral abdomen caudal to coxofemoral joint. Soft-shelled and shelled eggs are easily identified.
2) Manual palpation of the abdomen; detection of egg in fat hens is very difficult.
3) Radiograph of abdomen, dorsal/ventral and/or lateral views. Only eggs with shells are easily detected.
4) Manual examination of the oviduct via the cloaca.
5) History

C: Detection of bacterial infection within the oviduct
1) Culture of distal oviduct via a guarded culturette. The oviduct opening is at the 9 - 10 o'clock position in the left wall of the cloacal pouch. Contamination of the culture swab is common. Isolation of bacteria does not definitely indicate infection. It is normal for some actively producing hens to have bacteria in the distal oviduct, while the proximal oviduct is sterile. These hens still lay normal eggs, and have good hatchability and survivability of chicks.
2) Cytology of distal oviduct; identification of heterophils, mononuclear inflammatory cells, excessive bacteria or phagocytized bacteria, excessive mucous, and/or fibrin indicates a problem.
3) Ultrasound oviduct; identification of fluid in the oviduct indicates a problem.
4) History of contaminated eggs, poor shell quality, etc. Isolation of the same bacteria from the eggs and the oviduct is expected if the oviduct is the source of the contamination in the eggs.
5) Celiotomy with salpingostomy; bacterial and/or viral culture and biopsy.
6) Abdominocentesis using an 18-14g 1.5" needle often reveals inflammatory cells, fibrin, and occasional yolk material in severe infections and internal layers.
7) Complete blood count and serum chemistry values are often normal, except in cases with severe infections.

D: Prolapse of the oviduct
A common problem in immature ostriches seen primarily in Australia is hypersecretion of fluid into the oviduct, causing a prolapse into the cloaca. Correction is made by lancing the membrane over the oviduct opening, allowing the fluid to drain. Recurrence is not common. Current evidence points to a genetic predisposition.

COMMON TECHNIQUES AND REPRODUCTIVE DISORDERS OF MALE RATITES

A: Determination of fertility
At this time if a male is determined to have motile spermatozoa, he is considered fertile. Morphology and concentration of spermatozoa are not routinely evaluated. The spermatozoa can be visualized under light microscopy using a stained or unstained preparation. The motility of the spermatozoa is very sensitive to cold temperatures and exposure to air.

Male ostriches are very aggressive during breeding season, making samples difficult to collect. Both manual massage and electro-ejaculation have been used.

Male emus are very docile during the breeding season and most are easily collected by manual massage. Contamination with urine and feces is a problem. Volume collected varies from 0.05 to 1.0 ml in emus.

I have not had experience collecting rheas, but assume manual massage will work if you can catch the bird and hold him. Rhea males are very obnoxious during the breeding season.

B: Prolapsed phallus
1) Seen more in the ostrich
   a) Defined as an oversized phallus that will not fit into the cloacal pouch. Associated with high hormone levels.
   b) The phallus will regress in size and retract into the cloaca as hormone levels decrease.
   c) Supportive therapy may be needed to prevent frostbite, infection, sunburn, or physical trauma.
   d) Adminstration of dexamethasone will cause testicular regression and the phallus will reduce in size and retract back into the cloaca; however, a few days after administration, the phallus will enlarge again and prolapse. Dexamethasone is NOT recommended for long-term treatment, as continual treatment will cause the bird to become infertile and lose his libido.

- Brett A. Hopkins, DVM

MANAGEMENT-RELATED DISEASES AND DISORDERS OF RATITES

ENVIRONMENTAL DISEASES

Environmental diseases result from Mother Nature combined with management practices. With marginal management, even slight weather changes can set up disease. With good practices, greater change is necessary to create disease.

The type and frequency of environmental diseases vary according to the location in which the birds are raised. The most common are initially related to heat or cold, social stresses, and poor ventilation. These stresses can often lead to retained yolk sacs, weight loss, impactions, infections, growth retardation, intestinal disease, and respiratory disease.

Overheating is probably the most common cause of diarrhea, due to excessive drinking and increased motility of the intestines. Diarrhea can dehydrate a bird as well as decrease nutrient absorption and alter intestinal bacterial flora.

Reduced exercise and sunlight are very common predisposing factors of disease, especially diseases related to the musculoskeletal and immune systems and nutrition.

Several infections, including pneumonia, sinusitis, tracheitis, ophthalmitis, enteritis and septicemia can be caused by dirty drinking water. The soil, water and bedding can also be the home of several parasites, bacteria and fungi that can cause disease in susceptible birds.

Pneumonia and air sacculitis are always the result of poor management and environmental conditions. Heat or cold stress alone, or combined with dirty water, dusty straw or hay and poor ventilation, will cause respiratory disease. Affected birds are also commonly immunosuppressed. Overcrowded birds in the winter often acquire respiratory infections.

To reduce environmental disease, keep birds at a comfortable temperature with good ventilation, clean food and water, plenty of sunlight, exercise and space. Prevent exposure to items that cause trauma and/or impaction and do not overfeed.

NUTRITIONAL DEFICIENCIES

Nutritional deficiencies are quite common in ratites. The most commonly seen deficiencies in ostriches include those of the B complex vitamins. Mineral imbalances and vitamin A deficiencies are seen more commonly in rheas. Fewer nutritional disorders are seen in emus as a group, but B complex and mineral imbalances are still very common. Most of these deficiencies are diagnosed based on clinical signs and pathological workup. I am currently working to establish normal and abnormal values for several vitamins and minerals in the blood of live birds and livers in dead birds to help in formulating diets and the diagnosis of deficiency or excess.

HOW DEFICIENCIES CAN OCCUR

Nutritional imbalances and deficiencies occur primarily in chicks

1. The egg yolk is the source of nutrition for the developing embryo and the hatched chick. If the yolk is lacking in nutrients the embryo will develop with improper nutrition.
2. Hatched chicks that are normal can develop deficiencies if yolk sac absorption is delayed.
3. The least common way for deficiency to occur is after the yolk is absorbed and the chick cannot utilize the nutrition in its diet or the diet is deficient for an ingredient.

Many deficiencies can be medically corrected. The severity of the deficiency and therapy administered will determine the fate of the bird.

The breeder hen is responsible for the contents of the yolk.

1. If the hen does not consume enough nutrients to keep up with egg production, the yolks will begin to have reduced nutrient composition.
2. Adult hens and males are rarely diagnosed as having nutritional deficiencies.
3. Most vitamins are not stored in the hen's body; therefore they are required from the diet.
4. As a hen enters into egg production her total utilization of vitamins and minerals increase because extra nutrition is entering into the egg yolk in addition to her normal metabolic needs.
5. If her nutritional intake is not increased then the nutrient content of the yolks will be sacrificed, leading to eggs, embryos, and chicks which develop with nutritional deficiencies.

Common reasons why hens do not keep up with the added demands of egg production in relation to nutrition.

1. Most hens will go off feed for a few days and reduce feed consumption during laying season.
2. Most hens are pushed to lay more than one clutch of eggs.
3. Hens may not be able to utilize the diet formulation and get enough intestinal absorption as needed.
4. Many ostrich hens have excess gravel, grass or both in their stomachs. This alters the rate of passage and digestion.
5. Most diets are improperly formulated for laying hens. With genetic manipulation and improved diets many deficiencies will become very uncommon.

Brett A. Hopkins, DVM

COMMON PATHOLOGICAL CONDITIONS OF RATITES

Nutritional	mainly chicks
Infectious	once rare, becoming more common to find bird-to-bird transmission
Parasitic	lice, strongyles, giardia, tracheal worm in the emu
Traumatic	leg and toe fractures, dog attacks, fence running, pecking each other
Miscellaneous	volvulus, impactions, retained yolk sacs

CONDITIONS CAUSED BY COMBINED VITAMIN DEFICIENCIES

Embryonic death	Retarded growth	Muscle/skeleton abnormalities
Malpositioned chicks	Central nervous system	slipped tendons
Edematous chicks	(CNS) signs	rotated legs
Reduced hatchability	Scaly skin	rotated toes
Retained yolk sacs	Poor feathering	bowed legs
Weak chicks	Diarrhea	Others
Fading chicks		

SYMPTOMS ASSOCIATED WITH VITAMIN DEFICIENCY

VITAMINS	SYMPTOMS
Pantothenic Acid	Hyperkeratosis, ulceration, cracking of the skin and feet, crusty and/or exudative lesion of the eyelids, commissures of the mouth, severe cases may have yellow exudative dermatitis on non-feathered areas. Seen more often in ostriches. Fungal infections, biotin deficiency, niacin deficiency. Concrete lesions, if on feet only, is questionable.
Biotin	Resembles pantothenic acid.
Hock disorders	If just hyperkeratosis of the feet, probably biotin deficiency.
Niacin	Retarded growth, scaly dermatitis, poor feather quality, hock disorders.
Thiamine	Classical "stargazing" at time of hatch; treat aggressively 2 times daily for several days, then one time daily.
Riboflavin	Curly toe (emus, rheas), lateral rotation of greater toe (ostrich), edema (anasarca) in chicks, late embryonic death.
Choline	Leg deformities (slipped tendons, rotated legs), growth retardation.
Vitamin E, selenium	Torticollis, hemorrhagic cerebellum, encephalomalacia, subcutaneous edema with exudative diathesis.
Vitamin A	Squamous metaplasia of the esophagus and glands, embryonic death, dry eyes, sinusitis, possible role in blindness in hatchlings.
Vitamin B12	Hasn't been well documented, has been associated with edema in chicks, poor feather quality, anemia in chicks is common but it has NOT been determined if B12, folic acid, or iron etc. are involved.
Vitamin E	Associated with rolled head and somersault syndrome (emus and rheas).
Vitamin D	Rickets.
Any B-complex	Immunosuppressed, anemic, growth retardation.

SYMPTOMS ASSOCIATED WITH MINERAL DEFICIENCY

MINERALS	SYMPTOMS
Copper	Deficiencies implicated in some aortic rupture in ostriches by decreasing the copper-containing enzyme lysyl oxidase which is important in the cross-linking of elastin and collagen defects. Possible role in distal-limb edema of the adult ostrich.
Manganese	Embryonic bone and tendon deformities, especially the cranium and beak; emus and rheas.
Zinc	Poor doers; myopathy; osteogenic modalities; scaly skin or hyperkeratosis of the skin.
Selenium	Growth retardation; myopathy; exudative diathesis; edema in chicks. May or may not be associated with Vitamin E deficiency. Associated with muscle disorders leading to downed birds in young adult and adult ostriches. Both high and deficient levels are being investigated as to their role in the edematous chick syndrome.
Calcium-phosphorus imbalance	Leads to rickets (common in the rhea) and bowed metatarsal bones; levels and ratios are also commonly abnormal.
Iron	Common in ostrich chicks with anemia.

In general, mineral problems are more common in rheas.

NUTRITIONAL TOXICOSIS

MINERAL	SYMPTOMS	DIAGNOSIS
Zinc *	Pancreatic and liver fibrosis Proventriculus and gizzard ulcers May be associated with aortic rupture Chronic, severe weight loss Hypoproteinemia Anemia Hyperglycemia Poor feather quality	Analysis of zinc levels in the liver. Suggestive pathological lesions. Determine zinc levels in feed. Note: some feeds have high levels of zinc.
Iron	Poor doers Hepatopathy Often related to ingestion of foreign objects	
Lead	Central nervous system signs Ataxia Anorexia +/- Anemia Weight Loss	

* Zinc may possibly play a role in the embryonic bony deformities of the skull, beak, and spine commonly seen in rheas and emus. I plan to continue analyzing both vitamin and mineral levels that are considered normal, low or high and relate any pathological conditions associated with normal levels.

Brett A. Hopkins, DVM

VIRAL DISEASES

DISEASE	DESCRIPTION
Newcastle (paramyxovirus)	Diagnose using serology and culture (hasn't been isolated in the United States, yet). Has been isolated from ostriches overseas in Israel and Africa.
Fowl pox, ostrich pox, dry form (cutaneous), wet form	Diptheritic lesions in the oropharynx, esophagus, common to isolate in the cloaca. More common in birds in the coastal United States. Has been seen in Israel and Africa. Birds can be vaccinated.
Infectious bronchitis virus, corona virus	Infects the oviduct and uterus. Seen in thin eggs and rough shells in chickens. Not yet identified in ratites.
Influenza A (H7N1)	Rheas and emus in the USA, ostriches in South Africa.
H5N2, Western equine encephalitis (E, O)	Most common in Midwest, can vaccinate with the equine dosage and possibly get a protective antibiotic titer, detectable at 4-6 weeks. WEE seen in Missouri. Less mortality, more central nervous system symptoms. Compare to EEE. Usually seen in emus.
Eastern equine encephalitis, encephalomyelitis (E,O)	Usually fatal disease affecting younger birds during the vector (culicoides, horseflies and mosquitoes) season (spring and early summer). You may see a bloody diarrhea and hemorrhage out of the mouth and other organs. Seen in Louisiana, Texas and Florida. Primarily in emus.
Intestinal Viruses: Adeno, Astro, Entero, Corona, Rota, PMV, PMV II, Diminu Herpes, Picorn-like, Parvo-like, Birna-like, Myxoviridae, etc.	Sporadically isolated across the United States. Consistent pathology has not been related to any of the viruses, i.e. incidental findings. Some research on viral disease is currently being done.

IMPORTANT VIRUSES ISOLATED OVERSEAS

DISEASE	DESCRIPTION
Crimean-Congo hemorrhagic fever	Suspected to have been transmitted to a man via ticks that were present on an ostrich in South Africa.
Wesselbron virus	A flavivirus that has been isolated from dead ostriches. Positive serological titers have been identified in South Africa.
Borna disease	Identified in Israel associated with paresis in ostrich chicks two to six weeks of age.
Spongiform encephalopathy (BSE)	Similar lesions were identified in adult ostriches with neurologic disease in Germany.

BLOOD PARASITES

PARASITE	COMMENTS
Leucocozoon struthionis	Extremely rare in the United States, common in ostriches under 6 months of age in South Africa.
Aegyptianella pullorum	An anaplasma-like rickettsia, infecting red blood cells, identified in young ostriches in Chad.
Plasmodium struthionis	Identified in ostriches from Sudan.
Plasmodium spp.	Identified in ostriches from South Africa.
Plasmodium spp.	Unnamed; possible prelictum identified in a rhea in a zoo in Brazil.

INTERNAL PARASITES

PARASITE	SPECIES	COMMENTS
Cyanthostoma boularti, Cyanthostoma variegatum, Anatidae, Casuariidae, Ciconiidae, Dromiceiidae, Phasianidae Intermediate host- earthworm	Emu & Rhea	**TRACHEAL WORM** *CLINICAL SIGNS*: Emus exhibit hacking, coughing, and gasping, often shaking their heads from side to side or lowering their heads while shaking in an attempt to remove excess mucus and/or worms. The mucus is often blood tinged. Look for bloody mucus slung onto surfaces in their pens. Severely infected birds may have open-mouth breathing and dyspnea or labored breathing. Most birds will continue to eat and drink and appear healthy with only slight depression. Death is rare, but can be expected if treatment is not provided. *DIAGNOSIS*: The worms are red; females measure up to 3 cm in length and males 1 cm or less. Unlike *Syngamus* spp, males and females are not in permanent copulation, a major distinguishing trait. The ova measure 37.5 um x 24.3 um on average and are rarely operculated. If an operculum is seen, it is usually single. In the *C.variegatum* ovum, the operculum matures after leaving the host. If old or stored samples are examined, the presence of an operculum may be common. Ova can be seen in a mucus smear from the oral pharynx or trachea and in feces after routine flotation using light microscopy. Worms can often be found in the trachea and removed for examination using a culture swab. Females have a buccal cup with six teeth; maturing ova are nearest the buccal cup. *TREATMENT*: Ivermectin given subcutaneously at dosages of 0.45-0.9 mg/kg body weight has proven effective at eliminating clinical signs within 1-2 days after treatment. Most birds relapse with clinical signs approximately 30 days after the first treatment, thus requiring a second dose. Recurrence after the second treatment has been observed to be rare, although some farms are required to treat monthly throughout the year to keep infections controlled. Fenbendazole at 2.27 mg/kg body weight given orally is efficacious. Levamisol has been used in the water, but resistance appears to develop rapidly, necessitating the use of another anthelmintic. *EPIDEMIOLOGY*: The ova are spread through the oral mucus and feces, infecting soil, water, feed, bedding, and other birds. A very infectious disease and potentially difficult to control. Treatment appears to be able to control morbidity but the pens and birds are probably still infected. With the earthworm as a paratenic host, encysted larvae may live 4-5 years. This is a concern when considering placing juveniles in a pen or even on the farm where previous infection was evident. Migrating birds may be asymptomatic carriers. Incidence is greatest in the fall of the year. *CONTROL*: Since the soil is often contaminated and wild birds and domestic fowl can carry the disease, control is very difficult. On infected farms, these sources of infection should be removed and the emu chicks routinely de-wormed to aid in controlling the disease. These measures can also prevent the disease, along with scrutiny when purchasing emus. *NOTE*: Has been documented in emus in the US ranging in age 5-12 months and is much less common in adults.

INTERNAL PARASITES, Cont'd

PARASITE	SPECIES	COMMENTS
Amoebae	Rhea	Unknown identification.
Ascaridia orthocera	Rhea	
Balantidium coli, Balantidium spp.	Ostrich	Pathogenicity unknown.
Blastocystis spp.	Ostrich	In Japan.
Baylisascaris spp., Baylisascaris prozynosis	Emu	Aberrant migration to the brain, ataxia, paralysis, torticollis, etc. Very common in emus 2-6 months of age. TREATMENT: none effective. PREVENTION: Ivermectin. Prevent exposure to raccoon and opossum feces.
Capillaria spp.		Ova may only be transient passengers from prior ingestion.
Chandlerella quiscali	Emu	Microfilaria, aberrant migration to the brain. CNS signs, Culicoides vector. TREATMENT: none effective. PREVENTION: Ivermectin. More common in emus in the southern United States.
Chapmania tauricollis	Rhea	
Cittotaenia rheae	Rhea	
Codiostomum struthionis	Ostrich	Inhabits the colon.
Cotugnia collini	Emu	
Cryptosporidium spp.	Ostrich	Peritoneum, air sac.
Deletrocephalus dimidiatus	Rhea	
Dicheilonema spicularia	Ostrich	
Dicheilonema rheae	Rhea	
Dromaeostrongylus tricuspis	Emu	
Echinorhynchus reticulatus	Rhea	
Eimeria sp (coccidia)		Still need further research on coccidia.
Esthiopterum struthionis	Ostrich	
Giardia	Ostrich & rhea	Very common, possible role in B-complex deficiency. TREATMENT: 15-60 mg/kg Flagyl (metronidazole). CONTROL: Could come from feeding manure to chicks for gut stimulation. Usually no pathology. CLINICAL SIGNS: Can cause enteritis with liquid diarrhea in chicks. NOTE: Seen on every ostrich farm I have examined. Can be a serious problem in rheas.
Hexamita spp	Rhea	May be associated with malabsorption syndrome.
Histomonas meleagridis (blackhead)		Rare: identified in ostriches in The Netherlands.
Houttuynia struthionis	Ostrich	

INTERNAL PARASITES, Cont'd

PARASITE	SPECIES	COMMENTS
Isopora struthionis spp.		Commonly seen in feces, but rarely associated with disease.
Libyostrongylus douglassi (wire worm)	Ostrich	Hemorrhagic necrosis of the proventriculus and gizzard. Extremely rare in the United States.
Libyostrongylus magnus	Ostrich & rhea	
Odontospirura cetiopenis	Rhea	Proventriculus and ventriculus.
Paronchocerca struthionus	Ostrich	Lung, air sac, peritoneum.
Philophthalamus gralli	Ostrich	Filaria in the eye.
Railletina australis	Emu	
Spirura uncinipenis	Rhea	Proventriculus.
Spirura zschokkei	Rhea	Proventriculus.
Struthiofilaria megalocephala	Ostrich	
Trichomonas spp.		Oral and internal locations.
Versternema struthionis	Ostrich	
Other protozoa and helminths		

EXTERNAL PARASITES

PARASITE	SPECIES	COMMENTS
Feather mites Pterolichidae spp Quill mites		
Gabucinia sculpturata, bicaudata, paralges pachycnemis, abbreviata		
G. nouvela		From the skin, causing mange.
Lice		
Struthiolipeurus struthionis	Ostrich	
Dahlemhornia asymmetrica	Emu	
Struthiolipeurus renschi, stresemanni, nandu	Common rhea	
Meinertzhageniella lata, schubarti		
Ratitiphagus batocina		
Ticks		Several species, depending on geographic location, commonly attached to skin around head and the eyelids, probably because of more tender skin and greater superficial blood supply.
Flies and gnats		Can cause mental irritation and dermatitis of non-feathered areas, primarily the head and neck region.

Treat external parasites with a pinch of coumaphos (used in cattle), sevin dust, malathion spray, etc.

BACTERIAL AGENTS

BACTERIA	COMMENTS
Escherichia coli	Usually a secondary contaminant, but can be a primary infection in the yolk sac, wounds, oviduct, and in the ostrich, the proximal large intestine causing fibrinonecrotic colitis.
Klebsiella pneumoniae, K. oxytoxca, K. spp	Pneumonia, stomatitis, hepatitis, enteritis, encephalitis, meningitis, septicemia.
Salmonella spp Group D	A condemnable disease for chickens infected with S. pullorum, S. gallinarum, or S. enteritidis, egg transmitted. Not yet identified in ratites.
Salmonella enteritidis	Phage type 4 isolated from quarantine emus from the Netherlands. Not yet identified in the USA.
Salmonella spp. Group B Paratyphoid group, e.g. S. hadar, S. montevideo, S. agona, S. typhimurium (most common isolate), S. stanley, S. tuindrop, S. derby, etc.	Can cause only enteritis or hepatitis, but is usually seen as a systemic fibrinous serositis and fibrinonecrotic enteritis and colitis; one of the few diseases that routinely causes pyrexia. In the spring and summer of 1994, the incidence of salmonella isolation increased over 5 times from previous years.
Pseudomonas aeruginosa, P. maltophilia, P. alcaligenes, P. flourescens	Common pathogen involved in ocular pathologies (i.e. keratitis) and contaminants of eggs/embryos. Can cause septicemia in a healthy or compromised host as well as stomatitis, tracheitis, pneumonia, esophagitis, often with fibrinonecrotic cast, common to isolate from plastic products and water, especially in incubator or hatcher. Problem in crowded environments (pen mates pecking eyes), can be isolated from lungs that have aspirated stomach contents (cases of birds that have stomach tubed with large volumes of fluids).
Streptococcus viridans, Alpha s. spp.	Sinusitis, esophagitis, pharyngitis, often a secondary component of pneumonia, hepatitis, enteritis.
Alpha streptococcus	Seen with excessive use of probiotics, septicemia and eye infections.
Clostridium perfringens	Hemorrhagic ulcerations or congestion and hyperemia of the mucosa of the proventriculus, ventriculus or small intestine. Overgrowth in the gastrointestinal tract results in toxemia and ultimately death, (common in overfed and overheated chicks when the passage of ingesta has slowed). In adults, may be seen with rock or grass, etc. impaction or with acute anorexia and stress causing necrotizing enteritis and/or typhlitis (fibrinonecrotic cast may be seen in the feces). In South Africa, clostridium perfringens types A, B, and D, and in Israel type C appears to be the etiologic agent.
Clostridium chauveoi (blackleg), C. septicum, C. novyi, C. sordelli (pseudo blackleg)	The Blackleg organisms are identified as primary pathogens in the emu only. Disease is usually seen in 2-8 month old emus. One or a combination of these organisms are often associated with the disease. The disease does not spread from bird to bird. *CLINICAL SIGNS*: Blackleg, stumbling syndrome with head and neck tremors eventually progressing to recumbency and emaciation. Clinical course of the disease is very long. Anemia and ruptured livers are a common sequela in most cases. The livers become very friable and easily rupture causing exsanguination. Stumbling or rough handling may cause the rupture of the livers (do not sit on these birds for restraint). The oral mucosa is usually white in color if the liver has been ruptured. (Continued)

BACTERIAL AGENTS, Cont'd

Clostridium chauvoei (cont'd)	*LESIONS*: Hemorrhagic myositis, muscle cavitation, ruptured liver with excessive hemorrhage, old and fresh subcapsular hepatic hematomas, subcutaneous hemorrhage over the joints of the feet, legs and neck are common lesions. A toxin and/or DIC is suspected to cause blood-clotting deficits, creating a condition where the birds easily hemorrhage from minor contusions. The muscle lesions usually only occur on one side of the body. Skin the bird completely to see all possible lesions. Blackleg in cattle is more dry/gaseous in contrast to a more wet form in the emu. *DIAGNOSIS*: History, clinical signs, CBC, anemia, serum chemistries, muscle biopsy, anaerobic culture and/or fluorescent antibody stain of affected muscles. *Note*: Need to get samples for culture within 1 to 2 hours after death, because these organisms will spread rapidly throughout the carcass, giving a false etiology for the causative agent. Feathers can be cultured to confirm exposure. *PREVENTION*: Avoid muddy feedlot-like conditions. *Note*: You can vaccinate for clostridial infections using the cattle products and dosage. I prefer using the subcutaneous products with a 2 ml dosage. The subcutaneous injection may cause a lump, but this is covered by the feathers. *VACCINATING TECHNIQUE*: Part the feathers and wipe the exposed skin with disinfectant prior to injecting. Use a new, sterile needle for each bird. *Note*: The injection site I use is the right or left sacral region (I almost never place injections into the leg muscle). *POSSIBLE SOURCE*: Infected injectionsite, wounds, ingestion of spores (especially when preening); i.e. can have the organism on the feathers from contaminated soil (muddy feedlot, heavy rains, and disturbed soil from construction release buried spores). *NOTE*: I have not diagnosed "Blackleg" in emus in 1994, or to date in 1995, perhaps because of less rain, less construction and more vaccinations than previous years.
Clostridium tetani	Stiff neck, lockjaw, respiratory distress, ataxia, 3rd eyelid flutter, contracted toes, tonic/clonic contraction of thorax, legs and lumbar muscles. Note: Have seen only once - the victim was an emu.
Clostridium botulinum	Associated with ingestion of decaying plants or animal carcasses such as frogs, mice, birds or dead pen mates, etc. *SYMPTOMS*: Paralysis, with death occurring slowly or quickly. *NECROPSY FINDINGS*: Normal internal organs with vascular congestion. The esophagus is usually dilated and flaccid and contains ingested material and usually the incriminating material is still within the esophagus or proventriculus. The oral mucosa is often purple, indicating hypoxia/asphyxiation. Diagnosed in emus in Missouri and suspected in ostriches in the United States and Africa.
Enterobacter cloacae, E. agglomerans, E. spp.	Common contaminants of eggs/embryos, pneumonia, septicemia etc.
Serpulina hyodysenteriae	Extremely infectious disease in rheas. Fibrinonecrotic typhlitis, pyrexia, diarrhea (often with flecks of blood) off feed, depressed, poor doers, eventual death. Diagnose: antemortem by history, clinical symptoms and fecal culture and/or stain. Chicks often develop secondary pneumonia. *TREATMENT*: Flagyl and lincomycin (like swine dysentery). *TRANSMISSION*: Fecal/oral.

BACTERIAL AGENTS, Cont'd

BACTERIA	COMMENTS
Acinetobacter calcoaceticus wolffi	Tracheitis, septicemia, sinusitis contaminants of eggs, embryos, etc. Tracheitis, pneumonia.
Pasteurella pneumotropica, P. multocida (fowl cholera)	Isolated from ostriches in the Frankfurt Zoo in Germany and at Kano Zoo in Nigeria. Only positive serologic titers identified in the United States.
Edwardsiella tarda	Sinusitis and pneumonia, common water contaminant.
Aeromonas hydrophia	Sinusitis and pneumonia, common water contaminant.
Aeromonas caviae	Stomatitis, common water contaminant.
Bacillus anthracis	Anthrax.
Staphylococcus spp.	Joint, eye, yolk sac infection.
S. hyicus ss. hyicus	Conjunctivitis in ostrich in Saskatchewan.
S. aureus	Yolk sac infection, septicemia, egg/embryos.
Mycoplasma cloacae	Unknown mycoplasmas, not associated with pathology, can be isolated from the tracheas of ostriches.
Acholeplasma laidlowii	Trachea.
Mycobacterium avium	Visceral form occasionally seen. Genital and skin infections have also been seen. Ostriches and rheas.
Campylobacter jejunii ss. jejunii, C. jejunii ss. doylei, C. spp, C. jejunii	Serotype 8 was isolated from ostriches in Israel. Liver, necrotizing hepatitis. Commonly seen in rheas as hemorrhagic enteritis/typhilitis. Ingesta is liquid and has a characteristic orange-brown color.
Corynebacterium spp.	Tracheitis, sinusitis, stomatitis, etc.
Erysipethothris rhusiopathia, E. spp.	Pneumonia and septicemia from contaminated soil. Rare, but should always be considered if acute septicemia is present. Primarily an infection of emus, although also isolated from ostriches. Identified in ostriches and rheas in the Paris and Frankfurt zoos.
Chlamydia psittaci, C. spp.	Conjunctivitis, sinusitis, septicemia seen primarily in rheas in the United States; has been found in ostriches in France, Germany, South Africa and the United States.
Bordetella avium	Tracheitis, can live in water and water containers. Isolated most often in ostriches.
B. bronchiseptica	Pneumonia.
Proteus penneri, P. mirabilis, P. vulgaris	Septicemia, contaminant of eggs, embryos.
Morganella morganii	Septicemia.
Algaligenes denitrificans	Tracheitis, septicemia.
Flavobacterium spp.	Meningitis.
Actinomyces spp.	Wounds.
Altermonas putrifaciens	Septicemia.
Serratia liquefaciens, S. spp.	Pneumonia, sinusitis, septicemia.
Citrobacter freundii	Tracheitis and pneumonia, enteritis +/- septicemia, contaminant of eggs, embryos.

FUNGAL AGENTS

FUNGUS	COMMENTS
Candida albicans	Stomatitis which is associated with stress, immunosuppression and antibiotic misuse. Proventriculitis, ventriculitis where the stasis of ingesta overgrowth within the intestines is occasionally seen. Associated with pneumonia and septicemia. Primarily in chicks, sometimes adults. Drinking water can be a source of exposure.
Candida stellatoidea, C. krusei, Rhodococcus glutinis, Trichosporon cutaneum, Torulopsis glabrata	Other yeast isolated from ostriches in South Africa.
Aspergillus fumigatus, A. niger, A. spp.	Granulomatous air sacculitis, pneumonia and rarely, encephalitis. Very common in dusty environments, hay, and close confinement; affects lungs and air sacs. Organism grows in wet environments and sporulates when dried.
Mucor spp., Phycomyces spp., Scopulariopsis spp., Fusarium spp., Zygomyces spp	Pneumonia, air sacculitis, encephalitis, hepatitis, dermatitis, proventriculitis, ventriculitis, etc.
Geotrichium spp.	Stomatitis, proventriculitis, enteritis, dermatitis.
Penicillium spp.	Air sacculitis.
Cryptococcus spp.	
Nocardia spp.	Granulomatous air sacculitis.
Trichophyton spp.	Dermatitis of the beak, eyes and skin.
Unidentified fungi	Air sacculitis.

MISCELLANEOUS DISEASES AND AGENTS

DISEASE	COMMENTS
Adenocarcinoma of the proventriculus in a rhea	
Airsacculitis	Associated with poor ventilation and dust with fungal spores, or secondary to bacterial pneumonia or aspiration of food and/or water.
Antimicrobial toxicities: furazolidone, aminoglycosides, ketoconazole	Central nervous system signs with convulsions, ataxia, etc. Death is common. Renal tubular necrosis; gout, etc. Early in toxicity, birds have PU/PD.
Aortic rupture	May be associated with fast-growing birds, usually males. Some ostriches have had copper deficiency or elevated zinc levels. Other ruptures are from undetermined causes.
Arteriosclerosis	
Aspiration pneumonia, rhinitis	Usually occurs after esophageal tubing.
Atherosclerosis	Usually seen in fat zoo birds.
Cloacal prolapse	Multiple etiologies.

MISCELLANEOUS DISEASES AND AGENTS Cont'd

DISEASE	COMMENTS
Cold weather	Ostriches, young and adults, especially in upper midwest and northern states during winter. Some birds often become thin and can die due to inability to ingest enough potassium caloriess to meet metabolic demands of extreme ambient conditions. Need to increase potassium-calorie intake, monitor birds' weight, and provide warm areas for prevention.
Conjunctivitis (secondary to trauma)	Rule out Chlamydia spp.
Constipation	Dehydration, ingestion of dirt, etc. More common during cold weather.
Corneal edema	Blindness. Due to excessive ammonia build-up in the house. Rapid onset of blindness and the corneas are cloudy. Treatment is successful and blindness is temporary. Removing birds from the ammonia source is a must.

Edematous chicks	Incubator-hatcher problems. Chicks should lose about 15% body weight from incubator to hatcher.
	Conditions to consider in the incubator:
	    a) High humidity
	    b) Low air flow
	    c) Unequal airflow
	    d) High temperature.
	Nutritional considerations:
	    a) B-complex deficiency in the hen
	    b) See deficiency or toxicosis
	    c) Other nutritional anomalies.

Egg binding	
Feather loss	Feather picking vice of bird or pen mates, nutritional imbalance, breeding activity, external parasites, mechanical trauma, etc.
Fibroma, fibroma-like growths	Common in chronically down birds, in birds that sit most of the time, or post trauma, especially in the hock area or more distal.
Fractures	Pathologic, and traumatic; small doorways, falling down on slippery floors or ice-covered surfaces, etc.
Frostbite	Especially in birds with rotated limbs where leg or foot is not covered by the body.
Gout	Uric acid deposition, due to pre-renal, renal or post-renal insufficiency. You can see urate deposition anywhere in the bird, including the joints, tongue and brain. Calculi may clog the cloaca.
Hypoglycemia	Common in chicks; check glucose level.
Hypothermia	Common in young chicks, very thin or emaciated birds and most sick birds.
Intussusception	Irritation to the gut (parasites, foreign objects).
Lacerations	Fence rubbing, trauma from dogs, other birds, handling, buildings, etc.
Liver rupture	Especially seen in emus.
Opthalmitis	
Overgrown toenails	Sometimes related to mineral imbalances, but usually soft non-abrasive surfaces are the cause.
Pneumonia	More common in winter and in young chicks, or associated with ophthalmitis.

MISCELLANEOUS DISEASES AND AGENTS, Cont'd

DISEASE	COMMENTS
Prolapsed phallus	Primarily seen in male ostriches that are very active during breeding season.
Proventriculus, ventriculus impaction	Often seen after transfer of ownership or into a new environment. Ulcers, anemia, malnutrition (i.e., hypoproteinemia, hypoglycemia), and electrolyte imbalances are all common clinical abnormalities. Use of appropriate antibiotics is indicated with medical or surgical treatment. A change in bacterial flora is common with overgrowth of E. coli, Clostridium perfringens, Candida spp. or other fungi. Materials causing impaction are often rocks, sand, nails, bolts, wire, string, rope, plastic, grass, straw, hay, Astro-turf, carpet and occasionally feed.
Renal artery rupture	Especially seen in emus.

Retained yolk sac	The yolk should normally be gone or very small by 10 days of age. If the yolk is not properly absorbed it will become a large space-occupying lesion that will prevent nutritional absorption and normal internal function. The chick have a swollen abdomen that may or may not be infected (presence of a darkened umbilical region). Young chicks that have a foul or rotten odor almost always have an infected yolk sac.
	Some predisposing factors:
	  a) Vitamin/mineral deficiencies;
	  b) Too hot or too cold environments;
	  c) Dehydration;
	  d) Feeding chicks too soon. Don't need to full feed chicks until they are several days old; controlled exposure to feed is fine between 5-14 days of age;
	  e) Lack of proper exercise;
	  f) Bacterial infections; ascending infection through the umbilicus;
	  g) Other stressful conditions;
	  h) Improper incubation and hatching techniques (manually opening egg too early).
	The yolk can be surgically removed by tying off the vitelline arteries and the mekles diverticulum. Complications to the surgery include death from hypoglycemia and/or hypothermia. *NOTE*: I do not promote yolk removal. Post-surgical survival in chicks less than 10 days of age is 30% or less. In some older patients with inspissated yolks, the survival can be near 100%

Rotated legs	a) Greater tendency in males (slightly);
	b) Seen (slightly) more in the left leg, but right leg is also common;
	c) Rotated leg is longer; usually seen in the tibia, occasionally in the metatarsus, and rarely in the femur; gastrocnemius tendon under stress from leg growth or tendon contraction due to injury, nutritional imbalance or malposition in the egg;
	d) Always a lateral rotation; usually unilateral, but can be bilateral.
	May be associated with:
	  a) Trauma to limb, especially soft tissue injuries; non abrasive surfaces, i.e. slick floors causing slipping;
	  b) Any infection;
	  c) Being off feed or overfed; nutritional imbalance (i.e. high phosphorus levels in the diet);
	  d) Heavy body weight;
	  e) Stress;
	  f) Genetics (maybe in the ostrich);
	  g) Malposition in the egg.

MISCELLANEOUS DISEASES OR AGENTS, Cont'd

DISEASE	COMMENTS
Salpingitis	Can cause malformed eggs, or if severe, hen will stop laying, become depressed and die if not treated.
Septic arthritis	
Squamous cell carcinoma, myelomas, ovarian tumors	
Subcutaneous emphysema	Air under skin that has escaped from ruptured air sacs due to trauma or infection.
Thrombotic cardiomyopathy	
Thymic carcinoma (emu)	
Traumatic tendonitis	
Volvulus	Yolk sac commonly involved in chicks, other irritation to the intestines in adults.

SAVE THE SKIN

The diagrams below illustrate the incisions necessary to remove the skin from a ratite.

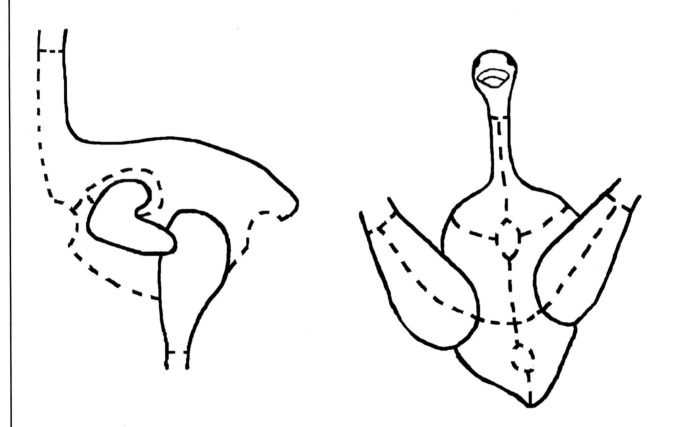

First make an incision on the inside of one leg, moving up the leg toward the body and across the lower chest, then back down the inside of the other leg. Cut around the lower part of each leg, at the beginning of the incision.

Next, cut around the breastplate, or sternum. Begin the next incision at the lower end of the breastplate and move downward toward the vent. Cut around the vent in a circle.

Go back to the breastplate and cut straight up the neck. Then, as you did with each leg, cut around the neck.

Beginning at the vent, start pulling off the skin. When you get to the wings, cut a circular incision around each one and pull the skin over it, leaving a hole where the wing was.

Instructions and diagrams courtesy of American Ostrich Tanning and Manufacturing, Fort Worth, Texas.

BIBLIOGRAPHY

Traditionally, a bibliography provides the reader with documentation of sources quoted or referred to in research material. Not all of the chapters in *The Ratite Encyclopedia* are of a nature to require this, so not all have sources listed. Those that do are listed in order of appearance.

HISTORY & GEOGRAPHY

(Drenowatz)

Anderson Brown, A. F. (1979). *The Incubation Book.* Exeter, England: The World Pheasant Association.

Bates, R. (1992). *The Dinosaurs!* Philadelphia: WHYY.

Bock, W. J. (1986). The arboreal origin of avian flight. In K. Padian (Ed), *The Origin of Birds and the Evolution of Flight: Memoirs of the California Academy of Sciences Number 8.* San Francisco: California Academy of Sciences.

Cracraft, J. (1973). Continental drift, paleoclimatology, and the evolution and biogeography of birds. *Journal of Zoology of London, 169,* 455-545.

Cracraft, J. (1974). Phylogeny and evolution of the ratite birds. *Ibis, 116,* 494-521.

Duewer, L., Madison, M., & Christensen, L. (1994). *Agricultural Outlook,* June 1994. USDA Economic Research Service.

Feduccia, A. (1980). *The Age of Birds.* Cambridge: Harvard University Press.

Gauthier, J. (1986). Saurischian monophyly and the origin of birds. In K. Padian (Ed), *The Origin of Birds and the Evolution of Flight: Memoirs of the California Academy of Sciences Number 8.* San Francisco: California Academy of Sciences.

Gill, F. P. (1995). *Ornithology* (2nd ed.). New York: W. H. Freeman and Company.

Goldie, F. (1968). *Ostrich Country.* Cape Town: Books of Africa, Ltd.

Gould, S. J. (1991). Justice Scalia's Misunderstanding. In *Bully for Brontosaurus,* 448-449. New York: W. W. Norton

Gould, S. J. (1993). Fall in the House of Ussher. In *Eight Little Piggies,* 181-193. New York: W. W. Norton.

Greenway, J. C. (1967). *Extinct and Vanishing Birds of the World.* New York: Dover Publications, Inc.

Heilmann, G. (1927). *The Origin of Birds.* New York: D. Appleton and Company.

Hindwood, K. (1966). *Australian Birds.* Honolulu: East-West Center Publishing.

Hou, L., Zhou, Z., Martin, L., & Feduccia, A. (1995). A beaked bird from the Jurassic of China. *Nature (337),* 616-618.

Huxley, T. H. (1870). Further evidence of the affinity between the dinosaurian reptiles and birds. *Quarterly Journal of the Geological Society of London, 26,* 12-31.

Lavine, S. A. (1981). *Wonders of Flightless Birds.* New York: Dodd, Mead & Company.

Marchant, S. & Higgins, P. J. (1990). *Handbook of Australian, New Zealand & Antarctic Birds,* (Vol. 1). Melbourne: Oxford University Press.

Martin, B. P. (1987). *World Birds*. Enfield, Middlesex, England: Guinness Superlatives, Ltd.

Medeiros, C. A. (1993). Types of ostrich and their potential use in ostrich farming. *Ostrich Update*, 1(1), 44-45.

Olson, S. L. (1985). The fossil record of birds. In D. S. Farner, J. R. King, & K. C. Parkes (Eds.), *Avian Biology* (Vol. VIII, pp. 79-217). Orlando, FL: Academic Press.

O'Malley, P. (1990). *The Emu Industry - Present and Potential*. Western Australia Department of Agriculture.

Ostrom, J. H. (1986). The cursorial origin of avian flight. In K. Padian (Ed), *The Origin of Birds and the Evolution of Flight: Memoirs of the California Academy of Sciences Number 8*. San Francisco: California Academy of Sciences.

Parker, W. K. (1864). Remarks on the skeleton *Archaeopteryx* and on the relations of the bird to the reptile. *Geology Magazine* (I) 1:55-57.

Pennycuick, C. J. (1986). Mechanical constraints on the evolution of flight. In K. Padian (Ed), *The Origin of Birds and the Evolution of Flight: Memoirs of the California Academy of Sciences Number 8*. San Francisco: California Academy of Sciences.

Perrins, C.M. (1990). *The Illustrated Encyclopedia of Birds*. New York: Prentice-Hall.

Peters, L. J. (1993). American ostrich experience: Progress by trial and error. *Ostrich Update*, 1,(1), 21.

Schreiner, C. A. C. (1898). *The Angora Goat and A Paper on the Ostrich*. London: Longmans, Green, and Co.

Sereno, P. C. & Chenggang, R. (1992). Early evolution of avian flight and perching: New evidence from the lower Cretaceous of China. *Science* 255, 845-848.

United States Department of Agriculture. Ostrich Farming in America. *Live Animal Trade & Transport Magazine*, June 1993.

Venn, K. (1994). *Free Range Emu Farming*. Seminar.

Wallace, G.J. (1963). *An Introduction to Ornithology* (2nd ed). New York: The MacMillan Company.

HISTORY & GEOGRAPHY

(Sales)

Anonymous (1993). Export control of birds to stay. *Farmer's Weekly Classified Section*, 5 November 1993, 1.

Appel, A. (1988). [*The District of Oudtshoorn till the 1880s: a Socio-Economic Study*]. State Press, Pretoria, South Africa, 178-191 [Afrikaans].

De Mosenthal, J. & Harting, J.E. (1879). *Ostriches and Ostrich Farming* (2nd ed). London: Truebner & Co.

Douglass, A. (1881). *Ostrich Farming in South Africa*. London: Cassell, Peter, Galpin & Co.

Holtzhausen, A. & Kotze, M. (1990). *The Ostrich*. Oudtshoorn, South Africa: C.P. Nel Museum.

Osterhoff, D.R. (1979). Ostrich Farming in South Africa. *World Review of Animal Production*, 15, 19-30.

Smit, D.J.v.Z. (1964). [*Ostrich Farming in the Little Karoo*] Pretoria: V and R Printers [Afrikaans].

Van Zyl, J. (1991). King of the Ostrich Industry. *Farmer's Weekly*, 27 September 1991, 18-19.

Wagner, P. (1986). *The Ostrich Story*. Cape Town: Chameleon Press.

RATITE GENETICS

Avise, J.C. (1994). *Molecular Markers, Natural History and Evolution*. New York: Chapman and Hall.

Cooke, F. & Buckley, P.A. (Eds.). (1987). *Avian Genetics, A Population and Ecological Approach*. Orlando, FL: Academic Press.

Etches, R.J. & Verrinder Gibbins, A. M. (Eds.). 1993. *Manipulation of the Avian Genome*. Boca Raton, FL: CRC Press, Inc.

THE RATITE EGG

(Further Reading)

Ar, A., Paganelli, C. V., Reeves, R. B., Greene, D. G. & Rahn, H. (1974). The avian egg: water vapour conductance, shell thickness and functional pore area. *Condor*, 76, 153-158.

Ar, A. & Rahn, H. (1978). Interdependence of gas conductance, incubation length and weight of the avian egg. In *Respiratory Function in Birds, Adult and Embryonic*. Ed. J.Piiper. pp. 227-236. Springer-Verlag, Heidelberg.

Ar, A. & Rahn, H. (1980). Water in the avian egg: overall budget of incubation. *American Zoologist*, 20, 373-384.

Bertram, B. C. R. (1992). *The Ostrich Communal Nesting System*. Princeton University Press, Princeton.

Bertram, B. C. R. & Burger, A. E. (1981a). Aspects of incubation in ostriches. *Ostrich*, 52: 36-43.

Burger, A. E. & Bertram, B. C. R. (1981). Ostrich eggs in artificial incubators: could their hatching success be improved? *South African Journal of Science*, 77: 188-189.

Buttemer, W. A., Astheimer, L. B. & Dawson, T. J. (1988). Thermal and water relations of emu eggs during natural incubation. *Physiological Zoology*, 59, 95-108.

Cannon, M. E., Carpenter, R. E. & Ackerman, R. A. (1986). Synchronous hatching and oxygen consumption of Darwin's rhea eggs (*Pterocnemia pennata*). *Physiological Zoology*, 59, 95-108.

Carey, C., Rahn, H. & Parisi, P. (1980). Calories, water, lipid and yolk in avian eggs. *Condor*, 82, 335-343.

Deeming, D. C. (1991). Water loss from ostrich eggs. *The Ostrich News*, 5(36), 19-20.

Deeming, D. C. (1992). Practical aspects of ratite incubation. *The Ostrich Report*, June issue, 12, 28, 30.

Deeming, D. C. (1994) The hatching sequence of ostrich (*Struthio camelus*) embryos with notes on development as observed by candling. *British Poultry Science*, in press.

Deeming, D. C., Ayres, L. & Ayres, F. J. (1993). Observations on the commercial production of Ostrich (*Struthio camelus*) in the UK: Incubation. *The Veterinary Record*, 132, 602-607.

Deeming, D. C., Ayres, L. & Ayres, F. J. (1993). Observations on the commercial production of Ostrich (*Struthio camelus*) in the UK: Rearing of chicks. *The Veterinary Record*, 132, 627-631.

Freeman, B. M. & Vince, M. A. (1974). *Development of the Avian Embryo*. Chapman & Hall, London.

Hoyt, D. F., Vleck, D. & Vleck, C. M. (1978). Metabolism of avian embryos: ontogeny and temperature effects in the ostrich. *Condor*, 80, 265-271.

Jarvis, M. J. F., Keffen, R. H. & Jarvis, C. (1985a). Some physical requirements for ostrich egg incubation. *Ostrich*, 56, 42-51.

Rahn, H. & Ar, A. (1974). The avian egg: incubation time and water loss. *Condor*, 76, 147-152.

Tullett, S. G. (1984). The porosity of avian eggshells. *Comparative Biochemistry and Physiology*, 78A, 5-13.

Vleck, C. M., Vleck, D. & Hoyt, D. F. (1980). Patterns of metabolism and growth in avian embryos. *American Zoologist*, 20, 405-416.

Vleck, D., Vleck, C. M. & Hoyt, D. F. (1980). Metabolism of avian embryos: ontogeny of oxygen consumption in the rhea and emu. *Physiological Zoology*, 53, 125-135.

INCUBATION & HATCHING

Brake, J., Walsh, T. J., and Vick, S. V. (1993). Relationship of egg storage time, storage conditions, flock age, eggshell and albumen characteristics, incubation conditions, and machine capacity to broiler hatchability: Review and model synthesis. *Zootechnica Int'l.* 16(1), 30-41.

Owen, J., (1991). Principles and problems of incubator design. In S. G. Tullett (Ed.), *Avian Incubation*, (pp 205-224). London: Butterworth-Heinemann.

Peebles, E. D., and Brake, J. (1987). Eggshell quality and hatchability in broiler breeder eggs. *Poultry Science*, 66, 596-604.

Stikeleather Swann, G., & Brake, J. (1990). Relationship of incubation dry bulb and wet bulb temperatures to time of hatch and chick weight at hatch. *Poultry Science*, 69, 887-897.

Vick, S. V., Brake, J., & Walsh, T. J. (1993). Effect of incubation humidity and flock age on hatchability of broiler hatching eggs. *Poultry Science*, 72, 251-258.

CANDLING

Burley, R.W. & Vadehra, D.V. (1989). *The Avian Egg: Chemistry and Biology*. New York: John Wiley and Sons.

Byerly, T.C. & Olsen, M.W. (1993). Time and manner of determination of malposition head-in-small-end-of-egg. *Poultry Science*, 12, 261-265.

Robertson, I.S. (1961). Studies of chick embryo orientation using x-rays. II. Malpositioned embryos and their subsequent hatchability. *British Poultry Science*, 2, 49-58.

Stern, C.D. (1994). The chick. In J.B.L. Bard (Ed), *Embryos, Color Atlas of Development*, pp. 167-182. Wolf Publishing, M.A. England.

Waters, N.F. (1935). Certain so-called malpositions a natural occurrence in the normal development of the chick embryo. *Poultry Science*, 14, 208-216.

FEATHERS

De Mosenthal, J. and Harting, J.E. (1879). *Ostriches and Ostrich Farming* (2nd ed.) London: Truebner & Co.

Douglass, A. (1881). *Ostrich Farming in South Africa*. London: Cassell, Peter, Galpin & Co.

Duerden, J.E. (1907a). Experiments with ostriches, III: The influence of climatic changes on feather growth. *The Agricultural Journal of the Cape of Good Hope*, 31, 31-35.

Duerden, J.E. (1907b). Experiments with ostriches, IV: The rate of growth of ostrich feathers. *The Agricultural Journal of the Cape of Good Hope*, 31, 435-438.

Duerden, J.E. (1908a). Experiments with ostriches, VII: Time of quilling. *The Agricultural Journal of the Cape of Good Hope* 32, 713-721.

Duerden, J.E. (1908b). Experiments with ostriches, V: Scaliness and unopened feathers in the ostrich. *The Agricultural Journal of the Cape of Good Hope*, 32, 355-359.

Duerden, J.E. (1909a). Experiments with ostriches, IX: The terminology of ostrich feathers. *The Agricultural Journal of the Cape of Good Hope*, 34, 513-524.

Duerden, J.E. (1909b). Experiments with ostriches, X: How the bars in ostrich feathers are produced. *The Agricultural Journal of the Cape of Good Hope, 35*, 474-487.

Duerden, J.E. (1910a). Experiments with ostriches, XIII: The influence of nutrition, season and quilling on the feather crop. *The Agricultural Journal of the Cape of Good Hope, 36*, 19-32.

Duerden, J.E. (1910b). Experiments with ostriches. Principles of Ostrich Breeding, Pamphlet No. 47. 1910.

Duerden, J.E. (1911). Experiments with ostriches, XVI: The plumages of the ostrich. *Agricultural Journal of the Union of South Africa, 1*, 29-37.

Duerden, J.E. (1913). Experiments with ostriches, XXII: The development of the feather, showing absence of cruelty in clipping and quilling. *Agricultural Journal of the Union of South Africa, 6*, 648-661.

Holtzhausen, A. and Kotze, M. (1990). *The Ostrich*. Oudtshoorn, South Africa: C.P. Nel Museum.

Osterhoff, D.R. (1979). Ostrich farming in South Africa. *World Review of Animal Production, 15*, 19-30.

Smit, D.J.v.Z. (1964). [Ostrich farming in the Little Karoo] Pretoria, South Africa: V and R Printers [Afrikaans].

Swart, D., 1979. [Replace sick feathers with show plumes]. *Landbouweekblad*, 16 March 1979 [Afrikaans].

Swart, D., Heydenrych, H.J. and Poggenpoel, D.G. (1984). [The relative economic importance of quality traits in ostrich feathers]. *South African Journal of Animal Science, 14*, 45-50. [Afrikaans with English summary].

Wagner, P. (1986). *The Ostrich Story*. Cape Town: Chameleon Press.

RHEA OIL

Allen, R.R., Formo, M. W., Krishnamurthy, R.G., McDermett, G.N., Norris, F.A., & Sonntag, N.O. (1982). *Bailey's Industrial Oil and Fat Products*, (Vol. 2). New York: John Wiley & Sons.

Body, D. (1988). The lipid composition of adipose tissue. *Progress in Lipid Research, 27*, 39-60.

Davies, P., & MacIntyre, D.E. (1992). Prostaglandins and inflammation. In J. Gallin, I.M. Goldstein, & R. Snyderman (Eds.), *Inflammation: Basic Principles & Clinical Correlates* (pp.123-137). New York: Raven Press, Ltd.

Dimand, R.J., Moonen, C.T., Chu, S.C., Bradbury, E.M., Kurland, G., & Cox, K.L. (1988). Adipose tissue abnormalities in cystic fibrosis: Noninvasive determination of mono and polyunsaturated fatty acids by carbon 13 topical magnetic resonance spectroscopy. *Pediatric Research, 24*, 243-246.

Fuji, Y. & Sakurai, J. (1989). Contraction of the rat isolated aorta caused by clostridium perfringens alpha toxin (phospolipase C): Evidence for the involvement of arachidonic acid metabolism. *British Journal of Pharmacology, 97*, 119-124.

Garner, A.A.A., Hunter, A.C., & Keogh, J.P. (1988). The gastroduodenal mucus barrier and the place of eicosanoids. In K. Hiller (Ed.), *Eiconsanoids and the Intestinal Tract*, (pp. 195-213). Boston: MTP Press Limited.

Goldstein, I.M. (1992). Agents that interfere with arachidonic acid metabolism. In J. Gallin, I.M. Goldstein, & R. Snyderman (Eds.), *Inflammation: Basic Principles & Clinical Correlates* (p. 1127). New York: Raven Press, Ltd.

Henderson, B. (1988). The role of eicosanoids in inflammatory diseases of the joints. In M. Church & C. Robinson (Eds.), *Eicosanoids in Inflammatory Conditions of the Lung, Skin, and Joints* (pp. 129-146). Boston: MTP Press.

Innis, S. (1991). Essential fatty acids in growth and development. *Progress in Lipid Research, 30*, 39-103.

Innis, S. (1992). Human milk and formula fatty acids. *Journal of Pediatrics, 120*, 556-561.

Institute of Advanced Manufacturing Sciences, Inc. (1994). *Performance of rhea-based cutting oil in drilling operations*. (IAMS Report No. APQ-414). Cincinnati: IAMS.

Lam, B.K., & Austen, K.F. (1992). Leukotrienes: Biosynthesis, release, and actions. In J. Gallin, I.M. Goldstein, & R. Snyderman (Eds.), *Inflammation: Basic Principles & Clinical Correlates* (p. 139). New York: Raven Press, Ltd.

Lindmark, D. G., Beach, D.H., Singh, B.H., & Holz, Jr., G.G. (1991). Lipids and lipid metabolism of trichomonads. In G.H. Coombs & M.J. North (Eds.), *Biochemical Protozoology* (pp. 329-335). Washington: Taylor & Francis.

Noble, R.C., & Cocchi, M. (1990). Lipid metabolism and the neonatal chicken. *Progress in Lipid Research, 29*, 107-140.

Vergroesen, A.J., & Crawford, M. (1989). *The Role of Fats in Human Nutrition* (2nd Ed.). London: Academic Press.

EMU MEAT

Australian Quarantine and Inspection Service (AQIS) (1993). *Register of approved emu cuts and items* (Bulletin 4266). The East Perth, WA, Department of Agriculture, Western Australia.

Berndt, R.M., & Berndt, C.H. (1964). *The World of the First Australians*. Chicago: The University of Chicago Press.

Emu Ranchers Incorporated (ERI) (1994). Unpublished meat study data collected in 1994. Personal communication.

Ford, C.R. (1994). Census and growth projection study announced at AEA convention. *AEA News*, 4(7), 1.

Forrest, J.C., Aberle, E.D., Hedrick, H.B., Judge, M.D., & Merkel, R.A. (1975). *Principles of Meat Science*. San Francisco: W. H. Freeman and Company.

Frapple, P. (1994). Preparing emu meat for the commercial market. *AEA News*, 4,(7) 1.

Huffman, K.L., Miller, M.F., Gilbert, S.Y., & Ramsey, C. B. (1994). Tenderness threshold of beef steaks by consumers in a retail environment. *Animal Science and Food Technology Research Report 1994*. (Agricultural Sciences and Natural Resources Technical Report No. T-5-342). Lubbock, TX: Texas Tech University.

Minnaar, P. & Minnaar, M. (1992). *The emu farmer's handbook*. Groveton, TX: Induna Company.

Moreng, R.E. & Avens, J.S. (1985). *Poultry science and production*. Prospect Heights, IL: Waveland Press, Inc.

Spencer, B. (1927). *The Arunta: A Study of a Stone Age People*. London: Macmillan and Company, Limited.

Steele, J.G. (1983). *Aboriginal Pathways in Southeast Queensland and the Richmond River*. St. Lucia, Queensland: University of Queensland Press.

Thompson, L.D., Daniel, D.R., Hoover, L. C., Adams, C., Miller, M.F., Butler, M., & Behrends, E. (1994). *Emu meat composition, palatability, and consumer acceptance*. Unpublished data.

USDA. (1992). *Composition of Foods: Pork Products*. Agricultural Handbook No. 8-10. Washington, DC: United States Department of Agriculture.

USDA. (1990). *Composition of Foods: Beef Products*. Agricultural Handbook No. 8-13. Washington, DC: United States Department of Agriculture.

USDA. (1989). *Composition of Foods: Lamb, Veal and Game Products*. Agricultural Handbook No. 8-17. Washington, DC: United States Department of Agriculture.

USDA. (1979). *Composition of Foods: Poultry Products*. Agricultural Handbook No. 8-5. Washington, DC: United States Department of Agriculture.

RATITE MEAT

Bradley, O.C. & Grahame, T. (1950). *The Structure of the Fowl*, (3rd Ed.). Philadelphia: J. B. Lippincott Co.

The Culinary Institute of America. (1991). *The New Professional Chef* (5th ed.). New York: Van Nostrand Reinhold.

Department of Agriculture of Western Australia (1993). *Register of approved emu cuts and items*. (Bulletin 4266). Perth, Western Australia.

Getty, R. (1975). *Sisson and Grossman's The Anatomy of the Domestic Animals*, (Vol. 2) (5th ed). Philadelphia: W. B. Saunders Company.

Gisslen, W. (1989). *Professional Cooking* (2nd ed.). New York: John Wiley & Sons.

Harris, S.D., Miller, R.K., Morris, C.A., Hale, D.S., Keeton, J.T., May, S.G. & Savell, J.W. (1994). Comparison of consumer acceptability of ostrich meat versus beef top sirloin steak. *Poultry Science*, 73(Supp. 1), 138.

Harris, S.D., Miller, R.K., Hale, D.S., Morris, C.A., Keeton, J.T., and Savell, J.W. (1994). Nutritional analysis of cooked ostrich meat. *Poultry Science*, 73(Supp. 1), 138.

Levie, A. (1970). *The Meat Handbook* (3rd ed.). Westport, CT: AVI Publishing Co.

McMillin, K. (1994). *Initial studies on characteristics of ostrich meat: A technical report*. Submitted to Pacesetter Premium Ostrich Farms, Folsom, LA.

Mellett, F. D. (1994). A note on the musculature of the prominal part of the pelvic limb of the ostrich. *Journal of the South African Veterinary Association*, 65, 5-9.

Morris, C. A. (1994) The birth of an industry. *Exclusively Ostrich*, 2(10), 68-73.

DISEASES

Blue-McClendon, A. (1992). An outbreak of cerebral nematodiasis in emus. *Proceedings Joint Meeting American Assocation of Zoological Veterinarians/American Association of Wildlife Veterinarians* (pp. 191-192). College Station, TX: Texas A & M University.

Craig, T. (1993). *Natural parasites of ratites*. Paper presented at the Symposium on Ratite Management and Medicine, Texas A&M University, College Station, TX.

Dorland, W.A. (Ed.) (1981). *Dorland's Illustrated Medical Dictionary* (26th Ed.). Philadelphia: W. B. Saunders Co.

Dorrestein, G.M. (1993). Avian chlamydiosis therapy. *Seminars in Avian and Exotic Pet Medicine*, 2(1), 23-29.

Fokema, A. (1985). Anthelmintic efficacy of fenbendazole against *Lybiostrongylus douglassi* and *Houttuynia struthionis* in Ostriches. *Journal of South African Veterinary Association*, 56(1), 47-48.

Grimes, J. (1994). Case reports of ratite chlamydias and update on the chlamydias. *Main conference proceedings of the Association of Avian Veterinarians*, Reno, NV.

Gruss, B. (1988). The anthelmintic efficacy of resorantel against *Houttuynia struthionis* in ostriches. *Journal of South African Veterinary Association, 59(4),* 207-208.

Harrison, G.J. & Harrison, L.R. (Eds.) (1986). *Clinical Avian Medicine and Surgery.* Philadelphia: W. B. Saunders Co.

Hoover, J.P. (1988). Quill mites in an ostrich with rhinitis, sinusitis, and airsacculitis. *Companion Animal Practice, 2(3),* 23-26.

Kwiecien, J.P. (1993). Encephalitis attributed to larval migration of *Baylisascaris* species in emus. *Canadian Veterinary Journal, 34(3),* 176-178.

Lublin, A. (1993). A paralytic-like disease of the ostrich (*Struthio camelus massaicus*) associated with *clostridium chauvoei* infection. *Veterinary Record, 132(II),* 273-275.

Mock, R. (1994). Results of equine encephalitis study. *Proceedings American Ostrich Association Convention and Annual Meeting,* San Diego, CA.

Nagaraja, K.V. (1991). Arizonosis. In B.W. Calnek, H.J. Barnes, C.W. Beard, W.M. Reid, & A.W. Yoder, Jr. (Eds.) *Diseases of Poultry,* (9th Ed.) (pp. 130-137). Ames: Iowa State University Press.

Raines, A.M. (1993). Adenovirus in the ostrich (*Struthio camelus*). *Proceedings of the Association of Avian Veterinarians,* Nashville, TN.

Raines, A.M. A study to determine the pathogenicity of adenovirus in the ostrich (*Struthio camelus*). Unpublished.

Ritchie, B., Harrison, G.J., and Harrison, L.R. (Eds.) (1994). *Avian Medicine Principles and Application.* Lake Worth, FL: Wingers Publishing, Inc.

Shah, N.M. (1987). A note on isolation of *salmonella weltevreden* from emu (*Dromaius novahollandiae*). *Indian Veterinary Journal, 64*(Sept.) 801-802.

Shavaprasad, H.L. (1994). *Ratite Pathology.* Annual Symposium for Veterinarians, Texas A&M University, College Station, TX.

Thoen, C. (1991). Tuberculosis. In B.W. Calnek, H.J. Barnes, C.W. Beard, W.M. Reid, and A.W. Yoder, Jr. (Eds.) *Diseases of Poultry* (9th Ed.), (pp. 172-185). Ames: Iowa University Press.

Tully, T. (1993). Multivalent equine encephalomyelitis vaccine to protect emus (*Dromaius novaehollandiae*). *Proceedings, Association of Avian Veterinarians,* (pp. 297-303). Nashville, TN.

Winterfield, R. W. Verminous encephalitis in the emu. *Avian Diseases, 22(2),* 336-339.

RECORD-KEEPING & MANAGEMENT

Angel, R. (1995). Least cost management. Paper presented at Ostrichfest 1995, Las Vegas, NV. *American Ostrich,* April 1995.

Kay, R. D., & Edwards, W. M. (1994). *Farm Management.* New York: McGraw-Hill.

North, M. O. & Bell, D. D. (1990). *Commercial Chicken Production Manual.* New York: Chapman and Hall.

Petitte, J. & Pardue, S. (1995). Selection of replacement stock. Paper presented at Ostrichfest 1995, Las Vegas, NV. *American Ostrich,* April 1995.

Taylor, R. E. (1992). *Scientific Farm Animal Production.* New York: MacMillan Publishing Company.

INDEX

A

Aborigines
   culture 209
   emu oil 223
   hunting emus 209
   Ngangganawili Community 223
accounting methods 300, 323
   reporting breeding stock 323
   reporting of inventory 323
   software 300
accrual method 323
acetabulum 38, 39
acoustic meatus 42
acts of God 318, 348
adenine 64
Adenovirus 279
adipose tissue 58
adrenal glands 52, 53
AEA, American Emu Association 25
Aepyornithidae dispersal 12
aggression 280
Ahlquist, Jon E. 65
air exchange 50
air sacs 32, 50, 51
   thoracic 51
   abdominal 51
   caudal thoracic 51
   cervical 51
   clavicular 51
albumen 94
   antibacterial properties 104
   degradation 104
   protein composition 95
   quality 105
   thick 84, 94
   thin 94

albumen quality
   and long-term storage 106
   storage conditions 106
all-inclusive operation 315
allantois 99
alleles 64, 65, 70
   dominant 64, 65, 69
   heterozygous 64, 69, 70
   homozygous 64, 69
   recessive 64, 65, 69, 70
American Emu Association (AEA) 25
American Ostrich Association (AOA) 20
American Ostrich Company 19
amino acid
   requirements 289
   sources 288
ammonia fumes
   danger to chicks 153, 193
amnion 99
amplified fragment length polymorphism
   AMPFLP 73
ampulla 54
ankle joint 38, 39
antibodies 58
AOA, American Ostrich Association 20
apteria 40, 175
arbitration 343, 349
arboreal origin of flight 6
Archaeopteryx lithographica 4, 5, 8, 11, 13
asternal ribs 34
Astrovirus 279
avian influenza 279

B

B-lymphocytes 58
bacteria 277, 296
   Chlamydia 278
   Clostridium 278
   Mycobacterium avium 278
   Salmonella 277
   tuberculosis 278
Balda, Russell 8
barbs, barbules 175
basilic vein 59
Baylisascaris 280
beak serrations 40
beak shape 40
behavior
   see also individual birds
   displaying 130
   fluttering 130
   observation 310
behavioral problems 280
bile 52
biochemistry of reproduction 86
biosecurity
   bacteria 296
   bacterial 295
   boots 296
   buyers 295
   disinfectants 114, 115
   disinfection 296
   Escherischia coli 296
   eggs 296
   employees 147
   fogging 115
   hatcher contamination 296
   hatchers 115
   incubators 115
   isolation 295
   isolation pens 147
   live-haul equipment 295
   moisture on surface of egg 296
   mycoplasmas 296
   new arrivals 147
   not advisable to wash eggs 115
   principles 295
   protective clothing 115
   Pseudomonas 296
   reducing hatcher bacteria 297
   Salmonella 296
   step pans 147
   successful hatching 114
   traffic flow 114, 147, 296
   viral diseases 295, 296
   visitors 114, 146, 295
   washing eggs 296
birds as living dinosaurs 9

Birnavirus 279
blacks (feathers) 176
blastoderm 83, 94, 98
blastoderm 83 94
blood cholesterol 160
blood samples
   appropriate tube 282
   chemistries 283
   collection 282
   complete blood counts 283
   instruction in proper procedures 282
   packaging 283
   smear 283
   stress 282
boarding agreement 345
   adverse external events 347
   allocation of costs 347
   basic elements 345
   communication 348
   compensation 346
   record keeping 223, 348
   standards of care 348
   visits 348
boarding facilities 324
Bock, Walter J. 7
boots, ostrich skin 167
   country and western singers 170
Borna disease 279
bracheal vein 59
brain 48
   cerebellum 49
   cerebrum 49
   medulla oblongata 49
   olfactory lobes 49
   optic lobes 49
breeder pens, *see also* facilities
   45-degree corners, 134, 261
   alleyway 134
   fencing 134, 135
   holding pen 134, 259, 261
   location 134
   nest site 136
   quarantine 136
   shade, shelter 134, 185, 260
   size 134, 185
   windbreak 134
breeders
   early 314
   marker-assisted selection 63
   nest site 136
   quarantine 136
breeding
   for specific traits 313
   good genetics vs. good management 313
   heritability percentages 313
   late breeders could cost 314
   older males with first-year hens 314

replacement stock   313
breeding coefficient   74, 76
   correlated to production parameters   74, 76
   RFLP fingerprints   74
   to better pair emus   76
breeding records   303
bronchi   49
brooder pens   141, 142
broodiness   88
browse   311
   see also grazing, forage
Buffon, Georges   3
bursa of Fabricius   48, 58
business or hobby   300, 325
business plan   299
buying and selling
   agreement   341
   contract   341
   general legal principles   341
   meeting of the minds   341
bycocks   175, 176

C

calamus   175
calcium ions   89
calcium metabolism   50
callosity   40
candling   94, 99, 100, 117, 139, 311
   advantages   118
   bacterial contamination   118, 183
   contamination   99, 119
   cracks   99
   dead or infertile   100
   defects   99
   detecting breathing or movement   120
   early deaths   183
   embryonic development   99
   emu eggs   117, 183
   expense   122
   fertility   183
   infrared lamps   99, 183
   internal pipping   183
   malpositioning   183
   pipping process   119
   position changes   119
   position of the air cell   119
   records   118
   rhea eggs   234
   size of the air space   99
   malpositions   121

reduce work load   122
capital gain   324
carbohydrate utilization   51
cash journal   301
cash method of accounting   323
cassowaries, dispersal of   12
catastrophe   3
catheterization   59
caudal renal portal vein   59
caudal vena cava   59
caudal vertebrae   34
Cawston, Edwin
   and Thomas Cockburn   20
ceca   47
central toe   39
cerebellum   49
cerebral hemispheres   49
cervical vertebrae   34
chalaza, chalazae   84, 94, 103
Chandlerella   280
chick barns   154
chick survival, critical period   149
chlamidosis   295
Chlamydia   278
chlorine fumes   286
choanal opening   41
cholesterol
   blood   159, 160, 161
   dietary   159, 160
   genetics   161
   heart disease   160
   high-density lipoprotein   160
   low-density lipoprotein   160
   saturated fat   160
choosing future breeders   129
   see also breeders, breeding
chorio-allantoic membrane   99, 106
chorion   99
chromosomes   64, 65
   diagnostic tests   65
circadian rhythm   49
CITES   28
   International Convention for
      the Trade in Endangered Species   25
clavicle   36
clitoris   55, 56
cloaca   48, 53, 55
Cockburn, Thomas
   and Edwin Cawston   20
      Hot Springs Ostrich Farm in Arkansas   20
      Los Angeles   20
      San Antonio, Texas   20
coccygeomesenteric vein   59
coitus   56
commercial growers   315
commodity wages
   disadvantages   327

exempt from payroll taxes 327
   title and risk of loss 328
common iliac vein 59
Compsognathus 4, 5, 13
conditioning 130
conformation
   defect 130
   ostrich 129
Confuciusornis sanctus 5, 11
consideration 341
continental drift 11, 66
   Africa and South America 11, 67
   Antarctica and Africa 11
   Antarctica and Australia 11
   Australia 67
   evolution of birds 11
contract 341
   arbitration 343, 349
   common provisions 342
   consideration 341
   delivery 342
   enforcement 349
   expiration 348
   general legal principles 341
   guarantees 349
   identification 342
   legal capacity 341
   mediation 343, 349
   meeting of the minds 341
   passage of title 344
   performance 341, 343
   remedies 344
   risk of loss 344
   standard forms 349
   terms of sale 342
   warranties 349
   written 341
coprodeum 48
coracoid 36
Corona virus 279
corporation 339
costal sternum 36
costal-chondral junction 36
county fairs
   ratites 123
coxofemoral joint 39
Cracraft, Joel 5, 11, 12
cranial renal portal vein 59
Cretaceous era 11, 12
Crimean-Congo hemorrhagic fever 279
crocodile
   divided ventricle 13
   homoiothermic 13
crop 43
cross breeding, wild birds from Barbary 17
crushed limestone 294
cultures
   contamination 283
   source 283
   transfer medium 283
cursorial origin of flight 6
custom hatching 315
cuticle 104
   barrier to microbial penetration 104
   egg shell 85
   first line of defense 90
   role in water loss 104
Cuvier, Georges 3
cytosine 64

D

Dallas Mavericks 217
Darwin, Charles 4
De Mosenthal, J. 173
deceptive trade practice 343
defective birds
   in a production market 156
   not passed on as breeders 156
deoxyribose nucleic acid 64
   see also DNA
dermis 177
detumescence 56
Diatrymas 9
digestive enzymes 46
digestive system 43
digits 36, 38
dimorphism 87
Dinosauria 4
dinosaurs 4
   cursorial 9
   small
dirty eggs 296
   contaminated 296
   discard 296
disease, *see* bacteria, infectious disease, fungi
   non-infectious disease, viruses
disinfectants 296
dispersal of ratites 13
divided ventricle
   crocodiles 9
   tall ancestor of ratites 9
DNA 64, 71
   double helix 64
   evolutionary history and taxonomy 65
   gender determination 184
   genetic relatedness 184

mitochondrial 67
parentage identification 184
permanent bird identification 184
DNA fingerprinting 63, 70
dominant allele 65
Douglass, Arthur
first incubator for ostrich eggs 16
drabs 176
drainage 310
drugs 281
improperly used 281
Duerden, J. E. 176, 180
duodenal loop 46
duodenum 45, 46

E

eastern equine encephalitis 279
edematous chicks 141
EEE 279
see also eastern equine encephalitis
egg
see also emu egg, ostrich egg, rhea egg
bacterial contamination 183
candling 99, 183
chemical composition 94, 95
collecting 136
defense mechanisms 90
development 98
dimensions 94
discard dirty eggs 296
fertilization 88
fertility 99
formation 88
hatching process 100
holding facility 106
increasing production 314
length of clutch in the wild 105
long-term storage 104, 106
nutritional influences 88
passive antibodies 90
pH barrier 117
production, increasing 314
quality 101
risk eggs 297
shape 94
shell 94
size 93, 303
storage 106
storage conditions 105
storage and quality chicks 105
structure 94, 117
timing mechanism 104
weight 93
weight loss 97
egg shell, see also emu egg shell, ostrich egg shell, rhea egg shell
abnormalities 96
amount of calcium 89
color 97
composed of 104
cuticle 85, 89, 97
functions 95
measuring thickness 303
membranes 104
oxygen exchange 104
pigment 85, 97
pores 89, 104
pore structure 96
porosity 96, 97
strength 101
structural layers 96
thickness 95, 303
washing 296
egg storage 310
egg tooth 41
eggshell thickness 303
ejaculatory fossa 55
embryo 94
development 97, 98, 106
mortality 106, 115, 121
embryo development
humidity 107
length of storage 107
respiration 107
temperature 106, 107
weight loss 107
embryology 97
embryos, communication between 104
emu chicks
ammonia fumes 193
barn 192
brooder 191, 195, 264
chick barn 192
DNA sexing 198
facilities 191, 192
farm management 196
feed 191, 193, 195, 198
fencing 192, 193, 262
flooring 192
grit 195
grow-out pens 193
handling 198, 202
hatching 190
heaters 191
herding 202
hiding illness 196

hobble   194, 195
huddle in corners   193
incubation problem   196
leg bands   194
microchip   194, 199
minerals   197
non-slip flooring   194
normal hatch   196
nutrition   197
pens   191, 193
playful   193
runs   192, 193
sexing   195, 198, 199, 206
similar-sized birds together   196
start hatching in December   193
stress   196
temperature   191, 193
transporting   199
vaccinate   195
vent sexing   198, 199
ventilation   193
vitamin/mineral supplements   198
water   191, 193, 195, 198
whistling   193
wind break   192
working pen   193
worming   195

emu egg, *see also* egg
   candling   183
   gathering   187, 188
   identification   187
   lay at dark   187
   size   183

emu farming, Australia   25

emu handling
   calf-roping   205
   emu chicks   202
   flipping   205
   herding   202
   practice   201
   prepare   201
   protective clothing   201
   restraining   204
   sexing   206
   skills   201
   wing walking   204, 205

emu meat   210
   cholesterol content   214
   classified as poultry   211
   color   213
   consumer perception   215
   cookery   216
   cuts   212
   dividing the carcass   212
   drum   213
   fabrication   212
   fat content   214
   federal regulations   211
   fore saddle   213
   frozen storage   213, 214
   hind quarter   213
   hind saddle   213
   inspection   211, 212
   maximize tenderness   211
   minerals   214
   nutritional composition   214
   packaging   213
   palatability attributes   216
   preparation   215
   processing plant sanitation   213
   protein source   214
   shelf life   213
   slaughter   210
   slaughter guidelines   212
   Texas Department of Health   212
   thigh   213
   vitamin content   215
   voluntary inspection   211

emu oil
   Aborigines   217, 223
   chemical composition   224
   clinical studies   218
   commercial products   224
   contusion   219
   Donna Karan   221
   fatty acids   218, 224
   grades   220
   injuries   218
   marketing   220, 226
   over the counter   222
   patents   226
   pro sports   219
   public reaction to
      animal-based compounds   221, 226
   purifying   220
   research   218, 224, 226
   shampoo   220
   sports   221
   swelling   219
   topical analgesic   217
   uses   217
   yield   223

emus
   Aboriginal culture   26, 209
   aggressive activity   186
   bonding technique   186
   booming   79, 186
   bounty on   24, 26
   breeding   187
   breeding season   183
   claiming territory   186
   classified as poultry   211
   coins   26
   colony, community pairing   185, 186

cooking 209
distinguish male and female 79
dominant females 187
drumming 79, 186
egg gathering 187
extinct 24
federal regulations 211
feeding 185, 188
Great Emu War 26
grunting 186
handling 201
hunting 209
incubation period 183
induced pairing 185
inspection 211
Kangaroo and King Islands 24
lay on an irregular cycle 188
mating process 187
meat 210
mid-season layoff 188
mortality rate 221
omnivores 185
pairing 184, 185
pecking order 185, 186, 187
reproduction 183
sexing 183, 206
sexual activity 81
sexual maturity 184, 185, 186
slaughter 210
slaughter market 222
Tasmania 24
territorial 187
tracheal slit 186
trademark 26
transporting 199
voluntary inspection 212
water 185, 188
winter breeders 187
emus and cassowaries, dispersal of 12
Enaliornis 11
encephalitis 279
endocrine 52
enforceable contract 341
entoglossal 32
epidermis 178
epididymis 82
esophagus 43
estrogen 53
evolution 5
   feathers from scales 7
   of birds and continental drift 11
evolutionary relationship
   DNA hybridization 65
exercise 294
exocrine 52
expense deductions 324
external ears 32, 42

external iliac vein 59
external parasites 310
   see also feather lice, feather mites
extinction 3
eye 42
eyelashes 42
eyelid, third 42
eyelids 42
eyesight 42

F

15-18 nm virus 279
facilities, *see* ranch design
fallopian tube 83
fancies 176
farm
   commodity wages 326, 327
   expense deductions 324
   general partnership 339
   joint venture 339
   landlord-tenant relationship 330
   laws governing 337
   laws to protect livestock 338
   leases 324
   limited liability company 340
   limited partnership 339
   meals and lodging 327
   partnership 338
   partnership agreement 339
   payment of rent to spouse 327
   registered limitedliability partnership 339
   rent payments to spouse 329
   S corporation 331
   safe harbor 325
   section 179 deduction 324
   sole proprietorship 338
   spousal wages 326
   state law 338
   tangible property 324
   tax considerations 340
   tax planning 326
farmer
   corporate 329
   first-time 325
   owners of existing farms 325
   passive 324
   preparatory period 325
   qualifying as 323
fat 58

fat-soluble vitamins   290
feather follicle   175
feather germ   175, 177
feather industry collapse   17
feather lice, feather mites   279
feather palaces   17
feather sheath   175, 178
feather socket   175, 178
feather, parts of   175-178
feather picking   280
feathers   5, 40
   aerodynamic   5
   as thermoregulators   7
   asymmetry   5
   auto bodies, preparation for painting   24
   camouflage   79
   coloring   79
   compared to aircraft wing   5
   contour   175
   crop   173
   cross breeding   17
   demand   16
   diagram   175
   electronics manufacturing   23
   expeditions, in 1886, 1888 and 1903   17
   exports from the Cape Colony   16
   fashion   16, 173
   feather dusters   24
   harvesting   17
   lack   40
   part of the skin   177
   prices   16
   procedure for the removal   17
   sex differences   177
   stress lines   130
Feduccia, A.   9, 10, 12
feed   154
   additives   155
   grit   155
   starter feeds   154
feed lots   315
feed storage   262, 294
feminas   175
femur   38, 39, 51
fertilization   54
fibula   38
first ostrich farmer in America   19
first stomach   44
flight
   arboreal origin theory   8
   body attitude   8
   cursorial origin theory   8
   energy for   7, 9
   flapping   7
   gliding   7, 8
   muscles   7
   origin of   6

   parachuting   8
   physics of   6
   powered   8
   roll, pitch, and yaw   8
   three-dimensional orientation 8
flightlessness
   body weight   10
   digestive system   10
   herbivorous   10
   ratites larger than flying ancestors   10
   more offspring   10
floating ribs   36
flock health records   305
flock purchase history   129, 308
floss   175
flue   175
fogging   115
follicle, feather   175, 178
follicle, ovarian   53, 83
follicle sheath   175
follicle-stimulating hormone (FSH)   88
foot   38
foot baths   115
forage   311
Freitag, Stefanie   68
FSH, follicle-stimulating hormone   88
fungi   278
   Aspergillas   279
Future Farmers of America   312
   at 1995 Houston Livestock Show 123-126

G

Gallaway, Benny J.   13
Gallimimus   9
Gallornis   11
gender identification   76
   accuracy   76
   DNA probes   76
   historical techniques   76
   intersexes   76
   sex-reversed   76
gene combinations   65
general partnership   339
generator, standby power   152
genes   64
genetic redundancy   64
genetic and history lineage chart   308
genetic load   69, 70
genetic markers
   RFLP probes   76

PCR alleles   76
genetic weakness   90
genotype distribution   65
germinal disc   83
gill   5, 6, 12
gizzard   292
   external palpation   45
glandular stomach   44
   gonadotropic releasing hormone (GnRH)   87
Gondwanaland
   breakup   11
   continental drift   66
   origin of the ratites   12
gout   280
grazing   142, 311
   see also browse, forage, free-range
greater toe   39
green feather   175
Greenway, J. C.   15
grit   155, 292, 294
grow-out pens, stress in crowded   142
Gruiformes   9
guanine   64
guarantees   349

H

hair feathers   176
hallux
   grasping   7
   reversed   7
handling
   emu chick   202, 268
   emus   204, 205, 270
   hood   268
   hook   268, 270
   ostrich chick   267
   ostriches   268
   procedures   267
   ratites   267
   rhea chick   268
   rheas   271
   safety   267
   using a hood   268
   using a hook   268
Harting, J. E.   173
hatcher, *see also* incubator, hatching
   disinfecting   297
   humidity & temperature   110

hatching, *see also* egg, emu chicks, emu eggs,
      incubation, ostrich chicks, ostrich eggs,
      rhea chicks, rhea eggs
   assistance   100
   excess moisture   110
   foot plays a major role   100
   gas exchange   110
   humidity   109
   interference   100
   malpositions   100, 115
   normal hatching position   115, 121
   normal length   120
   oxygen requirements   110
   pipping   100
   position   110, 120
   post hatch   115
   premature help   100
   time   100, 109
   retained yolk sacs   110
hazardous chemicals
   cleansers   286
   employee access   285
   mixing chlorine with ammonia   286
   warnings and instructions   286
heart   50
Heilmann, Gerhard   6
hen production analysis   304
heritability percentages   313
hip joint   38, 39
hobble
   edematous chicks   141
   splayed or weak legs   141
hobby-loss issue   300, 325
hock joint   38, 39
holding area, holding pen   134, 258-261
Holtzhausen, A.   173
homoiothermy
   arboreal lifestyle   7
   in crocodiles   13
hood   270
hook   270
Hou et al
   Confuciusornis sanctus   5
   Houston Livestock Show & Rodeo   123
   commercial winners   127
   FFA emu Winners   126
   FFA ostrich Winners   126
Houttuynia struthionis   280
humeral immunity   58
humerus   36
Hutton, James   3
Huxley, Thomas H.   3, 5
   and ratites   10
hybrid vigor, loss of   70
hygiene, *see* biosecurity
hyoid   32

I

identification
   microchip 273
   traditional 273
idiot-proofing
   hazardous chemicals 286
ileo-cecal junction 47
ileum 47
ilium 34
   cervical 32
impaction 45, 46, 144
improperly used drugs 281
inbreeding
   homozygosity 70
   reduce possible adverse effects 73
inbreeding depression 65, 69, 70, 90
increased light 87
increasing egg production 314
incubation
   air-flow 107
   batch cycle 310
   embryonic death 115
   excessive turning 111
   fresh air 108
   humidity 107, 233
   length 107
   machine operation 108
   optimum conditions 107
   rotation 110
   temperature 107, 233
   thick albumen 108
   turning 110
   ventilation 111
incubation and hatching information chart 303
incubation and hatching procedures 304
incubator, *see also* hatcher, incubation
   first for ostrich eggs 16
   humidity & temperature 107
indemnities 349
individual bird records 308

infectious disease
   Adenovirus 279
   aerobic 277
   anaerobic 277
   Aspergillas 279
   bacterial 277
   Chlamydia 278
   Clostridium 278
   eastern equine encephalitis (EEE) 279
   encephalitis 279
   fungal 278
   gram-negative bacteria 277
   gram-positive bacteria 277
   Mycobacterium avium 278
   Salmonella 277
   tuberculosis 278
   viruses 279
   western equine encephalitis (WEE) 279
influenza 295
infundibulum 54, 83
inner ear 42
installment sales of livestock 325
insulin 52
insurance 348
   accident 319
   acts of God 318
   all-risk coverage 319
   application 322
   causes of loss 317
   coverage 318
   examination by a veterinarian 321
   exclusions 319
   fraud 317, 319, 321
   indemnify 320
   industry's evolution 317
   loss experience 317
   losses caused by management mistakes 321
   microchip 317
   moral hazard 319
   named perils 318
   production market 322
   rates 322
   slaughter market 320
   theft 318
   three-month-old birds 318
   transit 320, 321
   veterinarian's examination certificate 322
insurers
   annual contracts 318
   foreign 317, 318
   front companies 318
   Lloyds of London 318
   new products 322
   protect the underwriter from fraud 319
   reinsurers 318
   three-month-old birds 318
intensive breeding 129
internal parasites 310
internal vertebral sinuses 59
Internet
   as a marketing tool 311
   web site 312
intravenous injection 59
ischium 34, 36
isolation pens 147
   see also quarantine
isthmus 45, 54, 84

J

jaw 31
jejunum 46
joint venture 339
jugal arch 32
jugular vein 58
Jurassic era 4, 5, 11

K

keratin 39, 40
kidney 52
kiwis and moas, dispersal of 12
Klein Karoo Agriculture Cooperative (KKLK)
    abattoir 18
    compared to DeBeers diamond cartel 18
    cooperative marketing system 18
    export of breeding stock and eggs 19
    lifting single channel marketing scheme 19
    marketing 19
    monopoly 18
    right to buy skins 19, 168
    stringently controlled sales 18
Kotze, M. 173

L

lack of feathers 40
lacrimal gland 42
large intestine 47, 48
larynx 32
late hatchers
    cost of maintaining for extra year 314
lateral toe 39
lawful purpose 341
leg 38
legal capacity 341
lengthening days 87
LH, luteinizing hormone 88
limb deformities
    diagnosis 145
    not allow birds to breed 145
    raise for leather, feathers, or meat 145
    surgical procedure 146
    trauma 145
limited liability company 340
limited partnership 339
link, missing 6
liver 46, 51
livestock shows
    4H, Future Farmers of America 123-126, 312
    ratites in 123
living dinosaurs, birds as 9
locus 64
losses
    basis and at-risk 324
    passive activity 324
    suspended 325
lower umbilicus 175
lumen 45
lung 50
luteinizing hormone (LH) 88
Lyell, Charles 4

M

magnum 54, 84
maintenance agreement 345
major minerals 289
malpositions 100, 115, 183
management agreement 345
management practices
    accounting program 300
    all-in all-out production 310
    bacterial build-up 310
    breeding for specific traits 313
    capital investment costs 314
    chick pens 310
    cleaning and disinfecting 310
    colony breeding 314
    control 300
    conversion of feed to weight gain 310
    cost-efficient 313
    culling 313
    early breeders 314
    evaluate egg production 305
    evaluation 299
    feed costs 310
    feed to egg production 310
    flock health records 305
    good-quality water 309

grazing 311
health management 309
hen production analysis 304
heritability percentages and 313
increasing egg production 314
keeping birds of the same age together 310
late hatchers 314
learning behavioral patterns 310
observation 310
pen areas 310
realistic planning 300
record-keeping systems 300
reduced internal costs 314
rotate pens 310
setting goals 300, 313
traffic flow 310
trios instead of pairs 314
ventilation 309
marketing 311, 349
focus 312
Internet 312
literature 312
meat processors 311
potential of the industry 312
speakers' group 311
to the public 311
traditional agricultural families 312
untapped market 312
mastodon 3
mating season 49
maxillae 31
meat
emu 209-216
ostrich 159-166
ratite 251-256
medial metatarsal vein 59
medial toe 39
mediation 343, 349
medical exams 137, 144, 281
medulla 175, 178
medulla oblongata 49
meeting of the minds 341
Mendel, Gregor Johan 64
metabolic processes 51
metabolizable energy 289
metacarpal bone 36
metasternum 36
metatarsal bones 38
microchip
accurate records 274
documents 276
health certificates 276
identification 273
insurance, insurance exams 276
laboratory tests 276
law enforcement agencies 276
medical records 275

reader 273, 274
register 275
remove 274
size 274
theft deterrence 276
tool for veterinarians 275
transponder 273
uses 274
verifying 275
veterinary certificate 276
working parts 274
microchip numbers
bills of sale 274
contracts and sales 274
hot sheets 275
permanent 274
register 275
registered 275
stolen 275
theft 275
unalterable 274
minerals 155
balance 289
deficiencies 289
imbalances 289
major 289
nutrition 289
trace 290
mitochondrial DNA
determining relatedness 67
inheritance pattern 67
maternal bloodlines 67
moas, dispersal of 12
mosasaur 3
mouth 43
mtDNA, mitochondrial DNA 67
Murphy's Law 285
muscular stomach 45
musk glands 48
mutations 69
mycloplasmas 296
Myxovirus 279

N

named perils 318
NARA, North American Rhea Association 29
nares 41
nasal cavity 41
national associations

home pages   312
Internet   312
National Ostrich Breeders Assn (South Africa)
   abattoirs and tanneries   19
natural selection   4
necropsy
   gross examination   283
   post-mortem changes   283
new arrivals
   adjust to the new environment   185
   blood work   137
   isolate   185
   isolation pens   147
   medical exams   137
   oviduct culture   137
   quarantine   136
   ultrasound   137
Newcastle disease   279, 295
nictitating membrane   42
non-infectious diseases   280
   gout   280
Nopcsa, Baron Franz   8
North American Rhea Association (NARA)   29
nucleotides   64
number of vertebrae   32
nutrition
   balanced diets   289
   breeders   293
   clinical tests   310
   energy   289
   feed costs   310
   feeding program   293
   feeding slaughter birds   293
   feedlot rations   292, 293
   finishing   292
   grower diet   292
   maintenance   292
   metabolizable energy   289
   protein   288
   requirements   310
   research   293, 310
   starter ration   292
   stress   293
   supplements   294
   water   287

O

Olson , Storrs T.   5, 6
oocyte   83

optic lobes   49
orbits   32, 42
orientation
   arboreal   7
   terrestrial   7
   three dimensional   7
   two-dimensional   7
origin of ratites   12
origin of flight   6
   arboreal   6
   cursorial   6
Origin of Species   4
Ornithischia   4
Osterhoff, D. R.   180
ostium   54
ostrich chicks
   ammonia fumes   153
   assisted hatching   140
   bacterial infection   144
   body temperature   141
   care of the navel   140, 150
   combining broods   142
   critical decisions   151
   deaths, peak period of   149
   deformities   156
   exposed yolk sacs   140
   feed   142, 151
   food additives   155
   fungal problems   145
   genetic history   139
   grazing   142
   grit   156
   grow-out pens   142
   hatcher to brooder   151
   heat lamps   152
   hobble   141
   identification   150
   immune system   150
   impaction   143, 144
   leg band   141
   limb deformities   145
   microchip   150
   normal hatching   139, 150
   normal vs. abnormal   156
   parasites   145
   peak period of deaths   149
   pig blankets   152
   pipping muscle   140
   post-hatch procedure   140
   rearing   139
   records   139, 141
   sexing   141
   shelter   152
   signs of health   143
   signs of sickness   143
   stable environment   154
   starter feeds   142, 154

substrate 151, 153
survival 149
temperature 151, 152
ventilation 152
water 142, 151, 156
weight 141
yolk sac retention 141, 143, 144
ostrich egg, *see also* egg
air cell membrane 140
as water vessel 15
assisted hatching 140
candling 139, 140
chick position 140
exposed yolk sacs 140
external pipping 140
internal pipping 140
normal hatching 139
pipping muscle 140
weight loss 140
ostrich farming
first ostrich farmer in America 19
KKLK, Klein Karoo Cooperative 18-19
ostrich feathers
bars 180
clipping 178, 179
crop 173
fashion 173
fashion must 173
improved by feed, breeding 173
plucking 178, 179
qualities 173
quilling 178, 179
rate of growth 178
sorting 179, 180
stumping 178
symbol of justice 173
uses 180
valuable characteristics 180
wrinkling 180
yield 173
ostrich meat
calories 159
cholesterol 159
consistent supply 164
consumeracceptance 161, 162
cooking methods 162
decrease in red-meat consumption 165
degree of doneness 162
healthy alternative 165
lean 161
marinades 162
market development 164
marketing 161
nutritional profile 159
price 161
processed ostrich meat 163
protein 159

recipes 161
retail 163
saturated fat 159
sauces 162
sausage 163
segmented industry 163
taste 161
total fat 159
wok cooking 162
ostrich skin
belts 168
boots 167
colors 169
durability 169
full quill 168
golf shoes 171
Klein Karoo 19, 168
prices 168
running shoes 171
South Africa 19, 168
supply 19, 167
tanning 169
ostriches
African black 19
among herds of grazing animals 21
behavior 130
booming 133
breeding season 131
cantling 133
characteristics 14
copulation 133
courtship ritual 80
displaying 130
domesticated 16
Eogruidae 12
Ergilornithidae 12
farming 16
feed 135
genetic diversity 68
Geranoididae 12
gruiforms 12
hunting 16
introduced to australia 23
introducing birds 133
laying pattern 131
maternal lineages 68
mating ritual 133
monitoring eating habits to detect illness 135
nest site 136
origin 12
pairing breeders 133
range 15
reputation for being mean 133
research 17
RFLP studies 68
sand bath 136
sexual display 80

    social life   23
    source of food   15
    taxonomy   14
    trios   133
    water   136
Ostrom, John H.   8
Oudtshoorn, hub of South African ostrich industry   17
ova   53
ovary   53, 54, 83
oviduct   53
oviposition   55, 85
ovulation   83
Owen, Sir Richard   5
    Archaeopteryx   5
    Dinosauria   4

P

palate   31
palatine   32
pancreas   46
pancreatic ducts   52
papilla   39
paraglossum   32
Paramyxovirus   279
parasites
    Baylisascaris   280
    chandlerella   280
    de-worming schedule   145
    external   279
    feather lice   279, 280
    feather mites   279, 280
    Houttuynia struthionis   280
    stool samples   145
parathormone   50
parathyroid   50
partnership   338
Patton, John C.   13
PCR   71, 73, 77
pecten   42
pelvic girdle   34, 39
pelvis   34
Pennycuick, C. J.   8, 9
pen check list   308
pericardial sac   50
pericardial space   50
pH barrier   117
phalangeal bones   36
phalanges   36, 39

phallus   55, 56, 82, 83
phenol   296
phorusrhacids   9
phosphorous metabolism   50
Picornavirus   279
pineal gland   49, 87
pipping   109
    chick's need for more oxygen   120
    external   100
    internal   100, 120
pipping muscle   43
pitch   175
pith   175, 178
pituitary gland   88
plate tectonics and evolution of ratites   11
plumage   176
    South African exports   16
plume   175
pneumatic   32
pneumatic bone   38, 51
pneumatic spaces   32
polymerase chain reaction   71
pores
    number and density   96
    structure   96
porosity   96, 97
power outages, standby generator for   152
Poxvirus   279
pre-purchase exam   315
premaxillae   31
prevailing winds   310
primaries   176
proctodeum   48
production records   303
protective clothing   115
protein
    amino acids   288
    critical amino acids   288
    crude   288
    percent   288
    requirements   289
    sources   288
    total   288
protobird   8
proventriculotomy   45
proventriculus   43, 44, 45, 291
pterygoid   32
pterylae   40, 175
pubic symphysis   36
pubis   34, 36
pulp   178
pygostyle   31, 34
pyloric valve   45, 46

Q

quadrate 32
quarantine, quarantine area 136, 147, 295
    see also isolation
quill 175

R

rachis 175
radius 36
ranch design
    access 257
    adapted from existing facilities 257
    barns 262
    breeder pens 261
    brooder barn, room 151, 194, 195, 235, 264
    chick barns 154, 191, 192
    chick pens, runs 191-193
    cleanliness 258
    climate 257
    community breeder pens 260
    controlled access 258
    design 257, 258
    drainage 257
    egg collection 260
    egg storage room 264
    existing facilities, adapting 263
    feed storage 262, 294
    fencing 134, 135, 228, 236, 262, 263
    generator, standby 152
    grow-out pens 142, 193, 236, 259
    hatching rooms 264
    heated waterers 260
    holding areas, pens 134, 258-261
    incubation room 264
    layout 257
    off-season pens 259
    office 263
    protection 257
    shelter 134, 185, 259, 260
    shipped 258
    soil 257
    ventilation 193
    wagon-wheel design 260
    water 257
rancher, *see* farm, farmer
    qualifying as 323
ratite, structure of 10

ratite egg
    dimensions 93, 94
    washing 296
ratite meat
    ageing 253
    cooking 254-255
    degree of tenderness 253
    inspection 254
    low-fat red meat 251
    marketing 253
    muscle cut 253
    muscle identification 251-252
    pan broiling 255
    processing 253
    tenderness 253
    yield 252, 253
ratites
    common ancestor 66
    DNA hybridization 66
    evolutionary relationship 65
    Huxley, T. H. 10
    too large to fly 9
recessive allele 65
record keeping 348
record-keeping, manual and computer 300
records
    accounting program or system 300
    breeding 303
    breeding values 309
    check lists 308
    chick survivability 305
    death 305
    early egg production 305
    egg production 305
    financial 301
    flock health performance 303
    flock purchase history 308
    incubation and hatching 303
    individual bird records 308
    local and national level 309
    measuring performance 300
    microchip numbers 308
    mortality 305
    parents 315
    production 303
    weather 308
registered limited liability partnership 339
remiges 175
renal portal veins 59
renal toxicity
    anesthetic agents 59
    therapeutics with potential of 59
renal vein 59
Reovirus 279
reporting of inventory 323
reproduction biochemistry 86
reproductive system

Index

female 85
male 81, 83
reproductive tract diseases 90
respiration 51
restriction enzymes 67
restriction fragment length
    polymorphism (RFLP) 68, 71, 77
    breeding coefficient 74
    maternal lineages 68
    ostrich 68
rhea chicks
    adapted to range conditions 239
    barn 236
    breeding season 240
    brood 231
    brooder boxes or pens 235
    defects 235
    dominant male 240
    feeding 236
    fence 236
    fiber 237
    free range 239, 240
    grow-out pens 236
    habitat 239
    hatches and environmental conditions 240
    hatching 231, 234
    heat 236
    house 236
    incubation 233
    microchip 233, 236
    minerals 237
    pens 236
    predators 232, 236, 240
    problems 237
    raising 230
    rearing 232
    shelter 236
    swim 231
    temperature 233
    tube-feeding 237
    ventilation 236
    vet for medical problems 237
    vitamins 237
    water 236
    whistle in the shell 235
    worming 235
rhea egg
    air cell 234
    candling 234
    clutch hatching 232
    contamination 232
    control of bacteria 232
    damage 232
    fertility 234
    gathering 232
    handling 232, 234
    hatching 234

humidity 233, 234
incubation 232
incubation time 234
infertile 234
normal vs. assisted hatch 235
pH barrier 233
pip the internal membrane 234
preparation 232
records 233
rotten 234
storing 233
temperature 233, 234
ventilation 233, 234
weight loss 234
rhea farming
    Argentina, South America 29
rhea oil
    cutting fluid 248
    fatty-acid content 248
    fatty-acid profile 246, 247
    grades 245, 246
    leather conditioning 247
    lipid nutrition 248
    perceived therapeutic qualities 245
    potential uses 245
    properties 247
    refining 245, 246
    standards 245
    uses 247
    yield 245
rheas
    adaptable 242
    association with other herd animals 29, 241
    Bariloche 29
    boleadora 27, 28
    breeding farms forming in Argentina 28
    booming 229
    breeder management 230
    breeders 228
    breeding season 229
    browsing brush 241
    capture 243
    chicks 228
    CITES 28
    colony 230
    compatible with other livestock 241
    dietary importance 27
    difficult to handle 227
    dispersal 12
    distinguishing features 79
    diverse diet 241
    dominant male 240
    feed 228
    fence 228
    free ranging 230
    gathered by helicopter 242
    graze in large groups 241

handling 242
harvest 245
hunting 27, 28
incubation 230
interactions 230
internal parasites 242
laying record 228
male aggression 240
male possessiveness 230
mating ritual 230
mineral supplement 242
ñandú 27
nesting site 230
orphaned chicks 240, 242
pairs 230
parasite control 242
pens 228, 230
potential uses 245
predators 241
pre-Hispanic 27
production 231
protecting their chicks 240
raising 227
range conditions 243
reduce predation in other herd animals 241
roundup 242
sexing 229
sexual activity 81
sexual maturity 230
shelter 228
studies 227
transport 243
trios 230
Uruguay 28, 29
water 228
ribs 36
risk of loss 348
Robinson, Terence 68
rock overload 46
routine procedures, written for employees 286

S

S corporation
   benefits 331
   corporate veil 331
   electing status 333
   income shifting 331
   liquidation 332
   reducing payroll taxes 331
   tax benefits 331

sacral vertebrae 32
sales journal 301
sales of livestock 323
Salmonella 277, 295
salt gland 42
sand bath, removing external parasites 136
sand nests 136
Saurischia 4
scapula 36
scapus 175
scutes 39, 40
secondaries 176
selection, natural 4
self-employment tax 323, 324
semen 55
seminal groove 55
Sereno and Chenggang 5
sesamoid bone 38
sex chromosomes 65
sexing 183
   by feel 184
   DNA examination 184
   emus 206
   rheas 229
   surgical 184
   visual 184
sexual dimorphism 87
shaft, feather 175
shell, *see* egg shell, emu shell,
   ostrich shell, rhea shell
shell gland 54, 84
shell membrane 94, 95
short days 88
Sibley, Charles G. 65
Sinornis santensis 5
site design 258
Sketchly, Charles J.
   first ostrich farmer in America 19
skin 39, 40
skull 31
small intestine 45, 292
Smit, D. J. vZ. 175
sole proprietorships 338
Solnhofen 4
southern blot method, RFLP 73
space density 309
spadonas 176, 178
sperm viability 84
spermatogenesis 82
spermatozoa 53, 82
spinal cord 49
spinal ribs 36
spleen 52
spongiform encephalopathy 279
spread sheets 300
standardized records 308
   evaluation for breeding characteristics 309

large databases 308
    scientific performance evaluation 308
standby generator 152
stargazing 280
starter feeds 154
state fairs, ratites in 123
stem, feather 175
sternal ribs 36
sternum 31, 36
stifle joint 38, 39
storage glands 54
storing eggs
    chest-type cooler 136
    humidity 106
    temperature 106, 136
stress 293, 309
substrate 153, 154
sulcus ejaculatorius 55
sulcus phalli 55
supplements 294
sutures 32
Swart, D. 180
synovial gout 280
synsacrum 34, 51
syrinx 49

T

35-40 nm virus 279
T-lymphocytes 50, 58
tail 34
tail quills 176
tall ancestor
    crocodile 13
    divided ventricle 9
tapeworm 280
tarsal bones 38
tarso-metatarsus 38
tax planning 326
territorial behavior 280
testes, testicles 53, 83
    sexual activity 81
    sexual maturity 82
testosterone 53
thecodont dinosaurs 12
theft 318
theropod dinosaurs 5, 13
third eyelid 42
third-eyelid gland 42
thoracic cavity 34, 36

thoracic vertebrae 32, 34, 36
thorax 36
thymine 64
thymus 50
thyroid 50
thyroxine 50
tibia 38
tibio-tarsus 39
toe claws 36, 39, 40
toes 38
tongue 32, 43
trace minerals 290
trachea 32, 41, 49
tracheal diverticulum in emus 50, 186
transit insurance
    fraud 321
    full-mortality 320
    named-perils 320
transponder, microchip 273
transportation insurance 348
transporting
    air transportation 272
    darkness 272
    distance 272
    eggs 271
    emus 199
    feed 272
    laying season 272
    loading 271
    loading ramp 271
    night 272
    physical stress 272
    ratites 267
    trailer 271
    unloading at night 272
    unloading 271, 272
    water 272
tuberculosis 278
tumescence 56
tympanic cavities 32
tympanic membrane 42

U

ulna 36
uncinate process 36
Uniform Commercial Code, 341
upper umbilicus 175
uric acid 52
urinary bladder 48

urodeum 48, 53, 55
uropygial gland 31, 43
uterus 54, 84

V

vagina 54, 55
vas deferens 55, 82
veins 58-59
ventilation 153, 309
   air flow patterns 113
   air turns per hour 113
   ammonia fumes 153
   carbon dioxide levels 114
   fan speeds 114
   fresh air CFM requirement 113
   incubation 111
   machine air flow 114
   machine CO^2 114
   machine embryo load 114
   oxygen deficiency 114
   rate for larger eggs 112
   rates 112
   removal of carbon dioxide 112
   removal of foul air 112
   removal of water vapor 112
   required percentage fresh air 114
   room static pressures 114
   stale air 153
   supply of oxygen 112
ventricular impactions 46
ventriculus 45, 46
verminous encephalitis 280
vertebrae
vestigial wings 36
veterinarian
   blood samples 282
   case history 285
   client-patient relationship 137, 281
   experienced in treating ratites 144, 281
   instruct producer in procedures 282
   plan of action 281
veterinarian's examination certificate 322
viruses 279, 296
visceral gout 280

vitamins 155
   B Vitamins 291
   deficiencies 291
   fat-soluble 290
   supplements 291
   water-soluble 291
vitelline membrane 94
vitreous body 42
vomer 32

W

warranties 349
water 294
   access 257
water quality
   farm wells 288
water-soluble vitamins 291
weather conditions 308
web site
   national associations 312
well water
   check for coliform bacteria 309
Wesselsbron virus 279
western equine encephalitis (WEE) 279
whites (feathers) 175
wing 36
wing coverts 176
wing quills 175
written contract 341

Y

yearly summary chart 304, 305
yolk 94
yolk sac retention 144
   surgery 144
yolk sac membrane 99

THE AUTHORS

We asked each of the contributors to *The Ratite Encyclopedia* to provide a brief biographical sketch and a photo, so that the reader could know a little bit about them.

If a bio or photo is missing, it was not provided, except in the case of Daniel V. Sarasqueta, which was due to a breakdown in communications between him and the publisher. We thank him for his contribution.

Richard L. Adams is Poultry Extension Specialist for the State of Indiana. While he works primarily in extension, Dr. Adams has done considerable research and teaching.

Kathy Bader lives with her husband Jim and their two daughters on the family ranch in Kinney County, Texas. They own and operate Lazy J Livestock, a combination cattle, sheep, and goat operation. They have been in the business for twenty-two years, following graduation from Texas A&M University. Kathy taught school for several years before starting a family, and now works with Jim in the daily operation of the ranch. Her main interests include the breeding management and sire selection for the Angora goats and the Rambouillet sheep. She is also very involved in wildlife management, which includes the study of the wild rhea population on the ranch.

Sharon Barron was born in Houston, Texas. She and her husband, Roland, have two sons and two grandsons. Sharon worked in the electronic industry for twenty years, the last seven of which she was involved in research and development.

While hosting a Memorial Day barbeque in 1989, a guest asked her if she had heard about people raising ostriches. They discussed it briefly during the afternoon, and Sharon could not stop thinking about ostriches. Within a week, she and Roland were on the road going from ranch to ranch in Texas and Oklahoma, looking at ostriches. For Sharon it was love at first sight, and she has never gotten over it.

They started by building a small facility in the Houston area. No sooner had the last nail been driven when they were asked to move to the Texas Hill Country and start an ostrich ranch for a friend. They completed that ranch and had two extremely successful years, when they were asked to move again. This time it was to the area of Stephenville, Texas, where they converted an existing cutting-horse ranch to an ostrich ranch. Sharon is currently the manager and vice president of Lucky W Farms, Inc.

The Authors

Joe G. Berry was born in Sayre, Oklahoma. He earned a BS in Poultry Science at Oklahoma State University in 1965, an MS in Poultry Science at OSU in 1967, and a Ph. D. in Food Science from Kansas State University in 1970.

He has been employed as research assistant, teaching assistant, assistant professor, and associate professor of poultry and animal science at Oklahoma State University, Kansas State University, and Purdue University. He is currently Extension Poultry Specialist in the Animal Science Department at Oklahoma State University. His duties are divided between teaching and extension services.

Dr. Berry serves on several department committees and the College of Agriculture Water Quality Task Force, and serves as faculty representative on the Student Conduct Committee.

His publications include more than a hundred extension fact sheets, journal articles, published abstracts, and popular articles. He has presented papers at many scientific meetings, and is active in industry-related associations and fraternities.

Vern E. Brackett was born and reared in Mobile, Alabama, and is a graduate of Auburn University School of Engineering. His emu ranch is in Creola, Alabama, near Mobile. Vern retired from his business of manufacturing, sales, and marketing in Atlanta to start a new career in ranching, small business consulting, writing, teaching, and motivational speaking.

Vern is a member of the Alabama Emu Association and is Director of Zone 4, State Zones Coordinator, a member of the research committee, and chair of the governmental affairs and ethics committee. Vern also serves as co-chair of American Emu Association's state affiliate training and development committee and serves as parliamentarian on the AEA state affiliate group.

John T. Brake is a North Carolina native and grew up on a small farm in Edgecombe County. He attended North Carolina State University at Raleigh and graduated Summa Cum Laude with a double major in Animal Science and Poultry Science in 1974. He completed the requirements for a Ph. D. in December, 1977. He has been a member of the faculty of Auburn University as well as North Carolina State University. He presently serves as Professor and Research Coordinator in the Department of Poultry Science at North Carolina State.

Dr. Brake has published more than 300 scientific and popular articles. His publications have been translated into six languages and he has spoken to scientific and industry groups in eighteen countries. He has received awards for both outstanding research and teaching. Dr. Brake travels extensively and werves as a consultant to a number of poultry integrators world-wide.

Dr. Brake has worked with a major manufacturer of ratite incubators for several years, dealing with design and operation questions. He regularly answers incubation trouble-shooting questions from producers and has spoken at several ratite industry meetings.

Teresa Coble graduated from Texas A&M University School of Veterinary Medicine in 1977. Dr. Coble and her husband began raising large hookbills (parrots, macaws, and cockatoos) in 1986, and maintain a large collection of threatened and endangered species. This has proven to be a major advantage in dealing with many ratite problems.

Several of Dr. Coble's clients were on the pioneering edge of the development of the ratite industry. She attributes much of her knowledge to these forward-thinking individuals who were willing to let her "try this" or "try that" with their valuable birds, and thanks them for their assistance and patience.

Ken Coldwell was a founding director of the Texas Emu Association as well as its first President. He also has served as TEA Zone II President, and authored the Student Education & Training Program (STEP). Presently he is Chairman of TEA Disease Prevention & Control Committee, one of the founders of the Emu Industry Council of America, and a member of AEA, TEA, ERI, EMU and Emu Industry Council of America.

Ken Coldwell and Wayne Sealey are partners in C&S Ranch and GenLab, Inc. the company they formed to market DNA ProFiles™ to the ratite industry. They were responsible for initiating and funding research studies of Emu genetics, much of which is first reported in this book. Both have been in the Emu ranching business since 1988-89.

Gheorghe M. Constantinescu is Professor of Veterinary Anatomy at the College of Veterinary Medicine, University of Missouri-Columbia. A native of Romania, he has been a United States citizen since 1989. He earned his DVM from the Faculty of Veterinary Medicine in Bucharest in 1955, and his Ph. D. in Veterinary Anatomy from the same institution in 1964.

Dr. Constantinescu served in several positions, including researcher, veterinarian, and professor in Bucharest and at the Agronomic Institute and the Faculty of Veterinary Medicine in Timisoara. He joined the faculty at University of Missouri in 1984 as an Associate Professor, and has been a full Professor since 1992.

Dr. Constantinescu has published, contributed to, or advised on hundreds of papers and articles on veterinary medicine and anatomy, and his illustrations appear in dozens of textbooks and articles worldwide. He has been a presenter at two dozen conferences or meetings since his arrival in the United States, and eleven prior to that time.

The Authors

D. C. Deeming has thirteen years of experience in research and practical aspects of incubation and resides in England. He graduated in 1984 with a Bachelor of Science degree in Applied Biology awarded by the University of Bath, England. During three years study at the University of Reading, Dr. Deeming studied the physiological effects of egg turning upon development for his Ph. D. thesis. He has worked with alligators and in a bird zoo. He has been involved in the ostrich industry, advising farmers in North America, Europe, and Africa for several years.

Since September 1993 Dr. Deeming has been full-time scientific advisor at Hangland Farm Ostriches, Ltd, the first ostrich farm in Europe. He is researching incubation and hatching, chick rearing and behavior, ostrich growth rates, and various other aspects related to the welfare of the birds.

Dr. Deeming has published numerous articles on incubation in the ostrich press, and has nine scientific papers on ostrich incubation and chick rearing published or in press.

Claire Drenowatz has been a writer and editor for twenty years, and a typographer for fifteen. She has worked as reporter, columnist, and editor for three newspapers, as columnist and editor for an aviation trade magazine, as managing editor for a computer trade magazine, and as technical editor on several scientific publications.

She is also an airline transport pilot, and until she established her own editing and graphic design company five years ago, divided her time between two avocations.

Claire is co-author of *Blueprint for Fundraising*, published in 1991.

Susan Dunn has a unique background, having been raised as a "military brat," all over the United States and in Germany. Her family eventually settled in Florida, and now hatches and raises alligators, crocodiles, cougars, bobcats, and snakes.

Susan's fascination with the animal world led her into the rodeo arena and on to jobs working with equine veterinarians and eventually into managing a horse ranch. With the large-animal veterinarian background, she decided to go into nursing. After graduating from nursing school, she spent ten years as a registered nurse in obstetrics and gynecology, and in emergency rooms.

Susan returned to non-human animals in 1989, founding Windwalker Exotics and raising ostriches and emus. She has been at the forefront of the development of the ratite industry in Central Texas, where she has published many articles, managed a very successful ratite ranch, and conducted numerous seminars on ratites throughout the United States.

Charley Elrod has ranched in Texas and Mexico, and has extensive experience in wildlife management. He has combined farm and ranch real estate experience with consulting on aspects of ranching such as soil science, brush control, wildlife management, stocking rates, water management, and production, primarily on cattle and wildlife ranches.

Charley has focused on the ratite industry for the last few years, and is co-author of *The Ratite Record Book*, published in 1992.

Alex Fairly's background is in computers, with a BS in Computer Information Systems. He spent seven years with a leading software developer, specializing in systems dedicated to the insurance industry. Alex began working with HRH in January of 1993, developing a nationwide ostrich program. In November 1993 he was awarded the first and only endorsement from the American Ostrich Association board of directors for the program that was developed. By year end 1994, HRH was the largest ostrich insurer in the United States. They currently specialize in the development of insurance programs for associations and large organizations.

Scotty Flowers was born and raised on a farm near Lubbock, Texas, and after achieving a BBA in Industrial Management from Texas Tech, has been in various successful businesses in Lubbock, including TTI Long Distance which was a multimillion dollar long distance company. He has been in the bird business since 1992, when Texas Longneck Ranch was incorporated with Scotty as president.

Benny J. Gallaway, President of the U.S. branch of LGL since 1974, also serves as President of LGL Ecological Genetics, Inc. He received his Ph.D. from Texas A&M University in 1978. The initial projects resulting in formation of the genetics group of LGL in 1989 came from his interest in the field and his observation that molecular genetics had many practical applications for ecology and aviculture.

Dr. Gallaway has been instrumental in the development of LGL's ratite genetics research program and is also well known for his aviculture and conservation expertise in regard to endangered new world parrots, the macaws, in particular.

Richard Ghiselli is an Assistant Professor in the Department of Restaurant, Hotel, Institutional and Tourism Management at Purdue University. Dr. Ghiselli teaches Quality Food Production, and his research interests include operational analysis and quality control.

Rollo Gurss moved to Lubbock in 1972 and moved to a farm in 1989. He has a degree in Architectural Engineering from Texas Techs and has owned a construction company since 1979. He has been in the bird business since 1989.

Lyle D. Hague was born and raised in Oklahoma and attended Northwestern Oklahoma State University. He received a bachelor of science degree in 1989, and then was commissioned an officer in the United States Marine Corps. He served on active duty for four years, including an eight-month tour in Saudi Arabia during Operation Desert Shield/Desert Storm. He now serves in the Marine Corps Reserves and in law enforcement.

By 1991, when Lyle was on active duty, his brother Frank had purchased twenty three-month-old pairs of ostriches, and was well on his way in the ostrich industry. In 1993, Frank convinced Lyle to come off active duty and join him in establishing what is now Vision Exotix Ostrich Ranch, LLC, in Lexington, Oklahoma.

In November of 1993 Lyle and Frank co-founded Vision Exotix Express, Inc., a nationwide ratite transportation company, also based in Lexington. Since that time, Lyle has personally handled and transported well over 2,000 ratites of various ages throughout the United States and Canada.

Brett A. Hopkins earned a BS in Biology at Missouri Southern State College in 1984, an MS in Poultry Diseases at the University of Arkansas in 1986, DVM at the College of Veterinary Medicine at the University of Missouri-Columbia in 1990. He is currently a Ph. D. candidate in Veterinary Pathology.

Dr. Hopkins is a member of the American Association of Avian Pathologists, and has served on several industry committees and councils, including chairing the Ratite Research Conference in 1993, the Ratite Nutrition Council in 1993, and the American Emu Association and North American Rhea Association research committees in 1994.

In October and November of 1994, Dr. Hopkins traveled to Zimbabwe to study and assist in ostrich production management as a member of Volunteers Overseas Cooperative Assistance. His research papers date back to 1985 and continue in scientific journals and industry publications.

He teaches in the Department of Veterinary Pathology at the University of Missouri-Columbia, and is in private practice as a veterinarian.

Pat Jodoin, with her husband Al, formed Jodoin Emu Ranch in 1987, starting out part-time with twelve yearling pairs, and have been working at it full time for the past seven years. They currently manage 700 emus on their place in Whitney, Texas, and are looking forward to setting up a new commercial operation on larger acreage in the near future.

Pat was secretary-treasurer and Al was charter president of American Emu Association, managing the office out of their home for a year and half, with Pat writing the newsletters, until AEA could hire professional staff. Pat has continued to write articles in all emu-related trade publications.

Pat's prime areas of responsibility today are incubation and hatching, nutrition and health. She works full-time approximately six months of the year and then travels extensively sharing with othe groups of emu ranchers in the United States and Canada. She is a member of United Emu Inc., Emu Ranchers Inc., Emu Marketing Unlimited, American Emu Association, Texas Emu Association, and Hill Country Emu Association.

The Authors

Lisa Kinder is a research specialist at the University of Arkansas at Fayetteville. She earned a BS in Animal Science in 1992, and an MS in Poultry Science in 1995, both at the University of Arkansas. She has received several scholarships and awards. Her publications include studies on selenium toxicity in emus, eggshell quality, and the early growth of emu chicks.

She is a member of the American Emu Association, American Ostrich Association, Poultry Science Association, and National Ratite Breeders Association, and has made presentations to their various national, state, and zone meetings and conventions for several years.

Jack W. Ledbetter is an attorney and emu rancher. He grew up in Texas and graduated with an engineering degree from the United States Naval Academy in 1951. After four years in the Navy, including a tour in Korea, he returned to civilian life and graduated from the University of Texas School of Law in 1957.

Ledbetter is licensed to practice law in the state of Texas and in all federal courts. He is a member of the law firm of Ledbetter & Benjamin, PC, in Austin, where he specializes in small business and estate planning.

He became an emu rancher in 1992, and is the owner of Ledbetter Emus of Austin. He has written a number of articles on legal topics related to emu ranching, which have appeared in Ratite Marketplace and Emu Today and Tomorrow. He frequently speaks at emu seminars and conventions on the topics of emu law and business.

Kenneth W. McMillin is a native of Indiana where he was active in 4-H, FFA, livestock and crop production, and operations in the family custom-meat plant. Dr. McMillin received a BS in Food Science from Purdue University in 1974, MS degree in Animal Science at Purdue in 1976, and the Ph. D. degree in Meat Science from Iowa State University in 1980, before joining the faculty at Louisiana State University in 1980.

Dr. McMillin is currently a Professor of Animal Science, with adjunct appointments in the Department of Food Science and Louisiana Cooperative Extension Service.

Dr. McMillin teaches courses on muscle food processing, meat science, growth and development, and muscle biology, and serves on national committees of the Institute of Food Technologists, American Meat Science Association, American Society of Animal Science, and International Meat and Poultry HACCP Alliance. Campus activities include offices and committees of the LSU Chapter of Sigma Xi, Gamma Sigma Delta Honor Society of Agriculture, and LSU Faculty Senate.

Walter G. Miller graduated cum laude with a BS in Accounting from Southwest Missouri State University in 1982. He has been a Certified Public Accountant since 1984, and a principal in the firm of Miller and Schroeder, CPAs, Ltd. since 1986. He is a member of the American Institute of Certified Public Accountants and the Arkansas Society of CPAs, serving as chairman of the Litigation Support Services Committee. He has taught accounting at the college level in Lubbock, Texas and Rogers, Arkansas.

Miller publishes the quarterly *Small Business Newsletter* and writes tax tip columns in publications with readers in more than twenty states. He has hosted several television specials on tax law changes and often presents prepared tax discussions for area organizations.

Craig Morris graduated from Iowa State University in 1992 with a BS in Animal Science, and earned his Ph. D. in Animal Science from Texas A&M University in 1995.

While a Regents Graduate Fellow at A&M, Dr. Morris published nearly two dozen papers and articles, participated in several conferences and research projects, and was active in professional and educational organizations.

The chapter on ostrich meat was written while Dr. Morris was at Texas A&M, but he is now Manager for Scientific and Technical Affairs at the American Meat Institute in Washington, DC.

John C. Patton, who directs all genetic laboratory research operations for LGL Ecological Genetics, Inc, received his Ph.D. from the University of Georgia in 1980. He has served as a member of the Board of Directors for the Wild Canid Survival and Research Center, and advisor to the Mexican Wolf Recovery Plan, the Elephant Species Survival Plan, and the Grevy's Zebra Species Survival Plan.

Dr. Patton's genetic work on elephants has been featured in *Science* magazine, and elements of his work will be the subject of a *NOVA* special. His work on red wolves has been featured on CNN. Dr. Patton has specialized in ratite genetics for the past two years and was instrumental in the discovery of PCR primers for emus.

The Authors

Amy Raines is a farm girl from Emerago, North Dakota. She completed her undergraduate work at North Dakota State University before attending veterinary school in Ames, Iowa. She received her DVM from Iowa State University in 1988. She worked in mixed practice in North Dakota and Texas before beginning her career with ratites in the winter of 1990. She currently owns Boondocks Ratite Hospital in Oklahoma City, a facility devoted 100% to ratites.

Dr. Raines is very interested in the ratite industry. She stresses to her clients the need for selection and improvements. She has been and is currently active in research and education for the benefit of the ratite industry. She has contributed to several leading ratite publications and has been published in veterinary journals and proceedings.

Dr. Raines has given presentations at seminars all over the United States, and has recently been named as a candidate for inclusion in *Who's Who in Executives and Professionals*.

Chris Ramsey was born and raised in Houston, Texas. He started in the exotic industry in 1978, and graduated from Sam Houston State University in 1981 with a degree in Wildlife Biology. On graduation, he married Judy Minton and started HuntClub Utopia, a hunting resort catering to small businesses. Exotic species were introduced for hunting and viewing from the start of the operation.

Chris entered the ratite industry in 1989, raising his own birds as well as working exotic sales. In 1994 he started a consulting business working with ratites and native and exotic hoofstock. He and his wife Judy and their two children currently work their birds as part of a family operation.

Kent Robinson has been an emu rancher since 1990. He started the first known emu education and training class at Tomball College in Tomball, Texas, in 1992, and spearheaded development of emu clinics with the Agriculture Science Department of Houston Community College.

Kent co-founded EmuScope, a consultant group formed for farm training and hands-on consultation serving the emu industry. He is an experienced sexer and handler, working local exotic auctions. He has contributed articles to several industry publications.

At the 1995 Houston Livestock Show & Rodeo, Kent was Emu Chairman for the Ostrich & Emu Show and Sale, and will repeat those jobs at the 1996 show.

Kent is a three-year member of Emu Ranchers, Inc., and a member of Emu Marketing Unlimited, American Emu Association, Texas Emu Association, and the Gulf Coast Agri-business Council.

James Sales is a researcher at the University of Stellenbosch in South Africa. He earned a BS in Agriculture in 1989, an MS in Agriculture in 1991, and a Ph. D. in Agriculture in 1994. His doctoral thesis was on the identification and improvements of quality characteristics of ostrich meat. He has been the recipient of several honors and awards for post-graduate study.

Dr. Sales has made presentations at scientific congresses in Transkei and France, and as either first author or co-author has published papers in several scientific journals in South Africa, Europe, and the United States. He has also been published in ostrich industry trade journals in Canada, the United States and Australia.

Hubert Schmieder is chef instructor in the Department of Restaurant, Hotel, Institutional and Tourism Management at Purdue University. Chef Schmieder holds six gold medals from the International Chefs' Competitions and was a member of the 1964 Chefs Olympic Team. He worked in product development for both egg and turkey companies.

Schmieder's involvement with ratite meat dates back t 1991, when he was introduced to the emerging ostrich industry by one of his students. He has served his ratite dishes at many banquets in the United States and Canada. He is frequently referred to as "The Big Bird Chef."

Chef Schmieder's many years of experience qualify him as an authoritative lecturer and demonstrator. He has lectured and demonstrated his culinary talent at many ratite seminars and conferences in fifteen states and Canada.

Wayne Sealey, a founding member of the Texas Emu Association, has served the organization as Chairman of the Marketing and Educational committee as well as chairman of the TEA-sponsored Zone II annual EMU seminar. Currently he is President of the South Central Texas EMU Association. In 1991 and 1992, he was a member of EMU Ranchers Incorporated, and is a current member of EMU Marketing Unlimited and the American Emu Association.

With Ken Coldwell, Wayne is a partner in C&S Ranch and GenLab, Inc., which markets DNA ProFiles™ to the ratite industry. They were responsible for initiating and funding research studies of emu genetics, much of which is first reported in *The Ratite Encyclopedia*. Both have been in the emu ranching business since 1988-89.

Dennis H. Sigler is currently a nutritionist for Muenster Milling Company in Muenster, Texas. He has been involved in researching, formulating, and developing feeds and nutritional products for ratites since 1989. Prior to that he was a professor of Animal Science at Kansas State Univerity.

Dr. Sigler received his Ph. D. from Texas A&M in 1980 and has published numerous scientific journal articles, book chapters, and other publications. He is well-respected across the country as an animal nutritionist and has been a featured speaker at many ratite seminars and conventions.

He holds professional memberships in the American Society of Animal Science and American Poultry Association, and currently serves as vice president of the Equine Nutrition and Physiology Society.

Dennis L. Sisson earned his BS in Accounting from the University of Arkansas in 1986, and has been a Certified Public Accountant since 1988. He worked for eight years as a Revenue Agent with the Internal Revenue Service, where he performed audits on individuals, corporations, and partnerships, ranging in size from very small to large multinational businesses.

Sisson joined Miller & Schroeder, CPAs, Ltd. in 1992. His work focuses primarily on the areas of federal taxation (including tax return preparation, tax research, IRS negotiations, and tax disputes) and new corporate formations for numerous firm clients located throughout the southern United States.

Sisson is a member of the American Institute of Certified Public Accountants and the Arkansas Society of CPAs. He is a contributing writer on many of the tax articles produced by the firm.

Paul C. Smith is a professor of Pathobiology at the College of Veterinary Medicine, Auburn University. He holds a Ph. D. in Veterinary Pathologh from Iowa State University, an MS in Virology from Ohio State University, and a DVM from Auburn University.

Dr. Smith served as Research Leader with the U. S. Department of Agriculture at the National Animal Disease Center and spent three years as the Professor of Food Animal Research at the University of Tennessee. He has been on the Veterinary faculty at Auburn University for the past fourteen years, and currently teaches Poultry Diseases, Advanced Avian Medicine, and Wildlife Diseases while coordinating ratite research.

William J. Stadelman is Professor Emeritus of Food Sciences at Purdue University. Dr. Stadelman works with poultry meat and eggs, processing, quality evaluation, and preservation.

Mary Lee Stropes and her husband have been breeding and raising rheas for thirteen years. Their goal has been to produce quality, large, high producing rheas to be used as breeding stock for potential rhea producers, in a habitat as close to nature as possible.

In 1993 Mary Lee had the opportunity to go to South America to learn all she could about birds in the wild, on a study program with Daniel Sarasqueta at INTA in Argentina.

She worked with the formation of the North American Rhea Association and served on the board of directors for two years.

Mary Lee has worked for the last nineteen years as a doctor's assistant at the Booneville Medical Clinic, but she considers her lifetime job to be the study of rheas, improving the quality of raising them for the future in a simple, but successful way.

Randall Wayne Sullivan earned a BS in Biomedical Science in 1980 at Texas A&M University, and received his DVM at Texas A&M in 1985.

Dr. Sullivan is a partner in Crossroads Veterinary Hospital in Seguin, Texas.

The Authors

William C. Sutton has been in private practice in Internal Medicine and Nuclear Medicine in Houston since 1961. Dr. Sutton has been director of the Department of Nuclear Medicine at Memorial City Hospital since 1972, and was elected Distinguished Fellow of the College of Nuclear Medicine in 1988. An active pilot with commercial license and multi-engine and instrument ratings, he is also an FAA Aviation Medical Examiner.

Dr. Sutton has been owner with his wife Pat of an exotic game ranch since 1974. They are currently involved in raising, buying, selling, trading, and showin more than forty different species of animals.

Rocky Terry earned an MS in Poultry Science, and DVM at Texas A&M University in 1973. He has spent eighteen years in the poulty business, and has worked for the last four years with ratites.

Dr. Terry is in private practice at Terry Veterinary Clinic in Glen Rose, Texas.

Leslie D. Thompson is an Assistant Professor of Food Technology in the Department of Animal Science and Food Technology at Texas Tech University in Lubbock. She teaches a variety of food science courses at the graduate and undergraduate level, and research in food safety, and quality and composition primarily in meat and dairy products.

She also serves as the Food Technology club advisor, the TTU Institute of Food Technologists Quiz Bowl Team coach, and is serving as a National IFT Student Association faculty advisor.

Dr. Thompson earned her Ph. D. degree in Food Science and Human Nutrition at the University of Florida, a well as her MS in Poultry Products Technology and BS in Poultry Science.

She has written or co-written eleven refereed scientific publications, twenty abstracts, and twelve technical reports, and has given numerous talks and seminars on food safety and food-related issues.

John R. Wade received his DVM from Louisiana State University in 1980. That same year he established and opened his own veterinary hospital where he operated a successful mixed animal and avian practice for ten years. Dr. Wade's interest in veterinary care of ostriches grew when several of his clients began to acquire these big birds.

In 1988, he became co-owner of Pacesetter Ostrich Farm in Folsom, Louisiana. In 1992, Pacesetter became a publicly-traded company and opened its second facility, now home to more than 100 breeding pairs, in Willcox, Arizona. Dr. Wade assumed the position of President and CEO of this operation, which was granted a USDA stamp for ostrich meat sales to begin in November of 1994.

In 1989, Dr. Wade became co-owner of Microchip Identification Systems by AVID®, located in Louisiana. Dr. Wade is a member of the American Ostrich Association, the American Emu Association, and the Association of Avian Veterinarians. As a board member of the AOA, he chaired the Membership Committee and the USDA Liaison Committee for future meat-market development.

Andy Weilbrenner was first introduced to the ostrich industry in 1986, when he and his partner were considering an ostrich operation on the family farm. At that time, Andy made his first trip to Africa to learn first-hand about the ostrich industry. In 1987, Southwind Ostrich Ranch became a reality. Andy has worked with most phases of the ranch over the years, and currently spends most of his time in domestic and international marketing.

Andy received his BS degree from Purdue University School of Agronomy. Following graduation, he returned to work on the family farm in Mt. Vernon, Indiana. Andy and his wife Dawn founded DNA Exotics, which imports, buys, and sells emus, rheas, cassowaries, and other exotic animals.

Andy serves as trustee for the Mt. Vernon Conservation Club and is currently president of the Black River Hunting Club and a member of Posey County Ducks Unlimited, Safari Club, and the Indiana Farm Bureau. *(Photo: Weilbrenner and President Masire of Botswana)*

Brian Wessels is a sophomore at Sam Houston State University, majoring in computer graphics design and minoring in Animal Science. He enjoys sports, hunting, fishing, and drawing.

Through his family's business, he is experienced in working with exotics and ranch work. Brian hopes to be able to combine his love of drawing with his desire to work with animals.

RESOURCES

ASSOCIATIONS

CALL YOUR NATIONAL ASSOCIATION FOR INFORMATION ABOUT STATE AND LOCAL GROUPS

American Ostrich Association
American Ostrich
3950 Fossil Creek Blvd, Suite 200
Fort Worth, TX 76137
817-232-1200 vox
817-232-1390 fax

American Emu Association
AEA News
P. O. Box 8174
Dallas, TX 75205
214-559-2321 vox
214-528-2359 fax

Australian Ostrich Association
P. O. Box 286
Jamison Centre, ACT 2614
Australia
+61 6 2531258 vox
+61 6 2516719 fax

Canadian Ostrich Association
66 Queenston Street
Winnipeg, Manitoba R3N 0W5
204-489-6443 vox
204-489-6521 fax

CoPro (Pvt) Ltd.
Trading Company of the Ostrich
    Producers Association
    of Zimbabwe
P. O. Box 1871
Harare, Zimbabwe
+263-4-754002 vox
+263-4-754008 fax

Emu Farmers Association
    of Australia, Inc.
P. O. Box 6291
East Perth, Western Australia 6004
+61 9 3252933 vox
+61 9 3254197 fax

European Ostrich Association
The Ostrich Update
P. O. Box 4 - Evere II
Belgium - 1140 Brussels
32/81/87.85.39

North American Rhea Association
The Rhea Reporter
11902 Elm Street, Suite 4
Omaha, NB 68144
402-697-5134 vox
402-333-4336 fax

Texas Animal Health Commission
Animal Health Matters
P. O. Box 12966
Austin, TX 78711-2966
512-719-0700 vox
512-719-0719 fax
Other states have similar government organizations or commissions which provide information on interstate and foreign shipping. Check your phone book.

PUBLICATIONS

CALEA News Update
18600 View Circle
Fiddletown, CA 95629
209-296-3802 vox/fax

Canadian Ostrich Magazine
Suite 204, 2915 19 Street NE
Calgary, Alberta T2E 7A2
403-250-1128 vox
403-250-1194 fax

Emu Today & Tomorrow
P. O. Box 7
Nardin, OK 74646-0007
405-628-2933 vox
405-628-2011 fax

Ostrich News
P. O. Box 860
Cache, OK 73527-0860
405-429-3765 vox
405-429-3935 fax

Ratite Journal
P. O. Box 161
Prineville, OR 97754
503-447-4902 vox
503-447-2578 fax

Ratite Marketplace
P. O. Box 1613
Bowie, TX 76230
800-972-7730 vox
817-872-3559 fax

COOPERATIVES

**THESE ARE THE CO-OPS WE'VE BEEN ABLE TO LOCATE.
CONTACT YOUR NATIONAL, STATE, OR LOCAL ASSOCIATION FOR OTHERS.**

American Ratite Marketing
 Cooperative
1690 South State Road 3261
Levelland, TX 79336
800-742-4440 vox
806-894-4799 fax

Cooperative for Ostrich, Rhea
 and Emu (CORE)
430 Guernsey Road
Biglerville, PA 17307
717-677-8010

CTC Advanced Processing
 & Marketing
P. O. Box 1077
Lockhart, TX 78644
210-875-3640 vox
210-875-2994 fax

Emu Marketing Unlimited (EMU)
P. O. Box K
Rosebud, TX 76570
800-791-2669 vox
817-583-4151 fax

Emu Ranchers Incorporated (ERI)
2210 N. Frazier, Suite 240
Conroe, TX 77303
800-473-6362 vox
409-826-8811 fax

Emu Producers Int'l Cooperative
P. O. Box 295
Jewett, TX 75846
903-626-6640

Emu Producers Cooperative
P. O. Box 66
Watkins, CO 80137
303-363-8597

REO National, Inc.
Route 2, Box 1971
Fredricksburg, TX 78624
210-997-4707

Ratite Ranchers Cooperative, Inc.
P. O. Box 307
Malvern, AR 72104
501-337-4425

Southwest Ratite Cooperative
6601 East Noyes
Sahuarita, AZ 85629
602-762-5449

United Emu, Inc.
P. O. Box 1118
Weatherford, TX 76086
800-806-4368

United Ratite Cooperative
13620 Lincoln Way, Suite 290
Auburn, CA 95603
916-885-9825 vox
916-885-9826 fax

VMG Ratite CoOp
P. O. Box 202768
Austin, TX 78720
512-331-7061 vox
512-331-2984 fax

SOURCES

DNA TESTING

GenLab, Inc
DNA ProFile™ (Emus)
P. O. Box 4647
Bryan, TX 77805-4647
409-779-8822

Zoogen, Incorporated
1105 Kennedy Place, Suite 4
Davis, CA 95616
800-995-2475

MICROCHIP SYSTEMS

Microchip Identification Systems
155 Woodside Drive
Mandeville, LA 70448
504-626-4167

RESEARCH

Ratite Research Foundation
P. O. Box 213
Cache, OK 73527-0213
405-429-8600

PRODUCTS & EQUIPMENT

Some of the companies which serve the ratite industry

NatureForm Hatchery Systems 474
1310 Tradeport Drive
Jacksonville, FL 32218 USA
904-354-7400 Phone
904-791-9590 Fax

InfraScope International, Inc. 475
P. O. Box 512
Bois D'Arc MO 65612 USA
800-364-8439 US
417-881-5203 International

The Ratite Record Book 475
Ratite Records, Inc.
P. O. Box 790365
San Antonio, TX 78279-0365 USA
210-308-8998 Phone
210-366-1657 Fax

American Exotic Tanning & Manufacturing 476
2358 North Main Street
Fort Worth, TX 76108 USA
800-827-3521 US
817-626-0089 International

RBE Software Development 476
5100 East Tecumseh Road
Norman, OK 73071 USA
405-360-3045 Phone/Fax

James Leddy Boots 477
915 Ambler
Abilene, TX 79601 USA
915-677-7811 Phone

BIO-TEK Industries, Inc. 478
P. O. Box 93746
Atlanta, GA 30318 USA
404-799-2050 Phone
404-799-2056 Fax

NatureForm® Incubator/Hatchers for Ostriches and Emus

NOM-125
Incubtor/Hatcher

A fully automatic incubator/hatcher that frees the operator from servicing of wet bulbs and also eliminates manual adjustments for humidity, temperature and air flow control.

NOM-125

NOM-45
Incubator/Hatcher

An incubator/hatcher designed for breeders new to the ratite industry. Although smaller in size, it contains the same quality controls and construction of more advanced models.

NOM-45

NatureForm®
HATCHERY SYSTEMS

InfraScope INTERNATIONAL, inc.

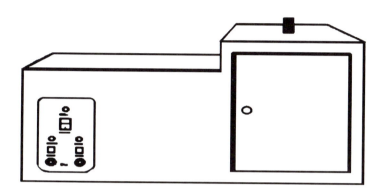

The Infrascope - an electronic egg viewer that displays the contents of all Ratite eggs on a TV monitor which can then be recorded for later viewing and study with the use of aVCR.

The Infrascope may be used in a lighted room and will help you determine fertility, shell death, mal-positioning exact location and size of air cell, internal pipping and even cracks in the egg.

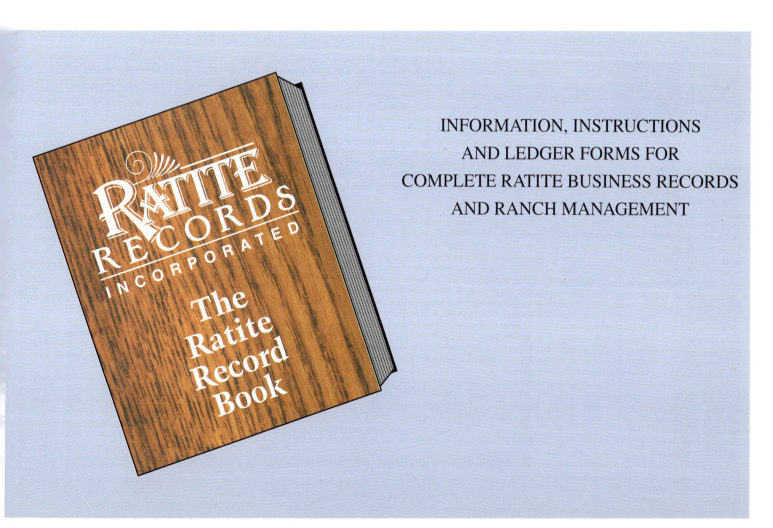

INFORMATION, INSTRUCTIONS AND LEDGER FORMS FOR COMPLETE RATITE BUSINESS RECORDS AND RANCH MANAGEMENT

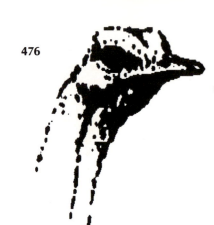

American Exotic Tanning and Manufacturing

Tanning of Exotic Hides
Custom Designed Leather Goods

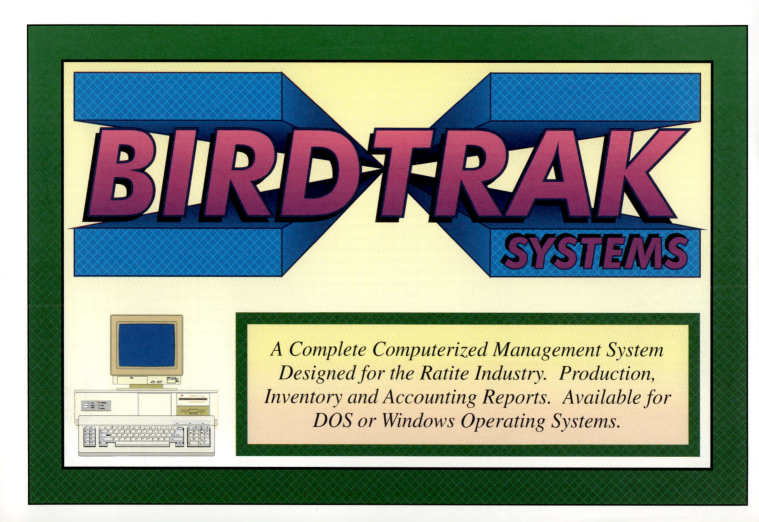

A Complete Computerized Management System Designed for the Ratite Industry. Production, Inventory and Accounting Reports. Available for DOS or Windows Operating Systems.

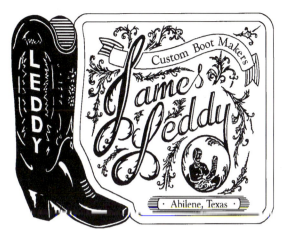

Custom Hand Made Boots

Buttercup Ostrich with kelly green top, 5 rows stitching

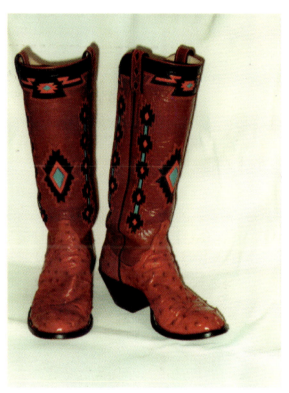

Rose Ostrich with inlay pattern

Black Ostrich, Black Kangaroo, Red Kangaroo Border

Gold Quill Ostrich golf, tennis or walking shoe

Custom Made Shoes

San-i-ta-tion ...The means by which **Health** is protected

- BROAD SPECTRUM KILL VS. AVIAN SPECIFIC DISEASES.
- RECOMMENDED FOR USE IN ALL DISINFECTING APPLICATIONS.

- HELPS ELIMINATE THE SPREAD OF DISEASE FROM MAN TO BIRD

- SPOT DISINFECTANT FOR BOOTS AND COVERALLS

Ordered By: ❏ *Individual* ❏ *Library* ❏ *School* ❏ *Government*
❏ *Medical* ❏ *Trade* ❏ *Other*

Name _____
Company _____
Address _____
City _____ State ____ Zip _____
Country _____

Important Ordering Information

If you have any questions regarding my order, my daytime phone and fax numbers are: Phone (____) _____
Fax (____) _____

Send me _____ copies of *The Ratite Encyclopedia* @ $84.95 plus shipping /handling and sales tax. (Texas only)
Texas $95.94 • Out of state $89.45 • International $92.45.
TOTAL _____
For volume discounts please call (210) 308-8998.

P.O. BOX 790365
San Antonio, TX 78279-0365
Call (210) 308-8998
Fax (210) 366-1657

Ship To:

Name _____
Company _____
Address _____ Div/Ste # _____
City _____ State ____ Zip _____
Country _____

Method of Payment
❏ Check (payable to Ratite Records, Inc)
❏ International - US currency / money order
❏ Visa ❏ M/C ❏ Amex ❏ Discover

☐☐☐☐☐☐☐☐☐☐☐☐☐☐☐☐

Exp. Date: _____ Signature _____

RATITE RECORDS

Ordered By: ❏ *Individual* ❏ *Library* ❏ *School* ❏ *Government*
❏ *Medical* ❏ *Trade* ❏ *Other*

Name _____
Company _____
Address _____
City _____ State ____ Zip _____
Country _____

Important Ordering Information

If you have any questions regarding my order, my daytime phone and fax numbers are: Phone (____) _____
Fax (____) _____

Send me _____ copies of *The Ratite Encyclopedia* @ $84.95 plus shipping /handling and sales tax. (Texas only)
Texas $95.94 • Out of state $89.45 • International $92.45.
TOTAL _____
For volume discounts please call (210) 308-8998.

P.O. BOX 790365
San Antonio, TX 78279-0365
Call (210) 308-8998
Fax (210) 366-1657

Ship To:

Name _____
Company _____
Address _____ Div/Ste # _____
City _____ State ____ Zip _____
Country _____

Method of Payment
❏ Check (payable to Ratite Records, Inc)
❏ International - US currency / money order
❏ Visa ❏ M/C ❏ Amex ❏ Discover

☐☐☐☐☐☐☐☐☐☐☐☐☐☐☐☐

Exp. Date: _____ Signature _____

RATITE RECORDS

Ordered By: ❏ *Individual* ❏ *Library* ❏ *School* ❏ *Government*
❏ *Medical* ❏ *Trade* ❏ *Other*

Name _____
Company _____
Address _____
City _____ State ____ Zip _____
Country _____

Important Ordering Information

If you have any questions regarding my order, my daytime phone and fax numbers are: Phone (____) _____
Fax (____) _____

Send me _____ copies of *The Ratite Encyclopedia* @ $84.95 plus shipping /handling and sales tax. (Texas only)
Texas $95.94 • Out of state $89.45 • International $92.45.
TOTAL _____
For volume discounts please call (210) 308-8998.

P.O. BOX 790365
San Antonio, TX 78279-0365
Call (210) 308-8998
Fax (210) 366-1657

Ship To:

Name _____
Company _____
Address _____ Div/Ste # _____
City _____ State ____ Zip _____
Country _____

Method of Payment
❏ Check (payable to Ratite Records, Inc)
❏ International - US currency / money order
❏ Visa ❏ M/C ❏ Amex ❏ Discover

☐☐☐☐☐☐☐☐☐☐☐☐☐☐☐☐

Exp. Date: _____ Signature _____

RATITE RECORDS